Welfare
Volume 1: Aggregate
Consumer Behavior

Welfare
Volume 1: Aggregate Consumer Behavior

Dale W. Jorgenson

The MIT Press
Cambridge, Massachusetts
London, England

This book was printed and bound in the United States of America.

Library of Congress Cataloging-in-Publication Data

Jorgenson, Dale Weldeau, 1933–
Welfare / Dale W. Jorgenson.
p. cm.
Includes bibliographical references and index.
Contents: v. 1. Aggregate consumer behavior. — v. 2. Measuring social welfare.
ISBN 0–262–10062–2 (v. 1: alk. paper). — ISBN 0–262–10063–0 (v. 2: alk. paper)
1. Income distribution. 2. Consumer behavior. 3. Economic policy.
4. Public welfare. I. Title.
HB523.J673 1997 96–44875
361.6′1—dc20 CIP

Contents

List of Tables	ix
Preface	xi
List of Sources	xxxi
1 Transcendental Logarithmic Utility Functions	**1**
L.R. Christensen, D.W. Jorgenson, and L.J. Lau	
1.1 Introduction	1
1.2 Transcendental Logarithmic Utility Functions	4
1.3 Testing the Theory of Demand	7
1.4 Empirical Results	13
1.5 Summary and Conclusion	26
2 The Structure of Consumer Preferences	**29**
D.W. Jorgenson and L.J. Lau	
2.1 Introduction	29
2.2 Transcendental Logarithmic Utility Functions with Time-Varying Preferences	32
2.3 Preference Structure	38
2.4 Empirical Results	58
3 Statistical Tests of the Theory of Consumer Behavior	**91**
D.W. Jorgenson and L.J. Lau	
3.1 Introduction	91
3.2 Integrability	92
3.3 Additive Demand Functions	93
3.4 Rotterdam Demand Functions	95
3.5 Conclusion	101

4 The Integrability of Consumer Demand Functions **103**
D.W. Jorgenson and L.J. Lau
4.1 Introduction 103
4.2 Integrability 106
4.3 Homogeneity and Summability 110
4.4 Symmetry 113
4.5 Nonnegativity and Monotonicity 120
4.6 Conclusion 123
Appendix 4A Symmetry 124
Appendix 4B Logarithmic Function 127
Appendix 4C Power Function 133

5 Testing the Integrability of Consumer Demand Functions, United States, 1947–1971 **137**
D.W. Jorgenson and L.J. Lau
5.1 Introduction 137
5.2 Integrability 139
5.3 Empirical Tests 143
5.4 Conclusion 150

6 The Structure of Consumer Preferences, Federal Republic of Germany, 1950–1973 **153**
K. Conrad and D.W. Jorgenson
6.1 Introduction 153
6.2 Transcendental Logarithmic Utility Functions with Time-Varying Preferences 154
6.3 Preference Structure 157
6.4 Statistical Tests 168
6.5 Empirical Results 171
6.6 Summary 177

7 Testing the Integrability of Consumer Demand Functions, Federal Republic of Germany, 1950–1973 **179**
K. Conrad and D.W. Jorgenson
7.1 Introduction 179
7.2 Direct and Indirect Systems 180
7.3 Integrability 182
7.4 Estimation and Testing 189
7.5 Conclusion 195
Appendix 196

8 **Transcendental Logarithmic Model of Aggregate Consumer Behavior** **203**
D.W. Jorgenson, L.J. Lau, and T.M. Stoker
8.1 Introduction 203
8.2 Exact Aggregation for Consumers with Identical Preferences 220
8.3 Exact Aggregation with Differences in Individual Preferences 242
8.4 Demands as Functions of Prices 258
8.5 Translog Model of Consumer Behavior 280
8.6 Econometrics of the Translog Model 301
8.7 Aggregate Consumer Behavior in the United States, 1958–1974 323
Appendix 8.1 Cross-Section Estimation Results 350
Appendix 8.2 Aggregate Instrumental Variables 353

9 **Aggregate Consumer Expenditures on Energy** **357**
D.W. Jorgenson and T.M. Stoker
9.I Aggregate Consumer Expenditures on Energy 357
9.I.1 Introduction 357
9.I.2 Translog Model of Consumer Behavior 359
9.I.3 Econometrics of Aggregate Energy Expenditures 369
9.II Individual Energy Expenditures 390
9.II.1 Introduction 390
9.II.2 Consumer Expenditure Survey of 1960/61 392
9.II.3 Consumer Expenditure Survey of 1972 400
9.II.4 Consumer Expenditure Survey of 1973 406
9.II.5 Lifestyle and Household Energy Use Survey of 1973 408
9.II.6 Lifestyle and Household Energy Use Survey of 1975 418
9.II.7 Summary and Conclusion 423
Appendix 425
9.III Aggregate Energy Expenditures 428
9.III.1 Introduction 428
9.III.2 Pooled Estimation Results 429
9.III.3 Consumer Expenditure Surveys 437
9.III.4 Separability of Transportation and Household Operations 440
9.III.5 Tests of Structural Change 442
9.III.6 Summary and Conclusion 445
Appendix 447

10 Nonlinear Three-Stage Least Squares Pooling of Cross-Section and Time-Series Observations **449**
D.W. Jorgenson and T.M. Stoker
10.1 Introduction 449
10.2 Stochastic Specification 452
10.3 The Nonlinear Three-Stage Least Squares Estimator 457
10.4 Parametric Hypothesis Tests 460
10.5 Estimation Subject to Inequality Restrictions 461
10.6 Illustration: Residential Demand for Energy 463
10.7 Conclusion 470
Appendix 10.A Technical Assumptions 471
Appendix 10.B Instrumental Variables, 1958–1978 473

11 Two-Stage Budgeting and Consumer Demand for Energy **475**
D.W. Jorgenson, D.T. Slesnick, and T.M. Stoker
11.1 Introduction 475
11.2 Translog Model of Consumer Behavior 476
11.3 Econometrics of Exact Aggregation 487
11.4 Empirical Results 498
11.A Appendix: Intrumental Variables, 1958–1978 509

References 511

Index 523

List of Tables

1.1 Estimates of the parameters of the direct translog utility function 19
1.2 Estimates of the parameters of the indirect translog utility function 21
1.3 Critical values of χ^2/degrees of freedom 25
1.4 Test statistics for direct and indirect tests of the theory of demand and tests of additivity and homotheticity 25
1.5 Test statistics for direct and indirect tests of restrictions on functional form, given additivity or homotheticity or both 26
2.1 Parameter estimates, direct translog utility function 66
2.2 Parameter estimates, indirect translog utility function 75
2.3 Critical values of χ^2/degrees of freedom 87
2.4 Test Statistics 88
5.1 Estimates of the parameters of the direct translog demand system 144
5.2 Estimates of the parameters of the indirect translog demand system 146
5.3 Critical values of χ^2/degrees of freedom and standard normal test statistics 150
5.4 Test statistics for direct and indirect translog demand systems 151
6.1 Critical values of χ^2/degrees of freedom 174
6.2 Test statistics 175
7.1 Critical values of χ^2/degrees of freedom and standard normal test statistics 191
7.2 Test statistics for direct and indirect translog demand systems 191
7.A.1 Estimates of the parameters of the indirect translog demand system 196
7.A.2 Estimates of the parameters of the direct translog demand system 199
8.1 Elements of B_{pp}^{-1} 297
8.2 Restrictions on the elements of $B_{pp} = LDL'$ 299
8.3 Pooled estimation results 330

8.4 Nonnegativity bounds, 1972 336
8.5 Estimated budget shares, price and expenditure elasticities, 1972 343
8.A1 Cross-section estimation results 350
9.II.1 Notation 393
9.II.2 Summary statistics, 1960/61 CES 395
9.II.3 Summary statistics, 1972 CES 401
9.II.4 Summary statistics, 1973 CES 407
9.II.5 Summary statistics, 1973 LHES 413
9.II.6 Summary statistics, 1975 LHES 419
9.II.A.1 Cross-section results, 1960/61 CES 425
9.II.A.2 Cross-section results, 1972 CES 426
9.II.A.3 Cross-section results, 1973 CES 426
9.II.A.4 Cross-section results, 1973 LHES 427
9.II.A.5 Cross-section results, 1973 LHES 427
9.III.1 Pooled estimation results: Five cross-section data sets 430
9.III.2 Estimated price elasticities, 1972 436
9.III.3 Pooled estimation results: 1972 CES 438
9.III.4 Pooled estimation results: Three CES cross-section data sets 439
9.III.5 Pooled estimation results for separability: Five cross-section data sets 441
9.III.6 Estimated price elasticities: Separability, 1972 443
9.III.7 Pooled estimation results for structural change: Five cross-section data sets 444
9.III.8 Estimated price elasticities: Structural change, 1972 446
9.III.A1 Instrumental variables, 1958–1978 447
10.1 Residential demand for energy 469
10.2 Residential demand for energy with gasoline separable from other types of energy 470
10.B.1 Instrumental variables, 1958–1978 473
11.1 Pooled estimation results for aggregate consumer behavior 501
11.2 Pooled estimation results for aggregate energy expenditures 504
11.3 Estimated own-price elasticities, 1972, holding total energy expenditure fixed 507
11.4 Estimated own-price elasticities, 1972, holding total expenditure fixed 508
11.A Instrumental variables, 1958–1978 509

Preface

Dale W. Jorgenson

This volume is the first of two volumes containing my empirical studies of consumer behavior. The centerpiece of the volume is an econometric model of demand obtained by aggregating over a population of consumers with heterogeneous preferences. Heterogeneity is captured by allowing preferences to depend on the demographic characteristics of individual households. The two principal streams of empirical research on consumer behavior are unified by implementing the model through pooling of aggregate time series data with cross section data for households.

The second volume, *Measuring Social Welfare,* presents a new conceptual framework for normative economics that exploits the model of aggregate consumer behavior presented in this volume. The model is a system of aggregate demand functions constructed from underlying individual demand functions. Measures of individual welfare are recovered from the individual demand functions and combined into an indicator of social welfare, reflecting concepts of horizontal and vertical equity. This approach has been successfully applied to the evaluation of economic policy, the measurement of poverty and inequality, and the assessment of the standard of living and its cost.

The exact aggregation approach to modeling aggregate consumer behavior presented in this volume, like the representative consumer approach that preceded it, rests on the foundations of the theory of individual consumer behavior.[1] The exact aggregation approach readily encompasses both the theory of the consumer and heterogeneity of preferences. The essential innovation in this approach is to incorporate the attributes of consumers, such as demographic characteristics, that reflect this heterogeneity into a model of aggregate demand through statistics of the joint distribution of attributes and total expenditures over the population.

The representative consumer approach has persisted for decades in the face of critical deficiencies. The first is that the theory of individual consumer behavior, applied to aggregate behavior, is essentially vacuous.[2] The second is that the main implication of the representative consumer model—the integrability of aggregate demand functions—does not adequately describe aggregate data. This is not surprising, since conditions required for validity of the representative consumer approach are totally at odds with evidence accumulated over more than a century of empirical research on the behavior of individual households. This evidence reveals heterogeneity of individual preferences that is inconsistent with the model of a representative consumer, but is perfectly consistent with the theory of individual consumer behavior.

The econometric model of aggregate consumer behavior presented in my 1982 paper with Lawrence Lau and Stoker, reprinted in chapter 8, has successfully extricated demand modeling from the procrustrean bed provided for more than half a century by the highly restrictive framework of a representative consumer. This model has provided a wholly new point of departure for subsequent empirical research, including my 1984 paper with Stoker, reprinted in chapter 9, my 1983 paper with Daniel Slesnick and Stoker, reprinted in chapter 11, and my 1987 paper with Slesnick, reprinted as chapter 5 of *Measuring Social Welfare.* Stoker (1993) provides a detailed survey of this rapidly growing literature.

The model presented in chapter 8 unifies two distinct lines of empirical research on consumer behavior. The first issues from the seminal contributions of Henry Schultz (1938), Richard Stone (1954b), and Herman Wold (1953) and focuses on prices and total expenditure as determinants of aggregate demand. The theory of consumer behavior is used to derive a model of a representative consumer. This model is implemented through time series data on prices and per capita quantities consumed and total expenditure.

A second line of research, represented by the classic studies of household budgets by Conrad Leser (1963), Sigmund Prais and Hendrik Houthakker (1955), and Holbrook Working (1943), has focused on demographic characteristics and total expenditure as determinants of household demand. The theory of consumer behavior is used to derive a model of the individual consumer. This model is implemented through cross section data on quantities consumed, total expenditure, and the characteristics of households.

Aggregate time series and individual cross section data have been combined by Stone (1954b) and Wold (1953) in models of aggregate demand based on the model of a representative consumer. Cross section data are used to estimate the effect of total expenditure and time series data to characterize the impact of prices. However, this pioneering research omits a crucial link between individual and aggregate demands arising from the fact that aggregate demand functions are sums of individual demand functions.

Aggregate demand functions depend on prices and total expenditure; however, aggregate demands depend on individual expenditures rather than aggregate expenditure. If individual expenditures are allowed to vary independently, the model of a representative consumer places restrictions on preferences that severely restrict the dependence of individual demands on total expenditure. Alternatively, if individual expenditures are functions of aggregate expenditure, for example, fixed proportions of expenditure, the implications of the theory of consumer behavior for aggregate demand are extremely limited.

One implication of the theory of consumer behavior is that aggregate expenditure is a weighted sum of aggregate demand functions with each function weighted by the corresponding price. A second implication is that aggregate demands are homogeneous of degree zero in prices and expenditures. Erwin Diewert (1977) and Sonnenschein (1973b) have shown that any system of demand functions that satisfies these two conditions, but is otherwise arbitrary, can be rationalized as the sum of individual demand functions with a fixed expenditure distribution.

The implications of aggregation over a population of consumers for the model of a representative consumer are summarized in Section 8.1.A of chapter 8. First, Terence Gorman (1953) has shown that individual demand functions must be linear in the total expenditure and attributes of households, such as demographic characteristics. Furthermore, if demands are equal to zero when expenditure is zero, all consumers must have identical, homothetic preferences.

Homothetic preferences are inconsistent with well-established empirical regularities in the behavior of consumers, such as Engel's Law, which states that the proportion of expenditure devoted to food is a decreasing function of total expenditure.[3] Identical preferences are inconsistent with empirical findings that expenditure patterns depend on the demographic characteristics of households.[4] Even the weaker form of Gorman's results, that demands are linear functions of expenditure with identical slopes for all individuals, is inconsistent with empirical evidence from budget studies.[5]

Despite the conflict between Gorman's characterization of individual behavior and empirical evidence on households, this characterization has been an important stimulus to empirical research. The linear expenditure system, proposed by Lawrence Klein and Herman Rubin (1947–1948) and implemented by Stone (1954b), has the property that individual demand functions are linear in total expenditure. This system has been widely used in modeling time series. Generalizations that retain the critical property of linearity in total expenditure have also been employed.[6]

John Muellbauer (1975, 1976a) has substantially generalized Gorman's concept of a representative consumer. In Muellbauer's approach individual preferences are identical, but not necessarily homothetic, and demands may be nonlinear functions of total expenditure. An implication of nonlinearity is that aggregate expenditure shares, interpreted as the shares of a representative consumer, depend on prices and a function of individual expenditures that is not restricted to aggregate or per capita expenditure.

Despite the conflict between Muellbauer's assumption of identical preferences and empirical evidence on households, his characterization of individual behavior, like Gorman's, has been an important stimulus to empirical research. Ernst Berndt, Masako Darrough, and Diewert (1977) and Angus Deaton and Muellbauer (1980a) have implemented models of aggregate demand conforming to Muellbauer's characterization. Both studies retain the assumption that preferences are identical for all individuals.

Lau's (1977b, 1982) theory of exact aggregation, summarized in Sections 8.2 and 8.3 of chapter 8, is the key to surmounting the limitations of the representative consumer model. One of the remarkable implications of Lau's theory is that individual demand functions can be recovered uniquely from a system of aggregate demand functions. This makes it possible to exploit the theory of the individual consumer in specifying a model of aggregate demand—the feature of the representative consumer model that accounts for its widespread application.

Lau permits aggregate demand functions to depend on one or more symmetric functions of individual expenditures and attributes of households such as demographic characteristics. These functions can be interpreted as statistics describing the population of consumers. Lau's (1977b, 1982) Fundamental Theorem of Exact Aggregation, Theorem 8.1 of chapter 8, provides a characterization of individual and aggregate demand functions that depends only on the existence of well-defined individual demand functions:

1. Individual demand functions for the same commodity must be identical up to the addition of a function that is independent of individual expenditure and attributes.

2. Individual demand functions must be the products of separate functions of prices and of individual expenditure and attributes.

3. Aggregate demand functions depend on statistics of the joint distribution of individual expenditures and attributes; the only admissible statistics are additive in functions of individual expenditures and attributes.

4. Aggregate demand functions are linear functions of these statistics.

Lau's theory of exact aggregation contains the models of a representative consumer of Gorman (1953) and Muellbauer (1975, 1976a) as special cases. For example, Gorman's model includes only one statistic describing the population of consumers, namely, aggregate expenditure. Muellbauer's model involves two such statistics, one of which must be aggregate expenditure. The assumption of identical preferences can be tested by eliminating the attributes of individual consumers from statistics that characterize the population of consumers in Lau's theory.

Gorman (1981) has shown that a system of individual demand functions that is linear in functions of total expenditure depends on at most three such functions. Although he motivates the condition of linearity by its connection with aggregation, he does not derive this condition from a theory of aggregation. Arthur Lewbel (1991) presents a test for determining the number of functions of total expenditure empirically and has applied this test to cross section data for individual households with a common set of demographic characteristics. Neither Gorman nor Lewbel deal with the issues raised by heterogeneity of preferences.

A system of individual demand functions that conforms to the theory of exact aggregation must be linear in one or more functions of total expenditure and the attributes of the individual consumer. In Section 8.3 we incorporate differences in preferences into aggregate demand functions. A simple, but relatively tractable, representation of individual demands involves three functions of the total expenditure and attributes of households. One of these is total expenditure, a second is nonlinear in expenditure and does not depend on attributes, and a third depends on both expenditure and attributes.

The second step in specifying a model of aggregate consumer behavior is to incorporate the properties of individual demand functions generated by utility maximization, subject to a budget constraint. Such demand functions are said to be *integrable.* A complete characterization of integrable demand functions is given, for example, by Hurwicz (1971) and summarized in Section 8.1.C of chapter 8 as follows:

1. *Homogeneity.* Individual demand functions are homogeneous of degree zero in prices and expenditure.
2. *Summability.* A weighted sum of the individual demand functions with each function multiplied by the price of the corresponding commodity is equal to total expenditure.
3. *Symmetry.* The matrix of compensated own- and cross-price effects must be symmetric.
4. *Nonnegativity.* The individual quantities demanded are nonnegative.
5. *Monotonicity.* The matrix of compensated own- and cross-price effects must be nonpositive definite for all prices and total expenditure.

Summability and homogeneity simplify the representation of individual demands considerably. The nonlinear function of expenditure must be the product of expenditure and either the logarithm or a power function of expenditure. Demands also depend on the attributes of individual households such as demographic characteristics. Aggregate demand functions depend on prices as well as the joint distribution of expenditures and attributes among individuals.

The theory of exact aggregation enables us to specify individual demands as functions of expenditure and attributes very precisely. To incorporate the implications of the theory of the individual consumer, we must also specify the dependence of these demands on prices. In Section 8.4 we show that only the transcendental logarithmic or translog indirect utility function introduced in my 1975 paper with Laurits Christensen and Lau (1975), reprinted as chapter 1, combines flexibility in the representation of preferences with parsimony in the number of parameters that must be estimated.[7]

In the model presented in chapter 1 we incorporate the implications of the integrability into the model of a representative consumer and test the resulting restrictions. Previous tests had employed additive and homothetic preferences in formulating these tests. As a consequence, rejections could be attributed either to failure of integrability or restrictions on preferences. We introduced the indirect translog utility function as a means of discriminating between these two alternative interpretations.

In chapter 1 we carry out a nested sequence of tests, beginning with tests of integrability and continuing with tests of additivity and homotheticity of preferences, jointly and in parallel, conditional on integrability. The tests reject integrability and, conditional on integrability, reject both additivity and homotheticity. The results have strongly adverse implications for models of consumer demand based on the model of a representative consumer and, more specifically, for models incorporating additive or homothetic preferences.

My 1975 paper with Lau, reprinted as chapter 2, introduced time-varying preferences into the model of a representative consumer and developed a detailed methodology for choosing an appropriate set of restrictions on preferences, including separability, homotheticity, and neutrality or independence of time. We consider fifty-four different combinations of these restrictions and, conditional on the validity of the representative consumer model, select a relatively parsimonious specification for the United States. We reject restrictions such as additivity, homotheticity, and neutrality. My 1978 paper with Klaus Conrad, reprinted in chapter 6, carries out a parallel set of tests for Germany with similar results.

My 1977 paper with Lau, reprinted as chapter 3, and Lau (1977a) show that integrable systems of demand functions in common use—such as the linear logarithmic demand system employed by Schultz (1938), Stone (1954b), and Wold (1953)—imply that expenditure shares are constant, so that underlying utility function is neutral and linear logarithmic. This utility function embodies the restrictions implied by additivity, homotheticity, and neutrality. Similar results obtain for the Rotterdam system of Anton Barten (1964a) and Henry Theil (1965). These systems can be used to test integrability only in conjunction with neutral linear logarithmic utility.

My 1979 paper with Lau, reprinted as chapter 4, considers tests for integrability for the model with time-varying preferences. These tests are based on precisely the same formulation of integrability as in

Section 8.4 of chapter 8; however, the implied restrictions are incorporated into the model of a representative consumer. By contrast with the approach of my 1975 paper with Christensen and Lau, tests of homogeneity and summability of demand functions are separated from the test of symmetry. In addition, my 1979 paper with Lau presents tests of nonnegativity and monotonicity. The monotonicity test is based on Lau's (1978) methodology for testing the semi-definiteness of a real symmetric matrix.

My 1986 paper with Lau, reprinted as chapter 5, carries out the tests of integrability proposed in our 1979 paper for U.S. aggregate time series for the period 1947–1971. We first test homogeneity and summability in parallel without imposing symmetry. We then test symmetry, nonnegativity, and monotonicity, given homogeneity and summability. We reject each of these implications of integrability. My 1979 paper with Conrad, reprinted in chapter 7, carries out a parallel system of tests for Germany with similar results.

My paper with Christensen and Lau and my four papers with Lau, reprinted as chapters 1–5, and my parallel studies with Conrad, reprinted as chapters 6 and 7, provide an exhaustive treatment of econometric modeling within the representative consumer framework. We made it possible to discriminate between the two possible interpretations of rejections of this framework. The first is that integrability must be rejected. The other is that functional form restrictions—such as additivity, homotheticity, or neutrality—must be rejected. Our results show that integrability must be rejected, setting the stage for development of the exact aggregation approach in chapter 8.

A key contribution of chapters 1–5 was to introduce and characterize the indirect translog utility function and the corresponding system of individual demand functions.[8] This system provided a flexible and parsimonious approach for modeling individual demand with the representative consumer framework. These advantages are immediately transferable to modeling individual and aggregate demands within the exact aggregation framework. The characterization of integrability in my 1979 paper with Lau and the analysis of the structure of preferences in our 1975 paper also carry over directly.

The final contribution of the papers presented in chapters 1–5 is the successful application of new statistical methods for systems of nonlinear simultaneous equations to modeling aggregate demand. These methods are essential for avoiding simultaneous equations bias in the estimation of price effects. Methods of estimation for the nonlinear simultaneous equations model are developed in my 1974 paper with Jean-Jacques Laffont and methods for statistical inference in my 1979 paper with Ronald Gallant. These methods are extended to the exact aggregation framework in my 1986 paper with Stoker, reprinted in chapter 10.

To incorporate differences in individual preferences into a model of aggregate consumer behavior in chapter 8 we allow the indirect translog utility function for each individual to depend on attributes, such as demographic characteristics, that vary among individuals. The theory of exact aggregation requires that individual demand functions must be linear in functions of the expenditure and attributes of the individual. We impose the resulting restrictions on the indirect utility function for each individual.

Integrability requires that the indirect utility function for each individual must be homogeneous, monotone, and quasiconvex. In Section 8.5 we impose the corresponding restrictions on the indirect translog utility functions for all individuals. To construct a system of individual demand functions we apply Rene Roy's (1943) Identity to these indirect utility functions.[9] The resulting demand functions express the shares of total expenditure allocated to each commodity group as linear functions of the logarithm of expenditure and the attributes of the individual.

Our model of aggregate consumer behavior is a weighted average of individual demand functions for the population as a whole. Weights are given by the share of each individual in aggregate expenditure. This model expresses the share of expenditure allocated to each commodity group as a function of prices. These shares also depend on weighted averages of the logarithms of individual expenditures and attributes.

We find it convenient to represent the attributes of individuals, such as demographic characteristics, by variables equal to unity for an individual with the corresponding attribute and zero otherwise. The weighted average of each attribute for the population as a whole is the share of individuals with that attribute in aggregate expenditure. Our model of aggregate demand includes these shares as explanatory variables to capture the effect of change in the demographic characteristics of the population. Similarly, we incorporate a weighted average of the logarithm of individual expenditures to encompass the impact of changes in the distribution of total expenditure over the population.

We could implement the model of aggregate demand presented in Section 8.5 from individual cross section data on expenditure shares, prices, total expenditure, and demographic characteristics. Alternatively, we could implement this model from aggregate time series on expenditure shares, prices, shares of demographic groups in aggregate expenditure, and a weighted average of the logarithms of expenditure. However, if prices take the same values for all individuals and cross section observations are limited to individual expenditure shares and total expenditure, the best estimation strategy is to pool aggregate time series with individual cross section data along the lines outlined in Section 8.6.

Econometric methodology for pooling aggregate time series with individual cross sections in models based on exact aggregation is presented in detail in my 1986 paper with Stoker, reprinted as chapter 10. Assuming that prices faced by all households are the same, the first step is to estimate the parameters of a model for a single cross section. This model can be estimated by ordinary least squares. Since the number of cross section observations is typically large, a considerable number of parameters associated with total expenditure and the demographic characteristics of individual households can be identified in this way.

The second step in pooling is to incorporate time series of prices and statistics describing the joint distribution of total expenditures and attributes over the population. Instrumental variables methods are essential for mitigating simultaneous equations bias in the estimation of price effects. Our inequality-constrained, nonlinear three-stage least squares estimator generalizes the nonlinear three-stage least squares estimator for simultaneous equations introduced in my 1974 paper with Laffont. Tests of equality and inequality restrictions generalize the tests of equality restrictions introduced in my 1979 paper with Gallant.[10]

Implementation of nonlinear three-stage least squares requires a sequence of iterations. Under exact aggregation these iterations are greatly simplified by the fact that individual cross section observations are not required for the pooled estimator. This estimator depends only on moments calculated in evaluating the least squares estimator at the initial step of the iterative process. Imposition of inequality constraints requires nonlinear programming techniques.

In Section 8.7 we estimate the parameters of the transcendental logarithmic model of aggregate consumer behavior for the United States.

We analyze the allocation of aggregate demand among five categories of goods and services—energy, food and clothing, consumer services, capital services, and other nondurable goods. We employ a breakdown of households by family size, age of head, region, race, and urban versus rural residence. We implement this model by pooling cross section data for U.S. households from the Consumer Expenditure Survey for 1972 with annual U.S. time series on aggregate demand for the period 1958–1974.

Our model of aggregate demand depends on eighty-two unknown parameters. Sixty-four of these describe the impact of attributes of individual households, four represent income effects, ten give price effects, and the remaining four are intercepts in equations for the expenditure shares. With a relatively modest number of time series observations these parameters could not be identified from aggregate data alone. Similarly, the absence of price variation in data for households makes it impossible to identify the price effects from cross section data. All eighty-two parameters can be identified through pooling of time series and cross section data.

As total expenditure increases, we find that the share of the consumer budget allocated to capital services rises, while shares of the other four commodity groups decline. Demographic effects are very important for all categories of consumer expenditures, ruling out both Gorman (1953) and Muellbauer (1975, 1976a) forms of the representative consumer model. Demographic effects are also very important in determining the impacts of total expenditure and prices.

Family size effects are almost a mirror image of total expenditure effects. As family size increases from one to seven or more, the shares of energy, food and clothing, and other nondurables increase, while shares of capital services and consumer services decrease. The difference between consumption patterns for families of size one, unrelated individuals, and larger families is substantial. Two person families, for example, spend a larger portion of their budget on necessities, such as energy and food and clothing. A similarly abrupt change occurs for families of size seven or more, a category that includes families of larger sizes, such as families with twelve or even fifteen members.

The impact of age reflects the high degree of correlation between age of head and the ages of children in the family. For example, the share of food and clothing rises until approximately age 40, levels off, and then declines. The pattern for the share of capital services is the opposite of that for food and clothing, while the share of consumer services declines relatively smoothly with age. Region and urban versus rural residence have substantial impacts on shares of capital services and energy with residents of North Central and Southern regions spending more on capital and energy. White-nonwhite differentials are not substantial, except for a smaller share devoted to capital services and a slightly larger share to consumer services for nonwhites.

Increases in total expenditures reduce expenditure elasticities and enlarge price elasticities, except for capital services. By contrast increases in family size for a given level of expenditure reduce price elasticities and enlarge expenditure elasticities. Differences in price and expenditure elasticities associated with age of head, region, race, and urban versus rural residence are also considerable. These differences are entirely neglected in models of aggregate demand based on the model of a representative consumer.

One of the most important features of our econometric model of aggregate demand is that individual demand functions can be recovered uniquely from the system of aggregate demand functions. This makes it possible to incorporate the implications of the theory of individual consumer behavior into our aggregate model. The same feature enables us to derive measures of welfare from individual demand functions in Section 8.5. These are the compensating and equivalent variations introduced by John Hicks (1942).

My 1987 paper with Slesnick, reprinted as chapter 5 of *Measuring Social Welfare,* implements the translog model of aggregate consumer expenditures for a greatly extended time series data set, including U.S. aggregate time series data for the period 1947–1985. This paper provides an alternative interpretation of the role of demographic characteristics by incorporating them into household equivalence scales. All households have identical indirect utility functions when total expenditure is expressed relative to the number of household equivalent members.

Under exact aggregation the translog indirect utility functions employed in Section 8.5 provide cardinal measures of welfare that are fully comparable among individuals. The compensating and equivalent variations of Hicks (1942) give only ordinal measures that are not interpersonally comparable. Cardinality and interpersonal comparability were not exploited in my 1982 paper with Lau and Stoker, but are the key to development of measures of social welfare in my 1983 paper with Slesnick, reprinted as chapter 2 of *Measuring Social Welfare.*

The translog indirect utility function used in generating our model of aggregate demand was originally introduced to test the implications of the framework of a representative consumer. The introduction of the attributes of households, such as demographic characteristics, made it possible to overcome the limitations of this framework. Our model of aggregate demand is obtained by exact aggregation over a population of consumers with heterogeneous preferences. An important remaining issue is aggregation over commodity groups.

The primary purpose of demand modeling is to determine price and expenditure elasticities empirically for specific commodities. These elasticities play a critical role in projecting future demands and evaluating the impact of economic policies on consumer welfare. For example, the own-price and cross-price elasticities of demand for energy and nonenergy commodities and specific types of energy are essential for the evaluation of energy policies. Unfortunately, the number of own- and cross-price elasticities increases with the square of the number of commodity groups.

The proliferation of elasticities as the number of commodity groups increases has necessitated the development of modeling strategies based on two-stage budgeting. At each stage the number of commodity groups can be reduced to manageable size. The usefulness of two-stage budgeting is considerably enhanced by Gorman's (1959) detailed characterization of the corresponding restrictions on preferences.[11] This characterization suggests two alternative approaches to modeling consumer behavior. The first is based on a utility function for each consumer that is additive in subutility functions for commodity groups.[12] The second, employed in chapter 8, is based on homothetic separability. The utility function is not required to be additive, but subutility functions for commodity groups must be homothetic.

The model of aggregate demand presented in chapter 8 includes five commodity groups—energy, food and clothing, consumer services, capital services, and other nondurable expenditure. The allocation of total expenditure embodies the restriction that the indirect utility function is homothetically separable in the commodities within each group. More specifically, we assume that the price of each commodity group is a homogeneous translog function of its components. The price index for the group has growth rate equal to a weighted average of growth rates of the components with weights given by the average value shares.[13]

The objective of my 1984 paper with Stoker, reprinted as chapter 9, is to model the allocation of energy expenditure among different types of energy within the exact aggregation framework. This model incorporates time series data on aggregate quantities of energy consumed and energy prices. It also includes time series data on the level and distribution of energy expenditure and the demographic characteristics of the population. Finally, the model incorporates individual cross section data on the allocation of energy expenditure among types of energy for households with different demographic characteristics. This model has been integrated into a model for the allocation of total expenditure between energy and nonenergy commodities in my 1983 paper with Slesnick and Stoker, reprinted as chapter 11.

The econometric model presented in chapter 9 is based on two-stage allocation of total expenditure. In the first stage total expenditure is allocated between energy and nonenergy commodities. The first-stage allocation depends on the price of energy, prices of all nonenergy commodities, and the level of total expenditure. In the second stage allocation energy expenditure is allocated among individual types of energy. The second-stage allocation depends on the prices of individual types of energy and the level of energy expenditure determined at the first stage.

The key assumption that underlies two-stage allocation, summarized in Section 9.1.2A of chapter 9, is homothetic separability in energy prices. Under homothetic separability the price of energy for each consumer is a function of the prices of different types of energy. This assumption was introduced in the model of aggregate demand presented in chapter 8. Our model of energy demand in chapter 9 allows the price of energy to depend on household attributes. Although the prices for individual types of energy faced by consumers are the same for all households, preferences are heterogeneous, so that the price for the energy aggregate differs among households.

We define a quantity index of energy is the ratio of energy expenditure to the price index for energy, so that the product of price and quantity indexes is equal to energy expenditure. This quantity index is an indirect subutility function representing preferences that are homothetically separable in energy. Given price and quantity indexes, we define a two-stage allocation process for each household. The allocation of total expenditure between energy and nonenergy commodities depends on the price index for energy and the prices of nonenergy commodities, as well as the level of total expenditure. Energy expenditure determined at the first stage is then allocated among types of energy at the second stage.

Our model of the two-stage allocation process results in two systems of individual demand functions. The first stage of the process generates a system for allocation between energy and nonenergy commodities. The second stage produces a system for allocation of energy expenditure among types of energy. Since preferences are homothetically separable in energy, demands for all types of energy are proportional to energy expenditure with proportions that depend on energy prices. The final step in formulating the two-stage model of individual demand for energy is to incorporate restrictions implied by integrability into both systems of demand functions.

Our model of aggregate demand is obtained by exact aggregation over each of the two systems of individual demand functions. This generates two systems of aggregate demand functions, each a weighted average of the corresponding system of individual demand functions. For the first stage the weights are the shares of each individual in aggregate expenditure. For the second stage these weights are shares in energy expenditure. The aggregate energy shares are linear in the logarithms of energy prices and the shares of demographic groups in aggregate energy expenditure.

The model of demand for energy presented in chapter 9 is implemented by pooling aggregate time series with five cross section surveys of individual demand for energy. These include the Consumer Expenditure Surveys (CES) of 1960/61, 1972, and 1973 and the Lifestyle and Household Energy Use Surveys (LHES) of 1973 and 1975. Altogether there are 34,424 household observations in these five surveys. This massive data set is used to characterize patterns of consumer demand for electricity, natural gas, gasoline, fuel oil and other fuels.

The three CES cross sections are reasonably balanced in terms of demographic composition, so that the cross section estimates can be considered representative of the underlying structure of energy expenditures. Our model of individual consumer behavior implies that estimates of demographic effects should be the same in all three surveys. Similarities should be taken as support for the model, while dissimilarities indicate violations of the underlying assumptions. In fact, the impacts of demographic characteristics on energy use are virtually identical. Similarities among the three surveys are striking, confirming that they are appropriate for pooling with aggregate time series.

Two important differences between the CES and LHES surveys are apparent. The 1973 CES and LHES surveys can be compared directly; substantial differences between average gasoline and fuel oil use are reported in these surveys. The differences can be attributed to alternative procedures for measuring consumption of these two forms of energy. Since the demographic effects estimated from the two surveys are similar, only moments that are unaffected by differences in measurement procedures are used in pooling these results with aggregate time series. Finally, the impacts of race and urban versus rural residence are reversed in the 1975 LHES, relative to the other surveys, so that we model structural change in these coefficients explicitly in pooling these data with time series.

In chapter 9 we present pooled time series and cross section estimates for all five surveys. Our most important finding is that there are strong demographic effects in the determination of aggregate energy expenditures, implying that an energy price index that does not incorporate the attributes of individual households results in errors of aggregation. Second, we test and reject the hypothesis that gasoline is separable from the other three types of energy, so that we are unable to disaggregate energy demand between transportation and household use. Finally, we find evidence for structural change in the final household survey, which occurred after the first oil crisis in 1975.

Our complete model of energy demand consists of two systems of aggregate demand functions. This model has been implemented by Jorgenson, Slesnick, and Stoker (1983), reprinted as chapter 11. An important link between the two systems of demand functions is provided by the aggregate price index for energy. This takes the simple and intuitively appealing form of a weighted average of price indexes for individual households with weights given by the relative share of each household in aggregate expenditure. This can be expressed in terms of the prices of individual types of energy and the shares of demographic groups in aggregate expenditure.

The second link between the two systems of demand functions is the shares of demographic groups in energy expenditure. Aggregate energy expenditure and expenditure for each demographic group are determined in the first stage of the two-stage allocation process. Shares of demographic groups in the aggregate can be substituted into the model for the second stage of the process. The complete model is estimated by pooling aggregate time series for the United States for the period 1958 to 1978 with cross section data from the 1972 Consumer Expenditure Survey. The pooling process incorporates both links between the two stages of the overall allocation process.

Our two-stage model of aggregate demand employs the same breakdown of energy and nonenergy commodity groups used by Jorgenson, Lau, and Stoker (1982) and the classification of individual types of energy employed by Jorgenson and Stoker (1984). The same classification of households by demographic characteristics is used in all three studies. The results for the first stage are similar to those of Jorgenson, Lau, and Stoker. Expenditure shares for energy and food increase with total expenditure, while the shares for consumer goods, capital services, and other consumer services decrease. The effects of an increase in family size are the reverse of those for total expenditure. The effects of age of head, region, race, and urban versus rural residence are very substantial for most commodity groups. Similarly, own- and cross-price effects are highly significant for all commodity groups, but differ considerably among demographic groups.

Results for the second stage of the two-stage model are similar to those of Jorgenson and Stoker (1984). The effects of family size are substantial only for gasoline. The addition of a second member of a family usually involves a second driver and increases the share of gasoline considerably. Additional members of the family are mainly children, so that the share of gasoline gradually declines. By contrast with family size, the impact of age of head of household is quite dramatic. The share of gasoline declines with age with corresponding increases in the shares of electricity, natural gas, and fuel oil. Effects of region, race, and rural versus urban residence are all quite substantial.

Finally, we compare own- and cross-price elasticities, first holding energy expenditure fixed and then holding total expenditure fixed. As expected, the price elasticities holding total expenditure fixed are uniformly larger, reflecting substitution not only among different types of energy, but also between energy and nonenergy commodities. Focusing on price elasticities with total expenditure constant, we find that gasoline is the least price elastic of the four types of energy, while electricity is the most price elastic form of energy. Price elasticities for natural gas are similar to those for gasoline, while price elasticities for fuel oil are intermediate between those for gasoline and electricity. Price elasticities vary substantially with demographic characteristics of households.

The main contribution of the econometric model of aggregate consumer behavior presented in chapter 8, was to implement the theory of exact aggregation, making it possible to dispense with the model of a representative consumer. The representative consumer framework was thoroughly tested and rejected in chapters 1–7. The key feature of the exact aggregation approach, recoverability of individual demand functions, made it possible to adapt the specifications of models of individual consumer behavior in chapters 1–7 to the exact aggregation framework. These specifications included integrability of demand functions and restrictions on preferences, such as those required by homothetic separability.

The second contribution of the model presented in chapter 8 was the successful implementation of a statistical methodology for pooling aggregate time series and individual cross sections. This grew out of the methodology for systems of nonlinear simultaneous equations developed by Jorgenson and Laffont (1974) and Gallant and Jorgenson (1979). While the model could be identified from either type of data, the relative paucity of time series data and the absence of price variation in cross sections mandated pooling the two data sources. The statistical methodology for pooling is presented in detail by Jorgenson and Stoker (1986) in chapter 10.

Finally, aggregation over individuals was successfully combined with aggregation over commodity groups in the models presented in chapters 9 and 11. Gorman (1959) provided the appropriate modeling framework for individual demand functions by introducing methods for two-stage allocation. This approach is employed in chapter 8 for constructing price indexes for commodity groups. The approach is extended to price indexes based on heterogeneous preferences in chapters 9 and 11. This implies links between the two stages of the allocation process that can be exploited in estimation and testing.

My papers with Lau and Stoker (1980, 1981, 1982) employed the exact aggregation framework to construct ordinal measures of individual welfare for households with stipulated characteristics and level of total expenditure and applied the results in analyzing the impact of economic policies. However, the exact aggregation framework implies cardinal and interpersonally comparable measures of individual welfare that can be incorporated into an indicator of social welfare. These implications were developed in a series of papers initiated by Jorgenson and Slesnick (1983), reprinted in chapter 2 of *Measuring Social*

Welfare and summarized in my Presidential Address to the Econometric Society in 1990, reprinted as chapter 1 of that volume.

The model of aggregate consumer behavior presented in chapter 8 is incorporated into an intertemporal general equilibrium model for the United States in a series of papers initiated by my 1990 paper with Peter Wilcoxen.[14] This general equilibrium model has been used to project aggregate consumer demand in the United States along with future prices and the future level and distribution of total expenditure. The model has also been used to generate projections for groups of individuals, classified by total expenditure and demographic characteristics. Finally, the model has been utilized in my 1992 paper with Slesnick and Wilcoxen, reprinted as chapter 9 of *Measuring Social Welfare,* for assessing the impact of alternative economic policies on social welfare and the welfare of individuals with given characteristics.

Much remains to be done to exploit the exact aggregation approach for modeling aggregate demand. One promising opportunity for extending the econometric models presented in this volume is to encompass labor-leisure choice as well as choice among goods. This will require the recognition of heterogeneity of abilities of different consumers in the labor market as well as heterogeneity of the preferences that underly labor-leisure choice. Another promising extension is to intertemporal choice. Econometric models encompassing heterogeneity of preferences can be used in projecting aggregate demand, labor supply, and saving.

Extensions of the exact aggregation approach offer exciting new possibilities for enriching normative economics as well as the econometric modeling of aggregate behavior. By recovering the underlying models of individual behavior, consumer preferences can be brought to bear on a wider and wider range of issues in economic policy. In addition, measures of economic performance—such as poverty and inequality and the cost and standard of living—can be extended to encompass leisure as well as goods and lifetime patterns of consumption of both goods and leisure.

I would like to thank June Wynn of the Department of Economics at Harvard University for her excellent work in assembling the manuscripts for this volume in machine-readable form. Renate d'Arcangelo of the Editorial Office of the Division of Engineering and Applied Sciences at Harvard edited the manuscripts, proofread the machine-readable versions and prepared them for typesetting. Warren Hrung, then a senior at Harvard College, checked the references and proofread successive versions of the typescript. William Richardson and his associates provided the index. Gary Bisbee of Chiron Incorporated typeset the manuscript and provided camera-ready copy for publication. The staff of The MIT Press, especially Terry Vaughn, Victoria Richardson, and Michael Sims, has been very helpful at every stage of the project. Financial support was provided by the Program on Technology and Economic Policy of the Kennedy School of Government at Harvard. As always, the author retains sole responsibility for any remaining deficiencies in the volume.

Notes

1. The canonical formulation of this theory is that of John Chipman, Leonid Hurwicz, Marcel Richter, and Hugo Sonnenschein (1971).
2. This perspective is presented, forcefully, by Alan Kirman (1992) along with references to the literature. See Thomas Stoker (1993) for a detailed discussion of the implications for demand modeling.
3. See, for example, Houthakker (1957) and the references given there.
4. Surveys of empirical evidence on the impact of demographic characteristics on demand are presented by Angus Deaton (1986) and Martin Browning (1992).
5. This evidence is surveyed by Deaton (1986).
6. See Charles Blackorby, Richard Boyce, and Robert Russell (1978) and the references given there.
7. Surveys of the representation of the effects of prices on demand are given by Deaton (1986), Lau (1986), and Richard Blundell (1988).
8. Translog price and production functions for modeling producer behavior were introduced by Christensen, Jorgenson, and Lau (1971, 1973). This functional form provides the basis for the econometric methodology for modeling producer behavior summarized by Jorgenson (1986).
9. The specification of a system of individual demand functions by means of Roy's Identity was introduced in a pathbreaking study by Houthakker (1960). Lau (1977a) provides a detailed survey of econometric models of consumer demand based on this approach.
10. A unified framework for tests of equality and inequality restrictions has been proposed by Frank Wolak (1989).
11. Gorman's theory of two-stage budgeting is discussed in detail by Blackorby, Primont and Russell (1978).
12. This approach is employed by Blackorby, Boyce, and Russell (1978), who provide extensive references to the literature.
13. Diewert (1976) has shown that this index number exactly reproduces a homogeneous translog price function.
14. Jorgenson and Wilcoxen (1993) provide a survey and detailed references.

List of Sources

1. Laurits R. Christensen, Dale W. Jorgenson, and Lawrence J. Lau. 1975. Transcendental Logarithmic Utility Functions. *American Economic Review* 65, no. 3 (June): 367–383. Reprinted by permission.

2. Dale W. Jorgenson and Lawrence J. Lau. 1975. The Structure of Consumer Preferences. *Annals of Social and Economic Measurement* 4, no. 1 (January): 49–101. Reprinted by permission.

3. Dale W. Jorgenson and Lawrence J. Lau. 1977. Statistical Tests of the Theory of Consumer Behavior. In *Quantitative Wirtschaftforschung*, ed. H. Albach. E. Helmstädter, and R. Henn, 383–394. Tübingen, J.C.B. Mohr. Reprinted by permission.

4. Dale W. Jorgenson and Lawrence J. Lau. 1979. The Integrability of Consumer Demand Functions. *European Economic Review* 12, no. 2 (April): 115–147. Reprinted by permission of Elsevier Science Publishers B.V.

5. Dale W. Jorgenson and Lawrence J. Lau. 1986. Testing the Integrability of Consumer Demand Functions, United States, 1947–1971. In *Advances in Econometrics,* vol. 5, ed. D. Slottje, 31–48. Greenwich, CT: JAI Press. Reprinted by permission.

6. Klaus Conrad and Dale W. Jorgenson. 1978. The Structure of Consumer Preferences, Federal Republic of Germany, 1950–1973. *Zeitshrift für Nationalekonomie* 38, nos. 1–2: 1–28. Reprinted by permission of Springer-Verlag Wien.

7. Klaus Conrad and Dale W. Jorgenson. 1979. Testing the Integrability of Consumer Demand Functions, Federal Republic of Germany, 1950–1973. *European Economic Review* 12, no. 2 (April): 149–169.

8. Dale W. Jorgenson, Lawrence J. Lau, and Thomas M. Stoker. 1982. The Transcendental Logarithmic Model of Aggregate Consumer Behavior. In *Advances in Econometrics,* vol. 1, eds. R. L. Basmann and G. Rhodes, 97–238. Greenwich, CT: JAI Press. Reprinted by permission.

9. Dale W. Jorgenson and Thomas M. Stoker. 1984. Aggregate Consumer Expenditures on Energy. In *Advances in the Economics of Energy and Resources,* vol. 5, ed. J. R. Moroney, 1–84. Greenwich, CT: JAI Press. Reprinted by permission.

10. Dale W. Jorgenson and Thomas M. Stoker. 1986. Nonlinear Three-Stage Least Squares Pooling of Cross-Section and Time-Series Observations. In

Advances in Statistical Analysis and Statistical Computing, vol. 1, ed. R. S. Mariano, 87–115. Greenwich, CT: JAI Press. Reprinted by permission.

11. Dale W. Jorgenson, Daniel T. Slesnick, and Thomas M. Stoker. 1987. Two-Stage Budgeting and the Consumer Demand for Energy. In *Advances in the Economics of Energy and Resources,* vol. 6, ed. J. R. Moroney, 125–162. Greenwich, CT: JAI Press. Reprinted by permission.

Welfare

Volume 1: Aggregate Consumer Behavior

1 Transcendental Logarithmic Utility Functions

Laurits R. Christensen,
Dale W. Jorgenson, and
Lawrence J. Lau

1.1 Introduction

The traditional starting point of econometric studies of consumer demand is a system of demand functions giving the quantity consumed of each commodity as a function of total expenditure and the prices of all commodities. Tests of the theory of demand are formulated by requiring that the demand functions be consistent with utility maximization. Additive and homothetic utility functions have played an important role in formulating tests of the theory of demand. If the utility function is homothetic, expenditure proportions are independent of total expenditure. If the utility function is additive and homothetic, elasticities of substitution among all pairs of commodities are constant and equal.[1]

An example of the traditional approach to demand analysis is the system of double logarithmic demand functions employed in the pioneering studies of consumer demand by Henry Schultz, Richard Stone, and Herman Wold. If the theory of demand is valid and demand functions are double logarithmic, the utility function is linear logarithmic.[2] Similarly, the Rotterdam system of demand functions employed by A. P. Barten and Henri Theil is consistent with utility maximization only if the utility function is linear logarithmic.[3] A linear logarithmic utility function is both additive and homothetic; all expenditure proportions are constant, and elasticities of substitution among all pairs of commodities are constant and equal to unity.

Hendrik Houthakker and Richard Stone have developed alternative approaches to demand analysis that retain the assumption of additivity while dropping the assumption of homotheticity.[4] Stone has employed a linear expenditure system, based on a utility function that is linear in the logarithms of quantity consumed less a constant for each commodity. The constants are interpreted as initial commitments; incremental expenditure proportions, derived from quantities consumed in excess of the initial commitments, are constant for all variations in total expenditure and prices. If all initial commitments are zero, the utility function is linear logarithmic in form. Nonzero commitments permit expenditure proportions to vary with total expenditure.

Houthakker has employed a direct addilog system, based on a utility function that is additive in functions that are homogeneous in the quantity consumed for each commodity. The degree of homogeneity may differ from commodity to commodity, permitting expenditure proportions to vary with total expenditure. If the degrees of homogeneity is the same for all commodities, the addilog utility function is additive and homothetic. Robert Basmann, Leif Johansen, and Kazuo Sato have combined the approaches of Houthakker and Stone, defining each of the homogeneous functions in the direct addilog utility function on the quantity consumed less a constant for each commodity. The resulting utility function is additive but not homothetic.[5]

Our first objective is to develop tests of the theory of demand that do not employ additivity or homotheticity as part of the maintained hypothesis. For this purpose we introduce new representations of the utility function in section 1.2. Our approach is to represent the utility function by functions that are quadratic in the logarithms of the quantities consumed. The resulting utility functions provide a local second-order approximation to any utility function. These utility functions allow expenditure shares to vary with the level of total expenditure and permit a greater variety of substitution patterns among commodities than functions based on constant and equal elasticities of substitution among all pairs of commodities.

Our second objective is to exploit the duality between prices and quantities in the theory of demand. A complete model of consumer demand implies the existence of an indirect utility function, defined on total expenditure and the prices of all commodities.[6] The indirect utility function is homogeneous of degree zero and can be expressed as a function of the ratios of prices of all commodities to total expenditure. The direct utility function is useful in characterizing systems of indirect demand functions, giving the ratios of prices to total expenditure as functions of the quantities consumed. The system consisting of direct utility function and indirect demand functions is dual to the system consisting of indirect utility function and direct demand functions.[7]

We represent the indirect utility function by functions that are quadratic in the logarithms of ratios of prices to total expenditure, paralleling our treatment of the direct utility function. The resulting indirect utility functions provide a local second-order approximation to any indirect utility function. These indirect utility functions are not required to be additive or homothetic. The duality between direct and indirect utility functions has been used extensively in Houthakker's pathbreaking studies of consumer demand. Paralleling the direct addilog demand system, Houthakker has employed an indirect addilog system, based on an indirect utility function that is additive in ratios of prices to total expenditure.[8]

We refer to our representation of the direct utility function as the direct transcendental logarithmic utility function, or more simply, the *direct translog utility function*. The utility function is a transcendental function of the logarithms of quantities consumed. Similarly we refer to our representation of the indirect utility function as the indirect transcendental logarithmic utility function, or, more simply, the *indirect translog utility function*. Earlier, we introduced transcendental logarithmic functions into the study of production.[9] The duality between direct and indirect translog utility functions is analogous to the duality between translog production and price frontier employed in our study of production.

For an additive direct utility function ratios of indirect demand functions, giving the ratios of prices, depend only on the quantities of the two commodities involved. The direct addilog and linear expenditure systems, together with the system employed by Basmann, Johansen, and Sato, have this property. Similarly, for an additive indirect utility function, ratios of direct demand functions giving the ratios of quantities depend only on the prices of the two commodities involved. The indirect addilog system has this property. For an additive and homothetic direct utility function the ratios of indirect demand functions depend only on the ratios of quantities. Furthermore, the indirect utility function is also additive and homothetic, so that ratios of direct demand functions depend only on ratios of prices. The use of direct and indirect translog utility functions permits us to test these restrictions on direct and indirect demand functions. We do not impose the restrictions as part of the maintained hypothesis.

We present statistical tests of the theory of demand in section 1.3. These tests can be divided into two groups. First, we test restrictions on the parameters of the direct translog utility function implied by the theory of demand. We test these restrictions without imposing the assumptions of additivity and homotheticity. We test precisely analogous restrictions on the parameters of the indirect translog utility function. Second, we test restrictions on the direct translog utility function corresponding to restrictions on the form of the utility function. In particular, we test restrictions corresponding to additivity and homotheticity of the direct translog utility function. Again, we test precisely analogous restrictions on the indirect translog utility function.

We present empirical tests of the theory of demand based on time-series data for the United States for 1929–1972 in section 1.4. The data include prices and quantities consumed of the services of consumers' durables, nondurable goods, and other services. For these data we present direct tests of the theory of demand based on the direct translog utility function, and indirect tests of the theory based on the indirect translog utility function. For both direct and indirect tests we first test the extensive set of restrictions implied by the theory of demand. Proceeding conditionally on the validity of the theory, we test restrictions on the form of the direct and indirect utility functions implied by the assumptions of additivity and homotheticity.

1.2 Transcendental Logarithmic Utility Functions

1.2.1 Direct Translog Utility Function

The *direct utility function* U can be represented in the form

$$\ln U = \ln U(X_1, X_2, \ldots, X_m) \tag{1.1}$$

where X_i is the quantity consumed of the ith commodity. The consumer maximizes utility subject to the budget constraint

$$\sum p_i X_i = M \tag{1.2}$$

where p_i is the price of the ith commodity and M is the value of total expenditure.

The first-order conditions for a maximum of utility can be written

$$\frac{\partial \ln U}{\partial \ln X_i} = \mu \frac{p_j X_j}{U}, \qquad (j = 1, 2, \ldots, m) \tag{1.3}$$

where μ is the marginal utility of income. From the budget constraint we obtain

$$\frac{\mu}{U} = \frac{1}{M} \sum \frac{\partial \ln U}{\partial \ln X_i} \tag{1.4}$$

so that

$$\frac{\partial \ln U}{\partial \ln X_j} = \frac{p_j X_j}{M} \sum \frac{\partial \ln U}{\partial \ln X_i}, \qquad (j = 1, 2, \ldots, m). \tag{1.5}$$

To preserve symmetry with our treatment of the indirect utility function given below, we approximate the negative of the logarithm of the direct utility function by a function quadratic in the logarithms of the quantities consumed

$$-\ln U = \alpha_0 + \sum a_i \ln X_i + \frac{1}{2} \sum\sum \beta_{ij} \ln X_i \ln X_j. \tag{1.6}$$

Using this form for the utility function we obtain

$$\alpha_j + \sum \beta_{ji} \ln X_i = \frac{p_j X_j}{M} \sum \left(\alpha_k + \sum \beta_{ki} \ln X_i \right), \qquad (j = 1, 2, \ldots, m). \tag{1.7}$$

To simplify notation we write

$$\alpha_M = \sum \alpha_k \tag{1.8}$$

$$\beta_{Mi} = \sum \beta_{ki}, \qquad (i = 1, 2, \ldots, m) \tag{1.9}$$

so that

$$\frac{p_j X_j}{M} = \frac{\alpha_j + \sum \beta_{ji} \ln X_i}{\alpha_M + \sum \beta_{Mi} \ln X_i}, \qquad (j = 1, 2, \ldots, m). \tag{1.10}$$

The budget constraint implies that

$$\sum \frac{p_i X_i}{M} = 1 \tag{1.11}$$

so that, given the parameters of any $m - 1$ equations for the budget shares $p_j X_j / M$ $(j = 1, 2, \ldots, m)$, the parameters of the mth equation α_m and β_{mj} $(j = 1, 2, \ldots, m)$, can be determined from the definitions of α_M and β_{Mj} $(j = 1, 2, \ldots, m)$.

Since the equations for the budget shares are homogeneous of degree zero in the parameters, a normalization of the parameters is required for estimation. A convenient normalization for the parameters of the direct translog utility function is

$$\alpha_M = \sum \alpha_i = -1 . \tag{1.12}$$

1.2.2 Indirect Translog Utility Function

The *indirect utility function* V can be represented in the form

$$\ln V = \ln V\left(\frac{p_1}{M}, \frac{p_2}{M}, \ldots, \frac{p_m}{M}\right). \tag{1.13}$$

We determine the budget share for the jth commodity from the identity[10]

$$\frac{p_j X_j}{M} = -\frac{\partial \ln V}{\partial \ln p_i} \Big/ \frac{\partial \ln V}{\partial \ln M}, \qquad (j = 1, 2, \ldots, m). \tag{1.14}$$

Preserving symmetry with the direct utility function, we approximate the logarithm of the indirect utility function by a function quadratic in the logarithms of the ratios of prices to the value of total expenditures

$$\ln V = \alpha_0 + \sum \alpha_i \ln \frac{p_i}{M} + \frac{1}{2} \sum \sum \beta_{ij} \ln \frac{p_i}{M} \ln \frac{p_j}{M} . \tag{1.15}$$

Using this form for the utility function we obtain

$$\frac{\partial \ln V}{\partial \ln p_j} = \alpha_j + \sum \beta_{ji} \ln \frac{p_i}{M}, \qquad (j = 1, 2, \ldots, m), \tag{1.16}$$

$$-\frac{\partial \ln V}{\partial \ln M} = \sum \left(\alpha_k + \sum \beta_{ki} \ln \frac{p_i}{M}\right). \tag{1.17}$$

As before, we simplify notation by writing

$$\alpha_M = \sum \alpha_k \tag{1.18}$$

$$\beta_{Mi} = \sum \beta_{ki} \quad (i = 1, 2, \ldots, m) \tag{1.19}$$

so that

$$\frac{p_j X_j}{M} = \frac{\alpha_j + \sum \beta_{ji} \ln \frac{p_i}{M}}{\alpha_M + \sum \beta_{Mi} \ln \frac{p_i}{M}}, \qquad (j = 1, 2, \ldots, m). \tag{1.20}$$

The budget constraint implies that given the parameters of any $m - 1$ equations for the budget shares, the parameters of the mth equation, α_m and β_{mj} $(j = 1, 2, \ldots, m)$, can be determined from the definitions of α_M and β_{Mj} $(j = 1, 2, \ldots, m)$. As before, we can normalize the parameters so that

$$\alpha_M = \sum \alpha_i = -1 . \tag{1.21}$$

1.3 Testing the Theory of Demand

1.3.1 Stochastic Specification

The first step in implementing an econometric model of demand based on the direct translog utility function is to add a stochastic specification to the theoretical model based on equations for the budget shares $p_j X_j / M$ $(j = 1, 2, \ldots, m)$. Given the disturbances in any $m - 1$ equations, the disturbance of the remaining equation can be determined from the budget constraint. Only $m - 1$ equations are required for a complete econometric model of demand.

1.3.2 Equality and Symmetry

We estimate $m - 1$ equations for the budget shares, subject to normalization of the parameter α_M appearing in each equation at minus unity. If the equations are generated by utility maximization, the parameters β_{Mj} $(j = 1, 2, \ldots, m)$ appearing in each equation must be the same. This results in a set of restrictions relating the m parameters appearing in each of the $m - 1$ equations, a total of $m(m - 2)$ restrictions. We refer to these as *equality restrictions*.

The logarithm of the direct translog utility function is twice differentiable in the logarithms of the quantities consumed, so that the Hessian of this function is symmetric. This gives rise to a set of restrictions relating the parameters of the cross-partial derivatives

$$\beta_{ij} = \beta_{ji}, \qquad (i \neq j ; i, j = 1, 2, \ldots, m). \tag{1.22}$$

There are $(1/2)(m-2)(m-1)$ restrictions of this type among the parameters of the $m-1$ equations we estimate directly and $m-1$ such restrictions among the parameters of the equations we estimate indirectly from the budget constraint. We refer to these as *symmetry restrictions*. The total number of symmetry restrictions is $(1/2)m(m-1)$.

If equations for the budget shares are generated by maximization of a direct translog utility function, the parameters satisfy equality and symmetry restrictions. There are $(1/2)m(3m-5)$ such restrictions.

1.3.3 Additivity

If the direct utility function U is *additive*, we can write

$$\ln U = F\left(\sum \ln U^i(X_i)\right) \tag{1.23}$$

where each of the functions U^i depends on only one of the commodities demanded X_i, and F is a real-valued function of one variable.

The parameters of the translog approximation to an additive direct utility function can be written

$$-\frac{\partial \ln U}{\partial \ln X_i} = -F' \frac{\partial \ln U^i}{\partial \ln X_i} = \alpha_i\,, \qquad (i = 1, 2, \ldots, m) \tag{1.24}$$

$$-\frac{\partial^2 \ln U}{\partial \ln X_i \partial \ln X_j} = -F'' \frac{\partial \ln U^i}{\partial \ln X_i} \frac{\partial \ln U^j}{\partial \ln X_j} = \beta ij\,, \quad (k \neq j,\, i, j = 1, 2, \ldots, m) \tag{1.25}$$

where the logarithmic derivatives,

$$F' = \frac{\partial \ln U}{\partial \ln U^i}\,, \qquad (i = 1, 2, \ldots, m) \tag{1.26}$$

$$F'' = \frac{\partial^2 \ln U}{\partial \ln U^i \partial \ln U^j}\,, \qquad (i, j = 1, 2, \ldots, m) \tag{1.27}$$

are independent of i and j.

Under additivity the parameters of the translog utility function satisfy the restrictions

$$\beta_{ij} = \theta\alpha_i\alpha_j\,, \qquad (i \neq j\,;\, i, j = 1, 2, \ldots, m) \tag{1.28}$$

where

$$\theta = -\frac{F''}{(F')^2}\,. \tag{1.29}$$

We refer to these as *additivity restrictions*. The total number of such restrictions is $(1/2)(m-2)(m-1)$.

The translog approximation to an additive utility function is not necessarily additive. The direct translog utility function is additive if and only if $\ln U$ can be written as the sum of m functions, each depending on only one of the quantities demanded. We refer to such a function as *explicitly additive*. Explicit additivity of the translog utility function implies the additivity restrictions given above and the additional restriction

$$\theta = 0\,. \tag{1.30}$$

We refer to this restriction as the *explicit additivity restriction*. We note that the translog approximation to an explicitly additive function is explicitly additive.

1.3.4 Homotheticity

If the direct utility function is *homothetic*, we can write

$$\ln U = F(\ln H(X_1, X_2, \ldots, X_m)) \tag{1.31}$$

where the function H is homogeneous of degree one.

The parameters of the translog approximation to a homothetic direct utility function can be written

$$-\frac{\partial \ln U}{\partial \ln X_i} = \frac{\partial F}{\partial \ln H}\frac{\partial \ln H}{\partial \ln X_i} = a_i\,, \qquad (i = 1, 2, \ldots, m) \tag{1.32}$$

$$\begin{aligned} -\frac{\partial^2 \ln U}{\partial \ln X_i \partial \ln X_j} &= \left[\frac{\partial F}{\partial \ln H}\frac{\partial^2 \ln H}{\partial \ln X_i \partial \ln X_j} + \frac{\partial^2 F}{\partial \ln H^2}\frac{\partial \ln H}{\partial \ln X_i}\frac{\partial \ln H}{\partial \ln X_j}\right] \\ &= \beta ij\,, \qquad (i, j = 1, 2, \ldots, m)\,. \end{aligned} \tag{1.33}$$

Homogeneity of degree one of the function H implies that

$$\sum \frac{\partial \ln H}{\partial \ln X_i} = 1 \tag{1.34}$$

$$\sum_{j=1}^{m} \frac{\partial^2 \ln H}{\partial \ln X_i \partial \ln X_j} = 0\,, \qquad (i = 1, 2, \ldots, m)\,. \tag{1.35}$$

Under homotheticity the parameters of the translog utility function satisfy the restrictions

$$\beta_{Mi} = \sigma\alpha_i\,, \qquad (i = 1, 2, \ldots, m) \tag{1.36}$$

where

$$\sigma = \frac{\partial^2 F}{\partial \ln H^2} \tag{1.37}$$

and we have used the normalization

$$\sum \alpha_i = -1\,. \tag{1.38}$$

We refer to these as *homotheticity restrictions*. There are $m - 1$ such restrictions.

The translog approximation to a homothetic utility function is not necessarily homothetic. A necessary and sufficient condition for homotheticity of the translog utility function is that it is homogeneous, so that

$$\sigma = 0\,. \tag{1.39}$$

We refer to this restriction as the *homogeneity restriction*. We note that the translog approximation to a homogeneous function is homogeneous.

1.3.5 Additivity and Homotheticity

The class of additive and homothetic direct utility functions coincides with the class of utility functions with constant elasticities of substitution among all commodities. If the direct utility function U is additive and homothetic, we can write

$$\ln U = F\left(\sum \delta_i X_i^{\rho}\right) \tag{1.40}$$

or

$$\ln U = F\left(\sum \delta_i \ln X_i\right). \tag{1.41}$$

The second form is a limiting case of the first corresponding to unitary elasticities of substitution among all commodities.

The parameters of the translog approximation to an additive and homothetic utility function satisfy the additivity and homotheticity restrictions given above, so that

$$\beta_{ij} = \theta\, \alpha_i\, \alpha_j\,, \qquad (i \neq j\,;\, i, j = 1, 2, \ldots, m) \tag{1.42}$$

$$\beta_{ii} = (\sigma + \theta)\alpha_i + \theta\alpha_i^2\,, \qquad (i = 1, 2, \ldots, m) \tag{1.43}$$

where we have used the normalization

$$\sum \alpha_i = -\,1\,. \tag{1.44}$$

The translog approximation to an additive and homothetic utility function is not necessarily additive and homothetic. We can, however, identify the parameters of a translog approximation with the parameters of the additive and homothetic utility function given above, as follows

$$\sigma + \theta = \rho \tag{1.45}$$

$$\alpha_i = \delta_i\,, \qquad (i = 1, 2, \ldots, m)\,. \tag{1.46}$$

As before, the parameter θ corresponds to

$$\theta = -\,\frac{F''}{(F')^2}\,. \tag{1.47}$$

The translog approximation to a utility function characterized by unitary elasticities of substitution among all commodities satisfies the restriction

$$\sigma + \theta = \rho = 0\,. \tag{1.48}$$

Under this restriction the expenditures shares are constant

$$\frac{p_j X_j}{M} = \frac{\alpha_j + \theta\alpha_j \sum \alpha_i \ln X_i}{-1 - \theta \sum \alpha_i \ln X_i} = -\alpha_j . \tag{1.49}$$

The value of the parameter θ is arbitrary so that we can let σ and θ be equal to zero. The translog approximation to a utility function with unitary elasticities of substitution has the same empirical implications as a linear logarithmic utility function, which is explicitly additive and homogeneous.

1.3.6 Duality

In implementing an econometric model of demand based on the indirect translog utility function the first step as before is to add a stochastic specification to the theoretical model based on equations for the budget shares $p_j X_j / M$ $(j = 1, 2, \ldots, m)$. Only $m - 1$ equations are required for a complete model. If equations for the budget shares are generated from the indirect translog utility function, the parameters satisfy equality and symmetry restrictions that are strictly analogous to the corresponding restrictions for the direct translog utility function.

Additivity and homotheticity restrictions for the indirect translog utility function are analogous to the corresponding restrictions for the direct translog function. The direct utility function is homothetic if and only if the indirect utility function is homothetic.[11] In general, an additive direct utility function does not correspond to an additive indirect utility function.[12] However, if the direct utility function is additive and homothetic, the indirect utility function is additive and homothetic. Direct and indirect utility functions corresponding to the same preferences are additive only if the direct utility function is homothetic[13] or the direct utility function is linear logarithmic in all but one of the commodities.[14] In this relationship the roles of direct and indirect utility functions can be interchanged.

A direct utility function is *self-dual* if the corresponding indirect utility function has the same form.[15] The only direct translog utility function which is self-dual is the linear logarithmic utility function. Linear logarithmic utility functions are the only additive and homothetic direct or indirect translog utility functions. Translog direct and indirect utility functions represent the same preferences if and only if they are self-dual; that is, if and only if they are linear logarithmic. Unless this stringent condition is met, the direct and indirect translog approximations to a given pair of direct and indirect utility functions represent different preferences.

1.4 Empirical Results

1.4.1 Summary of Tests

We have developed statistical tests of the theory of demand that do not employ the assumptions of additivity and homotheticity for individual commodities or for commodity groups. At this point we outline restrictions on equations for the budget shares corresponding to direct and indirect translog utility functions. First, we present restrictions derived from the theory of demand; that is, from the basic hypothesis of utility maximization. Second, we present restrictions derived from hypotheses about functional form such as additivity and homotheticity.

Our empirical tests are based on data for three commodity groups—services of consumers' durables, nondurable goods, and other services—so that we specialize our presentation of statistical tests of the theory of demand to the three-commodity case, $m = 3$. A complete econometric model for either direct or indirect translog utility functions is provided by any pair of equations for the budget shares. We consider the system of two equations

$$\frac{p_1 X_1}{M} = \frac{\alpha_1 + \beta_{11} \ln X_1 + \beta_{12} \ln X_2 + \beta_{13} \ln X_3}{-1 + \beta_{M1} \ln X_1 + \beta_{M2} \ln X_2 + \beta_{M3} \ln X_3} \tag{1.50}$$

$$\frac{p_2 X_2}{M} = \frac{\alpha_2 + \beta_{21} \ln X_1 + \beta_{22} \ln X_2 + \beta_{23} \ln X_3}{-1 + \beta_{M1} \ln X_1 + \beta_{M2} \ln X_2 + \beta_{M3} \ln X_3} \tag{1.51}$$

corresponding to the direct translog utility function and the system of equations,

$$\frac{p_1 X_1}{M} = \frac{\alpha_1 + \beta_{11} \ln \frac{p_1}{M} + \beta_{12} \ln \frac{p_2}{M} + \beta_{13} \ln \frac{p_3}{M}}{-1 + \beta_{M1} \ln \frac{p_1}{M} + \beta_{M2} \ln \frac{p_2}{M} + \beta_{M3} \ln \frac{p_3}{M}} \tag{1.52}$$

$$\frac{p_2 X_2}{M} = \frac{\alpha_2 + \beta_{21} \ln \frac{p_1}{M} + \beta_{22} \ln \frac{p_2}{M} + \beta_{23} \ln \frac{p_3}{M}}{-1 + \beta_{M1} \ln \frac{p_1}{M} + \beta_{M2} \ln \frac{p_2}{M} + \beta_{M3} \ln \frac{p_3}{M}} \tag{1.53}$$

corresponding to the indirect translog utility function. Restrictions for the two systems are perfectly analogous so that the following outline may be applied to either system. We emphasize the fact that the two systems represent the same preferences if and only if

$$\beta_{ij} = 0, \qquad (i, j = 1, 2). \tag{1.54}$$

1. *Equality Restrictions.* The parameters $\{\beta_{M1}, \beta_{M2}, \beta_{M3}\}$ occur in both equations and must take the same values. There are three equality restrictions.

2. *Symmetry Restrictions.* One restriction of this type is explicit in the two equations we estimate directly, namely,

$$\beta_{12} = \beta_{21}. \tag{1.55}$$

In addition, we estimate the parameters β_{31} and β_{32} from the equations

$$\beta_{31} = \beta_{M1} - \beta_{11} - \beta_{21} \tag{1.56}$$

$$\beta_{32} = \beta_{M2} - \beta_{12} - \beta_{22} \tag{1.57}$$

so that the two additional symmetry restrictions are implicity in the two equations we estimate. We write these restrictions in the form

$$\beta_{13} = \beta_{M1} - \beta_{11} - \beta_{21} \tag{1.58}$$

$$\beta_{23} = \beta_{M2} - \beta_{12} - \beta_{22}. \tag{1.59}$$

There are three symmetry restrictions altogether.

We can identify tests of the six equality and symmetry restrictions with tests of the theory of demand. We next consider tests of hypotheses about functional form.

3. *Additivity Restrictions.* Given the equality and symmetry restrictions, the additivity restrictions take the form

$$\beta_{12} = \theta \alpha_1 \alpha_2 \tag{1.60}$$

$$\beta_{13} = \theta\alpha_1(-1 - \alpha_1 - \alpha_2) \tag{1.61}$$

$$\beta_{23} = \theta\alpha_2(-1 - \alpha_1 - \alpha_2)\,. \tag{1.62}$$

We introduce the additional parameter θ, so that there are two independent restrictions of this type.

4. *Homotheticity Restrictions.* Given the equality and symmetry restrictions, the homotheticity restrictions take the form

$$\beta_{M1} = \sigma\alpha_1 \tag{1.63}$$

$$\beta_{M2} = \sigma\alpha_2 \tag{1.64}$$

$$\beta_{M3} = \sigma(-1 - \alpha_1 - \alpha_2)\,. \tag{1.65}$$

We introduce the additional parameter σ, so that the are two independent restrictions of this type.

5. *Explicity Additivity Restrictions.* Given the equality, symmetry, and additivity restrictions, a translog utility function is explicitly additive under the further restriction

$$\theta = 0\,. \tag{1.66}$$

6. *Homogeneity Restrictions.* Given the equality, symmetry, and homotheticity restrictions, the homogeneity restriction takes the form

$$\sigma = 0\,. \tag{1.67}$$

7. *Linear Logarithmic Utility Restrictions.* Given the equality, symmetry, additivity, and homotheticity restrictions, the translog utility function reduces to linear logarithmic form under the additional restrictions

$$\sigma = \theta = 0\,. \tag{1.68}$$

Tests of hypotheses about the form of the utility function can be carried out in a number of different sequences. We propose to test additivity and homotheticity in parallel. Each of these hypotheses consists of two independent restrictions. Our test procedure is presented in diagrammatic form in Figure 1.1. We also present alternative test procedures. For example, we could first test additivity and then test

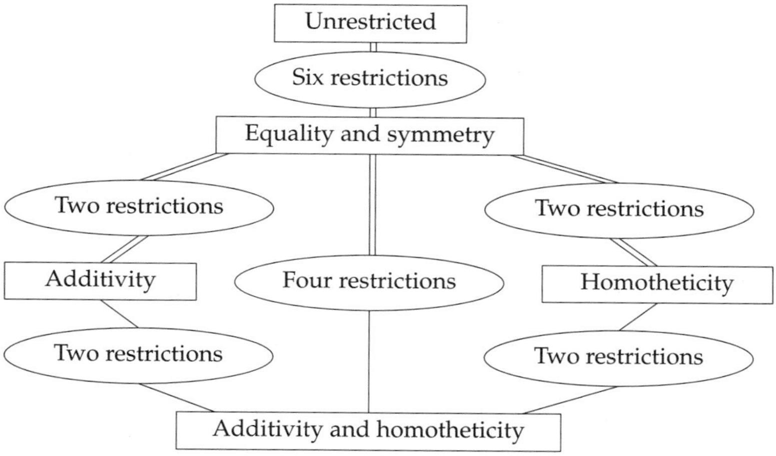

Figure 1.1
Tests of Additivity and Homotheticity.

homotheticity only if additivity is accepted. Our test procedure is indicated with double lines while possible alternative procedures are indicated with single lines.

The next step in our test procedure depends on the outcome of the tests of additivity and homotheticity. If we accept both additivity and homotheticity restrictions, we continue by testing explicit additivity and homogeneity in parallel. If we accept both hypotheses, we conclude that utility is linear logarithmic. A second possibility is that we accept additivity but reject homotheticity. In this case we continue by testing explicit additivity. The third possibility is that we accept homotheticity but reject additivity; we continue by testing homogeneity. If we reject both additivity and homogeneity, we terminate the sequence of tests. These tests are presented diagrammatically in Figure 1.2.

1.4.2 Estimation

Our empirical results are based on time-series data for U.S. personal consumption expenditures for 1929–1972. The data include prices and quantities of the services of consumers' durables, nondurable goods, and other services. We have fitted the equations for budget shares

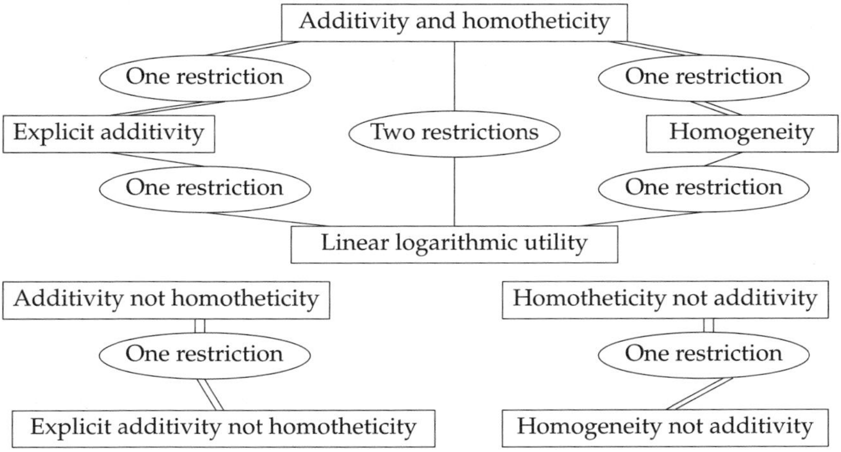

Figure 1.2
Tests Conditional on Additivity or Homotheticity.

generated by direct translog and indirect translog utility functions, employing the stochastic specification outlined above. Under this specification only two equations are required for a complete econometric model of demand. We have fitted equations for the services of consumers' durables (durables) and for nondurable goods (nondurables). There are forty-four observations for each behavioral equation, so that the number of degrees of freedom available for statistical tests of the theory of demand is eighty-eight for either direct or indirect specification.

For both direct and indirect specifications the maintained hypothesis consists of the unrestricted form of the two behavioral equations for the budget shares. We estimate the behavioral equations for durables and nondurables by the method of maximum likelihood and derive estimates of the parameters of the behavioral equation for services, using the budget constraint.[16] The maximum likelihood estimates of the parameters of all three behavioral equations are invariant with respect to the choice of the two equations to be estimated directly.

The unrestricted behavioral equations, normalized so that the parameter α_M is minus unity in each equation, involve fourteen unknown parameters or seven unknown parameters for each equation. Unrestricted estimates of these parameters for the direct translog utility function are presented in the first column of table 1.1. The first hypothesis to be tested is that the theory of demand is valid; to test this hypothesis we impose the six equality and symmetry restrictions. Restricted estimates of the fourteen unknown parameters are presented in the second column of table 1.1. Unrestricted and restricted estimates of the fourteen unknown parameters for the indirect translog utility function are presented in the first and second columns of table 1.2.

Given the validity of the theory of demand, the remaining hypotheses to be tested are restrictions on the functional form. First, we test the hypothesis that the direct utility function is additive; this hypothesis requires that we impose two additional restrictions. The corresponding restricted estimates of the unknown parameters for the direct translog utility function are given in the third column of table 1.1. Second, we test the hypothesis that the direct utility function is homothetic without imposing the additivity restrictions; this hypothesis requires two restrictions in addition to the equality and symmetry restrictions. The restricted estimates of the unknown parameters for the direct translog utility function are given in the fourth column of table 1.1. Finally, we impose both additivity and homotheticity restrictions, obtaining the restricted estimates presented in the fifth column of table 1.1. The corresponding restricted estimates for the direct translog utility function are given in the third, fourth, and fifth columns of table 1.2.

The next stage of our test procedure is contingent on the outcome of our tests of additivity and homotheticity. If we accept additivity, but not homotheticity, we test explicit additivity by imposing one further restriction. If we accept homotheticity, but not additivity, we test homogeneity by imposing one further restriction. The restricted estimates under these restrictions are given in the sixth and seventh columns of table 1.1. The corresponding estimates for the indirect translog utility function are given in the sixth and seventh columns of table 1.2.

If we accept both additivity and homotheticity hypotheses, we test the hypothesis that the direct utility function is explicitly additive by imposing one further restriction. Similarly, we test homogeneity by imposing one further restriction. Finally, we impose both restrictions under the hypothesis that utility is linear logarithmic. The restricted estimates under each of these sets of restrictions are given in the

Table 1.1
Estimates of the parameters of the direct translog utility function

Parameters	Unrestricted estimates	Equality and symmetry	Additivity	Homo- theticity	Additivity and homo- theticity	Explicit additivity, not homo- theticity	Homo- geneity not additivity	Explicit additivity and homo- theticity	Additivity and homo- geneity	Linear logarithmic utility
					Durables					
α_1	−0.145	−0.138	−0.144	−0.139	−0.146	−0.147	−0.140	−0.147	−0.147	−0.127
	(0.00302)	(0.00262)	(0.00357)	(0.00257)	(0.00328)	(0.00279)	(0.00220)	(0.00265)	(0.00280)	(0.00378)
β_{11}	0.0490	−0.0216	−0.137	−0.268	−0.123	−0.102	−0.317	−0.100	−0.121	—
	(0.0888)	(0.0129)	(0.00971)	(0.0140)	(0.00778)	(0.00694)	(0.0122)	(0.00637)		
β_{12}	0.500	0.139	0.142	0.170	0.0983	—	0.147	—	0.0671	—
	(0.194)	(0.0277)	(0.0227)	(0.0293)	(0.0219)		(0.0178)		(0.00386)	
β_{13}	−0.555	−0.0737	0.115	−0.139	0.0790	—	0.170	—	0.0543	—
	(0.206)									
β_{M1}	0.659	0.0440	0.120	0.0407	0.542	−0.102	—	−0.100	—	—
	(0.864)	(0.0356)		(0.0372)						
β_{M2}	3.53	0.165	0.213	0.136	0.176	−0.339	—	−0.323	—	—
	(1.76)	(0.113)								
β_{M3}	−3.94	0.265	0.209	−0.116	0.141	−0.275	—	−0.261	—	—
	(1.96)	(0.107)	(0.104)			(0.0318)				

Table 1.1 (continued)

Parameters	Unrestricted estimates	Equality and symmetry	Additivity	Homo-theticity	Additivity and homo-theticity	Explicit additivity, not homo-theticity	Homo-geneity not additivity	Explicit additivity and homo-theticity	Additivity and homo-geneity	Linear logarithmic utility
					Nondurables					
α_1	−0.467	−0.468	−0.472	−0.464	−0.473	−0.471	−0.461	−0.472	−0.471	−0.495
	(0.00420)	(0.00353)	(0.00345)	(0.00402)	(0.00385)	(0.00487)	(0.00328)	(0.00440)	(0.00336)	(0.00792)
β_{21}	0.272	0.139	0.142	0.170	0.0983	—	0.147	—	0.0671	—
	(0.299)	(0.0277)	(0.0227)	(0.0293)	(0.0219)		(0.0178)		(0.00386)	
β_{22}	−0.536	−0.334	−0.306	−0.168	−0.179	−0.339	−0.216	−0.323	−0.241	—
	(0.774)	(0.0563)	(0.0571)	(0.0619)		(0.0448)	(0.0326)			
β_{23}	0.259	0.361	0.377	0.133	0.256	—	0.0693	—	0.174	—
	(0.866)									
β_{M1}	0.282	0.0440	0.120	0.0407	0.0542	−0.102	—	−0.100	—	—
	(0.555)	(0.0356)		(0.0372)						
β_{M2}	−0.271	0.165	0.213	0.136	0.176	−0.339	—	−0.323	—	—
	(1.55)	(0.113)								
β_{M3}	0.105	0.265	0.209	0.116	0.141	−0.275	—	−0.261	—	—
	(1.69)	(0.107)	(0.104)			(0.0318)				

Table 1.2
Estimates of the parameters of the indirect translog utility function

Parameters	Unrestricted estimates	Equality and symmetry	Additivity	Homotheticity	Additivity and homotheticity	Explicit additivity, not homotheticity	Homogeneity not additivity	Explicit additivity and homotheticity	Additivity and homogeneity	Linear logarithmic utility
					Durables					
α_1	−0.141	−0.125	−0.128	−0.119	−0.119	−0.127	−0.120	−0.120	−0.120	−0.127
	(0.00215)	(0.00300)	(0.00279)	(0.00390)	(0.00370)	(0.00228)	(0.00392)	(0.00364)	(0.00370)	(0.00378)
β_{11}	−0.115	−0.0970	−0.0595	−0.131	−0.0930	−0.0662	−0.106	−0.105	−0.0796	—
	(0.0188)	(0.0188)	(0.00972)	(0.0273)	(0.00823)	(0.00684)	(0.0246)	(0.00618)		
β_{12}	0.695	0.0816	0.0188	0.100	0.0282	—	0.113	—	0.0454	—
	(0.0447)	(0.0300)	(0.0153)	(0.0403)	(0.0131)		(0.0379)		(0.00238)	
β_{13}	−0.473	−0.0174	0.0144	−0.334	0.0212	—	−0.00754	—	0.0342	—
	(0.0527)									
β_{M1}	−0.801	−0.0324	−0.0262	−0.0644	−0.0434	−0.0662	—	−0.105	—	—
	(0.172)	(0.0379)		(0.0216)						
β_{M2}	4.52	−0.489	−0.491	−0.273	−0.183	−0.631	—	−0.440	—	—
	(0.419)	(0.134)								
β_{M3}	−3.50	−0.280	−0.274	−0.202	−0.137	−0.393	—	−0.330	—	—
	(0.464)	(0.114)	(0.107)			(0.213)				

Table 1.2 (continued)

Parameters	Unrestricted estimates	Equality and symmetry	Additivity	Homo-theticity	Additivity and homo-theticity	Explicit additivity, not homo-theticity	Homo-geneity not additivity	Explicit additivity and homo-theticity	Additivity and homo-geneity	Linear logarithmic utility
					Nondurables					
α_1	−0.472	−0.499	−0.494	−0.506	−0.503	−0.497	−0.504	−0.503	−0.502	−0.495
	(0.00472)	(0.00533)	(0.00479)	(0.0576)	(0.00597)	(0.00383)	(0.00612)	(0.00576)	(0.00612)	(0.00792)
β_{21}	−0.872	0.0816	0.0188	0.100	0.282	—	0.113	—	0.454	—
	(0.120)	(0.0300)	(0.0153)	(0.0403)	(0.0131)		(0.0379)		(0.00238)	
β_{22}	1.11	−0.668	−0.565	−0.539	−0.300	−0.631	−0.348	−0.440	−0.189	—
	(0.247)	(0.0881)	(0.0715)	(0.0810)		(0.0307)	(0.0610)			
β_{23}	−0.227	0.0972	0.0560	0.166	0.0891	—	0.234	—	0.143	—
	(0.164)									
β_{M1}	−1.63	−0.0324	−0.0262	−0.0644	−0.0434	−0.0662	—	−0.0105	—	—
	(0.212)	(0.0379)		(0.0216)						
β_{M2}	2.98	−0.489	−0.491	−0.273	−0.183	−0.631	—	−0.440	—	—
	(0.464)	(0.134)								
β_{M3}	−1.11	−0.280	−0.274	−0.202	−0.137	−0.393	—	−0.330	—	—
	(0.334)	(0.114)	(0.107)			(0.213)				

eighth through tenth columns of table 1.1. The corresponding restricted estimates for the indirect translog utility function are given in the eighth through tenth columns of table 1.2. The direct and indirect translog utility functions are self-dual if they are linear logarithmic, so that restricted estimates for the two alternative econometric models given in the final columns of the two tables are identical.

1.4.3 Test Statistics

To test the validity of restrictions implied by the theory of demand and restrictions on the form of the utility functions, we employ test statistics based on the likelihood ratio λ, where

$$\lambda = \frac{\max\limits_{\omega} \mathcal{L}}{\max\limits_{\Omega} \mathcal{L}}. \tag{1.69}$$

The likelihood ratio is the ratio of the maximum value of the likelihood function $\mathcal{L}$ for the econometric model of demand ω subject to restriction to the maximum value of the likelihood function for the model Ω without restriction. For normally distributed disturbances the likelihood ratio is equal to the ratio of the determinant of the restricted estimator of the variance-covariance matrix of the disturbances to the determinant of the unrestricted estimator, each raised to the power $-(n/2)$.

Our test statistic for each set of restrictions is based on minus twice the logarithm of the likelihood ratio, or

$$-2 \ln \lambda = n(\ln |\hat{\Sigma}_{\omega}| - \ln |\hat{\Sigma}_{\Omega}|) \tag{1.70}$$

where $\hat{\Sigma}_{\omega}$ is the restricted estimator of the variance-covariance matrix and $\hat{\Sigma}_{\Omega}$ is the unrestricted estimator. Under the null hypothesis this test statistic is distributed, asymptotically, as chi-square with number of degrees of freedom equal to the number of restrictions to be tested.

To control the overall level of significance for each series of tests, direct and indirect, we set the level of significance for each series at 0.05. We allocate the overall level of significance among the various stages in each series. We first assign a level of significance of 0.01 to the test of equality and symmetry restrictions implied by the theory of demand. We then assign a level of significance of 0.04 to tests of restrictions on functional form. These two sets of tests are "nested";

under the null hypothesis the sum of levels of significance provides a close approximation to the level of significance for both sets of tests simultaneously.

We test additivity and homotheticity in parallel, proceeding conditionally on the validity of the theory of demand. These tests are not nested so that the sum of levels of significance for each of the two hypotheses is an upper bound for the level of significance of tests of the two hypotheses considered simultaneously. There are four possible outcomes of our parallel tests of additivity and homotheticity: Reject both, accept both, accept only additivity, and accept only homotheticity. If we reject both hypotheses, our test procedure terminates. If we accept either or both of these hypotheses, we proceed to test explicit additivity or homogeneity, or both.

If we accept both additivity and homotheticity, we test explicit additivity and homogeneity in parallel, conditional on the validity of additivity and homotheticity. Again, the tests are not nested, so that the sum of levels of significance for the two tests provides an upper bound for the tests considered simultaneously. If we accept only additivity, we proceed to test explicit additivity, conditional on additivity. Similarly, if we accept only homotheticity, we proceed to test homogeneity.

Since our three alternative procedures for testing explicit additivity and homogeneity are mutually exclusive, we carry out tests of these hypotheses one time at most. We assign levels of significance to the four hypotheses—additivity, explicit additivity, homotheticity, and homogeneity—with the assurance that the sum of levels of significance provides an upper bound for the level of significance for all four tests. We assign a level of significance of 0.01 to each of the four hypotheses. With the aid of critical values for our test statistics given in table 1.3 the reader can evaluate the results of our tests for alternative allocations of the overall levels of significance among stages of the test procedure.

Test statistics for both direct and indirect tests of the theory of demand and of restrictions on functional form are presented in tables 1.4 and 1.5. At a level of significance of 0.01 we reject the hypothesis that restrictions implied by the theory of demand are valid for either direct or indirect series of tests. With this conclusion we can terminate the test sequence, since these results invalidate the theory of demand.

One interesting alternative to our test procedure is to maintain the theory of demand and to test the validity of restrictions on the form of

Table 1.3
Critical values of χ^2/degrees of freedom

Degrees of freedom	Level of significance .10	.05	.025	.01	.005
1	2.71	3.84	5.02	6.63	7.88
2	2.30	3.00	3.69	4.61	5.30
4	1.94	2.37	2.79	3.32	3.72
6	1.77	2.10	2.41	2.80	3.09

the utility functions. Proceeding conditionally on the validity of the theory of demand, we could test the validity of restrictions on the form of the utility function. For the direct series of tests we would reject the restrictions implied by additivity and homotheticity. This conclusion would hold for our preferred procedure of testing these hypotheses in parallel, for a test of either hypothesis conditional on the validity of the other, or for a joint test of the two hypotheses.

For the indirect series of tests we would reject the restrictions implied by homotheticity, but we would accept the restrictions implied by additivity at a level of significance of 0.01. For the direct series of tests we could terminate the test sequence conditional on the theory of demand at this point. For the indirect series of tests, we could test the validity of explicit additivity, given additivity but not homotheticity. We would accept the hypothesis of explicit additivity,

Table 1.4
Test statistics for direct and indirect tests of the theory of demand and tests of additivity and homotheticity

Hypothesis	Degrees of freedom	Direct	Indirect
Theory of demand			
Equality and symmetry	6	5.64	10.25
Given the theory of demand			
Additivity	2	33.63	2.95
Homotheticity	2	13.71	22.68
Additivity and homotheticity	4	19.02	16.24
Additivity given homotheticity	2	24.33	9.81
Homotheticity given additivity	2	4.42	29.54

Table 1.5
Test statistics for direct and indirect tests of restrictions on functional form, given additivity or homotheticity or both

Hypothesis	Degrees of freedom	Direct	Indirect
Given additivity			
Explicit additivity	1	19.97	1.59
Given homotheticity			
Homogeneity	1	1.47	4.73
Given additivity and homotheticity			
Explicit additivity	1	11.25	4.02
Homogeneity	1	1.74	1.16
Linear logarithmic utility	2	29.67	48.31
Given explicit additivity and homotheticity			
Linear logarithmic utility	1	48.09	92.61
Given additivity and homogeneity			
Linear logarithmic utility	1	57.60	95.46

given additivity at a level of significance of 0.01, conditional on the validity of the theory of demand.

In previous econometric studies of demand, the theory of demand has been maintained together with the assumption of additivity. A second alternative to our test procedure is to maintain both the theory of demand and the restrictions implied by additivity. We can test homotheticity; for either direct or indirect series of tests we reject this hypothesis. Given additivity but not homotheticity, we would reject explicit additivity for the direct series of tests and accept explicit additivity for the indirect series of tests. Either of these sets of results would rule out linear logarithmic utility.

1.5 Summary and Conclusion

Our objective has been to test the theory of demand without imposing the assumptions of additivity and homotheticity as part of the maintained hypothesis. For either the direct or the indirect series of tests, we conclude that the theory of demand is inconsistent with the evidence. These results confirm the findings of Wold (in association with Lars Juréen) for the double logarithmic demand system and Barten for the Rotterdam demand system[17]. At the same time our results provide the basis for more specific conclusions.

If the theory of demand were valid, the double logarithmic form for the system of demand functions would imply that the utility function is linear logarithmic. Similarly, the validity of the theory of demand and the Rotterdam form of the system of demand functions would imply linear logarithmic utility. An equally valid interpretation of the results of Wold and Barten is that the theory of demand is valid, but that utility is not linear logarithmic. Our results rule out this alternative interpretation and make possible an unambiguous rejection of the theory of demand.

A possible alternative to our test procedure is to maintain the validity of the theory of demand. Proceeding conditionally on the validity of demand theory, we would reject the hypothesis of additivity for the direct series of tests. Additivity of the direct utility function is employed as a maintained hypothesis by Houthakker in the direct addilog demand system, by Stone in the linear expenditure system, and by Basmann, Johansen, and Sato in the demand system incorporating features of both.

Again, proceeding conditionally on the validity of the theory of demand, we would accept the hypothesis of additivity for the indirect series of tests. This hypothesis is maintained by Houthakker in the implementation of the indirect addilog demand system. Additivity of the direct and indirect utility functions is mutually consistent if and only if the direct utility function is homothetic, so that the acceptance of additivity of the indirect utility function and the rejection of homotheticity rule out acceptance of additivity for the direct utility function.

Notes

1. The class of additive and homothetic utility functions was first characterized by Bergson (1936).
2. See Schultz (1938), Stone (1954b), Wold (1953), and Basmann, Battalio, and Kagel (1973).
3. See Barten (1964a, 1967, 1969), McFadden (1964), and Theil (1965, 1967, 1971).
4. See Houthakker (1960) and Stone (1954a). The linear expenditure system was originally proposed by Klein and Rubin (1947–1948).
5. A recent survey of econometric studies of consumer demand is given by Brown and Deaton (1972).
6. The indirect utility function was introduced by Antonelli (1971), and independently by Hotelling (1932).
7. Indirect demand functions were introduced by Antonelli (1971). The duality between direct and indirect utility functions is discussed by Lau (1969a); the duality between

systems of direct and indirect demand functions is discussed by Wold (1953), Chipman (1971), and Hurwicz (1971).
8. See Houthakker (1960). This demand system was originally proposed by Leser (1941) and has also been employed by Somermeyer, Hillhorst, and Wit (1961).
9. See Christensen, Jorgenson, and Lau (1971, 1973).
10. This is the logarithmic form of René Roy's Identity (1943).
11. See, for instance, Samuelson (1965) and Lau (1969b).
12. See Lau (1969b).
13. See Houthakker (1960), Samuelson (1965), and Lau (1969b).
14. This is the special case introduced by Hicks (1969). See also Samuelson (1969).
15. See Samuelson (1965) and Houthakker (1965a). We may also mention the "self-dual addilog system" introduced by Houthakker (1965a). This system is not generated by additive utility functions except for special cases.
16. We employ the maximum likelihood estimator discussed, for example, by Malinvaud (1980, pp. 338–341). In the computations we use the Gauss-Newton method described by Malinvaud (1980, p. 343). For the direct series of tests we assume that the disturbances are independent of the quantities consumed. For the indirect series of tests we assume that the disturbances are independent of the ratios of prices to the value of total expenditure.
17. See Wold (1953, especially pp. 281–302); Barten (1969). A detailed review of tests of the theory of demand is given by Brown and Deaton (1972, pp. 1188–1195).

2 The Structure of Consumer Preferences

Dale W. Jorgenson and Lawrence J. Lau

2.1 Introduction

The purpose of this chapter is to present an econometric methodology for characterizing the structure of consumer preferences and changes in preferences over time.[1] For this purpose we introduce new representations of consumer preferences. Our approach is to represent the underlying utility function by functions that are quadratic in the logarithms of the quantities consumed and time. Similarly, we represent the underlying indirect utility function by functions that are quadratic in the logarithms of ratios of prices to total expenditure and time. These representations of consumer preferences do not require the assumptions of additivity, homotheticity, and stationarity of preferences implicit in the traditional approach to statistical demand analysis.

We refer to our representation of the utility function as the direct transcendental logarithmic utility function with time-varying preferences, or more simply, the *direct translog utility function.* The utility function is a transcendental function of the logarithms of the quantities consumed and of time.[2] Similarly, we refer to our representation of the indirect utility function as the indirect transcendental logarithmic utility function with time-varying preferences or, more simply, the *indirect translog utility function.* Direct and indirect translog utility functions without time-varying preferences were introduced by Christensen, Jorgenson, and Lau and used by them to test the theory of demand and to characterize substitution patterns among commodity groups.[3] Lau and Mitchell and Christensen and Manser have employed homothetic indirect translog utility functions to characterize substitution patterns.[4]

As an illustration of the traditional approach to demand analysis, we can consider the double logarithmic demand functions employed in the pioneering studies of consumer demand by Schultz, Stone, and Wold.[5] If the theory of demand is valid and demand functions are double logarithmic with time trends, the utility function is neutral linear logarithmic. A neutral linear logarithmic utility function is additive, homothetic, and stationary. Elasticities of substitution among all pairs of commodities are constant and equal to unity. All expenditure proportions are constant for all values of prices, total expenditure, and time. Similarly, the Rotterdam system of demand functions with time trends employed by Barten and Theil is consistent with utility maximization only if the utility function is neutral linear logarithmic.[6] We conclude that the double logarithmic and Rotterdam demand systems implicitly maintain the hypotheses of additivity, homotheticity, and stationarity.

Houthakker and Stone have developed alternative approaches to demand analysis that retain the assumption of additivity while dropping the assumption of homotheticity.[7] Stone has employed a linear expenditure system, based on a utility function that is linear in the logarithm of quantities consumed less a constant for each commodity, representing initial commitments of expenditure. Nonzero commitments permit expenditure proportions to vary with total expenditure. Houthakker has employed a direct addilog system, based on a utility function that is additive in functions that are homogenous in the quantity consumed for ech commodity. The degree of homogeneity may vary from commodity to commodity, again permitting expenditure proportions to vary with total expenditure. Parallelling the direct addilog demand system, Houthakker has also employed an indirect addilog system, based on an indirect utility function that is additive in the ratios of prices to total expenditure.

Basmann, Johansen, and Sato have combined the approaches of Houthakker and Stone, defining each of the homogeneous functions in the direct addilog utility function on the quantity consumed less a constant for each commodity.[8] The resulting utility function is additive but not homothetic. We conclude that the linear expenditure system, the direct and indirect addilog systems, and the combined systems introduced by Basmann, Johansen, and Sato maintain the hypotheses of direct or indirect additivity. By employing direct and indirect translog utility functions with time-varying preferences we can test additivity, homotheticity, and stationarity restrictions rather than maintaining these restrictions on preferences as part of our econometric model.

In the following section we introduce direct and indirect translog utility functions with time-varying preferences and the corresponding systems of indirect and direct demand functions. We consider restrictions on the demand functions implied by utility maximization. We impose these restrictions as part of our maintained hypothesis. In section 2.3 we consider demand systems associated with restrictions on the structure of consumer preferences and changes in preferences over time. We begin with groupwise separability and groupwise homotheticity of preferences. For each set of restrictions on preferences, we derive parametric restrictions on the corresponding system of demand functions. These parametric restrictions provide the basis for statistical test of alternative hypotheses about the structure of consumer preferences.

We consider two alternative sets of restrictions on the variation of consumer preferences over time. The first set corresponds to separability of goods and time; a commodity group is separable from time if the ratios of any pair of demand functions for all commodities within the group are independent of time. An alternative set of restrictions on changes in preferences is associated with commodity augmention; commodity augmentation by itself is not a testable hypothesis since any change in preferences over time can be regarded as commodity augmenting or commodity diminishing. We impose restrictions on the variation of preferences with time by imposing restrictions on rates of augmentation of commodities within a given group; in particular, we formulate tests of equality of rates of commodity augmentation within a group. Groupwise separability from time and groupwise equality of rates of commodity augmentation are not mutually exclusive; however, they coincide only under additional restrictions such as neutral linear logarithmic utility.

We present empirical results of tests of alternative sets of restrictions on consumer preferences and changes in preferences over time in section 2.4. Our tests are based on time series data for U.S. personal consumption expenditures of three commodity groups—durables, nondurables, and energy—for the period 1947–1971. Our concept of personal consumption expenditures differs from the corresponding concept in the U.S. national income and product accounts in the treatment of consumers' durables.[9] We treat expenditure on consumers' durables as part of gross private domestic investment rather than personal consumption expenditures. We add an imputed flow of services from consumers' durables to personal consumption expenditures, so that our concept of durables services is perfectly analogous to the national accounting concept of housing services.

2.2 Transcendental Logarithmic Utility Functions with Time-Varying Preferences

2.2.1 The Direct Translog Utility Function

A *direct utility function* U with time-varying preferences can be written in the form

$$-\ln U = F(X_1, X_2, X_3, t), \tag{2.2.1}$$

where X_i $(i = 1, 2, 3)$ is the quantity consumed of the ith commodity and t is time. At each time the consumer maximizes utility, subject to the budget constraint,

$$\sum p_i X_i = M, \tag{2.2.2}$$

where p_i $(i = 1, 2, 3)$ is the price of the ith commodity and M is the value of total expenditure.

Maximizing utility, subject to the budget constraint, we obtain the identity

$$\frac{\partial \ln U}{\partial \ln X_j} = \frac{p_j X_J}{M} \sum \frac{\partial \ln U}{\partial \ln X_i}, \qquad (j = 1, 2, 3). \tag{2.2.3}$$

This identity gives the ratios of prices to total expenditure as functions of the quantities consumed

$$\frac{P_j}{M} = \frac{\dfrac{\partial \ln U}{\partial \ln X_j}}{X_j \sum \dfrac{\partial \ln U}{\partial \ln X_i}}, \qquad (j = 1, 2, 3). \tag{2.2.4}$$

We refer to these functions as *indirect demand functions*.

Utility is nondecreasing in the quantities consumed, so that the negative of the logarithm of utility is nonincreasing in the logarithms of the quantities consumed. A necessary and sufficient condition for monotonicity of the negative of the logarithm of the utility function at a particular point is that the budget shares are nonnegative at that point. The utility function is quasiconcave, so that the negative of the logarithm of the utility function is quasiconvex. Monotonicity and quasiconvexity of the negative of the logarithm of the utility function are the basic assumptions of the theory of demand.

We approximate the negative of the logarithm of the utility function by a function quadratic in the logarithms of the quantities consumed and t

$$- \ln U = \alpha_0 + \sum \alpha_i \ln X_i + \alpha_t \cdot t + \frac{1}{2} \sum \sum \beta_{ij} \ln X_i \ln X_j + \sum \beta_{it} \ln X_i \cdot t + \frac{1}{2} \beta_{it} \cdot t^2 . \tag{2.2.5}$$

Using this form of the utility function we obtain

$$\alpha_j + \sum \beta_{ji} \ln X_i + \beta_{jt} \cdot t = \frac{p_j X_j}{M} \sum (\alpha_k + \sum \beta_{ki} \ln X_i + \beta_{kt} \cdot t) , \quad (j = 1, 2, 3) . \tag{2.2.6}$$

To simplify this notation we write

$$\alpha_M = \sum \alpha_k , \quad \beta_{Mi} = \sum \beta_{ki} , \quad \beta_{Mt} = \sum \beta_{kt} , \quad (i = 1, 2, 3) , \tag{2.2.7}$$

so that

$$\frac{p_j X_j}{M} = \frac{\alpha_j + \sum \beta_{ji} \ln X_i + \beta_{jt} \cdot t}{\alpha_M + \sum \beta_{Mi} \ln X_i + \beta_{Mt} \cdot t} , \quad (j = 1, 2, 3) . \tag{2.2.8}$$

We note that the parameters α_t and β_{tt} have no effect on the utility-maximizing quantities consumed. These two parameters cannot be identified from data on prices and quantities.

The budget constraints implies that

$$\sum \frac{p_i X_i}{M} = 1 , \tag{2.2.9}$$

so that, given the parameters of any two equations for the budget shares, $p_i X_j / M \ (j = 1, 2, 3)$, the parameters of the third equation can be determined from the definition α_M, β_{Mj} $(j = 1, 2, 3)$, and β_{Mt}.

Since the equations for the budget shares are homogeneous of degree zero in the parameters, normalization of the parameters is required for estimation. A convenient normalization for the direct translog utility function is

$$\alpha_M = \sum \alpha_i = -1 . \tag{2.2.10}$$

We estimate only two of the equations for the budget shares, subject to normalization of the parameter α_M appearing in each equation at minus unity. Unrestricted, there are eighteen unknown parameters to be estimated from the two equations. If the equations are generated by utility maximization, the parameters β_{Mj} $(j = 1, 2, 3)$ and β_{Mt} appearing in each equation must be the same. This results in a set of restrictions relating the four parameters appearing in each of the two equations, a total of four restrictions. We refer to these as *equality restrictions*.

The negative of the logarithm of the direct translog utility function is twice differentiable in the logarithms of the quantities consumed, so that the Hessian of this function is symmetric. This gives rise to a set of restrictions relating the parameters of the cross-partial derivatives

$$\beta_{ij} = \beta_{ji} , \qquad (i \neq j \, ; i, j = 1, 2, 3) . \tag{2.2.11}$$

There is one restriction of this type among the parameters of the two equations we estimate directly and two such restrictions among the parameters of the equation we estimate indirectly from the budget constraint. We refer to these as *symmetry restrictions*. The total number of symmetry restrictions is three.

If equations for the budget shares are generated by maximization of a direct translog utility function, the parameters satisfy equality and symmetry restrictions. There are seven such restrictions. Given the seven equality and symmetry restrictions, eleven unknown parameters remain to be estimated. Our approach to the analysis of consumer demand takes as assumptions the restrictions on expenditure allocation implied by utility maximization and the existence of the three commodity groups—durables, nondurables, and energy—as well-defined economic aggregates. Given these assumptions, we estimate the unknown parameters of our complete demand system simultaneously.

Given the hypothesis of consistency between our system of indirect demand functions and the maximization of utility and the grouping of commodities into three aggregates, we could proceed to impose further constraints on the allocation of personal consumption expenditures, such as constant price and income elasticities of demand or constant elasticities of substitution among commodity groups.[10] However, such an approach would frustrate our primary research objective of characterizing the pattern of consumer demand empirically. This approach would convert hypotheses about budget allocation and patterns of substitution into assumptions rather than hypotheses to be tested. Instead we propose to test all further restrictions on the structure of the direct utility function.

2.2.2 The Indirect Translog Utility Function

An *indirect utility function* V with time-varying preferences can be written in the form

$$\ln V = G\left(\frac{p_1}{M}, \frac{p_2}{M}, \frac{p_3}{M}, t\right), \tag{2.2.12}$$

where V is the maximum level of utility corresponding to the prices p_i $(i = 1, 2, 3)$ and the level of total expenditure M.

We can determine the budget share from the jth commodity from the identity[11]

$$\frac{\partial \ln V}{\partial \ln p_j/M} = \frac{p_j X_j}{M} \sum \frac{\partial \ln V}{\partial \ln p_i/M}, \qquad (j = 1, 2, 3). \tag{2.2.13}$$

This identity gives the quantities consumed as functions of the ratios of prices to total expenditures

$$X_j = \frac{\dfrac{\partial \ln V}{\partial \ln p_j/M}}{\dfrac{p_j}{M} \sum \dfrac{\partial \ln V}{\partial \ln p_i/M}}, \qquad (j = 1, 2, 3). \tag{2.2.14}$$

We refer to these functions as *direct demand functions*.

Utility is nonincreasing in the prices, so that the logarithm of utility is nonincreasing in the logarithms of the prices. A necessary and sufficient condition for monotonicity of the logarithm of the indirect utility function at a particular point is that the budget shares are nonnegative at that point. The indirect utility function is quasiconvex, so that the logarithm of this function is quasiconvex.

The system consisting of the negative of the logarithm of the direct utility function and the indirect demand functions is dual to the system consisting of the logarithm of the indirect utility function and the direct demand functions. One system can be obtained from the other by simply interchanging the quantities consumed X_i $(i = 1, 2, 3)$ with the ratios of prices to the total expenditure p_i/M $(i = 1, 2, 3)$. All the properties of one system carry over to the other system with the role of these two sets of variables interchanged.

We approximate the logarithm of the indirect utility function by a function quadratic in the logarithms of the ratios of prices to the value of total expenditure and t

$$\ln V = \alpha_0 + \sum \alpha_i \ln \frac{p_i}{M} + \alpha_t \cdot t + \frac{1}{2} \sum \sum \beta_{ij} \ln \frac{p_i}{M} \ln \frac{p_j}{M} + \sum \beta_{it} \ln \frac{p_i}{M} \cdot t + \frac{1}{2} \beta_{tt} \cdot t^2 . \tag{2.2.15}$$

Using this form of the indirect utility function we obtain

$$\alpha_j + \sum \beta_{ji} \ln \frac{p_i}{M} + \beta_{jt} \cdot t = \frac{p_j X_j}{M} \left(\sum \alpha_k + \sum \beta_{ki} \ln \frac{p_i}{M} + \beta_{kt} \cdot t \right), \quad (j = 1, 2, 3) . \tag{2.2.16}$$

As before, we simplify notation by writing

$$\alpha_M = \sum \alpha_k , \quad \beta_{Mi} = \sum \beta_{ki} , \quad \beta_{Mt} = \sum \beta_{kt} , \qquad (i = 1, 2, 3) , \tag{2.2.17}$$

so that

$$\frac{p_j X_j}{M} = \frac{\alpha_j + \sum \beta_{ji} \ln p_i/M + \beta_{jt} \cdot t}{\alpha_M + \sum \beta_{Mi} \ln p_i/M + \beta_{Mt} \cdot t} , \qquad (j = 1, 2, 3) . \tag{2.2.18}$$

The parameters α_t and β_{tt} cannot be identified.

The budget constraint implies that given the parameters of any two equations for the budget shares, the parameters of the third equation can be determined from the definitions of α_M, β_{Mj} $(j = 1, 2, 3)$, and β_{Mt}. As before, we normalize the parameters of the indirect translog utility function so that

$$\alpha_M = \sum \alpha_i = -1 \,. \tag{2.2.19}$$

As in the case of the direct translog utility function with time-varying preferences, we estimate only two of the equations for the budget shares, subject to normalization of the parameter α_M appearing in each equation at minus unity. We also maintain the assumptions of utility maximization and the existence of the three aggregates. The equality and symmetry restrictions resulting from these assumptions are strictly analogous to those for the direct translog utility function with time-varying preferences.

2.2.3 Stochastic Specification

The first step in implementing an econometric model of demand based on the direct translog utility function with time-varying preferences is to add a stochastic specification to the theoretical model based on equations for the budget shares $p_j X_j / M$ $(j = 1, 2, 3)$. Given the disturbances in any two equations, the disturbance in the remaining equation can be determined from the budget constraint. Only two equations are required for a complete econometric model of demand. We assume that the noncontemporaneous disturbances, whether from the same or different equations, have zero covariance. No additional restrictions are placed on the disturbances, other than the requirement that disturbances from the three equations must add up to zero. We also assume that the right-hand side variables of the equations for the budget shares are uncorrelated with the stochastic disturbances. This latter assumption facilitates the use of the method of maximum likelihood in estimation of the parameters.

In implementing an econometric model of demand based on the indirect utility function with time-varying preferences the first step, as before, is to add a stochastic specification to the theoretical model based on equations for the budget shares $p_j X_j / M$ $(j = 1, 2, 3)$. Only two equations are required for a complete model. The assumptions that we make here are strictly analogous to those for the direct translog utility function with time-varying preferences. We note, however, that the implications of the stochastic specification are different for the direct and indirect models and hence the results for the two models are not directly comparable.

To summarize: We have derived models for the allocation of personal consumption expenditures from direct and indirect translog utility functions with time-varying preferences. We take the hypothesis of utility maximization to be an assumption rather than a hypothesis to be tested. Utility maximization implies that the parameters of equations for the budget shares in each model satisfy seven equality and symmetry restrictions that enable us to reduce the number of unknown parameters from eighteen to eleven. These parameters are further constrained by certain inequalities that embody monotonicity and quasiconvexity restrictions on the negative of the logarithm of the direct utility function and the logarithm of the indirect utility function. We estimate the parameters of our models of consumption subject to the equality and symmetry restrictions; at a later stage we incorporate the monotonicity and quasiconvexity restrictions.[12]

2.3 Preference Structure

2.3.1 Approximation

The primary object of our research is to ascertain and characterize the structure of consumer preferences empirically, without maintaining restrictive assumptions on the specific form of the utility function other than monotonicity and quasiconvexity. We wish, first, to determine the effects of changes in total expenditures and changes in preferences over time on the allocation of the consumer budget among commodity groups and, second, to determine the effects of changes in relative prices on the allocation of the consumer budget, that is, to characterize the patterns of substitution among commodities.

In the remainder of this section, we develop tests of a series of possible restrictions on the underlying structure of consumer preferences. First, we consider groupwise separability of preferences in commodities and in time. Second, we consider overall homotheticity and groupwise homotheticity of preferences. Third, we consider groupwise linear logarithmic utility as a possible restriction on preferences. Finally, we consider groupwise equal rates of commodity augmentation as a possible restriction on changes in the structure of preferences over time.

The transcendental logarithmic utility function with time-varying preferences can be interpreted as a local second-order Taylor's series approximation of an arbitrary utility function with time-varying preferences that is differentiable at least up to the third order. In practical applications the latter condition is hardly any restriction as any utility function can be approximated arbitrarily closely by an infinitely differentiable function. Using this local approximation property, the translog utility function can be used to test specific hypotheses on the structure of the underlying utility function.

The parameters of the translog utility function can be identified with the coefficients in a Taylor's series expansion to the underlying utility function. They take the values of the first and second partial logarithmic derivatives of the negative of the logarithm of the underlying utility function at the point of expansion. Specific hypotheses on the structure of preferences imply restrictions on the Hessian of the negative of the logarithm of the utility function and can be tested by imposing these restrictions on the parameters of the translog utility function.

Restrictions on the structure of preferences do not necessarily imply the corresponding restrictions on the translog utility function itself. Properties of the underlying utility function and its translog approximation agree up to and including second-order derivatives at the point of approximation. We distinguish between situations where the translog utility function provides an approximation to an underlying utility function with a certain property and situations where the translog utility function also possesses that property. In the latter case, we say that the translog utility function possesses the property intrinsically.

2.3.2 Groupwise Separability

The first set of restrictions on consumer preferences that we propose to test are *groupwise separability* restrictions. A direct utility function U with time-varying preferences that is separable in X_1 and X_2 from X_3 can be written in the form

$$-\ln U = F(-\ln U^1(X_1, X_2, t), X_3, t), \qquad (2.3.1)$$

where the function $-\ln U^1$ depends only on X_1, X_2 and time and is nonincreasing and quasiconvex in X_1 and X_2. A necessary and sufficient condition for groupwise separability of the direct utility function in X_1 and X_2 from X_3 is that the ratio of the indirect demand functions for X_1 and X_2 is independent of the quantity of X_3. A direct utility function that is groupwise separable in X_1 and X_2 from time can be written in the form

$$-\ln U = F(-\ln U^1(X_1,\ X_2,\ X_3),\ X_3,\ t), \tag{2.3.2}$$

which is analogous to equation (2.3.1) with the roles of X_3 and t interchanged. A necessary and sufficient condition for groupwise separability of X_1 and X_2 from time is that the ratio of the indirect demand functions of X_1 and X_2 is independent of time. Groupwise separability in time is also referred to as *groupwise neutrality.*

Partially differentiating equation (2.3.1) first with respect to $\ln X_3$ and then with respect to $\ln X_1$ and in $\ln X_2$ separately, we obtain

$$\frac{\partial^2 - \ln U}{\partial \ln X_1 \partial \ln X_3} = \frac{\partial^2 F}{\partial - \ln U^1 \partial \ln X_3} \cdot \frac{\partial - \ln U^1}{\partial \ln X_1},$$

$$\frac{\partial^2 - \ln U}{\partial \ln X_2 \partial \ln X_3} = \frac{\partial^2 F}{\partial - \ln U^1 \partial \ln X_3} \cdot \frac{\partial - \ln U^1}{\partial \ln X_1}. \tag{2.3.3}$$

By observing that

$$\frac{\partial - \ln U}{\partial \ln X_1} = \frac{\partial F}{\partial - \ln U^1} \frac{\partial - \ln U^1}{\partial \ln X_1},$$

$$\frac{\partial - \ln U}{\partial \ln X_2} = \frac{\partial F}{\partial - \ln U^1} \frac{\partial - \ln U^1}{\partial \ln X_2}, \tag{2.3.4}$$

we can rewrite

$$\frac{\partial^2 - \ln U}{\partial \ln X_1 \partial \ln X_3} = \frac{\partial^2 F/(\partial - \ln U^1 \partial \ln X_3)}{\partial F/(\partial - \ln U^1)} \cdot \frac{\partial - \ln U}{\partial \ln X_1},$$

so that

$$\frac{\partial^2 - \ln U}{\partial \ln X_2 \partial \ln X_3} = \frac{\partial^2 F/(\partial - \ln U^1 \partial \ln X_3)}{\partial F/(\partial - \ln U^1)} \frac{\partial - \ln U}{\partial \ln X_2}. \tag{2.3.5}$$

Given groupwise separability, equation (2.3.5) must hold everywhere; in particular, they must hold at the point of approximation, in this case, $\ln X_i = 1\ (i = 1, 2, 3,),\ t = 0$, where we can identify the first and second partial derivatives with the parameters of the direct translog utility function with time-varying preferences

$$\frac{\partial^2 - \ln U}{\partial \ln X_1 \partial \ln X_3} = \beta_{13}\,, \qquad \frac{\partial^2 - \ln U}{\partial \ln X_2 \partial \ln X_3} = \beta_{23}\,,$$

$$\frac{\partial - \ln U}{\partial \ln X_1} = \alpha_1\,, \qquad \frac{\partial - \ln U}{\partial \ln X_2} = \alpha_2\,.$$

Thus, given groupwise separability of X_1 and X_2 from X_3, the parameters of the direct translog utility function must satisfy the restrictions

$$\beta_{13} = \rho_3 \alpha_1\,, \qquad \beta_{23} = \rho_3 \alpha_2\,, \tag{2.3.6}$$

where ρ_3 is a constant given by

$$\rho_3 = \frac{\partial^2 F/(\partial - \ln U^1 \partial \ln X_3)}{\partial F/(\partial - \ln U^1)}\,,$$

at the point of approximation.

Similarly, in a manner strictly analogous to the derivation of equation (2.3.6), it can be shown that given groupwise separability of X_1 and X_2 from time, the parameters of the direct translog utility function must satisfy the restrictions

$$\beta_{1t} = \rho_1 \alpha_1\,, \qquad \beta_{2t} = \rho_1 \alpha_2\,. \tag{2.3.7}$$

We note that there are no analogous restrictions on the direct translog parameters for groupwise separability of the type X_1 and time from X_2 because the parameter α_1 cannot be identified.

We distinguish among three commodity groups. Each pair of commodities, such as X_1 and X_2, can be separable from the remaining commodity, X_3 in this instance, and time. Corresponding to the three possible pairs of commodities, there are six possible sets of groupwise separability restrictions analogous to equation (2.3.6) or equation (2.3.7). Each set of two restrictions involves the introduction of one new parameters $-\rho_3$ and ρ_t in the examples given above. Under each set of such restrictions, maintaining the symmetry and equality restrictions, ten unknown parameters remain to be estimated.

The translog approximation to a groupwise separable utility function is not necessarily groupwise separable. For a direct translog utility function to be groupwise separable in X_1 and X_2 from X_3, the ratio of the indirect demand functions generated by the direct translog utility function must be independent of X_3. We refer to a direct translog utility function as *intrinsically groupwise separable* if it is groupwise separable. Two alternative sets of restrictions on the parameters of the direct translog utility function are jointly necessary and sufficient for intrinsic groupwise separability of the direct translog utility function. The first set consists of the restrictions given in equation (2.3.6) and the additional restriction

$$\rho_3 = 0 . \tag{2.3.8}$$

This restriction implies that the cross partial derivatives of the direct translog utility function with respect to X_1 and X_3 and X_2 and X_3, respectively, are identically zero at the point of approximation. Thus the indirect demands of X_1 and X_2 do not depend on X_3. We refer to this set of restrictions as *explicit groupwise separability* restrictions.

A second set of restrictions that implies intrinsic groupwise separability of the direct translog utility function is that ρ_3 is different from zero, but that the ratio of the budget shares of X_1 and X_2 is constant for all prices, total expenditure and time. This means that the parameters of the direct translog utility function must satisfy the restrictions

$$\alpha_1\beta_{12} = \alpha_2\beta_{11} , \quad \alpha_1\beta_{22} = \alpha_2\beta_{12} , \quad \alpha_1\beta_{23} = \alpha_2\beta_{13} , \quad \alpha_1\beta_{2t} = \alpha_2\beta_{1t} ,$$

that is, the second-order translog parameters corresponding to the first and second commodities must be in the same proportion as the first-order translog parameters. If the ratio of the optimal budget shares of X_1 and X_2 is constant, the direct utility function takes the form

$$-\ln U = F(\delta_1 \ln X_1 + \delta_2 \ln X_2 , X_3 , t) ,$$

where δ_1 and δ_2 are constants. This utility function is both *groupwise linear logarithmic* in X_1 and X_2 and *groupwise separable* in X_1 and X_2 from time. We say that such a utility function is *groupwise neutral linear logarithmic*. This condition is much more restrictive than groupwise separability or explicit groupwise separability; we will discuss it in more detail in section 2.3.4 below.

Similarly, two alternative sets of restrictions on the parameters of the direct translog utility function are jointly necessary and sufficient for the intrinsic groupwise separability of X_1 and X_2 from time. The first set consists of the restrictions given in equation (2.3.7) above and the additional restriction

$$\rho_t = 0 , \tag{2.3.10}$$

that is, the direct translog utility function is *explicitly groupwise separable* in X_1 and X_2 from time. A second set of restrictions that also implies *intrinsic groupwise separability* of X_1 and X_2 from time are restrictions of groupwise neutral linear logarithmic utility.

We can show that restrictions analogous to equations (2.3.8) and (2.3.10) must hold for any one of the six possible types of explicit groupwise separability, given groupwise separability. Under each set of explicit groupwise separability restrictions, nine unknown parameters remain to be estimated.

A direct utility function with time-varying preferences is *additive* in X_1, X_2 and X_3 if it can be written in the form

$$-\ln U = F(-(\ln U^1(X_1\,, t) + \ln U^2(X_2\,, t) + \ln U^3(X_3\,, t))\,, t)\,. \tag{2.3.11}$$

A necessary and sufficient condition for additivity in commodities is that the direct utility function is groupwise separable in any pair of commodities from the remaining commodity. In particular, since there are only three commodities, groupwise separability of any two pairs of commodities, from the third is sufficient for additivity. A direct translog utility function with time-varying preferences is *explicitly additive* if it can be written in the form

$$-\ln U = -\ln U^1(X_1\,, t) - \ln U^2(X_2\,, t) - \ln U^3(X_3\,, t)\,, \tag{2.3.12}$$

where each function $-\ln U^i (i = 1, 2, 3)$ is nonincreasing and convex. The translog approximation to an explicitly additive utility function is necessarily explicitly additive. A necessary and sufficient condition for explicit additivity in commodities is that the direct translog utility function is explicitly groupwise separable in any pair of commodities from the remaining commodity. Since there are only three commodities, explicit groupwise separability for any two pairs of commodities from a third commodity is sufficient for explicit additivity.

A direct utility function with time-varying preferences is *neutral* if it can be written in the form

$$-\ln U = F(-\ln U^1(X_1\,, X_2\,, X_3)\,, t)\,,$$

where $-\ln U^1$ is independent of time. A necessary and sufficient condition for neutrality is that the direct utility function is groupwise separable in any pair of commodities from time. In particular, since there are only three commodities, groupwise separability of any two pairs of commodities from time is sufficient for neutrality. A direct utility function with time-varying preferences is *explicitly neutral* if it can be written in the form

$$-\ln U = -\ln U^1(X_1, X_2, X_3) + F(t). \tag{2.3.13}$$

The translog approximation to an explicitly neutral utility function is necessarily explicitly neutral. A necessary and sufficient condition for explicit neutrality is that the direct translog utility function is explicitly groupwise separable in any pair of commodities from time. In particular, since there are only three commodities, explicit groupwise separability of any two pairs of commodities from time is sufficient for explicit neutrality.

2.3.3 Groupwise Homotheticity and Homogeneity

The second set of functional restrictions on consumer preferences that we propose to test are *homotheticity* restrictions. First, we consider overall homotheticity of preferences. A direct utility function with time-varying preferences that is *homothetic* can be written in the form

$$-\ln U = F(\ln H(X_1, X_2, X_3, t), t), \tag{2.3.14}$$

where H is homogeneous of degree one in the quantities X_1, X_2, and X_3. Under homotheticity, the optimal budget shares for all three commodities depend only on prices and time and are independent of total expenditure. An equivalent characterization of homotheticity is that the ratios of indirect demand functions are all homogeneous of degree zero in X_1, X_2 and X_3.

Partially differentiating equation (2.3.14) with respect to $\ln X_j$ $(j = 1, 2, 3)$, we obtain

$$\frac{\partial - \ln U}{\partial \ln X_j} = \frac{\partial F}{\partial \ln H} \frac{\partial \ln H}{\partial \ln X_j}, \qquad (j = 1, 2, 3). \tag{2.3.15}$$

Second, differentiating again with respect to $\ln X_k$ $(k = 1, 2, 3)$, we obtain

$$\frac{\partial^2 - \ln U}{\partial \ln X_k \partial \ln X_j} = \frac{\partial^2 F}{\partial \ln H} \frac{\partial \ln H}{\partial \ln X_k} \cdot \frac{\partial \ln H}{\partial \ln X_j}$$

$$+\frac{\partial F}{\partial \ln H}\frac{\partial^2 \ln H}{\partial \ln X_k \partial \ln X_j}, \qquad (j,k=1,2,3). \qquad (2.3.16)$$

Finally, summing over k and using homogeneity of degree one of the function H, we can write

$$\sum \frac{\partial^2 - \ln U}{\partial \ln X_k \partial \ln X_j} = \frac{\partial^2 F}{\partial \ln H}\frac{\partial \ln H}{\partial \ln X_j}, \qquad (j=1,2,3). \qquad (2.3.17)$$

Given homotheticity, equations (2.3.17) must hold everywhere; in particular, they must hold at the point of approximation, where we can identify the first and second partial derivatives with the parameters of the direct translog utility function with time-varying preferences

$$\sum \frac{\partial^2 - \ln U}{\partial \ln X_k \partial \ln X_j} = \sum \beta_{kj} = \beta_{Mj}, \qquad (j=1,2,3),$$

and

$$\frac{\partial - \ln U}{\partial \ln X_j} = \alpha_j, \qquad (j=1,2,3).$$

Given homotheticity, the parameters of the direct translog utility function must satisfy the restrictions

$$\beta_{M1} = \sigma\alpha_1, \quad \beta_{M2} = \sigma\alpha_2, \quad \beta_{M3} = \sigma\alpha_3, \qquad (2.3.18)$$

where σ is constant given by

$$\sigma = \frac{\partial^2 F/(\partial \ln H)}{\partial F/(\partial \ln H)}.$$

We introduce one new parameter, σ, so that these restrictions reduce the number of parameters by two, leaving nine unknown parameters to be estimated.

The translog approximation to a homothetic direct utility function is not necessarily homothetic, even though it must satisfy the restrictions given in equation (2.3.18) above. For a direct translog utility function to be homothetic, the ratios of the indirect demand functions generated by the direct translog utility function must be homogeneous of degree zero in the quantities consumed. We refer to a direct translog utility function as *intrinsically homothetic* if it is itself homothetic. Two alternative sets of restrictions on the parameters of the direct translog utility function are jointly necessary and sufficient for intrinsic homotheticity of the direct translog utility function. The first set consists of the restrictions given in equation (2.3.18) above and the additional restriction

$$\sigma = 0. \tag{2.3.19}$$

We refer to this set of restrictions as *explicit homotheticity* restrictions. Under the explicit homotheticity restrictions, only eight unknown parameters remain to be estimated.

A second set of restrictions that implies intrinsic homotheticity of the direct translog utility function is that σ is different from zero, but that the ratios of all pairs of optimal budget shares are constant for all prices, total expenditure and time. This means that the parameters of the direct translog utility function must satisfy

$$\begin{array}{lll} \alpha_1\beta_{12} = \alpha_2\beta_{11}, & \alpha_1\beta_{13} = \alpha_3\beta_{11}, & \alpha_2\beta_{13} = \alpha_3\beta_{12}, \\ \alpha_1\beta_{22} = \alpha_2\beta_{12}, & \alpha_1\beta_{23} = \alpha_3\beta_{12}, & \alpha_2\beta_{23} = \alpha_3\beta_{22}, \\ \alpha_1\beta_{23} = \alpha_2\beta_{13}, & \alpha_1\beta_{33} = \alpha_3\beta_{13}, & \alpha_2\beta_{33} = \alpha_3\beta_{23}, \\ \alpha_1\beta_{2t} = \alpha_2\beta_{1t}, & \alpha_1\beta_{3t} = \alpha_3\beta_{1t}, & \alpha_2\beta_{3t} = \alpha_3\beta_{2t}, \end{array} \tag{2.3.20}$$

not all of which are independent. In other words, the second-order parameters of each commodity must be in the same proportion as the first-order parameters. If the ratios of all pairs of optimal budget shares are constant, the direct utility function takes the form

$$-\ln U = F(\delta_1 \ln X_1 + \delta_2 \ln X_2 + \delta_3 \ln X_3, t) \tag{2.3.21}$$

where δ_1, δ_2, and δ_3 are constants. We refer to such a utility function as *neutral linear logarithmic*. This condition is much more restrictive than homotheticity or explicit homotheticity and we will discuss it in more detail in section 2.3.4.

A direct utility function with time-varying preferences is *homogeneous* if it can be written in the form

$$-\ln U = \ln H(X_1, X_2, X_3, t), \tag{2.3.22}$$

where H is a homogeneous function of degree one in X_1, X_2 and X_3. Homogeneity is, of course, a specialization of homotheticity. Under homogeneity the parameters of the direct translog utility function must satisfy the explicitly homotheticity restrictions given in equation (2.3.19) above and the additional restriction

$$\beta_{Mt} = 0 . \tag{2.3.23}$$

We refer to this set of restrictions as *homogeneity* restrictions. Under these restrictions only seven unknown parameters remain to be estimated. We note that the translog approximation to a homogeneous direct utility function is necessarily homogeneous.

An alternative form of homotheticity of preferences is *groupwise homotheticity*. A direct utility function with time-varying preferences that is groupwise homothetic in X_1 and X_2 can be written in the form

$$-\ln U = F(\ln H(X_1 , X_2 , X_3 , t) , X_3 , t) \tag{2.3.24}$$

where H is homogeneous of degree one in the quantities X_1 and X_2. Under groupwise homotheticity in X_1 and X_2 the ratio of the indirect demand functions of X_1 and X_2 is homogeneous of degree zero in X_1 and X_2. In other words, the ratio of the indirect demands remains invariant under proportional changes in the quantities consumed of X_1 and X_2. Under groupwise homotheticity the parameters of the direct translog utility function must satisfy the restrictions

$$\beta_{11} + \beta_{12} = \sigma_{12}\alpha_1 , \qquad \beta_{12} + \beta_{22} = \sigma_{12}\alpha_2 . \tag{2.3.25}$$

This set of two restrictions involves the introduction of one new parameter, σ_{12}, so that only ten unknown parameters remain to be estimated. Corresponding to the three possible pairs of commodities, there are three possible sets of groupwise homotheticity restrictions. Restrictions analogous to those given in equations (2.3.25) above must hold for any one of the three possible sets of groupwise homotheticity restrictions.

The translog approximation to a groupwise homothetic direct utility function is not necessarily groupwise homothetic. For a direct translog utility function to be groupwise homothetic, the ratio of the indirect demand functions of X_1 and X_2 generated by the direct translog utility function must be homogenous of degree zero in X_1 and X_2. We shall refer to a direct translog utility function as *intrinsically groupwise homothetic* if it is itself groupwise homothetic. Two alternative sets of restrictions on the parameters of the direct translog utility function are jointly necessary and sufficient for intrinsic groupwise homotheticity of the direct translog utility function. The first set consists of the restrictions given in equations (2.3.25) above and the additional restriction

$$\sigma_{12} = 0 . \tag{2.3.26}$$

We refer to this set of restrictions as *explicit groupwise homotheticity* restrictions. Under the explicit groupwise homotheticity restrictions, only nine unknown parameters remain to be estimated.

A second set of restrictions that implies intrinsic groupwise homotheticity of the direct translog utility function is that σ_{12} is different from zero, but that the ratio of the optimal budget shares of X_1 and X_2 is constant for all prices, total expenditure and time. This is precisely the case of groupwise neutral linear logarithmic utility discussed in section 2.3.2 above with the restrictions given in equation (2.3.9). Corresponding to the three possible pairs of commodities, there are three possible sets of explicit groupwise homotheticity restrictions. Restrictions analogous to those given in equation (2.3.26) above must hold for any one of the three possible sets of explicit groupwise homotheticity restrictions.

A direct utility function with time-varying preferences is *inclusively groupwise homothetic* in X_1 and X_2 if it can be written in the form

$$-\ln U = F(\ln H(X_1 , X_2 , X_3 , t) , t) , \tag{2.3.27}$$

where H is homogeneous of degree one in the quantities X_1 and X_2. Given groupwise homotheticity, this condition implies in addition that the ratios of all the indirect demand functions are homogeneous of degree zero in the quantities X_1 and X_2. Under *inclusive groupwise homotheticity* in X_1 and X_2 the parameters of the direct translog utility function must satisfy the groupwise homotheticity restrictions given in equation (2.3.25) above and the additional restriction

$$\beta_{13} + \beta_{23} = \sigma_{12}\alpha_3 . \tag{2.3.28}$$

Under the inclusive groupwise homotheticity restrictions, only nine unknown parameters remain to be estimated. Again, there are three possible sets of inclusive groupwise homotheticity restrictions corresponding to the three possible sets of groupwise homotheticity restrictions. Restrictions analogous to those give in equation (2.3.28) must hold for any one of the three possible sets of groupwise homotheticity restrictions.

The translog approximation to an inclusively groupwise homothetic direct utility function is not necessarily inclusively groupwise homothetic. For a direct translog utility function to be inclusively groupwise homothetic, the ratios of all pairs of indirect demand functions generated by the direct translog utility function must be homogeneous of degree zero in X_1 and X_2. As before, two alternative sets of restrictions on the parameters of the direct translog utility function are jointly necessary and sufficient for inclusive groupwise homotheticity of the direct translog utility function. The first set consists of the restrictions given in equations (2.3.28) above and the additional restriction

$$\sigma_{12} = 0 . \tag{2.3.29}$$

We refer to this set of restrictions as *explicit inclusive groupwise homotheticity* restrictions. Under this set of restrictions, only eight unknown parameters remain to be estimated.

A second set of restrictions that implies intrinsic inclusive groupwise homotheticity of the direct translog utility function is that σ_{12} is different from zero but that the direct utility function is groupwise neutral linear logarithmic. Corresponding to the three possible pairs of commodities, there are three possible sets of explicit inclusive groupwise homotheticity restrictions. Restrictions analogous to those given in equation (2.3.9) above must hold for any one of the three possible sets of explicit inclusive groupwise homotheticity restrictions.

Finally, direct utility function with time-varying preferences is *groupwise homogeneous* if it can be written in the form

$$-\ln U = \ln H(X_1 , X_2 , X_3 , t) , \tag{2.3.30}$$

where H is homogeneous of degree one in the quantities X_1 and X_2. Groupwise homogeneity is, of course, a specialization of inclusive groupwise homotheticity which is in turn a specialization of groupwise homotheticity. Under groupwise homogeneity the parameters of the direct translog utility function must satisfy the explicit inclusive groupwise homotheticity restrictions give in equation (2.3.29) above and the additional restriction

$$\beta_{1t} + \beta_{2t} = 0 . \tag{2.3.31}$$

We refer to this set of restrictions as *groupwise homogeneity* restrictions. Under these restrictions only seven unknown parameters remain to be estimated. We note that the translog approximation to a groupwise homogeneous direct utility function is not necessarily groupwise homogeneous. Corresponding to the three possible pairs of commodities, there are three possible sets of groupwise homogeneity restrictions. Restrictions analogous to those given in equation (2.3.31) must hold for any one of the three possible sets of groupwise homogeneity restriction.

We conclude this section by noting that groupwise homotheticity in all possible groups is neither necessary nor sufficient for homotheticity of the direct utility function. Even explicit groupwise homotheticity in all possible groups is not sufficient for homotheticity of the direct utility function. On the other hand, inclusive groupwise homotheticity in all possible groups is sufficient, but not necessary, for homotheticity. Inclusive groupwise homotheticity in all possible groups implies linear logarithmic utility. Finally, explicit inclusive groupwise homotheticity in all possible groups implies explicit linear logarithmic utility and groupwise homogeneity in all possible groups implies neutral linear logarithmic utility.

2.3.4 Groupwise Linear Logarithmic Utility

A direct utility function with time-varying preferences that is *groupwise homothetically separable* in X_1 and X_2 from X_3 can be written in the form

$$-\ln U = F(\ln H(X_1, X_2, t), X_3, t), \tag{2.3.32}$$

where H is a homogeneous function of degree one and depends only on X_1, X_2 and time. A necessary and sufficient condition for a direct utility function to be groupwise homothetically separable in X_1 and X_2 from X_3 is that the function is both groupwise separable and groupwise homothetic in X_1 and X_2.

Groupwise homothetic separability implies that the ratio of the indirect demand functions is independent of X_3 and is homogeneous of degree zero in X_1 and X_2. The translog approximation to a groupwise homothetically separable direct utility function is not necessarily groupwise homothetically separable. For a direct translog utility function to be itself groupwise homothetically separable, the ratio of the indirect demand functions of X_1 and X_2 generated from a direct translog utility function must be independent of X_3 and homogeneous of degree zero in X_1 and X_2. We refer to a direct translog utility function as *intrinsically groupwise homothetically separable* if it is groupwise homothetically separable.

As before, two alternative sets of restrictions on the parameters of the direct translog utility function are jointly necessary and sufficient for intrinsic groupwise homothetic separability of the direct translog utility function. The first consists of the combination of the explicit groupwise separability, given in equation (2.3.8) above, and explicit groupwise homotheticity, given in equation (2.3.26) above. We refer to the conjunction of these two sets of restrictions as the *explicit groupwise homothetic separability* restrictions. A second set of restrictions that implies intrinsic groupwise homothetic separability of the direct translog utility function is that of groupwise neutral linear logarithmic utility, given in equation (2.3.9) above.

A direct utility function U with time-varying preferences is *groupwise linear logarithmic* if it can be written in the form

$$-\ln U = F(\delta_1(t) \ln X_1 + \delta_2(t) \ln X_2 , X_3, t), \tag{2.3.33}$$

where $\delta_1(t)$ and $\delta_2(t)$ are functions only of time. A necessary and sufficient condition for groupwise linear logarithmic utility in X_1 and X_2 is that the ratio of the optimal budget shares of X_1 and X_2 is independent of all prices and total expenditure and depends only on time. Given groupwise homothetic separability in X_1 and X_2 from X_3, groupwise linear logarithmic utility in X_1 and X_2 requires the additional restriction

$$\alpha_1 \beta_{12} = \alpha_2 \beta_{11} . \tag{2.3.34}$$

Under these restrictions only eight unknown parameters remain to be estimated. There are three possible sets of groupwise logarithmic utility restrictions and restrictions analogous to those given in equation (2.3.34) must hold for any one of them.

The translog approximation of a groupwise linear logarithmic direct utility function is not necessarily groupwise linear logarithmic. For a direct translog utility function to be itself groupwise linear logarithmic, the ratio of the optimal budget shares of X_1 and X_2 generated from a direct translog utility function must depend only on time. We shall refer to a direct translog utility function as *intrinsically groupwise linear logarithmic* if it is itself groupwise linear logarithmic. As before, two alternative sets of restrictions on the parameters of the direct translog utility function are jointly necessary and sufficient for intrinsic groupwise linear logarithmic utility. The first consists of the explicit groupwise homothetic separability restrictions and the additional restriction

$$\beta_{12} = 0\,. \tag{2.3.35}$$

Under these restrictions only six unknown parameters remain to be estimated. We refer to these restrictions as *explicit groupwise linear logarithmic utility* restrictions. A second set of restrictions that implies intrinsic groupwise linear logarithmic utility is that of groupwise neutral linear logarithmic utility, given in equation (2.3.9) above. Corresponding to the three possible pairs of commodities, there are three possible sets of *explicit groupwise linear logarithmic utility* restrictions. Restrictions analogous to those given in equation (2.3.35) must hold for any one of them.

A direct utility function with time-varying preferences is *linear logarithmic* in X_1, X_2, and X_3 if it can be written in the form

$$-\ln U = F(\delta_1(t)\ln X_1 + \delta_2(t)\ln X_2 + \delta_3(t)\ln X_3\,,\, t)\,, \tag{2.3.36}$$

where $\delta_1(t)$, $\delta_2(t)$ and $\delta_3(t)$ are functions only of time. A necessary and sufficient condition for linear logarithmic utility is that the direct utility function is groupwise linear logarithmic in every pair of the three commodities. In particular, since there are only three commodities, groupwise linear logarithmic utility for any two pairs of commodities is sufficient for linear logarithmic utility.

A direct utility function U with time-varying preferences is *explicitly linear logarithmic* if it can be written in the form

$$-\ln U = F(\delta_1(t)\ln X_1 + \delta_2(t)\ln X_2 + \delta_3(t)\ln X_3 + F(t)\,. \tag{2.3.37}$$

The translog approximation to an explicitly linear logarithmic utility function is necessarily explicitly linear logarithmic. A necessary and sufficient condition for *explicit linear logarithmic utility* is that the direct translog utility function is explicitly groupwise linear logarithmic in every pair of the three commodities. In particular, since there are only three commodities, explicit groupwise linear logarithmic utility for any two pairs of commodities is sufficient. Given linear logarithmic utility, explicit groupwise linear logarithmic utility in any one of the three possible pairs implies that the direct utility function is explicitly linear logarithmic. For an explicitly linear logarithmic utility function the budget shares of all commodities are independent of prices and total expenditure, depending only on time.

Finally, a direct utility function U with time-varying preferences is *neutral linear logarithmic* if it can be written in the form

$$-\ln U = F(\delta_1 \ln X_1 + \delta_2 \ln X_2 + \delta_3 \ln X_3 , t), \tag{2.3.38}$$

where δ_1, δ_2 and δ_3 are constants. Two alternative sets of conditions are jointly necessary and sufficient for neutral linear logarithmic utility. First, the direct translog utility function is both neutral and linear logarithmic and it is either explicitly neutral, explicitly linear logarithmic, or both. Alternatively, the direct translog utility function satisfies the restrictions given in equation (2.3.20), that is, the neutral linear logarithmic utility restrictions. In either case, the empirical implications are identical—the budget shares of all commodities are constant.

2.3.5 Groupwise Equal Rates of Commodity Augmentation

As an alternative point of departure for the analysis of time-varying preferences, we suppose that the quantities consumes of X_1, X_2 and X_3 are augmented by factors $A_1(t)$, $A_2(t)$ and $A_3(t)$ respectively, where the augmentation factors are functions only of time. A direct utility function with commodity-augmenting time-varying preferences can be written in the form

$$-\ln U = F(A_1(t)X_1 , A_2(t)X_2 , A_3(t)X_3). \tag{2.3.39}$$

Without loss of generality, the augmentation factors can be normalized so that they all take the value unity for $t = 0$. Without further restrictions on the function F commodity augmentation is not a testable hypothesis, since it has no empirical implications that can be refuted. Even if one restricts each augmentation factor to be drawn from the family on one-parameter algebraic functions, commodity augmentation is still not a testable hypothesis since the parameters α_1 and β_{tt} are not identified.

A direct utility function with time-varying preferences that is characterized by *groupwise equal rates of commodity augmentation* can be written in the form

$$-\ln U = F(A(t)X_1 , A(t)X_2 , A_3(t)X_3). \tag{2.3.40}$$

The cross partial derivatives of $-\ln U$ with respect to time and $\ln X_1$, $\ln X_2$ or $\ln X_3$ are given by

$$\frac{\partial^2 - \ln U}{\partial \ln X_1 \partial t} = \frac{\partial^2 F}{\partial \ln X_1^2} \cdot \frac{\dot{A}}{A} + \frac{\partial^2 F}{\partial \ln X_1 \partial \ln X_2} \cdot \frac{\dot{A}}{A} + \frac{\partial^2 F}{\partial \ln X_1 \partial \ln X_3} \cdot \frac{\dot{A}_3}{A_3},$$

$$\frac{\partial^2 - \ln U}{\partial \ln X_2 \partial t} = \frac{\partial^2 F}{\partial \ln X_1 \partial \ln X_2} \cdot \frac{\dot{A}}{A} + \frac{\partial^2 F}{\partial \ln X_2^2} \cdot \frac{\dot{A}}{A} + \frac{\partial^2 F}{\partial \ln X_2 \partial \ln X_3} \cdot \frac{\dot{A}_3}{A_3}, \tag{2.3.41}$$

$$\frac{\partial^2 - \ln U}{\partial \ln X_3 \partial t} = \frac{\partial^2 F}{\partial \ln X_1 \partial \ln X_3} \cdot \frac{\dot{A}}{A} + \frac{\partial^2 F}{\partial \ln X_2 \partial \ln X_3} \cdot \frac{\dot{A}_3}{A} + \frac{\partial^2 F}{\partial \ln X_3^2} \cdot \frac{\dot{A}_3}{A_3}.$$

By observing that

$$\frac{\partial^2 F}{\partial \ln X_i \partial \ln X_j} = \frac{\partial^2 - \ln U}{\partial \ln X_i \partial \ln X_j}, \qquad (i, j = 1, 2, 3). \tag{2.3.42}$$

and the fact that equation (2.3.41) must hold everywhere, in particular, at the point of approximation where $t = 0$, we can identify the first and second partial derivatives of $-\ln U$ with the parameters of the direct translog utility function with time-varying preferences. Groupwise equal rates of commodity augmentation in X_1 and X_2 implies the following sets of restrictions

$$\beta_{1t} = \beta_{11}\lambda + \beta_{12}\lambda + \beta_{13}\lambda_3,$$
$$\beta_{2t} = \beta_{12}\lambda + \beta_{22}\lambda + \beta_{23}\lambda_3, \tag{2.3.43}$$
$$\beta_{3t} = \beta_{13}\lambda + \beta_{23}\lambda + \beta_{33}\lambda_3,$$

where

$$\lambda = \frac{\dot{A}}{A}, \qquad \lambda_3 = \frac{\dot{A}_3}{A_3},$$

are the rates of commodity augmentation at the point of approximation. We note that this set of three restrictions involves the introduction of two new parameters, λ and λ_3 in the example given above. Hence under groupwise equal rates of commodity augmentation only ten unknown parameters remain to be estimated. Restrictions analogous to those given in equation (2.3.43) must hold for the two remaining possible sets of groupwise equal rates of commodity augmentation restrictions.

A necessary and sufficient condition for groupwise equal rates of commodity augmentation of the direct utility function in X_1 and X_2 is that there exist two scalars η and η_3 for every t such that

$$\frac{[\partial U/\partial X_1](X_1, X_2, X_3, t)}{[\partial U/\partial X_2](X_1, X_2, X_3, t)} = \frac{[\partial U/\partial X_1](\eta X_1, \eta X_2, \eta_3 X_3, 0)}{[\partial U/\partial X_2](\eta X_1, \eta X_2, \eta_3 X_3, 0)}. \tag{2.3.44}$$

In other words, at every t there exists a proportional scaling of X_1 and X_2, and a scaling for X_3, so that the ratio of the indirect demands at time zero is the same as the ratio of the indirect demands at time t. We can verify directly that a translog approximation to a direct utility function with time-varying preferences characterized by groupwise equal rates of commodity augmentation is always characterized by groupwise equal rates of commodity augmentation.

A direct utility function U with time-varying preferences that is characterized by *groupwise zero rates of commodity augmentation* can be written in the form

$$-\ln U = F(X_1, X_2, A_3(t)X_3). \tag{2.3.45}$$

The corresponding restrictions on the parameters of the indirect translog utility function with time-varying preferences can be obtained from equation (2.3.43) above by setting λ equal to zero. Under groupwise zero rates of commodity augmentation the parameters must satisfy the restrictions

$$\beta_{1t} = \beta_{13}\lambda_3, \qquad \beta_{2t} = \beta_{23}\lambda_3, \qquad \beta_{3t} = \beta_{33}\lambda_3. \tag{2.3.46}$$

Under these restrictions, only nine unknown parameters remain to be estimated. Restrictions analogous to those given in equation (2.3.46) must hold for the two remaining possible sets of groupwise zero rates of commodity augmentation. As before, we can show that the translog approximation to a direct utility function with time-varying preferences characterized by groupwise zero rates of commodity augmentation is always characterized by groupwise zero rates of commodity augmentation.

A direct utility function with time-varying preferences is characterized by equal rates of commodity augmentation in X_1, X_2 and X_3 if it can be written in the form

$$-\ln U = G(A(t)X_1, A(t)X_2, A(t)X_3). \tag{2.3.47}$$

A necessary and sufficient condition for equal rates of commodity augmentation of the direct utility function is that the direct utility function is characterized by groupwise equal rates of commodity augmentation in every pair of the three commodities. In particular, since there are only three commodities, groupwise equal rates of commodity augmentation for any two pairs of commodities is sufficient for equal rates of commodity augmentation.

Finally, a direct utility function with time-varying preferences is characterized by *zero rates of commodity augmentation* if and only if it is characterized by groupwise zero rates of commodity augmentation in every pair of the three commodities. In particular, since there are only three commodities, groupwise zero rates of commodity augmentation for any two pairs of commodities is sufficient. In fact, given equal rates of commodity augmentation, zero rates of commodity augmentation for any pair of commodities implies zero rates of augmentation. In this case the direct utility function is also explicitly neutral.

2.3.6 Duality

The implications of separability, homotheticity, linear logarithmic utility and equal rates of commodity augmentation for the indirect utility function with time-varying preferences are strictly analogous to the corresponding properties for the direct utility function with time-varying preferences. They impose restrictions on the direct demand functions as opposed to the indirect demand functions. Similarly, the parametric restrictions implied by these properties of the indirect translog utility functions are strictly analogous to the parametric restrictions implied by the corresponding properties of the direct translog function. The roles of quantities consumed and ratios of prices to total expenditure are, of course, interchanged.

However, a given property of the direct utility function need not imply the same property of the indirect utility function. For example, a groupwise homothetic direct utility function does not correspond to a groupwise homothetic indirect utility function. The direct utility function is inclusively groupwise homothetic if and only if the indirect utility function is inclusively groupwise homothetic. Since homotheticity implies groupwise inclusive homotheticity for the group consisting of all commodities, direct homotheticity is equivalent to indirect homotheticity. An alternative sufficient condition for groupwise homotheticity of both the direct and indirect utility functions is groupwise separability (either direct or indirect) in the same group of commodities.

Similarly, a groupwise commodity separable direct utility function does not correspond to a groupwise commodity separable indirect utility function. Direct and indirect utility functions are groupwise commodity separable in the same group of commodities if and only if the utility function (either direct or indirect) is also groupwise homothetic in the same group of commodities. In addition, the direct utility function is groupwise homothetically commodity separable if and only if the indirect utility function is groupwise homothetically commodity separable.

In general, a groupwise time separable direct utility function does not correspond to a groupwise time separable indirect utility function. Two alternative sufficient conditions for groupwise time separability of both the direct and the indirect utility functions in the same group of commodities are, first, inclusive groupwise homotheticity of the utility function (either direct or indirect) in the same group of commodities and, second, groupwise homothetic commodity separability of the utility function (either direct or indirect) in the same group of commodities.

An additive direct utility function does not correspond to an additive indirect utility function. Direct and indirect utility functions are simultaneously additive only if the utility function (either direct or indirect) is homothetic or if the utility function (either direct or indirect) is linear logarithmic in all but one of the commodities.[13] In addition the direct utility function is additive and homothetic if and only if the indirect utility function is additive and homothetic. On the other hand, a neutral direct utility function always corresponds to a neutral indirect utility function. A groupwise linear logarithmic direct utility function always corresponds to a groupwise linear logarithmic indirect utility function. Since a groupwise linear logarithmic utility function is groupwise homothetically commodity separable, a groupwise neutral linear logarithmic direct utility function always corresponds to a groupwise neutral linear logarithmic indirect utility function.

Moreover, a direct utility function with time-varying preferences characterized by groupwise equal rates of commodity augmentation always corresponds to an indirect utility function with time-varying preferences characterized by groupwise equal rates of commodity augmentation. Likewise, a direct utility function with time-varying preferences characterized by groupwise zero rates of commodity augmentation always corresponds to an indirect utility function with time-varying preferences characterized by groupwise zero rates of commodity augmentation.[14]

Finally, a utility function is *self-dual* if both the direct and the indirect utility functions (corresponding to the same preferences) have the same functional form.[15] The only translog utility function which is self-dual is the neutral linear logarithmic utility function. Neutral linear logarithmic utility functions are the only intrinsically additive, homothetic, and stationary direct or indirect translog utility functions. Direct and indirect translog utility functions can represent the same preferences if and only if they are neutral linear logarithmic. Unless this stringent condition is met, the direct and indirect translog approximations to a given pair of direct and indirect utility functions correspond to different preferences, so that the properties of these approximations are not fully comparable.

2.4 Empirical Results

2.4.1 Summary of Tests

Tests of the restrictions on preferences we have considered can be carried out in many sequences. We propose to test restrictions on the structure of preferences, given equality and symmetry restrictions, but not monotonicity and quasiconvexity restrictions. Monotonicity and quasiconvexity restrictions take the form of inequalities rather than equalities, so that these restrictions do not affect the asymptotic distributions of our statistics for tests of restrictions on the structure of preferences.[16] These distributions are the same with or without imposing the restrictions associated with monotonicity and quasiconvexity. After the set of acceptable restrictions on the structure of preferences is determined, we can impose the constraints implied by monotonicity and quasiconvexity of the direct or indirect utility function.

Our proposed test procedure is presented in diagrammatic form in a series of five figures. We propose to test the restrictions derived from groupwise separability, homotheticity, groupwise homotheticity, and commodity augmenting change in preferences, in parallel. Given groupwise homothetic separability for any group, we proceed to test the additional restrictions implied by groupwise linear logarithmic utility, conditional on the restrictions implied by groupwise homothetic separability. Given the outcome of these tests we can determine the set of acceptable restrictions on the structure of preferences.

Beginning with separability, we recall that, first, groupwise separability for two of the three possible groups of two commodities from the third commodity implies groupwise separability for the third group and additivity of the utility function. Likewise, explicit groupwise separability for two of the three possible groups implies explicit groupwise separability for the third and explicit additivity of the utility function. Second, groupwise separability for two of the three possible groups of two commodities from time implies groupwise separability of the third group from time and neutrality of the utility function. Likewise, explicit groupwise separability for two of the three possible groups from time implies explicit groupwise separability of the third group from time and explicit neutrality of the utility function.

We first test groupwise separability restrictions for each possible group. If we accept groupwise separability for any group, we proceed to test explicit groupwise separability for that group. If we accept the hypothesis of groupwise separability from the third commodity for any two of the three possible groups, we accept the hypothesis of additivity. If we accept the hypothesis of explicit groupwise separability from the third commodity for any two of the three groups, we accept the hypothesis of explicit additivity. If we accept the hypothesis of groupwise separability from time for any two of the three possible groups, we accept the hypothesis of neutrality. If we accept the hypothesis of explicit groupwise separability from time for any two of the three groups, we accept the hypothesis of explicit neutrality.

Our test procedure for separability is presented diagrammatically in figure 2.1. There are three sets of tests of this type; the diagram gives only one set of such tests. For each group we test groupwise separability from the third commodity and from time. Conditional on the corresponding groupwise separability restrictions we proceed to test the hypothesis of explicit groupwise separability from the third commodity and from time. Combining results from the tests for each of the three commodity groups, we can test the hypotheses of additivity, explicit additivity, neutrality, and explicit neutrality.

Continuing with homotheticity, we first test groupwise homotheticity restrictions for each possible group. In parallel we test homotheticity restrictions for the group consisting of all three commodities. If we accept homotheticity for all three commodities, we proceed to test explicit homotheticity. If we accept explicit homotheticity for all three commodities, we proceed to test homogeneity. Our test procedure for

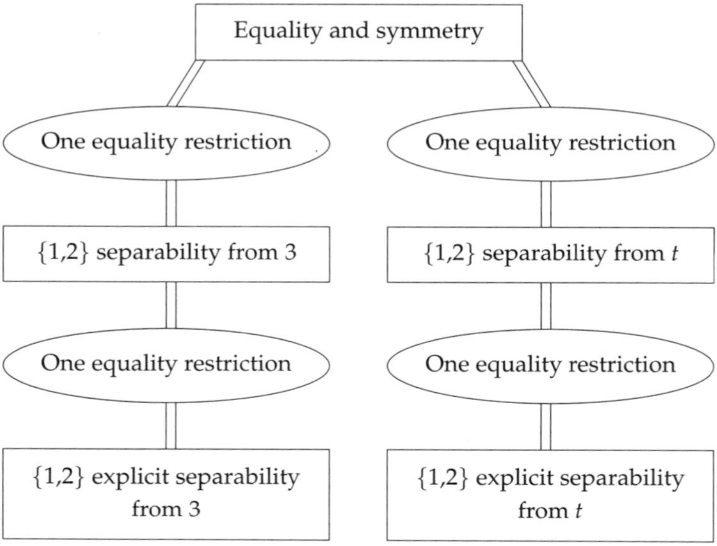

Figure 2.1
Tests of separability. (There are three sets of this type; this diagram gives only one set of such tests corresponding to the group {1,2}.)

homotheticity, explicit homotheticity, and homogeneity is presented diagrammatically in figure 2.2.

If we accept groupwise homotheticity for any group, we proceed to test explicit groupwise homotheticity and inclusive groupwise homotheticity for that group in parallel. If we accept both explicit groupwise homotheticity and inclusive groupwise homotheticity for any group, we accept the hypothesis of explicit groupwise inclusive homotheticity. Conditional on explicit groupwise homotheticity for any group, we proceed to test groupwise homogeneity for that group. Our test procedure for explicit and inclusive groupwise homotheticity is presented diagrammatically in figure 2.3. There are three sets of tests of this type; the diagram gives only one set of such tests.

We observe that a utility function with time-varying preferences is characterized by linear logarithmic utility if it is groupwise linear logarithmic in all three possible groups consisting of two commodities each. Inclusive groupwise homotheticity for all three groups implies that the utility function is linear logarithmic; if we accept inclusive groupwise homotheticity for all three groups, we accept the hypothesis of linear logarithmic utility. If we accept explicit inclusive group-

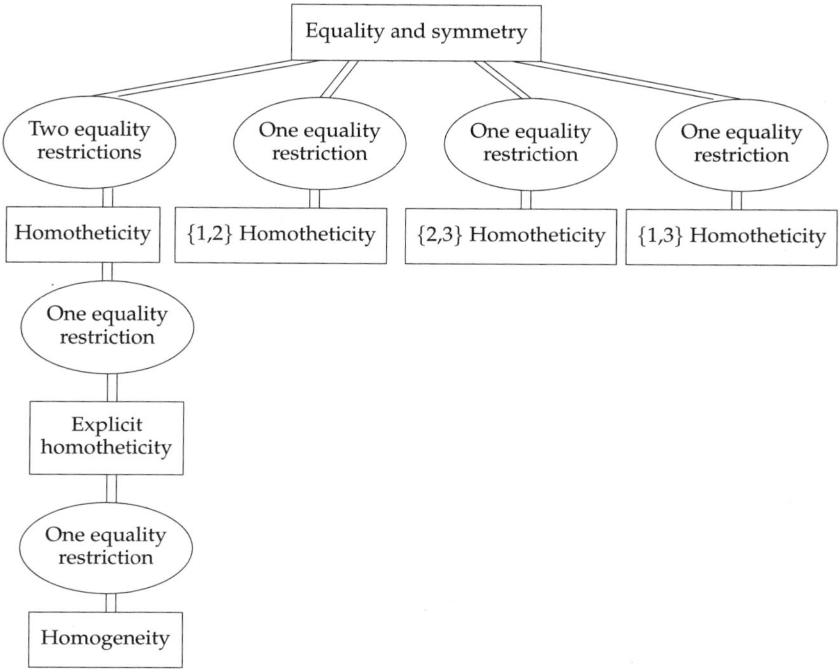

Figure 2.2
Tests of homotheticity.

wise homotheticity for all three groups, we accept the hypothesis of explicit linear logarithmic utility. Finally, if we accept groupwise homogeneity for all three groups, we accept the hypothesis of neutral linear logarithmic utility.

We can combine the results of our parallel tests of separability and homotheticity in order to draw conclusions about homothetic separability. If we accept the hypothesis of groupwise separability for a group consisting of two commodities from the third, and for the same group we accept the hypotheses of groupwise homotheticity, explicit groupwise homotheticity, inclusive groupwise homotheticity, or groupwise homogeneity, we accept the hypotheses of groupwise homothetic separability, groupwise explicitly homothetic separability, groupwise inclusive homothetic separability, or groupwise homogeneous separability, respectively, for that group. Similarly, if we accept the hypothesis of explicit groupwise separability for a given group, and for the same group we accept the hypothesis of groupwise

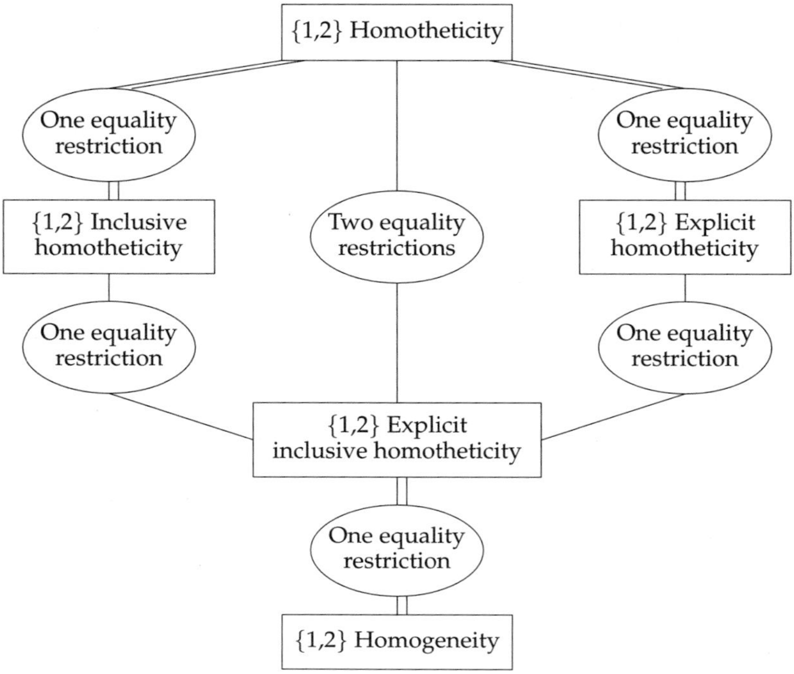

Figure 2.3
Tests of groupwise homotheticity. (There are three sets of this type; this diagram gives only one set of such tests corresponding to the group {1,2}.)

homotheticity, explicit groupwise homotheticity, inclusive groupwise homotheticity and groupwise homogeneity, we accept the hypotheses of groupwise homothetic explicit separability, explicit groupwise homothetic separability, groupwise inclusive homothetic explicit separability and explicit groupwise homogeneous separability, respectively, for that group. Finally, if we accept the hypotheses of additivity and homotheticity, we accept the hypothesis of homothetic additivity. If we accept the hypotheses of explicit additivity and either explicit homotheticity or homogeneity, we accept the hypotheses of explicit linear logarithmic utility and neutral linear logarithmic utility, respectively.

Proceeding under the hypothesis of additivity, if we accept inclusive groupwise homotheticity of any one of the three possible groups of two commodities each, we accept the hypothesis of groupwise linear logarithmic utility for that group. If we accept inclusive groupwise homotheticity of any two of the three possible groups of two commodities each, we accept linear logarithmic utility of the utility function. If we accept explicit inclusive groupwise homotheticity of any one of the three possible groups of two commodities each, we accept the hypothesis of explicit groupwise linear logarithmic utility for that group. If we accept explicit inclusive groupwise homotheticity of any two of the three possible groups of two commodities each, we accept the hypothesis of explicit linear logarithmic utility of the utility function.

Alternatively, proceeding under the hypothesis of explicit additivity, if we accept inclusive groupwise homotheticity of any one of the three possible groups of two commodities each, we also accept the hypothesis of explicit groupwise linear logarithmic utility for that group. If we accept inclusive groupwise homotheticity of any two of the three possible groups of two commodities each, we accept the hypothesis of explicit linear logarithmic utility.

If we accept the hypothesis of groupwise homothetic separability for all three possible groups of two commodities each and, in addition, we accept the hypothesis of inclusive groupwise homotheticity of any one of the three possible groups of two commodities each, we accept the hypothesis of linear logarithmic utility. If either of these two hypotheses are strengthened to hold explicitly, we accept the hypothesis of explicit linear logarithmic utility.

If we accept the hypothesis of groupwise homothetic separability for any group of two commodities from the third we proceed to test the hypothesis of groupwise linear logarithmic utility for that group, conditional on groupwise homothetic separability. If we accept the hypothesis of groupwise linear logarithmic utility for group consisting of two commodities, and for that group we accept any two of the three hypotheses of explicit groupwise separability, explicit groupwise homotheticity, and inclusive groupwise homotheticity, we accept the hypothesis of explicit linear logarithmic utility for that group. If, in addition, we accept the hypothesis of groupwise homogeneity for that group, we accept the hypothesis of explicit neutral linear logarithmic utility for that group. If we accept the hypothesis of groupwise linear logarithmic utility for any two of the three possible commodity groups, we accept the hypothesis of linear logarithmic utility. Our test procedure for groupwise linear logarithmic utility, given groupwise homothetic separability restrictions, is presented diagrammatically in figure 2.4.

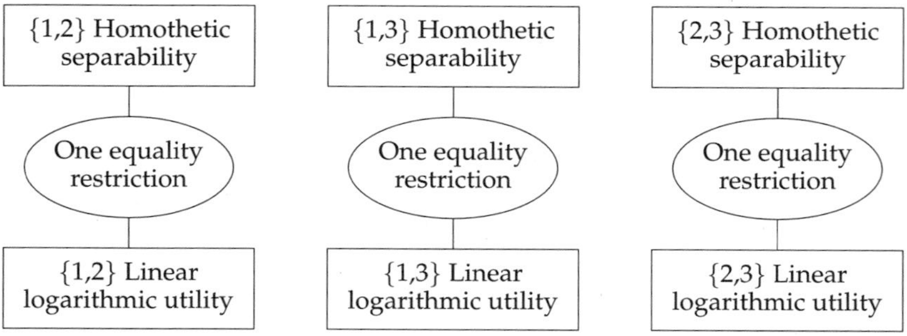

Figure 2.4
Tests of linear logarithmic utility.

Finally, we consider tests of restrictions associated with commodity augmenting changes of preferences over time. First we test the hypothesis of groupwise equal rates of commodity augmentation for all three possible groups of two commodities each. If we accept the hypothesis of equal rates of commodity augmentation for any two of the three groups, we accept the hypothesis of equal rates of augmentation for all three commodities, and hence for all three groups. There is then no need to test zero rates because equal zero rates for all commodities is implied by explicit neutrality, which has been tested under separability. If we accept the hypothesis of equal rates of commodity augmentation for only a single group of two commodities, we proceed to test the hypothesis that the rate of augmentation for that group is equal to zero. Our test procedure for equal rates of commodity augmentation is presented diagrammatically in figure 2.5.

2.4.2 Estimation

Our empirical results are based on time series data for prices and quantities of durables, nondurables, and energy and time. We have fitted the equations for budget shares generated by direct and indirect translog utility functions with time-varying preferences, using the stochastic specification outlined above. Under this specification only two equations are required for a complete econometric model of demand. We have fitted equations for durables and energy.[17] For both direct and indirect specifications we impose the hypothesis that the model of demand is consistent with utility maximization, so that the parameters of this model satisfy equality and symmetry restrictions.

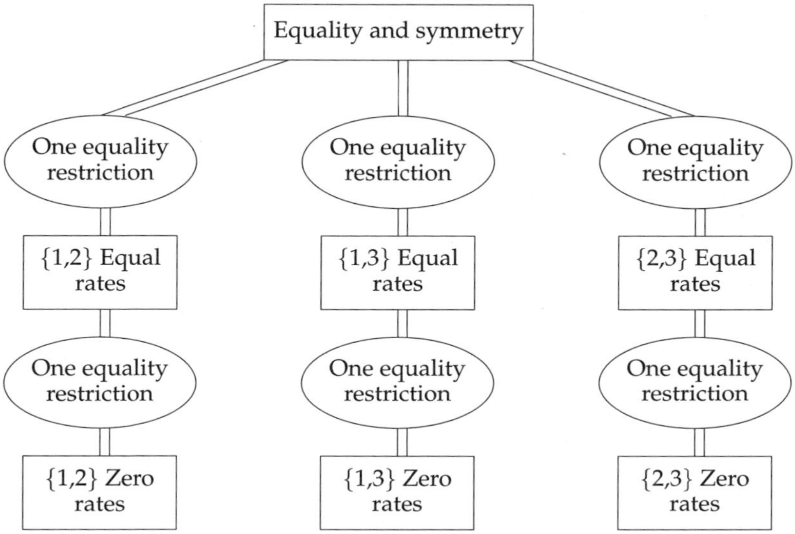

Figure 2.5
Tests of commodity-augmenting change in preferences.

Given these restrictions, and the normalization of α_M at minus unity, eleven unknown parameters remain to be estimated in our econometric model. Estimates of these parameters for the direct translog utility function with time-varying preferences are given in the first column of table 2.1. Estimates of these parameters for the indirect translog utility function with time-varying preferences are presented in the first column of table 2.2.

Given the validity of the theory of demand, we impose restrictions on the structure of consumer preferences for durables, nondurables, and energy. For each set of restrictions we impose the equality and symmetry restrictions. We then impose the additional restrictions associated with each hypothesis about the form of the utility function. The second column of table 2.1 gives estimates under equality and symmetry restrictions, reparameterized to provide estimates of the commodity augmentation factors without imposing further restrictions. The third column gives estimates under additivity restrictions; the fourth column gives estimates under explicit additivity, the fifth under neutrality, and the sixth under explicit neutrality. The seventh column gives estimates under homotheticity, the eighth under explicit homotheticity, the ninth under homogeneity; the tenth column gives

Table 2.1
Parameter estimates, direct translog utility function

Parameter	1. Equality and symmetry		2. Commodity augmentation		3. Additivity		4. Explicit additivity		5. Neutrality		6. Explicit neutrality	
α_1	−0.238	(0.00183)	−0.238	(0.00198)	−0.248	(0.00269)	−.238	(0.00244)	−0.237	(0.00174)	−0.225	(0.00549)
β_{11}	−0.962	(0.0414)	−0.961	(0.310)	0.0608	(0.0494)	.101	(0.768)	−1.03	(0.260)	−0.514	(0.0505)
β_{12}	−3.03	(0.102)	−3.03	(0.833)	−0.108	(0.101)			−3.08	(0.728)	−3.35	(0.298)
β_{13}	−0.203	(0.00890)	−0.202	(0.0684)	−0.00805	(0.00752)			−0.210	(0.0587)	−0.0992	(0.0219)
β_{1t}	−0.0705	(0.00253)	0.0705	(0.0705)	−0.0145	(0.00233)	−.0145	(0.00000)	0.0760	(0.0270)		
α_2	−0.710	(0.00193)	−0.710	(0.00203)	−0.700	(0.00266)	−.711	(0.00170)	−0.711	(0.00183)	−0.727	(0.00620)
β_{21}	−3.03	(0.102)	−3.03	(0.833)	−0.108	(0.101)			−3.08	(0.728)	−3.15	(0.298)
β_{22}	−8.35	(0.237)	−8.34	(0.236)	−1.51	(0.226)	.332	(0.105)	−8.37	(2.23)	−5.63	0.485
β_{23}	−0.509	(0.0202)	−0.508	(0.164)	−0.0227	(0.0213)			−0.556	(0.156)	−0.477	(0.0556)
β_{2t}	0.217	(0.00000)	0.217	(0.0885)	0.00281	(0.00000)	−.0481	(0.00523)	0.228	(0.0804)		
α_3	−0.0520	(0.000441)	−0.0520	(0.00047)	−0.0521	(0.00039)	−.527	(0.00441)	−0.0516	(0.00057)	−0.0484	(0.00111)
β_{31}	−0.203	(0.00890)	−0.202	(0.0684)	−0.00805	(0.00752)			−0.210	(0.0587)	−0.0992	(0.0219)
β_{32}	−0.509	(0.0202)	−0.508	(0.164)	−0.0227	(0.0213)			−0.556	(0.156)	−0.477	(0.0556)
β_{33}	−0.0360	(0.0131)	−0.0360	(0.0153)	−0.0152	(0.0105)	−.103	(0.0242)	−0.0750	(0.0171)	−0.0811	(0.0212)
β_{3t}	0.0132	(0.000575)	0.0186	(0.0143)	−0.00104	(0.00061)	−.00558	(0.00273)	0.0165	(0.00590)		
λ_1			−0.0403	(0.0520)								
λ_2			−0.0206	(0.0377)								
λ_3			0.152	(0.290)								
ρ					−0.623	(0.530)						
ρ_t									−0.320	(0.103)		

Table 2.1 (continued)

Parameter	7. Homotheticity		8. Explicit homotheticity		9. Homogeneity		10. Linear logarithmic utility		11. Explicit linear logarithmic utility		12. Neutral linear logarithmic utility	
α_1	−0.240	(0.00127)	−0.242	(0.00258)	−0.244	(0.00318)	−0.242	(0.00201)	−0.244	(0.00193)	−0.236	(0.00619)
β_{11}	−0.593	(0.226)	−0.0250	(0.0461)	−0.105	(0.0284)	−0.00057	(0.00076)				
β_{12}	−2.16	(0.623)	0.0352	(0.048)	0.131	(0.0275)	−0.0943	(0.0242)				
β_{13}	−0.141	(0.0594)	−0.0102	(0.0164)	−0.0251	(0.0118)	−0.00673	(0.00175)				
β_{1t}	0.0380	(0.0214)	−0.108	(0.00530)	−0.00148	(0.00053)	−0.0150	(0.00120)	−0.0166	(0.00102)		
α_2	−0.710	0.00121	−0.706	(0.00273)	−0.703	(0.00328)	−0.707	(0.00194)	−0.707	(0.00193)	−0.714	(0.00673)
β_{21}	−2.16	(0.623)	0.0352	(0.048)	0.131	(0.0275)	−0.0943	(0.0242)				
β_{22}	−5.99	(1.91)	−0.0711	(0.0610)	−0.178	(0.0284)	−0.275	(0.716)				
β_{23}	−0.417	(0.417)	0.0359	(0.00848)	0.0476	(0.00438)	−0.0197	(0.00519)				
β_{2t}	0.135	(0.0630)	−0.0208	(0.0126)	0.00068	(0.00053)	−0.0259	(0.00507)	−0.0365	(0.00366)		
α_3	−0.0506	(0.00058)	−0.519	(0.00063)	−0.0525	(0.00046)	−0.0505	(0.00049)	−0.0495	(0.00057)	−0.0488	(0.00077)
β_{31}	−0.141	(0.0594)	−0.0102	(0.0164)	−0.0251	(0.0118)	−0.00673	(0.00175)				
β_{32}	−0.417	(0.147)	0.0359	(0.00848)	0.0476	(0.00438)	−0.0197	(0.00519)				
β_{33}	−0.0531	(0.0148)	−0.0257	(0.0146)	−0.0225	(0.0130)	−0.00140	(0.00038)				
β_{3t}	0.00982	(0.00504)	−0.00085	(0.00104)	0.00081	(0.00022)	−0.00057	(0.00076)	−0.0560	(0.00514)		
σ	12.1	(3.76)										
ρ							−0.551	(0.134)				
ρ_t												

Table 2.1 (continued)

Parameter	13. {1, 2} Separability from 3		14. {1, 3} Separability from 2		15. {2, 3} Separability from 1		16. {1, 2} Separability from 3		17. {1, 3} Separability from 2		18. {2, 3} Separability from 1	
α_1	−0.239	(0.00153)	−0.248	(0.00298)	−0.238	(0.00220)	−0.242	(0.00242)	−0.248	(0.00278)	−0.242	(0.00255)
β_{11}	−0.652	(0.0345)	0.354	(0.0525)	−1.09	(0.337)	−0.00425	(0.0462)	0.0653	(0.0831)	0.0480	(0.0394)
β_{12}	−2.35	(0.0639)	0.920	(0.143)	−3.24	(1.05)	−0.366	(0.0864)				
β_{13}	−0.130	(0.00498)	0.0506	(0.00934)	−0.239	(0.0772)			−0.00957	(0.0167)		
β_{1t}	0.0417	(0.00171)	−0.0392	(0.00320)	0.0834	(0.0298)	−0.0139	(0.00266)	−0.0140	(0.00758)	−0.0168	(0.00229)
α_2	−0.709	(0.00159)	−0.699	(0.00302)	−0.710	(0.00230)	−0.706	(0.00254)	−0.699	(0.00277)	−0.705	(0.00266)
β_{21}	−2.35	(0.0639)	0.920	(0.143)	−3.24	(1.05)	−0.366	(0.0864)				
β_{22}	−6.51	(0.0900)	1.38	(0.358)	−9.00	(2.61)	−1.19	(0.196)	−1.27	(0.183)	−0.228	(0.290)
β_{23}	−0.384	(0.0147)	0.195	(0.0316)	−0.553	(0.184)					0.0737	(0.0146)
β_{2t}	0.146	(0.00000)	−0.0754	(0.00000)	0.248	(0.0835)	−0.0143	(0.00618	0.00178	(0.0156)	−0.0301	(0.00769)
α_3	−0.0515	(0.00039)	−0.0526	(0.00046)	−0.0523	(0.00040)	−0.0519	(0.00039)	−0.0523	(0.00051)	−0.0524	(0.00037)
β_{31}	−0.130	(0.00498)	0.0506	(0.00934)	−0.239	(0.0772)			−0.00957	(0.0167)		
β_{32}	−0.384	(0.0147)	0.195	(0.0316)	−0.553	(0.184)					0.0737	(0.0146)
β_{33}	−10.5	(0.442)	0.0105	(0.0144)	11.2	(0.626)	−0.0111	(0.00772)	−0.00910	(0.0140)	0.00967	(0.00863)
β_{3t}	0.00813	(0.00051)	−0.00688	(0.00064)	0.0155	(0.00669)	−0.00306	(0.00056)	−0.00117	(0.00149)	−0.00429	(0.00073)
ρ_3	−10.5	(0.397)										
ρ_2			5.30	(0.741)								
ρ_1					−19.2	(5.62)						

Table 2.1 (continued)

Parameter	19. {1,2} Separability from t		20. {1,3} Separability from t		21. {2,3} Separability from t		22. {1,2} Explicit separability from t		23. {1,3} Explicit separability from t		24. {2,3} Explicit separability from t	
α_1	−0.239	(0.00255)	−0.240	(0.00170)	−0.240	(0.00201)	−0.239	(0.00252)	−0.242	(0.00231)	−0.244	(0.00339)
β_{11}	−0.172	(0.0228)	−0.603	(0.184)	0.166	(0.0055)	−0.172	(0.0226)	−0.140	(0.0259)	−0.0898	(0.0676)
β_{12}	−0.450	(0.144)	−2.20	(0.523)	−0.150	(0.0627)	−0.449	(0.142)	−0.676	(0.168)	0.143	(0.0905)
β_{13}	−0.0381	(0.00685)	−0.128	(0.0435)	0.0117	(0.0112)	−0.0381	(0.00671)	−0.0381	(0.00703)	−0.0159	(0.0135)
β_{1t}	0.00000	(0.000012)	0.0388	(0.0192)	−0.0229	(0.00377)					−0.00334	(0.00414)
α_2	−0.708	(0.00276)	−0.708	(0.00171)	−0.708	(0.00212)	−0.708	(0.00273)	−0.706	(0.00243)	−0.703	(0.00350)
β_{21}	−0.450	(0.144)	−2.20	(0.523)	−0.150	(0.0627)	−0.449	(0.142)	−0.676	(0.168)	0.143	(0.0905)
β_{22}	−0.947	(0.215)	−6.24	(1.58)	0.0841	(0.0642)	−0.945	(0.212)	−2.20	(0.426)	−0.206	(0.0926)
β_{23}	0.00663	(0.0225)	−0.374	(0.111)	1.17	(0.227)	−0.00670	(0.0224)	−0.0723	(0.0288)	0.0203	(0.193)
β_{2t}	0.000000	(0.00035)	0.140	(0.0507)	−0.0953	(0.0128)				0.0255	(0.00626)	
α_3	−0.0523	(0.00048)	−0.0516	(0.00043)	−0.0520	(0.00046)	−0.0523	(0.00046)	−0.0522	(0.00045)	−0.0527	(0.00051)
β_{31}	−0.0381	(0.00685)	−0.128	(0.0435)	0.0117	(0.0112)	−0.0381	(0.00671)	−0.0381	(0.00703)	−0.0159	(0.0135)
β_{32}	0.00663	(0.0225)	−0.374	(0.111)	1.17	(0.0227)	−0.00670	(0.0224)	−0.0723	(0.0288)	0.0203	(0.193)
β_{33}	0.00659	(0.0135)	−0.0436	(0.0114)	−1.06	(0.231)	0.00652	(0.0132)	−0.0121	(0.0106)	0.0221	(0.190)
β_{3t}	−0.00173	(0.00047)	0.00834	(0.00415)	−0.00700	(0.00095)	−0.00173	(0.00044)				
ρ_t	0.00000	(0.0045)	−0.162	(0..0717)	0.135	(0.0162)						

Table 2.1 (continued)

Parameter	25. {1,2} Homotheticity		26. {1,3} Homotheticity		27. {2,3} Homotheticity		28. {1,2} Homotheticity		29. {1,3} Explicit homotheticity		30. {2,3} Explicit homotheticity	
α_1	−0.240	(.00145)	−0.239	(.00174)	−0.241	(.00176)	−0.241	(.00218)	−0.242	(.00251)	−0.243	(.00197)
β_{11}	−0.761	(.0250)	−0.754	(.224)	0.217	(.0439)	0.0159	(.0366)	0.00933	(.0101)	0.158	(.0661)
β_{12}	−2.5436	(.105)	−2.55	(.574)	0.214	(.0448)	−0.0159	(.0331)	−0.149	(.124)	0.136	(.0706)
β_{13}	−0.164	(.0821)	−0.158	(.0463)	−0.192	(.0500)	−0.00304	(.0129)	−0.00933	(.00911)	−0.115	(.0700)
β_{1t}	0.0536	(.00125)	0.0521	(.0185)	−0.0182	(.00414)	−0.0153	(.00391)	0.0133	(.00166)	0.0175	(.00680)
α_2	−0.708	(.00151)	−0.709	(.00180)	−0.656	(.0120)	−0.707	(.00231)	−0.706	(.00268)	−0.672	(.0181)
β_{21}	−2.54	(.105)	−2.55	(.574)	0.214	(.0448)	−0.0159	(.0331)	−0.149	(.124)	0.136	(.0706)
β_{22}	−7.21	(.256)	−7.08	(1.70)	0.620	(.121)	0.0159	(.0366)	−0.628	(.406)	−0.0444	(.00980)
β_{23}	−0.422	(.0218)	−0.426	(.120)	0.124	(.0129)	0.0817	(.00963)	0.0458	(.0213)	0.0444	(.00888)
β_{2t}	0.177	(.00000)	0.171	(.0543)	−0.0520	(.00838)	−0.0343	(.00866)	−0.0192	(.00968)	−0.828	(.0130)
α_3	−0.0520	(.00044)	−0.0518	(.00042)	−0.104	(.0125)	−0.0523	(.0043)	−0.0524	(.00045)	−0.0845	(.0192)
β_{31}	−0.164	(.00821)	−0.158	(.0463)	−0.192	(.0500)	−0.00304	(.0129)	−0.00933	(.00911)	−0.115	(.0700)
β_{32}	0.422	(.0218)	−0.426	(.120)	0.124	(.0129)	0.0817	(.00963)	0.0458	0.0213	0.0444	(.00888)
β_{33}	−0.0301	(.0130)	−0.0395	(.0127)	−0.00607	(.00940)	0.0895	(.0171)	0.00933	(.0101)	−0.0444	(.00980)
β_{3t}	0.0101	(.00051)	0.0102	(.00444)	−0.00541	(.00085)	−0.00438	(.00089)	0.00364	(.00041)	−0.00195	(.00143)
σ_{12}	13.8	(.464)										
σ_{13}			3.82	(1.03)								
σ_{23}					−1.13	(.167)						

Table 2.1 (continued)

Parameter	31. {1,2} Inclusive homotheticity		32. {1,3} Inclusive homotheticity		33. {2,3} Inclusive homotheticity		34. {1,2} Homogeneity		35. {1,3} Homogeneity		36. {2,3} Homogeneity	
α_1	−0.240	(.00122)	−0.239	(.00212)	−0.241	(.00138)	−0.243	(.00315)	−0.241	(.00358)	−0.241	(.00309)
β_{11}	−0.608	(.259)	−0.821	(.256)	−0.422	(.0222)	−0.106	(.0290)	0.0405	(.0113)	−0.163	(.0517)
β_{12}	−2.22	0.652	−2.53	(.703)	−1.74	(.0677)	0.106	(.0267)	−0.0300	(.0105)	0.0103	(.00900)
β_{13}	−0.159	(.0572)	−0.176	(.0509)	−0.0946	(.00818)	−0.0609	(.00853)	−0.0405	(.0105)	−0.0103	(.00970)
β_{1t}	0.0404	(.0223)	0.0596	(.0210)	0.0226	(.00113)	0.00064	(.00067)	0.00064	(.00026)	0.00077	(.00187)
α_2	−0.710	(.00122)	−0.709	(.00219)	−0.708	(.00117)	−0.704	(.00338)	−0.705	(.00384)	−0.707	(.00312)
β_{21}	−2.22	(.652)	−2.53	(.703)	−1.74	(.0677)	0.106	(.0267)	−0.0300	(.0105)	0.0103	(.00900)
β_{22}	−6.16	(2.18)	−7.14	(2.02)	−5.06	(.197)	−0.106	(.0290)	−1.53	(.294)	−0.0457	(.00660)
β_{23}	−0.436	(.148)	−0.430	(.159)	−0.330	(.0164)	0.0609	(.00921)	0.0300	(.0114)	0.0457	(.00660)
β_{2t}	0.140	(.0648)	0.187	(.0625)	0.0990	(.00000)	−0.00064	(.00071)	0.0424	(.00608)	−0.00122	(.00021)
α_3	−0.0504	(.00066)	−0.0522	(.00042)	0.0508	(.00050)	−0.0529	(.00053)	−0.0531	(.00055)	−0.0521	(.00044)
β_{31}	−0.159	(.0572)	−0.176	(.0509)	−0.0946	(.00818)	−0.0609	(.00854)	−0.0405	(.0105)	−0.0103	(.00970)
β_{32}	−0.436	(.148)	−0.430	(.159)	−0.330	(.0164)	0.0609	(.00921)	0.0300	(.0114)	0.0457	(.00660)
β_{33}	−0.0299	(.0155)	−0.0414	(.0165)	−0.0573	(.00918)	0.0310	(.0169)	0.0405	(.0113)	0.0457	(.00711)
β_{3t}	0.00957	(.00493)	0.0120	(.00498)	0.00688	(.00033)	−0.165	(.00115)	0.190	(.00640)	0.234	(.00193)
σ_{12}	11.8	(3.70)										
σ_{13}			4.17	(1.19)								
σ_{23}					7.62	(.273)						

Table 2.1 (continued)

Parameter	37. {1,2} Homothetic separability		38. {1,3} Homothetic separability		39. {2,3} Homothetic separability		40. {1,2} Linear logarithmic utility		41. {1,3} Linear logarithmic utility		42. {2,3} Linear logarithmic utility	
α_1	−0.239	(0.00122)	−0.252	(0.00294)	−0.241	(0.00226)	−0.242	(0.00165)	−0.252	(0.00284)	−0.235	(0.00172)
β_{11}	−0.650	(0.165)	0.229	(0.374)	−0.248	(0.0538)	−0.669	(0.264)	0.124	(0.403)	−0.780	(0.222)
β_{12}	−2.34	(0.444)	0.928	(0.998	−0.867	(0.165)	−1.95	(0.771)	0.725	(1.07)	−2.47	(0.693)
β_{13}	−0.130	(0.0337)	0.0316	(0.0739)	−0.0644	(0.0125)	−0.122	(0.0548)	0.0258	(0.0840)	−0.175	(0.0489)
β_{1t}	0.0417	(0.0133)	−0.0301	(0.0315)	0.00951	(0.00490)	0.0426	(0.0216)	0.0231	(0.0337)	0.0525	(0.0197)
α_2	−0.709	(0.00123)	−0.695	(0.00300)	−0.706	(0.00238)	−0.706	(0.00154)	−0.695	(0.00689)	−0.714	(0.00185)
β_{21}	−2.34	(0.444)	0.928	(0.998)	−0.867	(0.165)	−1.95	(0.771)	0.725	(1.07)	−2.47	(0.693)
β_{22}	−6.51	(1.45)	1.22	(2.76)	−2.59	(0.642)	−5.69	2.25	0.687	(2.95)	−6.09	1.94
β_{23}	0.383	(0.0996)	0.195	(0.209)	−0.0904	(0.0280)	−0.327	(0.160)	0.151	(0.223)	−0.430	(0.137)
β_{2t}	0.146	(0.0396)	−0.0598	(0.0921)	0.0437	(0.0169)	0.140	(0.0637)	−0.0424	(0.0974)	0.152	(0.0565)
α_3	−0.0516	(0.00036)	−0.0529	(0.00048)	−0.0525	(0.00039)	−0.0517	(0.00042)	−0.0527	(0.00041)	−0.0505	(0.00039)
β_{31}	−0.130	(0.0337)	0.0316	(0.0739)	−0.0644	(0.0125)	−0.112	(0.0548)	0.0258	(0.0840)	−0.0505	(0.00039)
β_{32}	−0.383	(0.0996)	0.195	(0.209)	−0.0904	(0.0280)	−0.327	(0.160)	0.151	(0.223)	−0.430	(0.137)
β_{33}	−0.0411	(0.00883)	0.0232	(0.0189)	−0.108	(0.0212)	−0.0606	(0.0142)	0.00539	(0.0175)	−0.0304	(0.00970)
β_{3t}	0.00814	(0.00307)	−0.00601	(0.00664)	0.00070	(0.00088)	0.00906	(0.00503)	0.261	(0.143)	0.0103	(0.00431)
σ_3	−10.5	(2.47)					−8.95	(4.03)				
σ_2			5.30	(5.16)					4.14	(5.59)		
σ_1					−5.09	(0.873)					−14.7	(3.80)
ρ_{12}	12.5	(2.47)					10.8	(3.92)				
ρ_{13}			−1.04	(1.63)					−5.93	(1.77)		
ρ_{23}					3.79	(0.868)					9.12	(2.67)

Table 2.1 (continued)

Parameter	43. {1,2} Explicit linear logarithmic utility		44. {1,3} Explicit linear logarithmic utility		45. {2,3} Explicit linear logarithmic utility		46. {1,2} Neutral linear logarithmic utility		47. {1,3} Neutral linear logarithmic utility		48. {2,3} Neutral linear logarithmic utility	
α_1	−0.242	(0.00199)	−0.254	(0.00273)	−0.242	(0.00166)	−0.234	(0.00670)	−0.248	(0.00357)	−0.238	(0.00129)
β_{11}					0.152	(0.0221)	−0.559	(0.399)	−0.861	(0.342)	−0.0698	(0.0399)
β_{12}							−1.70	(1.21)	−2.55	(0.965)	−0.591	(0.143)
β_{13}							−0.0934	(0.0838)	−0.178	(0.0703)	−0.0402	(0.00985)
β_{1t}	−0.0154	(0.00120)	−0.0145	(0.00133)	−0.0268	(0.00153)	0.0332	(0.0349)	0.0611	(0.0303)	−0.0122	(0.00404)
α_2	−0.707	(0.00194)	−0.694	(0.00274)	−0.708	(0.00170)	−0.714	(0.00644)	−0.700	(0.00340)	−0.713	(0.00213)
β_{21}							−1.70	(1.21)	−2.55	(0.965)	−0.591	(0.143)
β_{22}			−1.42	(0.167)			−5.18	(3.70)	−8.41	(2.59)	−0.966	(0.500)
β_{23}							−0.284	(0.255)	−0.526	(0.199)	−0.0290	(0.0141)
β_{2t}	−0.0318	(0.00418)	−0.00423	(0.00682)	−0.0514	(0.00304)	−0.101	(0.106)	0.204	(0.0864)	0.0290	(0.0141)
α_3	−0.0506	(0.00050)	−0.0519	(0.00036)	−0.0502	(0.00044)	−0.0520	(0.00045)	−0.0513	(0.00053)	−0.0485	(0.00166)
β_{31}							−0.0934	(0.0838)	−0.178	(0.0703)	−0.0402	(0.00985)
β_{32}							−0.284	(0.255)	−0.5226	(0.199)	−0.0657	(0.0341)
β_{33}	−0.0395	(0.00962)					1.84	(1.17)	−0.0366	(0.0145)	−0.00447	(0.00233)
β_{3t}	−0.00076	(0.00070)	−0.00248	(0.00030)	−0.00397	(0.00018)	0.00546	(0.00670)	0.0126	(0.00625)	−0.00197	(0.00096)
ρ_3							0.398	(0.332)				
ρ_2									10.3	(3.61)		
ρ_1											0.828	(0.187)
σ_{12}							9.64	(6.38)				
σ_{13}									−4.18	(1.54)		
σ_{23}											1.45	(0.695)
ρ_t							−0.142	(0.138)	−0.246	(0.113)	0.0408	(0.0184)

Table 2.1 (continued)

Parameter	49. {1,2} Equal rates		50. {1,3} Equal rates		51. {2,3} Equal rates		52. {1,2} Zero rates		53. {1,3} Zero rates		54. {2,3} Zero rates	
α_1	−0.242	(0.00249)	−0.242	(0.00260)	−0.242	(0.00277)	−0.241	(0.00248)	−0.243	(0.00257)	−0.242	(0.00272)
β_{11}	−0.0836	(0.0486)	−0.104	(0.189)	−0.00638	(0.0291)	−0.0756	(0.0529)	−0.374	(0.158)	−0.0469	(0.457)
β_{12}	−0.427	(0.0854)	−0.309	(0.384)	−0.00409	(0.0830)	−0.407	(0.101)	−0.896	(0.465)	−0.0866	(0.0617)
β_{13}	−0.0207	(0.00497)	−0.0322	(0.0403)	−0.00919	(0.0107)	−0.0187	(0.00574)	−0.0919	(0.0345)	−0.0155	(0.0188)
β_{1t}	−0.00604	(0.00382)	−0.00360	(0.0185)	−0.0124	(0.00311)	−0.00694	(0.00376)	0.0204	(0.0147)	−0.00923	(0.00667)
α_2	−0.706	(0.00261)	−0.705	(0.00275)	−0.705	(0.00293)	−0.706	(0.00259)	−0.704	(0.00269)	−0.705	(0.289)
β_{21}	−0.427	(0.0854)	−0.309	(0.384)	−0.00409	(0.0830)	−0.407	(0.101)	−0.896	(0.465)	−0.0866	(0.0617)
β_{22}	−1.33	(0.224)	−1.05	(1.09)	−2.01	(0.199)	−1.25	(0.147)	−2.77	(1.26)	−0.395	(0.371)
β_{23}	−0.00847	(0.00683)	0.0168	(0.0733)	0.0741	(0.00344)	−0.00400	(0.00957)	−0.0989	(0.0846)	0.0597	(0.0222)
β_{2t}	0.00157	(0.00795)	0.00136	(0.0463)	−0.0242	(0.0102)	−0.00148	(0.00442)	0.0630	(0.0410)	−0.0171	(0.0196)
α_3	−0.0523	(0.00041)	−0.0526	(0.00048)	−0.0525	(0.00045)	−0.0522	(0.00040)	−0.0529	(0.00041)	−0.0525	(0.00045)
β_{31}	−0.0207	(0.00497)	−0.0322	(0.0403)	−0.00919	(0.0107)	−0.0187	(0.00574)	−0.0919	(0.0345)	−0.0155	(0.0188)
β_{32}	−0.00847	(0.00683)	0.0168	(0.0733)	0.0741	(0.00344)	−0.00400	(0.00957)	−0.0989	(0.0846)	0.0597	(0.0222)
β_{33}	−0.00537	0.00282	0.0114	(0.0111)	0.0106	(0.0123)	−0.00544	(0.00313)	0.0140	(0.00950)	0.00879	(0.0116)
β_{3t}	−0.00184	(0.00071)	−0.00205	(0.00335)	−0.00362	(0.00053)	−0.00202	(0.00065)	0.00225	(0.00246)	−0.00305	(0.00152)
λ	−0.00261	(0.00385)	0.0794	(0.206)	0.137	(0.825)						
λ_1	1.97	(7.75)			1.66	(7.85)					1.97	(7.75)
λ_2			−0.0233	(0.0134)					−0.0227	(0.00343)		
λ_3	0.356	(0.249)					0.371	(0.276)				

Table 2.2
Parameter estimates, indirect translog utility function

Parameter	1. Equality and symmetry		2. Commodity augmentation		3. Additivity		4. Explicit additivity		5. Neutrality		6. Explicit neutrality	
α_1	−0.239	(.00083)	−0.239	(.00083)	−0.239	(.00080)	−0.236	(.00610)	−0.238	(.00063)	−0.237	(.00067)
β_{11}	0.109	(.133)	0.109	(.133)	0.164	(.123)	−0.0274	(.00204)	0.228	(.0837)	0.123	(.00793)
β_{12}	0.640	(.378)	0.638	(.378)	0.765	(.389)			0.929	(.253)	0.612	(.0150)
β_{13}	0.0143	(.0264)	0.0142	(.0246)	0.0537	(.0271)			0.0612	(.0185)	0.0385	(.00550)
β_{1t}	−0.00077	(.0106)	−0.00081	(.0120)	0.00398	(.00995)	−0.0157	(.00000)	0.00882	(.00759)		
α_2	−0.710	(.00091)	−0.710	(.711)	−0.711	(.00451)	−0.714	(.00095)	−0.714	(.00103)		
β_{21}	0.640	(.378)	0.638	(.378)	0.765	(.389)			0.929	(.253)	0.612	(.0150)
β_{22}	1.40	(.997)	1.40	(.997)	1.73	(.928)	0.0344	(.0390)	1.89	(.738)	0.960	(.0616)
β_{23}	0.0555	(.0720)	0.0553	(.0720)	0.160	(.0811)			0.217	(.0560)	0.151	(.0183)
β_{2t}	0.00599	(.0287)	0.00591	(.0325)	0.0183	(.0273)	−0.0381	(.00185)	0.0265	(.0239)		
α_3	−0.0513	(.00046)	−0.0513	(.00046)	−0.0499	(.00055)	−0.525	(.0116)	−0.0489	(.00059)	−0.0488	(.00058)
β_{31}	0.0143	(.264)	0.0142	(.0246)	0.0537	(.0271)			0.0612	(.0185)	0.0385	(.00550)
β_{32}	0.0555	(.0720)	0.0553	(.0720)	0.160	(.0811)			0.217	(.0560)	0.151	(.0183)
β_{33}	−0.0240	(.00834)	−0.0240	(.00833)	−0.0203	(.00788)	−0.0140	(.00624)	−0.0204	(.0119)	−0.0236	(.0109)
β_{3t}	−0.00259	(.00231)	−0.00013	(.00086)	0.00042	(.00222)	−0.00278	(.00053)	0.00182	(.00164)		
λ_1			0.0130	(.0136)								
λ_2			−0.00576	(.0120)								
λ_3			0.102	(.0432)								
ρ					4.50	(2.07)						
ρ_t									−0.0371	(.0303)		

Table 2.2 (continued)

Parameter	7. Homotheticity		8. Explicit homotheticity		9. Homogeneity		10. Linear logarithmic utility		11. Explicit Linear logarithmic utility		12. Neutral Linear logarithmic utility	
α_1	−0.240	(.00060)	−0.239	(.00059)	−0.225	(.00262)	−0.240	(.00188)	−0.244	(.00193)	−0.236	(.00619)
β_{11}	0.00771	(.0772)	−0.0819	(.00464)	−0.155	(.0356)	−0.0316	(.00346)				
β_{12}	0.358	(.234)	0.0880	(.00688)	0.157	(.0441)	−0.0933	(.0104)				
β_{13}	0.0137	(.0191)	−0.00611	(.00453)	−0.00241	(.00969)	−0.00666	(.00076)				
β_{1t}	−0.00780	(.00665)	−0.0154	(.00036)	−0.00271	(.00032)	−0.0157	(.00108)	−0.0166	(.00102)		
α_2	−0.717	(.00069)	−0.711	(.00073)	−0.726	(.00326)	−0.709	(.00208)	−0.7078	(.00193)	−0.714	(.00673)
β_{21}	0.358	(.234)	0.0880	(.00688)	0.157	(.0441)	−0.0933	(.0104)				
β_{22}	0.668	(.690)	−0.133	(.0154)	−0.191	(.0550)	−0.276	(.0317)				
β_{23}	0.0994	(.0542)	0.0453	(.0113)	0.0335	(.128)	−0.0197	(.00229)				
β_{2t}	−0.0106	(.0201)	−0.0333	(.00132)	0.00349	(.00040)	−0.0361	(.00352)	−0.0363	(.00366)		
α_3	−0.0496	(.00047)	−0.0496	(.00046)	−0.0488	(.00072)	−0.0506	(.00040)	−0.0495	(.0057)	−0.0488	(.00077)
β_{31}	0.0137	(.0191)	−0.00611	(.00453)	−0.00241	(.00969)	−0.00666	(.00076)				
β_{32}	0.0994	(.0542)	0.0453	(.0113)	0.0335	(.128)	−0.0197	(.00229)				
β_{33}	−0.00184	(.00153)	−0.0391	(.00861)	−0.0311	(.00538)	−0.00141	(.00017)				
β_{3t}	−0.0347	(.00948)	−0.00342	(.00014)	−0.00078	(.00012)	−0.00441	(.00028)	−0.0560	(.00514)		
σ	−1.58	(1.37)										
ρ							−0.0548	(.0582)				
ρ_t												

Table 2.2 (continued)

Parameter	13. {1,2} Separability from 3		14. {1,3} Separability from 2		15. {2,3} Separability from 1		16. {1,2} Explicit separability from 3		17. {1,3} Explicit separability from 2		18. {2,3} Explicit separability from 1	
α_1	−0.239	(.00078)	−0.239	(.00082)	−0.239	(.00083)	−0.239	(.00073)	−0.240	(.00075)	−0.240	(.00078)
β_{11}	0.159	(.116)	0.0414	(.126)	0.176	0.138	(.0394)	(.028)	−0.122	(.00994)	−0.103	(.0102)
β_{12}	0.772	(.334)	0.226	(.402)	0.802	(.436)	0.428	(.0624)				
β_{13}	0.0241	(.0257)	−0.00605	(.0265)	0.0564	(.0307)			−0.0225	(.00467)		
β_{1t}	0.00290	(.00941)	−0.0118	(.0102)	0.00496	(.0110)	−0.00682	(.00163)	−0.0182	(.00037)	−0.0175	(.00038)
α_2	−0.710	(.00087)	−0.710	(.00099)	−0.711	(.00100)	−0.710	(.00078)	−0.710	(.00086)	−0.710	(.00104)
β_{21}	0.772	(.334)	0.226	(.402)	0.802	(9.436)	0.428	(.0624)				
β_{22}	1.74	(.890)	0.323	(.949)	1.84	(1.037)	0.826	(.182)	−0.257	(.100)	−0.291	(.112)
β_{23}	0.0719	(.0765)	0.0474	(.0842)	0.162	(.0747)					0.00867	(.0244)
β_{2t}	0.772	(.334)	0.226	(.402)	0.802	(9.436)	0.428	(.0624)				
α_3	−0.0514	(.00041)	−0.0502	(.00044)	−0.0500	(.00070)	−0.0516	(.00038)	−0.0503	(.00039)	−0.0500	(.00071)
β_{31}	0.0241	(.0257)	−0.00605	(.0265)	0.0564	(.0307)			−0.00225	(.00467)		
β_{32}	0.0719	(.0765)	0.0474	(.0842)	0.162	(.0747)					0.00867	(.0244)
β_{33}	−0.0196	(.00533)	−0.0412	(.00746)	0.422	(.246)	−0.0227	(.00400)	−0.0435	(.00597)	−0.0303	(.00975)
β_{3t}	−0.00200	(.00210)	−0.00347	(.00234)	0.00055	(.00239)	−0.00397	(.0O015)	−0.00478	(.00027)	−0.00384	(.00046)
ρ_3	1.97	(1.89)										
ρ_2			1.33	(2.11)								
ρ_1					4.72	(2.30)						

Table 2.2 (continued)

Parameter	19. {1,2} Separability from t		20. {1,3} Separability from t		21. {2,3} Separability from t		22. {1,2} Explicit separability from t		23. {1,3} Explicit separability from t		24. {2,3} Explicit separability from t	
α_1	−0.238	(.00062)	−0.240	(.00081)	−0.237	(.00085)	−0.238	(.00066)	−0.240	(.00071)	−0.229	(.00179)
β_{11}	0.307	(.0884)	−0.00467	(.135)	−0.0252	(.0178)	0.143	(.00709)	0.105	(.0104)	0.0969	(.0357)
β_{12}	1.17	(.267)	0.330	(.383)	0.200	(.0333)	0.679	(.0139)	0.639	(.0136)	0.508	(.0539)
β_{13}	0.0511	(.0192)	0.0130	(.0290)	0.0135	(.00727)	0.0161	(.0416)	0.0363	(.00483)	0.0383	(.00911)
β_{1t}	0.0141	(.00842)	−0.00875	(.0121)	−0.0108	(.00117)					0.00268	(.00100)
α_2	−0.711	(.00066)	−0.710	(.00096)	−0.714	(.00120)	−0.711	(.00069)	−0.711	(.00084)	−0.723	(.00233)
β_{21}	1.17	(.267)	0.330	(.383)	0.200	(.0333)	0.679	(.0139)	0.639	(.0136)	0.508	(.0539)
β_{22}	2.70	(.775)	0.666	(1.02)	−0.276	(.0453)	1.26	(.0554)	1.48	(.103)	−0.616	(.0662)
β_{23}	0.141	(.0582)	0.0923	(.0782)	0.180	(.0723)	0.0367	(.0151)	0.154	(.0135)	0.665	(.0816)
β_{2t}	0.0420	(.0252)	−0.0117	(.0295)	−0.0282	(.00406)			0.0118	(.00272)		
α_3	−0.0514	(.00045)	−0.0495	(.00052)	−0.0487	(.00065)	−0.0515	(.00042)	−0.0495	(.00051)	−0.0485	(.00068)
β_{31}	0.0511	(.0192)	0.0130	(.0290)	0.0135	(.00727)	0.0161	(.00416)	0.0362	(.00483)	0.0383	(.00911)
β_{32}	0.141	(.0582)	0.0923	(.0782)	0.180	(.0723)	0.0367	(.0151)	0.154	(.0135)	0.665	(.0816)
β_{33}	−0.0136	(.00674)	−0.0289	(.0114)	−0.133	(.0728)	−0.0190	(.00532)	−0.0234	(.00935)	−0.0585	(.0817)
β_{3t}	−0.00003	(.00180)	−0.00180	(.00250)	−0.00192	(.0028)	−0.00296	(.00035)				
ρ_t	−0.0592	(.0317)	0.0364	(.0451)	0.0395	(.00510)						

Table 2.2 (continued)

Parameter	25. {1,2} Homotheticity		26. {1,3} Homotheticity		27. {2,3} Homotheticity		28. {1,2} Explicit homotheticity		29. {1,3} Explicit homotheticity		30. {2,3} Explicit homotheticity	
α_1	−0.239	(.00059)	−0.239	(.00084)	−0.237	(.00083)	−0.239	(.00060)	−0.239	(.00075)	−0.242	(.00075)
β_{11}	0.00618	(.0882)	0.0633	(.155)	−0.123	(.0137)	−0.0841	(.00541)	−0.00541	(.00438)	−0.125	(.0106)
β_{12}	0.359	(-0.239)	0.500	(.393)	0.0508	(.0171)	0.0841	(.00490)	0.307	(.0336)	−0.0186	(.0186)
β_{13}	−0.00531	(.0169)	0.0204	(.0290)	−0.702	(.0178)	−0.0241	(.00417)	0.00541	(.00397)	0.00375	(.0171)
β_{1t}	−0.00860	(.00676)	−0.00425	(.0111)	−0.0176	(.00052)	−0.0164	(.00039)	−0.00953	(.00091)	−0.0182	(.00041)
α_2	−0.709	(.00067)	−0.710	(.00105)	−0.701	(.00407)	−0.710	(.00066)	−0.710	0.00104	−0.713	(.00433)
β_{21}	0.359	(.239)	0.500	(.393)	0.0508	(.0171)	0.0841	(.00490)	0.307	(.0336)	−0.0186	(.0186)
β_{22}	0.723	(.786)	1.14	(1.04)	−0.578	(.0899)	−0.0841	(.00541)	0.628	(.176)	−0.0393	(.00808)
β_{23}	0.00607	(.0494)	0.0260	(.0762)	−0.00499	(.0108)	−0.0475	(.0169)	−0.0157	(.0233)	0.0393	(.00732)
β_{2t}	−0.0133	(.0204)	−0.0510	(.00068)	−0.0621	(.00465)	−0.0513	(.00043)	−0.0511	(.00067)	−0.0452	(.00498)
α_3	−0.0513	(.00044)	−0.0510	(.00068)	−0.0621	(.00465)	−0.0513	(.00043)	−0.0511	(.00067)	−0.0452	(.00498)
β_{31}	−0.00531	(.0169)	0.0204	(.0290)	−0.0702	(.0178)	−0.0241	(.00417)	0.00541	(.00397)	0.00375	(.0171)
β_{32}	0.00607	(.0494)	0.0260	(.0762)	−0.00499	(.0108)	−0.0475	(.0169)	−0.0157	(.0233)	0.0393	(.00732)
β_{33}	0.0282	(.00675)	−0.00256	(.00919)	−0.0466	(.00794)	−0.103	(.0195)	−0.00541	(.00438)	−0.0393	(.00808)
β_{3t}	−0.00402	(.00155)	−0.00235	(.00247)	−0.00471	(.00032)	−0.0556	(.00042)	−0.00394	(.00054)	−0.00372	(.00019)
σ_{12}	−1.53	(1.33)										
σ_{13}			−0.350	(.700)								
σ_{23}					0.831	(.126)						

Table 2.2 (continued)

Parameter	31. {1,2} Inclusive homotheticity		32. {1,3} Inclusive homotheticity		33. {2,3} Inclusive homotheticity		34. {1,2} Homogeneity		35. {1,3} Homogeneity		36. {2,3} Homogeneity	
α_1	−0.239	(.00059)	−0.237	(.00119)	−0.241	(.00069)	−0.225	(.00254)	−0.233	(.00492)	−0.231	(.00169)
β_{11}	−0.0303	(.0853)	0.385	(.130)	−0.184	(.0881)	−0.161	(.0416)	−0.0237	(.00209)	−0.233	(.0383)
β_{12}	0.257	(.234)	1.27	(.359)	−0.160	(.264)	0.161	(.0386)	0.0269	(.00570)	0.0226	(.0100)
β_{13}	−0.00209	(.0174)	0.0924	(.0245)	−0.0265	(.0216)	−0.00747	(.00829)	0.00079	(.00012)	−0.00923	(.00082)
β_{1t}	−0.0109	(.00667)	0.0185	(.0102)	−0.0226	(.00751)	−0.00299	(.00033)	0.00079	(.00012)	−0.00923	(.00082)
α_2	−0.710	(.00065)	−0.712	(.00179)	−0.709	(.00069)	−0.725	(.00327)	−0.715	(.00591)	−0.721	(.00209)
β_{21}	0.257	(.234)	1.27	(.359)	−0.160	(.264)	0.161	(.0386)	0.0269	(.00570)	0.0226	(.0108)
β_{22}	0.414	(.761)	2.94	(1.02)	−0.553	(.860)	−0.161	(.0416	0.807	(.610)	−0.0433	(.00824)
β_{23}	0.0496	(.0538)	0.170	(.0807)	0.00481	(.0552)	0.00747	(.00894)	−0.0268	(.00615)	0.0433	(.00764)
β_{2t}	−0.0188	(.0201)	0.527	(.0296)	−0.0461	(.0227)	0.00299	(.00035)	0.0318	(.0150)	0.00164	(.00024)
α_3	−0.0503	(.00038)	−0.0510	(.00088)	−0.0497	(.00042)	−0.0495	(.00060)	−0.0516	(.00108)	−0.0489	(.00054)
β_{31}	−0.00209	(.0174)	0.0924	(.0245)	−0.0265	(.0216)	−0.00747	(.00829)	0.0237	(.00194)	−0.0226	(.0108)
β_{32}	0.0496	(.0538)	0.170	(.0807)	0.00481	(.0552)	0.00747	(.00894)	0.0268	(.00615)	0.0433	(.00764)
β_{33}	−0.0387	(.00719)	0.0104	(.00861)	−0.0432	(.00900)	0.0322	(.00325)	−0.0237	(.00209)	0.0433	(.00824)
β_{3t}	−0.00729	(.00154)	0.00224	(.00232)	−0.00466	(.00174)	−0.00452	(.00030)	−0.0585	(.0162)	−0.00221	(.00070)
σ_{12}	0.945	(1.30)										
σ_{13}			−2.02	(.599)								
σ_{233}					0.773	(1.18)						

Table 2.2 (continued)

Parameter	37. {1,2} Homothetic separability		38. {1,3} Homothetic separability		39. {2,3} Homothetic separability		40. {1,2} Linear logarithmic utility		41. {1,3} Linear logarithmic utility		42. {2,3} Linear logarithmic utility	
α_1	−0.239	(.00058)	−0.241	(.00082)	−0.239	(.00082)	−0.241	(.00207)	−0.241	(.00087)	−0.238	(.000080)
β_{11}	−0.0305	(.0861)	0.0947	(.146)	0.175	(.136)	0.242	(.331)	0.138	(.144)	0.216	(.136)
β_{12}	0.422	(.238)	0.620	(.417)	0.794	(.426)	0.711	(.971)	0.705	(.409)	0.887	(.422)
β_{13}	0.00072	(.0184)	0.0391	(.0282)	0.0559	(.0300)	0.989	(.0367)	0.0279	(.0291)	0.0622	(.0297)
β_{1t}	−0.00686	(.00671)	−0.00097	(.0107)	0.0479	(.0109)	0.00613	(.0258)	0.00114	(.0106)	0.00752	(.0109)
α_2	−0.709	(.00063)	−0.710	(.00088)	−0.711	(.00085)	−0.708	(.00227)	−0.710	(.00088)	−0.712	(.00095)
β_{21}	0.422	(.238)	0.620	(.417)	0.794	(.426)	0.711	(.971)	0.705	(.409)	0.8787	(.422)
β_{22}	0.919	(.769)	1.53	(1.01)	1.81	(1.13)	2.09	(2.85)	1.72	(90.997)	1.99	(1.12)
β_{23}	0.00214	(.0544)	0.128	(.863)	0.156	(.0718)	0.108	(.197)	0.143	(.0829)	0.139	(.0787)
β_{2t}	−0.0889	(.0203)	0.00992	(.0293)	0.0201	(.0294)	0.0336	(.0778)	0.0160	(.0289)	0.0244	(.0296)
α_3	−0.0516	(.0039)	−0.0498	(.00053)	−0.0501	(.00048)	−0.0513	(.00041)	−0.0489	(.0071)	−0.0499	(.00057)
β_{31}	0.00072	(.0184)	0.0391	(.0282)	0.0559	(.0300)	0.989	(.0367)	0.0279	(.0291)	0.0622	(.0297)
β_{32}	0.00214	(.0544)	0.128	(.0863)	0.145	(.0718)	0.108	(.197)	0.143	(.0829)	0.139	(.0787)
β_{33}	−0.0222	(.00443)	−0.0114	(.00663	−0.0176	(.0112)	−0.0313	(.00921)	0.00566	(.00591)	0.00977	(.00553)
β_{3t}	−0.00384	(.00153)	−0.00021	(.00221)	0.00045	(.00229)	−0.00081	(.00561)	0.00058	(.00216)	0.00115	(.00225)
ρ_3	−0.0584	(1.35)					2.97	(4.98)				
ρ_2			3.63	(2.22)					4.12	(2.20)		
ρ_1					4.67	(2.28)					5.23	(2.29)
σ_{12}	−1.89	(1.32)					−3.96	(4.95)				
σ_{13}			−0.556	(.666)					−0.687	(.659)		
σ_{23}					−2.76	(1.54)					−2.99	(1.54)

Table 2.2 (continued)

Parameter	43. {1,2} Explicit linear logarithmic utility		44. {1,3} Explicit linear logarithmic utility		45. {2,3} Explicit linear logarithmic utility		46. {1,2} Neutral linear logarithmic utility		47. {1,3} Neutral linear logarithmic utility		48. {2,3} Neutral linear logarithmic utility	
α_1	−0.240	(.00201)	−0.240	(.00188)	−0.242	(.00070)	−0.236	(.00646)	−0.241	(.00105)	−0.235	(.00133)
β_{11}					−0.119	(.00820)	0.528	(.516)	0.202	(.143)	−0.0116	(.138)
β_{12}							1.60	(1.56)	0.884	(.408)	0.230	(.422)
β_{13}							0.107	(.108)	0.414	(.0293)	0.0156	(.0287)
β_{1t}	−0.0129	(.00127)	−0.0168	(.00088)	−0.0183	(.00039)	0.0434	(.0477)	0.00627	(.0115)	−0.00879	(.0119)
α_2	−0.709	(.00225)	−0.712	(.00211)	−0.708	(.00070)	−0.714	(.00724)	−0.710	(.00085)	−0.716	(.00226)
β_{21}							1.60	(1.56)	0.884	(.408)	0.230	(.422)
β_{22}			−0.685				−4.84	(4.73)	2.22	(1.01)	0.112	(1.13)
β_{23}							0.323	(.326)	0.181	(.0837)	0.00759	(.0767)
β_{2t}	−0.0233	(.00418)	−0.0531	(.00690)	−0.0357	(.00137)	0.131	(.145)	0.0296	(.0316)	−0.0248	(.0326)
α_3	−0.0508	(.00039)	−0.0486	(.00075)	−0.0496	(.00059)	−0.0508	(.00089)	−0.0493	(.00092)	−0.0487	(.00114)
β_{31}							0.107	(.108)	0.414	(.0293)	0.0156	(.0287)
β_{32}							0.323	(.326)	2.22	(1.01)	0.00759	(.0767)
β_{33}	−0.0426	(.00447)					−1.73	(1.51)	0.00848	(.00601)	−0.00052	(.00522)
β_{3t}	−0.00386	(.00028)	−0.00313	(.00023)	−0.00302	(.00012)	0.00675	(.00889)	0.00128	(.00236)	−0.00169	(.00222)
ρ_3							−0.453	(.423)				
ρ_2									−3.67	(1.58)		
ρ_1											−0.321	(.546)
σ_{12}							−9.02	(8.17)				
σ_{13}									−1.01	(.665)		
σ_{23}											−0.166	(1.56)
ρ_t							−0.184	(.188)	−0.0260	(.0444)	0.0347	(.0423)

Table 2.2 (continued)

Parameter	49. {1,2} Equal rates		50. {1,3} Equal rates		51. {2,3} Equal rates		52. {1,2} Zero rates		53. {1,3} Zero rates		54. {2,3} Zero rates	
α_1	–0.239	(.00085)	–0.240	(.00090)	–0.239	(.00060)	–0.238	(.00066)	–0.240	(.0079)	–0.238	(.00068)
β_{11}	–0.0353	(.0784)	0.104	(.154)	–0.0817	(.0473)	0.164	(.0164)	–0.0758	(.0371)	0.143	(.0125)
β_{12}	0.216	(.207)	0.659	(.437)	0.0822	(.0705)	0.748	(.0351)	0.148	(.0890)	0.714	(.0424)
β_{13}	–0.0152	(.0147)	0.0229	(.0307)	–0.00605	(.00423)	0.0200	(.00543)	–0.00971	(.00875)	0.0425	(.00694)
β_{1t}	–0.0127	(.00658)	0.00047	(.0138)	–0.0154	(.00041)	0.00207	(.00087)	–0.0140	(.00279)	0.00256	(.00133)
α_2	–0.710	(.00093)	–0.710	(.00104)	–0.711	(.00075)	–0.711	(.00065)	–0.709	(.00095)	–0.713	(.00089)
β_{21}	0.216	(.207)	0.6589	(.437)	0.0882	(.00705)	0.748	(.0351)	0.148	(.0890)	0.714	(.0424)
β_{22}	0.227	(.464)	1.62	(1.16)	–0.132	(.0158)	1.45	(.0884)	0.249	(.146)	1.41	(.201)
β_{23}	–0.0227	(.0417)	0.129	(.0824)	0.0453	(.0106)	0.0668	(.00123)	–0.0235	(.00252)	0.0128	(.00659)
β_{2t}	–0.0278	(.0153)	0.0162	(.0373)	–0.0333	(.00141)	0.00690	(.00123)	–0.0235	(.00252)	0.0128	(.00659)
α_3	–0.0513	(.00044)	–0.0503	(.00045)	–0.0496	(.00048)	–0.0512	(.00043)	–0.0502	(.00045)	–0.0488	(.00055)
β_{31}	–0.0152	(.0147)	0.0229	(.0307)	–0.00605	(.00423)	0.0200	(.00543)	–0.00971	(.00875)	0.0425	(.00694)
β_{32}	–0.0227	(.0417)	0.129	(.0824)	0.0453	(.0106)	0.0668	(.0115)	0.0387	(.0241)	0.186	(.0211)
β_{33}	–0.0302	(.00614)	–0.0348	(.00933)	–0.0391	(.00902)	–0.0226	(.00610)	–0.0405	(.00663)	–0.0254	(.0117)
β_{3t}	–0.00488	(.00126)	–0.00107	(.00264)	–0.00331	(.00078)	–0.00234	(.00043)	–0.000365	(.00067)	0.00076	(.00041)
λ	–0.0512	(.0789)	0.0315	(.00609)	–21.7	(.0448)						
λ_1					–21.6	(.00000) *41P*[a]					0.0179	(.00738)
λ_2			–0.00534	(.0130)					–0.0943	(.0736)		
λ_3	0.225	(.213)					0.103	(.0267)				

[a]Singular likelihood function.

estimates under linear logarithmic utility, the eleventh under explicit linear logarithmic utility, and the twelfth under neutral linear logarithmic utility. Corresponding estimates for the indirect translog utility function are presented in the second through twelfth columns of table 2.2. Estimates for neutral linear logarithmic utility are identical for direct and indirect translog utility functions.

Our next set of restrictions is associated with groupwise separability of the direct translog utility function with time-varying preferences. The thirteenth column of table 2.1 gives restricted estimates for groupwise separability of the group {1,2}. This group consists of durables and nondurables. The fourteenth column of table 2.1 gives estimates for the group {1,3}, consisting of durables and energy. The fifteenth column of table 2.2 gives estimates for the group {2,3}, nondurables and energy. We present restricted estimates for explicit groupwise separability in these same groups in the sixteenth through eighteenth columns of table 2.1. Corresponding estimates for the indirect translog utility function are given in the thirteenth through eighteenth columns of table 2.2.

The nineteenth column of table 2.1 gives restricted estimates for groupwise separability for the group {1,2} from time. The twentieth column of table 2.1 gives estimates for the group {1,3}, and the twenty-first column for the group {2,3}. We present restricted estimates for explicit groupwise separability from time in these same groups in the twenty-second through twenty-fourth columns of table 2.1. Corresponding estimates for the indirect translog utility function are given in the nineteenth through twenty-fourth columns of table 2.2.

Our third set of restrictions on functional form is associated with hypotheses of groupwise homotheticity of the direct translog utility function with time-varying preferences. The twenty-fifth column of table 2.1 gives restricted estimates for groupwise homotheticity for the group {1,2}. Restricted estimates for the groups {1,3} and {2,3} are given in the twenty-sixty and twenty-seventh columns. Columns twenty-eight through twenty-nine give the corresponding restricted estimates for explicit groupwise homotheticity. Columns thirty through thirty-two give the corresponding restricted estimates for inclusive groupwise homotheticity restrictions. Columns thirty-three through thirty-six give the corresponding restricted estimates for groupwise homogeneity. The corresponding restricted estimates for the indirect translog utility function are given in columns twenty-five through thirty-six of table 2.2.

Our fourth set of restrictions on functional form is associated with groupwise homothetic separability of the direct translog utility function with time-varying preferences. For each of these hypotheses we impose equality and symmetry restrictions and the corresponding groupwise separability and groupwise homotheticity restrictions. The thirty-seventh column of table 2.1 gives restricted estimates for groupwise homothetic separability for the group {1,2}. Corresponding estimates for groups {1,3} and {2,3} are given in columns thirty-eight and thirty-nine of table 2.1. Restricted estimates for groupwise linear logarithmic utility are given in columns forty through forty-two, for explicit groupwise linear logarithmic utility in columns forty-three through forty-five, and for groupwise neutral linear logarithmic utility in columns forty-six through forty-eight. The corresponding restricted estimates for the indirect translog utility function are given in columns thirty-seven through forty-eight of table 2.2.

The fifth and final set of restrictions on functional form is associated with restrictions on the form of commodity augmenting change in preferences for the direct translog utility function with time-varying preferences. We present restricted estimates corresponding to the hypotheses of groupwise equal rates of commodity augmentation in columns forty-nine through fifty-one of table 2.1 and restricted estimates corresponding to the hypotheses of zero rates of commodity augmentation in columns fifty-two through fifty-four. Corresponding estimates for the indirect translog utility function is given in columns forty-nine through fifty-four of table 2.2.

2.4.3 Test Statistics

To test the validity of equality restrictions implied by the theory of demand and restrictions on the form of the utility function, we employ test statistics based on the likelihood ratio Λ, where

$$\Lambda = \frac{\max\limits_{\omega} \mathcal{L}}{\max\limits_{\Omega} \mathcal{L}} .$$

The likelihood ratio is the ratio of the maximum value of the likelihood function for the econometric model of demand Ω without restriction to the maximum value of the likelihood function for the model ω subject to restriction.

We have estimated econometric models of demand from data on

U.S. personal consumption expenditures for 1947–1971. There are twenty-five observations for each behavioral equation, so that the number of degrees of freedom available for statistical tests of the theory of demand is fifty for either direct or indirect specification. For normally distributed disturbances like likelihood ratio is equal to the ratio of the determinant of the restricted estimator of the variance-covariance matrix of the disturbances to the determinant of the unrestricted estimator, each raised to the power $-(n/2)$.

Our test statistic for each set of restrictions is based on minus twice the logarithm of the likelihood ratio, or

$$-2 \ln \Lambda = n(\ln |\hat{\Sigma}_{\omega}| - \ln |\hat{\Sigma}_{\Omega}|),$$

where $\hat{\Sigma}_{\omega}$ is the restricted estimator of the variance-covariance matrix and $\hat{\Sigma}_{\Omega}$ is the unrestricted estimator. Under the null hypothesis the likelihood ratio test statistic is distributed, asymptotically, as chi-squared with a number of degrees of freedom equal to the number of restrictions to be tested.

To control the overall level of significance for each series of tests, direct and indirect, we set the level of significance for each series at 0.05. We then allocate the overall level of significance among the various stages in each series of tests. We test groupwise separability, homotheticity, groupwise homotheticity, groupwise linear logarithmic utility, and groupwise equal rates of commodity augmentation proceeding conditionally on the validity of the equality and symmetry restrictions implied by the theory of demand. These tests are not "nested" so that the sum of the levels of significance for each of the five sets of hypotheses is an upper bound for the level of significance of tests of the sets of hypotheses considered simultaneously. We assign a level of significance of 0.01 to each of the five sets of restrictions.

There are twelve restrictions associated with groupwise separability and explicit groupwise separability; we assign a level of significance of 0.0008 to each. There are three restrictions associated with homotheticity; we assign 0.0033 to each. There are twelve restrictions associated with groupwise homotheticity; we assign 0.0008 to each. There are three restrictions associated with groupwise linear logarithmic utility; we assign 0.033 to each of these restrictions. Finally, there are six restrictions associated with groupwise equal rates of commodity augmentation; we assign a level of significance of 0.0017 to each.

Table 2.3
Critical values of χ^2/degrees of freedom

Degrees of freedom	Level of significance					
	0.10	0.05	0.01	0.005	0.001	0.0005
1	2.71	3.84	6.64	7.88	10.83	12.12
2	2.30	3.00	4.61	5.30	6.91	7.60

For our econometric models of demand based on the direct and indirect translog utility functions with time-varying preferences we have assigned levels of significance to each of our tests of hypotheses about the structure of preferences so as to control the overall level of significance for all tests at 0.05. The probability of a false rejection for one test among the collection of all tests we consider is less than or equal to 0.05. With the aid of critical values for our test statistics given in table 2.3, the reader can evaluate the results of our tests for alternative significance levels or for alternative allocations of the overall level of significance among stages of our test procedure. Test statistics for each of the hypotheses we have considered about the structure of preferences are given in table 2.4.

The results of our tests of restrictions on preferences based on the direct translog utility functions, as presented in table 2.4, are, first, that the group {1,2}, durables and nondurables, is separable from commodity 2, energy, and that the group {2,3}, nondurables and energy, is separable from commodity 1, durables. These two sets of restrictions imply additivity. Second, the group {1,3}, durables and energy, and the group {2,3}, nondurables and energy, are separable from time. These two sets of restrictions imply neutrality. Third, all three possible groups of two commodities each are groupwise homothetic; hence, each of these groups is homothetically separable. Fourth, the group {1,3}, durables and energy, is explicitly inclusive groupwise homothetic, which implies explicit linear logarithmic utility. Finally, the group [1,3} is explicitly separable from time, which implies neutral linear logarithmic utility or constant budget shares. This specification is determined by only two unknown parameters.

Turning to the results of our tests of restrictions on preferences based on the indirect translog utility function, as presented in table 2.4, we find that the group {1,3}, consisting of durables and non-

Table 2.4
Test statistics

Hypothesis	Degrees of freedom	Critical values	Test statistics direct	Test statistics indirect
		Given equality and symmetry		
Groupwise separability				
{1, 2} from 3	1	11.35	4.40	0.55
{1, 3} from 2	1	11.35	27.52	15.14
{2, 3} from 1	1	11.35	1.86	30.35
{1, 2} from t	1	11.35	15.44	3.83
{1, 3} from t	1	11.35	7.08	27.96
{2, 3} from t	1	11.35	4.11	37.73
Homotheticity	2	5.98	28.24	25.37
Groupwise homotheticity				
{1, 2}	1	11.35	1.87	1.08
{1, 3}	1	11.35	1.90	24.68
{2, 3}	1	11.35	3.21	17.65
Groupwise equal rates				
{1, 2}	1	10.32	11.89	2.13
{1, 3}	1	10.32	12.45	16.50
{2, 3}	1	10.32	14.18	30.38
		Given groupwise separability		
Groupwise explicit separability				
{1, 2} from 3	1	11.35	12.61	1.39
{1, 3} from 2	1	11.35	0.88	0.38
{2, 3} from 1	1	11.35	11.61	5.27
{1, 2} from t	1	11.35	0.00	3.99
{1, 3} from t	1	11.35	4.97	0.67
{2, 3} from t	1	11.35	28.16	15.17
		Given homotheticity		
Explicit homotheticity	2	5.98	10.09	1.20
		Given groupwise homotheticity		
Groupwise inclusive homotheticity				
{1, 2}	1	11.35	29.25	13.04
{1, 3}	1	11.35	3.56	21.99
{2, 3}	1	11.35	20.77	13.11
Groupwise explicit homotheticity				
{1, 2}	1	11.35	12.70	1.63
{1, 3}	1	11.35	10.77	0.16
{2, 3}	1	11.35	26.20	13.99

Table 2.4 (continued)

Hypothesis	Degrees of freedom	Critical values	Test statistics direct	indirect
	Given groupwise equal rates			
Groupwise zero rates				
{1, 2}	1	10.32	0.23	5.12
{1, 3}	1	10.32	2.21	2.60
{2, 3}	1	10.32	0.08	4.90
	Given explicit homotheticity			
Homogeneity	1	9.13	3.21	45.40
	Given groupwise explicit inclusive homotheticity			
Groupwise homogeneity				
{1, 2}	1	11.35	3.69	38.89
{1, 3}	1	11.35	32.01	13.12
{2, 3}	1	11.35	13.82	52.24
	Given groupwise homothetic separability			
Groupwise linear logarithmic utility				
{1, 2}	1	9.13	15.72	27.06
{1, 3}	1	9.13	1.57	20.50
{2, 3}	1	9.13	16.02	10.35

durables, is explicitly groupwise separable from commodity 2, energy, and from time. This group is also explicitly groupwise homothetic and has equal rates of commodity augmentation equal to zero. The form of the system of equations corresponding to the indirect utility function is as follows

$$\frac{p_1 X_1}{M} = \frac{\alpha_1 + \beta_{11}(\ln[p_1/M] - \ln[p_2/M])}{-1 + \beta_{33}\ln(p_3/M) + \beta_{3t}\cdot t},$$

$$\frac{p_2 X_2}{M} = \frac{\alpha_2 - \beta_{11}(\ln[p_1/M] - \ln[p_2/M])}{-1 + \beta_{33}\ln(p_3/M) + \beta_{3t}\cdot t},$$

$$\frac{p_3 X_3}{M} = \frac{\alpha_3 + \beta_{33}\ln(p_3/M) + \beta_{3t}\cdot t}{-1 + \beta_{33}\ln(p_3/M) + \beta_{3t}\cdot t}.$$

This specification is determined by five unknown parameters. We recall that the direct and indirect utility function represent the same preferences only if they are self-dual. The dual of the neutral linear logarithmic direct utility function is the neutral linear logarithmic indirect utility function. We conclude that the test results for the two models do not coincide. This is not surprising since the stochastic specifications used in the two sets of tests are different.

Notes

1. Direct and indirect utility functions with time-varying preferences are discussed by Lau (1969a).
2. A function $U = F(X)$ is an algebraic function if U can be defined implicitly by an equation $G(U, X) = 0$, where G is a polynomial in U and X. All functions which are not algebraic are transcendental. See Courant (1936), p. 119.
3. See Christensen, Jorgenson and Lau (1975). Earlier Christensen, Jorgenson and Lau (1971, 1973) introduced transcendental logarithmic functions into the study of production.
4. See Lau and Mitchel (1971) and Christensen and Manser (1974, 1975).
5. See Schultz (1938), Stone (1954b), and Wold (1953). For a proof that an integrable system of double logarithmic demand functions with time trends implies neutral linear logarithmic utility, see Jorgenson and Lau (1979a).
6. See Barten (1964a, 1967, 1969), McFadden (1964), and Theil (1965, 1967, 1971). For a proof that an integrable Rotterdam system with time intercepts implies explicit neutral linear logarithmic utility, see Jorgenson and Lau (1979a).
7. See Houthakker (1960) and Stone (1954a). The linear expenditure system was originally proposed by Klein and Rubin (1947–1948).
8. See Basmann (1969), Johanson (1969) and Sato (1972). For an empirical application see Brown and Heien (1972). A recent survey of econometric studies of consumer demand is given by Brown and Deaton (1972).
9. A detailed reconciliation of our concept of personal consumption expenditures and the national accounting concept is given by Christensen and Jorgenson (1973), pp. 331–348.
10. Systems of direct and indirect demand functions with these properties are discussed by Christensen, Jorgenson and Lau (1975).
11. This is the logarithmic form of Roy's identity. See Roy (1943).
12. Monotonicity and quasiconvexity restrictions are discussed by Lau (1974). See also Jorgenson and Lau (1979).
13. This is the special case introduced by Hicks (1969). See also Samuelson (1969).
14. For some of these results on the duality of direct and indirect utility functions, see Houthakker (1960), Samuelson (1960) and Lau (1969b).
15. See Samuelson (1965) and Houthakker (1965a). We may also mention the "self-dual addilog system" introduced by Houthakker (1965a). This system is not generated by additive utility functions except for special cases.
16. See Malinvaud (1970), pp. 366–368.
17. We employ the maximum likelihood estimator discussed, for example, by Malinvaud (1970), pp. 338–341. For the direct series of tests we assume that the disturbances are independent of the quantities consumed. For the indirect series of tests we assume that the disturbances are independent of the ratios of prices to the value of total expenditure.

3 Statistical Tests of the Theory of Consumer Behavior

Dale W. Jorgenson and Lawrence J. Lau

3.1 Introduction

The traditional starting point for econometric studies of consumer behavior is a system of demand functions, giving quantities demanded as functions of prices and income. Tests of the theory of consumer behavior are formulated by interpreting the demand functions and the budget constraints as the solutions to a system of partial differential equations. If the system of demand functions is integrable, it can be generated by maximization of a utility function, subject to the budget constraint. The conditions for integrability imply restrictions on the system of demand functions that can be tested statistically.

Statistical tests of the theory of consumer behavior based on the integrability of consumer demand functions originated with the pioneering studies of Schultz (1938). Schultz's tests were based on the double-logarithmic system of demand functions with constant price and income elasticities of demand. This system of demand functions was subsequently employed in the classic studies of consumer demand by Stone (1954b) and by Wold (1953). An important stimulus to the development of tests of the theory of consumer demand has been provided by the pathbreaking work of Barten (1964a) and Theil (1965), based on the Rotterdam system of demand functions. A comprehensive review of empirical research on the integrability of systems of consumer demand function has been given by Brown and Deaton (1972).

The purpose of this chapter is to consider the selection of a parametric representation of consumer preferences in formulating statistical tests of the theory of consumer behavior. We find that a broad class of systems of demand functions that is linear in the parameters and includes the double logarithmic system of Schultz, Stone, and Wold is integrable if and only if it can be generated by a neutral linear logarithmic utility function.[1] For this utility function the proportion of the consumer budget allocated to each commodity is independent of prices, income, and time. Similarly, the Rotterdam system of Barten and Theil is integrable if and only if it can be generated by a neutral linear logarithmic utility function.[2] We conclude that for these demand systems the hypothesis of integrability can be tested only in conjunction with the hypothesis of neutral linear logarithmic utility.

3.2 Integrability

A complete system of demand functions can be written in the form

$$X_j = D^j(p_1, p_2, \ldots, p_m, M, t), \qquad (j = 1, 2, \ldots, m),$$

where X_j $(j = 1, 2, \ldots, m)$ is the quantity consumed of the jth commodity, p_j $(j = 1, 2, \ldots, m)$ is the price of the jth commodity, M is the value of the total expenditure, and t is time. We assume that the functions D^j $(j = 1, 2, \ldots, m)$ are continuously differentiable. A system of demand functions is *integrable* if it can be generated by maximization of a utility function $U(X_1, X_2, \ldots, X_m, t)$ subject to the budget constraint

$$\sum p_j X_j = M.$$

Utility is nondecreasing and quasi-concave in the quantities consumed.

The conditions for intergrability of a complete system of demand functions are the following:

(1) *Homogeneity*. The demand functions D^j $(j = 1, 2, \ldots, m)$ are homogeneous of degree zero in the prices p_j $(j = 1, 2 \ldots, m)$ and total expenditure M.

(2) *Summability*. The weighted sum of the demand functions with weights given by the prices is equal to total expenditure

$$\sum_{j=1}^{m} p_j D^j(p_1, p_2, \ldots, p_m, M, t) = M,$$

for all p_j $(j = 1, 2, \ldots, m)$, all M, and all t.

(3) *Symmetry*. The matrix of compensated own- and cross-price effects for the demand functions must be symmetric

$$\frac{\partial D^j}{\partial p_k} + X_k \frac{\partial D^j}{\partial M} = \frac{\partial D^k}{\partial p_j} + X_j \frac{\partial D^k}{\partial M}, \qquad (j, k = 1, 2, \ldots, m),$$

for all p_j $(j = 1, 2, \ldots, m)$, all M, and all t.[3]

(4) *Nonnegativity.* The quantities consumed are nonnegative

$$X_j = D^j\,(p_1, p_2, \ldots, p_m, M, t) \geqq 0, \qquad (j = 1, 2, \ldots, m),$$

for all p_j $(j = 1, 2, \ldots, m)$, all M, and all t.

(5) *Monotonicity.* We consider proportional variations in the prices

$$dp_j = \lambda_j dp, \qquad (j = 1, 2, \ldots, m);$$

we can define a composite demand function, say D, as a weighted sum of the demand functions[4]

$$D(p_1, p_2, \ldots, p_m, M, t; \lambda_1, \lambda_2, \ldots, \lambda_m) = \sum \lambda_j D^j\,(p_1, p_2, \ldots, p_m, M, t).$$

The compensated own-price substitution effect for the composite demand function is nonpositive

$$\sum \sum \lambda_j \lambda_k \left(\frac{\partial D^j}{\partial p_k} + X_k \frac{\partial D^j}{\partial M} \right) \leqq 0,$$

for all λ_j $(j = 1, 2, \ldots, m)$, and all M.

If a system of demand functions satisfied conditions (1)–(5), we say that it is *globally integrable.* If the system satisfies these conditions in the neighborhood of some p_j $(j = 1, 2, \ldots, m)$, M, and t, we say that it is *locally* integrable. Since global integrability implies local integrability for all p_j $(j = 1, 2, \ldots, m)$, all M, and all t, we focus attention on the implications of locate integrability for the selection of a parametric representation of consumer preferences.

3.3 Additive Demand Functions

We first consider the implications of local integrability for a system of demand functions giving the budget shares as additive functions of prices, total expenditure and time

$$w_j = f\left[\alpha_j + \sum_k \beta_{jk} g_k(p_k) + \beta_{jM} g_M(M) + \beta_{jt} g_t(t) \right], \qquad (j = 1, 2, \ldots, m),$$

where the parameters $\{\alpha_j, \beta_{jk}, \beta_{jM}, \beta_{jt}\}$ are constants, w_j $(j = 1, 2,...,m)$ is the budget share of the jth commodity

$$w_j = \frac{p_j X_j}{M}, \qquad (j = 1, 2, \ldots, m),$$

the functions $\{f, g_k, g_M, g_t\}$ are twice differentiable, increasing functions of a single variable and the second derivative of f is everywhere negative or everywhere positive. For $f(z) = \exp z$, $g_k(z) = g_M(z) = \ln z$, and $g_t(t) = t$, the system of additive demand functions reduces to the double-logarithmic demand system employed by Schultz (1938), Stone (1954b), and Wold (1953)[5]

$$w_j = \exp\left[\alpha_j + \sum_k \beta_{jk} \ln p_k + \beta_{jM} \ln M + \beta_{jt} \cdot t\right], \qquad (j = 1, 2, \ldots, m).$$

Summability implies that

$$\sum w_j = \sum_j f\left[\alpha_j + \sum_k \beta_{jk} g_k(p_k) + \beta_{jM} g_M(M) + \beta_{jt} g_t(t)\right] = 1,$$

for all p_j $(j = 1, 2, \ldots, m)$, all M, and all t. Differentiating this equation with respect to p_k $(k = 1, 2, \ldots, m)$, M, and t, we obtain

$$\sum_j f' \beta_{jk} = 0, \qquad (k = 1, 2, \ldots, m),$$
$$\sum_j f' \beta_{jM} = 0,$$
$$\sum_j f' \beta_{jt} = 0.$$

Differentiating a second time we obtain

$$\sum_j f'' \beta_{jk}^2 = 0, \qquad (k = 1, 2, \ldots, m),$$
$$\sum_j f'' \beta_{jM}^2 = 0,$$
$$\sum_j f'' \beta_{jt}^2 = 0.$$

Since f'' is everywhere negative or everywhere positive, we conclude that $\beta_{jt} = \beta_{jM} = \beta_{jk} = 0$ $(j, k = 1, 2, \ldots, m)$, so that

$$w_j = f(\alpha_j), \qquad (j = 1, 2, \ldots, m),$$

where

$$\sum f(\alpha_j) = 1.$$

For the double-logarithmic demand system[6]

$$w_j = \exp(\alpha_j), \qquad (j = 1, 2, \ldots, m),$$

where

$$\sum \exp(\alpha_j) = 1.$$

3.4 Rotterdam Demand Functions

We next consider the implications of local integrability for the Rotterdam demand functions employed by Barten (1964a) and Theil (1965).[7] If we permit time-varying preferences the Rotterdam demand system can be written in the form

$$w_j d \ln X_j = -\alpha_j \sum w_k (d \ln p_k) + \sum_k \beta_{jk} d \ln p_k + \beta_{jM} \, d \ln M + \beta_{jt} \, dt, \qquad (j = 1, 2, \ldots, m),$$

where the parameters $(\alpha_j, \beta_{jk}, \beta_{jM}, \beta_{jt})$ are constants. Under summability these parameters satisfy the restrictions

$$\sum \alpha_j = 0,$$
$$\sum \beta_{jk} = 0, \qquad (k = 1, 2, \ldots, m),$$
$$\sum \beta_{jM} = 1,$$
$$\sum \beta_{jt} = 0.$$

The logarithmic derivatives of the logarithms of the budget shares are given by

$$\frac{\partial \ln w_j}{\partial \ln p_k} = \begin{cases} \dfrac{\partial \ln X_j}{\partial \ln p_k}, & (j \neq k; j, k = 1, 2, \ldots, m), \\ 1 + \dfrac{\partial \ln X_j}{\partial \ln p_j}, & (j = k; j = 1, 2, \ldots, m), \end{cases}$$

the derivatives of the logarithms of the budget shares with respect to total expenditure and time are given by

$$\frac{\partial \ln w_j}{\partial \ln M} = \frac{\partial \ln X_j}{\partial \ln M} - 1\,, \qquad (j = 1, 2, \ldots, m)\,,$$

$$\frac{\partial \ln w_j}{\partial t} = \frac{\partial \ln X_j}{\partial t}\,, \qquad (j = 1, 2, \ldots, m)\,.$$

The Rotterdam demand system implies that

$$w_j \frac{\partial \ln X_j}{\partial \ln p_k} = -\alpha_j w_k + \beta_{jk}\,, \qquad (j, k = 1, 2, \ldots, m)\,;$$

$$w_j \frac{\partial \ln X_j}{\partial \ln M} = \beta_{jM}\,, \qquad (j = 1, 2, \ldots, m)\,,$$

$$w_j \frac{\partial \ln X_j}{\partial t} = \beta_{jt}\,, \qquad (j = 1, 2, \ldots, m)\,.$$

We can rewrite these conditions in the form

$$\begin{aligned} \frac{\partial w_j}{\partial \ln p_k} &= w_j \frac{\partial \ln X_j}{\partial \ln p_k} \\ &= -\alpha_j w_k + \beta_{jk}\,, \qquad (j \neq k;\, j, k = 1, 2, \ldots, m)\,; \end{aligned}$$

$$\begin{aligned} \frac{\partial w_j}{\partial \ln p_j} &= w_j \left(1 + \frac{\partial \ln X_j}{\partial \ln p_j}\right) \\ &= (1 - \alpha_j) w_j + \beta_{jj}\,, \qquad (j = 1, 2, \ldots, m)\,; \end{aligned}$$

$$\begin{aligned} \frac{\partial w_j}{\partial \ln M} &= w_j \left(-1 + \frac{\partial \ln X_j}{\partial \ln M}\right) \\ &= -w_j + \beta_{jM}\,, \qquad (j = 1, 2, \ldots, m)\,; \end{aligned}$$

$$\begin{aligned} \frac{\partial w_j}{\partial t} &= w_j \frac{\partial \ln X_j}{\partial t} \\ &= \beta_{jt}\,, \qquad (j = 1, 2, \ldots, m)\,. \end{aligned}$$

We first consider the implications of integrability for a Rotterdam demand system with three or more commodities; interchanging the order of differentiation, we obtain the conditions

$$\frac{\partial^2 w_j}{\partial \ln p_i \partial \ln p_k} = -\alpha_j \frac{\partial w_i}{\partial \ln p_k} = -\alpha_j \frac{\partial w_k}{\partial \ln p_i}\,, \quad (i \neq j \neq k\,;\, i, j, k = 1, 2, \ldots, m)\,.$$

If $\alpha_j \neq 0$ $(j = 1, 2, \ldots, m)$, then

$$-\alpha_i w_k + \beta_{ik} = -\alpha_k w_i + \beta_{ki}, \qquad (i \neq k; i, k = 1, 2, \ldots, m).$$

Combining $m - 1$ of these conditions with the condition for summability, we can construct a system of linear equations in the budget shares $\{w_i\}$ that has an unique solution. For example, letting $i = 1$ and $k = 2, 3, \ldots, m$, we obtain

$$\begin{bmatrix} 1 & 1 & 1 & \ldots & 1 \\ -\alpha_2 & \alpha_1 & 0 & \ldots & 0 \\ -\alpha_3 & 0 & \alpha_1 & \ldots & 0 \\ \vdots & \vdots & \vdots & & \vdots \\ -\alpha_m & 0 & 0 & \ldots & \alpha_1 \end{bmatrix} \begin{bmatrix} w_1 \\ w_2 \\ w_3 \\ \vdots \\ w_m \end{bmatrix} = \begin{bmatrix} 1 \\ \beta_{12} - \beta_{21} \\ \beta_{13} - \beta_{31} \\ \vdots \\ \beta_{1m} - \beta_{m1} \end{bmatrix}.$$

The determinant of the matrix of coefficients is

$$\alpha_1^{n-1} \cdot \sum_{j=1}^{m} \alpha_j = \alpha_1^{n-1} \neq 0,$$

so that this system of equations determines the budget shares uniquely and these shares are constant. This proof does not depend on homogeneity, symmetry, nonnegativity or monotonicity of the system of demand functions. A system with constant budget shares has all of these properties.

A Rotterdam demand system with only two commodities is not necessarily characterized by constant budget shares. We suppose, as before, that $\alpha_j \neq 0$ $(j = 1, 2)$. Interchanging the order of differentiation, we obtain

$$\frac{\partial^2 w_j}{\partial t \partial \ln p_j} = (1 - \alpha_j) \frac{\partial w_j}{\partial t} = (1 - \alpha_j)\beta_{jt} = 0, \qquad (j = 1, 2),$$

so that

$$\beta_{jt} = 0, \qquad (j = 1, 2).$$

Using these restrictions and the restrictions implied by summability, we can write the partial derivatives of the first budget share in the form

$$\frac{\partial w_1}{\partial \ln p_1} = (1 - \alpha_1)w_1 + \beta_{11},$$

$$\frac{\partial w_1}{\partial \ln p_2} = -\alpha_1(1 - w_1) + \beta_{12}\,,$$
$$= -\alpha_1(1 - w_1) - \beta_{11}\,,$$

$$\frac{\partial w_1}{\partial \ln M} = -w_1 + \beta_{1M}\,.$$

To derive an explicit form for the system of direct demand functions we can treat this system as the solution of a system of partial differential equations. Using $e^{-(1-\alpha_1)\ln p_1}$ as an integrating factor, we can write

$$\frac{\partial e^{-(1-\alpha_1)\ln p_1} w_1}{\partial \ln p_1} = \beta_{11} e^{-(1-\alpha_1)\ln p_1}\,,$$

so that

$$w_1 = \frac{-\beta_{11}}{1-\alpha_1} + \phi(\ln p_2, \ln M)e^{(1-\alpha_1)\ln p_1}\,.$$

Differentiating with respect to $\ln p_2$, we obtain

$$\frac{\partial w_1}{\partial \ln p_2} = \frac{\partial \phi}{\partial \ln p_2} e^{(1-\alpha_1)\ln p_1}$$
$$= -\alpha_1\left[1 + \frac{\beta_{11}}{1-\alpha_1} - \phi(\ln p_2, \ln M)e^{(1-\alpha_1)\ln p_1}\right] - \beta_{11}\,.$$

Since the function ϕ and its derivative are independent of p_1, the parameters must satisfy

$$\beta_{11} = -\alpha_1(1 - \alpha_1)\,,$$

and ϕ satisfies the partial differential equation

$$\frac{\partial \phi}{\partial \ln p_2} = \alpha_1 \phi(\ln p_2, \ln M)\,,$$

so that ϕ is an exponential function of $\ln p_2$

$$\phi(\ln p_2, \ln M) = \psi(\ln M)e^{a_1 \ln p_2},$$

where ψ is a function of $\ln M$ alone.

We can write the first budget share in the form

$$w_1 = \alpha_1 + \psi(\ln M)e^{(1-\alpha_1)\ln p_1 + \alpha_1 \ln p_2}.$$

Differentiating with respect to $\ln M$, we obtain

$$\begin{aligned}\frac{\partial w_1}{\partial \ln M} &= \frac{\partial \psi}{\partial \ln M}\, e^{(1-\alpha_1)\ln p_1 + \alpha_1 \ln p_2} \\ &= -\alpha_1 - \psi(\ln M)\, e^{(1-\alpha_1)\ln p_1 + \alpha_1 \ln p_2 + \beta_{1M}}.\end{aligned}$$

Since the function ψ and its derivative are independent of p_1 and p_2, the parameters must satisfy

$$-\alpha_1 + \beta_{1M} = 0,$$

and ψ satisfies the ordinary differential equation

$$\frac{d\psi}{d \ln M} = -\psi(\ln M)$$

so that

$$\psi(\ln M) = Ke^{-\ln M}$$

where K is a constant.

We conclude that the budget shares can be written in the form

$$\begin{aligned}w_1 &= \alpha_1 + Ke^{(1-\alpha_1)\ln p_1 + \alpha_1 \ln p_2 - \ln M}, \\ w_2 &= (1-\alpha_1) - Ke^{(1-\alpha_1)\ln p_1 + \alpha_1 \ln p_2 - \ln M}.\end{aligned}$$

This proof does not depend on homogeneity, symmetry, nonnegativity or monotonicity of the system of demand functions. The resulting system has all of these properties. If $K = 0$, the budget shares are constant.

Up to this point we have assumed that $\alpha_j \neq 0\ (j = 1, 2, \ldots, m)$. If $\alpha_j = 0$ for some j, the implications of integrability for the Rotterdam system are slightly different. Under this condition the Rotterdam system implies

$$\frac{\partial w_j}{\partial \ln \frac{p_i}{M}} = \beta_{ji}, \qquad (i \neq j; i = 1, 2, \ldots, m),$$

$$\frac{\partial w_j}{\partial \ln \frac{p_j}{M}} = w_j + \beta_{jj},$$

$$\frac{\partial w_j}{\partial t} = \beta_{jt}.$$

Interchanging the order of differentiation, as before, we obtain

$$\frac{\partial^2 w_j}{\partial \ln \frac{p_i}{M} \partial \ln \frac{p_j}{M}} = \frac{\partial w_j}{\partial \ln \frac{p_i}{M}} = \beta_{ji} = 0, \qquad (i \neq j; i = 1, 2, \ldots, m),$$

and

$$\frac{\partial^2 w_j}{\partial t \partial \ln \frac{p_j}{M}} = \frac{\partial w_j}{\partial t} = \beta_{jt} = 0.$$

Summability implies that

$$\beta_{jj} = 0,$$

so that

$$\frac{\partial w_j}{\partial \ln \frac{p_j}{M}} = w_j,$$

and

$$\frac{\partial \ln X_j}{\partial \ln \frac{p_j}{M}} = 0.$$

We conclude that the quantity X_j is independent of the ratios of prices to total expenditure and time, and must be constant.

For all commodities with α_j equal to zero, the quantities are constant. If there are three or more commodities remaining, we can express the budget shares as linear and homogeneous functions of the proportion of the budget remaining after expenditure on the fixed quantities is determined. Nonnegativity requires that the proportion of the budget remaining must be positive. If there are two commodities remaining, we can derive an explicit form for the two corresponding direct demand functions that is analogous to the form we have derived for a Rotterdam demand system with only two commodities. If there is only one commodity remaining, the budget share of that commodity is equal to the proportions of the budget remaining after expenditure on the fixed quantities as determined. As before, this proof does not depend on homogeneity, symmetry, nonnegativity, or monotonicity of the system of demand functions.[8]

3.5 Conclusion

We have considered the implications of local integrability for a system of additive demand functions that includes the double-logarithmic demand system as a special case and for the Rotterdam demand system. With the exceptions we have noted these systems are locally integrable if and only if they are characterized by constant budget shares. A demand system with constant budget shares can be generated by a neutral linear logarithmic utility function

$$U = F\left(\sum \alpha_j \ln X_j, t\right).$$

An alternative interpretation of the double-logarithmic and Rotterdam systems of demand functions is to regard each of these systems as first-order Taylor's series approximations to an arbitrary integrable demand system.[9] Integrability of the underlying demand system implies that the approximating system satisfies the conditions for integrability at the point of approximation, but not necessarily at other points. Wold (1953) present a test of symmetry based on the double-logarithmic system of demand functions. This test depends on estimated parameters of the double-logarithmic system and on average budget shares for commodity groups. By interpreting the fitted demand functions as approximations to an integrable demand system at the average ratios of prices to income, this test can be interpreted as a test of symmetry of the approximating system at the point of approximation.[10] Stone (1954b) presents a test of homogeneity based on the double-logarithmic system. A double-logarithmic approximation to a homogeneous demand system is homogeneous; this property of the approximating system is implied by the corresponding property of the underlying system.[11]

The double-logarithmic approximation to an arbitrary integrable demand system is not necessarily integrable, except at the point of approximation; however, the Rotterdam system, interpreted as an approximation, is integrable if the underlying system is integrable. Integrability of the Rotterdam system of demand functions implies that the system can be generated by a neutral linear logarithmic utility function. The Rotterdam system can be used to test integrability only in conjunction with neutral linear logarithmic utility, whether or not this system is interpreted as an approximation to an underlying demand system in the case of more than two commodities.

Notes

1. See below, section 3.3, "Additive Demand Functions." We generalize the results of Wold (1953), p. 106, and Basmann, Battalio, and Kagel (1973).
2. Except for demand systems with only two commodities or demand systems with constant components of the consumer budget. See below, section 3.4, "Rotterdam Demand Functions." We generalize the results of McFadden (1964).
3. Symmetry conditions for integrability based on the indirect demand functions can be traced to Antonelli (1971) and Slutsky (1952). For additional references and discussion, see Samuelson (1950) and Hurwicz (1971, especially pp. 188–210).
4. This construction is employed by Leontief (1936) and by Hicks (1939). For additional references and discussion, see Wold (1953, pp. 108–110).
5. The double-logarithmic demand system has also been used for tests of integrability by Byron (1968, 1970a,b, 1973), Court (1967), and Lluch (1971). For further discussion, see Brown and Deaton (1972, pp. 1193–1195).
6. For an alternative proof, see Basmann, Battalio, and Kagel (1973).
7. The Rotterdam system has also been used for tests of integrability by Barten (1967, 1969, 1974), Parks (1969), Theil (1971), Lluch (1971), and Deaton (1974).
8. For alternative proofs, see McFadden (1964), Goldberger (1969), and Barten (1974).
9. This interpretation of the double-logarithmic demand system has been proposed by Stone (1954b) and by Byron (1973); the corresponding interpretation of the Rotterdam system has been proposed by Barten (1969, 1974). For further discussion, see Brown and Deaton (1972, especially pp. 1190–1195).
10. See Wold (1953, chapter 17, especially pp. 281–302). A similar test is presented by Byron (1970b).
11. See Stone (1954b, table 107, p. 329). A similar test is presented by Byron (1970b).

4 The Integrability of Consumer Demand Functions

Dale W. Jorgenson and Lawrence J. Lau

4.1 Introduction

One of the primary objectives of statistical demand analysis, originating with the pioneering studies of Henry Schultz (1938), is to test the theory of consumer behavior. The traditional starting point for demand analysis is a system of consumer demand functions, giving quantities demanded as functions of prices, income, and time. If the system of demand functions can be generated by maximization of a utility function, subject to a budget constraint, the system is said to be *integrable*. Conditions for integrability imply the existence of an underlying utility function; these conditions imply restrictions on the system of demand functions that can be tested.

To implement statistical tests of the theory of consumer behavior, it is necessary to select a parametric representation of consumer demand functions. Despite the existence of an impressive array of empirical tests of the theory of consumer behavior, the selection of an appropriate parametric representation remains an unresolved issue. Schultz's tests were based on the double-logarithmic system of demand functions with constant price and income elasticities of demand. This system of demand functions was subsequently employed in the classic studies of consumer demand by Stone (1954b) and by Wold (1953).

The double-logarithmic system of Schultz, Stone, and Wold has proved to be very useful in descriptive studies of consumer expenditure. The system is linear in the unknown price and income elasticities and is easy to implement econometrically. The double-logarithmic system is less attractive as a vehicle for testing the theory of consumer demand, since this system is integrable if and only if it can be generated by a neutral linear logarithmic utility function.[1] For this utility function the proportion of the consumer budget allocated to each commodity is independent of prices, income, and time.

Income elasticities of demand are equal to unity, own-price elasticities are equal to minus unity, and cross-price elasticities are zero.

An important stimulus to the development of statistical tests of the theory of consumer demand has been provided by the path-breaking work of Barten (1964a) and Theil (1965), based on the Rotterdam system of demand functions. The Rotterdam system of Barten and Theil is linear in the unknown parameters and has proved to be useful in descriptive studies. Like the double-logarithmic system the Rotterdam system is integrable if and only if it can be generated by a neutral linear logarithmic utility function, so that the implications of integrability can be tested only in conjunction with the hypothesis of neutral linear logarithmic utility.[2]

To show that the double-logarithmic and Rotterdam systems of demand functions are integrable only if they can be generated by neutral linear logarithmic utility functions, it is sufficient to use only two of the implications of integrability, namely, that demand functions are nonnegative and that demand functions, weighted by prices, must sum to the value of total expenditure for all prices and all values of total expenditure. Jorgenson and Lau (1977) and Lau (1977a) have shown that a wider class of systems of consumer demand functions *linear in the unknown parameters* satisfies these two conditions if and only if budget shares are constant, so that the underlying utility function is neutral linear logarithmic.

The purpose of this chapter is to analyze the implications of integrability for an important class of consumer demand functions which are *nonlinear in the unknown parameters*. Specifically, we consider the following parametric representation of a system of direct demand functions

$$\begin{aligned} w_j &= p_j X_j / M \\ &= \frac{\alpha_j + \sum \beta_{jk} g(p_k/M) + \beta_{jM} g_M(M) + \beta_{jt} g_t(t)}{-1 + \sum \beta^j_{Mk} g(p_k/M) + \beta^j_{MM} g_M(M) + \beta^j_{Mt} g_t(t)}, \\ &\qquad j = 1, 2, \ldots, m, \end{aligned} \tag{4.1.1}$$

where the functions g, g_M, and g_t are arbitrary twice continuously differentiable and strictly monotone increasing functions of a single variable, p_i is the price and X_i is the quantity of the *ith* commodity $(i = 1, 2, \ldots, m)$, M is total expenditure and t is time. Taking the function in the denominator to be the sum of the numerators of the demand functions, the condition that the sum of the demand functions, weighted by prices, is equal to total expenditure is satisfied without imposing further restrictions on the unknown parameters $\{\alpha_j, \beta_{jk}, \beta_{jM}, \beta_{jt}\}$.

The representation (4.1.1) of systems of consumer demand functions was first proposed by Jorgenson and Lau (1975). This approach is based on the indirect transcendental logarithmic utility function introduced by Christensen, Jorgenson, and Lau (1975). Taking the indirect utility function to be translog in form with time-varying preferences, Roy's (1943) identity implies the direct translog system of consumer demand functions,

$$w_j = \frac{\alpha_j + \sum \beta_{jk} \ln(p_k/M) + \beta_{jt} t}{-1 + \sum \beta_{Mk} \ln(p_k/M) + \beta_{Mt} t}, \qquad j = 1, 2, \ldots, m. \tag{4.1.2}$$

In this demand system the function g in the representation (4.1.1) is logarithmic, the function g_M is constant, and the function g_t is linear. The parameters $\{\beta^j_{Mk}, \beta^j_{Mt}\}$ are the same for all demand functions and the parameters $\{\alpha_j, \beta_{jk}, \beta_{jt}\}$ satisfy integrability conditions implied by the indirect translog utility function.

In this chapter we consider the implications of integrability for the system of expenditure share functions (4.1.1). In particular, we characterize the class of functions g, g_M and g_t which are consistent with integrability. We show that the only functions g in this class are logarithmic functions and power functions; further, the only functions that allow the system of demand functions to model arbitrary own- and cross-substitution effects are the logarithmic functions.[3] Any other choice of g in eqs. (4.1.1) results in an integrable system of demand functions only if all expenditure shares are constants, that is, only if the utility function is neutral linear logarithmic. We also consider integrability of a system of *indirect demand functions*, that is, prices as functions of quantities. By analogy with the case of the direct demand functions, we choose the representation

$$\begin{aligned} w_j &= p_j X_j / M \\ &= \frac{\alpha_j + \sum \beta_{jk} g(X_k) + \beta_{jM} g_M(M) + \beta_{jt} g_t(t)}{-1 + \sum \beta^j_{Mk} g(X_k) + \beta^j_{MM} g_M(M) + \beta^j_{Mt} g_t(t)}. \end{aligned} \tag{4.1.3}$$

The implications of integrability for indirect demand functions are strictly analogous to those for direct demand functions.

In addition to restrictions on forms for the functions g, g_M and g_t, integrability implies restrictions on the unknown parameters. These restrictions on the parameters provide the basis for statistical tests of the theory of consumer behavior. An unresolved problem in implementing econometric tests of the theory of individual consumer behavior is to provide an appropriate methodology for testing the hypothesis of monotonicity of a system of demand functions. We present methods for testing the monotonicity of a complete system of demand functions; our approach is based on the Jacobian of the complete system and does not require symmetry.[4] This approach is an extension of the methods developed by Lau (1978) for testing the semi-definiteness of a real symmetric matrix; Lau's methods are based on the Cholesky factorization of the matrix.[5]

Our methodology for testing the theory of consumer behavior can be applied directly to the analysis of data based on observations of individual consumers or households. It can also be used to test the applicability of the theory of individual consumer behavior to the analysis of aggregate consumer demand functions in per capita form. We can test whether the system of per capita consumer demands, considered as functions of prices and per capita total expenditure, is itself integrable. One advantage of using the representation of the system of demand functions in the forms of eqs. (4.1.1) and (4.1.3) with g logarithmic in form lies in the fact that integrability does not imply that the demand systems are generated by neutral linear logarithmic utility functions. However, neutral linear logarithmic utility is a special case so that the hypothesis of neutral linear logarithmic utility can be tested separately from the hypothesis of integrability. A natural sequence of tests would be to test neutral linear logarithmic utility along with other restrictions on the structure of the utility function, proceeding conditionally on integrability.[6]

4.2 Integrability

We consider systems of direct and indirect demand functions without assuming that they can be generated by the indirect and direct utility functions. For this purpose we can regard the direct demand system as giving the quantities as functions of the ratios of prices to total expenditure, total expenditure, and time,

$$X_j = C^j(p_1/M, p_2/M, \ldots, p_m/M, M, t), \qquad j = 1, 2, \ldots, m. \tag{4.2.1}$$

We assume that the functions C^j, $(j = 1, 2, \ldots, m)$ are continuously differentiable. Similarly, we can regard the indirect demand system as giving the ratios of prices to total expenditure as functions of the quantities and total expenditure,

$$p_j/M = D^j(X_1, X_2, \ldots, X_m, M, t), \qquad j = 1, 2, \ldots, m. \tag{4.2.2}$$

We assume that the functions D^j, $(j = 1, 2, \ldots, m)$ are continuously differentiable. Two parallel and equivalent sets of conditions for integrability are the following:

4.2.1 Homogeneity

For the direct demand system the quantities are independent of total expenditure for *given* ratios of prices to total expenditure,

$$\partial X_j/\partial M = \partial C^j/\partial M(p_1/M, p_2/M, \ldots, p_m/M, M, t) = 0, \qquad j = 1, 2, \ldots, m, \tag{4.2.3}$$

for all p_j/M, $(j = 1, 2, \ldots, m)$, all M, and all t. Similarly, for the indirect demand system the ratios of prices to total expenditure are independent of total expenditure for given quantities,

$$\partial(p_j/M) / \partial M = \partial D^j/\partial M(X_1, X_2, \ldots, X_m, M, t) = 0, \qquad j = 1, 2, \ldots, m, \tag{4.2.4}$$

for all X_j, $(j = 1, 2, \ldots, m)$, all M, and all t.

4.2.2 Summability

The weighted sum of the direct demand functions with weights given by the corresponding ratios of prices total expenditure is equal to unity,

$$\sum p_j/M \cdot C^j(p_1/M, p_2/M, \ldots, p_m/M, M, t) = 1, \tag{4.2.5}$$

for all p_j/M $(j = 1, 2, \ldots, m)$, all M, and all t. Similarly, the weighted sum of the indirect demand functions with weights given by the corresponding quantities is equal to unity.

$$\sum D^j (X_1, X_2, \ldots, X_m, M, t) \cdot X_j = 1 , \tag{4.2.6}$$

for all X_j $(j = 1, 2, \ldots, m)$, all M, and all t.

4.2.3 Symmetry

The matrix of compensated own- and cross-price effects for the direct demand functions must be symmetric,

$$\partial C^j/\partial(p_k/M) - C_k \sum \partial C^j/\partial(p_i/M) \cdot p_i/M = \partial C^k/\partial(p_j/M) \\ - C_j \sum \partial C^k/\partial(p_i/M) \cdot p_i/M , \quad j, k = 1, 2, \ldots, m , \tag{4.2.7}$$

for all p_j/M, $(j = 1, 2, \ldots, m)$, all M, and all t. Similarly the matrix of compensated own- and cross-quantity effects for the indirect demand functions must be symmetric,

$$\partial D^j/\partial X_k - D_k \sum \partial D^j/\partial X_i \cdot X_i = \partial D^k/\partial X_j - D_j \sum \partial D^k/\partial X_i \cdot X_i , \\ j, k = 1, 2, \ldots, m , \tag{4.2.8}$$

for all X_j, $(j = 1, 2, \ldots, m)$, all M, and all t.[7]

4.2.4 Nonnegativity

For the direct demand system the quantities are nonnegative,

$$X_j = C^j(p_1/M, p_2/M, \ldots, p_m/M, M, t) \geqq 0, \quad j = 1, 2, \ldots, m , \tag{4.2.9}$$

for all p_j/M, $(j = 1, 2, \ldots, m)$, all M, and all t. Similarly, for the indirect demand system the ratios of prices to total expenditures are nonnegative,

$$p_j/M = D^j(X_1, X_2, \ldots, X_m, M, t) \geqq 0, \quad j = 1, 2, \ldots, m , \tag{4.2.10}$$

for all X_j, $(j = 1, 2, \ldots, m)$, all M, and all t.

4.2.5 Monotonicity

For the direct demand system we consider proportional variations in the ratios of prices to total expenditure,

$$d(p_j/M) = \lambda_j d(p/M), \quad j = 1, 2, \ldots, m. \tag{4.2.11}$$

We can define a composite direct demand function, say C, as a weighted sum of the direct demand functions,[8]

$$C(p_1/M, p_2/M, \ldots, p_m/M, M, t; \lambda_1, \lambda_2, \ldots, \lambda_m)$$
$$\equiv \sum \lambda_j C^j(p_1/M, p_2/M, \ldots, p_m/M, M, t). \tag{4.2.12}$$

The compensated own-price substitution effect for the composite direct demand function is nonpositive,

$$\sum \sum \lambda_j \lambda_k (\partial C^j/\partial(p_k/M) - X_k \sum \partial C^j/\partial(p_i/M) \cdot p_i/M) \leqq 0, \tag{4.2.13}$$

for all λ_j, $(j = 1, 2, \ldots, m)$ and all M. Similarly, for the indirect demand system we consider proportional variations in the quantities demanded,

$$dX_j = \mu_j dX, \quad j = 1, 2, \ldots, m. \tag{4.2.14}$$

We can define a composite indirect demand function, say D, as a weighted sum of the indirect demand functions,

$$D(X_1, X_2, \ldots, X_m, M, t; \mu_1, \mu_2, \ldots, \mu_m)$$
$$\equiv \sum \mu_j D^j(X_1, X_2, \ldots, X_m, M, t). \tag{4.2.15}$$

The compensated own-price substitution effect for the composite direct demand function is nonpositive,

$$\sum \sum \mu_j \mu_k \left(\partial D^j/\partial X_k - p_k/M \sum \partial D^j/\partial X_i \cdot X_i \right) \leqq 0, \tag{4.2.16}$$

for all μ_j, $(j = 1, 2, \ldots, m)$ and all M.

Given homogeneity, summability, and symmetry, the system of direct demand functions can be regarded as a system of partial differential equations,

$$\partial \ln V / \partial \ln (p_j/M) = w_j \sum \partial \ln V / \partial \ln (p_k/M), \quad j = 1, 2, \ldots, m. \tag{4.2.17}$$

The solution of this system defines a family of indirect utility functions V. Given nonnegativity and monotonicity these indirect utility functions can be obtained from each other by monotone increasing transformations.[9] Similarly, given homogeneity, summability, and symmetry, the system of indirect demand functions can be regarded as a system of partial differential equations,

$$\partial \ln U / \partial \ln X_j = w_j \sum \partial \ln U / \partial \ln X_k, \quad j = 1, 2, \ldots, m. \tag{4.2.18}$$

The solution of this system defines a family of direct utility functions U. Given nonnegativity and monotonicity these direct utility functions can be obtained from each other by monotone increasing transformations.[10]

In order to formulate tests of the theory of individual consumer behavior we derive restrictions on the parametric representation of the direct demand system in eq. (4.1.1) corresponding to each of the five properties of an integrable demand system—homogeneity, summability, symmetry, nonnegativity, and monotonicity. By duality we can obtain the corresponding restrictions on the parameters of the indirect demand system in eq. (4.1.3) by interchanging the role of ratios of prices to total expenditure and quantities.

4.3 Homogeneity and Summability

For the direct demand system homogeneity implies that the quantities are independent of total expenditure for given ratios of prices to total expenditure,

$$\begin{aligned}\partial \ln w_i / \partial M = {} & \frac{\beta_{jM} g'_M(M)}{\alpha_j + \sum \beta_{jk} g(p_k/M) + \beta_{jM} g_M(M) + \beta_{jt} g_t(t)} \\ & - \frac{\beta^j_{MM} g'_M(M)}{-1 + \sum \beta^j_{Mk} g(p_k/M) + \beta^j_{MM} g_M(M) + \beta^j_{Mt} g_t(t)} \\ = {} & 0, \quad j = 1, 2, \ldots, m.\end{aligned} \tag{4.3.1}$$

Sufficient conditions for independence are that $\beta_{jM} = \beta^j_{MM} = 0$, $(j = 1, 2, \ldots, m)$. Necessary and sufficient conditions for independence consists of the sufficient conditions or constant budget shares. We refer to the conditions

$$\beta_{jM} = \beta^{j}_{MM} = 0\,, \qquad j = 1, 2, \ldots, m\,, \tag{4.3.2}$$

as the *homogeneity restrictions*. There are $2(m - 1)$ of these restrictions corresponding to two parameters in each of the $m - 1$ equations we estimate.[11] Similarly, for the indirect demand system the ratios of prices to total expenditure are independent of total expenditure for given quantities if restrictions strictly analogous to the homogeneity restrictions given above are satisfied. Necessary and sufficient conditions consist of these conditions or constant budget shares.

For the direct demand system summability implies that the budget shares is equal to unity,

$$\sum w_j = \sum \left(\frac{\alpha_j + \sum \beta_{jk} g(p_k/M) + \beta_{jM} g_M(M) + \beta_{jt} g_t(t)}{-1 + \sum \beta^{j}_{Mk} g(p_k/M) + \beta^{j}_{MM} g_M(M) + \beta^{j}_{Mt} g_t(t)} \right) = 1. \tag{4.3.3}$$

This sum is independent of the ratios of prices to total expenditure p_i/M, $(i = 1, 2, \ldots, m)$, total expenditure M, and time t. Sufficient conditions for summability are that the parameters $\{\beta^{j}_{Mk}, \beta^{j}_{MM}, \beta^{j}_{Mt}\}$ are the same for all j and the conditions

$$\sum \alpha_j = -1\,, \tag{4.3.4}$$

$$\sum \beta_{jk} = \beta_{Mk}\,, \qquad k = 1, 2, \ldots, m\,. \tag{4.3.5}$$

$$\sum \beta_{jM} = \beta_{MM}\,, \tag{4.3.6}$$

$$\sum \beta_{jt} = \beta_{Mt}\,. \tag{4.3.7}$$

If the parameters $\{\beta^{j}_{Mk}, \beta^{j}_{MM}, \beta^{j}_{Mt}\}$ are the same for all j, these conditions are also necessary.

To derive a complete set of necessary and sufficient conditions for summability we consider values of the variables

$$g(p_k/M) = \lambda_k \tau\,, \qquad k = 1, 2, \ldots, m\,. \tag{4.3.8}$$

$$g_M(M) = \lambda_M \tau\,, \tag{4.3.9}$$

$$g_t(t) = \lambda_t \tau\,, \tag{4.3.10}$$

so that the sum of budget shares can be written as

$$\sum w_j = \sum \left(\frac{\alpha_j + (\sum \beta_{jk}\lambda_k + \beta_{jM}\lambda_M + \beta_{jt}\lambda_t)\tau}{-1 + (\sum \beta^j_{Mk}\lambda_k + \beta^j_{MM}\lambda_M + \beta^j_{Mt}\lambda_t)\tau} \right)$$
$$= 1 . \qquad (4.3.11)$$

This sum is independent of τ for all values of parameters $\{\lambda_k, \lambda_M, \lambda_t\}$. Differentiating repeatedly with respect to τ, we obtain the sequence of conditions

$$\frac{d^n \sum w_j}{d\tau^n} = - n! \sum \frac{(\gamma_j + \gamma^j_M \alpha_j)}{(-1 + \gamma^j_M \tau)^{n+1}} (-\gamma^j_M)^{n-1} = 0 , \qquad n = 1, 2, \ldots , \qquad (4.3.12)$$

where

$$\gamma_j = \sum \beta_{jk}\lambda_k + \beta_{jM}\lambda_M + \beta_{jt}\lambda_t , \qquad (4.3.13)$$

$$\gamma^j_M = \sum \beta^j_{Mk}\lambda_k + \beta^j_{MM}\lambda_M + \beta^j_{Mt}\lambda_t , \qquad j = 1, 2, \ldots , m . \qquad (4.3.14)$$

Considering the sequence of necessary conditions, we can partition the m commodities into p mutually exclusive and exhaustive groups such that the parameters $\{\gamma^j_M\}$ are the same for all j within each group for all possible values of the parameters $\{\lambda_k, \lambda_M, \lambda_t\}$. There may, of course, be as many groups as there are commodities. If there is more than one group, we denote the set of indexes of the commodities included in each group by S_l, $(l = 1, 2, \ldots , p)$. Setting $\tau = 0$, the sequence of necessary conditions becomes

$$\sum (\gamma_j + \gamma^j_M \alpha_j)(\gamma^j_M)^{n-1} = 0 , \qquad n = 1, 2, \ldots . \qquad (4.3.15)$$

Since the parameters $\{\gamma^j_M\}$ are the same for all commodities within each group for all values of the parameters $\{\lambda_k, \lambda_M, \lambda_t\}$, we can denote the value of these parameters for the lth group by λ^l_M $(l = 1, 2, \ldots , p)$. Using this notation we can rewrite the sequence of necessary condition in the form

$$\sum_l \left[\sum_{S_1} (\gamma_j + \gamma^l_M \ \alpha_j) \right] (\gamma^l_M)^{n-1} = 0, \qquad n = 1, 2, \ldots , \qquad (4.3.16)$$

so that for each group the coefficient corresponding to γ^l_M, $(l = 1, 2, \ldots , p)$ is zero,

$$\sum_{S_1}(\gamma_j + \gamma_M^l\ \alpha_j) = \sum_{S_1} \gamma_j + \gamma_M^l \sum_{S_1} \alpha_j = 0\,, \qquad l = 1, 2, \ldots, p\,. \tag{4.3.17}$$

Otherwise, we can make the term corresponding to the parameter γ_M^l largest in absolute value and having a nonzero coefficient larger in absolute value than the sum of all the remaining terms by choosing n sufficiently large. But this violates the necessary conditions for summability.

Summing the budget shares for each group, we obtain

$$\begin{aligned}
\sum_{S_1} w_j &= \sum_{S_1}\left(\frac{\alpha_j + \sum \beta_{jk}\, g(p_k/M) + \beta_{jM}\, g_M(M) + \beta_{jt} \cdot g_t(t)}{-1 + \sum \beta_{Mk}^l\, g(p_k/M) + \beta_{MM}^l\, g_M(M) + \beta_{Mt}^l \cdot g_t(t)}\right) \\
&= \frac{\sum_{S_l} \alpha_j \left[1 - \sum \beta_{Mk}^l\, g(p_k/M) - \beta_{MM}^l\, g_M(M) - \beta_{Mt}^l \cdot g_t(t)\right]}{-1 + \sum \beta_{Mk}^l\, g(p_k/M) + \beta_{MM}^l\, g_M(M) + \beta_{Mt}^l \cdot g_t(t)} \\
&= -\sum_{S_l} \alpha_j\,, \qquad l = 1, 2, \ldots, p.
\end{aligned} \tag{4.3.18}$$

Necessary and sufficient conditions for summability consist of the sufficient conditions or constant budget shares for p mutually exclusive and exhaustive groups of the m commodities. We refer to the conditions that the parameters $\{\beta_{Mk}^j, \beta_{MM}^j, \beta_{Mt}^j\}$ are the same for all j as the *equality restrictions*. There are $(m-2)(m+2)$ of these restrictions corresponding to $m+2$ parameters in each of the $m-1$ equations we estimate. For the case $m = 3$, there can be at most one group of two commodities with a constant budget share. But this implies that the budget share for the third commodity is also constant. There is always a way of writing the system of expenditure share functions so that the equality restrictions hold; thus, in this case these restrictions are necessary and sufficient for summability. Similarly, by interchanging the role of ratios of prices to total expenditure and quantities we can derive a strictly analogous set of necessary and sufficient conditions for summability of the indirect demand system.

4.4 Symmetry

To formulate a test of symmetry we first impose homogeneity and equality restrictions, so that the direct demand system can be written in the form[12]

$$w_j = \frac{\alpha_j + \sum \beta_{jk} g(p_k/M) + \beta_{jt} g_t(t)}{-1 + \sum \beta_{Mk} g(p_k/M) + \beta_{Mt} g_t(t)}, \qquad j = 1, 2, \ldots, m, \tag{4.4.1}$$

where

$$\sum \beta_{jk} = \beta_{Mk}, \qquad k = 1, 2, \ldots, m,$$

and

$$\sum \beta_j = \beta_M .$$

Similarly, the indirect demand system can be written in the form

$$w_j = \frac{\alpha_j + \sum \beta_{jk} g(X_k) + \beta_{jt} g_t(t)}{-1 + \sum \beta_{Mk} g(X_k) + \beta_{Mt} g_t(t)}, \qquad j = 1, 2, \ldots, m. \tag{4.4.2}$$

For the direct demand system the typical element of the matrix of uncompensated own- and cross-price substitution effects take the form

$$\frac{\partial X_j}{\partial (p_k/M)} = \frac{1}{p_j/M}\left[\frac{\beta_{jk} g'(p_k/M) - w_j \beta_{Mk} g'(p_k/M)}{-1 + \sum \beta_{Mk} g(p_k/M) + \beta_{Mt} g_t(t)}\right] - \delta_{jk} \frac{w_j}{(p_j/M)^2},$$
$$j = 1, 2, \ldots, m. \tag{4.4.3}$$

where

$$\delta_{jk} = 1 \text{ if } j = k,$$
$$\quad = 0 \text{ if } j \neq k, \qquad j, k = 1, 2, \ldots, m.$$

The corresponding element of the matrix of compensated own- and cross-price substitution effects takes the form

$$\frac{\partial X_j}{\partial (p_k/M)} - X_k \sum \partial X_j/\partial (p_i/M) \cdot \frac{p_i}{M}$$
$$= \frac{g'(p_k/M)}{p_j/M}\left[\frac{\beta_{jk} - w_j \beta_{Mk}}{-1 + \sum \beta_{Mi} g(p_i/M) + \beta_{Mt} g_t(t)}\right]$$
$$- \frac{w_k}{(p_j/M)(p_k/M)}\left[\frac{\sum \beta_{ji} g'(p_i/M) p_i/M - w_j \sum \beta_{Mi} g'(p_i/M) p_i/M}{-1 + \sum \beta_{Mi} g(p_i/M) + \beta_{Mt} g_t(t)}\right]$$
$$+ \frac{w_k w_j}{(p_k/M)(p_j/M)} - \delta_{jk} \frac{w_j}{(p_j/M)^2}, \qquad j, k = 1, 2, \ldots, m. \tag{4.4.4}$$

Symmetry of the matrix of compensated own- and cross-price substitution effects requires that

$$\frac{g'(p_k/M)}{p_j/M}[\beta_{jk} - w_j\beta_{Mk}] - \frac{w_k}{(p_j/M)(p_k/M)}$$

$$\cdot\left[\sum \beta_{ji} g'\left(\frac{p_i}{M}\right)\frac{p_i}{M} - w_j \sum \beta_{Mi} g'\left(\frac{p_i}{M}\right)\frac{p_i}{M}\right]$$

$$= \frac{g'(p_j/M)}{p_k/M}[\beta_{kj} - w_k\beta_{Mj}] - \frac{w_j}{(p_j/M)(p_k/M)}$$

$$\cdot\left[\sum \beta_{ki} g'\left(\frac{p_i}{M}\right)\frac{p_i}{M} - w_k \sum \beta_{Mi} g'\left(\frac{p_i}{M}\right)\frac{p_i}{M}\right],$$

$$j \neq k, \quad j,k = 1,2,\ldots,m, \tag{4.4.5}$$

which may be rewritten as

$$\frac{p_k}{M} g'\left(\frac{p_k}{M}\right)[\beta_{jk} - w_j\beta_{Mk}] - w_k\left[\sum \beta_{ji} g'\left(\frac{p_i}{M}\right)\frac{p_i}{M}\right]$$

$$= \frac{p_j}{M} g'\left(\frac{p_j}{M}\right)[\beta_{kj} - w_k\beta_{Mj}] - w_j\left[\sum \beta_{ki} g'\left(\frac{p_i}{M}\right)\frac{p_i}{M}\right],$$

$$j \neq k, \quad j,k = 1,2,\ldots,m. \tag{4.4.6}$$

In appendix A we show that in order for eq. (4.4.6) to hold identically for all p_k/M, $(k = 1,2,\ldots,m)$ and t there are only three possibilities: (1) the budget shares are constant; (2) the function g is logarithmic,

$$g(Z) = k \ln Z;$$

or (3)

$$(g''(Z)Z + g'(Z)) \,/\, g'(Z) = \sigma,$$

where σ is a constant. If the constant σ is equal to zero the function g is logarithmic, as before; if the constant σ is not equal to zero, then

$$g''(Z)Z = (\sigma - 1)g'(Z),$$

which integrates successively to

$$g(Z) = k * Z^{\sigma-1},$$

and

$$g(Z) = kZ^{\sigma} + k**,$$

so that g is a power function. Without loss of generality we can set the constant k equal to one and k^{**} equal to zero.

The rest of this section is devoted to the implications of symmetry of the Slutsky matrix for demand systems corresponding to (4.4.1) or (4.4.2), where the function g is logarithmic or a power function.[13] We first consider the case of a logarithmic function; eq. (4.4.6) takes the form

$$\left(\beta_{jk} - \beta_{kj}\right) - w_j\left(\beta_{Mk} - \sum \beta_{ki}\right) + w_k\left(\beta_{Mj} - \sum \beta_{ji}\right) = 0,$$

$$j \neq k, \quad j, k = 1, 2, \ldots, m. \tag{4.4.7}$$

An obvious sufficient condition for symmetry of the Slutsky matrix is symmetry of the matrix $\{\beta_{jk}\}$. This is equivalent to the condition that the parameters $\beta_{Mj} - \sum \beta_{ji}$ are zero for all j. If the parameter $\beta_{Mk} - \sum \beta_{ki}$ is not zero for some k, there must be at least one parameter $\beta_{Mj} - \sum \beta_{ji}$ not equal to zero for j not equal to k, since the sum of all these parameters is equal to zero. Further, any commodity for which the parameter $\beta_{Mj} - \sum \beta_{ji}$ is equal to zero must have a constant budget share. Finally, at least one of the parameters $\beta_{jk} - \beta_{kj}$ must be different from zero; otherwise, the parameters $\beta_{Mj} - \sum \beta_{ji}$ are equal to zero for all j. Without loss of generality we can consider only the case that all the parameters $\beta_{Mj} - \sum \beta_{ji}$ are different from zero and at least one of the parameters $\beta_{jk} - \beta_{kj}$ is different from zero.

In appendix B we show that there are three alternative sets of symmetry conditions in addition to symmetry of the matrix $\{\beta_{jk}\}$; the first condition is

$$\beta_{jk} = -\alpha_j \beta_{Mk} + K * \left(\beta_{Mj} + \alpha_j \sum \beta_{Mi}\right)\left(\beta_{Mk} + \alpha_k \sum \beta_{Mi}\right)$$

$$+ K ** \left(\beta_{Mj} + \alpha_j \sum \beta_{Mi}\right)\alpha_k, \quad j, k = 1, 2, \ldots, m,$$

and

$$\beta_{jt} = -\alpha_j\beta_{Mt} + \sigma_t^*\left(\beta_{Mj} + \alpha_j \sum \beta_{Mi}\right), \qquad j = 1, 2, \ldots, m.$$

The total number of independent unknown parameters is $2m + 3$. The second case is

$$\beta_{jk} = \alpha_j\alpha_k \sum \beta_{Mi} + K^*\rho_j(\rho_k + \alpha_k), \qquad j, k = 1, 2, \ldots, m,$$

where the parameter $\sum \rho_k$ is equal to zero and

$$\beta_{jt} = -\alpha_j\beta_{Mt} + \sigma_t^*\rho_j, \qquad j = 1, 2, \ldots, m,$$

where we have replaced the parameter $\sigma_j - \alpha_j$ derived in appendix B by ρ_j to facilitate empirical implementation. The total number of independent unknown parameters is $2m + 2$. The third case is

$$\beta_{jk} = \delta_j\alpha_k, \qquad j \neq k, \ j, k = 1, 2, \ldots, m,$$

and

$$\beta_{jt} = -\alpha_j\beta_{Mt} + \sigma_t^*\left(\delta_j + \alpha_j \sum \delta_i\right), \qquad j = 1, 2, \ldots, m.$$

The total number of independent unknown parameters is $2m + 1$.

We next consider the case in which one of the parameters $\beta_{Mk} - \sum \beta_{ki}$ is equal to zero. This implies that w_k is a constant equal to $-\alpha_k$. Without loss of generality, we take $k = 1$. Thus, by assumption,

$$\beta_{M1} - \sum \beta_{1i} = 0. \tag{4.4.8}$$

By eq. (4.4.7),

$$\left(\beta_{j1} - \beta_{1j}\right) - \alpha_1\left(\beta_{Mj} - \sum \beta_{ji}\right) = 0, \qquad j = 2, 3, \ldots, m. \tag{4.4.9}$$

By constancy of the budget share w_1,

$$\beta_{1j} = -\alpha_1\beta_{Mj}, \qquad j = 1, 2, \ldots, m; t. \tag{4.4.10}$$

Summing eq. (4.4.10) over j, and using eq. (4.4.8), we have

$$\beta_{M1} = -\alpha_1 \sum \beta_{Mi}.$$

Combining eqs. (4.4.9) and (4.4.10), we have

$$\beta_{j1} = -\alpha_1 \sum \beta_{ji}, \quad j = 1, 2, \ldots, m. \tag{4.4.11}$$

For the first specification given above we note that these restrictions are achieved by setting the parameter $\beta_{M1} + \alpha_1 \sum \beta_{Mi}$ equal to zero, in accord with eq. (4.B.19). The number of independent unknown parameters is thus decreased by one. For the second specification the restrictions are achieved by setting $\rho_1 = 0$. The number of independent unknown parameters is thus also decreased by one. For the third specification the restrictions are achieved by setting $\delta_1 + \alpha_1 \sum \delta_i$ equal to zero. The number of independent unknown parameters is again decreased by one. We conclude that setting one of the parameters $\beta_{Mk} - \sum \beta_{ki}$ equal to zero does not give rise to additional specifications to be tested.

The forms of the indirect utility functions that give rise to these integrable direct translog demand systems are monotone transformations of the functions[14]

$$\begin{aligned} \ln V = \ln &\left(\sum \gamma_j \ln (p_j/M) + \gamma_t g_t(t) + \gamma_0 \right) \\ &+ C \ln \left(\sum \delta_j \ln (p_j/M) + \delta_t g_t(t) + \delta_0 \right) + \ln V_0 , \end{aligned} \tag{4.4.12}$$

$$\begin{aligned} \ln V = &\sum \gamma_j \ln (p_j/M) + (C_0 + C_1 g_t(t)) \\ &\cdot \ln \left(\sum \delta_j \ln (p_j/M) + \delta_t g_t(t) + \delta_0 \right) + \ln V_0 , \end{aligned} \tag{4.4.13}$$

$$\begin{aligned} \ln V = \ln &\left(\sum \gamma_j \ln (p_j/M) + \gamma_t g_t(t) + \gamma_0 \right) - \frac{1}{2} \ln \Bigg(\delta_0 + \sum \delta_j \ln (p_j/M) \\ &+ \delta_t g_t(t) + \frac{C}{2} \Bigg(\sum\sum \gamma_j \gamma_k \ln (p_j/M) \ln (p_k/M) \\ &+ \sum_j (\gamma_j \gamma_t + \gamma_t \gamma_j) \ln (p_j/M) g_t(t) + \gamma_t^2 g_t(t)^2 \Bigg) \Bigg) + \ln V_0 . \end{aligned} \tag{4.4.14}$$

These functions give rise to expenditure share functions that are ratios of linear functions of logarithms of prices normalized by total expenditures. None of these functional forms can be generated as special cases of the indirect translog utility function.[15] However, the number of independent parameters for these alternative utility functions is proportional to m whereas the corresponding number of independent parameters for the indirect translog utility function is proportional to m^2. For a moderate size of m, say $m = 4$, the ability of these alternative demand systems to model an arbitrary pattern of own- and cross-price substitution effects is very limited.

In appendix C we consider the case where the function g takes the form of a power function. We show that the parameters must satisfy

$$\begin{aligned} \beta_{jk} &= \alpha_j \beta_k , && j \neq k, \ j,k = 1,2,\ldots,m , \\ \beta_{jj} &= (C\sigma + \alpha_j)\beta_j , && j = 1,2,\ldots,m , \\ \beta_{jt} &= \alpha_j \beta_l , && j = 1,2,\ldots,m . \end{aligned}$$

The total number of symmetry restrictions, given homogeneity and equality, is $m^2 - 2$. Strictly analogous restrictions apply to the indirect demand system. The indirect utility function takes the form

$$\ln V = \sum_j \alpha_j \ln (p_j/M) + C \ln \left(\sum_j \beta_j (p_j/M)^{\sigma} + \beta_t g_t(t) + 1 \right) + \ln V_0 ,$$

which has as a special case of the indirect utility function for the linear expenditure system.

We conclude that the only possible forms for the function g that are consistent with integrability and that allow nonconstant budget shares are logarithmic and power functions. For the logarithmic case, a sufficient condition for symmetry is symmetry of the matrix $\{\beta_{jk}\}$. Necessary and sufficient conditions for symmetry consists of the sufficient conditions or proportionality conditions which imply linear relationships among all pairs of the budget shares. There are at most $m - 1$ independent equations of this type, so that there are no restrictions in the case of only two commodities. Corresponding to each independent equation, there are $m + 2$ restrictions among the parameters of the $m - 1$ equations we estimate. We refer to the conditions

$$\beta_{jk} = \beta_{kj} , \quad j \neq k, \quad j,k = 1,2,\ldots,m ,$$

as *symmetry restrictions*. The total number of symmetry restrictions is $(1/2)m(m - 1)$. The number of restrictions for the *alternate symmetry conditions*, given homogeneity and equality, range from $m^2 - 4$ to $m^2 - 2$, depending on which of the three alternative systems of demand functions is being considered. For power functions there are $m^2 - 2$ symmetry restrictions, given homogeneity and equality. For the indirect demand system, symmetry of the matrix of compensated own- and cross-quantity substitution effects implies symmetry restrictions that are strictly analogous to those for the direct demand system.

4.5 Nonnegativity and Monotonicity

To formulate a test of nonnegativity for the direct demand system, we impose homogeneity and equality restrictions, as before. Setting the functions $g(p_j/M)$ $(j = 1, 2, \ldots, m)$ and $g_t(t)$ equal to zero (or some preassigned constant), we can evaluate the direct demand system

$$X_j = -\alpha_j, \quad j = 1, 2, \ldots, m.$$

Necessary conditions for nonnegativity are that the inequalities

$$\alpha_j \leqq 0, \quad j = 1, 2, \ldots, m,$$

must hold simultaneously. There are $m - 1$ inequality restrictions on the parameters of the equations we estimate directly, and one inequality restriction for the equation we estimate indirectly, or m inequality restrictions altogether. We employ simultaneous tests of these restrictions; if we reject one or more of the restrictions, we reject the hypothesis of nonnegativity. Similarly, we can derive strictly analogous restrictions for nonnegativity of the indirect demand system.

In formulating a test of monotonicity, we continue to impose homogeneity and equality restrictions. If we set the functions $g(p_j/M)$, $(j = 1, 2, \ldots, m)$ and $g(t)$ equal to zero, and $g'(p_j/M)p_j/M$, $(j = 1, 2, \ldots, m)$ equal to one, which can always be done since g is specified up to a scalar multiplication, a typical element of the matrix of compensated own- and cross-price substitution effects becomes

$$\begin{aligned}\frac{\partial X_j}{\partial(p_k/M)} - X_k \sum \frac{\partial X_j}{\partial(p_i/M)}\, p_i/M &= \frac{-1}{(p_j/M)(p_k/M)}\,[\beta_{jk} + \alpha_j\beta_{Mk}] - \frac{\alpha_k}{(p_j/M)(p_k/M)} \\ &\quad \cdot \left[\sum \beta_{ji} + \alpha_j \sum \beta_{Mi}\right] + \frac{\alpha_k\alpha_j}{(p_j/M)(p_k/M)} + \frac{\delta_{jk}\alpha_j}{(p_j/M)^2}\,.\end{aligned}$$

The full matrix of compensated own- and cross-price substitution effects, say S^*, becomes

$$S^* = P^{-1}[-B - \alpha(\iota' B) - (\iota' B)'\alpha' - \alpha\iota' B\iota\alpha' + \alpha\alpha' + \text{diag}\,\alpha]P^{-1} \equiv P^{-1}SP^{-1},$$

where

$$P^{-1} \equiv \begin{bmatrix} \frac{1}{p_1/M} & 0 & \cdots & 0 \\ 0 & \frac{1}{p_2/M} & \cdots & 0 \\ \vdots & \vdots & & \vdots \\ 0 & 0 & \cdots & \frac{1}{p_m/M} \end{bmatrix},$$

$$B = \begin{bmatrix} \beta_{11} & \beta_{12} & \cdots & \beta_{1m} \\ \beta_{21} & \beta_{22} & \cdots & \beta_{2m} \\ \vdots & \vdots & & \vdots \\ \beta_{m1} & \beta_{m2} & \cdots & \beta_{mm} \end{bmatrix}, \quad \alpha = \begin{bmatrix} \alpha_1 \\ \alpha_2 \\ \vdots \\ \alpha_m \end{bmatrix}, \quad \iota = \begin{bmatrix} 1 \\ 1 \\ \vdots \\ 1 \end{bmatrix},$$

and diag α is a diagonal matrix with the elements of α as its diagonal elements.

Monotonicity of the direct demand system implies that the matrix $1/2(S^* + S^{*\prime})$, or equivalently, the matrix $1/2(S + S')$ is negative semidefinite; under homogeneity the rank of this matrix is at most $m - 1$. To test monotonicity we represent the matrix $1/2(S + S')$ in the form of its Cholesky decomposition,

$$1/2(S + S') = -LDL',$$

where L is a unit lower triangular matrix and D is a diagonal matrix,

$$L = \begin{bmatrix} 1 & 0 & \cdots & 0 \\ \lambda_{21} & 1 & \cdots & 0 \\ \vdots & \vdots & & \vdots \\ \lambda_{m1} & \lambda_{m2} & \cdots & 1 \end{bmatrix}, \qquad D = \begin{bmatrix} \delta_1 & 0 & \cdots & 0 \\ 0 & \delta_2 & \cdots & 0 \\ \vdots & \vdots & & \vdots \\ 0 & 0 & \cdots & \delta_m \end{bmatrix}.$$

The matrix $1/2(S + S') = -LDL'$ can be represented in the form

$$1/2(S+S') = -\begin{bmatrix} \delta_1 & \lambda_{21}\delta_1 & \cdots & \lambda_{m1}\delta_1 \\ \lambda_{21}\delta_1 & \lambda_{21}^2\delta_1 + \delta_2 & \cdots & \lambda_{21}\lambda_{m1}\delta_1 + \lambda_{m2}\delta_2 \\ \vdots & \vdots & & \vdots \\ \lambda_{m1}\delta_1 & \lambda_{21}\lambda_{m1}\delta_1 + \lambda_{m2}\delta_2 & \cdots & \lambda_{m1}^2\delta_1 + \lambda_{m2}^2\delta_2 + \cdots + \delta_m \end{bmatrix}.$$

Necessary conditions for monotonicity are that the elements of the matrix D are nonnegative. Under homogeneity the parameter δ_m is equal to zero. We employ simultaneous tests of the hypotheses $\delta_j \geqq 0$ $(j = 1, l, \ldots, m-1)$; if we reject one or more of these hypotheses, we reject the hypothesis of monotonicity.

To derive a test of monotonicity for the indirect demand system (4.1.3), we consider the matrix of compensated own- and cross-quantity effects. This matrix can be represented in the form of its Cholesky decomposition. Necessary conditions for monotonicity of the indirect demand system are strictly analogous to those we have given for the direct demand system.[16]

Our test of monotonicity of the direct and indirect demand systems is independent of whether the demand systems satisfy the symmetry restrictions. If the demand systems satisfy the symmetry restrictions, thus implying that the function g must be either a logarithmic function or a power function and that an underlying utility function exists, our test of monotonicity of the demand system can be interpreted as a test on the definiteness of the Hessian matrix of the underlying utility function.

Let the matrix H be defined as follows:

$$H = B - \text{diag}\,\alpha\,.$$

The matrix $1/2(H + H')$ can be identified with the Hessian of the indirect utility function, setting the variables $g(p_j/M)$ $(j = 1, 2, \ldots, m)$ and $g_t(t)$ equal to zero, under homogeneity, summability, and symmetry.[17]

We next observe that

$$\iota' H = \iota' B - \alpha'\,,$$
$$\iota' H \iota = \iota' B \iota + 1\,.$$

Expressing the matrix S of compensated own- and cross-price substitution effects in terms of the matrix H, we obtain

$$S = -\,H - \alpha\iota' H - (\iota' H)'\alpha' - \iota' H \iota \alpha\alpha'\,,$$

so that

$$1/2(S + S') = -\,1/2(I + \alpha\iota')(H + H')(I + \iota\alpha')\,.$$

The matrix $1/2(S + S')$ is negative semi-definite if and only if the matrix $1/2(H + H')$ is positive semi-definite subject to a linear homogeneous constraint with coefficients given by the vector $\alpha \neq 0$.

A necessary and sufficient condition for the matrix $1/2(H + H')$ to be positive semi-definite subject to a linear homogeneous constraint with coefficients $\alpha \neq 0$ and for the matrix $1/2(S + S')$ to be negative semi-definite is that all the principal minors of the matrix

$$\begin{bmatrix} 0 & \alpha' \\ \alpha & 1/2(H + H') \end{bmatrix},$$

are nonpositive.[18] This matrix can be identified with the bordered Hessian of the indirect utility function, setting the variables $g(p_j/M)$, $(j = 1, 2, \dots, m)$, and $g_t(t)$ equal to zero, under homogeneity, summability, and symmetry of B. Since the vector α is the gradient of the indirect utility function and the matrix $1/2(H + H')$ is the Hessian of this function, the bordered Hessian has nonpositive principal minors if and only if the indirect utility function is quasi-convex at these values of the variables $g(p_j/M)$ $(j = 1, 2, \dots, m)$ and $g_t(t)$. Similarly, this matrix can be identified with the bordered Hessian of the negative of the direct utility function, setting the variables $g(X_j)$, $(j = 1, 2, \dots, m)$, and $g_t(t)$ equal to zero, under homogeneity, summability, and symmetry of B. Nonpositivity of the principal minors of this matrix is necessary and sufficient for quasi-concavity of the direct utility function at these values of the variables $g(X_j)$, $(j = 1, 2, \dots, m)$, and $g_t(t)$.

4.6 Conclusion

In this chapter, we have investigated the implications of the conditions for integrability of consumer demand functions for a system of expenditure share functions that is representable as ratios of first-order polynomial functions. Such share functions arise naturally in applications in which the summability condition is important. We have demonstrated that a large class of such demand systems can satisfy the summability condition locally, in contrast to those systems which are linear in the parameters as analyzed by Jorgenson and Lau (1977) and Lau (1977). However, symmetry imposes restrictions that imply that the polynomials are linear in logarithmic or power functions of the same power of the normalized prices (or quantities) and a function of time. The only such direct or indirect demand systems that are capable of attaining a preassigned set of own- and cross-demand elasticities are the systems corresponding to the indirect or direct transcendental logarithmic utility functions.

Appendix A: Symmetry

The purpose of this appendix is to show that symmetry of the Slutsky matrix implies that the function g is logarithmic, so that

$$g'(Z)Z = k \, ,$$

a constant, or a power function, so that

$$(g''(Z)Z + g'(Z)) \, / \, g'(Z) = \sigma \, ,$$

a constant, *or* the budget shares $\{w_j\}$ are constant. Equation (4.4.6) of the text implies

$$\begin{aligned} & p_k/M \; g'(p_k/M)\left[\beta_{jk}\left(-1 + \sum \beta_{Mi} g(p_i/M) + \beta_{Mt} g_t(t)\right)\right. \\ & \left. \quad - \beta_{Mk}\left(\alpha_j + \sum \beta_{ji} g(p_i/M) + \beta_{jt} g_t(t)\right)\right] \\ & \quad - \left(\alpha_k + \sum \beta_{ki} g(p_i/M) + \beta_{kt} g_t(t)\right)\left[\sum \beta_{ji} g'(p_i/M) \; p_i/M\right] \\ & = p_j/M \; g'(p_j/M)\left[\beta_{kj}\left(-1 + \sum \beta_{Mi} g(p_i/M) + \beta_{Mt} g_t(t)\right)\right. \\ & \left. \quad - \beta_{Mj}\left(\alpha_k + \sum \beta_{ki} g(p_i/M) + \beta_{kt} g_t(t)\right)\right] \\ & \quad - \left(\alpha_j + \sum \beta_{ji} g(p_i/M) + \beta_{jt} g_t(t)\right)\left[\sum \beta_{ki} g'(p_i/M) p_i/M\right], \\ & \qquad j \neq k \, , \quad j, k = 1, 2, \ldots, m \, . \end{aligned} \tag{4.A.1}$$

Differentiating eqs. (4.A.1) with respect to $g_t(t)$, we obtain

$$\begin{aligned} & p_k/M \; g'(p_k/M)(\beta_{jk}\beta_{Mt} - \beta_{Mk}\beta_{jt}) - \beta_{kt} \sum \beta_{ji} g'(p_i/M) p_i/M \\ & = p_j/M \; g'(p_j/M)(\beta_{kj}\beta_{Mt} - \beta_{Mj}\beta_{kt}) - \beta_{jt} \sum \beta_{ki} g'(p_i/M) \; p_i/M \, , \\ & \qquad j \neq k, \quad j, k = 1, 2, \ldots, m \, . \end{aligned} \tag{4.A.2}$$

These equations are satisfied if the parameters β_{jt} are equal to zero for all j. We first suppose that not all of these parameters are equal to zero. If we also suppose that the function g is not logarithmic, we can differentiate the eqs. (4.A.2) with respect to $p_i/M \; g'(p_i/M)$ obtaining

$$\beta_{kt}\beta_{ji} - \beta_{jt}\beta_{ki} = 0, \quad i \neq j \neq k, \quad i, j, k = 1, 2, \ldots, m, \tag{4.A.3}$$

and

$$\beta_{jk}\beta_{Mt} - \beta_{Mk}\beta_{jt} - \beta_{kt}\beta_{jk} + \beta_{jt}\beta_{kk} = 0, \; j \neq k, \; j, k = 1, 2, \ldots, m. \tag{4.A.4}$$

Any set of parameters that satisfies the eqs. (4.A.3) also satisfies (4.A.4). We conclude that unless the parameters β_{jt} are equal to zero for all j or the function g is logarithmic, the rows of the matrix $\{\beta_{jk}\}$ are proportional to one another, except for diagonal elements.

Differentiating eqs. (4.A.1) with respect to P_l/M, we obtain

$$\begin{aligned}
&\frac{p_k}{M}\, g'(p_k/M)(\beta_{jk}\beta_{Ml} - \beta_{Mk}\beta_{jl})g'(p_l/M) \\
&\quad - \beta_{kl}g'(p_l/M) \sum \beta_{ji}g'(p_i/M)p_i/M \\
&\quad - \left(\alpha_k + \sum \beta_{ki}g(p_i/M) + \beta_{kt}g_t(t)\right)\beta_{jl}(g''(p_l/M)\; p_l/M + g'(p_l/M)) \\
&= p_j/M\;\; g'(p_j/M)(\beta_{kj}\beta_{Ml} - \beta_{Mj}\beta_{kl})g'(p_l/M) \\
&\quad - \beta_{jl}g'(p_lM) \sum \beta_{ki}g'(p_i/M)\; p_i/M \\
&\quad - \left(\alpha_j + \sum \beta_{ji}g(p_i/M) + \beta_{jt}g_t(t)\right)\beta_{kl}(g''(p_l/M)\; p_l/M + g'(p_t/M)), \\
&\qquad\qquad\qquad j \neq k \neq l, \;\; j, k, l = 1, 2, \ldots, m.
\end{aligned} \tag{4.A.5}$$

Dividing both sides by $g'(p_l/M)$, eq. (4.A.5) simplifies into

$$\begin{aligned}
&p_k/M\;\; g'(p_k/M)(\beta_{jk}\beta_{Ml} - \beta_{Mk}\beta_{jl}) - \beta_{kl} \sum \beta_{ji}g'(p_i/M)p_i/M \\
&\quad - \left(\alpha_k + \sum \beta_{ki}g(p_i/M) + \beta_{kt}g_t(t)\right)\beta_{jt}\left(\frac{g''(p_l/M)p_l/M}{g'(p_l/M)} + 1\right) \\
&= p_j/M\;\; g'(p_j/M)(\beta_{kj}\beta_{Ml} - \beta_{Mj}\beta_{kl}) - \beta_{jl} \sum \beta_{ki}g'(p_i/M)\; p_i/M \\
&\quad - \left(\alpha_j + \sum \beta_{ji}g(p_i/M) + \beta_{jt}g_t(t)\right)\beta_{kl}\left(\frac{g''(p_l/M)\; p_l/M}{g'(p_l/M)} + 1\right), \\
&\qquad\qquad\qquad j \neq k \neq l, \;\; j, k, l = 1, 2, \ldots, m.
\end{aligned} \tag{4.A.6}$$

Using eq. (4.A.3), we obtain

$$
\begin{aligned}
&p_k/M \; g'(p_k/M)(\beta_{jk}\beta_{ll} - \beta_{jl}\beta_{lk} + \beta_{jk}\beta_{kl} - \beta_{jl}\beta_{kk}) \\
&\quad - \beta_{kl}(\beta_{jj} g'(p_j/M) p_j/M + \beta_{jk} g'(p_k/M) p_k/M) \\
&\quad - (\alpha_k + \beta_{kj} g(p_j/M) + \beta_{kk} g(p_k/M)\beta_{jl} \left(\frac{g''(p_l/M) p_l/M}{g'(p_l/M)} + 1 \right) \\
&= p_j/M \; g'(p_j/M)(\beta_{kj}\beta_{ll} - \beta_{lj}\beta_{kl} + \beta_{kj}\beta_{jl} - \beta_{jj}\beta_{kl}) \\
&\quad - \beta_{jl}(\beta_{kj} g'(p_j/M) p_j/M + \beta_{kk} g'(p_k/M) p_k/M) \\
&\quad - (\alpha_j + \beta_{jj} g(p_j/M) + \beta_{jk} g(p_k/M))\beta_{kl} \left(\frac{g''(p_l/M) p_l/M}{g'(p_l/M)} + 1 \right), \\
&\qquad\qquad\qquad\qquad j \neq k \neq l, \quad j, k, l = 1, 2, \ldots, m \,. \qquad (4.A.7)
\end{aligned}
$$

We next suppose that the function g is neither a logarithmic nor a power function, so that

$$
\left(\frac{g''(p_l/M) p_l/M}{g'(p_l/M)} + 1 \right)
$$

is not constant. Differentiating eqs. (4.A.7) with respect to p_l/M, we obtain

$$
\begin{aligned}
&\alpha_k \beta_{jl} - \alpha_j \beta_{kl} = 0 \,, \\
&\beta_{jk}\beta_{jl} - \beta_{jj}\beta_{kl} = 0 \,, \qquad j \neq k \neq l, \quad j, k, l = 1, 2, \ldots, m \,. \qquad (4.A.8)
\end{aligned}
$$

Equations (4.A.3) and (4.A.8) imply that the rows of the matrix $\{\beta_{jk}\}$ are proportional to one another, including diagonal elements, so that

$$
\begin{aligned}
&\beta_{jk} = \alpha_j \beta_{Mk} \,, \qquad j, k = 1, 2, \ldots, m \,, \\
&\beta_{jt} = \alpha_j \beta_{Mt} \,, \qquad j = 1, 2, \ldots, m \,. \qquad (4.A.9)
\end{aligned}
$$

The expenditure share functions have the form

$$
w_j = \frac{\alpha_j - \alpha_j \left(\sum \beta_{Mi} g(p_i/M) + \beta_{Mt} g_t(t)\right)}{-1 + \sum \beta_{Mi} g(p_i/M) + \beta_{Mt} g_t(t)} = -\,\alpha_j \,, \qquad j = 1, 2, \ldots, m, \qquad (4.A.10)
$$

so that the budget shares $\{w_j\}$ are constant. We conclude that unless the parameters β_{jt} are equal to zero for all j, the function g is logarithmic *or* a power function *or* the budget shares are constant.

We next suppose that all the parameters β_{jt} are equal to zero. Differentiating the eq. (4.A.5) with respect to p_i/M we obtain

$$\begin{aligned}
&\beta_{kl} g'(p_l/M)\beta_{ji}(g''(p_i/M)p_i/M + g'(p_i/M)) \\
&\quad + \beta_{ki} g'(p_i/M)\beta_{jl}(g''(p_l/M)p_l/M + g'(p_l/M)) \\
&= \beta_{jl} g'(p_l/M)\beta_{ki}(g''(p_i/M)p_i/M + g'(p_i/M)) \\
&\quad + \beta_{ji} g'(p_i/M)\beta_{kl}(g''(p_l/M)p_l/M + g'(p_l/M)), \\
&\qquad i \neq j \neq k \neq l, \quad i, j, k, l = 1, 2, \ldots, m. \qquad (4.A.11)
\end{aligned}$$

Rewriting eqs. (4.A.11),

$$\begin{aligned}
&(\beta_{ki}\beta_{jl} - \beta_{ji}\beta_{kl}) g'(p_i/M)(g''(p_l/M)p_l/M + g'(p_l/M)) \\
&\quad = (\beta_{ki}\beta_{jl} - \beta_{ji}\beta_{kl}) g'(p_l/M)(g''(p_i/M)\, p_i/M + g'(p_i/M)), \\
&\qquad i \neq j \neq k \neq l, \quad i, j, k, l = 1, 2, \ldots, m. \qquad (4.A.12)
\end{aligned}$$

Unless the function g is logarithmic or a power function, the parameters $\beta_{ki}\beta_{il} - \beta_{ji}\beta_{kl}$ are equal to zero. This fact together with eqs. (4.A.8) imply that the rows of the matrix $\{\beta_{jk}\}$ are proportional to each other, including diagonal elements, so that the budget shares $\{w_j\}$ are constant. We conclude, finally, that the function g is logarithmic *or* a power function *or* the budget shares are constant. We consider the implications of symmetry of the Slutsky matrix where g is logarithmic in appendix B and where g is a power function in appendix C.

Appendix B: Logarithmic Function

The purpose of this appendix is to show that if the function g is logarithmic, symmetry of the Slutsky matrix implies either that the matrix $\{\beta_{jk}\}$ is symmetric or that one of the three sets of alternative symmetry restrictions given in the text must hold. If g is logarithmic, eq. (4.4.6) of the text can be written as

$$(\beta_{jk} - \beta_{kj}) - w_j\left(\beta_{Mk} - \sum \beta_{ki}\right) + w_k\left(\beta_{Mj} - \sum \beta_{ji}\right) = 0,$$
$$j \neq k, \quad j, k + 1, 2, \ldots, m. \qquad (4.B.1)$$

An obvious sufficient condition for the validity of the eqs. (4.B.1) is that the matrix $\{\beta_{jk}\}$ is symmetric. This implies that the parameters $\beta_{Mj} - \sum \beta_{ji}$ are equal to zero for all j. We first suppose that all of these parameters $\beta_{jk} - \beta_{kj}$ is different from zero.

Substituting expressions for the budget shares $\{w_j\}$ into eqs. (4.B.1), we obtain

$$(\beta_{jk} - \beta_{kj})\left(-1 + \sum \beta_{Mi} \ln(p_i/M) + \beta_{Mt} g_t(t)\right)$$
$$-\left(\alpha_j + \sum \beta_{ji} \ln(p_i/M) + \beta_{jt} g_t(t)\right)\left(\beta_{Mk} - \sum \beta_{ki}\right)$$
$$+\left(\alpha_k + \sum \beta_{ki} \ln(p_i/M) + \beta_{kt} g_t(t)\right)\left(\beta_{Mj} - \sum \beta_{ji}\right) = 0,$$
$$j \neq k, \quad j,k = 1,2,\ldots,m. \tag{4.B.2}$$

Differentiating with respect to $\ln(p_l/M)$,

$$(\beta_{jk} - \beta_{kj})\beta_{Ml} - \beta_{jl}\left(\beta_{Mk} - \sum \beta_{ki}\right) + \beta_{kl}\left(\beta_{Mj} - \sum \beta_{ji}\right) = 0,$$
$$j \neq k, \quad j,k,l = 1,2,\ldots,m. \tag{4.B.3}$$

Differentiating with respect to $g_t(t)$,

$$(\beta_{jk} - \beta_{kj})\beta_{Mt} - \beta_{jt}\left(\beta_{Mk} - \sum \beta_{ki}\right) + \beta_{kt}\left(\beta_{Mj} - \sum \beta_{ji}\right) = 0,$$
$$j \neq k, \quad j,k = 1,2,\ldots,m. \tag{4.B.4}$$

Finally, using eqs. (4.B.3) and (4.B.4), the eqs. (4.B.2) imply:

$$(\beta_{jk} - \beta_{kj}) + \alpha_j\left(\beta_{Mk} - \sum \beta_{ki}\right) - \alpha_k\left(\beta_{Mj} - \sum \beta_{ji}\right) = 0,$$
$$j \neq k, \quad j,k = 1,2,\ldots,m. \tag{4.B.5}$$

Substituting the eqs. (4.B.5) into (4.B.3), we obtain

$$(\beta_{jl} + \alpha_j\beta_{Ml})\left(\beta_{Mk} - \sum \beta_{ki}\right) - \left(\beta_{kl} + \alpha_k\beta_{Ml}\right)\left(\beta_{Mj} - \sum \beta_{ji}\right) = 0,$$
$$j \neq k, \quad j,k,l = 1,2,\ldots,m. \tag{4.B.6}$$

so that

$$(\beta_{jl} + \alpha_j\beta_{Ml}) \big/ \left(\beta_{Mj} - \sum \beta_{ji}\right) = \sigma_l, \quad j,l = 1,2,\ldots,m, \tag{4.B.7}$$

where σ_l is a constant that is independent of j. Similarly, substituting the eqs. (4.B.5) into (4.B.4),

$$(\beta_{jt} + \alpha_j \beta_{Mt}) / \left(\beta_{Mj} - \sum \beta_{ji} \right) = \sigma_t, \quad j = 1, 2, \ldots, m, \tag{4.B.8}$$

a constant independent of j. Summing the eqs. (4.B.7) over l we obtain

$$\left(\sum \beta_{jl} + \alpha_j \sum \beta_{Ml} \right) \Big/ \left(\beta_{Mj} - \sum \beta_{ji} \right) = \sum \sigma_l, \quad j = 1, 2, \ldots, m. \tag{4.B.9}$$

If the parameter $\sum \sigma_l$ is not equal to minus unity,

$$\beta_{Mj} - \sum \beta_{jl} = \left(\beta_{Mj} + \alpha_j \sum \beta_{Ml} \right) \Big/ \left(1 + \sum \sigma_l \right), \quad j = 1, 2, \ldots, m. \tag{4.B.10}$$

If this parameter is equal to minus unity,

$$\beta_{Mj} = \alpha_j \sum \beta_{Ml}, \quad j = 1, 2, \ldots, m. \tag{4.B.11}$$

Substituting eqs. (4.B.7) back into eqs. (4.B.5), we have

$$- \left(\beta_{Mj} - \sum \beta_{ji} \right) \sigma_k + \left(\beta_{Mk} - \sum \beta_{ki} \right) \sigma_j + \alpha_j \sum \beta_{ki} - \alpha_k \sum \beta_{ji} = 0,$$
$$j \neq k, \quad j, k = 1, 2, \ldots, m.$$

By eq. (4.B.9) this is equivalent to

$$- \left(\beta_{Mj} - \sum \beta_{ji} \right) \sigma_k + \left(\beta_{Mk} - \sum \beta_{ki} \right) \sigma_j + \alpha_j \left(\sum \sigma_i \right) \left(\beta_{Mk} - \sum \beta_{ki} \right)$$
$$- \alpha_k \left(\sum \sigma_i \right) \left(\beta_{Mj} - \sum \beta_{ji} \right) = 0,$$
$$j \neq k, \quad j, k = 1, 2, \ldots, m. \tag{4.B.12}$$

so that

$$\left(\sigma_j + \alpha_j \left(\sum_l \sigma_l \right) \right) \Big/ \left(\beta_{Mj} - \sum_l \beta_{jl} \right) = K, \quad j = 1, 2, \ldots, m, \tag{4.B.13}$$

a constant independent of j.

First, we consider the case in which K is not equal to zero. If $\sum \sigma_l$ is not equal to minus unity, eqs. (4.B.10) and (4.B.13) imply that

$$\left(\beta_{Mj} + \alpha_j \sum \beta_{Ml} \right) \Big/ \left(1 + \sum \sigma_l \right) = \left(\sigma_j + \alpha_j \left(\sum \sigma_l \right) \right) \Big/ K, \quad j = 1, 2, \ldots, m,$$

so that

$$\sigma_j = K\left(\beta_{Mj} + \alpha_j \sum \beta_{Ml}\right) \Big/ \left(1 + \sum \sigma_l\right) - \left(\sum \sigma_l\right)\alpha_j ,$$
$$j = 1, 2, \ldots, m . \qquad (4.B.14)$$

Substituting (4.B.14) into eqs. (4.B.7) and (4.B.8), we obtain

$$\beta_{jk} + \alpha_j \beta_{Mk} = K\left(\beta_{Mj} + \alpha_j \sum \beta_{Mi}\right)\left(\beta_{Mk} + \alpha_k \sum \beta_{Mi}\right) \Big/ (1 + K^*)$$
$$+ K^*\left(\beta_{Mj} + \alpha_j \sum \beta_{Mi}\right)\alpha_k , \quad j \neq k,\ j, k = 1, 2, \ldots, m, \qquad (4.B.15)$$

and

$$\beta_{jt} + \alpha_j \beta_{Mt} = \sigma_t^*\left(\beta_{Mj} + \alpha_j \sum \beta_{Mi}\right), \quad j = 1, 2, \ldots, m . \qquad (4.B.16)$$

It can be verified by direct computation that the following parameterization is equivalent:

$$\beta_{ij} = \alpha_i \delta_j + C^* \delta_i \alpha_j + C^{**} \delta_i \delta_j , \quad i, j = 1, 2, \ldots, m .$$

$$\beta_{Mj} = -\delta_j + C^*\left(\sum_k \delta_k\right)\alpha_j + C^{**}\left(\sum_k \delta_k\right)\delta_j ,$$

$$\beta_{it} = \alpha_i \delta_t + \delta_i \rho_t ,$$

$$\beta_{Mt} = -\delta_t + \left(\sum_k \delta_k\right)\rho_t .$$

A system of expenditure share functions with these parameters can be derived from an indirect utility function of the form

$$\ln V = \ln\left(\sum_j (-\alpha_j^* - C\delta_j) \ln(p_j/M) + \gamma_t t + 1\right)$$
$$+ C \ln\left(\sum \delta_j \ln(p_j/M) + \delta_t t + 1\right), \quad C \neq 0,$$

or of the form

$$\ln V = \sum_i (-\alpha_i^* - \delta_i) \ln (p_i/M)$$
$$+ (1 + C_t t) \ln\left(\sum \delta_i \ln (p_i/M) + \delta_t t + 1 \right),$$

or of the form

$$\ln V = \ln\left(\sum (\alpha_i^* + \delta_i) \ln (p_i/M) + (\alpha_t + \delta_t)t + 2 \right)$$
$$- 1/2 \ln \left[1 + \sum \delta_i \ln (p_i/M) + \delta_t t \right.$$
$$+ (C/2) \left(\sum_i \sum_j (\alpha_i^* + \delta_i)(\alpha_j^* + \delta_j) \ln (p_i/M) \ln (p_j/M) \right.$$
$$\left.\left. + 2 \sum_j (\alpha_i^* + \delta_i)(\alpha_t + \delta_t) \ln (p_i/M) t + (\alpha_t + \delta_t)^2 t^2 \right) \right].$$

The second indirect utility function has one less independent parameter than the first. The parametrization of the expenditure share functions of the second indirect utility function can be obtained from that of the first by setting $C^* = 0$.

If $\sum \sigma_l$ is equal to minus unity, then, by eq. (4.B.13),

$$\sigma_j - \alpha_j = K\left(\beta_{Mj} - \sum \beta_{jl} \right), \quad j = 1, 2, \ldots, m. \tag{4.B.17}$$

Substituting (4.B.17) into eqs. (4.B.7) and (4.B.8), we obtain

$$\beta_{jk} = \alpha_j \alpha_k \sum \beta_{Mi} + K^* (\sigma_j - \alpha_j)\sigma_k, \quad j \neq k, \quad j, k = 1, 2, \ldots, m, \tag{4.B.18}$$

and

$$\beta_{jt} + \alpha_j \beta_{Mt} = \sigma_t^* (\sigma_j - \alpha_j), \quad j = 1, 2, \ldots, m. \tag{4.B.19}$$

Second, we consider the case in which K is equal to zero. If $\sum \sigma_l$ is not equal to minus unity,

$$\sigma_j = -\left(\sum \sigma_l \right) \alpha_j,$$

$$\beta_{jk} + \alpha_j\beta_{Mk} = -\left(\sum \sigma_k\right)\left(\beta_{Mj} + \alpha_j \sum \beta_{Mk}\right)\alpha_k \Big/ \left(1 + \sum \sigma_k\right),$$
$$j \neq k, \quad j,k = 1,2,\ldots,m\,, \tag{4.B.20}$$

and

$$\beta_{jt} + \alpha_j\beta_{Mt} = \sigma_t^*\left(\beta_{Mj} + \alpha_j \sum \beta_{Ml}\right), \qquad j = 1,2,\ldots,m\,. \tag{4.B.21}$$

If $\sum \sigma_l$ is equal to minus unity,

$$\sigma_j = \alpha_j\,, \qquad j = 1,2,\ldots,m\,,$$

and

$$\begin{aligned}\beta_{jk} &= -\,\alpha_j\beta_{Mk} + \left(\beta_{Mj} - \sum_i \beta_{ji}\right)\alpha_k \\ &= \alpha_j\alpha_k \sum \beta_{Mi} - \alpha_k\alpha_j \sum \beta_{Mi} + \left(-\sum_i \beta_{ji}\right)\alpha_k \\ &= \left(-\sum_i \beta_{ji}\right)\alpha_k\,, \qquad j \neq k, \quad j,k = 1,2,\ldots,m\,.\end{aligned}$$

Let

$$\delta_j \equiv \left(-\sum_i \beta_{ji}\right), \qquad j = 1,2,\ldots,m\,,$$

and we have

$$\beta_{jl} = \delta_j\alpha_i\,, \qquad j,l = 1,2,\ldots,m\,, \tag{4.B.22}$$

and

$$\beta_{jt} + \alpha_j\beta_{Mt} = \sigma_t^*\left(\delta_j + \alpha_j \sum_i \delta_i\right), \qquad j = 1,2,\ldots,m\,. \tag{4.B.23}$$

An examination of all four possibilities: $\sum \sigma_1$ equal or not equal to minus unity and K equal or not equal to zero reveals three independent sets of alternative symmetry conditions, namely, the conditions given in the text.

Appendix C: Power Function

The purpose of this appendix is to derive the implications of symmetry of the Slutsky matrix where the function g is a power function. Substituting expressions for the budget shares $\{w_j\}$ into eq. (4.4.6) of the text, we obtain

$$
\begin{aligned}
&(p_k/M)^\sigma\Big[\beta_{jk}\Big(-1+\sum\beta_{Mi}(p_i/M)^\sigma+\beta_{Mt}g_t(t)\Big)\\
&\quad-\beta_{Mk}\Big(\alpha_j+\sum\beta_{ji}(p_i/M)^\sigma+\beta_{jt}g_t(t)\Big)\Big]\\
&\quad-\Big(\alpha_k+\sum\beta_{ki}(p_i/M)^\sigma+\beta_{kt}g_t(t)\Big)\sum\beta_{ji}(p_i/M)^\sigma\\
&=(p_j/M)^\sigma\Big[\beta_{kj}\Big(-1+\sum\beta_{Mi}(p_i/M)^\sigma+\beta_{Mt}g_t(t)\Big)\\
&\quad-\beta_{Mj}\Big(\alpha_k+\sum\beta_{ki}(p_i/M)^\sigma+\beta_{kt}g_t(t)\Big)\Big]\\
&\quad-\Big(\alpha_j+\sum\beta_{ji}(p_i/M)^\sigma+\beta_{jt}g_t(t)\Big)\sum\beta_{ki}(p_i/M)^\sigma,\\
&\qquad\qquad j\neq k\neq l,\quad j,k=1,2,\ldots,m. \qquad (4.C.1)
\end{aligned}
$$

Differentiating with respect to $p_l/M)^\sigma$,

$$
\begin{aligned}
&(p_k/M)^\sigma(\beta_{jk}\beta_{Ml}-\beta_{Mk}\beta_{jl})-(\alpha_k+\beta_{kt}g_t(t))\beta_{jl}\\
&=(p_j/M)^\sigma(\beta_{kj}\beta_{Ml}-\beta_{Mj}\beta_{kl})-(\alpha_j+\beta_{jt}g_t(t))\beta_{kl},\\
&\qquad\qquad j\neq k\neq l,\quad j,k,l=1,2,\ldots,m. \qquad (4.C.2)
\end{aligned}
$$

Differentiating with respect to $(p_j/M)^\sigma$,

$$\beta_{kj}\beta_{Ml}-\beta_{Mj}\beta_{kl}=0,\qquad j\neq k\neq l,\quad j,k,l=1,2,\ldots,m. \qquad (4.C.3)$$

Similarly, differentiating with respect to $g_t(t)$,

$$\beta_{kt}\beta_{jl}-\beta_{jt}\beta_{kl}=0,\qquad j\neq k\neq l,\quad j,k,l=1,2,\ldots,m. \qquad (4.C.4)$$

Finally, using eqs. (4.C.3) and (4.C.4), the eqs. (4.C.2) imply

$$\alpha_k\beta_{jl}-\alpha_j\beta_{kl}=0,\qquad j\neq k\neq l,\quad j,k,l=1,2,\ldots,m. \qquad (4.C.5)$$

We conclude that

$$\beta_{jk} = \alpha_j \beta_k , \quad j \neq k, \quad j, k = 1, 2, \ldots, m , \tag{4.C.6}$$

and

$$\beta_{Mj} = \sum_i \beta_{ij} = (-1 - \alpha_j)\beta_j + \beta_{jj} , \quad j = 1, 2, \ldots, m . \tag{4.C.7}$$

Substituting eqs. (4.C.6) and (4.C.7) into eqs. (4.C.3),

$$\alpha_k \beta_j [(-1 - \alpha_l)\beta_l + \beta_{ll}] = [(-1 - \alpha_j)\beta_j + \beta_{jj}]\alpha_k \beta_l ,$$
$$j \neq k \neq l , \quad j, k, l = 1, 2, \ldots, m .$$

so that

$$(\beta_{ll} - \alpha_l \beta_l) \,/\, \beta_l = (\beta_{jj} - \alpha_j \beta_j) \,/\, \beta_j = \rho , \quad j, l = 1, 2, \ldots, m , \tag{4.C.8}$$

a constant that is independent of j and l. We conclude that

$$\beta_{jj} = (\rho + \alpha_j)\beta_j$$

$$\beta_{Mj} = (\rho - 1)\beta_j , , \quad j = 1, 2, \ldots, m . \tag{4.C.9}$$

Similarly, substituting eqs. (4.C.6) into eqs. (4.C.4),

$$\beta_{kt}\alpha_j \beta_l = \beta_{jt}\alpha_k \beta_l , \quad j \neq k \neq l, \quad j, k, l = 1, 2, \ldots, m .$$

so that

$$\beta_{kt}/\alpha_k = \beta_{jt}/\alpha_j = \beta_t , \quad j, k = 1, 2, \ldots, m , \tag{4.C.10}$$

a constant that is independent of j and k. We conclude that

$$\beta_{jt} = \alpha_j \beta_t , \quad j = 1, 2, \ldots, m . \tag{4.C.11}$$

We conclude that the expenditure share equations depend on the $2m + 1$ independent parameters $\{\alpha_j, \beta_j, \beta_t, \rho\}$.

Notes

1. See Wold (1953, p. 196), Basmann, Battalio, and Kagel (1973), and Jorgenson and Lau (1977).

2. Except for demand systems with only two commodities or demand systems with some constant components of the consumer demand. See Barten (1974), Goldberger (1969), Jorgenson and Lau (1977), and McFadden (1964).

3. Systems with logarithmic functions $g(Z)$ correspond to direct and indirect transcendental logarithmic demand functions, introduced by Christensen, Jorgenson, and Lau (1975) and used by them to test the equality and symmetry restrictions implied by integrability and discussed below. Earlier Christensen, Jorgenson, and Lau (1971, 1973) introduced transcendental logarithmic functions into the study of production. Applications of systems of transcendental logarithmic demand systems are given by Christensen and Manser (1975, 1977), Jorgenson and Lau (1975), and Lau and Mitchell (1971).
4. Tests of monotonicity for a single function are given by Stone (1954b, pp. 339–340), and by Wold (1953, p. 298). For further discussion see section 4.5, below.
5. Independently, Lau's methods have been adapted to provide a test of monotonicity for the Rotterdam system by Barten and Geyskens (1975). The approach of Barten and Geyskens requires symmetry of the system of demand functions. For further discussion see section 4.5, below.
6. This sequence of tests is employed by Jorgenson and Lau (1975) in testing restrictions on the form of consumer preferences and changes in preferences over time.
7. Symmetry conditions for integrability based on the indirect demand functions can be traced to Antonelli (1886); symmetry conditions for integrability based on the direct demand functions can be traced to Slutsky (1915). For additional references and discussion, see Samuelson (1950) and Hurwicz (1971, esp. pp. 188–210).
8. This construction is employed by Leontief (1936) for indirect demand functions and by Hicks (1939) for direct demand functions. For additional references and discussion, see Wold (1953, pp. 108–110).
9. Hurwicz (1971, p. 178), refers to a system of demand functions characterized by homogeneity, summability and symmetry as 'mathematically' integrable and a system also characterized by nonnegativity and monotonicity as 'economically' integrable.
10. For a discussion of duality between the system of partial differential equations defining a family of indirect utility functions and the system defining the direct utility functions, see Hurwicz (1971, esp. pp. 202–210). See also Hotelling (1935), Lau (1969a,b).
11. See Stone (1954b, table 107, p. 329). A similar test is presented by Byron (1970b).
12. Homogeneity and summability are properties of market demand functions, while symmetry, nonnegativity, and monotonicity are properties of individual demand functions. The properties of individual demand functions carry over to market demand functions only under additional assumptions on individual demand functions or on variation in the distribution of income. For further discussion of the properties of market demand functions, see Sonnenschein (1972, 1973a), Mantel (1974), Debreu (1974), and McFadden, Mantel, Mas-Colell, and Richter (1974). For discussion of aggregation over individual demand functions, see Gorman (1953), Samuelson (1956), Chipman (1974), and Diewert (1977).
13. This is similar to Lau's (1977a) finding for the linear-in-parameters class.
14. See Kamke (1950, pp. 138–139), for a discussion of a similar 'integration' problem.
15. This situation is not unique to the 'translog' function. For instance, a system of demand functions which are ratios of linear functions to quadratic functions, similar in form to the system derived from the quadratic utility function, can be integrated into an utility function which is not quadratic.
16. This approach to testing monotonicity we have presented is based on the Jacobian of the system of direct demand functions. This approach uses homogeneity and summability restrictions, but does not use symmetry restrictions. Under symmetry the Jacobian of the system can be derived from the Hessian of the indirect utility function and *vice versa*.
17. Recall that under symmetry restrictions, the function g is either a logarithmic func-

tion or a power function. The corresponding utility functions are either the translog utility function, one of the three special cases, or

$$\ln V = \sum_j \gamma_j \ln p_j + C\left(\sum_j \delta_j (p_j/M)^\sigma + \delta_0\right) + \ln V_0 .$$

With the exception of the translog utility function, the matrix B is subject to additional parametric restrictions and is not necessarily symmetric.

18. See, for example, Debreu (1952).

5 Testing the Integrability of Consumer Demand Functions, United States, 1947–1971

Dale W. Jorgenson and
Lawrence J. Lau

5.1 Introduction

The purpose of this chapter is to implement a new econometric methodology for testing the theory of consumer behavior. The traditional starting point for econometric studies of consumer behavior is a system of demand functions, giving quantities demanded as functions of prices and income. Tests of the theory of consumer behavior are formulated by interpreting the demand functions as a system of partial differential equations. If the system of demand functions is integrable, it can be generated by maximization of a utility function, subject to the budget constraint. Conditions for integrability imply restrictions on the system of demand functions that can be tested statistically.

An important unresolved issue in formulating tests of the theory of consumer behavior is the selection of an appropriate parametric representation of preferences. The double-logarithmic system of Schultz (1938), Stone (1954b), and Wold (1953) is integrable if and only if it can be generated by a neutral linear logarithmic utility function.[1] For this utility function the proportion of the consumer budget allocated to each commodity is independent of prices, income, and time. Income elasticities of demand are equal to unity, own-price elasticities are equal to minus unity, and cross-price elasticities are zero. Similarly, the Rotterdam system of Barten (1964a) and Theil (1965) is integrable if and only if it can be generated by a neutral linear logarithmic utility function.[2]

For a wide class of systems of consumer demand functions linear in the unknown parameters, including the double-logarithmic and Rotterdam systems, integrability implies that the system can be generated by a neutral linear logarithmic utility function.[3] Accordingly, we employ a parametric representation of consumer demand functions that is nonlinear in the parameters. Specifically, we employ the system of direct demand functions

$$w_j = \frac{p_j X_j}{M} = \frac{a_j + \sum \beta_{jk} g(p_k/M) + \beta_{jM} g_M(M) + \beta_{jt} g_t(t)}{-1 + \sum \beta^j_{Mk} g(p_k/M) + \beta^j_{MM} g_M(M) + \beta^j_{Mt} g_t(t)},$$

$$j = 1, 2, \ldots, m, \tag{5.1}$$

where X_j is the quantity of the *jth* commodity, p_j is the corresponding price, M is total expenditure, and t is time. The functions g, g_M, and g_t are twice continuously differentiable and strictly monotone increasing functions of a single variable. The only demand functions of this form that are integrable are those in which the function g_M is constant and the function g is either a logarithmic or a power function. Only the logarithmic form of the function g is capable of representing an arbitrary set of own-price and cross-price elasticities of demand.[4]

In formulating tests of the theory of consumer behavior we employ the system of direct demand functions (5.1) with logarithmic functions g and g_M and a linear function g_t. This system is an extension of the direct transcendental logarithmic or translog demand functions with time-varying preferences introduced by Jorgenson and Lau (1975).[5] We also consider tests of the theory of consumer behavior based on the system of indirect demand functions

$$w_j = \frac{\alpha_j + \sum \beta_{jk} g(X_j) + \beta_{jM} g_M(M) + \beta_{jt} g_t(t)}{-1 + \sum \beta^j_{Mk} g(X_j) + \beta^j_{MM} g_M(M) + \beta^j_{Mt} g_t(t)},$$

$$j = 1, 2, \ldots, m, \tag{5.2}$$

where the functions g, g_M, and g_t are twice continuously differentiable and strictly monotone increasing functions of a single variable, as before. Conditions for integrability of the system of direct demand functions (5.1) are precisely analogous to those for the system of indirect demand functions (5.2), so that we employ logarithmic functions g and g_M and a linear function g_t in formulating tests of the theory of consumer behavior.[6] The resulting system of indirect demand functions is an extension of the indirect translog demand functions with time-varying preferences introduced by Jorgenson and Lau (1975).

To test the theory of consumer behavior we fit direct and indirect translog demand systems without requiring that these systems are integrable. We then impose restrictions on the parameters of these demand systems implied by integrability. We test restrictions corresponding to homogeneity or absence of money illusion, summability or adding up, symmetry of the cross-price or cross-quantity substitution effects, nonnegativity of the demand functions, and monotonicity of systems of demand functions. Our methodology for testing the hypothesis of monotonicity of a system of demand functions is based on the Jacobian matrix for the complete system and does not require symmetry of the cross-price or cross-quantity substitution effects.[7] Our approach is an application of methods developed by Lau (1978) for testing the semi-definiteness of a real symmetric matrix; Lau's methods are based on the Cholesky factorization of the matrix.

5.2 Integrability

Our empirical results are based on indirect and direct translog demand systems for three commodity groups. For either demand system a complete econometric model of consumer behavior is provided by any two of the three equations for the budget shares. We estimate the parameters of the system of two equations

$$\frac{p_1 X_1}{M} = \frac{\alpha_1 + \beta_{11} \ln \frac{p_1}{M} + \beta_{12} \ln \frac{p_2}{M} + \beta_{13} \ln \frac{p_3}{M} + \beta_{1M} \ln M + \beta_{1t} \cdot t}{-1 + \beta_{M1}^1 \ln \frac{p_1}{M} + \beta_{M2}^1 \ln \frac{p_2}{M} + \beta_{M3}^1 \ln \frac{p_3}{M} + \beta_{MM}^1 \ln M + \beta_{Mt}^1 \cdot t},$$

$$\frac{p_2 X_2}{M} = \frac{\alpha_2 + \beta_{21} \ln \frac{p_1}{M} + \beta_{22} \ln \frac{p_2}{M} + \beta_{23} \ln \frac{p_3}{M} + \beta_{2M} \ln M + \beta_{2t} \cdot t}{-1 + \beta_{M1}^2 \ln \frac{p_1}{M} + \beta_{M2}^2 \ln \frac{p_2}{M} + \beta_{M3}^2 \ln \frac{p_3}{M} + \beta_{MM}^2 \ln M + \beta_{Mt}^2 \cdot t},$$

corresponding to the direct translog demand system and the system of two equations

$$\frac{p_1 X_1}{M} = \frac{\alpha_1 + \beta_{11} \ln X_1 + \beta_{12} \ln X_2 + \beta_{13} \ln X_3 + \beta_{1M} \ln M + \beta_{1t} \cdot t}{-1 + \beta_{M1}^1 \ln X_1 + \beta_{M2}^1 \ln X_2 + \beta_{M3}^1 \ln X_3 + \beta_{MM}^1 \ln M + \beta_{Mt}^1 \cdot t},$$

$$\frac{p_2 X_2}{M} = \frac{\alpha_2 + \beta_{21} \ln X_1 + \beta_{22} \ln X_2 + \beta_{23} \ln X_3 + \beta_{2M} \ln M + \beta_{2t} \cdot t}{-1 + \beta_{M1}^2 \ln X_1 + \beta_{M2}^2 \ln X_2 + \beta_{M3}^2 \ln X_3 + \beta_{MM}^2 \ln M + \beta_{Mt}^2 \cdot t},$$

corresponding to the indirect translog demand system.

To test the hypotheses of homogeneity, equality, symmetry, nonnegativity, and monotonicity we impose the corresponding restrictions on the parameters of the direct and indirect translog demand system. We first outline these restrictions for the case of three commodity groups; restrictions for the two systems are perfectly analogous, so that the following outline can be applied to either system.[8]

(1) *Homogeneity*. For the direct demand system the quantities are independent of total expenditure for given ratios of prices to total expenditure; for the indirect demand system the ratios of prices to total expenditure are independent of total expenditure for given quantities. These restrictions imply that the parameters $\{\beta_{1M}, \beta_{2M}, \beta_{MM}^1, \beta_{MM}^2\}$ are equal to zero or that the budget shares $\{w_1, w_2, w_3\}$ are constant. There are four *homogeneity* restrictions.[9]

(2) *Summability*. For the direct demand system the sum of the budget shares is equal to unity for all prices, total expenditure, and time; for the indirect demand system the sum of the budget shares is equal to unity for all quantities, total expenditure, and time. Sufficient conditions for summability are that the parameters appearing in the denominators of the two equations must take the same value

$$\beta_{M1}^1 = \beta_{M1}^2 = \beta_{M1} ,$$

$$\beta_{M2}^1 = \beta_{M2}^2 = \beta_{M2} ,$$

$$\beta_{M3}^1 = \beta_{M3}^2 = \beta_{M3} ,$$

$$\beta_{MM}^1 = \beta_{MM}^2 = \beta_{MM} ,$$

$$\beta_{Mt}^1 = \beta_{Mt}^2 = \beta_{Mt} .$$

There are five *equality* restrictions; in addition, the following restrictions must be satisfied

$$\alpha_1 + \alpha_2 + \alpha_3 = -1 ,$$

$$\beta_{11} + \beta_{21} + \beta_{31} = \beta_{M1} ,$$

$$\beta_{12} + \beta_{22} + \beta_{32} = \beta_{M2} ,$$

$$\beta_{13} + \beta_{23} + \beta_{33} = \beta_{M3} ,$$

$$\beta_{1M} + \beta_{2M} + \beta_{3M} = \beta_{MM} ,$$

$$\beta_{1t} + \beta_{2t} + \beta_{3t} = \beta_{Mt} .$$

This set of restrictions enables us to identify the parameters of the equation we do not estimate directly. Summability implies either that the sufficient conditions hold or that at least one commodity has a constant budget share.

(3) *Symmetry*. For the direct demand system the Slutsky matrix of own- and cross-price substitution effects must be symmetric; similarly, for the indirect demand system the Antonelli matrix of own- and cross-quantity substitution effects must be symmetric.[10] To formulate a test of symmetry we first impose the homogeneity and equality restrictions given above.[11] For demand systems capable of modeling arbitrary own- and cross-substitution effects, symmetry of the matrix of parameters $\{\beta_{jk}\}$ is necessary and sufficient for symmetry of the matrix of substitution effects.[12] One restriction of this type is explicit in the two equations we estimate directly, namely,

$$\beta_{12} = \beta_{21} .$$

In addition, we estimate the parameters β_{31} and β_{32} from the equations

$$\beta_{31} = \beta_{M1} - \beta_{11} - \beta_{21} ,$$

$$\beta_{31} = \beta_{M2} - \beta_{12} - \beta_{22} ,$$

so that two additional restrictions are implicit in the two equations we estimate. We write these restrictions in the form

$$\beta_{13} = \beta_{M1} - \beta_{11} - \beta_{21} ,$$

$$\beta_{23} = \beta_{M2} - \beta_{12} - \beta_{22} .$$

There are three *symmetry* restrictions altogether.

(4) *Nonnegativity*. For the direct demand system the quantities are nonnegative; for the indirect demand system the ratios of prices to total expenditure are nonnegative. Necessary conditions for nonnegativity are

$$\alpha_1 \leq 0 ,$$

$$\alpha_2 \leq 0 ,$$

$$\alpha_3 = -1 - \alpha_1 - \alpha_2 \leq 0 .$$

There are three *nonnegativity* restrictions altogether. The first two are explicit in the two equations we estimate. The third is implicit in these equations.

(5) *Monotonicity*. In formulating a test of monotonicity, we continue to impose homogeneity and equality restrictions. Setting the ratios of prices to total expenditure in the direct demand system equal to unity and time equal to zero, we can express the matrix of substitution effects, say S, where

$$S = \begin{bmatrix} \sigma_{11} & \sigma_{12} & \sigma_{13} \\ \sigma_{21} & \sigma_{22} & \sigma_{23} \\ \sigma_{31} & \sigma_{32} & \sigma_{33} \end{bmatrix},$$

in terms of the parameters—α_i, β_{ij} $(i, j = 1, 2, 3)$—of the equations for the budget shares

$$\sigma_{ij} = -\beta_{ij} - \alpha_i \beta_{Mj} - \alpha_j \beta_{Mi} - \alpha_i \alpha_j \left(\sum \beta_{Mk} \right) + \alpha_i \alpha_j + \delta_{ij} \alpha_i, \qquad i, j = 1, 2, 3.$$

Next, we express the parameters of the matrix $1/2(S + S')$ in terms of the parameters of the Cholesky factorization of this matrix

$$\frac{1}{2}(S + S') = -\begin{bmatrix} \delta_1 & \lambda_{21}\delta_1 & \lambda_{31}\delta_1 \\ \lambda_{21}\delta_1 & \lambda_{21}^2\delta_1 + \delta_2 & \lambda_{21}\lambda_{31}\delta_1 + \lambda_{32}\delta_2 \\ \lambda_{31}\delta_1 & \lambda_{21}\lambda_{31}\delta_1 + \lambda_{32}\delta_2 & \lambda_{31}^2\delta_1 + \lambda_{32}^2\delta_2 + \delta_3 \end{bmatrix}.$$

Under homogeneity the matrix $1/2(S + S')$ has rank at most two, so that the parameter δ_3 is zero. The remaining parameters are given by

$$\delta_1 = -\sigma_{11},$$

$$\lambda_{21} = -\frac{1}{2\delta_1}(\sigma_{12} + \sigma_{21}),$$

$$\lambda_{31} = -\frac{1}{2\delta_1}(\sigma_{13} + \sigma_{31}),$$

$$\delta_2 = -\sigma_{22} - \lambda_{21}^2\delta_1,$$

$$\lambda_{32} = -\frac{1}{2\delta_2}(\sigma_{23} + \sigma_{32}) - \frac{\delta_1}{\delta_2}\lambda_{21}\lambda_{31}.$$

In terms of these parameters the necessary conditions for monotonicity take the form

$$\delta_1 \geq 0, \quad \delta_2 \geq 0.$$

There are two *monotonicity* restrictions altogether.

We can derive a test of monotonicity for the indirect demand system by setting the quantities equal to unity and time equal to zero. We can express the matrix of substitution effects in terms of parameters of the equations for the budget shares, as before. Necessary conditions for monotonicity of the indirect demand system are precisely analogous to those we have given for the direct demand system.

5.3 Empirical Tests

Our empirical tests are based on annual time series data for U.S. personal consumption expenditures on three commodity groups—durables, nondurables, and energy—for the period 1947–1971. Our concept of personal consumption expenditures differs from the corresponding concept in the U.S. national income and product accounts in the treatment of consumers' durables. We treat expenditure on durables as part of gross private domestic investment rather than personal consumption expenditures. We add an imputed flow of services from consumers' durables to personal consumption expenditures, so that our concept of durables services is perfectly analogous to the national accounting concept of housing services.[13]

We have fitted equations for the budget shares corresponding to the direct and indirect translog demand systems. Under the two alternative stochastic specifications outlined in section 5.2 only two equations are required for a complete econometric model of consumer behavior. We have fitted equations for durables and for nondurables by the method of nonlinear three stage least squares introduced by Jorgenson and Laffont (1974). The nonlinear three stage least squares estimator is obtained by minimizing the criterion

$$S(\theta) = \frac{1}{n} e'(\hat{\Sigma}^{-1} \otimes Z(Z'Z)^{-1}Z')e\,,$$

where θ is a vector of unknown parameters, e is a vector of fitted residuals from both equations, Σ is the covariance matrix of the underlying disturbances and $\hat{\Sigma}$ is a consistent estimator of this matrix, and Z is a matrix of instrumental variables.[14] For both direct and indirect translog demand systems our maintained hypothesis consists of the unrestricted form of the two behavioral equations for the budget shares. The unrestricted equations involve 22 unknown parameters or 11 unknown parameters for each equation. Unrestricted estimates of these parameters for the direct translog demand system are presented in the first column of table 5.1. Corresponding estimates for the indirect translog demand system are given in the first column of table 5.2.

Table 5.1
Estimates of the parameters of the direct translog demand system

Parameters	Unrestricted		Homogeneity		Equality	
α_1	−0.237	(0.00166)	−0.236	(0.00130)	−0.239	(0.00142)
β_{11}	−0.127	(0.327)	0.486	(0.215)	−0.427	(0.269)
β_{12}	0.0993	(0.120)	−0.0160	(0.0919)	0.318	(0.0953)
β_{13}	−1.08	(1.16)	1.23	(0.526)	−2.15	(0.974)
β_{1M}	−0.167	(0.175)	—	—	−0.236	(0.158)
β_{1t}	−0.0483	(0.0475)	0.0451	(0.0268)	−0.0845	(0.0404)
β^1_{M1}	0.0920	(1.34)	2.47	(0.915)	−1.23	(1.10)
β^1_{M2}	0.607	(0.680)	−0.284	(0.460)	1.74	(0.513)
β^1_{M3}	−4.73	(4.56)	4.36	(2.11)	−8.99	(3.82)
β^1_{MM}	−0.312	(0.766)	—	—	−0.495	(0.697)
β^1_{Mt}	−0.183	(0.184)	0.175	(0.104)	−0.319	(0.157)
α_2	−0.0526	(0.00133)	−0.0525	(0.00102)	−0.0501	(0.000368)
β_{21}	−0.214	(0.295)	0.0388	(0.222)	−0.0948	(0.0547)
β_{22}	0.246	(0.162)	0.287	(0.142)	0.0211	(0.0209)
β_{23}	−0.831	(1.23)	0.734	(0.684)	−0.458	(0.195)
β_{2M}	−0.747	(0.708)	—	—	−0.0428	(0.0339)
β_{2t}	−0.00181	(0.0580)	0.0396	(0.0373)	−0.0205	(0.00805)
β^2_{M1}	−4.33	(5.93)	0.721	(4.41)	—	—
β^2_{M2}	6.06	(4.26)	8.22	(3.26)	—	—

Table 5.1 (continued)

Parameters	Unrestricted		Homogeneity		Equality	
β^2_{M3}	−16.2	(24.2)	14.7	(13.6)	—	—
β^2_{MM}	−16.2	(16.0)	—	—	—	—
β^2_{Mt}	0.0932	(1.17)	0.930	(0.753)	—	—
Parameters	**Homogeneity and equality**		**Symmetry**			
α_1	−0.239	(0.00109)	−0.238	(0.000762)		
β_{11}	0.238	(0.187)	0.110	(0.148)		
β_{12}	0.168	(0.0840)	0.00929	(0.0306)		
β_{13}	0.677	(0.454)	0.667	(0.424)		
β_{1t}	0.0262	(0.0242)	0.0136	(0.0225)		
α_2	−0.0500	(0.000357)	−0.0500	(0.000316)		
β_{21}	0.0340	(0.0382)	0.00929	(0.0306)		
β_{22}	−0.0147	(0.0166)	−0.0451	(0.00809)		
β_{23}	0.107	(0.0927)	0.105	(0.0853)		
β_{2t}	0.00142	(0.00488)	−0.00102	(0.00454)		
α_3	−0.711	(0.00121)	−0.712	(0.000797)		
β_{31}	1.01	(0.561)	0.667	(0.424)		
β_{32}	0.566	(0.290)	0.105	(0.0853)		
β_{33}	1.34	(1.26)	1.37	(1.15)		
β_{3t}	0.0790	(0.0657)	0.0457	(0.0621)		
δ_1	0.0897	(0.0155)	—	—		
δ_2	−0.0552	(0.0471)	—	—		
λ_{21}	−0.790	(0.371)	—	—		
λ_{31}	2.61	(4.70)	—	—		
λ_{32}	−7.45	(10.1)	—	—		

The first hypothesis to be tested is that the system of equations for the budget shares is homogeneous in prices and the value of total expenditure. To test this hypothesis we impose the four homogeneity restrictions. These restrictions eliminate the parameters corresponding to the value of total expenditure; estimates of the remaining parameters for the direct translog demand system are presented in the second column of table 5.1. Corresponding estimates for the indirect translog demand system are given in the first column of table 5.2. The

Table 5.2
Estimates of the parameters of the indirect translog demand system

Parameters	Unrestricted		Homogeneity		Equality	
α_1	−0.219	(0.0182)	−0.246	(0.0150)	−0.246	(0.00618)
β_{11}	−4.57	(10.3)	0.851	(2.61)	1.43	(0.747)
β_{12}	1.78	(3.07)	−1.36	(5.01)	−1.33	(1.46)
β_{13}	−11.0	(36.3)	−0.578	(2.83)	2.15	(2.14)
β_{1M}	1.69	(7.66)	—	—	−1.13	(0.580)
β_{1t}	0.132	(0.692)	0.0198	(0.212)	0.0215	(0.0888)
β_{M1}^1	−20.7	(40.8)	3.95	(14.1)	5.98	(3.31)
β_{M2}^1	10.7	(15.6)	−7.35	(26.3)	−5.30	(6.51)
β_{M3}^1	−39.9	(145.0)	−2.63	(13.7)	8.30	(8.51)
β_{MM}^1	6.18	(33.1)	—	—	−5.15	(2.30)
β_{Mt}^1	0.412	(2.82)	0.166	(1.07)	0.122	(0.373)
α_2	−0.0532	(0.000896)	−0.0533	(0.00169)	−0.0532	(0.000900)
β_{21}	0.0971	(0.467)	0.103	(0.264)	0.251	(0.169)
β_{22}	−0.284	(0.899)	−0.00203	(0.562)	−0.229	(0.288)
β_{23}	0.207	(0.378)	0.199	(0.741)	0.475	(0.411)
β_{2M}	−0.0778	(0.350)	—	—	−0.232	(0.109)
β_{2t}	0.0119	(0.0248)	−0.00765	(0.0319)	0.00361	(0.0177)
β_{M1}^2	3.13	(9.32)	2.65	(5.78)	—	—
β_{M2}^2	−6.17	(19.0)	−0.915	(12.8)	—	—
β_{M3}^2	3.13	(8.18)	2.11	(15.9)	—	—
β_{MM}^2	−1.95	(7.74)	—	—	—	—
β_{Mt}^2	0.263	(0.520)	−0.111	(0.693)	—	—

Parameters	Homogeneity and equality		Symmetry	
α_1	−0.245	(0.00830)	−0.242	(0.00539)
β_{11}	0.301	(1.05)	−0.503	(0.653)
β_{12}	−1.09	(1.79)	−0.121	(0.143)
β_{13}	−2.42	(2.82)	−1.51	(1.81)
β_{1t}	0.0608	(0.0944)	0.0344	(0.0586)
α_2	−0.0536	(0.00123)	−0.0527	(0.000714)
β_{21}	0.0337	(0.222)	−0.121	(0.143)
β_{22}	−0.174	(0.405)	−0.0123	(0.0265)
β_{23}	−0.374	(0.545)	−0.238	(0.349)
β_{2t}	0.00972	(0.0206)	0.00649	(0.0112)
α_3	−0.701	(0.00889)	−0.706	(0.00530)
β_{31}	1.13	(3.79)	−1.51	(1.81)

Table 5.2 (continued)

Parameters	Homogeneity and equality		Symmetry	
β_{32}	−3.25	(7.18)	−0.238	(0.349)
β_{33}	−7.07	(8.24)	−4.72	(5.00)
β_{3t}	0.192	(0.342)	0.118	(0.162)
δ_1	0.138	(0.496)	—	—
δ_2	0.00155	(1.14)	—	—
λ_{21}	0.887	(6.55)	—	—
λ_{31}	−0.0118	(1.25)	—	—
λ_{32}	102	(75038)	—	—

second hypothesis to be tested is that the system of equations satisfies the summability condition. To test this hypothesis we impose the five equality restrictions. Estimates of the parameters of the direct translog demand system under these restrictions are presented in the third column of table 5.1. Corresponding estimates for the indirect translog demand system are given in the third column of table 5.2.

To test the remaining hypotheses we impose the homogeneity and equality restrictions on both direct and indirect demand systems. Estimates of the parameters of the direct translog demand system under these restrictions are presented in the fourth column of table 5.1. Corresponding estimates for the indirect translog demand system are presented in the fourth column of table 5.2. We test the hypothesis of symmetry by imposing the three restrictions implied by symmetry of the matrix $\{\beta_{jk}\}$. The resulting estimates for direct and indirect translog demand systems are presented in the fifth columns of tables 5.1 and 5.2, respectively.

To test the hypothesis of nonnegativity we consider estimates of the parameters α_1 and α_2 from the two equations we estimate and the estimate of α_3 implicit in these two equations. Estimates of these parameters under homogeneity and equality restrictions for the direct and indirect translog demand systems are given in the fourth columns of tables 5.1 and 5.2, respectively. The final hypothesis to be tested is the hypothesis of monotonicity. Estimates of the parameters δ_1 and δ_2 under homogeneity and equality restrictions for the direct and indirect translog demand systems are also given in the fourth columns of tables 5.1 and 5.2, respectively. These estimates are obtained by reparametrizing the direct and indirect translog demand system so as to exhibit the monotonicity restrictions.

Tests of integrability can be carried out in a number of different sequences. We test homogeneity and equality restrictions in parallel without imposing any additional restrictions. We test the remaining restrictions—symmetry, nonnegativity, monotonicity—in parallel, given homogeneity and equality. Our test procedure is presented in diagrammatic form in figure 5.1. We also present alternative procedures. For example, we could test equality given homogeneity or homogeneity given equality. Our test procedure is indicated with double lines while alternative procedures are indicated with single lines.

To test the validity of restrictions on the direct and indirect translog demand systems that take the form of equalities, we employ the following test statistic[15]

$$T = n(S_\omega - S_\Omega) .$$

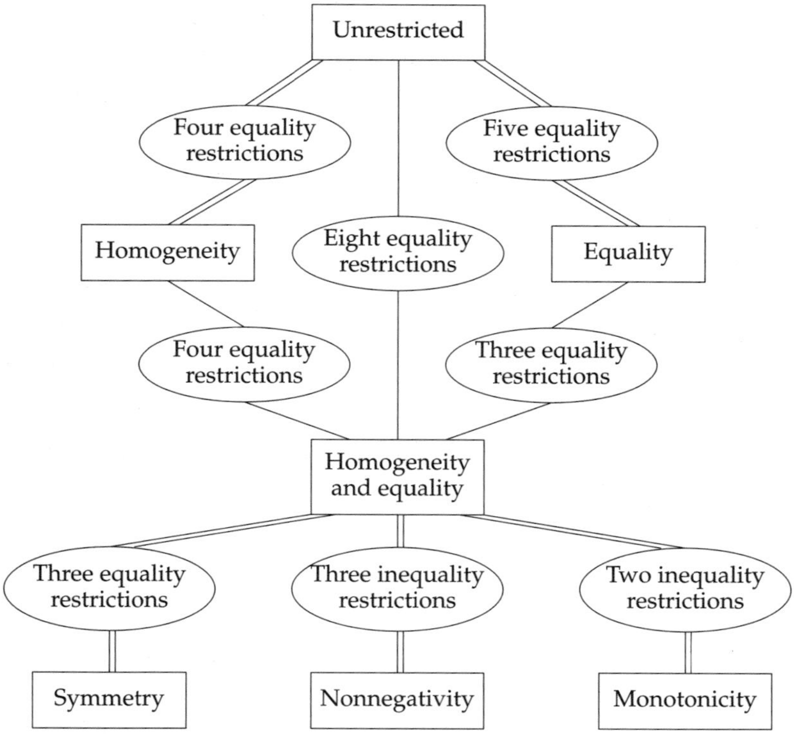

Figure 5.1
Tests of integrability.

This test statistic is based on the difference between the minimum value of the criterion used in construction of the nonlinear three stage least squares estimator subject to restriction S_{ω} and the minimum value without restriction S_{Ω}. We have estimated direct and indirect translog demand systems from annual data for U.S. personal consumption expenditures for the period 1947–1971. There are 25 observations for each behavioral equation, so that the number of degrees of freedom available for statistical tests of integrability is 50 for both direct and indirect translog demand systems.

Under the null hypothesis our test statistic is distributed, asymptotically, as chi-squared with a number of degrees of freedom equal to the number of restrictions to be tested. We employ the asymptotic distribution of the test statistic for tests of hypotheses that take the form of equality restrictions. To test the validity of inequality restrictions implied by the hypotheses of nonnegativity and monotonicity, we employ test statistics based on the ratio of each inequality constrained coefficient to its standard error. We employ a one-sided critical region to test the validity of each of the inequality restrictions. The ratio of each coefficient to its standard error is distributed, asymptotically, as a standard normal random variable. We employ this asymptotic distribution to test inequality restrictions.

To control the overall level of significance for each series of tests, based on direct and indirect translog demand systems, we set the level of significance for each series at 0.05. We allocate the overall level of significance among the various stages in each series. We first assign levels of significance of 0.01 to each of the tests of homogeneity and equality restrictions. We then assign levels of significance of 0.01 to each of the three sets of restrictions that are conditional on the homogeneity and equality restrictions—symmetry, nonnegativity, and monotonicity. The set of restrictions associated with nonnegativity includes three inequality restrictions; there are two restrictions associated with monotonicity. We assign a level of significance of 0.0033 to the test associated with each of the three restrictions for nonnegativity and 0.0050 to the test associated with each of the two restrictions for monotonicity. The tests for all five sets of restrictions—homogeneity, equality, symmetry, nonnegativity, and monotonicity—are not "nested" so that the sum of the levels of significance for each of these five sets of restrictions provides an upper bound for the level of significance of all five tests considered simultaneously.

Table 5.3
Critical values of χ^2/degrees of freedom and standard normal test statistics

	Level of significance				
Degrees of freedom	0.10	0.05	0.01	0.005	0.001
Standard normal					
1	1.28	1.65	2.33	2.58	3.09
χ^2/Degrees of freedom					
3	2.08	2.60	3.78	4.28	5.42
4	1.94	2.37	3.32	3.72	4.62
5	1.85	2.21	3.02	3.35	4.10
8	1.67	1.94	2.51	2.74	3.27

For the econometric model based on the direct translog demand system we have assigned levels of significance to all tests of hypotheses so as to control the overall level of significance for all tests at 0.05. This implies that the probability of a false rejection of the null hypothesis for one test among the collection of all tests we consider is less than or equal to 0.05. Similarly, we have assigned levels of significance for the model based on the indirect translog demand system so as to control the overall level of significance at 0.05. With the aid of critical values for our test statistics given in table 5.3, the reader can evaluate the results of our tests for alternative levels of significance or alternative allocations of the overall levels of significance among stages of the test procedure.

5.4 Conclusion

The results of our tests of the theory of consumer behavior, as presented in table 5.4, are that the set of restrictions on the parameters of the direct translog demand system implied by integrability must be rejected. For the direct demand system we reject equality; the sum of the budget shares is not independent of the ratios of prices to total expenditure, total expenditure, and time. If we were to test homogeneity and equality jointly rather than in parallel, we would reject the combined hypothesis for the direct demand system; we would also reject equality given homogeneity for this system.

We have provided a new econometric methodology for testing the monotonicity of a complete system of demand functions. The resulting tests of monotonicity do not require symmetry of the system of demand functions. If we were to proceed conditionally, taking homo-

Table 5.4
Test statistics for direct and indirect translog demand systems

Hypothesis	Degrees of freedom	Direct	Indirect
Homogeneity	4	6.99	5.62
Equality	5	26.8	1.72
Homogeneity and equality	8	35.4	8.65
Given homogeneity			
Equality	4	28.4	3.03
Given equality			
Homogeneity	3	8.62	6.93
Given homogeneity and equality			
Symmetry	3	4.88	3.69
Nonnegativity			
$-\alpha_1 \geq 0$	1	–219	–29.5
$-\alpha_2 \geq 0$	1	–140	–43.5
$1 + \alpha_1 + \alpha_2 \geq 0$	1	–586	–78.9
Monotonicity			
$\delta_1 \geq 0$	1	5.78	0.277
$\delta_2 \geq 0$	1	–1.17	0.00136

geneity and equality as given, we would accept the restrictions implied by symmetry and the restrictions implied by nonnegativity and monotonicity for both direct and indirect systems.

From the original studies of Henry Schultz (1938) through the present time market demand functions have been constructed by replacing the quantities demanded and income of the theory of behavior of the individual consumer by per capita quantities demanded and per capita income. The conditions under which market demand functions can be represented as strictly analogous to the individual demand functions in per capita form are very stringent.[16] On the basis of our empirical results, we can conclude that these conditions are in conflict with the empirical evidence.

Notes

1. See Basmann *et al.* (1973), Jorgenson and Lau (1977), and Wold (1953, p. 106). The double-logarithmic demand system has been used for tests of integrability by Byron (1968, 1970a, b, 1973), Court (1967), and Lluch (1971). For further discussion, see Barten (1977, pp. 51–53) and Brown and Deaton (1972, pp. 1193–1195).

2. Except for demand systems with only two commodities or demand systems with constant components of the consumer budget. See Barten (1974), Goldberger (1969), Jorgenson and Lau (1977), and McFadden (1964). The Rotterdam system has been used for tests of integrability by Barten (1967, 1969, 1974), Barten and Geyskens (1975), Deaton (1974), Lluch (1971), and Theil (1971, 1975). For further discussion, see Barten (1977, p. 51–53) and Brown and Deaton (1972, pp. 1193–1195).
3. See Jorgenson and Lau (1977) and Lau (1977).
4. See Jorgenson and Lau (1979).
5. Systems of demand functions based on direct and indirect transcendental logarithmic utility functions were introduced by Christensen *et al.* (1975) and used by them to test implications of integrability. Earlier, Christensen *et al.* (1971, 1973) introduced transcendental logarithmic functions into the study of production. Applications of demand systems based on transcendental logarithmic utility functions are given by Christensen and Manser (1975, 1977), Conrad and Jorgenson (1979), Jorgenson and Lau (1975), and Lau and Mitchell (1971).
6. For discussion of duality between direct and indirect demand functions see Chipman (1971). Hotelling (1935), Hurwicz (1971), Lau (1969a, b), and Wold (1953).
7. Tests of monotonicity for a single demand function are given by Stone (1954b, pp. 339–340), and by Wold (1953, p. 298). A test of monotonicity for the Rotterdam system is given by Barten and Geyskens (1975); this test requires symmetry of the system of demand functions.
8. The restrictions given have been derived in a form appropriate for any number of commodities by Jorgenson and Lau (1979).
9. Stone (1954b, table 107, p. 329), presents a test of homogeneity based on the double-logarithmic system of demand functions; a similar test is presented by Byron (1970b).
10. Symmetry conditions for integrability based on the indirect demand functions can be traced to Antonelli (1886, transl. 1971); symmetry conditions for integrability based on the direct demand functions can be traced to Slutsky (1915, transl. 1952). For additional references and discussion, see Hurwicz (1971, esp. pp. 188–210), and Samuelson (1950). Wold (1953, chapter 17, especially pp. 281–302) present a test of symmetry based on the double-logarithmic system of demand functions; a similar test is presented by Byron (1970b).
11. Homogeneity and summability are properties of market demand functions, while symmetry, nonnegativity, and monotonicity are properties of individual demand functions. The properties of individual demand functions carry over to market demand functions only under additional assumptions on individual demand functions or on variation in the distribution of income. Fur further discussion of the properties of market demand functions, see Debreu (1974), Mantel (1974), McFadden *et al.* (1974), and Sonnenschein (1972, 1973a). For discussion of aggregation over individual demand functions, see Chipman (1974), Diewert (1977), Gorman (1953), and Samuelson (1956).
12. See Jorgenson and Lau (1979).
13. A detailed reconciliation of our concept of personal consumption expenditures and the national accounting concept is given by Christensen and Jorgenson (1973, pp. 331–348).
14. The nonlinear three stage least squares estimator has also been discussed by Amemiya (1977), Gallant (1977), and Gallant and Jorgenson (1979).
15. This test statistic is based on the criterion for minimization employed in the construction of the nonlinear three stage least squares estimator; it was introduced and characterized by Gallant and Jorgenson (1979).
16. See, for example, the references on aggregation over individual demand functions given in note 11 above.

6 The Structure of Consumer Preferences, Federal Republic of Germany, 1950–1973

Klaus Conrad and
Dale W. Jorgenson

6.1 Introduction

In a recent paper, Christensen, Jorgenson and Lau (1975) have introduced systems of indirect and direct logarithmic demand functions to test restrictions on patterns of substitution implied by the theory of consumer behavior. They represent consumer preferences by translog utility functions that are quadratic in the logarithms of their arguments. These representations of consumer preferences do not require the assumptions of additivity and homotheticity implicit in the traditional approach to statistical demand analysis. In another paper, Jorgenson and Lau (1979) have introduced translog utility functions with time-varying preferences to test restrictions on the corresponding system of demand functions implied by integrability of these functions. They reject the hypothesis that the system of demand functions under consideration is integrable. By employing their methodology and by using German data for the same commodity groups, Conrad and Jorgenson (1979) accept the hypothesis of an integrable system of demand functions.

The objective of this chapter is to analyze the structure of consumer preferences and changes in preferences over time by using the same set of data as in Conrad and Jorgenson (1979). Our research is based on the methodology introduced by Jorgenson and Lau (1975) for analyzing the structure of consumer preferences. In the following section we briefly summarize the basic relationships between direct and indirect utility functions and the direct demand system. In section 6.3 we consider demand systems associated with restrictions on the structure of consumer preferences and changes in preferences over time. We begin with groupwise separability and groupwise homotheticity of preferences. For each set of restrictions on preferences, we derive parametric restrictions on the corresponding system of demand functions. In section 6.4 we present a summary of our alternative sets of tests and in section 6.5 we present empirical results of the tests, based on time series data for FRG consumption expenditures of three commodity groups—durables, nondurables, and energy—for the period 1950–1973. Finally, we compare our structure of consumer preferences with the structure obtained by Jorgenson and Lau (1975) for U.S. data.

6.2 Transcendental Logarithmic Utility Functions with Time-Varying Preferences

A quasi-concave direct utility function U with time-varying preferences can be written in the form

$$\ln U = F(X_1, X_2, X_3, t), \qquad (6.2.1)$$

where X_i $(i = 1, 2, 3)$ is the quantity consumed of the ith commodity and t is time. The theory of consumer behavior can be derived by maximizing utility, subject to the budget constraint

$$\sum \frac{P_i}{M} X_i = 1, \qquad (6.2.2)$$

where P_i $(i = 1, 2, 3)$ is the price of the ith commodity and M is the value of total expenditure.

Expressing the maximum level of utility, say V, as a function of ratios of prices to total expenditure P_i/M $(i = 1, 2, 3)$[1] and time t, we can write the indirect utility function in the form

$$\ln V = G\left(\frac{P_1}{M}, \frac{P_2}{M}, \frac{P_3}{M}, t\right), \qquad (6.2.3)$$

where V is a quasi-convex.[2] From the logarithmic form of Roy's identity,[3]

$$\frac{\partial \ln V}{\partial \ln \frac{P_j}{M}} = \frac{P_j X_j}{M} \sum_i \frac{\partial \ln V}{\partial \ln \frac{P_i}{M}}, \qquad (j = 1, 2, 3), \qquad (6.2.4)$$

we obtain the quantities consumed as functions of the "real" prices

$$X_i = \frac{\dfrac{\partial \ln V}{\partial \ln \dfrac{P_i}{M}}}{\dfrac{P_j}{M} \sum_i \dfrac{\partial \ln V}{\partial \ln \dfrac{P_i}{M}}}, \qquad (j = 1, 2, 3). \tag{6.2.5}$$

These direct demand functions provide a relationship between utility theory and empirical demand analysis.

We approximate the logarithm of the indirect utility function (6.2.3) by a function quadratic in the logarithms of the "real" prices and t[4]

$$\ln V = \alpha_0 + \sum_i \alpha_i \ln \frac{P_i}{M} + \alpha_t \cdot t + \frac{1}{2} \sum_{i,j} \beta_{ij} \ln \frac{P_i}{M} \ln \frac{P_j}{M}$$
$$+ \sum \beta_{it} \cdot t \cdot \ln \frac{P_i}{M} + \frac{1}{2} \beta_{tt} \cdot t^2 . \tag{6.2.6}$$

For the system of direct demand functions we obtain from (6.2.7) the following equations for the budget shares

$$\frac{P_j X_j}{M} = \frac{\alpha_j + \sum_i \beta_{ji} \dfrac{P_i}{M} + \beta_{jt} \cdot t}{\alpha_M + \sum \beta_{Mi} \ln \dfrac{P_i}{M} + \beta_{Mt} \cdot t}, \qquad (j = 1, 2, 3), \tag{6.2.7}$$

where

$$\alpha_M = \sum_k \alpha_{k,}$$
$$\beta_{Mi} = \sum_k \beta_{ki}, \tag{6.2.8}$$
$$\beta_{Mt} = \sum_k \beta_{kt}.$$

The budget constraint implies that the shares sum to unity so that, given the parameters of any two equations for the budget shares, the parameters of the third equation can be determined from the definitions of α_M, β_{Mi} and β_{Mt} in (6.2.8).

Since the equations for the budget shares (6.2.7) are homogeneous of degree zero in the parameters, normalization of the parameters is required for estimation; we choose the normalization $\alpha_M = -1$. To construct econometric tests of the theory of consumer behavior the system of the budget equations can be regarded as a system of demand functions without assuming that they can be generated by a utility function. Tests of integrability of these consumer demand functions answer the question of whether restrictions on the parameters derived from the theory are consistent with the empirical data. Jorgenson and Lau (1979) have formulated sets of conditions for integrability of the demand system.[5] They derive restrictions on the parameters of the translog demand systems corresponding to the properties of an integrable demand system—homogeneity, summability, symmetry, nonnegativity, and monotonicity.

The empirical results obtained by Jorgenson and Lau (1979), Conrad and Jorgenson (1979) and Conrad (1977) are based on time series of three commodity groups—durables, nondurables, and energy—for the U.S. and the FRG, respectively. For the direct demand system, Jorgenson and Lau (1979) accept homogeneity but reject summability; they reject the hypothesis that the direct demand system is integrable. Conrad and Jorgenson (1979), however, accept the hypothesis of integrability of the direct demand system whereas Conrad (1977) rejects symmetry by employing a dynamic version of the direct translog demand system. It is useful to compare these results with similar findings for the FRG. The recent book by Gollnick (1975) includes an analysis of the dynamic structure of household expenditures in the FRG, classifying consumption expenditures into 46 individual product groups. However, Gollnick's primary interest is empirical rather than theoretical so that he ignores integrability conditions or a relationship between his dynamic demand system and a dynamic utility function. Barten and Geyskens (1975) have tested integrability by means of the Rotterdam system of demand functions. They conclude that the hypothesis is not inconsistent with FRG data for four commodity groups for the period 1950–1968.[6]

The remaining problem is to get a deeper insight into the structure of consumer preferences by analyzing the structure of the corresponding utility function. This is the problem of groupwise separability and homotheticity of the utility function studied first by Sono (1961)[7] and Leontief (1947) and later by Strotz (1959), Gorman (1959), and Goldman and Uzawa (1964). Given the grouping of commodities into three aggregates we can test the possibility of separating the utility function into subfunctions, where the variables of the subfunctions consist of highly aggregated commodities like consumer durables and energy, for instance. By employing the mathematical correspondence between an integrable demand system and the corresponding utility function, Christensen, Jorgenson and Lau (1975) and Jorgenson and

Lau (1975) test a set of parameter restrictions on the translog demand system to characterize the pattern of consumer demand empirically. This approach does not employ hypotheses about budget allocation and patterns of substitution as assumptions but as hypotheses to be tested. We impose integrability conditions on the parameters of the demand system and use the resulting demand system to test restrictions on the structure of the indirect utility function.

6.3 Preference Structure

6.3.1 Introduction

Our econometric model of consumer behavior is provided by any two of the three equations for the budget shares, say

$$\frac{P_1 X_1}{M} = \frac{\alpha_1 + \beta_{11} \ln \dfrac{P_1}{M} + \beta_{12} \ln \dfrac{P_2}{M} + \beta_{13} \ln \dfrac{P_3}{M} + \beta_{1t} \cdot t}{-1 + \beta_{M1} \ln \dfrac{P_1}{M} + \beta_{M2} \ln \dfrac{P_2}{M} + \beta_{M3} \ln \dfrac{P_3}{M} + \beta_{Mt} \cdot t}$$

$$\frac{P_2 X_2}{M} = \frac{\alpha_2 + \beta_{21} \ln \dfrac{P_1}{M} + \beta_{22} \ln \dfrac{P_2}{M} + \beta_{23} \ln \dfrac{P_3}{M} + \beta_{2t} \cdot t}{-1 + \beta_{M1} \ln \dfrac{P_1}{M} + \beta_{M2} \ln \dfrac{P_2}{M} + \beta_{M3} \ln \dfrac{P_3}{M} + \beta_{Mt} \cdot t} .$$

This system is homogeneous of degree zero in prices and total expenditure. Equality restrictions imply that the parameters β_{M1}, β_{M2}, β_{m3}, and β_{Mt} are the same in both equations. Symmetry requires that

$$\beta_{12} = \beta_{21} ,$$
$$\beta_{13} = \beta_{31} = \beta_{M1} - \beta_{11} - \beta_{21} ,$$
$$\beta_{23} = \beta_{32} = \beta_{M2} - \beta_{12} - \beta_{22} .$$

If $P_1 X_1 / M$ is the budget share for durables and $P_2 X_2 / M$ the budget share for nondurables, the parameters of the equation for the budget share for energy, $P_3 X_3 / M$, can be determined from the definitions of α_M, β_{Mi} $(i = 1, 2, 3)$, and β_{Mt} in (6.2.8). Under homogeneity, equality and symmetry restrictions, eleven parameters remain to be estimated.

Our objective is to ascertain and characterize the structure of consumer preferences empirically without maintaining restrictive assumptions on the specific form of the utility function. We wish first to determine the effects of changes in total expenditures and changes in preferences over time on the allocation of the consumer budget among commodity groups and second to determine the effects of changes in relative prices on the allocation of the consumer budget, that is, to characterize the patterns of substitution among commodities.

In this section we test hypotheses on particular structures for consumer preferences by formulating restrictions on the parameters derived from grouping commodities. We consider groupwise separability of preferences in commodities and in time. For instance, an indirect translog utility function is groupwise separable in durables and energy from nondurables if the ratio of the budget shares of durables and energy is independent of the price of nondurables. Second, we consider overall homotheticity and groupwise homotheticity of preferences. For instance, an indirect translog utility function is homothetic if the income elasticity of demand is equal to one for all commodities. Third, we consider groupwise linear logarithmic utility as a possible restriction on preferences. For instance, an indirect translog utility function is groupwise linear logarithmic in durables and energy, if the ratio of the budget shares of durables and energy is independent of all prices and total expenditure and depends only on time.

6.3.2 Groupwise Separability

An indirect utility function V with time-varying preferences that is *groupwise separable* in X_1 and X_2 from X_3 can be written in the form

$$\ln V = F\left[\ln V^1\left(\frac{P_1}{M}, \frac{P_2}{M}, t\right), \frac{P_3}{M}, t\right] \tag{6.3.1}$$

where the function $\ln V^1$ depends only on P_1/M, P_2/M and time and is nonincreasing and quasi-convex in P_1/M and P_2/M. A necessary and sufficient condition for groupwise separability of the indirect utility function in P_1/M and P_2/M from P_3/M is that the ratio of the budget shares for X_1 and X_2 is independent of the price P_3 of X_3. An indirect utility function that is groupwise separable in P_1/M and P_2/M from time can be written in an analogous form with the roles of P_3/M and time t interchanged. A necessary and sufficient condition for groupwise separability of P_1/M and P_2/M from time is that the ratio of the budget shares for X_1 and X_2 is independent of time.

Partially differentiating eq. (6.3.1), first with respect to $\ln(P_3/M)$ and then with respect to $\ln(P_1/M)$ and $\ln(P_2/M)$ separately, we obtain

$$\frac{\partial^2 \ln V}{\partial \ln \frac{P_1}{M}\, \partial \ln \frac{P_3}{M}} = \frac{\dfrac{\partial^2 F}{\left(\partial \ln V^1\, \partial \ln \dfrac{P_3}{M}\right)}}{\dfrac{\partial F}{\partial \ln V^1}} \cdot \frac{\partial \ln V}{\partial \ln \frac{P_1}{M}} \tag{6.3.2}$$

and

$$\frac{\partial^2 \ln V}{\partial \ln \frac{P_2}{M}\, \partial \ln \frac{P_3}{M}} = \frac{\dfrac{\partial^2 F}{\left(\partial \ln V^1\, \partial \ln \dfrac{P_3}{M}\right)}}{\dfrac{\partial F}{\partial \ln V^1}} \cdot \frac{\partial \ln V}{\partial \ln \frac{P_2}{M}}\,. \tag{6.3.3}$$

Given groupwise separability, eqs. (6.3.2) and (6.3.3) must hold everywhere; in particular, they must hold at the point of approximation, in this case, $\ln(P_i/M) = 0$ $(i = 1, 2, 3)$, $t = 0$, where we can identify the second partial derivatives of the left-hand side of (6.3.2) and (6.3.3) with the parameters β_{13} and β_{23} of the indirect translog utility function. Similarly, we can identify the first partial derivatives of $\ln V$ with respect to $\ln(P_1/M)$ and $\ln(P_2/M)$ respectively with the parameters α_1 and α_2 of the indirect translog utility function. Thus, given groupwise separability of P_1/M and P_2/M from P_3/M, the parameters of the indirect translog utility function must satisfy the restrictions

$$\beta_{13} = \rho_3\, \alpha_1\,, \qquad \beta_{23} = \rho_3\, \alpha_2\,, \tag{6.3.4}$$

where ρ_3 is a constant given by

$$\rho_3 = \frac{\dfrac{\partial^2 F}{\partial \ln V^1\, \partial \ln \dfrac{P_3}{M}}}{\dfrac{\partial F}{\partial \ln V^1}}$$

at the point of approximation.

Similarly, given groupwise separability of P_1/M and P_2/M from time, the parameters must satisfy

$$\beta_{1t} = \rho_t \alpha_1\,, \qquad \beta_{2t} = \rho_t \alpha_2\,. \tag{6.3.5}$$

Each pair of commodities, such as P_1/M and P_2/M, can be separable from the remaining commodities, P_3/M in this instance, or from time. Corresponding to the three possible pairs of commodities, there are six possible sets of groupwise separability restrictions analogous to eqs. (6.3.4) and (6.3.5). Each set of two restrictions involves the introduction of one new parameter—ρ_3 and ρ_t in the examples given above. Maintaining the equality, homogeneity and symmetry restrictions, the number of unknown parameters, eleven, is reduced by one under each set of such restrictions.

The translog approximation to a groupwise separable indirect utility function is not necessarily groupwise separable. If the indirect translog utility function itself is groupwise separable then it is called *explicitly groupwise separable*.[8] For the explicit groupwise separability of P_1/M and P_2/M from P_3/M, we require the groupwise separability restrictions given in (6.3.4) and the additional restriction

$$\rho_3 = 0\,. \tag{6.3.6}$$

This restriction implies that the cross partial derivatives of the indirect translog utility function with respect to $\ln(P_1/M)$ and $\ln(P_3/M)$, and $\ln(P_2/M)$ and $\ln(P_3/M)$ respectively, are identically zero at the point of approximation. Thus the ratio of the expenditures on X_1 and X_2 is independent of P_3/M.

Similarly, explicitly groupwise separability of P_1/M and P_2/M from time requires the additional restriction

$$\rho_t = 0\,. \tag{6.3.7}$$

Thus the ratio of the expenditures on X_1 and X_2 is independent of time. Analogous restrictions must hold for any one of the six possible types of explicit groupwise separability. Under each set of restrictions there are nine unknown parameters remaining to be estimated.

An indirect utility function with time-varying preferences is *additive* in P_1/M, P_2/M and P_3/M if it can be written in the form

$$\ln V = F\left[\ln V^1\left(\frac{P_1}{M}, t\right) + \ln V^2\left(\frac{P_2}{M}, t\right) + \ln V^3\left(\frac{P_3}{M}, t\right), t\right]. \tag{6.3.8}$$

A necessary and sufficient condition for additivity in three commodities is that the indirect utility function is groupwise separable in any two pairs of commodities from the third. An indirect utility function is *explicitly additive* if it can be written in the form

$$\ln V = \ln V^1\left(\frac{P_1}{M}, t\right) + \ln V^2\left(\frac{P_2}{M}, t\right) + \ln V^3\left(\frac{P_3}{M}, t\right). \tag{6.3.9}$$

The translog approximation to an explicitly additive utility function is necessarily explicitly additive. A necessary and sufficient condition for explicit additivity in three commodities is that the indirect translog utility function is explicit groupwise separable in any two pairs of commodities from a third commodity.

An indirect utility function V with time-varying preferences that is *neutral* can be written in the form

$$\ln V = F\left[\ln V^1\left(\frac{P_1}{M}, \frac{P_2}{M}, \frac{P_3}{M}\right), t\right] \tag{6.3.10}$$

where the function V^1 depends on the "real" prices of the three commodities, but is independent of time. Groupwise separability for two of the three possible groups of two commodities from time implies groupwise separability of the third group from time and neutrality of the indirect utility function. The translog approximation to a neutral indirect utility functions not necessarily neutral. A neutral indirect translog utility function is called *explicitly neutral* and can be written in the form

$$\ln V = \ln V^1\left(\frac{P_1}{M}, \frac{P_2}{M}, \frac{P_3}{M}\right) + F(t). \tag{6.3.11}$$

Explicit groupwise separability for two of the three possible groups from time implies explicit groupwise separability of the third group from time and explicit neutrality of the indirect utility function.

6.3.3 Groupwise Homotheticity and Homogeneity

The second type of restrictions on preferences we will test are homotheticity restrictions. First, we consider overall homotheticity of preferences. An indirect utility function V with time-varying preferences that is *homothetic* can be written in the form

$$\ln V = F\left[\ln H\left(\frac{P_1}{M}, \frac{P_2}{M}, \frac{P_3}{M}, t\right), t\right] \tag{6.3.12}$$

where H is homogeneous of degree minus one in the ratios of prices to total expenditure. Under homotheticity the budget shares for all three commodities depend only on prices and time and are independent of total expenditure.

Partially differentiating eq. (6.3.12), first with respect to $\ln(P_j/M)$ $(j = 1,2,3)$ and then with respect to $\ln(P_k/M)$ $(k = 1,2,3)$, we obtain

$$\frac{\partial^2 \ln V}{\partial \ln \frac{P_k}{M}\, \partial \ln \frac{P_j}{M}} = \frac{\partial^2 F}{\partial \ln H^2}\, \frac{\partial \ln H}{\partial \ln \frac{P_k}{M}} \cdot \frac{\partial \ln H}{\partial \ln \frac{P_j}{M}} + \frac{\partial F}{\partial \ln H}\, \frac{\partial^2 \ln H}{\partial \ln \frac{P_k}{M}\, \partial \ln \frac{P_j}{M}}, \qquad (j,k = 1,2,3). \qquad (6.3.13)$$

Summing over k and using homogeneity of degree minus one of the function H, we can write

$$\sum_k \frac{\partial^2 \ln V}{\partial \ln \frac{P_k}{M}\, \partial \ln \frac{P_j}{M}} = -\frac{\partial^2 F}{\partial \ln H^2}\, \frac{\partial \ln H}{\partial \ln \frac{P_j}{M}}, \qquad (j = 1,2,3). \qquad (6.3.14)$$

Given homotheticity, eq. (6.3.14) must hold everywhere; in particular, they must hold at the point of approximation, where we can identify the first and second partial derivatives with the parameters of the indirect translog utility function which must satisfy the restrictions

$$\beta_{M1} = \sigma\, \alpha_1, \qquad \beta_{M2} = \sigma\, \alpha_2, \qquad \beta_{M3} = \sigma\, \alpha_3, \qquad (6.3.15)$$

where $\beta_{Mj} = \sum_k \beta_{kj}$ and σ is a constant given by

$$\sigma = -\frac{\dfrac{\partial^2 F}{\partial \ln H^2}}{\dfrac{\partial F}{(\partial \ln H)}}.$$

We introduce one new parameter, σ, so that these restrictions reduce the number of parameters by two, leaving nine parameters to be estimated.

The translog approximation to a homothetic indirect utility function is not necessarily homothetic. If the parameters of the indirect translog utility function satisfy the homotheticity restrictions (6.3.15) and the additional restriction

$$\sigma = 0 \,, \tag{6.3.16}$$

this function is homothetic. We refer to this set of restrictions as *explicit homotheticity* restrictions. Under these restrictions, only eight unknown parameters remain to be estimated.[9]

An indirect utility function V with time-varying preferences is *homogeneous* if it can be written in the form

$$\ln V = \ln H\left(\frac{P_1}{M}, \frac{P_2}{M}, \frac{P_3}{M}, t\right) \tag{6.3.17}$$

where H is a homogenous function of degree minus one in the "real" prices P_i/M $(i = 1, 2, 3)$. Under homogeneity the parameters of the indirect translog utility function must satisfy the explicit homotheticity restrictions (6.3.16) and the additional restrictions[10]

$$\beta_{Mt} = 0 \,. \tag{6.3.18}$$

Under this set of *homogeneity* restrictions only seven unknown parameters remain to be estimated.

A weaker form of homotheticity of preferences is *groupwise homotheticity*. An indirect utility function with time-varying preferences that is groupwise homothetic in P_1/M and P_2/M can be written in the form

$$\ln V = F\left[\ln H\left(\frac{P_1}{M}, \frac{P_2}{M}, \frac{P_3}{M}, t\right), \frac{P_3}{M}, t\right] \tag{6.3.19}$$

where H is homogenous of degree minus one in the real prices P_1/M and P_2/M. Under groupwise homotheticity in P_1/M and P_2/M the ratio of expenditures for X_1 and X_2 is homogeneous of degree zero in P_1/M and P_2/M.

Under groupwise homotheticity the parameters of the indirect translog utility function satisfy the restrictions

$$\beta_{11} + \beta_{12} = \sigma_{12}\,\alpha_1 \,, \qquad \beta_{12} + \beta_{22} = \sigma_{12}\,\alpha_2 \,. \tag{6.3.20}$$

This set of two restrictions involves the introduction of one new parameters, σ_{12}, so that the number of unknown parameters, eleven, is reduced by one. Corresponding to the three possible pairs of commodities, there are three possible sets of groupwise homotheticity restrictions, analogous to those given in (6.3.20).

The translog approximation to a groupwise homothetic indirect utility function is not necessarily groupwise homothetic. If the parameters of the indirect translog utility function satisfy the groupwise homotheticity restrictions given in (6.3.20) and the additional restriction

$$\sigma_{12} = 0\,, \tag{6.3.21}$$

this function is groupwise homothetic and the restrictions are called *explicit groupwise homotheticity* restrictions. Under these restrictions nine unknown parameters remain to be estimated. There are three possible sets of explicit groupwise homotheticity restrictions corresponding to the three possible pairs of commodities. Restrictions analogous to those outlined above must hold for any one of the three possible types of explicit groupwise homotheticity.

An indirect utility function with time-varying preferences is *inclusively groupwise homothetic* in P_1/M and P_2/M if it can be written in the form

$$\ln V = F\left[\ln H\left(\frac{P_1}{M}, \frac{P_2}{M}, \frac{P_3}{M}, t\right), t\right] \tag{6.3.22}$$

where H is homogeneous of degree minus one in the "real" prices P_1/M and P_2/M. Given groupwise homotheticity, this condition implies in addition that the ratios of all budget shares are homogeneous of degree zero in the "real" prices P_1/M and P_2/M. Under *inclusive groupwise homotheticity* in P_1/M and P_2/M the parameters of the indirect translog utility function satisfy the groupwise homotheticity restrictions given in (6.3.20) and the additional restriction

$$\beta_{13} + \beta_{23} = \sigma_{12}\,\alpha_3\,. \tag{6.3.23}$$

Under this additional restriction, nine parameters remain to be estimated. Again, there are three possible sets of inclusive groupwise homotheticity restrictions corresponding to the three possible sets of groupwise homotheticity restrictions.

The translog approximation to an inclusively groupwise homothetic indirect utility function is not necessarily inclusively groupwise homothetic. If the parameters of the indirect translog utility function satisfy the inclusive groupwise homotheticity restrictions given in (6.3.20) and (6.3.23) and the additional restriction

$$\sigma_{12} = 0\,, \tag{6.3.24}$$

this function is inclusively groupwise homothetic and the restrictions are called *explicit inclusive groupwise homotheticity* restrictions. Under this set of restrictions, only eight unknown parameters remain to be estimated.

Finally, an indirect utility function with time-varying preferences is *groupwise homogeneous* if it can be written in the form

$$\ln V = \ln H\left(\frac{P_1}{M}, \frac{P_2}{M}, \frac{P_3}{M}, t\right) \tag{6.3.25}$$

where H is homogeneous of degree minus one in the "real" prices P_1/M and P_2/M. Under groupwise homogeneity the parameters of the indirect translog utility function must satisfy the explicit inclusive groupwise homotheticity restrictions consisting of (6.3.20), (6.3.23), and (6.3.24) above and the additional restriction

$$\beta_{1t} + \beta_{2t} = 0\,. \tag{6.3.26}$$

Under these so-called *groupwise homogeneity* restrictions seven unknown parameters remain to be estimated. There are three possible sets of groupwise homogeneity restrictions and analogous restrictions must hold for any of them. We conclude this section by noting that inclusive groupwise homotheticity in all possible groups implies linear logarithmic utility and explicit inclusive groupwise homotheticity in all possible groups implies explicit linear logarithmic utility.

6.3.4 Groupwise Linear Logarithmic Utility

We next combine groupwise homotheticity and separability restrictions. An indirect utility function that is *groupwise homothetically separable* in P_1/M and P_2/M from P_3/M can be written in the form

$$\ln V = F\left[\ln H\left(\frac{P_1}{M}, \frac{P_2}{M}, t\right), \frac{P_3}{M}, t\right] \tag{6.3.27}$$

where H is a homogeneous function of degree minus one and depends only on $P_1/M, P_2/M$, and time. Groupwise homothetic separability implies that the ratio of the expenditures from X_1 and X_2 is independent of P_3/M and is homogeneous of degree zero in P_1/M and P_2/M. Again, the translog approximation to a groupwise homothetically separable utility function is not necessarily groupwise homothetically separable. If the parameters of the indirect translog utility function satisfy the combined restrictions of explicit groupwise separability, given in (6.3.6) above, and the explicit groupwise homotheticity restrictions, given in (6.3.21) above, this function is groupwise homothetic separable and the joint restrictions are the *explicit groupwise homothetic* separability restrictions.

An indirect utility function with time-varying preferences is *groupwise linear logarithmic* if it can be written in the form

$$\ln V = F\left[\delta_1(t)\ln\frac{P_1}{M} + \delta_2(t)\ln\frac{P_2}{M}, P_3, t\right] \tag{6.3.28}$$

where $\delta_1(t)$ and $\delta_2(t)$ are functions of time. A necessary and sufficient condition for groupwise linear logarithmic utility in P_1/M and P_2/M is that the ratio of the expenditure for X_1 and X_2 is independent of all prices and total expenditure and depends only on time. Given groupwise homothetic separability in P_1/M and P_2/M from P_3/M groupwise linear logarithmic utility in P_1/M and P_2/M requires the additional restriction

$$\alpha_1 \beta_{12} = \alpha_2 \beta_{11}\,. \tag{6.3.29}$$

Under these restrictions only eight unknown parameters remain to be estimated. There are three possible sets of groupwise linear logarithmic utility restrictions and analogous restrictions must hold for any one of them.

The translog approximation of a groupwise linear logarithmic utility function is not necessarily groupwise linear logarithmic. If the parameters of the indirect translog utility function satisfy the explicit groupwise homothetic separability restrictions and the additional restriction

$$\beta_{12} = 0\,, \tag{6.3.30}$$

this function is groupwise linear logarithmic and the restrictions are the explicit *groupwise linear logarithmic utility* restrictions. Corresponding to the three possible pairs of commodities, there are three possible sets of restrictions of this type.

An indirect utility function with time-varying preferences is *linear logarithmic* in P_1/M, P_2/M, and P_3/M if it can be written in the form

$$\ln V = F\left[\delta_1\,(t)\ln\frac{P_1}{M} + \delta_2\,(t)\ln\frac{P_2}{M} + \delta_3\,(t)\ln\frac{P_3}{M}, t\right]. \tag{6.3.31}$$

A necessary and sufficient condition for linear logarithmic utility is that the indirect utility function is groupwise linear logarithmic in every pair of the three commodities.

Finally, an indirect utility function V is *explicitly linear logarithmic* if it can be written in the form

$$\ln V = \sum_{i=1}^{3} \delta_i(t)\ln\frac{P_i}{M} + F(t). \tag{6.3.32}$$

Given linear logarithmic utility, explicit groupwise linear logarithmic utility in any one of the three possible pairs implies that the indirect utility function is explicitly linear logarithmic. For an explicitly linear logarithmic utility function the budget shares of all commodities are independent of prices and total expenditure, depending only on time.

Finally, an indirect utility function V is *neutral linear logarithmic* if it can be written in the form

$$\ln V = F\left(\sum_{i=1}^{3} \delta_i \ln\frac{P_i}{M}, t\right) \tag{6.3.33}$$

where δ_1, δ_2 and δ_3 are constants. A necessary and sufficient condition for neutral linear logarithmic utility is that the indirect translog utility function is both neutral and linear logarithmic, or both. For a neutral linear logarithmic utility function the budget shares of all commodities are constant.

To summarize: Starting with the assumption—tested and not falsified in a previous paper—that our model for the allocation of consumption expenditures can be generated by utility maximization, we have outlined tests of a series of possible restrictions on the underlying structure of consumer preferences. First, we have considered groupwise separability of preferences in commodities and in time. Second, we have considered overall homotheticity and groupwise homotheticity restrictions on preferences. Finally, we have considered groupwise linear logarithmic utility as a possible restriction on preferences.

6.4 Statistical Tests

We propose to test restrictions on the structure of preferences, given equality, homogeneity and symmetry restrictions. The tests we have carried out are presented in diagrammatic form in a series of four figures. We test the restrictions derived from groupwise separability, homotheticity, and groupwise homothecity in parallel. Given groupwise homothetic separability for any group, we proceed to test the additional restrictions implied by groupwise linear logarithmic utility, conditional on the restrictions implied by groupwise homothetic separability. Given the outcome of these tests we can determine the set of acceptable restrictions on the structure of preferences.

We first test groupwise separability for each possible group presented diagrammatically in figure 6.1 for the group {1, 2}. If we accept the hypothesis of groupwise separability from the third group for any two of the three possible groups, we accept the hypothesis of additivity. If we accept groupwise separability for any group, we proceed to test explicit groupwise separability for that group. If we accept the hypothesis of explicit groupwise separability from the third commodity for any two of the three groups, we accept the hypothesis of explicit additivity. If we accept the hypothesis of groupwise separabil-

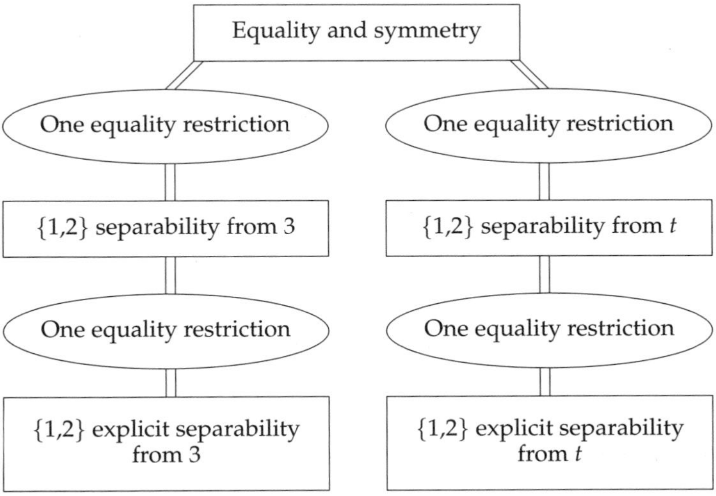

Figure 6.1
Tests of separability. (There are three sets of tests of this type; this diagram gives only one set of such tests corresponding to the group [1,2]).

ity from time for any two of the three possible groups, we accept the hypothesis of neutrality. Conditional on the groupwise separability restriction from time we test the hypothesis of explicit groupwise separability from time. Combining results from the tests for each of the three commodity groups, we can test the hypothesis of explicit neutrality.

In figure 6.2 our test procedure for homotheticity is presented diagrammatically. We first test groupwise homotheticity restrictions for each possible group. In parallel we test homotheticity restrictions for the group consisting of all three commodities. If we accept homotheticity for the group consisting of all commodities, we proceed to test explicit homotheticity. If we accept explicit homotheticity for the group of three commodities, we proceed to test homogeneity.

If we accept groupwise homotheticity for any group, we proceed to test explicit groupwise homotheticity and inclusive groupwise homotheticity for that group in parallel. If we accept both explicit groupwise homotheticity and inclusive groupwise homotheticity for any

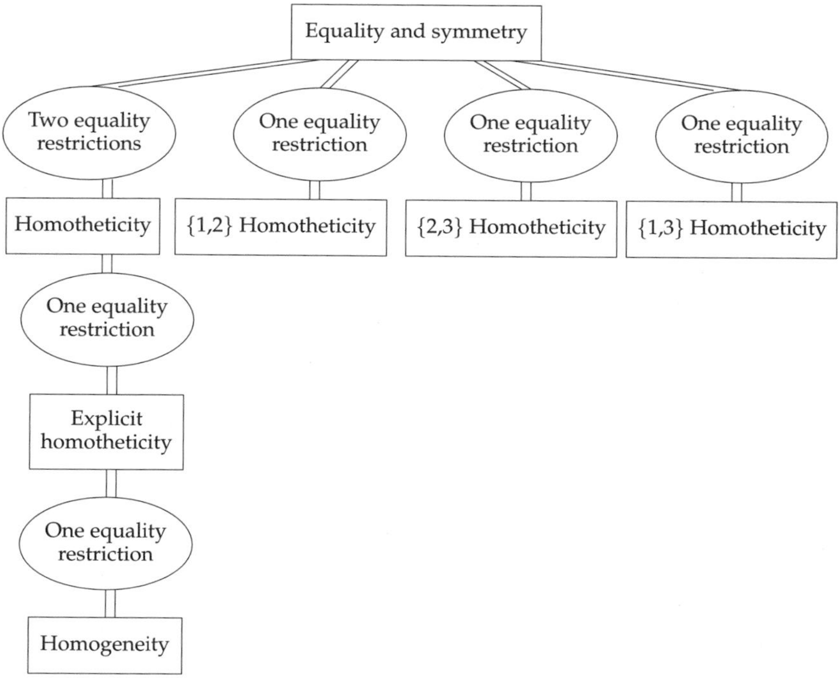

Figure 6.2
Tests of homotheticity.

group, we proceed to test groupwise homogeneity for that group. Our test procedure for explicit and inclusive groupwise homotheticity is presented diagrammatically in figure 6.3. We recall that inclusive groupwise homotheticity for all three groups implies that the utility function is linear logarithmic. If we accept explicit inclusive groupwise homotheticity for all three groups, we accept the hypothesis of explicit linear logarithmic utility. Finally, if we accept groupwise homogeneity for all three groups, we accept the hypothesis of neutral linear logarithmic utility.

We can combine the results of our tests of separability and homotheticity in order to draw conclusions about homothetic separability. If we accept the hypothesis of groupwise separability for a group consisting of two commodities, and for the same group we accept the hypothesis of groupwise homotheticity, we accept the hypothesis of groupwise homothetic separability.[11] If we accept the hypothesis of groupwise homothetic separability for any group of two commodities

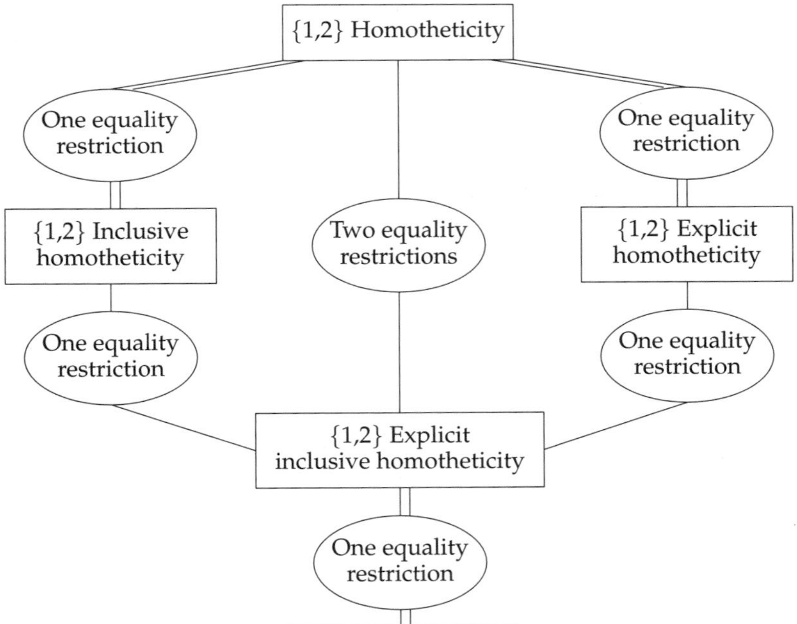

Figure 6.3
Tests of groupwise homotheticity. (There are three sets of tests of this type; this diagram gives only one set of such tests corresponding to the group [1,2]).

from the third, we proceed to test the hypothesis of groupwise linear logarithmic utility for that group, conditional on groupwise homothetic separability. An indirect utility function is characterized by linear logarithmic utility if it is groupwise linear logarithmic in all three possible groups consisting of two commodities each. Finally, if we accept the hypothesis of groupwise linear logarithmic utility for any group, we proceed to test the hypothesis of explicit groupwise linear logarithmic utility for that group. If in addition, we accept the hypothesis of groupwise homogeneity for that group, we accept the hypothesis of explicit neutral linear logarithmic utility for that group. Our test procedure for linear logarithmic utility is presented diagrammatically in figure 6.4.

6.5 Empirical Results

6.5.1 Estimation and Test Statistics

The first step in implementing an econometric model of demand based on the indirect translog utility function is to add a stochastic specification to the theoretical model based on equations for the three budget shares. Given the disturbances for any two equations, the disturbance for the remaining equation can be determined from the

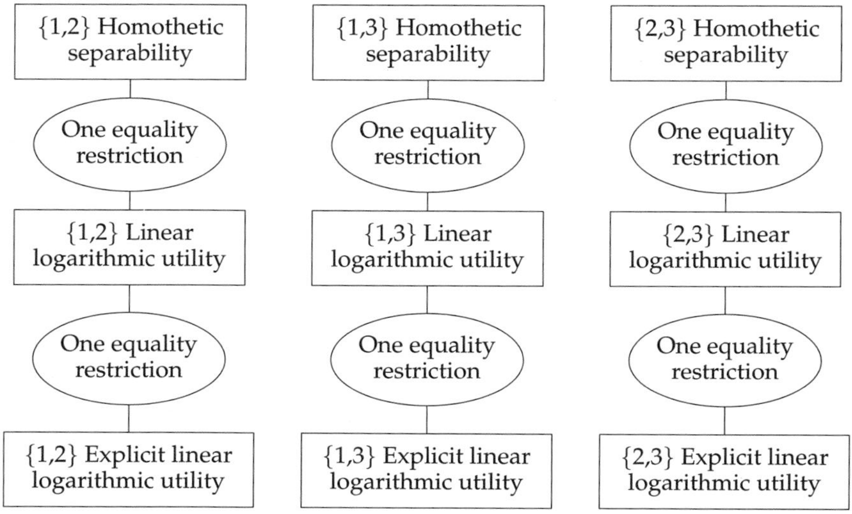

Figure 6.4
Tests of linear logarithmic utility.

budget constraint. Only two of the equations are required for a complete model of consumer demand. We have fitted the equations for durables and nondurables.[12] Our empirical results are based on time series data for prices and quantities of durables (X_1), nondurables (X_2), and energy (X_3) and time.[13] We impose the hypothesis that the model of demand is consistent with utility maximization, so that the parameters of this model satisfy homogeneity, equality and symmetry restrictions. Given these restrictions, and the normalization of α_M at minus unity, eleven unknown parameters remain to be estimated in our econometric model.

Given the validity of the theory of demand, we proceed to test hypotheses about possible restrictions on the structure of preferences of durables, nondurables, and energy. First, we test hypotheses associated with groupwise separability. Our second set of restrictions on the structure of preferences is associated with homotheticity—groupwise homotheticity, explicit groupwise homotheticity, inclusive groupwise homotheticity, groupwise homogeneity, homotheticity and homogeneity. Combining separability and homotheticity restrictions, we obtain estimates under groupwise homothetic separability. We also test the additional restrictions of groupwise and explicit groupwise linear logarithmic utility.[14]

To test the validity of restrictions on the structure of preferences, we employ test statistics based on the likelihood ratio λ, where

$$\lambda = \frac{\max_{\omega} L}{\max_{\Omega} L} .$$

The likelihood ratio is the ratio of the maximum value of the likelihood function L for the econometric model of demand ω subject to restriction to the maximum value of the likelihood function for the model Ω without restriction.

We have estimated econometric models of demand from data on FRG private consumption expenditures for 1950–1973. There are twenty-four observations for each behavioral equation, so that the number of degrees of freedom available for tests of hypotheses about the structure of preferences is forty-eight. Our test statistic for each set of restrictions is based on minus twice the logarithm of the likelihood ratio, which is distributed, asymptotically, as chi-squared with a number of degrees of freedom equal to the number of restrictions to be tested.

To control the overall level of significance for each series of tests, we set the level of significance at 0.05. We then allocated the overall level of significance among the various stages in each series of tests. We test groupwise separability from commodities, groupwise separability from time, homotheticity, groupwise homotheticity, and groupwise linear logarithmic utility proceeding conditionally on the validity of equality, homogeneity and symmetry restrictions implied by the theory of demand and on the restrictions implied by homothetic separability. These tests are not "nested" so that the sum of the levels of significance for each of the five sets of hypotheses is an upper bound for the level of significance of tests of the sets of hypotheses considered simultaneously. We assign a level of significance of 0.01 to each of the five sets of restrictions.

There are six restrictions associated with groupwise separability and explicit groupwise separability from commodities. We assign a level of significance of 0.0017 to each. We assign the same level of significance to restrictions associated with separability from time. There are three restrictions associated with homotheticity. We assign 0.0033 to each. There are twelve restrictions associated with groupwise homotheticity. We assign the level of significance 0.00083 to each. Finally, there are six restrictions associated with groupwise linear logarithmic utility. We assign 0.0017 to each of these restrictions.

For our econometric model of demand based on the indirect translog utility function we have assigned levels of significance to each of our tests of hypotheses about the structure of preferences so as to control the overall level of significance for all tests at 0.05. With the aid of critical values for our test statistics given in table 6.1, the reader can evaluate the results of our tests for alternative significance levels or for alternative allocations of the overall level of significance among stages of our test procedure. Test statistics for each of the hypotheses we have considered about the structure of preferences are given in table 6.2.

The results of our tests of restrictions on preferences based on the indirect translog utility function, as presented in table 6.2, are first that the indirect utility function is groupwise separable in any pair of commodities from the remaining commodity; this result implies additivity. The indirect translog utility function is even explicitly additive as we accept explicitly groupwise separability in all three groups of two commodities from the remaining commodity. This implies, for instance, that the ratio of the expenditures on durables (X_1) and

Table 6.1
Critical values of χ^2/degrees of freedom

Degrees of freedom	Level of significance					
	.10	.05	.01	.005	.001	.0005
1	2.71	3.84	6.64	7.88	10.83	12.12
2	2.30	3.0	4.61	5.30	6.91	7.60

nondurables (X_2) is independent from the price of energy (P_3). Second, the group {1.3}, durables and energy, is separable from time. Turning to the results of the corresponding tests by Jorgenson and Lau (1975) with U.S. data, we observe that they also found that the group {1, 2}, durables and nondurables, is explicitly separable from commodity 3, energy. This group is also explicitly groupwise separable from time, a result we strongly reject with FRG data due to the postwar situation.

We next turn to our results of tests of homotheticity, and observe that the group {1, 3}, durables and energy, is groupwise homothetic; the ratio of the expenditures for durables and energy is homogeneous of degree zero in the "real" prices of these two goods. Further tests of homotheticity are rejected. Treating groupwise homotheticity in P_2/M and P_3/M nondurables and energy, as an assumption we accept inclusive groupwise homotheticity, explicit groupwise homotheticity, and therefore, explicit inclusive homotheticity in P_2/M and P_3/M. We consider however a series of tests as terminated if we reject a hypothesis.

Finally, as we accept the hypothesis of groupwise homothetic separability for the group {1, 3}, durables and energy, we can proceed to test hypothesis of groupwise linear logarithmic utility. Just for that group, we reject this hypothesis so that further simplifications are not possible. We accept groupwise linear logarithmic utility for the groups {1, 2} and {2, 3}, but had to reject on the preceding stage of the series of tests groupwise homothetic separability for these groups. Comparing these results with the tests of homotheticity by Jorgenson and Lau with U.S. data, we notice that they accept the hypothesis of groupwise homotheticity for the group {1, 2}, durables and nondurables. This group is also explicitly groupwise homothetic, a hypothesis we strongly reject with FRG data.

Employing the restrictions corresponding to explicit additivity, we can reduce the number of parameters to be estimated from eleven to

Table 6.2
Test statistics

Hypothesis	Degrees of freedom	Critical values	Test statistics FRG	U.S.
Groupwise separability	Given equality and symmetry			
{1,2} from 3	1	10.32	0.61	0.55
{1,3} from 2	1	10.32	1.00	15.14
{2,3} from 1	1	10.32	0.48	30.35
{1,2} from t	1	10.32	40.56	3.83
{1,3} from t	1	10.32	1.06	27.96
{2,3} from t	1	10.32	23.75	37.13
Homotheticity	2	5.98	11.42	25.37
Groupwise homotheticity				
{1,2}	1	11.35	20.40	1.08
{1,3}	1	11.35	0.44	24.68
{2,3}	1	11.35	12.66	17.65
Given groupwise separability	Groupwise explicit separability			
{1,2} from 3	1	10.32	0.55	1.39
{1,3} from 2	1	10.32	0.12	0.38
{2,3} from 1	1	10.32	0.24	5.27
{1,2} from t	1	10.32	12.59	3.99
{1,3} from t	1	10.32	12.30	0.67
{2,3} from t	1	10.32	8.70	15.17
	Given homotheticity			
Explicit homotheticity	1	9.13	18.36	1.20
Groupwise inclusive homotheticity	Given groupwise homotheticity			
{1,2}	1	11.35	2.59	13.04
{1,3}	1	11.35	23.60	21.99
{2,3}	1	11.35	0.28	13.11
Groupwise explicit homotheticity				
{1,2}	1	11.35	22.16	1.63
{1,3}	1	11.35	25.84	0.16
{2,3}	1	11.35	1.22	13.99
	Given explicit homotheticity			
Homogeneity	1	9.13	14.87	45.50
Groupwise homogeneity	Given groupwise explicit inclusive homotheticity			
{1,2}	1	11.35	16.60	38.89
{1,3}	1	11.35	27.69	13.12
{2,3}	1	11.35	36.18	52.24

Table 6.2 (continued)

Hypothesis	Degrees of freedom	Critical values	Test statistics FRG	U.S.
Groupwise linear logarithmic utility	Given groupwise homothetic separability			
{1,2}	1	10.32	7.75	27.06
{1,3}	1	10.32	30.28	20.50
{2,3}	1	10.32	2.60	10.35
Explicit groupwise linear logarithmic utility	Given groupwise linear logarithmic utility			
{1,2}	1	10.32	23.21	—
{1,3}	1	10.32	27.0	—
{2,3}	1	10.32	1.04	—

eight. Under these restrictions the estimated form of our econometric model of consumer demand is as follows

$$\frac{P_1X_1}{M} = \frac{\underset{(0.001)}{-0.148} - \underset{(0.021)}{0.196} \ln \frac{P_1}{M} - \underset{(0.001)}{0.012} \cdot t}{-1 - \underset{(0.021)}{0.196} \ln \frac{P_1}{M} + \underset{(0.223)}{0.430} \ln \frac{P_2}{M} - \underset{(0.011)}{0.044} \ln \frac{P_3}{M} + \underset{(0.004)}{0.023} \cdot t}$$

$$\frac{P_2X_2}{M} = \frac{\underset{(0.001)}{-0.803} + \underset{(0.223)}{0.430} \ln \frac{P_2}{M} + \underset{(0.006)}{0.038} \cdot t}{-1 - 0.196 \ln \frac{P_1}{M} + 0.430 \ln \frac{P_2}{M} - 0.044 \ln \frac{P_3}{M} + 0.023 \cdot t}$$

$$\frac{P_3X_3}{M} = \frac{\underset{(0.0006)}{-0.049} - \underset{(0.001)}{0.044} \ln \frac{P_3}{M} - \underset{(0.0007)}{0.003} \cdot t}{-1 - 0.196 \ln \frac{P_1}{M} + 0.430 \ln \frac{P_2}{M} - 0.044 \ln \frac{P_3}{M} + 0.023 \cdot t}.$$

Employing the restrictions corresponding to explicit groupwise homothetic separability and to explicit separability from time for the group {1, 2}, Jorgenson and Lau (1975) can reduce the number of parameters to be estimated from eleven to five. The estimated form of their econometric model of consumer demand is as follows

$$\frac{P_1X_1}{M}=\frac{\underset{(0.005)}{-0.229}-\underset{(0.010)}{0.132}\left(\ln\frac{P_1}{M}-\ln\frac{P_2}{M}\right)}{-1-\underset{(0.0024)}{0.0307}\ln\frac{P_3}{M}-\underset{(0.0001)}{0.00094}\cdot t}$$

$$\frac{P_2X_2}{M}=\frac{\underset{(0.0006)}{-0.721}+\underset{(0.01)}{0.132}\left(\ln\frac{P_1}{M}-\ln\frac{P_2}{M}\right)}{-1-0.0307\ln\frac{P_3}{M}-0.00094\cdot t}$$

$$\frac{P_3X_3}{M}=\frac{\underset{(0.0007)}{-0.0503}-0.0307\ln\frac{P_3}{M}-\underset{(0.0001)}{0.0009}\cdot t}{-1-0.0307\ln\frac{P_3}{M}-0.00094\cdot t}.$$

We conclude that the structure of consumer preferences in the FRG, analyzed on the assumption of three aggregates and on per capita data differs from the structure of preferences analyzed by Jorgenson and Lau with the corresponding data for the U.S.A.

6.6 Summary

The objective of this chapter is to analyze the structure of consumer preferences and changes in preferences over time. Consumer preferences are represented by an indirect translog utility function with time-varying preferences that is quadratic in the logarithms of its arguments. We consider a system of demand functions associated with parameter restrictions consistent with the theory. We characterize groupwise separability and groupwise homotheticity of preferences and derive for each set of restrictions on preferences parametric restrictions on the corresponding system of demand functions. Empirical results of the tests, based on time series aa for FRG consumption expenditures on three commodity groups—durables, nondurables, and energy—are presented.

Notes

1. P_i $(i = 1, 2, 3)$ are called money prices and P_i/M $(i = 1, 2, 3)$ "real" prices.
2. For a discussion of duality of the direct utility function U and the indirect utility function V, see Lau (1977a) and the references given there.
3. See Roy (1943).

4. See Christensen, Jorgenson and Lau (1975).
5. See also an earlier paper by Christensen, Jorgenson and Lau (1975).
6. Barten (1977) presents a review of tests of integrability of systems of demand functions for countries including the U.S. and FRG. A critique of tests based on the Rotterdam system and systems linear in the parameters is presented by Jorgenson and Lau (1977). A series of comprehensive papers by Göttinger (1969, 1969/70) generalizes recent results in demand analysis and utility theory, emphasizing the usefulness of the theory for generating restrictions on preferences; these papers are of primarily theoretical interest.
7. The original paper was published in Japanese in 1945.
8. See Jorgenson and Lau (1975).
9. For a second set of restrictions that implies homotheticity of the translog utility function itself see Jorgenson and Lau (1975).
10. The condition for groupwise homogeneity of degree -1, $\sum_{k=1}^{3} (\partial \ln V/\partial \ln (P_k/M))$ implies that

$$\sum_{k=1}^{3} \frac{\partial^2 \ln V}{\partial \ln \frac{P_k}{M} \, \partial \ln \frac{P_j}{M}} = 0\,, \qquad (j = 1, 2, 3)\,,$$

and

$$\sum_{k=1}^{3} \frac{\partial^2 \ln V}{\partial \ln \frac{P_k}{M} \, \partial t} = 0\,.$$

11. For further combinations of tests see Jorgenson and Lau (1975).
12. We employ the maximum likelihood estimator discussed, for example, by Malinvaud (1980), pp. 338–341.
13. For a description of the data see Conrad and Jorgenson (1979) and Conrad (1977), p. 480.
14. Restricted estimates of the parameters under all these specifications will be provided on request.

7 Testing the Integrability of Consumer Demand Functions, Federal Republic of Germany, 1950–1973

Klaus Conrad and Dale W. Jorgenson

7.1 Introduction

In order to formulate tests of the theory of consumer behavior a parametric representation of consumer preferences must be chosen. This can be done either for the system of demand functions or for the utility function. Most approaches start with a formulation of the demand system by selection of 'appropriate' functional forms. Under integrability, that is, under the restrictions implied by homogeneity, summability, symmetry, nonnegativity and monotonicity, many well-known systems of demand functions imply that the corresponding utility functions must be additive in order to be consistent with the theory.[1] The double logarithmic systems and the Rotterdam system of demand functions are integrable if and only if they are characterized by constant budget shares so that the underlying utility function is linear logarithmic.

The purpose of this chapter is to employ the econometric methodology developed by Jorgenson and Lau (1986) to test the theory of consumer behavior. In an earlier approach to formal testing Christensen, Jorgenson and Lau (1975) employed a parametric representation of consumer preferences based on a utility function that is quadratic in the logarithms of its arguments.[2] This approach makes it possible to test the theory of demand without using additivity or homotheticity of the utility function as part of the maintained hypothesis. Jorgenson and Lau (1979) start from a system of consumer demand functions that is represented as ratios of first-order polynomial functions. They then impose restrictions on the parameters of the demand systems implied by integrability. We make use of this new econometric methodology to test the theory of consumer behavior with annual time series data for German personal consumption expenditures on three commodity groups—durables, nondurables, and energy—for the period 1950–1973. The services of durable goods include housing services and the services of consumers' durables. The stock of housing and consumers' durables corresponds to the stock of energy-using equipment and structures.

A possible objection to testing the theory of consumer behavior with aggregate data is that the conditions on the individual demand functions that imply integrability of the aggregate system of demand functions are unrealistic. While the rejection of the integrability hypothesis on the aggregate level does not imply that micro-theory is empirically irrelevant, acceptance of this hypothesis in many investigations provides empirical justification for applying micro-theory to derive restrictions on the system of aggregate demand functions. A methodology for testing integrability makes it possible to assess empirical results obtained from models which start their analysis by treating this hypothesis as an assumption.

7.2 Direct and Indirect Systems

In testing integrability of consumer demand functions one can start the discussion with the specification of a utility function and the corresponding system of demand functions generated by the utility function. Under parameter restrictions derived from the nature of the utility function such a system of demand functions is integrable, as it has been obtained as the solution of a utility maximization problem. Alternatively, we can consider a system of demand functions, regarded as a system of partial differential equations, the solution of which defines a family of utility functions. The problem of integrability arises in using the specification of the system of demand functions to derive the specification of a corresponding utility function.

We begin with a specification of consumer demand functions as ratios of two first-order polynomials in prices, income, and time. We then impose successively the restrictions implied by homogeneity, summability, symmetry, nonnegativity, and monotonicity. As shown by Jorgenson and Lau (1979) we can choose for the expenditure share functions ratios of first-order polynomials in either the logarithms or power functions of the same power of the prices (or quantities) and a function of time. As we want to exclude any restrictive condition on the matrix of uncompensated cross-price substitution effects such as row proportionality, a ratio of log-linear functions is the only possible candidate.

For our empirical implementation we choose three commodities—durables, nondurables, and energy. The direct translog demand system in terms of expenditure shares is as follows:

$$w_j = \frac{p_j X_j}{M}$$

$$= \frac{\alpha_j + \beta_{j1} \ln\left(\frac{p_1}{M}\right) + \beta_{j2} \ln\left(\frac{p_2}{M}\right) + \beta_{j3} \ln\left(\frac{p_3}{M}\right) + \beta_{jM} \ln M + \beta_{j1} \cdot t}{-1 + \beta^j_{M1} \ln\left(\frac{p_1}{M}\right) + \beta^j_{M2} \ln\left(\frac{p_2}{M}\right) + \beta^j_{M3} \ln\left(\frac{p_3}{M}\right) + \beta^j_{MM} \ln M + \beta^j_{Mt} \cdot t},$$

$$j = 1, 2, 3, \tag{7.1}$$

where X_j $(j = 1, 2, 3)$ is the quantity consumed of durables, nondurables, and energy, respectively, $p_j(j = 1, 2, 3)$ is the corresponding prices, M is the value of total expenditure and t is time.

We also consider integrability of the indirect translog system, that is, expenditure shares as functions of quantities,

$$w_j = p_j X_j / M$$

$$= \frac{\alpha_j + \beta_{j1} \ln X_1 + \beta_{j2} \ln X_2 + \beta_{j3} \ln X_3 + \beta_{jM} \ln M + \beta_{jt} \cdot t}{-1 + \beta^j_{M1} \ln X_1 + \beta^j_{M2} \ln X_2 + \beta^j_{M3} \ln X_3 + \beta^j_{MM} \ln M + \beta^j_{Mt} \cdot t}$$

$$j = 1, 2, 3. \tag{7.2}$$

For testing the integrability hypothesis the systems of indirect demand functions have to be considered without the assumption that they can be generated by direct and indirect utility functions. We then derive restrictions on the parameters of the direct translog demand system corresponding to each of the properties of an integrable demand system—homogeneity, summability, symmetry, nonnegativity, and monotonicity. By duality we can obtain the corresponding restrictions on the parameters of the indirect translog demand system by interchanging the role of ratios of prices to total expenditure and quantities.

7.3 Integrability

To formulate tests of the theory of consumer behavior the direct translog demand system (7.1) and the indirect translog demand system (7.2) have been presented in a form that does not imply that any of the restrictions implied by integrability are satisfied. We begin by incorporating a stochastic specification into each of the demand systems. For each system we assume that the equations for the expenditure shares are characterized by additive disturbances that are independent of the right-hand side variables in the equation. Summability implies that the expenditure shares add to unity, so that for any given values of the right-hand side variables, the sum of the disturbances is nonstochastic. One of the disturbances can therefore be determined from the remaining two disturbances. Given the parameters of any two equations for the expenditure shares, the parameters of the third equation can be determined from parameter conditions implied by the summability property. For both direct and indirect translog demand systems a complete econometric model of consumer behavior is provided by any two of the three equations for the expenditure shares.

We estimate the parameters of the system of two equations for the expenditure share of durables and of nondurables,

$$w_1 = \frac{\alpha_1 + \beta_{11} \ln \frac{p_1}{M} + \beta_{12} \ln \frac{p_2}{M} + \beta_{13} \ln \frac{p_3}{M} + \beta_{1M} \ln M + \beta_{1t} \cdot t}{-1 + \beta^1_{M1} \ln \frac{p_1}{M} + \beta^1_{M2} \ln \frac{p_2}{M} + \beta^1_{M3} \ln \frac{p_3}{M} + \beta^1_{MM} \ln M + \beta^1_{Mt} \cdot t} \tag{7.3}$$

$$w_2 = \frac{\alpha_2 + \beta_{21} \ln \frac{p_1}{M} + \beta_{22} \ln \frac{p_2}{M} + \beta_{23} \ln \frac{p_3}{M} + \beta_{2M} \ln M + \beta_{2t} \cdot t}{-1 + \beta^2_{M1} \ln \frac{p_1}{M} + \beta^2_{M2} \ln \frac{p_2}{M} + \beta^2_{M2} \ln \frac{p_3}{M} + \beta^2_{MM} \ln M + \beta^2_{Mt} \cdot t} \tag{7.4}$$

corresponding to the direct translog demand system, and

$$w_1 = \frac{\alpha_1 + \beta_{11} \ln X_1 + \beta_{12} \ln X_2 + \beta_{13} \ln X_3 + \beta_{1M} \ln M + \beta_{1t} \cdot t}{-1 + \beta^1_{M1} \ln X_1 + \beta^1_{M2} \ln X_2 + \beta^1_{M3} \ln X_3 + \beta^1_{MM} \ln M + \beta^1_{Mt} \cdot t}, \tag{7.5}$$

$$w_2 = \frac{\alpha_2 + \beta_{21} \ln X_1 + \beta_{22} \ln X_2 + \beta_{23} \ln X_3 + \beta_{2M} \ln M + \beta_{2t} \cdot t}{-1 + \beta^2_{M1} \ln X_1 + \beta^2_{M2} \ln X_2 + \beta^2_{M3} \ln X_3 + \beta^2_{MM} \ln M + \beta^2_{Mt} \cdot t}, \tag{7.6}$$

corresponding to the indirect translog demand system. We next proceed to impose the restrictions implied by the five properties of an integrable system. The set of integrability restrictions for the two systems are perfectly analogous, so that the following restrictions on the parameters can be applied to either system.

7.3.1 Homogeneity

For the direct translog demand system the quantities (or budget shares) are independent of total expenditure for given normalized prices. Necessary and sufficient conditions for independence consist of the *homogeneity restrictions*,

$$\beta_{1M} = \beta_{2M} = \beta^1_{MM} = \beta^2_{MM} = 0\,, \tag{7.7}$$

or of constant budget shares. There are four restrictions corresponding to two parameters in each of the two equations we estimate. Similarly, for the indirect translog demand system the ratios of prices to total expenditure (or expenditure shares) are independent of total expenditure for given quantities if the parameters in (7.5) and (7.6) satisfy restriction (7.7).

7.3.2 Summability

For the direct translog demand system the sum of budget shares is equal to unity,

$$\sum_{j=1}^{3} w_j = \sum_{j=1}^{3} \left(\frac{\alpha_j + \sum \beta_{ji} \ln (p_i/M) + \beta_{jM} \ln M + \beta_{jt} \cdot t}{-1 + \sum \beta^j_{Mi} \ln (p_i/M) + \beta^j_{MM} \ln M + \beta^j_{Mt} \cdot t} \right) = 1. \tag{7.8}$$

In principle, one can always define one expenditure share as the residual of unity minus the sum of $n - 1$ share functions in order to fulfill the summability condition. However, the residual share function will in general then have an algebraic form different from that of the other shares which excludes a symmetric treatment of all quantities. Therefore 'uniformity' (see Lau, 1977a) is desirable, that is, each single demand function of the system should have the same algebraic form.

Under the uniformity property, sufficient conditions for summability are equality restrictions and summability conditions. The restrictions on the parameters to take the same value in all denominators are called the *equality restrictions*,

$$\beta^1_{M1} = \beta^2_{M1} = \beta_{M1}, \qquad \beta^1_{MM} = \beta^2_{MM} = \beta_{MM},$$
$$\beta^1_{M2} = \beta^2_{M2} = \beta_{M2}, \qquad \beta^1_{Mt} = \beta^2_{Mt} = \beta_{Mt}.$$
$$\beta^1_{M3} = \beta^2_{M3} = \beta_{M3}, \tag{7.9}$$

Corresponding to the five parameters in each of the two equations we estimate there are five of these restrictions. If the equality restrictions hold, necessary conditions for summability are the conditions

$$\alpha_1 + \alpha_2 + \alpha_3 = -1, \qquad \beta_{11} + \beta_{21} + \beta_{31} = \beta_{M1},$$
$$\beta_{1M} + \beta_{2M} + \beta_{3M} = \beta_{MM}, \qquad \beta_{12} + \beta_{22} + \beta_{32} = \beta_{M2}, \tag{7.10}$$
$$\beta_{1t} + \beta_{2t} + \beta_{3t} = \beta_{Mt}, \qquad \beta_{13} + \beta_{23} + \beta_{33} = \beta_{M3}.$$

From these conditions we obtain the parameters of the third equation for the energy share given the parameters of the first two share functions. Similarly, by interchanging the role of the variables p_i/M and X_i a strictly analogous set of necessary and sufficient conditions for summability of the indirect translog demand system can be derived.

7.3.3 Symmetry

The matrix of compensated own- and cross-price effects for the direct demand functions must be symmetric. To formulate a test of symmetry we first impose homogeneity and equality restrictions, so that the direct translog demand system can be written in the form

$$w_j = \frac{\alpha_j + \beta_{j1} \ln(p_1/M) + \beta_{j2} \ln(p_2/M) + \beta_{j3} \ln(p_3/M) + \beta_{jt} \cdot t}{-1 + \beta_{M1} \ln(p_1/M) + \beta_{M2} \ln(p_2/M) + \beta_{M3} \ln(p_3/M) + \beta_{Mt} \cdot t}$$
$$j = 1, 2, 3. \tag{7.11}$$

Similarly, the indirect translog demand system can be written in the form

$$w_j = \frac{\alpha_j + \beta_{j1} \ln X_1 + \beta_{j2} \ln X_2 + \beta_{j3} \ln X_3 + \beta_{jt} \cdot t}{-1 + \beta_{M1} \ln X_1 + \beta_{M2} \ln X_2 + \beta_{M3} \ln X_3 + \beta_{Mt} \cdot t},$$
$$j = 1, 2, 3. \tag{7.12}$$

As shown by Jorgenson and Lau (1979) there are four independent sets of alternative conditions for symmetry of the Slutsky terms:

A.0. *Symmetry of the matrix of parameters* β_{ij}. One restriction of this type is explicit in the two equations we estimate directly, namely,

$$\beta_{12} = \beta_{21} .$$

The parameters β_{31} and β_{32} we estimate from the equations

$$\beta_{31} = \beta_{M1} - \beta_{11} - \beta_{21}, \quad \beta_{32} = \beta_{M2} - \beta_{12} - \beta_{22},$$

so that two additional restrictions are implicit in the two equations we estimate. We write these restrictions in the form

$$\beta_{13} = \beta_{M1} - \beta_{11} - \beta_{21}, \quad \beta_{23} = \beta_{M2} - \beta_{12} - \beta_{22},$$

There are three symmetry restrictions altogether.

A.1. *We reparametrize as follows* ($j = 1, 2$):

$$\beta_{j1} = -\alpha_j \beta_{M1} + K^* \left(\beta_{Mj} + \alpha_j \sum_i \beta_{Mi}\right)\left(\beta_{M1} + \alpha_1 \sum_i \beta_{Mi}\right) + K^{**}\left(\beta_{Mj} + \alpha_j \sum_i \beta_{Mi}\right)\alpha_1 ,$$

$$\beta_{j2} = -\alpha_j \beta_{M2} + K^* \left(\beta_{Mj} + \alpha_j \sum_i \beta_{Mi}\right)\left(\beta_{M2} + \alpha_2 \sum_i \beta_{Mi}\right) + K^{**}\left(\beta_{Mj} + \alpha_j \sum_i \beta_{Mi}\right)\alpha_2 ,$$

$$\beta_{j3} = -\alpha_j \beta_{M3} + K^* \left(\beta_{Mj} + \alpha_j \sum_i \beta_{Mi}\right)\left(\beta_{M3} - (1 + \alpha_1 + \alpha_2) \sum_i \beta_{Mi}\right) - K^{**}\left(\beta_{Mj} + \alpha_j \sum_i \beta_{Mi}\right)(1 + \alpha_1 + \alpha_2),$$

$$\beta_{jt} = -\alpha_j \beta_{Mt} + \sigma_t^* \left(\beta_{Mj} + \alpha_j \sum_i \beta_{Mi}\right).$$

There are nine unknown parameters under this specification: α_1, α_2, β_{M1}, β_{M2}, β_{M3}, β_{Mt}, $K*$, $K**$, σ_t^*. As the specification of homogeneity and equality involves fourteen unknown parameters, we conclude that under this type of symmetry there are five symmetry restrictions.

A.2. *We reparametrize as follows* $(j = 1, 2)$:

$$\beta_{j1} = \alpha_j \alpha_1 K** + K* \rho_j(\rho_1 + \alpha_1),$$

$$\beta_{j2} = \alpha_j \alpha_2 K** + K* \rho_j(\rho_2 + \alpha_2),$$

$$\beta_{j3} = -\alpha_j(1 + \alpha_1 + \alpha_2)K** - K* \rho_j(\rho_1 + \rho_2 + (1 + \alpha_1 + \alpha_2)),$$

$$\beta_{jt} = -\alpha_j \beta_{M1} + \sigma_t^* \rho_j,$$

$$\beta_{M1} = -\alpha_1 K**,$$

$$\beta_{M2} = -\alpha_2 K**,$$

$$\beta_{M3} = (1 + \alpha_1 + \alpha_3)K**.$$

There are eight unknown parameters under this specification: α_1, α_2, $K**$, $K*$, ρ_1, ρ_2, β_{Mt}, σ_t^*. Therefore, under this type of symmetry there are six symmetry restrictions.

A.3. *We reparametrize as follows* $(j = 1, 2)$:

$$\beta_{j1} = \delta_j \alpha_1,$$

$$\beta_{j2} = \delta_j \alpha_2,$$

$$\beta_{j3} = -\delta_j(1 + \alpha_1 + \alpha_2),$$

$$\beta_{jt} = -\alpha_j \beta_{Mt} + \sigma_t^* \left(\delta_j + \alpha_j \sum_i \delta_i\right),$$

$$\beta_{M1} = \alpha_1 \left(\sum_i \delta_i\right),$$

$$\beta_{M2} = \alpha_2 \left(\sum_i \delta_i\right),$$

$$\beta_{M3} = -(1 + \alpha_1 + \alpha_2)\left(\sum_i \delta_i\right).$$

There are seven unknown parameters under this specification: α_1, α_2, δ_1, δ_2, $(\sum \delta_i)$ (or δ_3), β_{Mt}, σ_t^*. Therefore, under this type of symmetry there are seven symmetry restrictions.

7.3.4 Nonnegativity

To formulate a test of nonnegativity for the direct translog demand system we impose homogeneity and equality restrictions, as before. With values of the variables in $\ln p_j/M$ $(j = 1, 2, 3)$ and t scaled to be equal to zero in 1962, we can evaluate the direct translog demand system

$$X_j = -\alpha_j, \qquad j = 1, 2, 3.$$

Therefore, necessary conditions for nonnegativity are

$$\alpha_1 \leqq 0, \qquad \alpha_2 \leqq 0, \qquad \alpha_3 = -1 - \alpha_1 - \alpha_2 \leqq 0.$$

There are three nonnegativity restrictions altogether. The first two are explicit in the two equations we estimate. The third is implicit in these equations. We employ simultaneous tests of these restrictions; if we reject one or more of the restrictions, we reject the hypothesis of nonnegativity. Similarly, we can derive strictly analogous restrictions for nonnegativity of the indirect translog demand system.

7.3.5 Monotonicity

In formulating a test of monotonicity we continue to impose homogeneity and equality restrictions. To derive the monotonicity restrictions, we set the variables $\ln p_j/M$ $(j = 1, 2, 3)$ and t equal to zero, the scaled value for 1962, and express the parameters of the Slutsky substitution matrix $S = (\sigma_{ij})$ in terms of the parameters—α_i, β_{ij} $(i, j = 1, 2, 3)$—of the equations for the budget shares,

$$\sigma_{ij} = -\beta_{ij} - \alpha_i \beta_{Mj} - \alpha_j \sum \beta_{ik} - \alpha_i \alpha_j \left(\sum \beta_{Mk} \right) + \alpha_i \alpha_j + \delta_{ij} \alpha_i,$$

$$i, j = 1, 2, 3.$$

To test monotonicity we next express the parameters of the matrix $1/2(S + S')$ in terms of the parameters of the Cholesky factorization of this matrix,[3]

$$1/2(S + S') = -\begin{bmatrix} \delta_1 & \lambda_{21}\delta_1 & \lambda_{31}\delta_1 \\ \lambda_{21}\delta_1 & \lambda_{21}^2\delta_1 + \delta_2 & \lambda_{21}\lambda_{31}\delta_1 + \lambda_{32}\delta_2 \\ \lambda_{31}\delta_1 & \lambda_{21}\lambda_{31}\delta_1 + \lambda_{32}\delta_2 & \lambda_{31}^2\delta_1 + \lambda_{32}^2\delta_2 + \delta_3 \end{bmatrix}.$$

Under homogeneity the matrix $1/2(S + S')$ has rank at most two, so that the parameter δ_3 is zero. The remaining parameters are given by

$$\delta_1 = -\sigma_{11},$$

$$\lambda_{21} = -\frac{1}{2\delta_1}(\sigma_{12} + \sigma_{21}),$$

$$\lambda_{31} = -\frac{1}{2\delta_1}(\sigma_{13} + \sigma_{31}),$$

$$\delta_2 = -\sigma_{22} - \lambda_{21}^2\delta_1,$$

$$\lambda_{32} = -\frac{1}{2\delta_2}(\sigma_{23} + \sigma_{32}) - \frac{\delta_1}{\delta_2}\lambda_{21}\lambda_{31}.$$

Furthermore, we observe

$$\sigma_{33} = \lambda_{31}^2\delta_1 - \lambda_{32}^2\delta_2.$$

In terms of these parameters the necessary conditions for monotonicity take the form

$$\delta_1 \geqq 0, \quad \delta_2 \geqq 0.$$

There are two monotonicity restrictions altogether. We employ simultaneous tests of these hypotheses; if we reject one or both of them, we reject the hypothesis of monotonicity. If the parameters δ_1 and δ_2 satisfy the inequality restrictions we obtain a number of inequality constraints on the elements of the matrix S of compensated substitution effects, the most familiar being that $\sigma_{11} \leqq 0$, $\sigma_{22} \leqq 0$, and $\sigma_{33} \leqq 0$. For the direct demand system this verifies the 'law of demand' that compensated own-price effects are negative or that compensated demand curves slope downwards. To derive a test of monotonicity for the indirect translog demand system, we consider the matrix of compensated own- and cross-quantity effects, setting the variables $\ln X_j$ $(j = 1, 2, 3)$ and t equal to zero in 1962. This matrix can be represented in the form of its Cholesky decomposition. Necessary conditions for monotonicity of the indirect translog demand system are strictly analogous to those we have given for the direct translog demand system.

7.4 Estimation and Testing

Our empirical tests are based on annual time series data for the Federal Republic of Germany (FRG) personal consumption expenditures on three commodity groups in per capita terms—durables, nondurables, and energy—for the period 1950–1973. Our concept of personal consumption expenditures differs from the corresponding concept in the FRG national income and product accounts in the treatment of consumers' durables. Consumers' durables purchased in one period are not fully consumed in that period and so are still partially present in subsequent periods to affect future purchases and consumption. We treat expenditure on durables as part of gross private domestic investment rather than personal consumption expenditures. We then add an imputed flow of services from consumers' durables to personal consumption expenditures to allow stocks of goods to affect current consumer behavior.[4] In our model of consumer expenditure allocation the services of capital include housing services and the services of consumers' durables.

In the FRG income and product accounts private consumption expenditures are classified by use so that purchases of gasoline are part of traffic expenditures. Annual household surveys conducted for four-person households with medium income show the percentage of expenditure for gasoline as part of the expenditure for traffic. We use this information to compute from the traffic expenditures in the national accounts a time series for expenditures on gasoline. We add these data to the expenditures on electricity, heating oil, coal and gas to obtain the energy data. Nondurables consumption includes all other items in the consumer budget. To compute price and quantity index numbers we employ the retail price index for gasoline as published in the statistical yearbook for the FRG. The prices of the three commodity groups are equal to one in 1962 and the quantities of the three groups are per capita quantities.

We have fitted equations for the budget shares corresponding to the direct and indirect translog demand systems. Under the stochastic specification outlined above only two equations are required for a complete econometric model of consumer behavior. We have fitted equations for durables and for nondurables.[5] For both direct and indirect translog demand systems our maintained hypothesis consists of the unrestricted form of the two behavioral equations for the budget shares. The unrestricted equations involve twenty-two unknown parameters of eleven unknown parameters for each equation. Unrestricted estimates of these parameters for the direct translog demand system are presented in table 7.A.1 of the appendix. Corresponding estimates for the indirect translog demand system are given in table 7.A.2 of the appendix.

The first hypothesis to be tested is that the system of equations for the budget shares is homogeneous in prices and the value of total expenditure. To test this hypothesis we impose the four homogeneity restrictions. These restrictions eliminate the parameters corresponding to the value of total expenditure; estimates of the remaining parameters for the direct and indirect translog demand system are given in the second column of tables 7.A.1 and 7.A.2 of the appendix. The second hypothesis to be tested is that the system of equations satisfies the summability condition. To test this hypothesis we impose the five equality restrictions (third column of tables 7.A.1 and 7.A.2, respectively, of the appendix). To test the remaining hypotheses we impose the homogeneity and equality restrictions on both direct and indirect demand systems (fourth column of tables 7.1 and 7.2).

We first test the hypothesis of symmetry-type A.0 by imposing the three symmetry restrictions. We then test the three alternate hypotheses of symmetry by reparametrizing the translog demand systems. Symmetry of type A.1 requires the introduction of three new parameters, so that the eight restrictions reduce the number of parameters by five, leaving nine unknown parameters to be estimated. Symmetry of type A.2 requires the introduction of five new parameters, so that the eleven restrictions reduce the number of parameters by six, leaving eight unknown parameters to be estimated. Finally, symmetry of type A.3 requires the introduction of four new parameters, so that the eleven restrictions reduce the number of parameters by seven, leaving seven unknown parameters to be estimated. Columns five to eight in tables 7.A.1 and 7.A.2 of the appendix show the resulting estimates for the alternate symmetry restrictions.

To test the hypothesis of nonnegativity we consider estimates of the parameters α_1 and α_2 from the two equations we estimate and the estimate of α_3 implicit in these two equations (fourth column of tables 7.1 and 7.2, respectively). The final hypothesis to be tested is the hypothesis of monotonicity. The estimates of the parameters δ_1 and δ_2 under homogeneity and equality restrictions (fourth columns of tables 7.1 and 7.2, respectively) are obtained by reparametrizing the direct

Table 7.1
Critical values of χ^2/degrees of freedom and standard normal test statistics

Degrees of freedom	Level of significance				
	0.10	0.05	0.01	0.005	0.001
Standard normal					
1	1.28	1.65	2.33	2.58	3.09
χ^2/degrees of freedom					
3	2.08	2.60	3.78	4.28	5.42
4	1.94	2.37	3.32	3.72	4.62
5	1.85	2.21	3.02	3.35	4.10
6	1.77	2.10	2.80	3.09	3.78
7	1.72	2.01	2.64	2.90	3.53

Table 7.2
Test statistics for direct and indirect translog demand systems

Hypothesis	Degrees of freedom	Direct	Indirect
Homogeneity	4	1.67	9.74
Equality	5	1.37	7.78
Homogeneity and equality	8	1.39	9.30
Given homogeneity			
Equality	4	1.10	8.86
Given equality			
Homogeneity	3	1.40	11.83
Given homogeneity and equality			
A.0. Symmetry	3	1.75	0.90
A.1. Symmetry	5	7.15	6.12
A.2. Symmetry	6	8.34	23.90
A.3. Symmetry	7	18.20	5.48
Nonnegativity			
$-\alpha_1 \geqq 0$	1	133.8	91.4
$-\alpha_2 \geqq 0$	1	582.6	557.8
$1 + \alpha_1 + \alpha_2 \geqq 0$	1	61.0	75.1
Monotonicity			
$\delta_1 \geqq 0$	1	−0.38	1.42
$\delta_2 \geqq 0$	1	0.42	−0.89

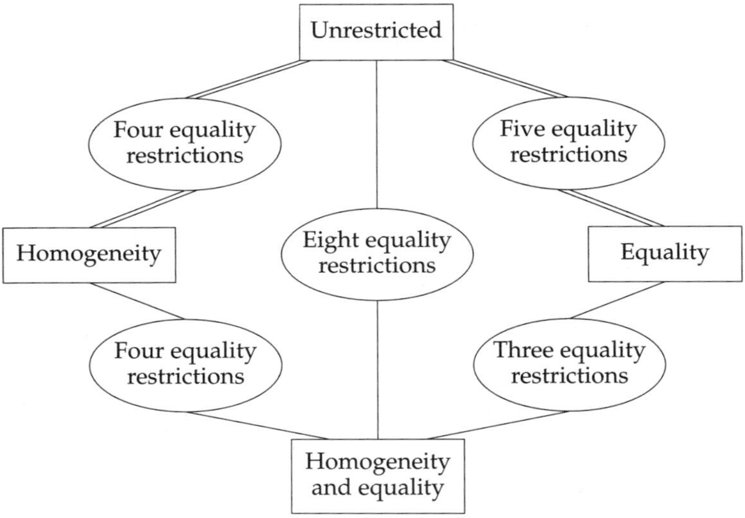

Figure 7.1
Tests of homogeneity and equality.

and indirect translog demand systems so as to exhibit the monotonicity restrictions.

Tests of integrability can be carried out in a number of different sequences. We test homogeneity and equality restrictions in parallel without imposing any additional restrictions. We test the remaining restrictions—alternative symmetry, nonnegativity, monotonicity—in parallel, given homogeneity and equality. Our test procedure is presented in diagrammatic form in figures 7.1 and 7.2. We also present alternative procedures. For example, we could test equality given homogeneity or homogeneity given equality. Our test procedure is indicated with double lines while alternative procedures are indicated with single lines.

To test the validity of restrictions on the direct and indirect translog demand systems that take the form of equalities, we employ test statistics based on the likelihood ratio λ, where

$$\lambda = \max_{\omega} \mathcal{L} / \operatorname*{Max}_{\Omega} \mathcal{L} .$$

The likelihood ratio is the ratio of the maximum value of the likelihood for the econometric model ω subject to restrictions to the maxi-

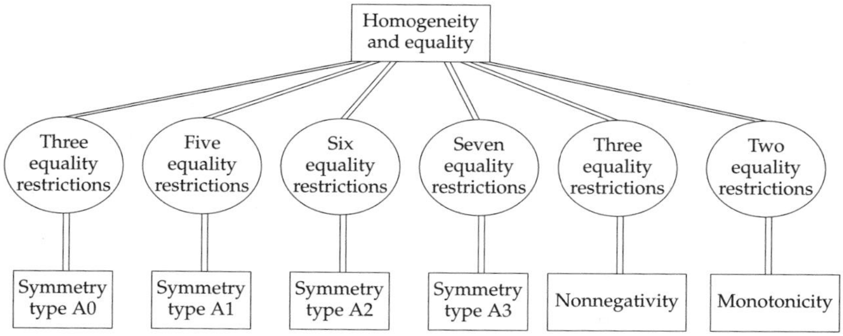

Figure 7.2
Tests of symmetry, nonnegativity, and monotonicity.

mum value of the likelihood function for the econometric model Ω without restrictions.

We have estimated direct and indirect translog demand systems from annual data for FRG personal consumption expenditures for the period 1950–1973. There are twenty-four observations for each behavior equation, so that the number of degrees of freedom available for statistical tests of integrability is forty-eight for both direct and indirect translog demand systems. For normally distributed disturbances the likelihood ratio is equal to the ratio of the determinant of the restricted estimator of the variance-covariance matrix of the disturbances to the determinant of the unrestricted estimator, each raised to the power $-(n/2)$.

Our test statistic for each set of restrictions is based on minus twice the logarithm of the likelihood ratio, or

$$-2\ln\lambda = n(\ln|\hat{\Sigma}_\omega| - \ln|\hat{\Sigma}_\Omega|),$$

where $\hat{\Sigma}_\omega$ is the restricted estimator of the variance-covariance matrix and Σ_Ω is the unrestricted estimator. Under the null hypothesis the likelihood ratio test statistic is distributed, asymptotically, as chi-squared with a number of degrees of freedom equal to the number of restrictions to be tested. We employ the asymptotic distribution of the likelihood ratio test statistic for tests of hypotheses that take the form of equality restrictions.

To test the validity of inequality restrictions implied by the hypotheses of nonnegativity and monotonicity, we employ test statistics based on the ratio of each inequality constrained coefficient to its standard error. We employ a one-sided critical region to test the validity of each of the inequality restrictions. For normally distributed disturbances the ratio of each coefficient to its standard error is distributed, asymptotically, as a standard normal random variable. We employ this asymptotic distribution to test inequality restrictions.

To control the overall level of significance for each series of tests, based on direct and indirect translog demand systems, we set the level of significance for each series at 0.05. We allocate the overall level of significance among the various stages in each series. We first assign levels of significance of 0.01 to each of the tests of homogeneity and equality restrictions. We then assign levels of significance of 0.005 to each of the six sets of restrictions that are conditional on the homogeneity and equality restrictions—four types of symmetry, nonnegativity, and monotonicity. The set of restrictions associated with nonnegativity includes three inequality restrictions; there are two restrictions associated with monotonicity. We assign a level of significance of 0.0017 to the test associated with each of the three restrictions for nonnegativity and 0.0025 to the test associated with each of the two restrictions for monotonicity. The tests for all eight sets of restrictions—homogeneity, equality, four types of symmetry, nonnegativity, and monotonicity—are not 'nested' so that the sum of the levels of significance for each of these eight sets of restrictions provides an upper bound for the level of significance of all eight tests considered simultaneously.

For the econometric model based on the indirect translog demand system we have assigned levels of significance to all tests of hypotheses so as to control the overall level of significance for all tests at 0.05. This implies that the probability of a false rejection of the null hypothesis for one test among the collection of all tests we consider is less than or equal to 0.05. Similarly, we have assigned levels of significance for the model based on the direct translog demand system so as to control the overall level of significance at 0.05. With the aid of critical values for our test statistics given in table 7.1, the reader can evaluate the results of our tests for alternative levels of significance or alternative allocations of the overall levels of significance among stages of the test procedure.

7.5 Conclusion

The results of our tests of the theory of consumer behavior, as presented in table 7.2, are that the set of restrictions on the parameters of the direct translog demand systems implied by integrability cannot be rejected. However, for the indirect translog demand system the set of restrictions implied by integrability must be rejected. For the direct system we accept homogeneity, that is we reject the presence of money illusion. We also accept equality, that is summability. The sum of the budget shares is independent of the ratios of prices to total expenditure, to total expenditure, and time. If we test homogeneity and equality jointly rather than in parallel, we would also accept the combined hypothesis for the direct demand system. We would also accept summability given homogeneity and homogeneity given summability. Homogeneity and summability are properties of market demand functions, while symmetry, nonnegativity, and monotonicity are properties of individual demand functions.

For the indirect translog demand system we reject homogeneity, that is the ratios of prices to total expenditure are not independent of total expenditure for given quantities demanded. We also reject the hypothesis of summability, that is the sum of the budget shares is not independent of the quantity demanded, total expenditure, and time. We also would reject the combined hypothesis of homogeneity and equality, and the hypothesis of summability given homogeneity and homogeneity given summability.

For the direct demand system we can proceed immediately to test symmetry, nonnegativity and monotonicity in parallel, given homogeneity and equality. We cannot reject the hypothesis of symmetry of type A.0 imploying that the direct translog demand system is integrable and corresponds to the indirect transcendental logarithmic utility function. We reject all three types of alternate symmetry conditions. Finally, we accept the hypothesis of nonnegativity and also the hypothesis of monotonicity as a hypothesis of negative values for the δ's must be rejected (see the size of the standard errors for δ_1 and δ_2 in column 4 of table 7.A.2 of the appendix). To carry out a similar test procedure for the indirect demand system, we have to proceed conditionally, taking homogeneity and equality as given. In this case we would also accept symmetry of type A.0, nonnegativity and monotonicity.

The results obtained by Barten and Geyskens (1975) in using Dutch and German per capita data are also consistent with the postulates of the theory of consumer behavior. For the German four-commodity model (food, clothing, rent, other) they had to reject however the hypothesis of monotonicity. But all restrictions jointly tested, the data did not allow rejection. Jorgenson and Lau (1979) using U.S. per capita data for durables, nondurables and energy had to reject the theory of consumer behavior on the aggregate level. As we employ the same parametric representation of consumer preferences, the same group of commodities, the same estimation procedure and about the same time periods these reasons are excluded to explain the different findings with U.S. data. Jorgenson and Lau reject summability for the direct and indirect demand system, that is they reject the uniformity property of the same algebraic form for the demand functions. A demand system seems to be appropriate which does not treat the three commodity groups symmetrically. Perhaps the special role of energy in the U.S. consumer budget accounts for the different results.

Appendix

Table 7.A.1
Estimates of the parameters of the indirect translog demand system

Parameters	(1) Unrestricted	(2) Homogeneity	(3) Equality
α_1	–0.145 (.001)	–0.148 (0.001)	–.145 (.001)
β_{11}	–0.116 (.90)	–0.272 (0.166)	–.068 (.06)
β_{12}	0.158 (.068)	0.228 (0.106)	–.047 (.038)
β_{13}	–0.010 (.06)	0.098 (0.105)	–.072 (.043)
β_{1M}	–0.051 (.116)	—	.053 (.067)
β_{1t}	0.004 (.011)	–0.001 (0.016)	.004 (.008)
β^1_{M1}	0.067 (.633)	–1.20 (1.19)	.279 (.416)
β^1_{M2}	0.867 (.502)	0.768 (0.958)	–.795 (.318)
β^1_{M3}	–0.153 (.370)	0.473 (0.697)	–.514 (.250)
β^1_{MM}	–1.13 (.50)	—	–.639 (.287)
β^1_{Mt}	0.789 (.066)	0.038 (0.107)	.103 (.043)
α_2	–0.805 (.001)	–0.803 (0.001)	–.806 (.0008)
β_{21}	0.351 (.384)	–0.474 (0.657)	.324 (.345)

Table 7.A.1 (continued)

Parameters	(1) Unrestricted	(2) Homogeneity	(3) Equality
β_{22}	−0.486 (.312)	−0.72 (0.558)	−.724 (.28)
β_{23}	−0.311 (.221)	0.16 (0.397)	−.372 (.197)
β_{2M}	−0.716 (.239)	—	−.646 (.209)
β_{2t}	0.082 (.038)	0.056 (0.061)	.091 (.034)
β^2_{M1}	0.311 (.464)	−0.667 (0.779)	.279 (.416)
β^2_{M2}	−0.506 (.357)	−0.675 (0.649)	−.795 (.318)
β^2_{M3}	−0.433 (.28)	0.176 (0.493)	−.514 (.25)
β^2_{MM}	−0.739 (.329)	—	−.639 (.287)
β^2_{Mt}	−0.092 (.048)	0.059 (0.074)	.103 (.043)

Parameters	(4) Homogeneity and equality	(5) A.0 symmetry
α_1	−0.145 (0.001)	−0.144 (.001)
β_{11}	−0.194 (0.066)	−0.112 (.031)
β_{12}	−0.112 (0.047)	−0.061 (.05)
β_{13}	0.026 (0.057)	−0.005 (.013)
β_{1t}	0.009 (0.008)	0.003 (.004)
α_2	−0.805 (0.001)	−0.805 (.001)
β_{21}	−0.776 (0.464)	−0.061 (.05)
β_{22}	−2.05 (0.386)	−1.62 (.375)
β_{23}	0.153 (0.284)	−0.059 (.018)
β_{2t}	0.117 (0.044)	0.064 (.015)
α_3	−0.049 (0.0006)	−0.049 (.0006)
β_{31}	−0.044 (0.030)	−0.005 (.013)
β_{32}	−0.081 (0.022)	−0.059 (.018)
β_{33}	−0.028 (0.024)	−0.042 (.009)
β_{3t}	0.007 (0.003)	0.004 (.002)
δ_1	0.158 (0.111)	
δ_2	−0.596 (0.665)	
λ_{21}	−1.37 (0.435)	
λ_{31}	0.064 (0.211)	
λ_{32}	0.828 (1.15)	

Table 7.A.1 (continued)

Parameters	(6) A.1. symmetry		(7) A.2. symmetry
α_1	−0.147 (.001)	α_1	−0.177 (0.008)
α_2	−0.801 (.005)	α_2	−0.767 (0.01)
K^*	0.004 (.005)	K^*	5.06 (0.16)
K^{**}	0.348 (.19)	K^{**}	−5.08 (4.5)
β_{M1}	−1.09 (.58)	ζ_1	0.14 (0.05)
β_{M2}	−0.86 (.69)	ζ_2	−0.17 (0.06)
β_{M3}	−0.183 (.11)	σ^*	−0.135 (0.024)
σ^*	0.025 (.013)	β_{Mt}	0.44 (0.16)
β_{Mt}	0.124 (.06)		

Parameters	(8) A.3. symmetry
α_1	−.149 (.001)
α_2	−.802 (.001)
δ_1	−.192 (.09)
δ_2	.37 (.74)
δ_3	.147 (.86)
σ_t^*	.079 (.009)
β_M	.0023 (.03)

Table 7.A.2
Estimates of the parameters of the direct translog demand system

Parameters	(1) Unrestricted	(2) Homogeneity	(3) Equality
α_1	−.148 (0.001)	−0.147 (0.001)	−0.147 (0.001)
β_{11}	−.050 (0.189)	−0.049 (0.128)	−0.083 (0.158)
β_{12}	.042 (0.160)	0.032 (0.172)	0.152 (0.128)
β_{13}	.098 (0.072)	0.083 (0.069)	0.074 (0.055)
β_{1M}	.065 (0.173)	—	0.029 (0.139)
β_{1t}	−.003 (0.012)	−0.0002 (0.008)	0.001 (0.01)
β^1_{M1}	.151 (1.14)	0.551 (0.588)	0.065 (0.98)
β^1_{M2}	.684 (1.33)	0.844 (1.36)	1.79 (1.07)
β^1_{M3}	.373 (0.412)	0.279 (0.397)	0.171 (0.323)
β^1_{MM}	−.235 (1.18)	—	−0.33 (1.00)
β^1_{MT}	.091 (0.078)	0.086 (0.054)	0.125 (0.065)
α_2	−.803 (0.001)	−0.803 (0.001)	−0.803 (0.001)
β_{21}	−.446 (1.03)	0.42 (0.428)	0.139 (0.782)
β_{22}	.879 (1.29)	1.17 (1.25)	1.57 (0.917)
β_{23}	.071 (0.315)	0.007 (0.30)	0.122 (0.258)
β_{2M}	−.887 (1.07)	—	−0.359 (0.833)
β_{2t}	.108 (0.072)	0.081 (0.053)	0.123 (0.053)
β^2_{M1}	.655 (1.29)	0.350 (0.583)	0.065 (0.98)
β^2_{M2}	.968 (1.53)	1.27 (1.49)	1.79 (1.07)
β^2_{M3}	.075 (0.403)	0.003 (0.384)	0.171 (0.323)
β^2_{MM}	−.971 (1.30)	—	−0.33 (1.0)
β^2_{Mt}	.105 (0.089)	0.077 (0.067)	0.125 (0.065)

Parameters	(4) Homogeneity and equality	(5) A.0 symmetry
α_1	−0.147 (0.001)	−.148 (.001)
β_{11}	−0.107 (0.093)	−.197 (.029)
β_{12}	0.195 (0.123)	.016 (.097)
β_{13}	0.059 (0.052)	−.007 (.016)
β_{1t}	0.003 (0.006)	−.012 (.005)
α_2	−0.804 (0.001)	−.803 (.001)
β_{21}	0.413 (0.327)	.016 (.097)
β_{22}	1.96 (0.839)	.607 (.767)
β_{23}	0.041 (0.246)	.015 (.031)

Table 7.A.2 (continued)

Parameters	(4) Homogeneity and equality	(5) A.0 symmetry
β_{2t}	0.117 (0.034)	.045 (.034)
α_3	−0.048 (0.0008)	−.049 (.0007)
β_{31}	0.009 (0.035)	−.007 (.016)
β_{32}	0.082 (0.049)	.015 (.031)
β_{33}	−0.027 (0.023)	−.046 (.012)
β_{3t}	−0.001 (0.002)	−.003 (.003)
δ_1	−0.017 (0.045)	
δ_2	0.644 (1.54)	
λ_{21}	−4.93 (8.51)	
λ_{31}	1.13 (4.12)	
λ_{32}	−0.872 (2.08)	

Parameters	(6) A.1. symmetry		(7) A.2. symmetry
α_1	−0.17 (0.008)	α_1	−0.149 (0.001)
α_2	−0.766 (0.01)	α_2	−0.8 (0.002)
K^*	0.07 (0.03)	K^*	1.37 (0.4)
K^{**}	13.29 (5.2)	K^{**}	−0.36 (1.2)
β_{M1}	0.09 (0.05)	ρ_1	0.165 (0.009)
β_{M2}	−0.37 (0.19)	ρ_2	−0.187 (0.006)
β_{M3}	−0.013 (0.014)	σ_t^*	−0.108 (0.018)
σ_t^*	0.56 (0.029)	β_{Mt}	0.014 (0.04)
β_{Mt}	−0.405 (0.06)		

Parameters	(8) A.3. symmetry
α_1	−0.143 (0.007)
α_2	−0.80 (0.008)
δ_1	−1.6 (0.7)
δ_2	−20.9 (3.9)
δ_3	23.3 (4.7)
σ_t^*	−0.045 (0.008)
β_M	0.775 (0.2)

Notes

1. See Brown and Deaton (1972), Barten (1977), Lau (1977a) and Jorgenson and Lau (1977, 1979) for a detailed discussion and a comprehensive review of empirical research on the integrability problem.
2. Applications of systems of transcendental logarithmic demand systems are given by Christensen and Manser (1975, 1977), Jorgenson and Lau (1975), Lau and Mitchell (1971), Conrad and Jorgenson (1978) and Conrad (1978). Tests of the integrability hypothesis employing a dynamic translog demand system with habit formation have been given by Conrad (1977).
3. For a detailed discussion of tests of monotonicity, see Jorgenson and Lau (1979) and Lau (1978).
4. A detailed reconciliation of our concept of personal consumption expenditures and the national accounting concept is given to Conrad and Jorgenson (1975, p. 91); time series of price and quantity of consumers' durable are given in their table 4 on p. 21.
5. Our estimator of the unknown parameters of the two alternative models of consumer behavior is based on the maximum likelihood method presented by Malinvaud (1970).

8 The Transcendental Logarithmic Model of Aggregate Consumer Behavior

Dale W. Jorgenson,
Lawrence J. Lau and
Thomas M. Stoker

8.1 Introduction

The objective of this chapter is to present a new econometric model of aggregate consumer behavior and to implement this model for the United States for the period 1958–1974. The model incorporates aggregate time-series data on quantities consumed, prices, the level and distribution of total expenditures, and demographic characteristics of the population. It also incorporates individual cross-section data on the allocation of consumer expenditures among commodities for households with different demographic characteristics.

Our econometric model can be applied to the generation of projections of aggregate consumer demand in the United States. Projected future prices, the future level and distribution of total expenditures, and the future demographic development of the population are required for projections. The model can also be used to make projections for groups of individuals within the United States, classified by total expenditure and by demographic characteristics. Finally, it can be employed in assessing the impacts of alternative economic policies on the welfare of individuals with common demographic characteristics.

Our model of aggregate consumer behavior unifies two distinct lines of empirical research on consumer behavior. The first line of research, issuing from the seminal contributions of Schultz (1938), Stone (1954b), and Wold (1953), has focused on the role of prices and total expenditure as determinants of the pattern of consumer expenditures. The theory of consumer behavior is used to derive a model of the representative consumer. This model is implemented on the basis of aggregate time-series data on prices, per capita quantities consumed, and per capita total expenditure.

A second line of research, represented by the classic studies of family budgets by Leser (1963), Prais and Houthakker (1955), and Working (1943), has focused on the role of demographic characteristics and total expenditures of individual households as determinants of the pattern of consumer expenditures. The theory of consumer behavior is used to derive a model of the individual consumer. This model is implemented on the basis of cross-section data on quantities consumed, total expenditure, and demographic characteristics of individual households.

Time series and cross-section data have been combined by Stone (1954b) and Wold (1953) in aggregate models of consumer behavior based on a model of the representative consumer. Cross-section data are used to estimate the impact of per capita total expenditure and time-series data are used to estimate the impact of prices within a model that determines per capita quantities consumed. This pioneering research omits an important link between individual and aggregate consumer behavior arising from the fact that aggregate demand functions can be represented as the sum of individual demand functions.

Aggregate demand functions depend on prices and total expenditures, as in the theory of individual consumer behavior. However, aggregate demand functions depend on individual total expenditures rather than aggregate expenditure. If individual expenditures are allowed to vary independently, models of aggregate consumer behavior based on aggregate expenditure or per capita expenditure imply restrictions that severely limit the dependence of individual demand functions on individual expenditure. Alternatively, if individual expenditures are functions of aggregate expenditure, for example, if each individual expenditure is a fixed proportion of aggregate expenditure so that the expenditure distribution is fixed, the implications of the theory of consumer behavior for aggregate demand functions are extremely limited.

One consequence of the theory of individual consumer behavior is that the weighted sum of aggregate demand functions with each function multiplied by the price of the corresponding commodity is equal to aggregate expenditure. A second consequence is that aggregate demand functions are homogeneous of degree zero in prices and individual expenditures. For a fixed expenditure distribution aggregate demand functions are homogeneous of degree zero in prices and aggregate expenditure. Diewert (1977) and Sonnenschein (1973b) have shown that any system of aggregate demand functions that satisfies these two conditions, but is otherwise arbitrary, can be rationalized as the sum of systems of individual demand functions with a fixed expenditure distribution.

8.1.A Representative Consumer

We now turn to the implication of models of aggregate consumer behavior based on per capita expenditure and quantities consumed. Before proceeding with the presentation, we first set down some notation. There are K consumers, indexed by $k = 1, 2, \ldots, K$. There are N commodities in the economy, indexed by $n = 1, 2, \ldots, N$; p_n is the price of the nth commodity, assumed to be the same for all consumers. We denote by $p = (p_1, p_2, \ldots, p_N)$ the vector of prices of all commodities. The quantity of the nth commodity demanded by the kth consumer is x_{nk}, and total expenditure of the kth consumer is $M_k = \sum_{n=1}^{N} p_n x_{nk}$. Finally, A_k is a vector of individual attributes of the kth consumer.[1]

We assume that the demand for the nth commodity by the kth consumer x_{nk} can be expressed as a function f_{nk} of the price vector p, total expenditure M_k and the vector of attributes A_k

$$x_{nk} = f_{nk}(p, M_k, A_k). \tag{8.1}$$

Aggregate demand for the nth commodity is given by

$$\sum_{k=1}^{K} x_{nk} = \sum_{k=1}^{K} f_{nk}(p, M_k, A_k).$$

In models of consumer behavior based on aggregate quantities consumed, the aggregate demand function depends on the price vector p, aggregate expenditure $\sum_{k=1}^{K} M_k$, and possibly some index of aggregate attributes, say $\sum_{k=1}^{K} A_k$. Thus, we may write

$$\sum_{k=1}^{K} f_k(p, M_k, A_k) = F\left(p, \sum_{k=1}^{K} M_k, \sum_{k=1}^{K} A_k\right) \tag{8.2}$$

where f_k is a vector-valued function

$$f_k = \begin{bmatrix} f_{1k} \\ f_{2k} \\ \vdots \\ f_{Nk} \end{bmatrix}, \qquad (k = 1, 2, \ldots, K),$$

giving the vector of demands for all N commodities by the kth consumer, and F is a vector-valued aggregate demand function giving the vector of demands for all N commodities by all K consumers.

The conditions under which equation (8.2) holds for all expenditures $M_k (k = 1, 2, \ldots, K)$, all prices, and all possible attributes, have been derived by Gorman (1953) under the assumption of utility maximization by individual consumers. Gorman's conditions imply

$$(1) \quad f_k(p, M_k, A_k) = h_1(p)M_k + h_2(p)A_k + C_k(p), \quad (k = 1, 2, \ldots, K)$$

$$(2) \quad F\left(p, \sum_{k=1}^{K} M_k, \sum_{k=1}^{K} A_k\right) = h_1(p) \sum_{k=1}^{K} M_k + h_2(p) \sum_{k=1}^{K} A_k + \sum_{k=1}^{K} C_k(p)$$

where the vector-valued function $h_1(p)$ is homogeneous of degree minus one and the vector-valued functions $h_2(p)$ and $C_k(p)$, $(k = 1, 2, \ldots, K)$ are homogeneous of degree zero. In other words, the individual demand functions are linear in expenditure and attributes. They are identical up to the addition of a function that is independent of expenditure and attributes. Furthermore, if aggregate demands are equal to zero when aggregate expenditure is equal to zero, individuals must have identical homothetic preferences.

We can illustrate Gorman's results by considering the case of two individuals. The aggregate demand function F is the sum of two individual demand functions

$$f_1(p, M_1, A_1) + f_2(p, M_2, A_2) = F(p, M_1 + M_2, A_1 + A_2).$$

Since interchanging M_1 and M_2 and interchanging A_1 and A_2 leaves the right-hand side unaffected, it must also leave the left-hand side unaffected. Thus

$$f_1(p, M_1, A_1) + f_2(p, M_2, A_2) = f_1(p, M_2, A_2) + f_2(p, M_1, A_1)$$

which upon rearrangement becomes

$$f_1(p, M_1, A_1) - f_2(p, M_1, A_1) = f_1(p, M_2, A_2) - f_2(p, M_2, A_2).$$

The left-hand side is independent of M_2 and A_2; the right-hand side is independent of M_1 and A_1. In order for the two sides to be equal, they must both depend only on prices. Therefore

$$f_1(p, M_k, A_k) - f_2(p, M_k, A_k) = C(p)$$

or

$$f_k(p_k M_k, A_k) = f(p, M_k, A_k) + C_k(p), \quad (k = 1, 2).$$

This shows that f_1 (p, M_1, A_1) and f_2 (p, M_2, A_2) are identical up to the addition of a vector-valued function $C_k(p)$ independent of expenditure.

Next we consider

$$f(p, M_1, A_1) + C_1(p) + f(p, M_2, A_2) + C_2(p) = F(p, M_1 + M_2, A_1 + A_2).$$

Under the assumption of differentiability of the aggregate demand function we can differentiate this equation with respect to one of the individual expenditures, so that

$$\frac{\partial f}{\partial M_1}(p, M_1, A_1) = \frac{\partial F}{\partial M_1}(p, M_1 + M_2, A_1 + A_2).$$

(We will see later that it is not essential to assume differentiability.) In order for this equation to hold for all M_1 and M_2 and all A_1 and A_2, the function $\partial F/\partial M$ must be independent of its second and third arguments, so that

$$\frac{\partial f}{\partial M_1}(p, M_1, A_1) = h_1(p).$$

Similarly,

$$\frac{\partial f}{\partial A_1}(p, M_1, A_1) = h_2(p)$$

so that the aggregate demand function is linear in expenditure and attributes

$$F(p, M_1 + M_2, A_1 + A_2) = h_1(p)[M_1 + M_2] + h_2(p)[A_1 + A_2] + C(p)$$

as Gorman has shown under the assumption that the individual attributes are fixed. If aggregate demands are zero when aggregate expenditure is equal to zero, then

$$C(p) = 0$$

individuals must have identical homothetic preferences.[2]

Homothetic preferences are inconsistent with well-established empirical regularities in the behavior of individual consumers, such as Engel's law, which states that the proportion of expenditure devoted to food is a decreasing function of total expenditure.[3] Identical preferences for individual households are inconsistent with empirical findings that expenditure patterns depend on demographic characteristics of individual households.[4] Even the weaker form of Gorman's results, that quantities consumed are linear functions of expenditure with identical slopes for all individuals, is inconsistent with empirical evidence from budget studies.[5]

Despite the conflict between Gorman's characterization of individual consumer behavior and the empirical evidence from cross-section data, this characterization has provided an important stimulus to empirical research based on aggregate time-series data. The linear expenditure system, proposed by Klein and Rubin (1947–1948) and implemented by Stone (1954a), has the property that individual demand functions are linear in total expenditure. The resulting system of aggregate demand functions has been used widely as the basis for econometric models of aggregate consumer behavior. Generalizations of the linear expenditure system that retain the critical property of linearity of individual demand functions in total expenditure have also been employed in empirical research.[6]

Muellbauer (1975, 1976a) has substantially generalized Gorman's characterization of the representative consumer model. Aggregate expenditure shares, interpreted as the expenditure shares of a representative consumer, may depend on prices and on a function of individual expenditures not restricted to aggregate or per capita expenditure. In Muellbauer's model of the representative consumer individual preferences are identical but not necessarily homothetic. Furthermore, quantities consumed may be nonlinear functions of expenditure rather than linear functions, as in Gorman's characterization. An important consequence of this nonlinearity is that aggregate demand functions depend on the distribution of expenditure among individuals. Berndt, Darrough, and Diewert (1977) and Deaton and Muellbauer (1980a) have implemented aggregate models of consumer behavior that conform to Muellbauer's characterization of the representative consumer model, retaining the assumption that preferences are identical among individuals.

8.1.B Exact Aggregation

Lau (1977b) has developed a theory of exact aggregation that makes it possible to incorporate differences in individual preferences. One of the most remarkable implications of Lau's theory of exact aggregation is that systems of demand functions for individuals with common demographic characteristics can be recovered uniquely from the system of aggregate demand functions. This feature makes it possible to exploit all of the implications of the theory of the individual consumer in specifying a model of aggregate consumer behavior. The corresponding feature of the model of a representative consumer accounts for the wide-spread utilization of this model in previous empirical research.

We first generalize the concept of an aggregate demand function to that of a function that depends on general symmetric functions of individual expenditures and attributes

$$\sum_{k=1}^{K} f_k(p, M_k, A_k) = F[p,\, g_1(M_1, M_2, \ldots, M_K,\, A_1, A_2, \ldots, A_K),\\ g_2(M_1, M_2, \ldots, M_K,\, A_1, A_2, \ldots, A_K), \ldots,\\ g_L(M_1, M_2, \ldots, M_K,\, A_1, A_2, \ldots, A_K)] \tag{8.3}$$

where each function g_l $(l = 1, 2, \ldots, L)$ is symmetric in individual expenditures and attributes, so that the value of this function is independent of the ordering of the individuals. For example, g_1 may be $\sum_{k=1}^{K} M_k$, g_2 may be $\sum_{k=1}^{K} [M_k - \sum_{j=1}^{K} M_j/K]^2$, and g_3 may be $\sum_{k=1}^{K} M_k A_k$.

We refer to the functions g_l $(l = 1, 2, \ldots, L)$ as index functions. These functions can be interpreted as statistics describing the population. To avoid triviality we assume also that the set of functions g_l $(l = 1, 2, \ldots, L)$ is functionally independent; there is no nonconstant function G such that

$$G[g_1(M_1, M_2, \ldots, M_K, A_1, A_2, \ldots, A_K),\\ g_2(M_1, M_2, \ldots, M_K, A_1, A_2, \ldots, A_K),\\ \ldots, g_L(M_1, M_2, \ldots, M_K, A_1, A_2, \ldots, A_K)] = 0$$

for all $\{M_k, A_k\}$. We note that the representation in equation (8.3) is not unique. Given any function F and a set of L functions g_l $(l = 1, 2, \ldots, L)$, we can represent the same aggregate demand function by

$$\sum_{k=1}^{K} f_k(p, M_k, A_k) = F * [p,\ g_1^*(M_1, M_2, \ldots, M_K, A_1, A_2, \ldots, A_K),$$
$$g_2^*(M_1, M_2, \ldots, M_K, A_1, A_2, \ldots, A_K), \ldots,$$
$$g_L^*(M_1, M_2, \ldots, M_K, A_1, A_2, \ldots, A_K)]$$

where the functions g_l^* $(l = 1, 2, \ldots, L)$ are obtained by a nonsingular transformation of the original L functions g_l $(l = 1, 2, \ldots, L)$ and $F*$ is chosen so that

$$F * = F$$

for all prices, expenditures, and attributes $\{p,\ M_k,\ A_k\}$.

The first result we discuss provides the foundation for the theory of exact aggregation. We consider the conditions under which the sum of individual demand functions can be represented in the form of equation (8.3). The Fundamental Theorem of Exact Aggregation establishes conditions for equation (8.3) to hold for all prices, individual expenditures and individual attributes. In our notation, this theorem can be stated as

Theorem 8.1. An aggregate demand function can be written in the form

$$\sum_{k=1}^{K} f_k(p, M_k, A_k) = F[p,\ g_1(M_1, M_2, \ldots, M_K, A_1, A_2, \ldots, A_K),$$
$$g_2(M_1, M_2, \ldots, M_K, A_1, A_2, \ldots, A_K), \ldots,$$
$$g_L(M_1, M_2, \ldots, M_K, A_1, A_2, \ldots, A_K)],$$

where

(1) each function g_l $(l = 1, 2, \ldots, L)$ is nonconstant and symmetric with respect to the individuals $\{1, 2, \ldots, K\}$;

(2) there exists no functional relationship among the functions g_l $(l = 1, 2, \ldots, L)$, that is, there exists no nonconstant function G such that $G(g_1, g_2, \ldots, g_L) = O$;

(3) there exist prices vectors $p^1, p^2, \ldots, p^L$ such that the system of functions $F(p^l, g_1, g_2, \ldots, g_L)$, $(l = 1, 2, \ldots, L)$, is invertible in $g_1, g_2, \ldots, g_L$ and the range of each $F(p^l, g_1, g_2, \ldots, g_L)$ is an interval of the nonnegative real line $(l = 1, 2, \ldots, L)$;

(4) the function $F(p, g_1, g_2, \ldots, g_L)$ is nonnegative if and only if

$$\text{(a)}\ f_k(p, M_k, A_k) = \sum_{l=1}^{L} h_l(p) g_l^*(M_k, A_k) + C_k^*(p), \quad (k = 1, 2, \ldots, K) \quad (8.4)$$

$$\text{(b)}\ g_l(M_1, M_2, \ldots, M_K, A_1, A_2, \ldots, A_K) = \sum_{k=1}^{K} g_l^*(M_k, A_k) \quad (l = 1, 2, \ldots, L) \quad (8.5)$$

$$\begin{aligned} \text{(c)}\ F[p,\ & g_1(M_1, M_2, \ldots, M_K, A_1 A_2, \ldots, A_K), \\ & g_2(M_1, M_2, \ldots, M_K, A_1, A_2, \ldots, A_K), \ldots, \\ & g_L(M_1, M_2, \ldots, M_K, A_1, A_2, \ldots, A_K)] \\ & = \sum_{l=1}^{L} h_l(p) \sum_{k=1}^{K} g_l^*(M_k, A_k) + \sum_{k=1}^{K} C_k^*(p) \end{aligned} \quad (8.6)$$

where the functions h_l and g_l^* $(l = 1, 2, \ldots, L)$ are two sets of linearly independent functions.

If, in addition, it is assumed that

$$\begin{aligned} F[p,\ & g_1(M_1, M_2, \ldots, M_K, A_1, A_2, \ldots, A_K), \\ & g_2(M_1, M_2, \ldots, M_K, A_1, A_2, \ldots, A_K), \ldots, \\ & g_L(M_1, M_2, \ldots, M_K, A_1, A_2, \ldots, A_K)] = 0 \end{aligned} \quad (8.7)$$

if $\sum_{k=1}^{K} M_k = 0$, we have

$$\begin{aligned} F[p,\ & g_1(M_1, M_2, \ldots, M_K, A_1, A_2, \ldots, A_K), \\ & g_2(M_1, M_2, \ldots, M_K, A_1, A_2, \ldots, A_K), \ldots, \\ & g_L(M_1, M_2, \ldots, M_K, A_1, A_2, \ldots, A_K)] = \sum_{l=1}^{L} h_l(p) \sum_{k=1}^{K} g_l^{**}(M_k, A_k) \end{aligned} \quad (8.8)$$

where

$$g_l^{**}(M_k, A_k) = g_l^*(M_k, A_k) - g_l^*(0, A_k), \quad (l = 1, 2, \ldots, L).$$

Finally, if we add the assumption that

$$f_k(p, M_k, A_k) \geqq 0, \quad (k = 1, 2, \ldots, K) \quad (8.9)$$

then we have[7]

$$f_k(p, M_k, A_k) = \sum_{l=1}^{L} h_l(p) g_l^{**}(M_k, A_k), \quad (k = 1, 2, \ldots, K). \quad (8.10)$$

From an economic point of view, Theorem 8.1 has the following very striking implications:

1. All the individual demand functions for the same commodity are identical up to the addition of a function independent of individual expenditure and attributes.

2. All the individual demand functions must be sums of products of separate functions of the prices and of the individual expenditure and attributes.

3. The aggregate demand functions depend on certain index functions of individual expenditures and attributes. The only admissible index functions are additive in functions of individual expenditures and attributes.

4. The aggregate demand functions can be written as linear functions of the index functions.

Our results imply that an index function such as the Gini coefficient is not admissible as an argument in an aggregate demand functions since it is not additive in individual expenditures. Our results also apply to cases in which one or more of the index functions depend only on the individual attributes. An index function of the age distribution, such as the average age of the population in the highest quantile, is not admissible as an index in the aggregate demand function, since it is not additive in the individual ages. On the other hand, the proportion of population above age 65 is admissible because it is the sum of the following functions

$$g(A) = \begin{cases} 1, & A \geqq 65 \\ 0, & A < 65 \end{cases}$$

$$g(A_1, A_2, \ldots, A_K) = \sum_{k=1}^{K} g(A_K)\,.$$

The proportion of the population that is above age 65 is $\sum_{k=1}^{K} g(A_k)/K$.

We note that these very strong conclusions follow from relatively weak restrictions on the individual demand functions. The only restrictions that have been placed on the individual demand functions are that they exist and are well defined. We have not assumed that the individual demand functions are generated by utility maximization. The invertibility assumption rules out the possibility that the aggregate demand function $F(p, g_1, g_2, \ldots, g_L)$ can be written in terms of a smaller number of functions g_l, $(l = 1, 2, \ldots, L)$ even though there is no relationship among these functions. For example, consider the aggregate demand function $F[p, G(g_1, g_2), g_3, \ldots, g_L]$; then there exists no set of L price vectors such that the corresponding values of the aggregate demand function $F_n (n = 1, 2, \ldots, N)$ are invertible in the functions $\{g_1, g_2, \ldots, g_L\}$. The difficulty is with g_1 and g_2; the two of them are effectively only a single index functions, namely, the function G.

Specializations of Theorem 8.1 have appeared earlier in the literature. For example, if there is only one index function and we take $g_1 = \sum_{k=1}^{K} M_k$, aggregate expenditure for the economy, then Theorem 8.1 implies that for given prices, all consumers must have parallel linear Engel curves. Restricting demands to be nonnegative for all prices and expenditures implies that for priven prices, all consumers have identical linear Engel curves. These are the results of Gorman (1953). Lau (1977b) has shown that if there is only one index function g_1 and the individual demand functions satisfy individual budget constraints, then g_1 must be aggregate expenditure $\sum_{k=1}^{K} M_k$, weakening the assumptions required for the validity of Gorman's results.

Our approach can be clearly distinguished from that of Muellbauer (1975, 1976a,b) in that we do not require the notion of a representative consumer. Muellbauer's condition for the existence of a representative consumer

$$\sum_{k=1}^{K} f_{nk}(p, M_k) = F_n[g_2(M_1, M_2, \ldots, M_K), p]\left(\sum_{k=1}^{K} M_k\right), \qquad (n = 1, 2, \ldots, N)$$

can be viewed as a special case of equation (8.3) with the number of indexes L equal to two and the first index function $g_1(M_1, M_2, \ldots, M_K) = \sum_{k=1}^{K} M_k$, equal to aggregate expenditure. The representative consumer interpretation fails for the case in more than two index functions. We show in section 8.2 that summability of the individual demand functions implies that for two index functions one can always choose $g_1(M_1, M_2, \ldots, M_k) = \sum_{k=1}^{K} M_k$ in equation (8.3). For two indexes our approach coincides with the approach of Muellbauer with identical implications under the assumption of individual utility maximization. However, our approach encompasses more than two indexes and can be applied to individual consumers with different preferences.

8.1.C Integrability

In this article we develop an econometric model of aggregate consumer behavior based on the theory of exact aggregation. In this theory the assumption that the impact of individual expenditures on aggregate demand can be represented by a single function of individual expenditures, such as aggregate or per capita expenditure, is replaced by the assumption that there may be a number of such functions. These functions may depend not only on individual expenditures but also on attributes of individuals, such as demographic characteristics, that give rise to differences in preferences.

By permitting aggregate quantities demanded to depend on a number of functions of individual expenditures and by allowing explicitly for differences in preferences among individuals we are able to overcome the limitations of the model of a representative consumer. At the same time we can test the model of a representative consumer as a special case within the framework provided by the theory of exact aggregation. Eliminating differences in preferences among individuals and suitably restricting the dependence of aggregate demands on individual expenditures, our model of aggregate consumer behavior can be reduced to the model of a representative consumer.

To specify a model of aggregate consumer behavior based on the theory of exact aggregation, we must first specify a model of the individual consumer. A complete characterization of the behavior of an individual consumer can be given in terms of the properties of the corresponding system of individual demand functions. If the system of individual demand functions can be generated by maximization of a utility function, subject to a budget constraint, the system is said to be *integrable*. If the individual demand functions are continuously differentiable, integrability implies the following restrictions:

1. *Homogeneity*. The individual demand functions are homogeneous of degree zero in prices and expenditure

$$x_{nk} = f_{nk}(\lambda p, \lambda M_k, A_k) = f_{nk}(p, M_k, A_k), \qquad (k = 1, 2, \ldots, K; \; n = 1, 2, \ldots, N)$$

for all prices p, expenditure M_k, and positive λ.

2. *Summability*. A weighted sum of the individual demand functions with each function multiplied by the price of the corresponding commodity is equal to expenditure

$$\sum_{n=1}^{N} p_n f_{nk}(p, M_k, A_k) = M_k \,, \qquad (k = 1, 2, \ldots, K)$$

for all prices p and expenditure M_k.

3. *Symmetry.* The matrix of compensated own- and cross-price effects must be symmetric

$$\frac{\partial f_{nk}}{\partial p_m} - x_{nk} \sum_{l=1}^{N} \frac{\partial f_{nk}}{\partial p_l} \cdot \frac{p_l}{M_k} = \frac{\partial f_{mk}}{\partial p_n} - x_{mk} \sum_{l=1}^{N} \frac{\partial f_{mk}}{\partial p_l} \cdot \frac{p_l}{M_k}$$
$$(k = 1, 2, \ldots, K; \;\; m, n = 1, 2, \ldots, N)$$

for all prices p and all expenditure M_k.

4. *Nonnegativity.* The individual quantities demanded are nonnegative

$$x_{nk} = f_{nk}(p, M_k, A_k \geqq 0 \,, \qquad (k = 1, 2, \ldots, K; \;\; n = 1, 2, \ldots, N)$$

for all prices p and all expenditure M_k.

5. *Monotonicity.* The matrix of compensated own- and cross-price effects must be nonpositive definite for all prices p and all expenditure M_k.

A useful interpretation of the monotonicity condition is provided by composite demand functions. First, we consider proportional variations in prices

$$dp_n = \lambda_n \, dp \,, \qquad (n = 1, 2, \ldots, N) \,.$$

We can define a composite demand function, say c_k, as a weighted sum of the demand functions

$$c_k(p, M_k, A_k; \;\; \lambda_1, \lambda_2, \ldots, \lambda_N) = \sum \lambda_n f_{nk} \, (p, M_k, A_k) \,.$$

The compensated own-price substitution effect for the composite demand function is nonpositive

$$\sum \sum \lambda_n \, \lambda_m \left(\frac{\partial x_{nk}}{\partial p_m} - x_{nk} \sum \frac{\partial x_{nk}}{\partial p_l} \cdot \frac{p_l}{M_k} \right) \leqq 0$$

for all λ_n $(n = 1, 2, \ldots, N)$ and all expenditure M_k.

Given homogeneity, summability, and symmetry, the system of individual demand functions can be generated as the solutions of the system of partial differential equations

$$\frac{\partial \ln V_k}{\partial \ln p_n} = \frac{p_n \, x_{nk}}{M_k} \sum \frac{\partial \ln V_k}{\partial \ln p_l}, \qquad (k = 1, 2, \ldots, K; \; n = 1, 2, \ldots, N)$$

defining a family of indirect utility functions V_k. Given nonnegativity and monotonicity these indirect utility functions can be obtained from one another by means of monotonically increasing transformations. An alternative and equivalent characterization of the behavior of an individual consumer can be given in terms of the following properties of the indirect utility function:

1. *Homogeneity.* The indirect utility function is homogeneous of degree zero in prices and expenditure

$$V_k = V_k(\lambda p, \lambda M_k, A_k) = V_k(p, M_k, A_k), \qquad (k = 1, 2, \ldots, K)$$

for all prices p, expenditure M_k, and positive λ.

2. *Monotonicity.* The indirect utility function is nonincreasing in prices and nondecreasing in expenditure

$$\frac{\partial V_k}{\partial p} \leqq 0, \qquad \frac{\partial V_k}{\partial M_k} \geqq 0, \qquad (k = 1, 2, \ldots, K)$$

for all prices p and expenditure M_k.

3. *Quasiconvexity.* The indirect utility function is quasiconvex in prices and expenditure for all prices p and expenditure M_k.

8.1.D Overview

The theory of exact aggregation can be employed to derive restrictions on individual demand functions that allow aggregate demand functions to be expressed in terms of index functions that depend on individual expenditures and attributes. We first derive the conditions under which an aggregate demand function can be obtained as the sum of individual demand functions. We then impose the restrictions implied by utility maximization by individual consumers on the individual demand functions.

A system of individual demand functions that conforms to the theory of exact aggregation must be linear in a number of functions of total expenditure and attributes of the individual. If the individual demand functions are summable, one of the functions of individual expenditure and attributes must be independent of attributes and must reduce to expenditure itself. If there is only a single function of individual expenditure and attributes, this characterization of individual preferences reduces to Gorman's model of a representative consumer. Demand functions are linear in expenditure with identical slopes for all individuals.

In section 8.2 we consider the dependence of individual and aggregate demand functions on individual expenditures. We first assume that preferences are identical for all individuals, but allow the system of individual demand functions to depend on two linearly independent functions of expenditure. The first function must reduce to expenditure itself, but the second must be nonlinear in expenditure. If the individual demand functions are summable and homogeneous of degree zero, the nonlinear function of individual expenditure must be the product of expenditure and either the logarithm of expenditure or a power function of expenditure. This characterization of individual demand functions reduces to Muellbauer's model of a representative consumer. Although the system of demand functions is identical for all individuals, the system of aggregate demand functions depends on the distribution of expenditures among individuals as well as the level of per capita expenditure.

In section 8.3 we dispense with the model of a representative consumer in order to incorporate differences in preferences among individuals. If we allow individual demand functions to depend on two linearly independent functions of the attributes and expenditure of individuals, one of these functions is independent of attributes and reduces to expenditure itself, while the second function involves an arbitrary function of the individual attributes and a logarithmic or power function of individual expenditure. While this specification is consistent with evidence from budget studies that individual preferences depend on demographic characteristics and Engel curves are nonlinear, the impact of differences in demographic characteristics and the impact of differences in functions of expenditure are related to each other.

We conclude our discussion of the theory of exact aggregation by considering a representation of individual demand functions that depends on attributes as well as expenditures of individuals and does not require Engel curves to be linear. In this representation we allow the system of individual demand functions to depend on three linearly independent functions of the expenditures and attributes of individuals. One of these functions is independent of attributes and reduces to expenditure itself. A second function is nonlinear in expenditure and does not depend on attributes. A third function depends on both expenditure and attributes. This specification does not impose restrictions on the impact of differences in attributes and the impact of differences in expenditure.

Under summability and homogeneity the nonlinear function of expenditure that occurs in the system of individual demand functions must be the product of expenditure and either the logarithm of expenditure or a power function of expenditure. The individual demand functions also depend on attributes of individuals, such as demographic characteristics. By representing aggregate demand functions as the sum of these individual demand functions, the aggregate demand functions depend on the distribution of expenditures among individuals as well as the level of aggregate expenditure and prices. The aggregate demand functions also depend on the joint distribution of demographic characteristics and expenditures over the population.

The theory of exact aggregation enables us to specify the dependence of systems of individual demand functions on expenditure and attributes. To incorporate the implications of the theory of the individual consumer we must also specify the dependence of systems of individual demand functions on prices. In section 8.4 we show that only the transcendental logarithmic or translog indirect utility functions is capable of combining flexibility in the representation of preferences with parsimony in the number of parameters that must be estimated.[8]

To incorporate differences in individual preferences into a model of aggregate consumer behavior we allow the indirect translog utility function for each individual to depend on attributes, such as demographic characteristics, that vary among individuals. The theory of exact aggregation requires that the individual demand functions must be linear in a number of functions of the expenditure and attributes of the individual. We impose the resulting parametric restrictions on the indirect translog utility function for each individual.

Integrability of systems of individual demand functions requires that the indirect utility function for each individual must be homogeneous, monotone, and quasiconvex. In section 8.5 we impose the corresponding restrictions on the indirect translog utility functions for all individuals. To construct a system of individual demand functions we apply Roy's (1943) Identity to the indirect translog utility function.[9] The resulting models of individual consumer behavior consist of systems of demand functions giving the shares of total expenditure allocated to each commodity group. For given values of prices the expenditure shares are linear in the logarithm of expenditure and the attributes of individuals.

To construct a model of aggregate consumer behavior we first multiply the expenditure shares for each individual by expenditure for that individual and divide by expenditure for the population as a whole. We then sum the resulting weighted individual demand functions across the whole population. The resulting model of aggregate consumer behavior gives the share of aggregate expenditure allocated to each commodity group as a function of prices. The aggregate expenditure shares also depend on averages of the logarithms of individual expenditures and the attributes, weighted by the share of expenditure for each individual in expenditure for the population.

We find it convenient to represent the attributes of individuals, such as demographic characteristics, by variables equal to unity for an individual with the corresponding attribute and zero otherwise. For this representation the appropriate weighted average for each attribute is simply the share of all individuals with that attribute in aggregate expenditure. To incorporate the impact of changes in the demographic characteristics of the population on the allocation of aggregate expenditure among commodity groups, we include the shares of aggregate expenditure for all demographic groups as explanatory variables. Similarly, the weighted average of the logarithm of individual expenditures has weights equal to the shares of all individuals in expenditure for the population as a whole. To incorporate the impact of the distribution of expenditure on the allocation of aggregate expenditure, we include the weighted average of the logarithm of expenditure for the population as an explanatory variable.

A model of aggregate consumer behavior based on the theory of exact aggregation can be implemented from individual cross-section data on expenditure shares, prices, total expenditure, and demographic characteristics. Alternatively, since the system of demand functions for an individual with given demographic characteristics can be recovered uniquely from the system of aggregate demand functions, a model of aggregate consumer behavior can be implemented from time-series data on aggregate expenditure shares, prices, shares of demographic groups in aggregate expenditure, and a weighted average of the logarithms of expenditure. If cross-section data are limited to individual expenditure shares and total expenditure, with prices taking the same values for all individuals, a model of aggregate consumer behavior can be implemented by pooling aggregate time-series data with individual cross-section data along the lines discussed in section 8.6.

In section 8.7 we present a transcendental logarithmic model of aggregate consumer behavior for the United States for the period 1958–1974. We analyze the allocation of aggregate consumer expenditures among five categories of goods and services—energy, food and clothing, consumer services, capital services, and other nondurable goods. We employ a breakdown of individual consumer units by family size, age of head of household, region, race, and urban versus rural residence. We implement this model from a cross-section survey of individual consumer expenditures for the United States for the year 1972 and annual time series observations on aggregate consumer expenditure for the period 1958–1974.

We find that at total expenditure increases, the share of the consumer budget allocated to capital services increases substantially, while the shares allocated to the other four groups of goods and services decline. Demographic effects are very important for all categories of consumer expenditures. The impact of changes in total expenditures on the allocation of the consumer budget depends strongly on demographic characteristics. These characteristics also have a substantial effect on the impact of changes in relative prices on budget allocation.

8.2 Exact Aggregation for Consumers with Identical Preferences

In section 8.1 we have stated the Fundamental Theorem of Exact Aggregation. Under this Theorem all the individual demand functions for the same commodity are identical up to the addition of a function that is independent of individual attributes and expenditure. The individual demand functions must be sums of products of separate functions of prices and of individual expenditure and attributes. The aggregate demand functions depend on index functions that are additive in functions of expenditure and attributes for individuals. Finally, the aggregate demand functions can be written as linear functions of the index functions.

In this section we combine the theory of exact aggregation with restrictions on individual consumer behavior implied by maximization of a utility function, subject to a budget constraint. We first consider consumers with identical preferences, so that individual expenditures on all commodity groups depend on total expenditure, but not on attributes of the individual consumer such as demographic characteristics. We impose the restrictions on individual demand functions implied by utility maximization and derive the resulting restrictions on aggregate demand functions. For systems of individual demand functions that are integrable, we can summarize these restrictions in terms of an indirect utility function for each consumer.

We begin with the case of two index functions of individual expenditures. Under exact aggregation the individual demand functions take the form

$$f_k(p, M_k) = h_1(p)g_1^*(M_k) + h_2(p)g_2^*(M_k) + C_k(p), \quad (k = 1, 2, \ldots, K) \tag{8.11}$$

where without loss of generality we take $g_1^*(0) + g_2^*(0) = 0$. The index functions of individual expenditures take the form

$$g_l(M_1, M_2, \ldots, M_K) = \sum_{k=1}^{K} g_l^*(M_k), \quad (l = 1, 2) \tag{8.12}$$

and the aggregate demand function takes the form

$$F[p, g_1(M_1, M_2, \ldots, M_K), g_2(M_1, M_2, \ldots, M_K)] \\ = h_1(p) \sum_{k=1}^{K} g_1^*(M_k) + h_2(p) \sum_{k=1}^{K} g_2^*(M_k) + \sum_{k=1}^{K} C_k(p). \tag{8.13}$$

8.2.A Summability

We assume that the individual demand functions are summable, that is

$$\sum_{n=1}^{N} p_n f_{nk}(p, M_k) = M_k \tag{8.14}$$

or

$$\sum_{n-1}^{N} p_n h_{n1}(p)g_1^*(M_k) + \sum_{n=1}^{N} p_n h_{n2}(p)g_2^*(M_k) + \sum_{n=1}^{N} p_n C_{nk}(p) = M_k. \tag{8.15}$$

Let $M_k = 0$, then $\sum_{n=1}^{N} p_n C_{nk}(p) = 0$. Let $h_1^*(p) \equiv \sum_{j=1}^{N} p_n h_{n1}(p)$ and $h_2^*(p) \equiv \sum_{n=1}^{N} p_n h_{n2}(p)$; then equation (8.15) may be rewritten as

$$h_1^*(p)g_1^*(M_k) + h_2^*(p)g_2^*(M_k) = M_k \,. \tag{8.16}$$

By Theorem 8.1 above $g_1^*(M_k)$ and $g_2^*(M_k)$ are linearly independent functions.

Now consider any two price vectors, say p^1 and p^2; by equation (8.16), we have

$$h_1^*(p^1)g_1^*(M_k) + h_2^*(p^1)g_2^*(M_k) = M_k \tag{8.17}$$

and

$$h_1^*(p^2)g_1^*(M_k) + h_2^*(p^2)g_2^*(M_k) = M_k \tag{8.18}$$

so that

$$[h_1^*(p^1) - h_1^*(p^2)]g_1^*(M_k) + [h_2^*(p^1) - h_2^*(p^2)]g_2^*(M_k) = 0$$

for all p^1 and p^2. But $g_1^*(M_k)$ and $g_2^*(M_k)$ are linearly independent functions, which implies that

$$h_1^*(p^1) - h_1^*(p^2) = 0$$

and

$$h_2^*(p^1) - h_2^*(p^2) = 0$$

for all p^1 and p^2, so that

$$h_1^*(p) = \bar{h}_1^*, h_2^*(p) = \bar{h}_2^*$$

both constants.

Substituting the constants $\bar{h}_1^*$ and $\bar{h}_2^*$ into equation (8.16) we have

$$\bar{h}_1^* g_1^*(M_k) + \bar{h}_2^* g_2^*(M_k) = M_k \,.$$

We cannot have both $\bar{h}_1^* = 0$ and $\bar{h}_2^* = 0$, otherwise any positive M_k leads to a contradiction. Suppose $\bar{h}_1^* \neq 0$; then we can solve for $g_1^*(M_k)$ as follows

$$g_1^*(M_k) = \frac{1}{\bar{h}_1^*} M_k - \frac{\bar{h}_2^*}{\bar{h}_1^*} g_2^*(M_k) \,.$$

By defining

$$h_{n1}^*(p) \equiv h_{n1}(p)\,\frac{1}{\bar{h}_1^*}$$

$$h_{n2}^*(p) \equiv -\,h_{n1}(p)\,\frac{\bar{h}_2^*}{\bar{h}_1^*} + h_{n2}(p) \qquad (n = 1, 2, \ldots, N)$$

each individual demand function may be written as

$$f_{nk}(p, M_k) = h_{n1}^*(p)M_k + h_{n2}^*(p)g_2^*(M_k) + C_{nk}(p)\,, \qquad (n = 1, 2, \ldots, N;\ k = 1, 2, \ldots, K)$$

with the restrictions that

$$\sum_{n=1}^{N} p_n h_{n1}^*(p) = 1\ ; \qquad \sum_{n=1}^{N} p_n h_{n2}^*(p) = 0\ ; \qquad \sum_{n=1}^{N} p_n C_{nk}(p) = 0\,.$$

The argument used here is perfectly general and can be easily extended to the case of an arbitrary finite number of index functions of expenditures. Thus, we have proved

Theorem 8.2. Under the assumption that the individual demand functions are summable, a system of aggregate demand functions can be written in the form

$$\sum_{k=1}^{K} f_{nk}(p, M_k) = F_n[p, g_1(M_1, M_2, \ldots, M_K), g_2(M_1, M_2, \ldots, M_K), \ldots, g_L(M_1, M_2, \ldots, M_K)]\,, \qquad (n = 1, 2, \ldots, N)$$

where the functions g_l $(l = 1, 2, \ldots, L)$ and $F_n(n = 1, 2, \ldots, N)$ satisfy assumptions (1) through (4) in Theorem 8.1, if and only if

(1) $$f_{nk}(p, M_k) = h_{n1}(p)M_k + \sum_{l=2}^{L} h_{n1}(p)g_l^*(M_k) + C_{nk}(p)\,, \qquad (n = 1, 2, \ldots, N;\ k = 1, 2, \ldots, K)$$

where $h_{n1}(p)$ and $C_{nk}(p)$ are arbitrary functions of p satisfying

$$\sum_{n=1}^{N} p_n h_{nl}(p) = 1\ ; \qquad \sum_{n=1}^{N} p_n h_{nl}(p) = 0\,, \qquad (l = 2, 3, \ldots, L)$$

$$\sum_{n=1}^{N} p_n C_{nk}(p) = 0\,, \qquad (k = 1, 2, \ldots, K)$$

and

(2) $$g_1(M_1, M_2, \ldots, M_K) = \sum_{k=1}^{K} M_k$$

$$g_l(M_1, M_2, \ldots, M_K) = \sum_{k=1}^{K} g_l^*(M_k), \qquad (l = 2, 3, \ldots L)$$

(3) $$F_n[p, g_1(M_1, M_2, \ldots, M_K), g_2(M_1, M_2, \ldots, M_K), \ldots, g_L(M_1, M_2, \ldots, M_K)] = h_{n1}(p) \sum_{k=1}^{K} M_k + \sum_{l=2}^{L} h_{nl}(p) \sum_{k=1}^{K} g_l^*(M_k) + \sum_{k=1}^{K} C_{nk}(p), \quad (n = 1, 2, \ldots, N).$$

Theorem 8.2 implies that the individual demand function for at least one commodity must have a term that is linear in expenditure. If there is only one demand function with a term that is linear in expenditure, then the corresponding function $h_{nl}(p)$ must be equal to one. All other such functions must be equal to zero. We note further that index functions that are not linear in expenditures must appear in the demand functions of more than one commodity; otherwise, $\sum_{n=1}^{N} p_n h_{nl}(p) \neq 0$ for some $l \neq 1$. It is possible that the individual demand functions for some commodities do not have the linear expenditure term.

8.2.B Homogeneity

Next, we consider the implications of zero degree homogeneity, given summability, for the individual demand functions. Under summability, Theorem 8.2 implies for two index functions that the individual demand function has the form

$$f(p, M) = h_1(p)M + h_2(p)g(M) + C(p) \tag{8.19}$$

where $g(0) = 0$. Homogeneity of degree zero of the individual demand function implies that

$$h_1(\lambda p)\lambda M + h_2(\lambda p)g(\lambda M) + C(\lambda p) = h_1(p)M + h_2(p)g(M) + C(p). \tag{8.20}$$

Let $M = 0$ and equation (8.20) becomes

$$C(\lambda p) = C(p),$$

so that $C(p)$ is homogeneous of degree zero in p.

Subtracting $C(p)$ from both sides of equation (8.20) we obtain

$$h_1(\lambda p)\lambda M + h_2(\lambda p)g(\lambda M) = h_1(p)M + h_2(p)g(M). \tag{8.21}$$

Dividing both sides by M, we obtain

$$h_1(\lambda p)\lambda + h_2(\lambda p)\lambda \frac{g(\lambda M)}{\lambda M} = h_1(p) + h_2(p)\frac{g(M)}{M}. \tag{8.22}$$

By a change of the dependent variable $g*(M) \equiv g(M)/M$ with the requirement that $\lim_{M\to 0} M \cdot g*(M) = 0$, equation (8.22) becomes

$$h_2(\lambda p)\lambda g*(\lambda M) - h_2(p)g*(M) = h_1(p) - h_1(\lambda p)\lambda. \tag{8.23}$$

Equation (8.23) holds for all M, and in particular one can choose $M = M_1$ and M_2 so that

$$h_2(\lambda p)\lambda g*(\lambda M_1) - h_2(p)g*(M_1) = h_2(\lambda p)\lambda g*(\lambda M_2) - h_2(p)g*(M_2)$$

which upon rearrangement becomes

$$\frac{h_2(\lambda p)\lambda}{h_2(p)}[g*(\lambda M_1) - g*(\lambda M_2)] = g*(M_1) - g*(M_2). \tag{8.24}$$

Equation (8.24), which must hold for all p, M_1, M_2 and λ implies that $h_2(\lambda p)\lambda/h_2(p)$ is at most a function of λ, say $k(\lambda)$

$$\frac{h_2(\lambda p)\lambda}{h_2(p)} = k(\lambda)$$

or

$$h_2(\lambda p) = k*(\lambda)h_2(p) \tag{8.25}$$

where $k*(\lambda) \equiv k(\lambda)/\lambda$. This is the generalized Euler's equation for a homogeneous function with the solution

$$h_2(\lambda p) = \lambda^{-\sigma}h_2(p). \tag{8.26}$$

In other words, $h_2(p)$ is a homogeneous of degree $-\sigma$ function. It follows that

$$k(\lambda) = \lambda^{-\sigma+1}.$$

Substituting equation (8.26) and $k(\lambda)$ into equation (8.23) we obtain

$$\lambda^{-\sigma+1} g * (\lambda M) - g * (M) = \frac{h_1(p) - h_1(\lambda p)\lambda}{h_2(p)}. \tag{8.27}$$

Each side of equation (8.27) must be a function of λ only, say $l(\lambda)$. Thus we have

$$\lambda^{-\sigma+1} g * (\lambda M) - g * (M) = l(\lambda) \tag{8.28}$$

with $l(1) = 0$. By setting $M = 1$, we have

$$\lambda^{-\sigma+1} g * (\lambda) - g * (1) = l(\lambda). \tag{8.29}$$

Substituting equation (8.29) into equation (8.28), we obtain

$$\lambda^{-\sigma+1} g * (\lambda M) - g * (M) = \lambda^{-\sigma+1} g * (\lambda) - g * (1). \tag{8.30}$$

By interchanging the roles of λ and M in equation (8.30), we obtain

$$M^{-\sigma+1} g * (\lambda M) - g * (\lambda) = M^{-\sigma+1} g * (M) - g * (1). \tag{8.31}$$

By equating the values of $g * (\lambda M)$ in equations (8.30) and (8.31), we obtain

$$\lambda^{\sigma-1} g * (M) + g * (\lambda) - \lambda^{\sigma-1} g * (1) = M^{\sigma-1} g * (\lambda) + g * (M) - M^{\sigma-1} g * (1)$$

which may be rearranged as

$$\begin{aligned} &\lambda^{\sigma-1} g * (M) - g * (M) - \lambda^{\sigma-1} g * (1) + g * (1) \\ &\quad = M^{\sigma-1} g * (\lambda) - g * (\lambda) - M^{\sigma-1} g * (1) + g * (1) \end{aligned}$$

which, if $\sigma \neq 1$ may be factorized as

$$(\lambda^{\sigma-1} - 1)[g * (M) - g * (1)] = (M^{\sigma-1} - 1)[g * (\lambda) - g * (1)]$$

so that

$$g * (M) - g * (1) = D[M^{\sigma-1} - 1] \tag{8.32}$$

where D is a constant.

If $\sigma = 1$, then by equation (8.28) we have

$$g * (\lambda M) = g * (M) + l(\lambda)$$

a functional equation with the well-known general solution

$$g * (M) = D_1 \ln M + D_2 \tag{8.33}$$

where D_1, D_2 are constants. Since $g(M) = g * (M)M$, we have, either

$$g(M) = D_1 M^{\sigma} + D_2 M \tag{8.34}$$

where D_1, D_2 are constants. The condition that $g(0) = 0$ requires that $\sigma \geqq 0$, or

$$g(M) = D_1 M \ln M + D_2 M , \tag{8.35}$$

where D_1, D_2 are constants.

If we substitute equation (8.34) into equation (8.22) and make use of the homogeneity of degree $-\sigma$ of $h_2(p)$, we obtain

$$\begin{aligned} h_1(\lambda p)\lambda + h_2(p)\lambda^{-\sigma}(D_1\lambda^{\sigma}M^{\sigma-1} + D_2\lambda) \\ = h_1(p) + h_2(p)(D_1 M^{\sigma-1} + D_2) , \end{aligned} \tag{8.36}$$

which results in

$$h_1(\lambda p)\lambda + D_2 h_2(p)\lambda^{1-\sigma} = h_1(p) + D_2 h_2(p) \tag{8.37}$$

or

$$h_1(\lambda p)\lambda + D_2 h_2(\lambda p)\lambda = h_1(p) + D_2 h_2(p) \tag{8.38}$$

or $h_1(p) + D_2 h_2(p)$ is homogeneous of degree minus one.

By defining $h_1^*(p) \equiv h_1(p) + D_2 h_2(p)$, $h_2^*(p) \equiv D_1 h_2(p)$ we can write the individual demand function as

$$f(p, M) = h_1^*(p)M + h_2^*(p)M^{\sigma} + C(p) \tag{8.39}$$

where $h_1^*(p)$ is homogeneous of degree minus one, $h_2^*(p)$ is homogeneous of degree $-\sigma$ and $C(p)$ is homogeneous of degree zero and $\sigma > 0$.

If we substitute equation (8.35) into equation (8.22) we obtain

$$\begin{aligned} h_1(\lambda p)\lambda + h_2(p)\lambda^{-1}[D_1\lambda(\ln M + \ln\lambda) + D_2\lambda] \\ = h_1(p) + h_2(p)[D_1 \ln M + D_2] , \end{aligned} \tag{8.40}$$

which simplifies into

$$\lambda h_1(\lambda p) + D_1 h_2(p) \ln\lambda = h_1(p)$$

or

$$\lambda h_1(\lambda p) - h_1(p) + D_1 h_2(p) \ln \lambda = 0 \tag{8.41}$$

or

$$\frac{h_1(\lambda p)}{D_1 h_2(\lambda p)} - \frac{h_1(p)}{D_1 h_2(p)} + \ln \lambda = 0\,. \tag{8.42}$$

Exponentiating equation (8.42) we obtain

$$\exp[h_1(\lambda p)/D_1 h_2(\lambda p)] = \lambda^{-1} \exp[h_1(p)/D_1 h_2(p)]$$

so that $h_1^*(p) \equiv \exp[h_1(p)/D_1 h_2(\lambda p)]$ is homogeneous of degree minus one in p. Let $h_2^*(p) \equiv D_1 h_2(p)$. Thus, we can write the individual demand function as

$$\begin{aligned} f(p, M) &= h_1(p)M + h_2^*(p)[M \ln M + (D_2/D_1)M] + C(p) \\ &= h_2^*(p) \ln h_1^{**}(p)M + h_2^*(p)M \ln M + C(p) \end{aligned} \tag{8.43}$$

where $h_1^{**}(p) \equiv \exp(D_2/D_1)h_1^*(p)$ and $h_2^*(p)$ are homogeneous of degree minus one and $C(p)$ is homogeneous of degree zero.

If an aggregate demand function exists with two index functions that depend on individual expenditure alone, equations (8.39) and (8.43) are the only possible forms for the individual demand function under the assumptions of summability and zero degree homogeneity. Equations (8.39) are (8.43) are precisely the forms proposed by Muellbauer (1975, 1976a,b). We have shown that these forms are necessary within a much more general framework.[10] Thus, we have proved

Theorem 8.3. Under the assumption that the individual demand functions are summable and zero degree homogeneous in prices and expenditure, a system of aggregate demand functions can be written in the form

$$\sum_{k=1}^{K} f_{nk}(p, M_k) = F_n[p, g_1(M_1, M_2, \dots, M_K), g_2(M_1, M_2, \dots, M_K)]\,, \qquad (n = 1, 2, \dots, N)$$

where $g_l(l = 1, 2)$ and F satisfy assumptions (1) through (4) in Theorem 8.1, if and only if

$$(1)\qquad f_{nk}(p, M_k) = \begin{cases} h_{n1}(p)M_k + h_{n2}(p)M_k^{\sigma} + C_{nk}(p), & (n = 1, 2, \ldots, N) \\ h_{n2}^{*}(p) \ln h_{n1}^{*}(p)M_k + h_{n2}^{*}(p)M_k \ln M_k + C_{nk}(p), & (n = 1, 2, \ldots, N) \end{cases}$$

where $h_{n1}(p)$, $h_{n2}^{*}(p)$ and $h_{n1}^{*}(p)$ are homogeneous of degree minus one, $h_{n2}(p)$ is homogeneous of degree $-\sigma$, $\sigma > 0$, $\sigma \neq 1$, and $C_{nk}(p)$ is homogeneous of degree zero, $(n = 1, 2, \ldots, N)$; furthermore

$$\sum_{n=1}^{N} p_n h_{n1}(p) = \sum_{n=1}^{N} p_n h_{n2}^{*}(p) \ln h_{n1}^{*}(p) = 1$$

$$\sum_{n=1}^{N} p_n h_{n2}(p) = \sum_{n=1}^{N} p_n h_{n2}^{*}(p) = 0$$

$$\sum_{n=1}^{N} p_n C_{nk}(p) = 0$$

$$(2)\qquad g_1(M_1, M_2, \ldots, M_K) = \sum_{k=1}^{K} M_k$$

$$(3)\qquad F_n[p, g_1(M_1, M_2, \ldots, M_K), g_2(M_1, M_2, \ldots, M_K)]$$

$$= \begin{cases} h_{n1}(p) \sum_{k=1}^{K} M_k + h_{n2}(p) \sum_{k=1}^{K} M_k^{\sigma} + \sum_{k=1}^{K} C_{nk}(p), & (n = 1, 2, \ldots, N) \\ h_{n2}^{*}(p) \ln h_{n1}^{*}(p) \sum_{k=1}^{K} M_k + h_{n2}^{*}(p) \sum_{k=1}^{K} M_k \ln M_k + \sum_{k=1}^{K} C_{nk}(p), & (n = 1, 2, \ldots, N). \end{cases}$$

We also have

Corollary 8.1. If, in addition to the assumption of the theorem, $\sum_{k=1}^{K} M_k = 0$ implies that

$$(4)\quad F_n[p, g_1(M_1, M_2, \ldots, M_K), g_2(M_1, M_2, \ldots, M_K)] = 0, \qquad (n = 1, 2, \ldots, N)$$

then $\sum_{k=1}^{K} C_{nk}(p) \equiv 0$. The proof of this corollary is obvious.

Corollary 8.2. If in addition to the assumptions of the theorem and Corollary 8.1 we have

(5) $f_{nk}(p, M_k) \geqq 0\,, \quad (k = 1, 2, \ldots, K;\ n = 1, 2, \ldots, N)$

then

$$f_{nk}(p, M_k) = \begin{cases} h_{n1}(p)M_k + h_{n2}(p)M_k^{\sigma} \quad (n = 1, 2, \ldots, N) \\ h_{n2}^*(p) \ln h_{n1}^*(p)M_k + h_{n2}^*(p)M_k \ln M_k \\ \qquad\qquad (k = 1, 2, \ldots, K;\ n = 1, 2, \ldots N) \end{cases}$$

where $h_{n1}(p) \geqq 0$, $h_{n2}(p) \geqq 0$, $h_{n2}^*(p) \ln h_{n1}^*(p) \geqq 0$.
Proof: It is obvious that

$$C_{nk}(p) = 0\,, \quad (k = 1, 2, \ldots, K;\ n = 1, 2, \ldots, N)\,.$$

To see that $h_{n1}(p) \geqq 0$ and $h_{n2}(p) \geqq 0$ are necessary for the nonnegativity of $h_{n1}(p)M_k + h_{n2}(p)M_k^{\sigma}$, suppose $\sigma > 1$. Then for large M_k, the second term dominates, which implies $h_{n2}(p) \geqq 0$; and for $M_k < 1$, the first term dominates, which implies $h_{n1}(p) \geqq 0$. The same argument works in reverse if $\sigma < 1$.[11] To see that $h_{n2}^*(p) \ln h_{n1}^*(p) \geqq 0$ is necessary and sufficient for the nonnegativity of $h_{n2}^*(p) \ln h_{n1}^*(p)M_k + h_{n2}^*(p)M_k \ln M_k$, rewrite the individual demand function as

$$f_{nk}(p, M_k) = h_{n2}^*(p) \ln h_{n1}^*(p/M_k)M_k\,, \quad (k = 1, 2, \ldots, K;\ n = 1, 2, \ldots, N)$$

where we have made use of the fact that $h_{n1}^*(p)$ is homogeneous of degree minus one. The condition we have stated is necessary as well as sufficient.[12]

8.2.C Symmetry

If a system of aggregate demand functions with two index functions of expenditures exists, Theorem 8.2 implies that under summability, zero degree homogeneity, and nonnegativity, the systems of individual demand functions must have one of the two following forms

$$f_{nk}(p, M_k) = h_{n1}(p)M_k + h_{n2}(p)M_k^{\sigma}\,, \ (k = 1, 2, \ldots, K; n = 1, 2, \ldots, N) \quad (8.44)$$

or

$$f_{nk}(p, M_k) = h_{n2}^*(p) \ln h_{n1}^*(p)M_k + h_{n2}^*(p)M_k \ln M_k\,, \quad (k = 1, 2, \ldots, K;\ n = 1, 2, \ldots, N) \quad (8.45)$$

where $h_{n1}(p)$, $h^*_{n2}(p)$ and $h^*_{n1}(p)$ are homogeneous of degree minus one and $h_{n2}(p)$ is homogeneous of degree $-\sigma$, $\sigma > 0$.

We first take up the case of equation (8.44). Symmetry of the Slutsky substitution matrix, under the additional assumption of continuous differentiability of the individual demand functions, implies

$$\frac{\partial f_{jk}(p, M_k)}{\partial p_n} + f_{nk}(p, M_k)\frac{\partial f_{jk}(p, M_k)}{\partial M_k} = \frac{\partial f_{nk}(p, M_k)}{\partial p_j} + f_{jk}(p, M_k)\frac{\partial f_{nk}(p, M_k)}{\partial M_k}.$$

When applied to equation (8.44), this yields

$$\begin{aligned}
&\frac{\partial}{\partial p_n} h_{j1}(p)M_k + \frac{\partial}{\partial p_n} h_{j2}(p)M_k^\sigma \\
&\quad + [h_{n1}(p)M_k + h_{n2}(p)M_k^\sigma][h_{j1}(p) + \sigma h_{j2}(p)M_k^{\sigma-1}] \\
&\quad = \frac{\partial}{\partial p_j} h_{n1}(p)M_k + \frac{\partial}{\partial p_i} h_{n2}(p)M_k^\sigma \\
&\quad + [h_{j1}(p)M_k + h_{j2}(p)M_k^\sigma][h_{n1}(p) + \sigma h_{n2}(p)M_k^{\sigma-1}]
\end{aligned}$$

which simplifies into

$$\begin{aligned}
&h_{j1n}(p)M_k + h_{j2n}(p)M_k^\sigma + \sigma h_{n1}(p)h_{j2}(p)M_k^\sigma + h_{n2}(p)h_{j1}(p)M_k^\sigma \\
&\quad = h_{n1j}(p)M_k + h_{n2j}(p)M_k + \sigma h_{j1}(p)h_{n2}(p)M_k^\sigma + h_{j2}(p)h_{n1}(p)M_k^\sigma
\end{aligned}$$

or

$$\begin{aligned}
&h_{j1n}(p)M_k + [h_{j2n}(p) - (1-\sigma)h_{j2}(p)h_{n1}(p)]M_k^\sigma \\
&\quad = h_{n1j}(p)M_k + [h_{n2j}(p) - (1-\sigma)h_{n2}(p)h_{j1}(p)]M_k^\sigma. \qquad (8.46)
\end{aligned}$$

Equation (8.46) must hold for all M_k, and thus

$$h_{j1n}(p) - h_{nlj}(p) = 0, \quad (j, n = 1, 2, \ldots, N).$$

This implies that

$$h_{n1}(p) = \frac{\partial \ln H^*(p)}{\partial p_n}, \quad (n = 1, 2, \ldots, N)$$

where $\ln H^*(p)$ is a function of p. By the summability condition, $\sum_{n=1}^N p_n h_{n1}(p) = 1$, so that $H^*(p)$ is homogeneous of degree one. Similarly

$$h_{j2n}(p) - (1 - \sigma)h_{j2}(p)h_{n1}(p) = h_{n2j}(p) - (1 - \sigma)h_{n2}(p)h_{j1}(p). \tag{8.47}$$

Multiplying equation (8.47) through by $H^*(p)^{-(1-\sigma)}$ we obtain

$$\frac{\partial}{\partial p_n}[H^*(p)^{-(1-\sigma)}h_{j2}(p)] = \frac{\partial}{\partial p_j}[H^*(p)^{-(1-\sigma)}h_{n2}(p)]$$

so that

$$H^*(p)^{-(1-\sigma)}h_{n2}(p) = \frac{\partial H^{**}(p)}{\partial p_n}$$

where $H^{**}(p)$ is another function of p. By the summability condition, $\sum_{n=1}^N p_n h_{n2}(p) = 0$, so that $H^{**}(p)$ is homogeneous of degree zero.

Let the indirect utility function of the kth consumer be given by

$$V_k(p, M_k) = \frac{1}{(\sigma - 1)} H^*(p)^{(\sigma-1)} M_k^{-(\sigma-1)} + H^{**}(p) \tag{8.48}$$

where $H^*(p)$ is homogeneous of degree one and $H^{**}(p)$ is homogeneous of degree zero. Application of Roy's Identity then yields

$$\begin{aligned} f_{nk}(p, M_k) &= \frac{-\partial V_k(p, M_k)/\partial p_n}{\partial V_k(p, M_k)/\partial M_k} \\ &= \frac{-\left\{ H^*(p)^{(\sigma-2)} \dfrac{\partial H^*(p)}{\partial p_n} M_k^{-(\sigma-1)} + \dfrac{\partial H^{**}(p)}{\partial p_n} \right\}}{-H^*(p)^{(\sigma-1)} M_k^{-\sigma}} \\ &= \frac{\partial \ln H^*(p)}{\partial p_n} M_k + H^*(p)^{-(\sigma-1)} \frac{\partial H^{**}(p)}{\partial p_n} M_k^{\sigma} \end{aligned}$$

which is precisely the same form as equation (8.44) after taking into account symmetry of the Slutsky substitution matrix.

We next take up the case of equation (8.45).

$$f_{nk}(p, M_k) = h_{n2}^*(p) \ln h_{n1}^*(p) M_k + h_{n2}^*(p) M_k \ln M_k\,, \qquad (k = 1, 2, \ldots, K;\ n = 1, 2, \ldots, N). \tag{8.49}$$

Symmetry of the Slutsky substitution matrix, under the additional assumption of continuous differentiability of the individual demand functions implies

$$h^*_{j2n}(p)[\ln h^*_{j1}(p)M_k + M_k \ln M_k] + \frac{h^*_{j2}(p)h^*_j \ln(p)}{h^*_{j1}(p)} M_k$$
$$+ h^*_{n2}(p)[\ln h^*_{n1}(p)M_k + M_k \ln M_k]h^*_{j2}(p)[\ln h^*_{j1}(p) + \ln M_k + 1]$$
$$= h^*_{n2j}(p)[\ln h^*_{n1}(p)M_k + M_k \ln M_k] + \frac{h^*_{n2}(p)h^*_{nlj}(p)}{h^*_{n1}(p)} M_k$$
$$+ h^*_{j2}(p)[\ln h^*_{j1}(p)M_k + M_k \ln M_k]\, h^*_{n2}(p)[\ln h^*_{n1}(p) + \ln M_k + 1]$$
$$(j, n = 1, 2, \ldots, N)$$

which simplifies into

$$h^*_{j2n}(p)[\ln h^*_{j1}(p) + \ln M_k] + \frac{h^*_{j2}(p)h^*_{j1n}(p)}{h^*_{j1}(p)} + h^*_{n2}(p) \ln h^*_{n1}(p)h^*_{j2}(p)$$
$$= h^*_{n2j}(p)[\ln h^*_{n1}(p) + \ln M_k] + \frac{h^*_{n2}(p)h^*_{nlj}(p)}{h^*_{n1}(p)}$$
$$+ h^*_{j2}(p) \ln h^*_{j1}(p)h^*_{n2}(p). \tag{8.50}$$

Equation (8.50) must hold for all M_k, implying that the coefficients for the $\ln M_k$ term and the constant term must be identically zero. Thus, we have

$$h^*_{j2n}(p) = h^*_{n2j}(p), \qquad (j, n = 1, 2, \ldots, N), \tag{8.51}$$

and

$$h^*_{j2n}(p) \ln h^*_{j1}(p) + \frac{h^*_{j2}(p)h^*_{j1n}(p)}{h^*_{j1}(p)} + h^*_{n2}(p) \ln h^*_{n1}(p)h^*_{j2}(p)$$
$$= h^*_{n2j}(p) \ln h^*_{n1}(p) + \frac{h^*_{n2}(p)h^*_{nlj}(p)}{h^*_{n1}(p)} + h^*_{j2}(p) \ln h^*_{l1}(p)h^*_{n2}(p)$$
$$(j, n = 1, 2, \ldots, N). \tag{8.52}$$

Equation (8.51) implies that

$$h^*_{n2}(p) = \frac{-\partial \ln H^*(p)}{\partial p_n}, \qquad (n = 1, 2, \ldots, N) \tag{8.53}$$

where $-\ln H^*(p)$ is a function of p. By the summability condition

$$\sum_{n=1}^{N} p_n h_{n2}^*(p) = 0 .$$

Thus $-\ln H^*(p)$ and, equivalently, $H^*(p)$ must be homogeneous of degree zero. Zero degree homogeneity of $-\ln H^*(p)$ or, equivalently, $H^*(p)$ is sufficient to imply that $h_{n2}^*(p)$ is homogeneous of degree minus one as required. Given equation (8.53), equation (8.52) may be rewritten as

$$\frac{\partial}{\partial p_n}\left[H^*(p)\frac{\partial \ln H^*(p)}{\partial p_j}\ln h_{j1}^*(p)\right] = \frac{\partial}{\partial p_j}\left[H^*(p)\frac{\partial \ln H^*(p)}{\partial p_n}\ln h_{n1}^*(p)\right] \quad (j, n = 1, 2, \dots, N)$$

so that

$$\frac{\partial H^*(p)}{\partial p_n}\ln h_{n1}^*(p) = \frac{\partial \ln H^{**}(p)}{\partial p_n}, \qquad (n = 1, 2, \dots, N) \tag{8.54}$$

where $\ln H^{**}(p)$ is another function of p.

By the summability condition,

$$\sum_{n=1}^{N} p_n h_{n2}^*(p) \ln h_{n1}^*(p) = 1 .$$

Thus

$$\sum_{n=1}^{N} p_n \left(\frac{-\partial \ln H^*(p)}{\partial p_n}\right) \ln h_{n1}^*(p) = \frac{-1}{H^*(p)} \sum_{n=1}^{N} \frac{\partial \ln H^{**}(p)}{\partial \ln p_n} = 1$$

or

$$H^*(p) = -\sum_{n=1}^{N} \frac{\partial \ln H^{**}(p)}{\partial \ln p_n} . \tag{8.55}$$

Given any $H^{**}(p)$, $H^*(p)$ is uniquely determined by equation (8.55). Since $H^*(p)$ is homogeneous of degree zero, it follows that $\sum_{n=1}^{N} (\partial \ln H^{**}(p)/\partial \ln p_n)$ is a homogeneous function of degree zero, which implies that

$$\sum_{j=1}^{N} \sum_{n=1}^{N} \frac{\partial^2 \ln H^{**}(p)}{\partial \ln p_j \, \partial \ln p_n} = 0 . \tag{8.56}$$

If $H^{**}(p)$ were a homogeneous function, then $H^{*}(p)$ would be constant. This also implies, by equation (8.53), that

$$h_{n2}^{*}(p) = \frac{-\sum_{j=1}^{N} \dfrac{\partial^2 \ln H^{**}(p)}{\partial p_n \partial \ln p_j}}{\sum_{j=1}^{N} \dfrac{\partial \ln H^{**}(p)}{\partial \ln p_j}}, \qquad (n = 1, 2, \dots, N)$$

which is identically zero under homogeneity of $H^{**}(p)$.

Further, by equations (8.53), (8.54) and (8.55)

$$\begin{aligned} h_{n2}^{*}(p) \ln h_{n1}^{*}(p) &= - \frac{\partial \ln H^{*}(p)}{\partial p_n} \cdot \frac{\partial \ln H^{**}(p)}{\partial p_n} \Big/ \frac{\partial H^{*}(p)}{\partial p_n} \\ &= - \frac{1}{H^{*}(p)} \cdot \frac{\partial \ln H^{**}(p)}{\partial p_n} \\ &= \frac{\partial \ln H^{**}(p)}{\partial p_n} \Big/ \sum_{j=1}^{N} \frac{\partial \ln H^{**}(p)}{\partial \ln p_j} \end{aligned} \tag{8.57}$$

and

$$\begin{aligned} \ln h_{n1}^{*}(p) &= \left\{ \frac{\partial \ln H^{**}(p)}{\partial p_n} \Big/ \sum_{j=1}^{N} \frac{\partial \ln H^{**}(p)}{\partial \ln p_j} \right\} \Big/ - \frac{\partial \ln H^{*}(p)}{\partial p_n} \\ &= \left\{ \frac{\partial \ln H^{**}(p)}{\partial p_n} \Big/ \sum_{j=1}^{N} \frac{\partial \ln H^{**}(p)}{\partial \ln p_j} \right\} \\ &\qquad \Big/ \left\{ \sum_{j=1}^{N} \frac{\partial^2 \ln H^{**}(p)}{\partial p_n \partial \ln p_j} \Big/ - \sum_{j=1}^{N} \frac{\partial \ln H^{**}(p)}{\partial \ln p_j} \right\} \\ &= - \frac{\partial \ln H^{**}(p)}{\partial \ln p_n} \Big/ \sum_{j=1}^{N} \frac{\partial^2 \ln H^{**}(p)}{\partial \ln p_n \, \partial \ln p_j} \end{aligned} \tag{8.58}$$

assuming that $h_{n2}^{*}(p) \neq 0$.

But then, $h_{n1}^{*}(p)$ must be homogeneous of degree minus one, which implies and is implied by

$$\sum_{j=1}^{N} \frac{\partial \ln h_{n1}^{*}(p)}{\partial \ln p_j} = -1 .$$

But

$$\sum_{j=1}^{N} \frac{\partial \ln h_{n1}^{*}(p)}{\partial \ln p_j} = \sum_{j=1}^{N} \frac{\partial^2 \ln H^{**}(p)}{\partial \ln p_j \partial \ln p_n} \Big/ - \sum_{j=1}^{N} \frac{\partial^2 \ln H^{**}(p)}{\partial \ln p_n \partial \ln p_j}$$
$$- \frac{\partial \ln H^{**}(p)}{\partial \ln p_n} \cdot \sum_{j=1}^{N} \frac{\partial}{\partial \ln p_j}$$
$$\times \left[- \sum_{j=1}^{N} \frac{\partial^2 \ln H^{**}(p)}{\partial \ln p_n \partial \ln p_j} \right] \Big/ \left[- \sum_{j=1}^{N} \frac{\partial^2 \ln H^{**}(p)}{\partial \ln p_n \partial \ln p_j} \right]^2 . \quad (8.59)$$

The first term is equal to minus one. The second term is identically zero because of equation (8.56). Thus, by Euler's equation, $h_{n1}^{*}(p)$ is homogeneous of degree minus one. We conclude that there are no additional conditions on $H^{**}(p)$ other than that $\sum_{j=1}^{N} \partial \ln H^{**}(p)/\partial \ln p_j$ must be homogeneous of degree zero.

We note that the individual demand function may be rewritten as

$$f_{nk}(p, M_k) = h_{n2}^{*}(p) \ln h_{n1}^{*}(p) M_k + h_{n2}^{*}(p) M_k \ln M_k$$
$$= \frac{\partial \ln H^{**}(p)/\partial p_n}{\sum_{j=1}^{N} \partial \ln H^{**}(p)/\partial \ln p_j} M_k$$
$$- \frac{\sum_{j=1}^{N} \partial^2 \ln H^{**}(p)/\partial p_n \partial \ln p_j}{\sum_{j=1}^{N} \partial \ln H^{**}(p)/\partial \ln p_j} M_k \ln M_k . \quad (8.60)$$

Consider now an indirect utility function of the form

$$V_k(p, M_k) = \ln H^{**}(p/M_k) \quad (8.61)$$

where $\sum_{j=1}^{N} \partial \ln H^{**}(p)/\partial \ln p_j$ is homogeneous of degree zero. The individual demand function may be derived by using Roy's Identity as

$$f_{nk}(p, M_k) = \frac{- \partial V_k(p, M_k)/\partial p_n}{\partial V_k(p, M_k)/\partial M_k}$$
$$= \frac{\partial \ln H^{**}(p/M_k)/\partial (p_n/M_k)}{\sum_{j=1}^{N} \partial \ln H^{**}(p/M_k)/\partial \ln (p_j/M_k)}$$

$$= \left[\frac{\sum_{j=1}^{N} \frac{\partial^2 \ln H^{**}(p/M_k)}{\partial(p_n/M_k)\partial \ln(p_j/M_k)}}{\sum_{j=1}^{N} \frac{\partial \ln H^{**}(p/M_k)}{\partial \ln(p_j/M_k)}} \right] \left[\frac{\frac{\partial \ln H^{**}(p/M_k)}{\partial(p_n/M_k)}}{\sum_{j=1}^{N} \frac{\partial^2 \ln H^{**}(p/M_k)}{\partial(p_n/M_k)\partial \ln(p_j/M_k)}} \right]$$

assuming the $H^{**}(p)$ is not homogeneous. The term in the first square bracket is homogeneous of degree minus one. By equation (8.58) the exponential of the term in the second square bracket with adjustment of sign if necessary is also homogeneous of degree minus one. Thus

$$f_{nk}(p, M_k) =$$

$$\frac{\partial \ln H^{**}(p)/\partial p_n}{\sum_{j=1}^{N} \partial \ln H^{**}(p)/\partial \ln p_j} M_k - \frac{\sum_{j=1}^{N} \partial^2 \ln H^{**}(p)/\partial p_n \partial \ln p_j}{\sum_{j=1}^{N} \partial \ln H^{**}(p)/\partial \ln p_j} M_k \ln M_k$$

which is identical to equation (8.60).

We conclude that any system of individual demand functions which satisfies summability, zero degree homogeneity, nonnegativity and symmetry must be derivable from an indirect utility function of the form in equation (8.61) where $\sum_{j=1}^{N} \partial \ln H^{**}(p)/\partial \ln p_j$ is homogeneous of degree zero.

We wish to characterize the class of functions $H^{**}(p)$ further; the sums of the partial logarithmic derivatives of these functions are zero degree homogeneous but not constant. We thus seek the general solution of the partial differential equation

$$\sum_{n=1}^{N} \frac{\partial \ln H^{**}(\ln p_l, \ln p_2, \ldots, \ln p_N)}{\partial \ln p_n} = f(\ln p_1, \ln p_2, \ldots, \ln p_N) \qquad (8.62)$$

where the function f is nonconstant and zero degree homogeneous in p, that is

$$f(\ln p_1 + \ln \lambda, \ln p_2 + \ln \lambda, \ldots, \ln p_N + \ln \lambda) = f(\ln p_1, \ln p_2, \ldots, \ln p_N).$$

We note, first, that any homogeneous of degree zero function can be rewritten as $f^*(\ln p_2 - \ln p_1, \ln p_3 - \ln p_1, \ldots, \ln p_N - \ln p_1)$. We can transform both the dependent and independent variables by the nonsingular transformation

$$z_1 = \ln p_1$$
$$z_2 = \ln p_2 - \ln p_1$$
$$\ldots$$
$$z_N = \ln p_N - \ln p_1\,,$$
$$G(z_1, z_2, \ldots, z_N) = \ln H^{**}(\ln p_1, \ln p_2, \ldots, \ln p_N)\,.$$

The partial differential equation then becomes

$$\begin{aligned}\sum_{n=1}^{N} \frac{\partial \ln H^{**}(\ln p_1, \ldots, \ln p_N)}{\partial \ln p_n} &= \sum_{n=1}^{N} \sum_{j=1}^{N} \frac{\partial G}{\partial z_j} \cdot \frac{\partial z_j}{\partial \ln p_n} \\ &= \frac{\partial G}{\partial z_1} - \sum_{j=2}^{N} \frac{\partial G}{\partial z_j} + \sum_{n=2}^{N} \frac{\partial G}{\partial z_n} \\ &= f(\ln p_1, \ln p_2, \ldots, \ln p_N) \\ &= f^*(z_2, z_3, \ldots, z_N)\,.\end{aligned}$$

Thus, we have

$$\frac{\partial G}{\partial z_1}(z_1, \ldots, z_N) = f^*(z_2, \ldots, z_N)$$

which can be immediately integrated to yield

$$G(z_1, z_2, \ldots, z_n) = f^*(z_2, z_3, \ldots, z_N) z_1 + f_0^*(z_2, z_3, \ldots, z_N)\,.$$

We conclude that the general solution to the partial differential equation (8.62) is

$$\ln H^{**}(\ln p_1, \ln p_2, \ldots, \ln p_N) = H_1^{**}(p) \ln p_1 + H_2^{**}(p)$$

where $H_1^{**}(p)$ and $H_2^{**}(p)$ are both homogeneous of degree zero. Any function $H^{**}(p)$ satisfying equation (8.62) can be written in this form. We can verify by direct computation that

$$\begin{aligned}\sum_{j=1}^{N} \frac{\partial \ln H^{**}(p)}{\partial \ln p_j} &= \ln p_1 \sum_{j=1}^{N} \frac{\partial H_1^{**}(p)}{\partial \ln p_j} + H_1^{**}(p) + \sum_{j=1}^{N} \frac{\partial H_2^{**}(p)}{\partial \ln p_j} \\ &= H_1^{**}(p)\end{aligned}$$

by zero degree homogeneity of $H_1^{**}(p)$ and $H_2^{**}(p)$. We can therefore rewrite the indirect utility function as

$$V_k(p, M_k) = H_1^{**}(p) \ln (p_1/M_k) + H_2^{**}(p) .$$

We note further that the indirect utility function can be rewritten in a more symmetric form

$$\begin{aligned} V_k(p, M_k) &= - H_1^{**}(p) \ln M_k + H_1^{**}(p) \ln p_1 + H_2^{**}(p) \\ &= - H_1^{**}(p) \ln M_k + \ln \left[p_1^{H_1^{**}(p)} \, e^{H_2^{**}(p)} \right]. \end{aligned}$$

The term in square brackets satisfies

$$(\lambda p_1)^{H_1^{**}(\lambda p)} e^{H_2^{**}(\lambda p)} = \lambda^{H_1^{**}(p)} e^{H_2^{**}(p)}$$

and is homogeneous of degree $H_1^{**}(p)$. Moreover, any such function can be written as $H^*(p)^{H_1^{**}(p)}$, where $H^*(p)$ is homogeneous of degree one. Thus, we can write

$$V_k(p, M_k) = - H_1^{**}(p) \ln M_k + H_1^{**}(p) \ln H^*(p) , \qquad (k = 1, 2, \ldots, K)$$

where $H^*(p)$ is homogeneous of degree one and $H_1^{**}(p)$ is homogeneous of degree zero.

We conclude that the individual demand functions can be written as

$$\begin{aligned} f_{nk} &= \frac{- \partial V_k(p, M_k)/\partial p_n}{\partial V_k(p, M_k)/\partial M_k} \\ &= \frac{[\partial H_1^{**}(p)/\partial p_n] \ln H^*(p) + H_1^{**}(p) \partial \ln H^*(p)/\partial p_n}{H_1^{**}(p)} M_k \\ &\quad - \frac{\dfrac{\partial H_1^{**}(p)}{\partial p_n}}{H_1^{**}(p)} M_k \ln M_k , \qquad (n = 1, 2, \ldots, N; \; k = 1, 2, \ldots K) . \end{aligned}$$

Given the existence of an indirect utility function from which the system of individual demand functions may be derived, nonpositive definiteness of the Slutsky substitution matrix implies and is implied by quasiconvexity of the indirect utility function. It is clear that these curvature conditions will imply restrictions on the aggregate demand functions. Thus, we have proved

Theorem 8.4. Under the assumption that the individual demand functions are continuously differentiable and integrable, a system of aggregate demand functions can be written in the form

$$\sum_{k=1}^{K} f_{nk}(p, M_k) = F_n(p, g_1(M_1, M_2, \ldots, M_K), g_2(M_1, M_2, \ldots, M_K),$$
$$(n = 1, 2, \ldots, N)$$

where the functions $g_l \ (l = 1, 2,)$ and $F_n \ (n = 1, 2, \ldots, N)$ satisfy assumptions (1) through (4) of Theorem 8.1, and the assumption of zero aggregate demand for zero aggregate expenditure, if and only if

(1) $f_{nk}(p, M_k)$

$$= \begin{cases} \dfrac{\partial \ln H^*(p)}{\partial p_n} M_k + H^*(p)^{-(\sigma-1)} \dfrac{\partial H_1^{**}(p)}{\partial p_n} M_k^{\sigma}, \quad (n = 1, 2, \ldots, N) \\ \left[\dfrac{\partial \ln H_1^{**}(p)}{\partial p_n} \ln H^*(p) + \dfrac{\partial \ln H^*(p)}{\partial p_n} \right] M_k \\ - \dfrac{\partial \ln H_1^{**}(p)}{\partial p_n} M_k \ln M_k, \qquad (n = 1, 2, \ldots, N) \end{cases}$$

where $H^*(p)$ is positive and homogeneous of degree one and $H_1^{**}(p)$ is homogeneous of degree zero.

(2) $g_1(M_1, M_2, \ldots, M_K) = \sum_{k=1}^{K} M_k$

$$g_2(M_1, M_2, \ldots, M_K) = \begin{cases} \sum_{k=1}^{K} M_k^{\sigma} & \sigma > 0, \ \sigma \neq 1 \\ \sum_{k=1}^{K} M_k \ln M_k \end{cases}$$

(3) $F_n[p, g_1(M_1, M_2, \ldots, M_K), g_2(M_1, M_2, \ldots, M_K)]$

$$= \begin{cases} \dfrac{\partial \ln H^*(p)}{\partial p_n} \sum_{k=1}^{K} M_k + H^*(p)^{-(\sigma-1)} \dfrac{\partial H_1^{**}(p)}{\partial p_n} \sum_{k=1}^{K} M_k^{\sigma} \\ \left[\dfrac{\partial \ln H_1^{**}(p)}{\partial p_n} \ln H^*(p) + \dfrac{\partial \ln H^*(p)}{\partial p_n} \right] \sum_{k=1}^{K} M_k \\ - \dfrac{\partial \ln H_1^{**}(p)}{\partial p_n} \sum_{k=1}^{K} M_k \ln M_k, \qquad (n = 1, 2, \ldots, N) \end{cases}$$

(4) The indirect utility function is defined as

$$V_k(p, M_k) = \begin{cases} \dfrac{1}{(\sigma - 1)} H^*\left(\dfrac{p}{M_k}\right)^{\sigma-1} + H_1^{**}\left(\dfrac{p}{M_k}\right) \\ H_1^{**}\left(\dfrac{p}{M_k}\right) \ln H^*\left(\dfrac{p}{M_k}\right) \end{cases}.$$

This function is nonincreasing in prices, nondecreasing in expenditures, and quasiconvex in prices and expenditure.

8.2.D Summary and Conclusion

In this section we have considered the implications of the theory of exact aggregation under further restrictions implied by the theory of individual consumer behavior. First, if we assume that systems of individual demand functions are summable, one of the functions of individual expenditure must be individual expenditure itself and one of the index functions for aggregate demand functions must be aggregate expenditure. These conclusions hold for any number of index functions.

We next consider individual demand functions that depend on only two functions of individual expenditure. If we assume that the individual demand functions are summable and homogeneous of degree zero in prices and expenditure, one of the functions must be expenditure itself and the other must be either a power function of expenditure or the product of expenditure and the logarithm of expenditure. The corresponding aggregate demand functions depend on two index functions. One of these functions must be aggregate expenditure and the other must be either a sum of power functions of individual expenditures with the same power for all individuals or the sum of products of expenditure and the logarithm of expenditure for all individuals.

Finally, we consider individual demand functions that are integrable, that is, summable, homogeneous of degree zero in prices and expenditure, and nonnegative, with a Slutsky substitution matrix that is symmetric and nonpositive definite. These conditions imply that the individual demand functions can be derived from an indirect utility function that is nonincreasing in prices, nondecreasing in expenditure, and quasiconvex in prices and expenditure. The indirect utility function for each consumer can be represented in one of two possible ways. In either case the indirect utility function depends on a function that is positive and homogeneous of degree one in ratios of prices to expenditure and another function that is homogeneous of degree zero in these ratios.

Our overall conclusion is that the theory of exact aggregation and the theory of individual consumer behavior imply strong restrictions on systems of individual and aggregate demand functions. These restrictions can be used to simplify the specifications of individual and aggregate models of consumer behavior. Up to this point we have not admitted index functions that depend on both individual attributes and individual expenditures. In the following section we derive the implications of the theory of exact aggregation for individual demand functions that incorporate differences in individual preferences.

8.3 Exact Aggregation with Differences in Individual Preferences

In section 8.2 we have shown that exact aggregation and integrability impose restrictions on the dependence of demand functions on individual expenditures. However, we have limited consideration to consumers with identical preferences. In this section we derive the implications of the theory of exact aggregation for index functions that depend on individual attributes and expenditures, so that preferences may differ among individuals. We begin by stating a theorem that if an index function incorporating individual attributes has a nontrivial effect on aggregate demand, the index function must depend nontrivially on individual expenditures.

Theorem 8.5. Under the assumptions (1) through (4) of Theorem 8.1 and the assumptions of zero aggregate demand for zero aggregate expenditure and nonnegativity of the individual demand functions, an aggregate demand function can be written in the form

$$\begin{aligned}\sum_{k=1}^{K} f_k(p, M_k, A_k) = F[&p, g_1(M_1, M_2, \ldots, M_K, A_1, A_2, \ldots, A_K),\\ &g_2(M_1, M_2, \ldots, M_K, A_1, A_2, \ldots, A_K), \ldots,\\ &g_L(M_1, M_2, \ldots, M_K, A_1, A_2, \ldots, A_K),\\ &g_{L^*+1}(A_1, A_2, \ldots, A_K), \ldots, g_L(A_1, A_2, \ldots, A_K)]\end{aligned}$$

so that the last $(L - L^*)$ index functions $g_l(l = 1, 2, \ldots, L)$ do not depend on individual expenditures if and only if

$$(1)\quad f_k(p, M_k, A_k) = \sum_{l=1}^{L^*} h_l(p) g_l^*(M_k, A_k)\,, \qquad (k = 1, 2, \ldots, K)$$

$$(2)\quad F[p, g_1(M_1, M_2, \ldots, M_K, A_1, A_2, \ldots, A_K), g_2(M_1, M_2, \ldots, M_K, A_1, A_2, \ldots, A_K), \ldots, g_L(A_1, A_2, \ldots, A_K)] = \sum_{l=1}^{L^*} h_l(p) \sum_{k=1}^{K} g_l^*(M_k, A_k)$$

where $g_l^*(0, A_k) = 0$, $(l = 1, 2, \ldots, L^*)$ and the functions h_l and $g_l^*(M_k, A_k)$, $(l = 1, 2, \ldots, L^*)$ are linearly independent functions.

In other words, an index function with nontrivial effects on aggregate demand must depend on individual expenditures. For example, an index function which depends only on the age distribution is not an admissible index function under our assumptions. In order for a change in the distribution of individual attributes to affect aggregate demand, it must affect the distribution of individual expenditures.

8.3.A Two Index Functions

We now specialize to the case of two index functions that depend on individual expenditures and attributes. We consider the restrictions implied by utility maximization by individual consumers. By Theorem 8.1, the individual demand functions take the form

$$f_{nk}(p, M_k, A_k) = h_{n1}(p) g_1^{**}(M_k, A_k) + h_{n2}(p) g_2^{**}(M_k, A_k) \qquad (n = 1, 2, \ldots, N;\ k = 1, 2, \ldots, K)$$

where $g_l^{**}(0, A_k) = 0$, $(l = 1, 2)$.

Under the additional assumption of summability the individual demand functions must sum to M_k, so that

$$\sum_{n=1}^{N} p_n h_{n1}(p) g_1^{**}(M_k, A_k) + \sum_{n=1}^{N} p_n h_{n2}(p) g_2^{**}(M_k, A_k) = M_k\,.$$

As in section 8.2 we can show that

$$\sum_{n=1}^{N} p_n h_{n1}(p) = \bar{h}_1^*, \qquad \sum_{n=1}^{N} p_n h_{n2}(p) = \bar{h}_2^*\,.$$

This implies that

$$g_1^{**}(M_k, A_k) = \frac{M_k}{\bar{h}_1^*} - \frac{\bar{h}_2^*}{\bar{h}_1^*} g_2^{**}(M_k, A_k)$$

so that

$$f_{nk}(p, M_k, A_k) = h_{n1}^*(p)M_k + h_{n2}^*(p)g_2^{**}(M_k, A_k)$$
$$\sum_{n=1}^{N} p_n h_{n1}^*(p) = 1 \; ; \qquad \sum_{n=1}^{N} p_n h_{n2}^*(p) = 0 \, .$$

Under the additional assumption of zero degree homogeneity, we have

$$h_{n1}^*(\lambda p)\lambda M_k + h_{n2}^*(\lambda p)g_2^{**}(\lambda M_k, A_k) = h_{n1}^*(p)M_k + h_{n2}^*(p)g_2^{**}(M_k, A_k)\, .$$

The implications of zero degree homogeneity can be analyzed by using an argument strictly analogous to that presented in section 8.2.B.

First, we show, as in equation (8.26), that

$$h_2(\lambda p) = \lambda^{-\sigma} h_2(p)\, .$$

Then, from equation (8.28), we have

$$\lambda^{-\sigma+1} \frac{g_2^{**}(\lambda M_k, A_k)}{\lambda M_k} - \frac{g_2^{**}(M_k, A_k)}{M_k} = l(\lambda)\, . \tag{8.63}$$

Equation (8.63) must hold for all A_k and in particular for $A_k = 0$ or, equivalently, some reference level. Thus

$$\lambda^{-\sigma+1}\left[\frac{g_2^{**}(\lambda M_k, A_k)}{\lambda M_k} - \frac{g_2^{**}(\lambda M_k, 0)}{\lambda M_k}\right] = \frac{g_2^{**}(M_k, A_k)}{M_k} - \frac{g_2^{**}(M_k, 0)}{M_k}\, .$$

We conclude that

$$\frac{g_2^{**}(M_k, A_k)}{M_k} - \frac{g_2^{**}(M_k, 0)}{M_k}$$

is homogeneous of degree $\sigma - 1$ in M_k for all values of A_k. Thus, $g_2^{**}(M_k, A_k)$ must have the form

$$g_2^{**}(M_k, A_k) = g_2^{**}(M_k, 0) + l^*(A_k)M_k^{\sigma}\, .$$

Substituting the function $g_2^{**}(M_k, A_k)$ into equation (8.63), we obtain

$$\lambda^{-\sigma+1}\left[\frac{g_2^{**}(\lambda M_k,0)}{\lambda M_k}+\frac{l^*(A_k)\lambda^\sigma M_k^\sigma}{\lambda M_k}\right]-\left[\frac{g_2^{**}(M_k,0)}{M_k}+\frac{l^*(A_k)M_k^\sigma}{M_k}\right]=l(\lambda)$$

which reduces to

$$\lambda^{-\sigma+1}\,\frac{g_2^{**}(\lambda M_k,0)}{\lambda M_k}-\frac{g_2^{**}(M_k,0)}{M_k}=l(\lambda)\,. \tag{8.64}$$

Equation (8.64) has the same form as equation (8.28), with solution given by

$$g_2^{**}(M_k,0)=\begin{cases}D_1M_k^\sigma+D_2M_k\,, & \sigma\neq 1,\ \sigma>0\\ D_1M_k\ln M_k+D_2M_k & \sigma=1\end{cases}$$

where D_1 and D_2 are constants. This implies

$$g_2^{**}(M_k,A_k)=\begin{cases}[D_1+l^*(A_k)]\,M_k^\sigma+D_2M_k, & \sigma\neq 1,\ \sigma>0\\ D_1M_k\ln M_k+[D_2+l^*(A_k)]M_k & \sigma=1\end{cases}.$$

We conclude that under the additional assumption of zero degree homogeneity, the individual demand functions must take the form either

$$f_{nk}(p,M_k,A_k)=h_{n1}^*(p)M_k+h_{n2}^*(p)l^{**}(A_k)M_k^\sigma$$
$$\sum_{n=1}^N p_nh_{n1}^*(p)=1\,;\qquad \sum_{n=1}^N p_nh_{n2}^*(p)=0 \tag{8.65}$$

or

$$f_{nk}(p,M_k,A_k)=h_{n1}^*(p)M_k+h_{n2}^*(p)[l^{**}(A_k)M_k+M_k\ln M_k]$$
$$\sum_{n=1}^N p_nh_{n1}^*(p)=1\,;\qquad \sum_{n=1}^N p_nh_{n2}^*(p)=0\,. \tag{8.66}$$

The aggregate demand functions are given by either

$$\begin{aligned}&F_n[p,g_1(M_1,M_2,\ldots,M_K,A_1,A_2,\ldots,A_K),\\&\qquad g_2(M_1,M_2,\ldots,M_K\,,A_1,A_2,\ldots,A_K)]\\&\qquad =h_{n1}^*(p)\sum_{k=1}^K M_k+h_{n2}^*(p)\sum_{k=1}^K l^{**}(A_k)M_k^\sigma\,,\\&\qquad\qquad\qquad\qquad (n=1,2,\ldots,N)\end{aligned}$$

or

$$F_n[p, g_1(M_1, M_2, \ldots, M_K, A_1, A_2, \ldots, A_K),$$
$$g_2(M_1, M_2, \ldots, M_K, A_1, A_2, \ldots, A_K)]$$
$$= h^*_{n1}(p) \sum_{k=1}^{K} M_k + h^*_{n2}(p) \sum_{k=1}^{K} [l^{**}(A_k)M_k + M_k \ln M_k], \quad (n = 1, 2, \ldots, N)$$

where the appropriate homogeneity conditions must be satisfied by the functions $h^*_{nl}(p)$, $(l = 1, 2)$.

Finally, the consider the implications of symmetry of the Slutsky substitution matrix of the system of individual demand functions. Using the results of section 8.2.C, symmetry implies for equation (8.65) that the individual demand functions take the form

$$f_{nk}(p, M_k, A_k) = \frac{\partial \ln H^*(p)}{\partial p_n} M_k + H^*(p)^{-(\sigma-1)} \frac{\partial H_1^{**}(p)}{\partial p_n} l^{**}(A_k)M_k^{\sigma}$$

where $H^*(p)$ is homogeneous of degree one and $H_1^{**}(p)$ is homogeneous of degree zero.

For equation (8.66), we can write the individual demand functions as

$$f_{nk}(p, M_k, A_k) = [h^*_{n1}(p) + h^*_{n2}(p)l^{**}(0)]M_k + h^*_{n2}(p)M_k \ln M_k + h^*_{n2}(p)[l^{**}(A_k) - l^{**}(0)]M_k .$$

Let $A_k = 0$. By the results of section 8.2.C, symmetry implies that the individual demand functions take the form

$$f_{nk}(p, M_k, 0) = \left[\frac{\partial \ln H_1^{**}(p)}{\partial p_n} \ln H^*(p) + \frac{\partial \ln H^*(p)}{\partial p_n}\right] M_k - \frac{\partial \ln H_1^{**}(p)}{\partial p_n} M_k \ln M_k, \quad (n = 1, 2, \ldots, N)$$

where $H^*(p)$ is homogeneous of degree one and $H_1^{**}(p)$ is homogeneous of degree zero. This implies that

$$f_{nk}(p, M_k, A_k) = \left[\frac{\partial \ln H_1^{**}(p)}{\partial p_n} \ln H^*(p) + \frac{\partial \ln H^*(p)}{\partial p_n}\right] M_k$$
$$- \frac{\partial \ln H_1^{**}(p)}{\partial p_n} M_k \ln M_k + \frac{\partial \ln H_1^{**}(p)}{\partial p_n} l^{***}(A_k) M_k$$
$$(n = 1, 2, \ldots, N; \;\; k = 1, 2, \ldots, K).$$

For both forms of the individual demand functions the total expenditure effect and the attribute effect on the expenditure shares are related; for the power form

$$\frac{\partial}{\partial M_k} \cdot \frac{p_n f_{nk}(p, M_k, A_k)}{M_k} = (\sigma - 1) H^*(p)^{-(\sigma-1)} \frac{\partial H_1^{**}(p)}{\partial p_n} l^{**}(A_k) A_k^{(\sigma-2)} p_n$$

and

$$\frac{\partial}{\partial l^{**}(A_k)} \cdot \frac{p_n f_{nk}(p, M_k, A_k)}{M_k} = H^*(p)^{-(\sigma-1)} \frac{\partial H_1^{**}(p)}{\partial p_n} M_k^{(\sigma-1)} p_n$$

so that

$$\frac{\dfrac{\partial}{\partial M_k} \cdot \dfrac{p_n f_{nk}(p, M_k, A_k)}{M_k}}{\dfrac{\partial}{\partial l^{**}(A_k)} \cdot \dfrac{p_n f_{nk}(p, M_k, A_k)}{M_k}} = (\sigma - 1) M_k^{-1}, \qquad (n = 1, 2, \ldots, N)$$

for the logarithmic form

$$\frac{\partial}{\partial M_k} \cdot \frac{p_n f_{nk}(p, M_k, A_k)}{M_k} = - \frac{\partial \ln H_1^{**}(p)}{\partial p_n} M_k^{-1} p_n$$

and

$$\frac{\partial}{\partial l^{***}(A_k)} \cdot \frac{p_n f_{nk}(p, M_k, A_k)}{M_k} = \frac{\partial \ln H_1^{**}(p)}{\partial p_n} p_n$$

so that

$$\frac{\dfrac{\partial}{\partial M_k} \cdot \dfrac{p_n f_{nk}(p, M_k, A_k)}{M_k}}{\dfrac{\partial}{\partial l^{***}(A_k)} \cdot \dfrac{p_n f_{nk}(p, M_k, A_k)}{M_k}} = - M_k^{-1}, \qquad (n = 1, 2, \ldots, N).$$

Restrictions on the expenditure and attribute effects limit the degree of generality of the systems of individual demand functions with different attributes. If the expenditure term enters as a power function and if $l^{**}(A_k)$ is equal to zero for some A_k, the Engel curves for all individual consumers with attributes equal to A_k will be linear and homogeneous in expenditure for all commodities. Empirical evidence on Engel curves is inconsistent with this restriction. Note that this restriction does not apply if the expenditure term enters as expenditure times the natural logarithm of expenditure. We conclude that the case of two index functions does not provide an adequate representation of individual and aggregate demand functions when there are consumers with different expenditures and attributes. We therefore consider the case of three index functions in order to obtain a more satisfactory representation.

8.3.B Three Index Functions

An aggregate demand function with two index functions of individual expenditures alone and one index function of individual expenditures and attributes takes the form

$$\sum_{k=1}^{K} f_k(p, M_k, A_k) = F[p, g_1(M_1 M_2, \ldots, M_K), g_2(M_1, M_2, \ldots, M_K),$$
$$g_3(M_1, M_2, \ldots, M_K, A_1, A_{2,\ldots,} A_K)]$$

where we can assume without loss of generality that

$$g_1(0, 0, \ldots, 0) = 0$$

$$g_2(0, 0, \ldots, 0) = 0$$

$$g_3(0, 0, \ldots, 0;\ \ A_1, A_2, \ldots, A_K) = 0$$

and

$$g_3(M_1, M_2, \ldots, M_K;\ \ 0, 0, \ldots, 0) = 0\,.$$

This aggregate demand function implies that the individual demand functions have the form

$$f_{nk}(p, M_k, A_k) = h_{n1}(p)g_1^*(M_k) + h_{n2}(p)g_2^*(M_k) + h_{n3}(p)g_3^*(M_k, A_k) + C_{nk}(p)$$
$$(n = 1, 2, \ldots, N;\ k = 1, 2, \ldots, K)$$

where without loss of generality, $g_1^*(0) = g_2^*(0) = g_3^*(0, A_k) = g_3^*(M_k, 0) = 0$.

Under the assumption of zero aggregate demand for zero aggregate expenditure and nonnegativity

$$C_{nk}(p) = 0\,, \quad (n = 1, 2, \ldots, N;\ k = 1, , 2, \ldots, K)\,.$$

Under the assumption of summability the individual demand functions must sum to M_k, so that

$$f_{nk}(p, M_k, A_k) = h_{n1}(p)M_k + h_{n2}(p)g_2^*(M_k) + h_{n3}(p)g_3^*(M_k, A_k)$$

where

$$\sum_{n=1}^{N} p_n h_{n1}(p) = 1\,; \quad \sum_{n=1}^{N} p_n h_{nl}(p) = 0\,; \quad (l = 2, 3)\,.$$

Under the additional assumption of zero degree homogeneity, we have

$$h_{n1}(\lambda p)\lambda M_k + h_{n2}(\lambda p)g_2^*(\lambda M_k) + h_{n3}(\lambda p)g_3^*(\lambda M_k, A_k)$$
$$= h_{n1}(p)M_k + h_{n2}(p)g_2^*(M_k) + h_{n3}(p)g_3^*(M_k, A_k)\,. \qquad (8.67)$$

Letting $A_k = 0$, equation (8.67) reduces to equation (8.21) with the solutions given by Theorem 8.4. Subtracting both sides of equation (8.21) from equation (8.67) we obtain

$$h_{n3}(\lambda p)g_3^*(\lambda M_k, A_k) = h_{n3}(p)g_3^*(M_k, A_k)$$

or

$$\frac{h_{n3}(\lambda p)}{h_{n3}(p)} = l(\lambda)\,.$$

In other words, $h_{n3}(p)$ must be a homogeneous of degree $-\sigma_2$ function. It follows that $g_3^*(M_k, A_k)$ must be homogeneous of degree σ_2 in M_k, and $g_3^*(0, A_k) = 0$ implies that $\sigma_2 \geqq 0$. Hence

$$g_3^*(M_k, A_k) = l^*(A_k)M_k^{\sigma_2}\,.$$

The individual demand functions take the form

$$f_{nk}(p, M_k, A_k) = \begin{cases} h_{n1}(p)M_k + h_{n2}(p)M_k^{\sigma_1} + h_{n3}(p)l^*(A_k)M_k^{\sigma_2} \\ \qquad (k = 1, 2, \ldots, K;\ n = 1, 2, \ldots, N) \\ h^*_{n2}(p) \ln h^*_{n1}(p)M_k + h^*_{n2}(p)M_k \ln M_k + h^*_{n3}(p)l^*(A_k)M_k^{\sigma_2} \\ \qquad (k = 1, 2, \ldots, K; n = 1, 2, \ldots, N) \end{cases}$$

where $h_{n1}(p)$, $h^*_{n2}(p)$ and $h^*_{n1}(p)$ are homogeneous of degree -1, $h_{n2}(p)$ is homogeneous of degree $-\sigma_1$. The functions $h_{n3}(p)$ and $h^*_{n3}(p)$ are homogeneous of degree $-\sigma_2$, $\sigma_1, \sigma_2 \geqq 0$, $\sigma_1 \neq 1$ and $l^*(0) = 0$.

The assumption of symmetry implies additional restrictions on the form of the individual demand functions. First, let $A_k = 0$, then the results of section 8.2.D apply. Now supppose A_k is arbitrary. Symmetry of the Slutsky substitution matrix, under the additional assumption of once continuous differentiability of the individual demand functions, implies for the first case considered above

$$\begin{aligned} h_{j1n}(p)M_k &+ h_{j2n}(p)M_k^{\sigma_1} + h_{j3n}(p)l^*(A_k)M_k^{\sigma_2} \\ &+ [h_{n1}(p)M_k + h_{n2}(p)M_k^{\sigma_1} + h_{n3}(p)l^*(A_k)M_k^{\sigma_2}] \\ &\times [h_{j1}(p) + \sigma_1 h_{j2}(p)M_k^{\sigma_1-1} + \sigma_2 h_{j3}(p)l^*(A_k)M_k^{\sigma_2-1}] \\ = h_{n1j}(p)M_k &+ h_{n2j}(p)M_k^{\sigma_1} + h_{n3j}(p)l^*(A_k)M_k^{\sigma_2} \\ &+ [h_{j1}(p)M_k + h_{j2}(p)M_k^{\sigma_1} + h_{j3}(p)l^*(A_k)M_k^{\sigma_2}] \\ &\times [h_{n1}(p) + \sigma_1 h_{n2}(p)M_k^{\sigma_1-1} + \sigma_2 h_{n3}(p)l^*(A_k)M_k^{\sigma_2-1}] \end{aligned}$$

which simplifies into

$$\begin{aligned} h_{j1n}(p)M_k &+ h_{j2n}(p)M_k^{\sigma_1} + h_{j3n}(p)l^*(A_k)M_k^{\sigma_2} \\ &+ \sigma_1 h_{n1}(p)h_{j2}(p)M_k^{\sigma_1} + \sigma_2 h_{n1}(p)h_{j3}(p)l^*(A_k)M_k^{\sigma_2} \\ &+ h_{n2}(p)h_{j1}(p)M_k^{\sigma_1} + \sigma_2 h_{n2}(p)h_{j3}(p)l^*(A_k)M_k^{\sigma_1+\sigma_2-1} \\ &+ h_{n3}(p)h_{j1}(p)l^*(A_k)M_k^{\sigma_2} + \sigma_1 h_{n3}(p)h_{j2}(p)l^*(A_k)M_k^{\sigma_1+\sigma_2-1} \\ = h_{n1j}(p)M_k &+ h_{n2j}(p)M_k^{\sigma_1} + h_{n3j}(p)l^*(A_k)M_k^{\sigma_2} \\ &+ \sigma_1 h_{j1}(p)h_{n2}(p)M_k^{\sigma_1} + \sigma_2 h_{j1}(p)h_{n3}(p)l^*(A_k)M_k^{\sigma_2} \\ &+ h_{j2}(p)h_{n1}(p)M_k^{\sigma_1} + \sigma_2 h_{j2}(p)h_{n3}(p)l^*(A_k)M_k^{\sigma_1+\sigma_2-1} \\ &+ h_{j3}(p)h_{n1}(p)l^*(A_k)M_k^{\sigma_2} + \sigma_1 h_{j3}(p)h_{n2}(p)l^*(A_k)M_k^{\sigma_1+\sigma_2-1}. \end{aligned}$$

By setting $A_k = 0$, the above equation reduces to equation (8.46), which has been solved. By subtracting equation (8.46) from the above equation we obtain

$$\begin{aligned}[(\sigma_2 - 1)h_{j3}(p)h_{n1}(p) + h_{j3n}(p)]l * (A_k)M_k^{\sigma_2} \\ + (\sigma_2 - \sigma_1)h_{j3}(p)h_{n2}(p)l^*(A_k)M_k^{\sigma_1 + \sigma_2 - 1} \\ = [(\sigma_2 - 1)h_{n3}(p)h_{j1}(p) + h_{n3j}(p)]l^*(A_k)M_k^{\sigma_2} \\ + (\sigma_2 - \sigma_1)h_{n3}(p)h_{j2}(p)l^*(A_k)M_k^{\sigma_1 + \sigma_2 - 1}.\end{aligned} \tag{8.68}$$

Equation (8.68) must hold identically in M_k. Note that $\sigma_2 \neq \sigma_1 + \sigma_2 - 1$, for otherwise $\sigma_1 = 1$, which is ruled out. Thus

$$(\sigma_2 - 1)h_{j3}(p)h_{n1}(p) + h_{j3n}(p) = (\sigma_2 - 1)h_{n3}(p)h_{j1}(p) + h_{n3j}(p) \tag{8.69}$$

and

$$(\sigma_2 - \sigma_1)h_{j3}(p)h_{n2}(p) = (\sigma_2 - \sigma_1)h_{n3}(p)h_{j2}(p). \tag{8.70}$$

Now from section 8.2.C

$$h_{n1}(p) = \frac{\partial \ln H^*(p)}{\partial p_n}$$

so that equation (8.69) becomes

$$\frac{\partial}{\partial p_n} H^*(p)^{\sigma_2 - 1} h_{j3}(p) = \frac{\partial}{\partial p_j} H^*(p)^{\sigma_2 - 1} h_{n3}(p)$$

which implies that

$$H^*(p)^{\sigma_2 - 1} h_{n3}(p) = \frac{\partial}{\partial p_n} H^{***}(p). \tag{8.71}$$

By summability

$$\sum_{n=1}^{N} p_n h_{n3}(p) = \sum_{n=1}^{N} \frac{\partial H^{***}(p)}{\partial \ln p_n} H^*(p)^{1-\sigma_2} = 0.$$

Thus, $H^{***}(p)$ is homogeneous of degree zero in p.

If $\sigma_2 - \sigma_1 = 0$, equation (8.70) is trivially satisfied, so that the individual demand functions must take the form

$$f_{nk}(p, M_k, A_k) = \frac{\partial \ln H^*(p)}{\partial p_n} M_k + H^*(p)^{-(\sigma_1 - 1)} \frac{\partial H^{**}(p)}{\partial p_n} M_k^{\sigma_1} + H^*(p)^{-(\sigma_1-1)} \frac{\partial H^{***}(p)}{\partial p_n} l^*(A_k) M_k^{\sigma_1}$$

$$(n = 1, 2, \ldots, N;\ k = 1, 2, \ldots, K) \tag{8.72}$$

where $H^*(p)$ is homogeneous of degree one, $H^{**}(p)$ and $H^{***}(p)$ are homogeneous of degree zero.

Suppose $\sigma_2 - \sigma_1 \neq 0$. Then by making use of the fact from section 8.2.C that

$$h_{n2}(p) = \frac{\partial H^{**}(p)}{\partial p_n} \cdot H^*(p)^{-(\sigma_1-1)}$$

equation (8.70) becomes

$$h_{j3}(p) \frac{\partial H^{**}(p)}{\partial p_n} = h_{n3}(p) \frac{\partial H^{**}(p)}{\partial p_j}$$

which by using equation (8.71) leads to

$$\frac{\partial H^{**}(p)}{\partial p_n} \bigg/ \frac{\partial H^{***}(p)}{\partial p_n} = \frac{\partial H^{**}(p)}{\partial p_j} \bigg/ \frac{\partial H^{***}(p)}{\partial p_j}, \qquad (n, j = 1, 2, \ldots, N).$$

This implies that

$$H^{***}(p) = t[H^{**}(p)]$$

where $t(\cdot)$ is a function of a single variable.

We conclude that the individual demand functions must take the form

$$f_{nk}(p, M_k, A_k) = \frac{\partial \ln H^*(p)}{\partial p_n} M_k + H^*(p)^{-(\sigma_1-1)} \frac{\partial H^{**}(p)}{\partial p_n} M_k^{\sigma_1} + H^*(p)^{-(\sigma_2-1)} \frac{\partial}{\partial p_n} t(H^{**}(p)) l^*(A_k) M_k^{\sigma_2}$$

$$(n = 1, 2, \ldots, N;\ k = 1, 2, \ldots, K) \tag{8.73}$$

where $H^*(p)$ is homogeneous of degree one, $H^{**}(p)$ is homogeneous of degree zero and $t(\cdot)$ is a function of a single variable. This form implies that

$$\frac{h_{n2}(p)}{h_{n3}(p)} = \frac{H^*(p)^{-(\sigma_1-\sigma_2)}}{t'[H^{**}(p)]} \qquad (n = 1, 2, \ldots N).$$

In other words, the ratio of the nonlinear expenditure effect to the attribute expenditure effect is the same for all commodities.

Symmetry of the Slutsky substitution matrix implies for the second case considered above

$$\begin{aligned} & h^*_{j2n}(p)[\ln h^*_{j1}(p)M_k + M_k \ln M_k] + \frac{h^*_{j2}(p)h^*_{j1n}(p)}{h^*_{j1}(p)} \cdot M_k \\ &\quad + h^*_{j3n}(p)l^*(A_k)M_k^{\sigma_2} + \{h^*_{n2}(p)[\ln h^*_{n1}(p)M_k + M_k \ln M_k] \\ &\quad + h^*_{n3}(p)l^*(A_k)M_k^{\sigma_2}\}\{h^*_{j2}(p)[\ln h^*_{j1}(p) + \ln M_k + 1] \\ &\quad + \sigma_2 h^*_{j3}(p)l^*(A_k)M_k^{\sigma_2-1}\} \\ &= h^*_{n2j}(p)[\ln h^*_{n1}(p)M_k + M_k \ln M_k] + \frac{h^*_{n2}(p)h^*_{n1j}(p)}{h^*_{n1}(p)} \cdot M_k \\ &\quad + h^*_{n3j}(p)l^*(A_k)M_k^{\sigma_2} + \{h^*_{j2}(p)[\ln h^*_{j1}(p)M_k \\ &\quad + M_k \ln M_k] + h^*_{j3}(p)l^*(A_k)M_k^{\sigma_2}\}\{h^*_{n2}(p)[\ln h^*_{n1}(p) \\ &\quad + \ln M_k + 1] + \sigma_2 h^*_{n3}(p)l^*(A_k)M_k^{\sigma_2-1}\}. \qquad (8.74) \end{aligned}$$

By setting $A_k = 0$ the equation given above reduces to equation (8.50), which has been solved. Subtracting M_k times equation (8.50) from equation (8.74), we obtain

$$\begin{aligned} & h^*_{j3n}(p)l^*(A_k)M_k^{\sigma_2} + (\sigma_2 - 1)h^*_{j3}(p)l^*(A_k)h^*_{n2}(p)M_k^{\sigma_2}[\ln h^*_{n1}(p) + \ln M_k] \\ &\quad - h^*_{j3}(p)h^*_{n2}(p)l^*(A_k)M_k^{\sigma_2} \\ &= h^*_{n3j}(p)l^*(A_k)M_k^{\sigma_2} + (\sigma_2 - 1)h^*_{n3}(p)l^*(A_k)h^*_{j2}(p)M_k^{\sigma_2}[\ln h^*_{j1}(p) + \ln M_k] \\ &\quad - h^*_{n3}(p)h^*_{j2}(p)l^*(A_k)M_k^{\sigma_2}. \end{aligned}$$

To hold identically, this implies for $\sigma_2 = 1$

$$h^*_{j3n}(p) - h^*_{j3}(p)h^*_{n2}(p) = h^*_{n3j}(p) - h^*_{n3}(p)h^*_{j2}(p)$$

which, by making use of equation (8.53), can be written as

$$\frac{\partial}{\partial p_n} h^*_{j3}(p)\, H^*_1(p) = \frac{\partial}{\partial p_j} h^*_{n3}(p)H^*_1(p)$$

where $H^*_1(p)$ is homogenous of degree zero, so that

$$h_{n3}^*(p)H_1^*(p) = \frac{\partial}{\partial p_n} H^{***}(p) .$$

By summability, $\sum_{n=1}^{N} p_n h_{n3}^*(p) = 0$, which implies that $H^{***}(p)$ is homogeneous of degree zero. We conclude that

$$h_{n3}^*(p) = \frac{\partial H^{***}(p)}{\partial p_n} \bigg/ H_1^*(p) ,$$

which is homogeneous of degree minus one as required.

For $\sigma_2 \neq 1$, symmetry implies

$$h_{j3}^*(p)h_{n2}^*(p) = h_{n3}^*(p)h_{j2}^*(p) , \tag{8.75}$$

and

$$\begin{aligned} &h_{j3n}^*(p) + (\sigma_2 - 1)h_{j3}^*(p)h_{n2}^*(p) \ln h_{n1}^*(p) \\ &\quad = h_{n3j}^*(p) + (\sigma_2 - 1)h_{n3}^*(p)h_{j2}^*(p) \ln h_{j1}^*(p) . \end{aligned} \tag{8.76}$$

From equation (8.53)

$$h_{n2}^*(p) = \frac{\partial H_1^*(p)}{\partial p_n} .$$

From equation (8.75)

$$h_{n3}^*(p) = \frac{\partial t[H_1^*(p)]}{\partial p_n}$$

where $t(\cdot)$ is a function of a single variable.

By summability,

$$\sum_{n=1}^{N} p_n h_{n3}^*(p) = t'[H_1^*(p)] \sum_{n=1}^{N} p_n \frac{\partial H_1^*(p)}{\partial p_n} = 0$$

which is identically satisfied by zero degree homogeneity of $H_1^*(p)$. Moreover, $h_{n3}^*(p)$ is homogeneous of degree $-\sigma_2$ which implies that $t[H_1^*(p)] + D$, D a constant, must be homogeneous of degree $-\sigma_2 + 1$ so that

$$t'[H_1^*(p)] \sum_{n=1}^{N} p_n \frac{\partial H_1^*(p)}{\partial p_n} = (-\sigma_2 + 1)(t + D) .$$

But the left-hand-side is equal to zero. Hence the right-hand-side must also equal zero. Since $h_{n3}^{*}(p) \neq 0$, for all n and all p, $\sigma_2 = 1$.

We conclude that the individual demand functions must take the form

$$f_{nk}(p, M_k, A_k) = \left[\frac{\partial \ln H_1^{**}(p)}{\partial p_n} \ln H^{*}(p) + \frac{\partial \ln H^{*}(p)}{\partial p_n} \right] M_k$$
$$- \frac{\partial \ln H_1^{**}(p)}{\partial p_n} M_k \ln M_k + \left[\frac{\partial H_2^{**}(p)}{\partial p_n} \bigg/ H_1^{**}(p) \right] l^{*}(A_k) M_k ,$$
$$(n = 1, 2, \ldots N;\ k = 1, 2, \ldots K) \tag{8.77}$$

where $H^{*}(p)$ is homogeneous of degree one, the functions $H_l^{**}(p)$ $(l = 1, 2)$ are homogeneous of degree zero, and $l^{*}(0) = 0$. We note that in this case the ratio of the nonlinear expenditure effect to the attribute expenditure effect need not be the same for all commodities. Thus, for the second of the two cases considered above, the only admissible mixed index of expenditures and attributes is of the form

$$\sum_{k=1}^{K} g_3^{*}(M_k, A_k) = \sum_{k=1}^{K} l^{*}(A_k) M_k .$$

The individual demand function of the form in equation (8.77) may be derived from an indirect utility function of the form

$$V_k(p, M_k, A_k) = H_1^{**}(p) \ln H^{*}(p/M_k)$$
$$+ H_2^{**}(p) l^{*}(A_k), \quad (k = 1, 2, \ldots, K) \tag{8.78}$$

where $H^{*}(p)$ is homogeneous of degree one and the functions $H_t^{**}(p)$ $(l = 1, 2)$ are homogeneous of degree zero and $l^{*}(0) = 0$.

Equations (8.72) and (8.77) are superior to equation (8.73) in that they allow the attribute expenditure effect to be different from the expenditure effect for different commodities. By contrast equation (8.73) requires that the two effects be proportional. We therefore remove equation (8.73) from further consideration as the basis for the selection of a functional form for our empirical application.

8.3.D Summary and Conclusion

In this section we have considered the implications of the theory of exact aggregation under restrictions implied by the theory of individual consumer behavior. In order to allow for differences in preferences among individuals we have admitted index functions that depend on individual attributes as well as individual expenditures. We first observe that if an index function has a nontrivial effect on aggregate demand functions, the index function must depend on individual expenditures and not on individual attributes alone. This conclusion holds for any number of index functions.

We next consider individual demand functions that depend on only two functions of individual attributes and expenditure. If we assume that the individual demand functions are summable, one of the functions must depend on individual expenditure alone and must be individual expenditure itself. As before, one of the index functions for aggregate demand functions must be aggregate expenditure. These conclusions hold for index functions that depend on both individual attributes and expenditures as well as index functions that depend on individual expenditures alone.

If we assume that the individual demand functions are summable and homogeneous of degree zero in prices and expenditure, one of the two functions of individual expenditure and attributes must be expenditure itself. The other function must take one of two possible forms. First, the function may be equal to the product of a function of individual attributes alone and a power function of expenditure. Second, the function may be the product of expenditure and the sum of a function of the individual attributes alone and the logarithm of expenditure. The aggregate demand functions depend on two index functions—aggregate expenditure and the sum of the corresponding functions of individual attributes and expenditures for all individuals.

Finally, we consider individual demand functions that are integrable. As before, integrability implies that the individual demand functions can be derived from an indirect utility function that is nonincreasing in prices, nondecreasing in expenditure, and quasiconvex in prices and expenditure. The indirect utility function for each consumer can be represented in one of two possible ways. In either case the indirect utility function depends on a function that is positive and homogeneous of degree one in ratios of prices to expenditure and another function that is homogeneous of degree zero in these ratios.

In both cases the indirect utility function also depends on a function of individual attributes alone.

Examination of the form of the individual demand functions under the assumption that these functions are integrable reveals a relationship between the impact of changes in expenditure and the impact of changes in attributes. The ratio of these effects on individual expenditure shares depends only on expenditure and not on prices or individual attributes. We conclude that it is necessary to consider the case of three functions of individual attributes and expenditure in order to obtain a satisfactory representation of individual and aggregate demand functions.

In considering individual demand functions that depend on two functions of individual attributes and expenditure, we have found that summability implies that one of the two functions is equal to expenditure. Under homogeneity of degree zero in prices and expenditure, the second function must take one of two possible forms, but may depend on both individual attributes and expenditure. In considering individual demand functions that depend on three functions, we add a third function that depends on expenditure alone in order to simplify the specification of individual and aggregate demand functions. As before, summability implies that one of the three functions must be equal to expenditure.

If we assume that individual demand functions are homogeneous of degree zero in prices and expenditure, we find that the function of attributes and expenditure must be equal to the product of a function of attributes alone and a power function of individual expenditure. The second function of expenditure alone must take one of two possible forms. First, the function may be a power function of individual expenditure. Second, the function may be the product of expenditure and the logarithm of expenditure. The corresponding aggregate demand functions depend on index functions that are sums of these functions for all individuals.

Finally, if we assume that individual demand functions are integrable, these functions can be derived from an indirect utility function, as before. Considering the second functions of expenditure alone, we find either that the power function of expenditure must be the same as in the function of attributes and expenditure or the power function in the function of attributes and expenditure must be equal to expenditure itself. Otherwise, the impact of changes in expenditure and the impact of changes in attributes are related.

Consideration of index functions that depend on individual attributes and expenditure reinforces the conclusion we reached in section 8.2, namely, that the theory of exact aggregation and the theory of individual consumer behavior can be employed to simplify the specifications of individual and aggregate models of consumer behavior. In this section we have derived restrictions on the ways in which functions of individual attributes and individual expenditures can enter individual and aggregate models. We turn next to the dependence of individual and aggregate demand functions on prices.

8.4 Demands as Functions of Prices

In sections 8.2 and 8.3 we have shown that exact aggregation and integrability impose severe restrictions on the dependence of demand functions on individual attributes and expenditures. These restrictions can be used to simplify the specifications of models of individual and aggregate consumer behavior. Complete models of consumer behavior also require the specification of the role of prices in determining the allocation of consumer expenditures. In this section we consider the dependence of the individual demand functions on prices.

For three index functions—two index functions of individual expenditures alone and one index function of individual attributes and expenditure—we have shown that only two forms can be considered for individual demand functions. The first is the power form

$$f_{nk}(p, M_k, A_k) = \frac{\partial \ln H^*(p)}{\partial p_n} M_k + H^*(p)^{-(\sigma-1)} \frac{\partial H_1^{**}(p)}{\partial p_n} M_k^{\sigma} + H^*(p)^{-(\sigma-1)} \frac{\partial H_2^{**}(p)}{\partial p_n} l^*(A) M_k^{\sigma}$$

$$(n = 1, 2, \ldots, N; \; k = 1, 2, \ldots, K) \tag{8.79}$$

where $H^*(p)$ is homogeneous of degree one and the functions $H_l^{**}(p)$ $(l = 1, 2)$ are homogeneous of degree zero, $l^*(0) = 0$, and $\sigma \neq 1$, since $\sigma = 1$ is equivalent to homothetic preferences for all individuals.

Equation (8.79) can be derived from an indirect utility function of the form

$$V_k(p, M_k, A_k) = \frac{H^*(p)^{\sigma-1}}{(\sigma-1)} M_k^{-(\sigma-1)} + H_1^{**}(p) + H_2^{**}(p)l^*(A_k),$$
$$(k = 1, 2, \ldots, K). \tag{8.80}$$

An indirect utility function of this form can be characterized as the solution to the partial differential equation

$$\sum_{n=1}^{N} \frac{\partial V_k(p/M_k, A_k)}{\partial \ln(p_n/M_k)} = f(p/M_k, A_k) \tag{8.81}$$

where $f(p/M_k, A_k)$ is a homogeneous of degree $(\sigma - 1)$ function in p/M_k.

The second functional form for individual demand functions is the logarithmic form

$$f_{nk}(p, M_k, A_k) = \left[\frac{\partial \ln H_1^{**}(p)}{\partial p_n} \ln H^*(p) + \frac{\partial \ln H^*(p)}{\partial p_n}\right] M_k$$
$$- \frac{\partial \ln H_1^{**}(p)}{\partial p_n} M_k \ln M_k + \frac{\frac{\partial H_2^{**}(p)}{\partial p_n}}{H_1^{**}(p)} l^*(A_k) M_k,$$
$$(n = 1, 2, \ldots, N; \; k = 1, 2, \ldots, K) \tag{8.82}$$

where $H^*(p)$ is homogeneous of degree one and the functions $H_l^{**}(p)$ $(l = 1, 2)$ are homogeneous of degree zero and $l^*(0) = 0$.

Equation (8.82) can be derived from an indirect utility function of the form

$$V_k(p, M_k, A_k) = - H_1^{**}(p) \ln M_k + H_1^{**}(p) \ln H^*(p) + H_2^{**}(p)l^*(A_k)$$
$$(k = 1, 2, \ldots, K). \tag{8.83}$$

An indirect utility function of this form can be characterized as the solution to the partial differential equation

$$\sum_{n=1}^{N} \frac{\partial V_k(p/M_k, A_k)}{\partial \ln(p_n/M_k)} = f(p/M_k, A_k) \tag{8.84}$$

where $f(p/M_k, A_k)$ is a homogeneous of degree zero function in p/M_k.

To estimate the unknown parameters of a system of individual demand functions given by equations (8.79) or (8.82), it is necessary to specify the algebraic form of the demand functions. There are at least three possible approaches. First, we can specify a class of indirect utility functions $V_k(p, M_k, A_k)$ and select from it a member which satisfies equation (8.81) or equation (8.84). Second, we can specify a class of homogeneous functions and select from it the functions $H^*(p)$ and $H_l^{**}(p)$ $(l = 1, 2)$. Third, we can specify a class of systems of demand functions directly and select from it a system which has the form of equation (8.79) or equation (8.82). We discuss each of these approaches in turn. To simplify the notation we set the vector of individual attributes equal to zero. Our conclusions hold for arbitrary individual attributes.

8.4.A Polynomial Specification of the Indirect Utility Function

First, we consider the specification of the indirect utility function of $V_k(p, M_k)$, subject to the conditions given by equation (8.81) or equation (8.84). It is desirable to restrict the choice of $V_k(p, M_k)$ to a parametric class of functions that can provide an adequate approximation to arbitrary functions satisfying these equations. We confine our choices of $V_k(p, M_k)$ to the class of second-order generalized polynomials, that is

$$V_k(p, 1) = \alpha_0 + \sum_{i=1}^{N} \alpha_i t_i(\ln p_i) + \frac{1}{2} \sum_{i=1}^{N} \sum_{i=1}^{N} \beta_{ij} t_i(\ln p_i) t_j(\ln p_j) \tag{8.85}$$

where the functions t_n $(n = 1, 2, \ldots, N)$ are monotonic and the parameters (α_i, β_{ij}) are arbitrary constants, possibly depending on the vector of individual attributes A_k. We assume further that the functions t_n $(n = 1, 2, \ldots, N)$ are at least three times continuously differentiable.

From equation (8.85)

$$\sum_{n=1}^{N} \frac{\partial V_k}{\partial \ln p_n} = \sum_{n=1}^{N} \left(\alpha_n + \sum_{j=1}^{N} \beta_{nj} t_j(\ln p_j) \right) t_n'(\ln p_n) .$$

Differentiating $\sum_{n=1}^{N} \partial V_k / \partial \ln p_n$ with respect to $\ln p_m$, we obtain

$$\left[\alpha_m + \sum_{j=1}^{N} \beta_{mj} t_j(\ln p_j) \right] t_m''(\ln p_m) + \sum_{n=1}^{N} \beta_{mn} t_m'(\ln p_m) t_m'(\ln p_n) . \tag{8.86}$$

Summing equation (8.86) over m $(m = 1, 2, \ldots, N)$, we obtain

$$\sum_{m=1}^{N}\left[\alpha_m + \sum_{j=1}^{N}\beta_{mj}t_j(\ln p_j)\right]t_m''(\ln p_m) + \sum_{m=1}^{N}\sum_{n=1}^{N}\beta_{mn}t_m'(\ln p_m)t_n'(\ln p_n).$$

If $\sum_{n=1}^{N}\partial V_k/\partial \ln p_n$ is homogeneous of degree $(\sigma-1)$, $\sigma \neq 1$, then the above expression must be equal to

$$(\sigma-1)\sum_{n=1}^{N}\left[\alpha_n + \sum_{j=1}^{N}\beta_{nj}t_j(\ln p_j)\right]t_n'(\ln p_n)$$

or

$$\sum_{n=1}^{N}\left[\alpha_n + \sum_{j=1}^{N}\beta_{nj}t_j(\ln p_j)\right][t_n''(\ln p_n) - (\sigma-1)t_n'(\ln p_n)] + \sum_{m=1}^{N}\sum_{n=1}^{N}\beta_{mn}t_m'(\ln p_m)t_n'(\ln p_n) = 0. \quad (8.87)$$

Differentiating equation (8.87) with respect to $\ln p_k$, we obtain

$$\left[\alpha_k + \sum_{j=1}^{N}\beta_{kj}t_j(\ln p_j)\right][t_k'''(\ln p_k) - (\sigma-1)t_k''(\ln p_k)] + \sum_{n=1}^{N}\beta_{nk}t_k'(\ln p_k)[t_n''(\ln p_n) - (\sigma-1)t_n'(\ln p_n)] + 2\sum_{n=1}^{N}\beta_{kn}t_n'(\ln p_n)t_k''(\ln p_k) = 0. \quad (8.88)$$

Differentiating equation (8.88) with respect to $\ln p_l$, $l \neq k$, we obtain

$$\beta_{kl}t_l'(\ln p_l)[t_k'''(\ln p_k) - (\sigma-1)t_k''(\ln p_k)] + \beta_{lk}t_k'(\ln p_k) \times [t_l'''(\ln p_l) - (\sigma-1)t_l''(\ln p_l)] + 2\beta_{kl}t_l''(\ln p_l)t_k''(\ln p_k) = 0. \quad (8.89)$$

Either $\beta_{kl} = 0$, for all l, $l \neq k$, in which case we obtain from equation (8.87)

$$[\alpha_k + \beta_{kk}t_k(\ln p_k)][t_k''(\ln p_k) - (\sigma-1)t_k'(\ln p_k)] + \beta_{kk}t_k'(\ln p_k)^2 = C_k \quad (8.90)$$

a constant, or $\beta_{kl} \neq 0$ for some l, $l \neq k$, which implies

$$t_l'(\ln p_l)[t_k'''(\ln p_k) - (\sigma-1)t_k''(\ln p_k)] + t_k'(\ln p_k)[t_l'''(\ln p_l) - (\sigma-1)t_l''(\ln p_l)] + 2t_l''(\ln p_l)t_k''(\ln p_k) = 0. \quad (8.91)$$

If $\beta_{kl} = 0$, for all l, $l \neq k$, and $\beta_{kk} \neq 0$, then by the transformation

$$t_k^*(\ln p_k) \equiv \alpha_k + \beta_{kk} t_k(\ln p_k)$$

so that

$$t_k^{*\prime}(\ln p_k) = \beta_{kk} t_k'(\ln p_k)$$
$$t_k^{*\prime\prime}(\ln p_k) = \beta_{kk} t_k''(\ln p_k)$$

equation (8.90) may be rewritten as

$$t_k^*(\ln p_k)t_k^{*\prime\prime}(\ln p_k) + t_k^{*\prime}(\ln p_k)^2 - (\sigma - 1)t_k^*(\ln p_k)t_k^{*\prime}(\ln p_k) = C_k \tag{8.92}$$

or

$$\frac{d}{d \ln p_k} [t_k^*(\ln p_k)t_k^{*\prime}(\ln p_k)] - (\sigma - 1)t_k^*(\ln p_k)t_k^{*\prime}(\ln p_k) = C_k .$$

This implies

$$t_k^*(\ln p_k)t_k^{*\prime}(\ln p_k) = C_{kl} e[(\sigma - 1) \ln p_k] + C_{k2}$$

where C_{k1} and C_{k2} are constants, or

$$\frac{d}{d \ln p_k} 1/2\ t_k^*(\ln p_k)^2 = C_{k1} e[(\sigma - 1) \ln p_k] + C_{k2} .$$

Hence

$$t_k^*(\ln p_k) = \{C_{k1}^* e[(\sigma - 1) \ln p_k] + C_{k2}^* \ln p_k + C_{k3}^*\}^{1/2}$$

where C_{k1}^*, C_{k2}^*, and C_{k3}^* are constants.

We conclude that

$$t_k(\ln p_k) = \frac{\{C_{k1}^* e[(\sigma - 1) \ln p_k] + C_{k2}^* \ln p_k + C_{k3}^*\}^{1/2} - \alpha_k}{\beta_{kk}}$$

which implies that

$$\begin{aligned}\frac{\partial V_k}{\partial \ln p_k} &= [\alpha_k + \beta_{kk} t_k(\ln p_k)] t_k'(\ln p_k) \\ &= \{C_{k1}^* e[(\sigma-1)\ln p_k] + C_{k2}^* \ln p_k + C_{k3}^*\}^{1/2} \\ &\quad \times \frac{1}{2\beta_{kk}} \{C_{k1}^* e[(\sigma-1)\ln p_k] + C_{k2}^* \ln p_k + C_{k3}^*\}^{-1/2} \\ &\quad \times \{(\sigma-1) C_{k1}^* e[(\sigma-1)\ln p_k] + C_{k2}^*\} \\ &= \frac{1}{2\beta_{kk}} \{(\sigma-1) C_{k1}^* e[(\sigma-1)\ln p_k] + C_{k2}^*\}\,.\end{aligned}$$

Hence, $\sum_{n=1}^{N} \partial V_k/\partial \ln p_n$ is homogeneous of degree $(\sigma-1)$ if and only if $\sum_{n=1}^{N} C_{n2}^*/\beta_{nn} = 0$. Thus

$$\begin{aligned}V_k(p,1) &= \alpha_0 + \sum_{i=1}^{N} \alpha_i \frac{(\{C_{i1}^* e[(\sigma-1)\ln p_i] + C_{i2}^* \ln p_i + C_{i3}^*\}^{1/2} - \alpha_i)}{\beta_{ii}} \\ &\quad + 1/2 \sum_{i=1}^{N} \beta_{ii} \frac{(\{C_{i1}^* e[(\sigma-1)\ln p_i] + C_{i2}^* \ln p_i + C_{i3}^*\}^{1/2} - \alpha_i)^2}{\beta_{ii}^2} \\ &= \alpha_0^* + 1/2 \sum_{i=1}^{N} \frac{1}{\beta_{ii}} \{C_{i1}^* e[(\sigma-1)\ln p_i] + C_{i2}^* \ln p_i\} \\ &= \alpha_0^* + \sum_{i=1}^{N} \alpha_i^* (p_i^{(\sigma-1)} + \beta_i^* \ln p_i)\end{aligned}$$

where $\sum_{i=1}^{N} \alpha_i^* \beta_i^* = 0$. If $\beta_{kk} = 0$, then by equation (8.90)

$$t_k'(\ln p_k) = C_{k1} e[(\sigma-1)\ln p_k]$$

and

$$t_k(\ln p_k) = C_{k1}^* e[(\sigma-1)\ln p_k] + C_{k2}^*$$

a case that we shall consider later.

Equation (8.91) may be rewritten as

$$\begin{aligned}t_k'''(\ln p_k) &+ \left[\frac{2t_l''(\ln p_l)}{t_l'(\ln p_l)} - (\sigma-1)\right] t_k''(\ln p_k) \\ &+ \left[\frac{t_l'''(\ln p_l)}{t_l'(\ln p_l)} - (\sigma-1)\frac{t_l''(\ln p_l)}{t_l'(\ln p_l)}\right] t_k'(\ln p_k) = 0\end{aligned}$$

this may be regarded as a second-order ordinary differential equation in the function $t_k'(\ln p_k)$. In order that the solution of this differential equation is independent of $\ln p_l$, it is necessary that the coefficients be constants. Thus

$$\frac{2t_l''(\ln p_l)}{t_l'(\ln p_l)} - (\sigma - 1) = k_1$$

and

$$t_l'''(\ln p_l) - (\sigma - 1)\, t_l''(\ln p_l) = k_2$$

which, to be consistent, require

$$\frac{(\sigma - 1) + k_1}{2} = (\sigma - 1)$$

and

$$k_2 = 0 .$$

Hence, the constant

$$k_1 = (\sigma - 1)$$

and

$$t_l'(\ln p_l) = C_{l1} e[(\sigma - 1) \ln p_l]$$
$$t_l(\ln p_l) = C_{l1}^* e[(\sigma - 1) \ln p_l] + C_{l2}^*$$

the same as in the case $\beta_{kl} = 0$, for all k, l. By symmetry, $t_k(\ln p_k)$ must have the same form.

Substituting the results given above into equation (8.85), we obtain

$$V_k(p, 1) = \alpha_0^* + \sum_{i=1}^{N} \alpha_i^* e[(\sigma - 1) \ln p_i] + 1/2 \sum_{i=1}^{N} \sum_{j=1}^{N} \beta_{ij}^* \exp[(\sigma - 1)(\ln p_i + \ln p_j)] .$$

By differentiating this expression with respect to $\ln p_n$ and summing over n, we obtain

$$\sum_{n=1}^{N} \frac{\partial V_k}{\partial \ln p_n} = (\sigma - 1) \left\{ \sum_{n=1}^{N} \alpha_n^* e[(\sigma - 1) \ln p_n] + \sum_{n=1}^{N} \sum_{j=1}^{N} \beta_{nj}^* \exp[(\sigma - 1)(\ln p_n + \ln p_j)] \right\} .$$

Differentiating this expression with respect to $\ln p_m$ we obtain

$$\sum_{n=1}^{N} \frac{\partial^2 V_k}{\partial \ln p_m \partial \ln p_n} = (\sigma-1)^2 \Bigg[\alpha_m^* e[(\sigma-1)\ln p_m] + 2\sum_{n=1}^{N} \beta_{nm}^* e[(\sigma-1)(\ln p_n + \ln p_m)]\Bigg].$$

Summing over m, we obtain

$$\sum_{m=1}^{N}\sum_{n=1}^{N} \frac{\partial^2 V_k}{\partial \ln p_m \partial \ln p_n} = (\sigma-1)^2 \left\{\sum_{n=1}^{N} \alpha_n^* \exp[(\sigma-1)\ln p_n] + 2\sum_{n=1}^{N}\sum_{m=1}^{N} \beta_{nm}^* \exp[(\sigma-1)(\ln p_n + \ln p_m)]\right\}.$$

We see that homogeneity of degree $(\sigma-1)$ of $\sum_{n=1}^{N} \partial V_k/\partial \ln p_n$, which implies

$$\sum_{m=1}^{N} \frac{\partial}{\partial \ln p_m}\left(\sum_{n=1}^{N} \frac{\partial V_k}{\partial \ln p_n}\right) = (\sigma-1)\left(\sum_{n=1}^{N} \frac{\partial V_k}{\partial \ln p_n}\right)$$

requires that

$$\beta_{nm}^* = 0$$

for all n, m, so that

$$V_k(p, 1) = \alpha_0^* + \sum_{i=1}^{N} \alpha_i^* \exp[(\sigma-1)\ln p_i].$$

We conclude that the only second-order generalized polynomial form that satisfies equation (8.81) is the following

$$V_k(p, 1) = \alpha_0 + \sum_{i=1}^{N} \alpha_i(p_i^{\sigma-1} + \beta_i \ln p_i) \tag{8.93}$$

where $\sum_{i=1}^{N} \alpha_i\beta_i = 0$.

If $\sum_{n=1}^{N} \partial V_k/\partial \ln p_n$ is homogeneous of degree zero, then the counterpart to equation (8.89) becomes

$$\beta_{kl} t_l'(\ln p_l) t_k'''(\ln p_k) + 2\beta_{kl} t_l''(\ln p_l) t_k''(\ln p_k) + \beta_{lk} t_l'''(\ln p_l) t_k'(\ln p_k) = 0.$$

Either $\beta_{kl} = 0$, for all l, $l \neq k$, in which case we obtain from equation (8.87)

$$[\alpha_k + \beta_{kk} t_k(\ln p_k)] t_k''(\ln p_k) + \beta_{kk} t_k'(\ln p_k)^2 = C_k \tag{8.94}$$

a constant, or $\beta_{kl} \neq 0$ which implies for some l, $l \neq k$,

$$t_k'''(\ln p_k) + \frac{2t_l''(\ln p_l)}{t_l'(\ln p_l)} t_k''(\ln p_k) + \frac{t_l'''(\ln p_l)}{t_l'(\ln p_l)} t_k'(\ln p_k) = 0\,. \tag{8.95}$$

Equation (8.94) may be rewritten, using the same transformation as before

$$t_k^*(\ln p_k) t_k^{*\prime\prime}(\ln p_k) + [t_k^{*\prime}(\ln p_k)]^2 = C_k$$

or

$$\frac{d}{d \ln p_k} [t_k^*(\ln p_k) t_k^{*\prime}(\ln p_k)] = C_k$$

or

$$\frac{d^2}{d^2 \ln p_k} 1/2[t_k^*(\ln p_k)]^2 = C_k$$

so that

$$\frac{d}{d \ln p_k} 1/2[t_k^*(\ln p_k)]^2 = C_{k1} \ln p_k + C_{k2}.$$

and

$$1/2[t_k^*(\ln p_k)]^2 = C_{k1} \frac{(\ln p_k)^2}{2} + C_{k2} \ln p_k + C_{k3}\,.$$

Thus

$$t_k^*(\ln p_k) = [C_{k1}^*(\ln p_k)^2 + C_{k2}^* \ln p_k + C_{k3}^*]^{1/2}$$

where C_{k1}^*, C_{k2}^* and C_{k3}^* are constants.

We conclude that

$$t_k(\ln p_k) = \frac{[C_{k1}^*(\ln p_k)^2 + C_{k2}^* \ln p_k + C_{k3}^*]^{1/2} - \alpha_k}{\beta_{kk}}$$

and

$$V_k(p,1) = \alpha_0^* + \frac{1}{2}\sum_{i=1}^{N}\frac{1}{\beta_{ii}}[C_{i1}^*(\ln p_i)^2 + C_{i2}^*\ln p_i]$$
$$= \alpha_0^* + \sum_{i=1}^{N}\alpha_i^*\ln p_i + \frac{1}{2}\sum_{i=1}^{N}\beta_{ii}^*(\ln p_i)^2$$

where $\sum_i \beta_{ii}^* = 0$.

Now suppose $\beta_{kl} \neq 0$. Equation (8.95) may be regarded as a second-order ordinary differential equation in the function $t_k'(\ln p_k)$. In order that the solution of this differential equation is independent of $\ln p_l$, it is necessary that the coefficients are constants. Thus

$$\frac{2t_l''(\ln p_l)}{t_l'(\ln p_l)} = k_1$$
$$\frac{t_l'''(\ln p_l)}{t_k'(\ln p_l)} = k_2\,.$$

Thus, for $k_1 \neq 0$

$$t_l'(\ln p_l) = C_1\exp[(k_1/2)\ln p_l]$$
$$t_l''(\ln p_l) = \frac{k_1C_1}{2}\exp[(k_1/2)\ln p_l]$$
$$t_l'''(\ln p_l) = \frac{k_1^2}{4}C_1\exp[(k_1/2)\ln p_l]$$

or

$$k_2 = \frac{k_1^2}{4}\,.$$

This implies that

$$t_l(\ln p_l) = C_{1l}\exp[(k_1/2)\ln p_l] + C_{2l}\,. \tag{8.96}$$

For $k_1 = 0$

$$t_l(\ln p_l) = C_{1l}\ln p_l + C_{2l}\,. \tag{8.97}$$

For equation (8.96), $\sum_{n=1}^{N} \partial V_k/\partial \ln p_k$ being homogeneous of degree zero implies that $V_k(p,1)$ must be a homogeneous of degree zero polynomial but this implies that $V_k(p,1)$ is a constant. For equation (8.97)

$$V_k(p, 1) = \alpha_0 + \sum_{i=1}^{N} \alpha_i^* \ln p_i + \frac{1}{2} \sum_{i=1}^{N} \sum_{j=1}^{N} \beta_{ij}^* \ln p_i \ln p_j$$

which satisfies equation (8.84) if and only if $\sum_{i=1}^{N} \sum_{j=1}^{N} \beta_{ij}^* = 0$.

We have therefore proved

Theorem 8.6. The only nonhomothetic second-order generalized polynomial function form that satisfies the exact aggregation condition for an indirect utility function in equation (8.81) is

$$V_k(p, 1) = \alpha_0 + \sum_{i=1}^{N} \alpha_i (p_i^{\sigma} + \beta_i \ln p_i)$$

where $\sum_{i=1}^{N} \alpha_i \beta_i = 0$.

Theorem 8.7. The only nonhomothetic second-order generalized polynomial functional form which satisfies the exact aggregation condition for an indirect utility function in equation (8.84) is

$$V_k(p, 1) = \alpha_0 + \sum_{i=1}^{N} \alpha_i \ln p_i + \frac{1}{2} \sum_{i=1}^{N} \sum_{j=1}^{N} \beta_{ij} \ln p_i \ln p_j$$

where $\sum_{i=1}^{N} \sum_{j=1}^{N} \beta_{ij} = 0$.

Thus, if we restrict our choice of functional forms for the indirect utility functions satisfying equation (8.81) or (8.84) to second-order generalized polynomial functions that are not themselves homothetic, the only admissible functional forms are the sum of a constant-elasticity of substitution function and a linear logarithmic function and the transcendental logarithmic function.

8.4.B Polynomial Specification of the Functions $H^*(p)$ and $H_l^{**}(p)$

Second, we consider the specification of the functions $H^*(p)$ and $H_l^{**}(p)$ in equations (8.80) and (8.83). The individual demand functions can then be derived by applying Roy's Identity to equations (8.80) or (8.83); the aggregate demand function can be obtained by summing over the individual demand functions. The functions $H^*(p)$ and $H_l^{**}(p)$ must satisfy homogeneity restrictions; it is desirable to choose forms for these functions that can provide an adequate approximation to an arbitrary function. As before, we restrict consideration to second-order generalized polynomials

$$H^*(p) = T\left[\alpha_0 + \sum_{i=1}^{N} \alpha_i t_i(p_i) + \frac{1}{2}\sum_{i=1}^{N}\sum_{j=1}^{N} \beta_{ij} t_i(p_i) t_j(p_j)\right] \quad (8.98)$$

where the functions T and t_n, $(n = 1, 2, \ldots, N)$, are three times continuously differentiable monotonic functions and the parameters $\{\alpha_i, \beta_{ij}\}$ are arbitrary constants.

We state first the following lemma due to Jorgenson and Lau (1979)

Lemma 8.1. All homogeneous functions with the generalized polynomial form in equation (8.98) can be written as

$$H^*(p) = T\{P[t_1(p_1), \ldots, t_N(p_N)]\}$$

with either

$$(1) \quad T(Z) = Z^{\sigma_1}\ ; \qquad t_n(p_n) = p_n^{\sigma_2}, \qquad (n = 1, 2, \ldots, N)$$

where $P\,(\cdot)$ is a generalized bilinear form with each term consisting of a constant coefficient times the product of two functions $t_n(p_n)$; alternatively

$$(2) \quad T(Z) = e^Z\ ; \qquad t_n(p_n) = \ln p_n, \qquad (n = 1, 2, \ldots, N)$$

and P is a second-order polynomial in $t_n(p_n)$ whose coefficients satisfy

$$\sum_{j=1}^{N} \beta_{ij} = 0$$

for all i. In the special case of homogeneity of degree zero, $\sum_{i=1}^{N} \alpha_i = 0$, but $T(Z)$ can be arbitrary. We shall not prove this lemma here.

It is obvious that the form (1) cannot be homogeneous of degree zero without being constant, so that the functions $H_l^{**}(p)$ have the form

$$\ln H_l^{**}(p) = \alpha_0 + \sum_{i=1}^{N} \alpha_i \ln p_i + \frac{1}{2}\sum_{i=1}^{N}\sum_{j=1}^{N} \beta_{ij} \ln p_i \ln p_j \quad (8.99)$$

where in addition to the restrictions given above the parameters must satisfy $\sum_{i=1}^{N} \alpha_i = 0$. This is precisely the form of the transcendental logarithmic indirect utility function.

We now present the forms of $f_{nk}(p, M_k)$ based on alternative specifications of the functions $H^*(p)$ and $H_l^{**}(p)$ $(l = 1, 2)$. By Lemma 8.1, if we restrict our choices of these functions to second-order generalized polynomial forms, $H^*(p)$ can take only one of the two forms

$$H^*(p) = \begin{cases} \left(\frac{1}{2} \sum_{i=1}^{N} \sum_{j=1}^{N} \beta_{ij} p_i^{r/2} p_j^{r/2} \right)^{1/r} \\ \exp\left(\alpha_0 + \sum_{i=1}^{N} \alpha_i \ln p_i + \frac{1}{2} \sum_{i=1}^{N} \sum_{j=1}^{N} \beta_{ij} \ln p_i \ln p_j \right) \end{cases}$$

where

$$\sum_{i=1}^{N} \alpha_i = 1$$

and

$$\sum_{j=1}^{N} \beta_{ij} = 0$$

for all i; we refer to the first of the generalized polynomial forms as the power form and the second as the logarithmic form.

The functions $H_l^{**}(p)$ are homogeneous of degree zero and can take only the logarithmic form

$$\ln H_l^{**}(p) = \alpha_0^l + \sum_{i=1}^{N} \alpha_i^l \ln p_i + \frac{1}{2} \sum_{i=1}^{N} \sum_{j=1}^{N} \beta_{ij}^l \ln p_i \ln p_j$$

where

$$\sum_{i=1}^{N} \alpha_i^l = 0$$

and

$$\sum_{j=1}^{N} \beta_{ij}^l = 0$$

for all i.

Starting with equation (8.79), the form of $f_{nk}(p, M_k)$, corresponding to the power form of the generalized polynomial $H^*(p)$

is

$$f_{nk}(p, M_k) = \frac{1}{2} \frac{\sum_{j=1}^{N} \beta_{nj} p_j^{r/2} p_n^{r/2-1}}{\frac{1}{2} \sum_{i=1}^{N} \sum_{j=1}^{N} \beta_{ij} p_i^{r/2} p_j^{r/2}} M_k + \left(\frac{1}{2} \sum_{i=1}^{N} \sum_{j=1}^{N} \beta_{ij} p_i^{r/2} p_j^{r/2} \right)^{-(\sigma-1)/r}$$
$$\times \left(\alpha_n^l + \sum_{j=1}^{N} \beta_{nk}^l \ln p_j \right) \frac{M_k^\sigma}{p_n} \tag{8.100}$$

or

$$\frac{p_n f_{nk}(p, M_k)}{M_k} = \frac{\frac{1}{2} \sum_{j=1}^{N} \beta_{nj} p_j^{r/2} p_n^{r/2}}{\frac{1}{2} \sum_{i=1}^{N} \sum_{j=1}^{N} \beta_{ij} p_i^{r/2} p_j^{r/2}} + \left(\frac{1}{2} \sum_{i=1}^{N} \sum_{j=1}^{N} \beta_{ij} p_i^{r/2} p_j^{r/2} \right)^{-(\sigma-1)/r}$$
$$\times \left(\alpha_n^l + \sum_{j=1}^{N} \beta_{nj}^l \ln p_j \right) M_k^{\sigma-1} .$$

Even if r and σ were known *a priori*, this equation would be highly nonlinear. A further simplification is possible if it is assumed that $\sigma - 1 = r$. In that case

$$\frac{p_n f_{nk}(p, M_k)}{M_k} = \frac{\frac{1}{2} \sum_{j=1}^{N} \beta_{nj} p_j^{r/2} p_n^{r/2} + \left(\alpha_n^l + \sum_{j=1}^{N} \beta_{nj}^l \ln p_j \right) M_k^r}{\frac{1}{2} \sum_{i=1}^{N} \sum_{j=1}^{N} \beta_{ij} p_i^{r/2} p_j^{r/2}} .$$

For given r, this equation is the ratio of two forms which are linear in parameters and can be readily estimated. However, in general, σ and r will be unknown; if $(\sigma - 1) \neq r$, estimation will be very difficult.

If we let $H^*(p)$ be a first-order homogeneous generalized polynomial, then equation (8.99) becomes

$$f_{nk}(p, M_k) = \frac{\alpha_n p_n^{r-1} M_k}{\sum_{i=1}^{N} \alpha_i p_i^r} + \left(\sum_{i=1}^{N} \alpha_i p_i^r \right)^{-(\sigma-1)/r} \left(\alpha_n^l + \sum_{j=1}^{N} \beta_{nj}^l \ln p_j \right) \frac{M_k^\sigma}{p_n} \tag{8.101}$$

which under the assumption of $\sigma - 1 = r$ simplifies to

$$\frac{p_n f_{nk}(p, M_k)}{M_k} = \frac{\alpha_n p_n^r + \left(\alpha_n^l + \sum_{j=1}^{N} \beta_{nj}^l \ln p_j\right) M_k^r}{\sum_{i=1}^{N} \alpha_i p_i^r}.$$

For given r, this equation is the ratio of two forms that are linear in parameters and can easily be estimated. In general, this will not be the case and estimation will be difficult.

Again starting from equation (8.79), the form of $f_{nk}(p, M_k)$ corresponding to the logarithmic form of the generalized polynomial $H^*(p)$ is

$$\begin{aligned} f_{nk}(p, M_k) = {} & \left(\alpha_n + \sum_{j=1}^{N} \beta_{nj} \ln p_j\right) \frac{M_k}{p_n} \\ & + \left[\exp\left(\alpha_0 + \sum_{i=1}^{N} \alpha_i \ln p_i + \frac{1}{2} \sum_{i=1}^{N} \sum_{j=1}^{N} \beta_{ij} \ln p_i \ln p_j\right)\right]^{-(\sigma-1)} \\ & \times \left(\alpha_n^l + \sum_{j=1}^{N} \beta_{nj}^l \ln p_j\right) \frac{M_k^\sigma}{p_n} \end{aligned} \tag{8.102}$$

or

$$\begin{aligned} \frac{p_n f_{nk}(p, M_k)}{M_k} = {} & \left(\alpha_n + \sum_{j=1}^{N} \beta_{nj} \ln p_j\right) \\ & + \exp\left[-(\sigma-1)\left(\alpha_0 + \sum_{i=1}^{N} \ln p_i + \frac{1}{2} \sum_{i=1}^{N} \sum_{j=1}^{N} \beta_{ij} \ln p_i \ln p_j\right)\right] \\ & \times \left(\alpha_n^l + \sum_{j=1}^{N} \beta_{nj}^l \ln p_j\right) M_k^{\sigma-1}. \end{aligned}$$

Even if σ were known *a priori*, this equation would be highly nonlinear and is likely to be intractable from the point of view of estimation.

If we let $H^*(p)$ be a first-order homogeneous generalized polynomial, then equation (8.101) becomes

$$f_{nk}(p, M_k) = \alpha_n \frac{M_k}{p_n} + \left(\prod_{i=1}^{N} p_i^{\alpha_i}\right)^{-(\sigma-1)} \left(\alpha_n^l + \sum_{j=1}^{N} \beta_{nj}^l \ln p_j\right) \frac{M_k^\sigma}{p_n} \tag{8.103}$$

which may be rewritten as

$$\frac{p_n f_{nk}(p, M_k)}{M_k} = \alpha_n + \left(\prod_{i=1}^{N} p_i^{\alpha_i}\right)^{-(\sigma-1)} \left(\alpha_n^l + \sum_{j=1}^{N} \beta_{nj}^l \ln p_j\right) M_k^{\sigma-1}.$$

This equation is slightly more tractable than equation (8.101) although estimation of the parameters $\{\alpha_i\}$ is likely to be difficult.

Starting with equation (8.82), the form of $f_{nk}(p, M_k)$, corresponding to the power form of the generalized polynomial $H^*(p)$ is

$$f_{nk}(p, M_k) = \left\{ \frac{1}{r}\left(\alpha_n^l + \sum_{j=1}^{N} \beta_{nj}^l \ln p_j\right)\left(\ln\left[\frac{1}{2}\sum_{i=1}^{N}\sum_{j=1}^{N} \beta_{ij} p_i^{r/2} p_j^{r/2}\right]\right) \frac{\left(\sum_{j=1}^{N} \beta_{nj} p_j^{r/2}\right)\beta_{nn} p_n^{r/2}}{\sum_{i=1}^{N}\sum_{j=1}^{N} p_i^{r/2} p_j^{r/2}} \right\} \times \frac{M_k}{p_n} - \left(\alpha_n^l + \sum_{j=1}^{N} \beta_{nj}^l \ln p_j\right) \frac{M_k \ln M_k}{p_n}. \tag{8.104}$$

If we let $H^*(p)$ be a first-order homogeneous generalized polynomial, then equation (8.104) becomes

$$f_{nk}(p, M_k) = \left\{ \frac{1}{r}\left(\alpha_n^l + \sum_{j=1}^{N} \beta_{nj}^l \ln p_j\right)\left[\ln \sum_{i=1}^{N} \alpha_i p_i^r\right] + \frac{\alpha_n p_n^r}{\sum_{i=1}^{N} \alpha_i p_i^r} \right\} \frac{M_k}{p_n} - \left(\alpha_n^l + \sum_{j=1}^{N} \beta_{nj}^l \ln p_j\right) \frac{M_k \ln M_k}{p_n}. \tag{8.105}$$

Even if r were known, estimation of equations (8.104) and (8.105) is likely to be difficult because the term $\sum_{i=1}^{N} \alpha_i p_i^r$ occurs as both a logarithm and a reciprocal.

The form of $f_{nk}(p, M_k)$ corresponding to the logarithmic form of the generalized polynomial $H^*(p)$ is

$$\begin{aligned} f_{nk}(p, M_k) &= \left[\left(\alpha_n^l + \sum_{j=1}^N \beta_{nj}^l \ln p_j \right) \left(\alpha_0 + \sum_{i=1}^N \alpha_i \ln p_i + \sum_{i=1}^N \sum_{j=1}^N \beta_{ij} \ln p_i \ln p_j \right) \right. \\ &\quad \left. + \left(\alpha_n + \sum_{j=1}^N \beta_{nj} \ln p_j \right) \right] \frac{M_k}{p_n} - \left(\alpha_n^l + \sum_{j=1}^N \beta_{nj}^l \ln p_j \right) \frac{M_k \ln M_k}{p_n} \\ &= \left(\alpha_n^l + \sum_{j=1}^N \beta_{nj}^l \ln p_j \right) \left[\alpha_0 + \sum_{i=1}^N \alpha_i \ln p_i + \frac{1}{2} \sum_{i=1}^N \sum_{j=1}^N \beta_{ij} \ln p_i \ln p_j - \ln M_k \right] \\ &\quad \times \frac{M_k}{p_n} + \left(\alpha_n + \sum_{j=1}^N \beta_{nj} \ln p_j \right) \frac{M_k}{p_n} \end{aligned} \tag{8.106}$$

which can be written as

$$\begin{aligned} \frac{p_n f_{nk}(p, M_k)}{M_k} &= (\alpha_n^l + \alpha_n) + \sum_{j=1}^N (\beta_{nj}^l + \beta_{nj}) \ln p_j + \left(\alpha_n^l + \sum_{j=1}^N \beta_{nj}^l \ln p_j \right) \\ &\quad \times \left(\sum_{i=1}^N \alpha_i \ln p_i + \frac{1}{2} \sum_{i=1}^N \sum_{j=1}^N \beta_{ij} \ln p_i \ln p_j - \ln M_k \right) \end{aligned}$$

where

$$\alpha_0 = 1, \quad \sum_{i=1}^N \alpha_i = 1, \quad \sum_{i=1}^N \alpha_j^l = 0, \quad \sum_{j=1}^N \beta_{ij} = 0, \quad \sum_{j=1}^N \beta_{ij}^l = 0$$

for all i. If we let $\beta_{nj}^l = 0$, for all n, j, then this system of individual demand reduces to the AIDS system of Deaton and Muellbauer (1980a,b).

If we let $H^*(p)$ be a first-order homogeneous generalized polynomial, then equation (8.106) becomes

$$\begin{aligned} f_{nk}(p, M_k) &= \left(\alpha_n^l + \sum_{j=1}^N \beta_{nj}^l \ln p_j \right) \left(\alpha_0 + \sum_{i=1}^N \alpha_i \ln p_i - \ln M_k \right) \frac{M_k}{p_n} \\ &\quad + \alpha_n \frac{M_k}{p_n} \end{aligned} \tag{8.107}$$

which can be written as

$$\frac{p_n f_{nk}(p, M_k)}{M_k} = \alpha_n + \left(\alpha_n^l + \sum_{j=1}^{N} \beta_{nj}^l \ln p_j\right)\left(1 + \sum_{i=1}^{N} \alpha_i \ln p_i - \ln M_k\right).$$

To recapitulate, we note that equation (8.100) is intractable as far as estimation is concerned. For each equation the number of parameters is on the order of $N(N + 1)/2 + N$. The total number of parameters in the system is of the order of $N(N + 1)$. Equation (8.101) is somewhat more tractable although there are still some unavoidable nonlinearities involving the unknown parameters r and σ. The number of parameters in the system is on the order of $N(N + 1)/2 + N$. Equation (8.102) is just as intractable as equation (8.100). Equation (8.103) is much simpler, although there are still some unavoidable nonlinearities.

Equation (8.104) is quite intractable with equation (8.105) somewhat better. Equation (8.106) has the remarkable property that it is linear in polynomials of the logarithms of prices p_n and expenditures M_k. Unless we impose cross equation constraints, there will be a large number of unknown parameters in each equation, on the order of $N(N+1)/2+N$. In addition, there are nonlinear constraints among the parameters within the same equation. These nonlinear constraints remain even under the specialization to the AIDS system. Equation (8.107) is a simplified version of equation (8.106) and has each expenditure share equal to a transcendental logarithmic function of special structure.

We next consider the choices of the functions $H^*(p)$ and $H_l^{**}(p)$ that give rise to an indirect utility function $V_k(p, M_k)$ of the transcendental logarithmic form. Let

$$\ln H^*(p) = \frac{\alpha_0 + \sum_{i=1}^{N} \alpha_i \ln p_i + \frac{1}{2} \sum_{i=1}^{N} \sum_{j=1}^{N} \beta_{ij} \ln p_i \ln p_j}{\sum_{i=1}^{N} \alpha_i + \sum_{j=1}^{N} \sum_{i=1}^{N} \beta_{ij} \ln p_j}.$$

It can be verified directly that

$$\ln H^*(\lambda p) = \ln H^*(p) + \ln \lambda$$

that is $H^*(p)$ is homogeneous of degree one. Let

$$H_1^{**}(p) \equiv \sum_{i=1}^{N} \alpha_i + \sum_{j=1}^{N} \sum_{i=1}^{N} \beta_{ij} \ln p_j$$

with $\sum_{i=1}^{N} \sum_{j=1}^{N} \beta_{ij} = 0$. It can be verified directly that $H_1^{**}(p)$ is homogeneous of degree zero. The product $H_1^{**}(p) \ln H^*(p)$ has precisely the transcendental logarithmic form.

8.4.C Rational Specification of Individual Demand Functions

Third, we consider the specifications of $f_{nk}(p, M_k)$ in equations (8.79) and (8.82) directly. We shall restrict our choices of the expenditure share functions to the ratio of two first-order generalized polynomials in ratios of prices to expenditure, that is

$$\frac{p_n f_{nk}(p, M_k)}{M_k} = \frac{\alpha_n + \sum_j \beta_{nj} g(p_j/M_k)}{-1 + \sum_j \beta_{Mj} g(p_j/M_k)}, \quad (n = 1, 2, \ldots, N) \tag{8.108}$$

where the function g is monotonic in a single variable. We consider this form since expenditure share functions that are linear in the unknown parameters have been shown by Jorgenson and Lau (1977) and Lau (1977) and Lau (1977a) to satisfy the conditions of summability and nonnegativity if and only if the expenditure shares are constants. The systems of equations (8.107) with the restrictions

$$\sum_{n=1}^{N} \alpha_n = 1, \quad \sum_{n=1}^{N} \beta_{nj} = \beta_{Mj}$$

for all j satisfies summability identically.

The implications of symmetry for a system of individual demand functions of the form in equation (8.108) have been analyzed by Jorgenson and Lau (1977). They imply that either:

(1) the expenditure shares are constant

or

(2) $g(Z) = Z^{-(\sigma-1)}$

or

(3) $g(Z) = Z \ln Z$.

Constant expenditure shares are not an interesting specification. For a power function (2)

$$\frac{p_n f_{nk}(p, M_k)}{M_k} = \frac{\alpha_n + \sum_{j=1}^{N} \beta_{nj} p_j^{-(\sigma-1)} M_k^{\sigma-1}}{-1 + \sum_{j=1}^{N} \beta_{Mj} p_j^{-(\sigma-1)} M_k^{(\sigma-1)}} . \tag{8.109}$$

Equation (8.109) takes the form of equation (8.79) only if

$$\beta_{Mj} = 0$$

for all j. This restriction implies, under symmetry of the Slutsky substitution matrix, that [13]

$$\beta_{nj} = \alpha_n \beta_j \qquad n \neq j$$

$$\beta_{nn} = (1 + \alpha_n)\beta_n$$

for all n, j. Equation (8.109) then takes the form

$$\frac{p_n f_{nk}(p, M_k)}{M_k} = - \alpha_n - \left[\alpha_n \sum_{j=1}^{N} \beta_j p_j^{-(\sigma-1)} + \beta_n p_n^{-(\sigma-1)} \right] M_k^{(\sigma-1)} . \tag{8.110}$$

This system of individual demand functions can be derived from an indirect utility function of the form

$$\ln V_k(p, M_k) = \alpha_0 + \sum_{n=1}^{N} \alpha_n \ln (p_n/M_k) + \frac{1}{\sigma} \ln \left[\sum_{n=1}^{N} \beta_n (p_n/M_k)^{\sigma} + 1 \right] .$$

This system of individual demand equation has only $2N$ parameters and lacks the second-order interpolation property. It is obvious that equation (8.109) cannot take the form of equation (8.82).

For the logarithmic case (3), we have

$$\frac{p_n f_{nk}(p, M_k)}{M_k} = \frac{\alpha_n + \sum_{j=1}^{N} \beta_{nj} \ln p_j - \sum_{j=1}^{N} \beta_{nj} \ln M_k}{-1 + \sum_{j=1}^{N} \sum_{n=1}^{N} \beta_{nj} \ln p_j + \sum_{j=1}^{N} \sum_{n=1}^{N} \beta_{nj} \ln M_k} . \tag{8.111}$$

Equation (8.110) cannot take the form of equation (8.79). It takes the form of equation (8.82) only if

$$\sum_{j=1}^{N} \sum_{n=1}^{N} \beta_{nj} = 0 .$$

A transcendental logarithmic indirect utility function satisfying this restriction will give rise to equation (8.81). Other possible indirect utility functions lack the second-order interpolation property.[14]

8.4.D Summary and Conclusion

In this section we have analyzed systems of individual demand functions that can be generated from an indirect utility function and that satisfy the restrictions implied by the theory of exact aggregation. For three index functions of individual attributes and expenditures, where two of these functions depend on expenditures alone, only two forms can be considered for the individual demand functions. The first of these involves a power function of individual expenditures. We refer to this as the power form of the system of individual demand functions. The second involves a logarithmic function of individual expenditures; we refer to this as the logarithmic form.

We have considered three alternative approaches to specification of the dependence of the individual demand functions on prices. First, we specify a class of indirect utility functions that can be used to generate power and logarithmic forms of systems of individual demand functions. We restrict consideration to indirect utility functions that are second-order generalized polynomials. Second, we consider alternative specifications of certain homogeneous functions that occur in the representation of the indirect utility functions. Again, we restrict consideration to homogeneous functions that are first-order and second-order generalized polynomials. Third, we consider specifications of the power and logarithmic forms of a system of individual demand functions that are ratios of first-order generalized polynomials.

We find that the indirect utility function that generates the power form of the system of individual demand functions, restricting consideration to second-order generalized polynomials, can be written

$$V_k(p, 1) = \alpha_0 + \sum_{i=1}^{N} \alpha_i (p_i^{\sigma} + \beta_i \ln p_i)$$

where $\sum_{i=1}^{N} \alpha_i \beta_i = 0$. This indirect utility function lacks the second-order interpolation property. Similarly, we find that the indirect utility function that generates the logarithmic form of the system of individual demand function can be written

$$V_k(p, 1) = \alpha_0 + \sum_{i=1}^{N} \alpha_i \ln p_i + \frac{1}{2} \sum_{i=1}^{N} \sum_{j=1}^{N} \beta_{ij} \ln p_i \ln p_j$$

where $\sum_{i=1}^{N} \sum_{j=1}^{N} \beta_{ij} = 0$. This is the transcendental logarithmic indirect utility function and has the second-order interpolation property.

Our second approach to specifying systems of individual demand functions is to specify the homogeneous functions $H^*(p)$ and $H_l^{**}(p)$ that occur in the representation of the indirect utility functions that generate the power and logarithm forms of the system of individual demand functions. As before, we restrict consideration to representations of these homogeneous functions as first-order and second-order generalized polynomials. We find that the functional forms involving a power function of individual expenditures are intractable. The functional forms involving a logarithmic function of individual expenditures, including the AIDS system of Deaton and Muellbauer, are more tractable.

Finally, our third approach to specifying systems of individual demand functions is to consider power and logarithmic forms that can be represented as ratios of first-order generalized polynomials. The indirect utility function that generates the power form of the individual demand functions can be written

$$V_k(p, 1) = \alpha_0 + \sum_{n=1}^{N} \alpha_n \ln p_n + \frac{1}{\sigma} \ln\left(\sum_{n=1}^{N} \beta_n p_n^{\sigma} + 1 \right).$$

This indirect utility functions lacks the second-order interpolation property. The indirect utility function that generates the logarithmic form is the transcendental logarithmic indirect utility function.

Both the transcendental logarithmic demand system and equation (8.106) are nonlinear in the unknown parameters. In the absence of additional constraints equation (8.106) has many more parameters than the transcendental logarithmic system. The number of constraints that must be imposed for equation (8.106) is on the order of N^3, even under the restrictions required for the AIDS system, while the number of constraints that must be imposed is on the order of N^2 for the transcendental logarithmic system. We therefore use the transcendental logarithmic indirect utility function as a point of departure for our empirical application of the theory of exact aggregation.

8.5 Translog Model of Consumer Behavior

In this section we present individual and aggregate models of consumer behavior based on the theory of exact aggregation. The theory of exact aggregation requires that the individual demand functions must be linear in a number of functions of individual attributes and expenditure. Representing aggregate demand functions as the sum of individual demand functions, we find that the aggregate demand functions depend on the distribution of expenditure among individuals as well as the level of per capita expenditure and prices. The aggregate demand functions also depend on the joint distribution of expenditures and demographic characteristics among individuals.

In our model of consumer behavior the individual consuming units are households. We assume that household expenditures on commodity groups are allocated so as to maximize a household welfare function. As a consequence, the household behaves in the same way as an individual maximizing a utility function.[15] We require that the individual demand functions are integrable, so that these demand functions can be generated by Roy's Identity from an indirect utility function for each consuming unit. We assume that these indirect utility functions are homogeneous of degree zero in prices and expenditure, nonincreasing in prices and nondecreasing in expenditure, and quasiconvex in prices and expenditure.

To allow for differences in preferences among consuming units, we allow the indirect utility functions for the kth unit to depend on a vector of attributes A_k; each attribute is represented by a dummy variable equal to unity when the consuming unit has the corresponding characteristics and zero otherwise. In our model of consumer behavior there are several groups of attributes. Each consuming unit is assigned one of the attributes in each of the groups.

8.5.A Exact Aggregation

To represent our model of consumer behavior we require the following additional notation

$w_{nk} = p_n x_{nk}/M_k$	Expenditure share of the nth commodity group in the budget of the kth consuming unit $(k = 1, 2, \ldots, K)$.

$w_k = (w_{1k,}\ w_{2k} \dots w_{Nk})$ Vector of expenditure shares for the kth consuming unit $(k = 1, 2, \dots, K)$.

$\ln \frac{p}{M_k} = \left(\ln \frac{p_l}{M_k}, \ln \frac{p_2}{M_k}, \dots, \ln \frac{p_n}{M_k} \right)$ Vector of logarithms of ratios of prices to expenditure by the kth consuming unit $(k = 1, 2, \dots, K)$.

$\ln p = (\ln p_1, \ln p_2, \dots, \ln p_N)$ Vector of logarithms of prices.

We assume that the kth consuming unit allocates its expenditures in accord with the transcendental logarithmic or translog indirect utility function, say V_k, where

$$\ln V_k = F(A_k) + \ln \frac{p'}{M_k} \alpha_p + \frac{1}{2} \ln \frac{p'}{M_k} B_{pp} \ln \frac{p}{M_k} + \ln \frac{p'}{M_k} B_{pA} A_k\,, \qquad (k = 1, 2, \dots, K)\,. \tag{8.112}$$

In this representation the function F depends on the attribute vector A_k but is independent of the prices p and expenditure M_k. The vector α_p and the matrices B_{pp} and B_{pA} are constant parameters that are the same for all consuming units.

The expenditure shares of the kth consuming unit can be derived by the logarithmic form of Roy's Identity

$$w_{nk} = \frac{\partial \ln V_k}{\partial \ln (p_n/M_k)} \Big/ \sum \frac{\partial \ln V_k}{\partial \ln (p_n/M_k)}\,, \qquad (n = 1, 2, \dots, N;\ k = 1, 2, \dots, K)\,. \tag{8.113}$$

Applying this Identity to the translog indirect utility function, we obtain the system of individual expenditure shares

$$w_k = \frac{1}{D_k} \left(\alpha_p + B_{pp} \ln \frac{p}{M_k} + B_{pA} A_k \right) \quad (k = 1, 2, \dots, K) \tag{8.114}$$

where the denominators $\{D_k\}$ take the form

$$D_k = \iota' \alpha_p + \iota' B_{pp} \ln \frac{p}{M_k} + \iota' B_{pA} A_k\,, \quad (k = 1, 2, \dots, K) \tag{8.115}$$

and ι is a vector of ones.

We first observe that the function F that appears in the translog indirect utility function does not enter into the determination of the individual expenditure shares. This function is not identifiable from observed patterns of individual expenditure allocation. Second, since the individual expenditure shares can be expressed as ratios of functions that are homogeneous and linear in the unknown parameters α_p, B_{pp}, B_{pA} these shares are homogeneous of degree zero in the parameters. By multiplying a given set of the unknown parameters by a constant we obtain another set of parameters that generates the same system of individual budget shares. Accordingly, we can choose a normalization for the parameters without affecting observed patterns of individual expenditure allocation. We find it convenient to employ the normalization

$$\iota'\alpha_p = -1 .$$

Under this restriction any change in the set of unknown parameters will be reflected in changes in individual expenditure patterns.

The conditions for exact aggregation are that the individual expenditure shares are linear in functions of the attributes $\{A_k\}$ and total expenditures $\{M_k\}$ for all consuming units.[16] These conditions will be satisfied if and only if the terms involving the attributes and expenditures do not appear in the denominators of the expressions given above for the individual expenditure shares, so that

$$\iota' B_{pp}\, \iota = 0$$
$$\iota' B_{pA} = 0 .$$

These restrictions imply that the denominators $\{D_k\}$ reduce to

$$D = -1 + \iota'\, B_{pp} \ln p$$

where the subscript k is no longer required, since the denominator is the same for all consuming units. Under these restrictions the individual expenditure shares can be written

$$w_k = \frac{1}{D}\,(\alpha_p + B_{pp} \ln p - B_{pp}\, \iota \cdot \ln M_k + B_{pA}\, A_k)\,, \quad (k = 1, 2, \ldots, K)\,. \qquad (8.116)$$

The individual expenditure shares are linear in the logarithms of expenditures $\{\ln M_k\}$ and the attributes $\{A_k\}$, as required by exact aggregation.

Under the exact aggregation condition the indirect utility function for each consuming unit takes the form

$$\ln V_k = \ln p'(\alpha_p + 1/2\, B_{pp} \ln p + B_{pA} A_k) - \ln M_k \cdot D\,, \qquad (k = 1, 2, \ldots, K)\,. \tag{8.117}$$

The indirect utility function is additive in functions of the attributes and total expenditure of the individual consuming unit. This property is invariant with respect to affine transformations of the indirect utility function, but is not preserved by arbitrary monotonic transformations. We conclude that the translog indirect utility function provides a cardinal measure of individual welfare as well as an ordinal measure. Given the indirect utility function for each unit, we can solve explicitly for the expenditure function

$$\ln M_k = \frac{1}{D} [\ln p'(\alpha_p + 1/2\, B_{pp} \ln p + B_{pA} A_k) - \ln V_k]\,, \qquad (k = 1, 2, \ldots, K)\,. \tag{8.118}$$

The expenditure function gives the minimum expenditure required for the consuming unit to achieve the utility level V_k, given prices p.

The expenditure function and the indirect utility function can be employed in assessing the impacts of alternative economic policies on the welfare of consuming units with common demographic characteristics. For this purpose we can employ the equivalent variation in total expenditure required for each consuming unit to achieve the level of utility after a change in economic policy at prices prevailing before the policy change. To analyze the impact of a change in economic policy on the welfare of the kth household, we first evaluate the indirect utility function after the change in policy has taken place. Suppose that prices are p^1 and expenditure for the kth household is M_k^1. The level of individual welfare for the kth consuming unit after the policy change V_k^1 is given by

$$\ln V_k^1 = \ln p^{1'}(\alpha_p + 1/2 B_{pp} \ln p^1 + B_{pA} A_k) - \ln M_k^1 \cdot D(p^1)\,, \qquad (k = 1, 2, \ldots, K)\,. \tag{8.119}$$

Next, we suppose that the prices prevailing before the change in policy are p^0. We can define the equivalent variation in total expenditure for the kth household, say E_k, as the additional expenditure required to achieve the level of utility after the change in policy V_k^1 at the old prices p^0

$$E_k = M_k^1 - M_k(p^0, V_k^1, A_k), \quad (k = 1, 2, \ldots, K). \tag{8.120}$$

The equivalent variation depends on the attributes A_k of the kth consuming unit, on the final expenditure and prices, which enter through the indirect utility function of the kth consuming unit $V_k^1(p^1, A_k, M_k^1)$, on the prices p^0 prevailing before the policy change, and on expenditure M_k^1 after the policy change. If the equivalent variation is positive, the total expenditure of the consuming unit must be increased in order to compensate for the policy change. If the equivalent variation is negative, the total expenditure of the consuming unit must be decreased to compensate for the change.

Alternative economic policies result in differences in the prices facing the individual consuming units. They also result in differences in total expenditures for the individual units. Differences in equivalent variations among consuming units reflect the fact that preferences and economic circumstances differ among units. To evaluate the impact of alternative policies on individual welfare, we must compare the equivalent variation in total expenditure required to achieve the level of utility resulting from each policy with the change in total expenditure that actually takes place. For this purpose we define the net equivalent variation in total expenditure for the kth household, say N_k^E, as the difference between the equivalent variation and the change in total expenditure

$$N_k^E = E_k - (M_k^1 - M_k^0) = M_k^0 - M_k(p^0, V_k^1, A_k) \quad (k = 1, 2, \ldots, K) \tag{8.121}$$

where M_k^0 is total expenditure before the policy change. If the net equivalent variation is negative, the welfare of the consuming unit is increased by the policy change; if the net equivalent variation is positive, the welfare of the consuming unit is decreased.

Alternatively, we can assess the impacts of economic policies on the welfare of individual consuming units by means of the compensating variation in total expenditure. This is the change in expenditure required for each consuming unit to achieve the level of utility before a change in economic policy at prices prevailing after the policy change. To analyze the impact of a change in economic policy on the welfare of the kth household, we first evaluate the indirect utility function before the change in policy has taken place. The level of individual welfare for the kth consuming unit before the policy change V_k^0 is given by

$$\ln V_k^0 = \ln p^{0\prime}\left(\alpha_p + \frac{1}{2} B_{pp} \ln p^0 + B_{pA} A_k\right) - \ln M_k^0 \cdot D(p^0)$$
$$(k = 1, 2, \ldots, K). \tag{8.122}$$

We can define the compensating variation in total expenditure for the kth household, say C_k, as the additional expenditure required to achieve the level of utility before the change in policy V_k^0 at the new prices p^1

$$C_k = M_k(p^1, V_k^0, A_k) - M_k^0, \quad (k = 1, 2, \ldots, K). \tag{8.123}$$

The compensating variation depends on the attributes A_k of the kth consuming unit, on the initial expenditure and prices, which enter through the indirect utility function of the kth consuming unit $V_k^0(p^0, A_k, M_k^0)$, on the prices p^1 prevailing after the policy change, and on expenditure M_k^0 before the policy change. If the compensating variation is positive, the total expenditure of the consuming unit must be increased in order to compensate for the policy change. If the compensating variation is negative, the total expenditure of the consuming unit must be decreased to compensate for the change.

To evaluate the impact of alternative economic policies on individual welfare, we must compare the compensating variation in total expenditure required to achieve the level of utility resulting from each policy with the change in total expenditure that actually takes place. For this purpose we define the net compensating variation in total expenditure for the kth household, say N_k^C, as the difference between the compensating variation and the change in total expenditure

$$N_k^C = C_k - (M_k^1 - M_k^0) = M_k(p^1, V_k^0, A_k) - M_k^1 \quad (k = 1, 2, \ldots, K). \tag{8.124}$$

If the net compensating variation is negative, the welfare of the consuming unit is increased by the policy change; if the net compensating variation is positive, the welfare of the consuming unit is decreased.[17]

Given the initial prices p^0 and initial expenditure M_k^0 for the kth consuming unit, determining the initial welfare for this unit V_k^0, the net equivalent variation provides a monotonic transformation of the final value of the indirect utility function V_k^1. However, this transformation is not invariant with respect to changes in the initial prices and initial expenditure and does not provide a cardinal measure of individual welfare. Similarly, given the final prices p^1 and the final expenditure M_k^1 for the kth consuming unit, determining the final welfare

V_k^1, the net compensating variation provides a monotonic transformation of the final value of the indirect utility function V_k^1. This transformation also fails to provide a cardinal measure of individual welfare. Net equivalent variations based on a given initial policy can be used to provide a unique ordering among a number of alternative economic policies, while net compensating variations can be used only for binary ordering of each policy relative to the initial policy.[18]

Aggregate expenditure shares, say w, are obtained by multiplying individual expenditure shares by expenditure for each consuming unit, adding over all consuming units, and dividing by aggregate expenditure

$$w = \frac{\sum M_k w_k}{\sum M_k}. \tag{8.125}$$

The aggregate expenditure shares can be written

$$w = \frac{1}{D}\left(\alpha_p + B_{pp} \ln p - B_{pp} \iota \frac{\sum M_k \ln M_k}{\sum M_k} + B_{pA} \frac{\sum M_k A_k}{\sum M_k}\right). \tag{8.126}$$

Aggregate expenditure shares depend on prices p. They also depend on the distribution of expenditures over all consuming units through the function $\sum M_k \ln M_k / \sum M_k$, which may be regarded as a statistic of the distribution. This single statistic summarizes the impact of changes in the distribution of expenditures among individual consuming units on aggregate expenditure allocation. Finally, aggregate expenditure shares depend on the distribution of expenditures among demographic groups through the function $\{\sum M_k A_k / \sum M_k\}$, which may be regarded as statistics of the joint distribution of expenditures and attributes. Since the attributes are represented as dummy variables, equal to one for a consuming unit with that characteristic and zero otherwise, these functions are equal to the shares of the corresponding demographic groups in aggregate expenditure. We conclude that aggregate expenditure patterns depend on the distribution of expenditure over all consuming units through the statistic $\sum M_k \ln M_k / \sum M_k$ and the distribution among demographic groups through the statistics $\{\sum M_k A_k / \sum M_k\}$.

8.5.B Integrability

Under exact aggregation systems of individual expenditure shares for consuming units with identical demographic characteristics can be recovered in one and only one way from the system of aggregate expenditure shares. This makes it possible to employ all of the implications of the theory of individual consumer behavior in specifying an econometric model of aggregate expenditure allocation. If a system of individual expenditure shares can be generated from an indirect utility function by means of the logarithmic form of Roy's Identity, we say that the system is *integrable*. A complete set of conditions for integrability, expressed in terms of the system of individual expenditure shares, is the following:

1. *Homogeneity*. The individual expenditure shares are homogeneous of degree zero in prices and expenditure.

We can write the individual expenditure shares in the form

$$w_k = \frac{1}{D}\,(\alpha_p + B_{pp} \ln p - B_{pM} \ln M_k + B_{pA} A_k), \qquad (k = 1, 2, \ldots K)$$

where the parameter vector β_{pM} is constant and the same for all consuming units. Homogeneity implies that this vector must satisfy the restrictions

$$\beta_{pM} = B_{pp}\, \iota\,. \tag{8.127}$$

Given the exact aggregation restrictions there are $N-1$ restrictions implied by homogeneity.

2. *Summability*. The sum of the individual expenditure shares over all commodity groups is equal to unity

$$\sum w_{nk} = 1\,, \qquad (k = 1, 2, \ldots, K)\,.$$

We can write the denominator D in the form

$$D = -1 + \beta_{Mp} \ln p$$

where the parameters $\{\beta_{Mp}\}$ are constant and the same for all commodity groups and all consuming units. Summability implies that these parameters must satisfy the restrictions

$$\beta_{Mp} = \iota' B_{pp}\,. \tag{8.128}$$

Given the exact aggregation restrictions, there are $N-1$ restrictions implied by summability.

3. *Symmetry.* The matrix of compensated own- and cross-price effects must be symmetric.

Imposing homogeneity and summability restrictions, we can write the individual expenditure shares in the form

$$w_k = \frac{1}{D}\left(\alpha_p + B_{pp} \ln \frac{p}{M_k} + B_{pA} A_k\right) \quad (k = 1, 2, \ldots, K)$$

where the denominator D can be written

$$D = -1 + \iota' B_{pp} \ln p\,.$$

The typical element of the matrix of uncompensated own- and cross-price effects takes the form

$$\frac{\partial x_{nk}}{\partial(p_m/M_k)} = \frac{1}{(p_n/M_k)(p_m//M_k)}\left[\frac{1}{D}\left(\beta_{nm} - w_{nk}\,\beta_{Mn}\right) - \delta_{nm}\, w_{nk}\right]$$
$$(n, m = 1, 2, \ldots, N;\, k = 1, 2, \ldots, K)$$

where

$$\beta_{Mm} = \sum \beta_{mn} \quad (m = 1, 2, \ldots, N)$$

and

$$\delta_{nm} = \begin{cases} 0 & \text{if} \quad n \neq m \\ 1 & \text{if} \quad n = m \end{cases} \quad (n, m = 1, 2, \ldots, N)\,.$$

The corresponding element of the matrix of compensated own- and cross-price effects takes the form

$$\frac{\partial x_{nk}}{\partial(p_m/M_k)} - x_{mk} \sum \frac{\partial\, x_{nk}}{\partial(p_l/M_k)} \cdot \frac{p_l}{M_k}$$
$$= \frac{1}{(p_n/M_k)(p_m/M_k)}\left[\frac{1}{D}\,(\beta_{nm} - w_{nk}\,\beta_{Mm}) - \delta_{nm}\, w_{nk}\right]$$
$$- x_{mk} \sum \frac{1}{(p_n/M_k)(p_l/M_k)}\left[\frac{1}{D}\,(\beta_{nl} - w_{nk}\beta_{Ml}) - \delta_{nl}\, w_{nk}\right]\frac{p_l}{M_k}$$
$$(n, m = 1, 2, \ldots, N;\;\; k = 1, 2, \ldots, K)\,.$$

The full matrix of compensated own- and cross-price effects, say S_k, becomes

$$S_k = P_k^{-1}\left[\frac{1}{D}(B_{pp} - w_k \iota' B_{pp} - B_{pp}\iota w_k' + w_k \iota' B_{pp} \iota w_k') + w_k w_k' - W_k\right] P_k^{-1}, \qquad (k = 1, 2, \ldots, K) \qquad (8.129)$$

where

$$P_k^{-1} = \begin{bmatrix} \frac{1}{p_1/M_k} & 0 & \cdots & 0 \\ 0 & \frac{1}{p_2/M_k} & \cdots & 0 \\ \vdots & \vdots & & \vdots \\ 0 & 0 & \cdots & \frac{1}{p_N/M_k} \end{bmatrix}, \quad W_k = \begin{bmatrix} w_{1k} & 0 & \cdots & 0 \\ 0 & w_{2k} & \cdots & 0 \\ \vdots & \vdots & & \vdots \\ 0 & 0 & \cdots & w_{Nk} \end{bmatrix}$$

$$(k = 1, 2, \ldots, K).$$

The matrix S_k, $(k = 1, 2, \ldots, K)$, must be symmetric for all consuming units.

If the system of individual expenditure shares is to be generated from a translog indirect utility function, a necessary and sufficient condition for symmetry is that the matrix B_{pp} must be symmetric. Without imposing the condition that this matrix is symmetric we can write the individual expenditure shares in the form

$$w_k = \frac{1}{D}\left(\alpha_p + B_{pp} \ln \frac{p}{M_k} + B_{pA} A_k\right), \qquad (k = 1, 2, \ldots, K).$$

Symmetry implies that the matrix of parameters B_{pp} must satisfy the restrictions

$$B_{pp} = B_{pp}'. \qquad (8.130)$$

The total number of symmetry restrictions is $1/2\, N(N-1)$.

4. *Nonnegativity*. The individual expenditure shares must be nonnegative

$$w_{nk} \geqq 0, \qquad (n = 1, 2, \ldots, N;\; k = 1, 2, \ldots, K).$$

By summability the individual expenditure shares sum to unity, so that we can write

$$w_k \geq 0\,, \quad (k = 1, 2, \ldots, K)$$

where $w_k \geq 0$ implies $w_{nk} \geqq 0$, $(n = 1, 2, \ldots, N)$, and $w_k \neq 0$.

Nonnegativity of the individual expenditure shares is implied by monotonicity of the indirect utility function

$$\frac{\partial \ln V_k}{\partial \ln (p/M_k)} \leqq 0\,, \quad (k = 1, 2, \ldots, K)\,.$$

For the translog indirect utility function the conditions for monotonicity take the form

$$\frac{\partial \ln V_k}{\partial \ln (p/M_k)} = \alpha_p + B_{pp} \ln \frac{p}{M_k} + B_{pA} A_k \leqq 0\,, \ (k = 1, 2, \ldots, K)\,. \qquad (8.131)$$

Summability implies that not all the expenditure shares are zero, so that

$$D = -1 + \iota' \beta_{pp} \ln p < 0\,. \qquad (8.132)$$

Since the translog indirect utility function is quadratic in the logarithms of prices ln p, we can always choose the prices so that the individual expenditure shares violate the nonnegativity conditions. Alternatively, we can say that it is possible to choose the prices so the monotonicity of the indirect utility function is violated. Accordingly, we cannot impose restrictions on the parameters of the translog indirect utility function that would imply nonnegativity of the individual expenditure shares or monotonicity of the indirect utility function for all prices and expenditure. Instead we consider restrictions on the parameters that imply quasiconvexity of the indirect utility functions or monotonicity of the system of individual demand functions for all nonnegative expenditures shares.

5. *Monotonicity*. The matrix of compensated own- and cross-price effects must be nonpositive definite.

We first impose homogeneity, summability, and symmetry restrictions on the expenditure shares. We restrict consideration to values of the prices p, expenditure M_k, $(k = 1, 2, \ldots, K)$, and attributes A_k, $(k = 1, 2, \ldots, K)$ for which the individual expenditure shares satisfy the nonnegativity restrictions, so that $w_k \geqq 0$, $(k = 1, 2, \ldots, K)$. The summability restrictions imply that $\iota' w_k = 1$, $(k = 1, 2, \ldots, K)$. We can write the matrix of price effects in the form

$$S_k = P_k^{-1}\left[\frac{1}{D}(I - \iota w_k')'B_{pp}(I - \iota w_k') + w'w_k' - W_k\right]P_k^{-1}, \qquad (k = 1, 2, \ldots, K).$$

A necessary and sufficient condition for monotonicity of the system of individual expenditure shares is that the matrix $D^{-1}(I - \iota w_k')B_{pp}(I - \iota w_k') + w_k w_k' - W_k$, $(k = 1, 2, \ldots, K)$, is nonpositive definite for all expenditure shares satisfying the nonnegativity and summability conditions.

8.5.C Restrictions Implied by Monotonicity

We next consider restrictions on the parameters of the translog indirect utility function implied by monotonicity of the individual expenditure shares. If $\iota' B_{pp} = 0$, the denominator D is independent of prices and the translog indirect utility function is homothetic; otherwise, for a given value of the individual expenditure shares we can make the denominator D as large or as small as we wish by a suitable choice of prices p and expenditure M_k $(k = 1, 2, \ldots, K)$. A necessary and sufficient condition for monotonicity of the system of individual expenditure shares is that the matrices $D^{-1}(I - \iota w_k')' - B_{pp}(I - \iota w_k')$ and $w_k w_k' - W_k$, $(k = 1, 2, \ldots, K)$ are both nonpositive definite.

The matrix $w_k w_k{}' - W_k$, $(k =, 1, 2, \ldots, K)$, is nonpositive definite for all expenditure shares satisfying the nonnegativity and summability restrictions. A sufficient condition for nonpositive definiteness of the matrix $D^{-1}(I - \iota w_k')'B_{pp}(I - \iota w_k')$ is that the matrix B_{pp} is nonnegative definite. However, if the quadratic form $z'B_{pp}z$ achieves the value zero, which must be a minimum, for any vector z not equal to zero, then z is a characteristic vector of B_{pp} corresponding to a zero characteristic value. Since $\iota' B_{pp}\iota = 0$ by exact aggregation, ι is a characteristic vector of B_{pp} corresponding to a zero characteristic value if B_{pp} is nonnegative definite. Hence, $B_{pp}\iota = 0$ and the translog indirect utility function is homothetic. If B_{pp} is not nonnegative definite, then there is a vector z such that

$$z'B_{pp}z < 0$$

where z cannot be written in the form

$$z = (I - \iota\, w_k')x\,, \qquad (k = 1, 2, \ldots, K)$$

for some x and for individual expenditure shares such that $w_k \geqq 0$, $\iota' w_k = 1$, $(k = 1, 2, \ldots, K)$.

To characterize all vectors z that can be represented in the form given above, we first observe that these vectors can be written

$$z = x - (w_k' x)\iota\,, \quad (k = 1, 2, \ldots, K)$$

so that the vector z is equal to a vector x less a vector with elements equal to a weighted average of the elements x. Unless all the elements of x are the same, so that $z = 0$ or unless $w_k' x = 0$, $(k = 1, 2, \ldots, K)$, so that $z = x$, the vector z has at least one positive element and one negative element. Furthermore, if $w_k' x = 0$, $(k = 1, 2, \ldots, K)$, then the vector x has at least one positive and one negative element or complementary slackness obtains

$$\left.\begin{array}{l} x_n > 0 \text{ implies } w_{nk} = 0 \\ w_{nk} > 0 \text{ implies } x_n = 0 \end{array}\right\}, \quad (n = 1, 2, \ldots, N;\ k = 1, 2, \ldots, K)\,.$$

We conclude that either the vector z will have at least one positive and one negative element or the vector $z \geq 0$ or $z \leq 0$ with at least one zero element. These conditions rule the possibilities that $z > 0$ or $z < 0$, so that if B_{pp} is not nonnegative definite, then

$$z' B_{pp} z < 0$$

implies $z > 0$ or $z < 0$. We next consider the class of all matrices B_{pp} that satisfy this condition.

First, we introduce the definition due to Martos (1969) of a *merely positive subdefinite matrix*. A merely positive subdefinite matrix, say M, is a real symmetric matrix such that

$$x' Mx < 0$$

implies $Mx \geq 0$ or $Mx \leq 0$ and M is not nonnegative definite. Similarly, a *strictly merely positive subdefinite* matrix is a real symmetric matrix such that

$$x' Mx < 0$$

implies $Mx > 0$ or $Mx < 0$. A complete characterization of merely positive subdefinite matrices has been provided by Cottle and Ferland (1972), who have shown that such matrices must satisfy the conditions:

1. M consists of only nonpositive elements.
2. M has exactly one negative characteristic value.

A complete characterization of strictly merely positive subdefinite matrices has been provided by Martos (1969), who has shown that a strictly merely positive subdefinite matrix must satisfy the additional condition:

3. M does not contain a row (or column) of zeros.

We observe that this condition does not imply in itself that a strictly merely positive subdefinite matrix is nonsingular.

We are now in a position to characterize completely the class of matrices B_{pp} such that

$$z' B_{pp} z < 0$$

implies $z > 0$ or $z < 0$. A necessary and sufficient condition is that B_{pp}^{-1} exists and is strictly merely positive subdefinite. First, if B_{pp}^{-1} exists and is strictly merely positive subdefinite, then

$$x' B_{pp}^{-1} x < 0$$

implies $B_{pp}^{-1} x > 0$ or $B_{pp}^{-1} x < 0$. But then

$$x' B_{pp}^{-1} \, B_{pp} \, B_{pp}^{-1} x = z' \, B_{pp} z < 0$$

implies $z > 0$ or $z < 0$, where $z = B_{pp}^{-1} x$.

Conversely, if the condition on the matrix B_{pp} given above is satisfied, then B_{pp} has exactly one negative characteristic value. This matrix has at least one negative characteristic value, otherwise it would be nonnegative definite. If there were two negative characteristic values with characteristic vectors, say z_1 and z_2, then $z_1' \, B_{pp} z_1 < 0$ and $z_2' \, B_{pp} z_2 < 0$, so that $z_1 > 0$, $z_2 > 0$, and $z_1' \, z_2 > 0$, contradicting the orthogonality of the characteristic vectors of a real, symmetric matrix. Second, the matrix B_{pp} has no zero characteristic values; otherwise

$$(z_- + \alpha \, z_0)' \, B_{pp}(z_- + \alpha \, z_0) + z_-' B_{pp} z_- < 0$$

where z_- is a characteristic vector corresponding to the negative characteristic value, z_0 is a characteristics vector corresponding to a zero characteristic value, and α is a scalar. The scalar α can be chosen so as to make $z_- + \alpha z_0$ violate the conditions that $z_- + \alpha z_0 > 0$ or $z_- + \alpha z_0 < 0$. We conclude that the matrix B_{pp} has no zero characteristic values and is nonsingular.

Since the matrix B_{pp} is nonsingular, the inverse matrix B_{pp}^{-1} exists and we can write

$$x' B_{pp}^{-1} x = x' B_{pp}^{-1} B_{pp} B_{pp}^{-1} x = z' B_{pp} z < 0$$

implies $z > 0$ or $z < 0$, where $z = B_{pp}^{-1} x$, so that $B_{pp}^{-} x > 0$ or $B_{pp}^{-1} x < 0$ and B_{pp}^{-1} is strictly merely positive subdefinite. We conclude that the inverse matrix B_{pp}^{-1} consists of only nonpositive elements, has exactly one negative characteristic value, and does not contain a row (or column) of zeros.

To impose restrictions on the matrix B_{pp} implied by monotonicity of the systems of individual expenditure shares, we first provide a Cholesky factorization of this matrix

$$B_{pp} = LDL'$$

where L is a unit lower triangular matrix and D is a diagonal matrix. As an illustration, we can write the matrix B_{pp} in terms of its Cholesky factorization for a model of consumer behavior with five commodity groups as follows

$$B_{pp} = \begin{bmatrix} \delta_1 & \delta_1\lambda_{21} & \delta_1\lambda_{31} & \delta_1\lambda_{41} & \delta_1\lambda_{51} \\ \delta_l\lambda_{21} & \delta_1\lambda_{21}^2 + \delta_2 & \delta_1\lambda_{31}\lambda_{21} + \delta_2\lambda_{32} & \delta_1\lambda_{41}\lambda_{21} + \delta_2\lambda_{42} & \delta_1\lambda_{51}\lambda_{21} + \delta_2\lambda_{52} \\ \delta_1\lambda_{31} & \delta_1\lambda_{21}\lambda_{31} + \delta_2\lambda_{32} & \delta_1\lambda_{31}^2 + \delta_2\lambda_{32}^2 + \delta_3 & \delta_1\lambda_{41}\lambda_{31} + \delta_2\lambda_{42}\lambda_{32} + \delta_3\lambda_{43} & \delta_1\lambda_{51}\lambda_{31} + \delta_2\lambda_{52}\lambda_{32} + \delta_3\lambda_{53} \\ \delta_1\lambda_{41} & \delta_1\lambda_{21}\lambda_{41} + \delta_2\lambda_{42} & \delta_1\lambda_{31}\lambda_{41} + \delta_2\lambda_{32}\lambda_{42} + \delta_3\lambda_{43} & \delta_1\lambda_{41}^2 + \delta_2\lambda_{42}^2 + \delta_3\lambda_{43}^2 + \delta_4 & \delta_1\lambda_{51}\lambda_{41} + \delta_2\lambda_{52}\lambda_{42} + \delta_3\lambda_{53}\lambda_{43} + \delta_4\lambda_{54} \\ \delta_1\lambda_{51} & \delta_1\lambda_{21}\lambda_{51} + \delta_2\lambda_{52} & \delta_1\lambda_{31}\lambda_{51} + \delta_2\lambda_{32}\lambda_{52} + \delta_3\lambda_{53} & \delta_1\lambda_{41}\lambda_{51} + \delta_2\lambda_{42}\lambda_{52} + \delta_3\lambda_{43}\lambda_{53} + \delta_4\lambda_{54} & \delta_1\lambda_{51}^2 + \delta_2\lambda_{52}^2 + \delta_3\lambda_{53}^2 + \delta_4\lambda_{54}^2 + \delta_5 \end{bmatrix}$$

where

$$L = \begin{bmatrix} 1 & 0 & 0 & 0 & 0 \\ \lambda_{21} & 1 & 0 & 0 & 0 \\ \lambda_{31} & \lambda_{32} & 1 & 0 & 0 \\ \lambda_{41} & \lambda_{42} & \lambda_{43} & 1 & 0 \\ \lambda_{51} & \lambda_{52} & \lambda_{53} & \lambda_{54} & 1 \end{bmatrix}, \qquad D = \begin{bmatrix} \delta_1 & 0 & 0 & 0 & 0 \\ 0 & \delta_2 & 0 & 0 & 0 \\ 0 & 0 & \delta_3 & 0 & 0 \\ 0 & 0 & 0 & \delta_4 & 0 \\ 0 & 0 & 0 & 0 & \delta_5 \end{bmatrix}.$$

It is important to note that not every matrix with an inverse that is strictly merely positive subdefinite is Cholesky factorizable. For example, it the matrix B_{pp} for a model of consumer behavior with two commodity groups were to take the form

$$B_{pp} = \begin{bmatrix} 0 & -1 \\ -1 & 0 \end{bmatrix},$$

then the inverse matrix B_{pp}^{-1} would take the form

$$B_{pp}^{-1} = \begin{bmatrix} 0 & -1 \\ -1 & 0 \end{bmatrix},$$

which is strictly merely positive subdefinite with a negative characteristics value -1 and a positive characteristic value $+1$. The formulas for the Cholesky factorization

$$B_{pp} = \begin{bmatrix} \delta_1 & \delta_1\lambda_{21} \\ \delta_1\lambda_{21} & \delta_1\lambda_{21}^{1} + \delta_2 \end{bmatrix},$$

reveal that the condition $\delta_1 = 0$ contradicts the condition $\delta_1\lambda_{21} = -1$. However, the set of real symmetric matrices that are not Cholesky factorizable has measure zero in the set of all real symmetric matrices.

Next for a model of consumer behavior with five commodity groups we can derive an appropriate expression for B_{pp}^{-1}

$$B_{pp}^{-1} = (L')^{-1}\ D^{-1}\ L^{-1}$$

where

$$L^{-1} = \begin{bmatrix} 1 & 0 & 0 & 0 & 0 \\ -\lambda_{21} & 1 & 0 & 0 & 0 \\ -\lambda_{31} + \lambda_{32}\lambda_{21} & -\lambda_{32} & 1 & 0 & 0 \\ \begin{array}{l} -\lambda_{41} + \lambda_{42}\lambda_{21} + \lambda_{43}\lambda_{32} \\ \quad - \lambda_{43}\lambda_{32}\lambda_{21} \end{array} & -\lambda_{42} + \lambda_{43}\lambda_{32} & -\lambda_{43} & 1 & 0 \\ \begin{array}{l} -\lambda_{51} + \lambda_{52}\lambda_{21} + \lambda_{53}\lambda_{31} + \lambda_{54}\lambda_{41} \\ \quad - \lambda_{53}\lambda_{32}\lambda_{21} - \lambda_{54}\lambda_{42}\lambda_{21} - \lambda_{54}\lambda_{43}\lambda_{31} \\ \quad + \lambda_{54}\lambda_{43}\lambda_{32}\lambda_{21} \end{array} & \begin{array}{l} -\lambda_{52} + \lambda_{53}\lambda_{32} + \lambda_{54}\lambda_{42} \\ \quad - \lambda_{54}\lambda_{43}\lambda_{32} \end{array} & -\lambda_{53} + \lambda_{54}\lambda_{43} & -\lambda_{54} & 1 \end{bmatrix}$$

and

$$D^{-1} = \begin{bmatrix} \frac{1}{\delta_1} & 0 & 0 & 0 & 0 \\ 0 & \frac{1}{\delta_2} & 0 & 0 & 0 \\ 0 & 0 & \frac{1}{\delta_3} & 0 & 0 \\ 0 & 0 & 0 & \frac{1}{\delta_4} & 0 \\ 0 & 0 & 0 & 0 & \frac{1}{\delta_5} \end{bmatrix}.$$

Representing B_{pp}^{-1} in the form (β_{pp}^{ij}) where β_{pp}^{ij} is the element of the ith row and jth column of B_{pp}^{-1}, we obtain the expressions for these elements in table 8.1 for a model of consumer behavior with five commodity groups.

Since the matrix B_{pp}^{-1} is strictly merely positive subdefinite, all the elements of this matrix are nonpositive. Expressing the nonpositivity constraints on these elements in terms of the elements of the Cholesky factorization of the matrix B_{pp}, where

$$B_{pp} = LDL'$$

we obtain the restrictions given in table 8.2 for a model of consumer behavior with five commodity groups. In deriving these restrictions we make use of the fact that B_{pp} has exactly one negative Cholesky value, δ_5, and four positive Cholesky values δ_1, δ_2, δ_3, δ_4.

The exact aggregation condition

$$\iota' B_{pp} \iota = 0$$

implies that

$$\begin{aligned} &\delta_1(1 + \lambda_{21} + \lambda_{31} + \lambda_{41} + \lambda_{51})^2 + \delta_2(1 + \lambda_{32} + \lambda_{42} + \lambda_{52})^2 \\ &\quad + \delta_3(1 + \lambda_{43} + \lambda_{53})^2 + \delta_4(1 + \lambda_{54})^2 + \delta_5 = 0 \end{aligned}$$

so that we can use this restriction to eliminate the parameter δ_1 from the expression for β_{pp}^{11}, obtaining the inequality

$$\begin{aligned} &\delta_2\delta_3\delta_4\delta_5(1 + \lambda_{21} + \lambda_{31} + \lambda_{41} + \lambda_{51})^2 \\ &\qquad - [\delta_2(1 + \lambda_{32} + \lambda_{42} + \lambda_{52})^2 + \delta_3(1 + \lambda_{43} + \lambda_{53})^2 + \delta_4(1 + \lambda_{54})^2 + \delta_5] \\ &\qquad \times [\delta_3\delta_4\delta_5(-\lambda_{21})^2 + \delta_2\delta_4\delta_5(-\lambda_{31} + \lambda_{32}\lambda_{21})^2 \\ &\qquad + \delta_2\delta_3\delta_5(-\lambda_{41} + \lambda_{42}\lambda_{21} + \lambda_{43}\lambda_{31} - \lambda_{43}\lambda_{32}\lambda_{21})^2 \\ &\qquad + \delta_2\delta_3\delta_4(-\lambda_{31} + \lambda_{52}\lambda_{21} + \lambda_{53}\lambda_{31} + \lambda_{54}\lambda_{42} - \lambda_{53}\lambda_{32}\lambda_{21} \\ &\qquad - \lambda_{54}\lambda_{42}\lambda_{21} - \lambda_{54}\lambda_{43}\lambda_{31} + \lambda_{54}\lambda_{43}\lambda_{32}\lambda_{21})] \geqq 0 . \end{aligned} \tag{8.133}$$

Table 8.1
Elements of B_{pp}^{-1}

β_{pp}^{11}	$\frac{1}{\delta_1} + \frac{1}{\delta_2}(-\lambda_{21})^2 + \frac{1}{\delta_3}(-\lambda_{31} + \lambda_{32}\lambda_{21})^2 + \frac{1}{\delta_4}(-\lambda_{41} + \lambda_{42}\lambda_{21} + \lambda_{43}\lambda_{31} - \lambda_{43}\lambda_{32}\lambda_{21})^2 + \frac{1}{\delta_5}(-\lambda_{51} + \lambda_{52}\lambda_{21} + \lambda_{53}\lambda_{31} + \lambda_{54}\lambda_{41} - \lambda_{53}\lambda_{32}\lambda_{21} - \lambda_{54}\lambda_{42}\lambda_{21} - \lambda_{54}\lambda_{43}\lambda_{31} + \lambda_{54}\lambda_{43}\lambda_{32}\lambda_{21})^2$
β_{pp}^{12}	$\frac{1}{\delta_2}(-\lambda_{21}) + \frac{1}{\delta_3}(-\lambda_{32})(-\lambda_{31} + \lambda_{32}\lambda_{21}) + \frac{1}{\delta_4}(-\lambda_{42} + \lambda_{43}\lambda_{32})(-\lambda_{41} + \lambda_{42}\lambda_{21} + \lambda_{43}\lambda_{31} - \lambda_{43}\lambda_{32}\lambda_{21}) + \frac{1}{\delta_5}(-\lambda_{52} + \lambda_{53}\lambda_{32} + \lambda_{54}\lambda_{42} - \lambda_{54}\lambda_{43}\lambda_{32})(\lambda_{51} + \lambda_{52}\lambda_{21} + \lambda_{53}\lambda_{31} + \lambda_{54}\lambda_{41} - \lambda_{53}\lambda_{32}\lambda_{21} - \lambda_{54}\lambda_{42}\lambda_{21} - \lambda_{54}\lambda_{43}\lambda_{31} + \lambda_{54}\lambda_{43}\lambda_{32}\lambda_{21})$
β_{pp}^{13}	$\frac{1}{\delta_3}(-\lambda_{31} + \lambda_{32}\lambda_{21}) + \frac{1}{\delta_4}(-\lambda_{43})(-\lambda_{41} + \lambda_{42}\lambda_{21} + \lambda_{43}\lambda_{31} - \lambda_{43}\lambda_{32}\lambda_{21}) + \frac{1}{\delta_5}(-\lambda_{53} + \lambda_{54}\lambda_{43})(-\lambda_{51} + \lambda_{52}\lambda_{21} + \lambda_{53}\lambda_{31} + \lambda_{54}\lambda_{41} - \lambda_{53}\lambda_{32}\lambda_{21} - \lambda_{54}\lambda_{43}\lambda_{31} - \lambda_{54}\lambda_{43}\lambda_{31} + \lambda_{54}\lambda_{43}\lambda_{32}\lambda_{21})$
β_{pp}^{14}	$\frac{1}{\delta_4}(-\lambda_{41} + \lambda_{42}\lambda_{21} + \lambda_{43}\lambda_{31} - \lambda_{43}\lambda_{32}\lambda_{21}) + \frac{1}{\delta_5}(-\lambda_{54})(-\lambda_{51} + \lambda_{52}\lambda_{21} + \lambda_{53}\lambda_{31} + \lambda_{54}\lambda_{41} - \lambda_{53}\lambda_{32}\lambda_{21} - \lambda_{54}\lambda_{42}\lambda_{21} - \lambda_{54}\lambda_{43}\lambda_{31} + \lambda_{54}\lambda_{43}\lambda_{32}\lambda_{21})$
β_{pp}^{15}	$\frac{1}{\delta_5}(-\lambda_{51} + \lambda_{52}\lambda_{21} + \lambda_{53}\lambda_{31} + \lambda_{54}\lambda_{41} - \lambda_{53}\lambda_{32}\lambda_{21} - \lambda_{54}\lambda_{43}\lambda_{31} + \lambda_{54}\lambda_{43}\lambda_{32}\lambda_{21})$
β_{pp}^{22}	$\frac{1}{\delta_2} + \frac{1}{\delta_3}(-\lambda_{32})^2 + \frac{1}{\delta_4}(-\lambda_{42} + \lambda_{43}\lambda_{32})^2 + \frac{1}{\delta_5}(-\lambda_{52} + \lambda_{53}\lambda_{32} + \lambda_{54}\lambda_{42} - \lambda_{54}\lambda_{43}\lambda_{32})^2$
β_{pp}^{23}	$\frac{1}{\delta_3}(-\lambda_{32}) + \frac{1}{\delta_4}(-\lambda_{43})(-\lambda_{42} + \lambda_{43}\lambda_{32}) + \frac{1}{\delta_5}(-\lambda_{53} + \lambda_{54}\lambda_{43})(-\lambda_{52} + \lambda_{53}\lambda_{32} + \lambda_{54}\lambda_{42} - \lambda_{54}\lambda_{43}\lambda_{32})$
β_{pp}^{24}	$\frac{1}{\delta_4}(-\lambda_{42} + \lambda_{43}\lambda_{32}) + \frac{1}{\delta_5}(-\lambda_{54})(-\lambda_{52} + \lambda_{53}\lambda_{32} + \lambda_{54}\lambda_{42} - \lambda_{54}\lambda_{43}\lambda_{32})$
β_{pp}^{25}	$\frac{1}{\delta_5}(-\lambda_{52} + \lambda_{53}\lambda_{32} + \lambda_{54}\lambda_{42} - \lambda_{54}\lambda_{43}\lambda_{32})$

Table 8.1 (continued)

β_{pp}^{33}	$\frac{1}{\delta_3} + \frac{1}{\delta_4}(-\lambda_{43})^2 + \frac{1}{\delta_5}(-\lambda_{53} + \lambda_{54}\lambda_{43})^2$
β_{pp}^{34}	$\frac{1}{\delta_4}(-\lambda_{43}) + \frac{1}{\delta_5}(-\lambda_{54})(-\lambda_{53} + \lambda_{54}\lambda_{43})$
β_{pp}^{35}	$\frac{1}{\delta_5}(-\lambda_{53} + \lambda_{54}\lambda_{43})$
β_{pp}^{44}	$\frac{1}{\delta_4} + \frac{1}{\delta_5}(-\lambda_{54})^2$
β_{pp}^{45}	$\frac{1}{\delta_5}(-\lambda_{54})$
β_{pp}^{55}	$\frac{1}{\delta_5}$

Finally, we must include restrictions on the Cholesky values; for a model of consumer behavior with five commodity groups these take the form

$$\begin{aligned} &\delta_5 \leqq 0 \\ &\delta_4 \geqq 0 \\ &\delta_3 \geqq 0 \\ &\delta_2 \geqq 0 \\ &\delta_1 \geqq 0 . \end{aligned} \tag{8.134}$$

Combining these restrictions with the restrictions on the elements of B_{pp}^{-1} given in table 8.2, we obtain a complete set of restrictions implied by the monotonicity of the systems of individual expenditure shares.

8.5.D Summary and Conclusion

In this section we have presented a model of aggregate consumer behavior based on transcendental logarithmic or translog indirect utility functions for all consuming units. These indirect utility functions incorporate restrictions on individual behavior that result from maximization of a utility function subject to a budget constraint. Each consuming unit has an indirect utility function that is homogeneous of degree zero in prices and expenditure, nonincreasing in prices

Table 8.2
Restrictions on the elements of $B_{pp} = LDL'$

$\beta^{55}_{pp} \leqq 0$	$-\delta_5 \geqq 0$
$\beta^{45}_{pp} \leqq 0$	$-\lambda_{54} \geqq 0$
$\beta^{44}_{pp} \leqq 0$	$\delta_5 + \delta_4(-\lambda_{54})^2 \geqq 0$
$\beta^{35}_{pp} \leqq 0$	$-\lambda_{53} + \lambda_{54}\lambda_{43} \geqq 0$
$\beta^{34}_{pp} \leqq 0$	$\delta_5(-\lambda_{43}) + \delta_4(-\lambda_{54})(-\lambda_{53} + \lambda_{54}\lambda_{43}) \geqq 0$
$\beta^{33}_{pp} \leqq 0$	$\delta_5\delta_4 + \delta_3\delta_5(-\lambda_{43}) + \delta_3\delta_4(-\lambda_{53} + \lambda_{54}\lambda_{43})^2 \geqq 0$
$\beta^{25}_{pp} \leqq 0$	$-\lambda_{52} + \lambda_{53}\lambda_{32} + \lambda_{54}\lambda_{42} - \lambda_{54}\lambda_{43}\lambda_{32}) \geqq 0$
$\beta^{24}_{pp} \leqq 0$	$\delta_5(-\lambda_{42} + \lambda_{43}\lambda_{32}) + \delta_4(-\lambda_{54})(-\lambda_{52} + \lambda_{53}\lambda_{32} + \lambda_{54}\lambda_{42} - \lambda_{54}\lambda_{43}\lambda_{32}) \geqq 0$
$\beta^{23}_{pp} \leqq 0$	$\delta_4\delta_5(-\lambda_{32}) + \delta_3\delta_5(-\lambda_{43})(-\lambda_{42} + \lambda_{34}\lambda_{32})$ $+ \delta_3\delta_4(-\lambda_{53} + \lambda_{54}\lambda_{43})(-\lambda_{52} + \lambda_{53}\lambda_{32} + \lambda_{54}\lambda_{42} - \lambda_{54}\lambda_{43}\lambda_{32}) \geqq 0$
$\beta^{22}_{pp} \leqq 0$	$\delta_3\delta_4\delta_5 + \delta_2\delta_4\delta_5(-\lambda_{32})^2 + \delta_2\delta_3\delta_5(-\lambda_{42} + \lambda_{43}\lambda_{32})^2$ $+ \delta_2\delta_3\delta_4(-\lambda_{52} + \lambda_{53}\lambda_{32} + \lambda_{54}\lambda_{42} - \lambda_{54}\lambda_{43}\lambda_{32})^2 \geqq 0$
$\beta^{15}_{pp} \leqq 0$	$-\lambda_{51} + \lambda_{52}\lambda_{21} + \lambda_{53}\lambda_{31} + \lambda_{54}\lambda_{41} - \lambda_{53}\lambda_{32}\lambda_{21} - \lambda_{54}\lambda_{42}\lambda_{21} - \lambda_{54}\lambda_{43}\lambda_{31}$ $+ \lambda_{54}\lambda_{43}\lambda_{32}\lambda_{21} \geqq 0$
$\beta^{14}_{pp} \leqq 0$	$\delta_5(-\lambda_{41} + \lambda_{42}\lambda_{21} + \lambda_{43}\lambda_{31} - \lambda_{43}\lambda_{32}\lambda_{21}) + \delta_4(-\lambda_{54})(-\lambda_{51} + \lambda_{52}\lambda_{21}$ $+ \lambda_{53}\lambda_{31} + \lambda_{54}\lambda_{41} - \lambda_{53}\lambda_{32}\lambda_{21} - \lambda_{54}\lambda_{42}\lambda_{21} - \lambda_{54}\lambda_{43}\lambda_{31} + \lambda_{54}\lambda_{43}\lambda_{32}\lambda_{21}) \geqq 0$
$\beta^{13}_{pp} \geqq 0$	$\delta_4\delta_5(-\lambda_{31} + \lambda_{32}\lambda_{21}) + \delta_3\delta_5(-\lambda_{43})(-\lambda_{41} + \lambda_{42}\lambda_{21} + \lambda_{43}\lambda_{31} - \lambda_{43}\lambda_{32}\lambda_{21})$ $+ \delta_3\delta_4(-\lambda_{53} + \lambda_{54}\lambda_{43})(-\lambda_{51} + \lambda_{52}\lambda_{21} + \lambda_{53}\lambda_{31} + \lambda_{54}\lambda_{41}$ $- \lambda_{53}\lambda_{32}\lambda_{21} - \lambda_{54}\lambda_{42}\lambda_{21} - \lambda_{54}\lambda_{43}\lambda_{31} + \lambda_{54}\lambda_{43}\lambda_{32}\lambda_{21}) \geqq 0$
$\beta^{12}_{pp} \leqq 0$	$\delta_3\delta_4\delta_5(-\lambda_{21}) + \delta_2\delta_4\delta_5(-\lambda_{32})(-\lambda_{31} + \lambda_{32}\lambda_{21})$ $+ \delta_2\delta_3\delta_5(-\lambda_{42} + \lambda_{43}\lambda_{32})(-\lambda_{41} + \lambda_{42}\lambda_{21} + \lambda_{43}\lambda_{31} - \lambda_{43}\lambda_{32}\lambda_{21})$ $+ \delta_2\delta_3\delta_4(-\lambda_{52} + \lambda_{53}\lambda_{32} + \lambda_{54}\lambda_{42} - \lambda_{54}\lambda_{43}\lambda_{32})(-\lambda_{51} + \lambda_{52}\lambda_{21}$ $+ \lambda_{54}\lambda_{41} - \lambda_{53}\lambda_{32}\lambda_{21} - \lambda_{54}\lambda_{42}\lambda_{21} - \lambda_{56}\lambda_{43}\lambda_{31} + \lambda_{54}\lambda_{43}\lambda_{32}\lambda_{21}) \geqq 0$
$\beta^{11}_{pp} \geqq 0$	$\delta_2\delta_3\delta_4\delta_5 + \delta_1\delta_3\delta_4\delta_5(-\lambda_{21})^2$ $+ \delta_1\delta_2\delta_4\delta_5(-\lambda_{31} + \delta_{32}\lambda_{21})^2 + \delta_1\delta_2\delta_3\delta_5(-\lambda_{41} + \lambda_{42}\lambda_{21} + \lambda_{43}\lambda_{31} - \lambda_{43}\lambda_{32}\lambda_{21})^2$ $+ \delta_1\delta_2\delta_3\delta_4(-\lambda_{51} + \lambda_{52}\lambda_{21} + \lambda_{53}\lambda_{31} + \lambda_{54}\lambda_{41} - \lambda_{53}\lambda_{32}\lambda_{21}$ $- \lambda_{54}\lambda_{43}\lambda_{31} + \lambda_{54}\lambda_{43}\lambda_{32}\lambda_{21}) \geqq 0$

and nondecreasing in expenditure, and quasiconvex in prices and expenditure.

To incorporate differences in individual preferences into our model of aggregate consumer behavior we allow the indirect utility functions for all consuming units to depend on attributes, such as demographic characteristics, that vary among individuals. Each attribute is represented by a dummy variable equal to unity when the consuming unit has the corresponding characteristic and zero otherwise.

Given a translog indirect utility function for each consuming unit, we derive the expenditure shares for that unit by means of Roy's Identity. This results in expenditure shares that can be expressed as ratios of two functions that are linear in the logarithms of ratios of prices for all commodities to total expenditure and in attributes. The denominators of these ratios are functions that are the same for all commodity groups. Under exact aggregation the individual expenditure shares are linear in functions of attributes and total expenditure, so that the denominators are independent of total expenditure and attributes and are the same for all individuals.

Under the exact aggregation condition the translog indirect utility function is additive in functions of the attributes and total expenditure of the individual consuming unit and provides a cardinal measure of individual welfare as well as an ordinal measure. Given the indirect utility function for each unit, we can solve explicitly for the expenditure function, giving the minimum expenditure required to achieve a stipulated level of individual welfare for given prices.

The expenditure function and indirect utility function can be employed in assessing the impacts of alternative economic policies on the welfare of individual consuming units. For this purpose we introduce equivalent and compensating variations in expenditure. The equivalent variation gives the additional expenditure required to achieve the level of utility after the change in policy. The compensating variation gives the additional expenditure required to achieve the level of utility before the change in policy.

To derive aggregate expenditure shares we multiply the individual expenditure shares by total expenditure for each consuming unit, sum over all consuming units, and divide by aggregate expenditure. The aggregate expenditure shares, like the individual shares, can be expressed as ratios of two functions. The denominators are the same as for individual expenditure shares. The numerators are linear in the logarithms of prices, in a statistic of the distribution of expenditure over all consuming units $\sum M_k \ln M_k / \sum M_k$, and in the shares of all demographic groups in aggregate expenditure $\{\sum M_k \; A_k / \sum M_k\}$.

The individual expenditure shares are homogeneous of degree zero in prices and expenditure. Given the restrictions implied by exact aggregation, this implies an additional $N - 1$ restriction on the parameters of the translog indirect utility functions, where N is the number of commodities. Second, the sum of individual expenditure shares over all commodity groups is equal to unity. Again, given the exact aggregation restrictions, there are N additional restrictions implied by summability. Third, the matrix of compensated own- and cross-price effects must by symmetric. This implies $1/2 \; N \; (N - 1)$ restrictions on the parameters of the translog indirect utility functions.

Monotonicity of the indirect utility functions implies that the individual expenditure shares must be nonnegative. Similarly, quasiconvexity of the indirect utility functions implies that the individual expenditures shares must be monotonic or, equivalently, that the matrix of compensated own- and cross-price substitution effects must be nonpositive definite. It is always possible to choose prices so that monotonicity of the indirect utility functions or nonnegativity of the individual expenditure shares is violated. Accordingly, we consider restrictions that imply monotonicity of the expenditure shares wherever they are nonnegative.

To impose monotonicity of the system of individual expenditure shares we represent the matrix of price coefficients B_{pp} in terms of its Cholesky factorization. There is a one-to-one transformation between the elements of this matrix and the parameters of the Cholesky factorization. To impose the restrictions implied by monotonicity we can fit the parameters of the Cholesky factorization with the constraints on these parameters implied by strict mere positive subdefiniteness of the inverse matrix B_{pp}^{-1}; there are $1/2 \; (N^2 + 3N) - 1$ such restrictions. This completes our discussion of the specification of a model of consumer behavior based on the theory of exact aggregation.

8.6 Econometrics of the Translog Model

In this section we outline the econometric implementation of the translog model of aggregate consumer behavior presented in section 8.5. Our observations on individual expenditure patterns are limited to a single cross section, providing data on expenditure shares, total expenditure, and demographic characteristics for individual consuming units at a given point of time. We assume that prices are the same for all consuming units, while expenditures and demographic characteristics vary among units. By analyzing individual cross-section data we can obtain estimates of expenditure and demographic effects on individual expenditure patterns.

Our observations on aggregate expenditure patterns include time-series data on expenditure shares, the level of aggregate expenditure, a weighted average of the logarithms of expenditures for individual consuming units, shares of demographic groups in aggregate expenditure, and prices. It is important to note that our econometric model can be implemented from aggregate time-series data alone, provided that the number of demographic groups is small by comparison with the number of observations. By combining time series and cross-section data we can obtain more precise estimates of the effects of variations in expenditures and demographic characteristics on patterns of aggregate expenditure allocation.

We begin our discussion of econometrics of the translog model by presenting the stochastic structure employed for cross-section and time-series data. We next discuss the identification and estimation of unknown parameters for a single cross section, assuming that prices are the same for all consuming units. We then discuss identification and estimation for aggregate time series and the pooling of time series and cross-section data. This section provides the link between the theoretical model described in section 8.5 above and the empirical results to be presented in section 8.7.

8.6.A Stochastic Structure

The model of consumer behavior presented in section 8.5 is generated from a translog indirect utility function for each consuming unit. To formulate an econometric model of consumer behavior we add a stochastic component to the equations for the individual expenditure shares. We associate this component with unobservable random disturbances at the level of the individual consuming unit. The consuming unit maximizes utility, but the expenditure shares are chosen with a random disturbance. This disturbance may result from errors in implementation of consumption plans, random elements in the determination of consumer preferences not reflected in our list of attributes of consuming units, or errors of measurement of the individual expenditure shares. We assume that each of the equations for the individual shares has two additive components. The first is a nonrandom function of prices, expenditure and demographic characteristics. The second is an unobservable random disturbance that is functionally independent of these variables.

To represent our econometric model of consumer behavior we introduce some additional notation. We consider observations on expenditure patterns by K consuming units, indexed by $k = 1, 2, \ldots, K$, for T time periods, indexed by $t = 1, 2, \ldots, T$. The vector of expenditure shares for the kth consuming unit in the tth time period is denoted w_{kt}, $(k = 1, 2, \ldots, K;\ t = 1, 2, \ldots, T)$. Similarly, expenditure for the kth unit on all commodity groups in the tth time period is denoted M_{kt}, $(k = 1, 2, \ldots, K;\ t = 1, 2, \ldots, T)$. The vector of prices faced by all consuming units in the tth time period is denoted p_t, $(t = 1, 2, \ldots, T)$. Similarly, the vector of logarithms of prices in the tth time period is denoted $\ln p_t$, $(t = 1, 2, \ldots, T)$. The vector of logarithms of ratios of prices to expenditure for the kth consuming unit in the tth time period is denoted $\ln p_t/M_{kt}$, $(k = 2, 3, \ldots, K;\ t = 1, 2, \ldots, T)$.

Using our new notation, the individual expenditure shares can be written

$$w_{kt} = \frac{1}{D_t}\left(\alpha_p + B_{pp} \ln \frac{p_t}{M_{kt}} + B_{pA} A_k\right) + \varepsilon_{kt}, \quad (k = 1, 2, \ldots, K;\ t = 1, 2, \ldots, T) \tag{8.135}$$

where

$$D_t = -1 + \iota' B_{pp} \ln p_t \quad (t = 1, 2, \ldots, T)$$

and ε_{kt} $(k = 1, 2, \ldots, K;\ t = 1, 2, \ldots, T)$ is the vector of unobservable random disturbances for the kth consuming unit and the tth time period. Since the individual expenditure shares for all commodities sum to unity for each consuming unit in each time period, the unobservable random disturbances for all commodities sum to zero for each unit in each time period

$$\iota' \varepsilon_{kt} = 0, \quad (k = 1, 2, \ldots, K;\ t = 1, 2, \ldots, T). \tag{8.136}$$

These disturbances are not distributed independently.

We assume that the unobservable random disturbances for all commodities have expected value equal to zero for all observations

$$E(\varepsilon_{kt}) = 0\,, \quad (k = 1, 2, \ldots, K;\ t = 1, 2, \ldots, T)\,. \tag{8.137}$$

We also assume that these disturbances have the same covariance matrix for all observations

$$V(\varepsilon_{kt}) = \Omega_\varepsilon\,, \quad (k = 1, 2, \ldots, K;\ t = 1, 2, \ldots, T)\,.$$

Since the disturbances sum to zero for each observation, this matrix is nonnegative definite with rank at most equal to $N - 1$, where N is the number of commodities. We assume that the covariance matrix has rank equal to $N - 1$.

Finally, we assume that disturbances corresponding to distinct observations are uncorrelated. Under this assumption the covariance matrix of the disturbances for all consuming units at a given point of time has the Kronecker product form

$$V\begin{pmatrix} \varepsilon_{1t} \\ \varepsilon_{2t} \\ \vdots \\ \varepsilon_{Kt} \end{pmatrix} = \Omega_\varepsilon \otimes I\,. \tag{8.138}$$

The covariance matrix of the disturbances for all time periods for a given individual has an analogous form. The unknown parameters of the system of equations determining the individual expenditure shares can be estimated from time-series data on individual expenditure shares, prices, total expenditure, and demographic characteristics.

At any point of time the aggregate expenditure shares are equal to the individual expenditure shares multiplied by the ratios of individual expenditure to aggregate expenditure and summed over all individual consuming units. Although the data for individual consuming units and for the aggregate of all consuming units are based on the same definitions, the aggregate data are not obtained by summing over the data for individuals. Observations on individual consuming units are based on a random sample from the population of all consuming units. Observations for the aggregate of all consuming units are constructed from data on production of commodities and on consumption of these commodities by households and by other consuming units such as businesses, governments, and the rest of the world. Accordingly, we must introduce an additional source of random error in the equations for the aggregate expenditure shares, corresponding to unobservable errors of measurement in the observations that underly the aggregate expenditure shares.

We assume that each of the equations for the aggregate expenditure shares has three additive components. The first is a weighted average of the nonrandom functions of prices, expenditure and demographic characteristics that determine the individual expenditure shares. The second is a weighted average of the unobservable random disturbances in equations for the individual expenditure shares. The third is a weighted average of the unobservable random errors of measurement in the observations on the aggregate expenditure shares.

Denoting the vector of aggregate expenditure shares at time t by w_t $(t = 1, 2, \ldots, T)$, we can express these shares in the form

$$w_t = \frac{1}{D_t}(\alpha_p + B_{pp} \ln p_t) - \frac{1}{D_t} B_{pp}\iota \frac{\sum_{k=1}^{K} M_{kt} \ln M_{kt}}{\sum_{k=1}^{K} M_{kt}}$$

$$+ \frac{1}{D_t} B_{pA} \frac{\sum_{k=1}^{K} M_{kt} A_k}{\sum_{k=1}^{K} M_{kt}} + \varepsilon_t\,, \quad (t = 1, 2, \ldots, T) \tag{8.139}$$

where

$$D_t = -1 + \iota' B_{pp} \ln p_t\,, \quad (t = 1, 2, \ldots, T)$$

as before, and $\varepsilon_t (t = 1, 2, \ldots, T)$ is the vector of unobservable random disturbances for the tth time period.

The aggregate disturbances ε_t can be expressed in the form

$$\varepsilon_t = \frac{\sum_{k=1}^{K} M_{kt}\, \varepsilon_{kt}}{\sum_{k=1}^{K} M_{kt}} + \frac{\sum_{k=1}^{K} M_{kt} \nu_{kt}}{\sum_{k=1}^{K} M_{kt}}\,, \quad (t = 1, 2, \ldots, T) \tag{8.140}$$

where $\nu_{kt} (k = 1, 2, \ldots, K;\ T = 1, 2, \ldots, T)$ is the vector of errors of measurement that underly the data on the aggregate expenditure shares. Since the random disturbances for all commodities sum to zero in each time period

$$\iota' \varepsilon_t = 0\,, \quad (k = 1, 2, \ldots, K;\ t = 1, 2, \ldots, T) \tag{8.141}$$

these disturbances are not distributed independently.

We assume that the errors of measurement that underly the data on the aggregate expenditure shares have expected value equal to zero for all observations

$$E(\nu_{kt}) = 0\,, \qquad (k = 1, 2, \dots, K;\ t = 1, 2, \dots, T)\,.$$

We also assume that these errors have the same covariance matrix for all observations

$$V(\nu_{kt}) = \Omega_{\nu}\,, \qquad (k = 1, 2, \dots, K;\ t = 1, 2, \dots, T)$$

and that the rank of this matrix is equal to $N - 1$.

If the errors of measurement are distributed independently of expenditure and of the disturbances in the equations for the individual expenditure shares, the aggregate disturbances have expected value equal to zero for all time periods

$$E(\varepsilon_t) = 0 \qquad (t = 1, 2, \dots, T) \tag{8.142}$$

and have a covariance matrix given by

$$V(\varepsilon_t) = \frac{\sum_{k=1}^{K} M_{kt}^2}{\left(\sum_{k=1}^{K} M_{kt}\right)^2}\,\Omega_{\varepsilon} + \frac{\sum_{k=1}^{K} M_{kt}^2}{\left(\sum_{k=1}^{K} M_{kt}\right)^2}\,\Omega_{\nu}\,, \qquad (t = 1, 2, \dots, T)$$

so that the aggregate disturbances for different time periods are heteroscedastic.

We can correct for heteroscedasticity of the aggregate disturbances by transforming the observations on the aggregate expenditure shares as follows

$$\rho_t\, w_t = \frac{\rho_t}{D_t}\,(\alpha_p + B_{pp} \ln p_t) - \frac{\rho_t}{D_t}\, B_{pp}\, \iota\, \frac{\sum_{k=1}^{K} M_{kt} \ln M_{kt}}{\sum_{k=1}^{K} M_{kt}}$$

$$+ \frac{\rho_t}{D_t}\, B_{pA}\, \frac{\sum_{k=1}^{K} M_{kt} A_k}{\sum_{k=1}^{K} M_{kt}} + \rho_t\, \varepsilon_t\,, \qquad (t = 1, 2, \dots, T)$$

where

$$\rho_t^2 = \frac{\left(\sum_{k=1}^{K} M_{kt}\right)^2}{\sum_{k=1}^{K} M_{kt}^2}, \qquad (t = 1, 2, \ldots, T).$$

The covariance matrix of the transformed disturbances, say Ω, becomes

$$V(\rho_t \varepsilon_t) = \Omega_\varepsilon + \Omega_v = \Omega .$$

This matrix is nonnegative definite with rank equal to $N - 1$. Finally, we assume that the errors of measurement corresponding to distinct observations are uncorrelated. Under this assumption the covariance matrix of the transformed disturbances at all points of time has the Kronecker product form

$$V \begin{pmatrix} \rho_1 \varepsilon_1 \\ \rho_2 \varepsilon_2 \\ \vdots \\ \rho_T \varepsilon_T \end{pmatrix} = \Omega \otimes I \qquad (8.143)$$

8.6.B Identification and Estimation

We next discuss the estimation of the translog model of aggregate consumer behavior, combining a single cross section of observations on individual expenditure patterns with several time series observations on aggregate expenditure patterns. We first discuss application of the translog model to cross section data only. We then present methods for pooling individual cross-section and aggregate time-series data.

Suppose first that we have a random sample of observations on individual expenditure patterns at a given point of time. Prices for all consumers are the same. The translog model (8.134) takes for form

$$w_k = \gamma_1 + \gamma_2 \ln M_k + \Gamma_3 A_k + \varepsilon_k , \qquad (k = 1, 2, \ldots, K) \qquad (8.144)$$

where we drop the time subscript. In this model γ_1 and γ_2 are vectors of unknown parameters and Γ_3 is a matrix of unknown parameters. Random sampling implies that disturbances for different individuals are uncorrelated. We assume that the data matrix with $(1, \ln M_k, A_k)$ as its kth row is of full rank.

The parameters of γ_1, γ_2 and Γ_3 are identified in the cross section. Moreover, the model (8.144) is a multivariate regression model, except that the vector of disturbances ε_k has a singular distribution. If the vector ε_k is normally distributed,[19] the maximum likelihood estimator of the unknown parameters in the complete model is equivalent to the estimator obtained by dropping one equation, estimating the remaining $N - 1$ equations by maximum likelihood, and then deriving estimates of the parameters of the omitted equation from estimates of the parameters for the $N - 1$ equations not omitted.[20] Consider a model where one equation has been dropped; this reduced model is a linear multivariate regression model so that the unique, minimum variance, unbiased estimator of the unknown parameters γ_1, γ_2 and Γ_3 is obtained by applying ordinary least squares to each equation separately.

To link the parameters γ_1, γ_2 and Γ_3 to the parameters of the translog model of aggregate consumer behavior we first observe that the parameters of the translog model can be identified only up to a normalization, since multiplying all of the parameters by the same nonzero constant leaves the expenditure shares unchanged. The usual normalization is $\iota'\alpha_p = -1$, giving the unknown parameters the same sign as those in the translog indirect utility function. Second, without loss of generality we can take the prices of all goods to be equal to unity for a particular period of time. In the application to a single cross-section we take all prices at the date of the survey to be equal to unity. The prices for all other time periods are expressed relative to prices of this base period.

Given the normalization of the parameters and the choice of base period for measurement of the prices, we obtain the following correspondence between the unknown parameters of the cross-section model and the parameters of the translog model of aggregate consumer behavior

$$\begin{aligned} \gamma_1 &= -\alpha_p \\ \gamma_2 &= B_{pp}\iota \\ \Gamma_3 &= -B_{pA} . \end{aligned} \tag{8.145}$$

The constants α_p and the parameters associated with demographic characteristics of individual households B_{pA} can be estimated from a single cross section. The parameters associated with total expenditure

$B_{pp}\iota$ can also be estimated from a single cross section. The remaining parameters, those associated with prices, can be estimated from time-series data on aggregate expenditure patterns.

Since the model is linear in parameters for a cross section, we can use ordinary least squares regression to estimate the impact of the demographic structure on aggregate expenditure patterns. This feature characterizes exact aggregation models in general, as indicated in section 8.2. The resulting linearity greatly simplifies computations.

After correction for heteroscedasticity the translog model of aggregate consumer behavior is given by

$$\rho_t w_t = \frac{\rho_t}{D_t}(\alpha_p + B_{pp} \ln p_t) - \frac{\rho_t}{D_t} B_{pp}\iota \frac{\sum_{k=1}^{K} M_{kt} \ln M_{kt}}{\sum_{k=1}^{K} M_{kt}}$$

$$+ \frac{\rho_t}{D_t} B_{pA} \frac{\sum_{k=1}^{K} M_{kt} A_k}{\sum_{k=1}^{K} M_{kt}} + \rho_t \varepsilon_t, \quad (t = 1, 2, \ldots, T) \tag{8.146}$$

where

$$D_t = -1 + \iota' B_{pp} \ln p_t, \quad (t = 1, 2, \ldots, T)$$

and ε_t is a vector of unobservable random disturbances. We have time series observations on prices p_t, the expenditure statistic $\sum M_{kt} \ln M_{kt} / \sum M_{kt}$, the vector of attribute-expenditure statistics $\{\sum M_{kt} A_{kt} / \sum M_{kt}\}$, and the heteroscedasticity correction $\rho_t (t = 1, 2, \ldots, T)$.

The translog model in (8.146) might appear to be a nonlinear regression model with additive errors, so that nonlinear regression techniques could be employed.[21] However, the existence of supply functions for all commodities makes it more appropriate to treat some of the right side variables as endogenous. For example, due to demand-supply interactions shifts in prices should be treated as endogenous. To obtain a consistent estimator for this model we could specify supply functions for all commodities and estimate the complete model by full information maximum likelihood.

Alternatively, to estimate the model in (8.146) we can consider limited information techniques utilizing instrumental variables. In particular, we can introduce a sufficient number of instrumental variables to identify all parameters. We estimate the model by nonlinear three stage least squares (NL3SLS).[22] Application of NL3SLS to our model would be straightforward except for the fact that the covariance matrix of the disturbances is singular. We obtain NL3SLS estimators of the complete system by dropping one equation and estimating the resulting system of $N-1$ equations by NL3SLS; we derive an estimator for parameters of the remaining equation from the conditions for summability. The parameter estimates are invariant to the choice of the equation omitted in the model for aggregate time-series data and the model for individual cross-section data.

In the analysis of the model to be applied to cross-section data on individual expenditure patterns, we have assumed that individual disturbances and individual total expenditure are uncorrelated. If aggregate demand-supply interactions induce shifts in the distribution of expenditure, the zero correlation assumption cannot be strictly valid for all consumers at the individual level. However, the cross section is a random sample that includes a minute percentage of the total population, so that it is reasonable to assume that the correlations between total expenditure and disturbances at the individual level are negligible.

The NL3SLS estimator can be employed to estimate all parameters of the model of aggregate expenditures, provided that these parameters are identified. Since we wish to obtain a detailed characterization of the impact of changes in the demographic structure of the population, the model (8.146) contains a large number of parameters and requires a large number of time series observations for identification. The technical conditions for identification are quite complicated. A sufficient condition for underidentification is that the number of instruments is less than the number of parameters. For the translog model of aggregate consumer behavior, this occurs if

$$(N-1)(1+S)\,x\,\frac{(N+1)N}{2}-1>(N-1)x\,\min(V,T) \tag{8.147}$$

where N is the number of commodities, S is the number of components of A_{kt} and V is the number of instruments. The left-hand side of (8.147) is the number of free parameters of the translog model under symmetry of the matrix B_{pp} and the right-hand side is the number of instruments, assuming that no collinearity exists among the instruments.

Condition (8.147) is met in our application, so that not all parameters are identified in the model for aggregate time-series data.

We next consider methods utilizing individual cross-section data together with aggregate time-series data to obtain identification. As we have seen, cross-section data can be used to identify the constant α_p, the coefficients of total expenditure $- B_{pp}\iota$ and the demographic coefficients B_{pA}. Only the price coefficients B_{pp} must be identified from aggregate time-series data. A necessary condition for identification of these parameters is

$$\frac{(N-1)N}{2} < (N-1)\min(V,T) \tag{8.148}$$

or

$$\frac{N}{2} < \min(V,T)\,. \tag{8.149}$$

This condition is met in our application. Sufficient conditions are given in the next section; these amount to the nonlinear analogue of the absence of multicollinearity. These conditions are quite weak and hold in our application.

In order to pool cross-section and time-series data, we combine the model for individual expenditures and the model for aggregate expenditures and apply the method of NL3SLS to the whole system. The instruments for the cross-section model are the micro data themselves; for the aggregate model the instruments are variables that can be taken to be distributed independently of the aggregate disturbances. A list of the aggregate instrumental variables is given in appendix 8.2. The data sets are pooled statistically, where estimates of the covariance matrix of the aggregate disturbances from time-series data and the covariance matrix of the individual disturbances from cross-section data are used to weight aggregate and cross-section data, respectively. The resulting estimator is consistent and asymptotically efficient in the class of instrumental variable estimators utilizing the instruments we have chosen. We next describe the pooled estimation procedure, together with the simplification of computations that results from exact aggregation.

8.6.C Pooling Time Series and Cross Section

The pooled estimation of the translog model of aggregate consumer behavior requires application of the method of nonlinear three stage least squares (NL3SLS). The linearity of the cross-section model results in a number of simplifications of the NL3SLS estimator. Our objective is to estimate the unknown parameters α_p, B_{pp}, B_{pA} subject to the restrictions implied by summability, symmetry, monotonicity, the exact aggregation conditions, and the normalization $\iota'\alpha_p = -1$. By dropping the equation for one commodity in both cross-section and time-series models, we can eliminate the restrictions implied by summability. We employ these restrictions in estimating the parameters that occur in the equation that has been dropped.

We impose the restrictions implied by the exact aggregation conditions and the normalization $\iota'\alpha_p = -1$ by imposing these restrictions on the function D_t is expression (8.135) for the individual expenditure shares. Second, we impose the restrictions implied by symmetry by requiring that the matrix B_{pp} is symmetric. The restrictions implied by summability, symmetry, exact aggregation, and the normalization take the form of equalities. The restrictions implied by monotonicity take the form of inequalities. The matrix B_{pp} has an inverse B_{pp}^{-1} that is strictly merely positive subdefinite, so that all the elements of this inverse matrix are nonpositive and the matrix B_{pp} has exactly one negative Cholesky value, δ_5, and four positive Cholesky values—δ_1, δ_2, δ_3, δ_4. In section 8.5.C we have expressed these restrictions in terms of the Cholesky factorization of the matrix B_{pp}. We discuss the estimation of the unknown parameters α_p, B_{pp}, B_{pA} subject to monotonicity restrictions below.

Since we have taken the base period for all prices and time as the period corresponding to the cross-section survey, we can write the cross-section model in the form

$$\begin{aligned} y_1 &= X\beta_1 + \varepsilon_1 \\ y_2 &= X\beta_2 + \varepsilon_2 \\ &\cdots \\ y_{N-1} &= X\beta_{N-1} + \varepsilon_{N-1} \end{aligned} \tag{8.150}$$

where y_i, $(i = 1, 2, \ldots, N-1)$ is the vector of observations on the individual expenditure shares of the ith commodity for all individuals, X is a matrix of observations on $2 + S$ independent variables, including a dummy variable corresponding to the constant term in each equation, the logarithm of total expenditure, and dummy variables corresponding to individual attributes and ε_i, $(i = 1, 2, \ldots, N-1)$ is a vector of unobservable random disturbances.

We can stack the equations in (8.150) in the usual way, obtaining

$$y = [I \otimes X]\beta + \varepsilon \tag{8.151}$$

where

$$y = \begin{bmatrix} y_1 \\ y_2 \\ \vdots \\ y_{n-1} \end{bmatrix}, \quad I \otimes X = \begin{bmatrix} X & 0 & \dots & 0 \\ 0 & X & \dots & 0 \\ \vdots & \vdots & & \vdots \\ 0 & 0 & \dots & X \end{bmatrix}, \quad \beta = \begin{bmatrix} \beta_1 \\ \beta_2 \\ \vdots \\ \beta_{N-1} \end{bmatrix}, \quad \varepsilon = \begin{bmatrix} \varepsilon_1 \\ \varepsilon_2 \\ \vdots \\ \varepsilon_{N-1} \end{bmatrix}.$$

By the assumptions listed in section 8.6.B, above, the matrix X is of full rank and the random vector ε is distributed normally with mean zero and covariance matrix $\Sigma_\varepsilon \otimes I$, where Σ_ε is obtained from the covariance matrix Ω_ε in (8.138) by striking the row and column corresponding to the omitted equation.

Similarly, we can write the time series model in the form

$$\begin{aligned} v_1 &= f_1(\beta, \gamma) + \nu_1 \\ v_2 &= f_2(\beta, \gamma) + \nu_2 \\ &\dots \\ v_{N-1} &= f_{N-1}(\beta, \gamma) + \nu_{N-1} \end{aligned} \tag{8.153}$$

where v_i, $(i = 1, 2, \dots, N-1)$ is the vector of observations on the aggregate expenditure shares of the ith commodity for all time periods, transformed to eliminate heteroscedasticity, f_i, $(i = 1, 2, \dots, N-1)$ is a vector of nonlinear functions of the parameters β that enter the cross-section model and the remaining parameters γ that enter the time series model, and ν_i, $(i = 1, 2, \dots, N-1)$ is a vector of unobservable random disturbances, transformed to eliminate heteroscedasticity.

As before, we can stack the equations in (8.153), obtaining

$$\begin{aligned} v &= f(\beta, \gamma) + \nu \\ &= f(\delta) + \nu \end{aligned} \tag{8.154}$$

where

$$v = \begin{bmatrix} v_1 \\ v_2 \\ \vdots \\ v_{N-1} \end{bmatrix}, \quad f = \begin{bmatrix} f_1 \\ f_2 \\ \vdots \\ f_{N-1} \end{bmatrix}, \quad \delta = \begin{bmatrix} \beta \\ \\ \gamma \end{bmatrix}, \quad \nu = \begin{bmatrix} \nu_1 \\ \nu_2 \\ \vdots \\ \nu_{N-1} \end{bmatrix}.$$

By the assumptions listed in section 8.6.B the random vector ν is distributed normally with mean zero and covariance matrix $\Sigma_v \otimes I$, where Σ_v is obtained from the covariance matrix Ω in (8.143) by striking the row and column corresponding to the omitted equation.

The maximum likelihood estimator of β from the cross-section model is

$$\hat{\beta} = [I \otimes (X'X)^{-1} X'] \, y \tag{8.155}$$

or

$$\hat{\beta}_i = (X'X)^{-1} X' y_i \qquad (i = 1, 2, \ldots, N-1)$$

which is equivalent to the least squares estimator applied to each equation individually. This estimator has covariance matrix

$$V(\hat{\beta}) = \Sigma \otimes (X'X)^{-1} . \tag{8.156}$$

The least squares estimator is a consistent estimator of the vector of unknown parameters β; the probability limit of this estimator as the number of cross-section observations K tends to infinity is equal to β.

The nonlinear three-stage least squares (NL3SLS) estimator for the aggregate model is obtained by minimizing the weighted sum of squared residuals

$$\mathrm{SSR}(\delta) = [v - f(\delta)]'[\hat{\Sigma}_v^{-1} \otimes Z(Z'Z)^{-1} Z'][v - f(\delta)] \tag{8.157}$$

with respect to the vector of unknown parameters δ, where Z is the matrix of time series observations on the R instrumental variables. Provided that the parameters are identified from the aggregate model, we can apply the Gauss-Newton method to minimize (8.157). First, we can linearize the model, obtaining

$$v = f(\delta_0) + \frac{\partial f}{\partial \delta} (\delta_0) \, \Delta \, \delta + u \tag{8.158}$$

where δ_0 is the initial value of the vector of unknown parameters δ and

$$\Delta \, \delta = \delta_1 - \delta_0$$

where δ_1 is the revised value of this vector. The fitted residuals u depend on the initial and revised values.

To revise the initial values we apply Zellner and Theil's (1962) three stage least squares method to the linearized model, obtaining

$$\Delta\delta = \left\{ \frac{\partial f}{\partial \delta}(\delta_0)'(\hat{\Sigma}_v^{-1} \otimes Z(Z'Z)^{-1}Z') \frac{\partial f}{\partial \delta}(\delta_0) \right\}^{-1}$$
$$\times \frac{\partial f}{\partial \delta}(\delta_0)'\{\hat{\Sigma}_v^{-1} \otimes Z(Z'Z)^{-1}Z'\}[v - f(\delta_0)]\,. \qquad (8.159)$$

If $SSR(\delta_0) > SSR(\delta_1)$, a further iteration is performed by replacing δ_0 by δ_1 in (8.158) and (8.159), resulting in a further revised value, say δ_2, and so on. If this condition is not satisfied, we divide the revision $\Delta\delta$ by two and evaluate the criteria $SSR(\delta)$ again; we continue reducing the revision $\Delta\delta$ until the criterion improves or the consequence criterion $\max_j \Delta\delta_j/\delta_j$ is less than some prespecified limit. If the criterion improves, we continue with further iterations. If not, we stop the iterative process and employ the current value of the vector of unknown parameters δ as our NL3SLS estimator.

The final step in estimation of the aggregate model is to minimize the criterion function (8.157) subject to the restrictions implied by monotonicity of the individual expenditure shares. We have eliminated the restrictions implied by summability, symmetry, the exact aggregation conditions, and the normalization $\iota'\alpha_p = -1$; these restrictions take the form of equalities. Monotonicity of the individual expenditure shares implies the inequality restrictions given in table 8.2 and the restrictions (8.133) and (8.134). We can represent these restrictions in the form

$$\phi_r(\delta) \geqq 0\,, \quad (r = 1, 2, \ldots, R) \qquad (8.160)$$

where R is the number of restrictions. We obtain the inequality constrained nonlinear three stage least squares estimator for the aggregate model by minimizing the criterion function subject to the constraints (8.160). This estimator corresponds to a saddlepoint of the Lagrangian functions

$$\pounds = SSR(\delta) + \lambda'\phi \qquad (8.161)$$

where λ is a vector of R Lagrange multipliers and ϕ is a vector of R constraints. The Kuhn-Tucker (1951) conditions for a saddlepoint of this Lagrangian are the first-order conditions

$$\frac{\partial \pounds}{\partial \delta} = \frac{\partial \mathrm{SSR}(\delta)}{\partial \delta} + \lambda' \frac{\partial \phi}{\partial \delta} = 0 \tag{8.162}$$

and the complementary slackness condition

$$\lambda' \phi = 0, \qquad \lambda \geq 0. \tag{8.163}$$

To find a saddlepoint of the Lagrangian (8.161) we begin by linearizing the aggregate model (8.154) as in (8.158). Second, we linearize the constraints as

$$\phi(\delta) = \frac{\partial \phi}{\partial \delta}(\delta_0)\Delta\delta + \phi(\delta_0) \tag{8.164}$$

where δ_0 is a vector of initial values of the unknown parameters. We apply Liew's (1976) inequality constrained three stage least squares method to the linearized model, obtaining

$$\Delta\delta^* = \Delta\delta + \left\{ \frac{\partial f}{\partial \delta}(\delta_0)'(\hat{\Sigma}_v^{-1} \otimes Z(Z'Z)^{-1}Z') \frac{\partial f}{\partial \delta}(\delta_0) \right\}^{-1} \frac{\partial \phi}{\partial \delta}(\delta_0)'\lambda^* \tag{8.165}$$

where $\Delta\delta$ is the change in the value of the parameters (8.159) and λ^* is the solution of the linear complementarity problem

$$\begin{aligned} &\frac{\partial \phi}{\partial \delta}(\delta_0) \left\{ \frac{\partial f}{\partial \delta}(\delta_0)'(\hat{\Sigma}_v^{-1} \otimes Z(Z'Z)^{-1}Z') \frac{\partial}{\partial \delta}(\delta_0) \right\}^{-1} \frac{\partial \phi}{\partial \delta}(\delta_0)\lambda \\ &\qquad + \frac{\partial \phi}{\partial \delta}(\delta_0)\Delta\delta - \phi(\delta_0) \geq 0 \end{aligned}$$

where

$$\begin{aligned} &\left\{ \frac{\partial \phi}{\partial \delta}(\delta_0) \left[\frac{\partial f}{\partial \delta}(\delta_0)'(\hat{\Sigma}_v^{-1} \otimes Z(Z'Z)^{-1}Z') \frac{\partial f}{\partial \delta}(\delta_0) \right]^{-1} \frac{\partial \phi}{\partial \delta}(\delta_0) \right\} \lambda \\ &\qquad + \frac{\partial \phi}{\partial \delta}(\delta_0)\Delta\delta - \phi(\delta_0)'\lambda = 0, \qquad \lambda \geq 0. \end{aligned}$$

Given an initial value of the unknown parameters δ_0 that satisfies the R constraints (8.160), if $\mathrm{SSR}(\delta_1) < \mathrm{SSR}(\delta_0)$ and δ_1 satisfies the constraints, the iterative process continues by linearizing the model (8.154) as in (8.159) and the constraints (8.160) as in (8.164) at the revised value of the vector of unknown parameters $\delta_1 = \delta_0 + \Delta\delta$. If not, we shrink $\Delta\delta$ as before continuing until an improvement is found subject to the constraints or $\max_j \Delta\delta_j/\delta_j$ is less than a convergency criterion.

The conditions for identifiability of the vector of unknown parameters δ in the aggregate model are equivalent to the nonsingularity of the following matrix in a neighborhood of the true parameter vector

$$\frac{\partial f}{\partial \delta}(\delta)'(\Sigma_v^{-1} \otimes Z(Z'Z)^{-1}Z')\frac{\partial f}{\partial \delta}(\delta). \tag{8.166}$$

The condition (8.147) given above is sufficient for the singularity of this matrix, as well as the singularity of the matrix evaluated at each iteration in (8.159).

The pooled NL3SLS estimator is found by minimizing the following function with respect to δ

$$\begin{aligned} \mathrm{SSR}(\delta) = {} & (y - Y\delta)'(\hat{\Sigma}_\varepsilon^{-1} \otimes I)(y - Y\delta) \\ & + [v - f(\delta)]'[\hat{\Sigma}_v^{-1} \otimes Z(Z'Z)^{-1}Z'][v - f(\delta)] \end{aligned} \tag{8.167}$$

where

$$Y = \begin{bmatrix} I \otimes X & 0 \\ 0 & 0 \end{bmatrix} \tag{8.168}$$

is a matrix of observations on the variables that determine the individual expenditure shares in the cross-section model.

To find a minimum of the criterion function $\mathrm{SSR}(\delta)$ in (8.167) we began by linearizing the pooled system (8.151) and (8.153) as

$$y - Y\delta_0 = Y\Delta\delta + e \tag{8.169}$$

$$v - f(\delta_0) = \frac{\partial f}{\partial \delta}(\delta_0)\Delta\delta + u$$

where δ_0 is a vector of initial values of the unknown parameters. As before, we apply ordinary three stage least squares to the linearized model, obtaining

$$\Delta\delta = \left\{ Y'(\hat{\Sigma}_\varepsilon^{-1} \otimes I)Y + \frac{\partial f}{\partial \delta}(\delta_0)'[\hat{\Sigma}_\nu^{-1} \otimes Z(Z'Z)^{-1}Z'] \frac{\partial f}{\partial \delta}(\delta_0) \right\}^{-1}$$
$$\times \left\{ Y'(\hat{\Sigma}_\varepsilon^{-1} \otimes I)(y - Y\delta_0) + \frac{\partial f}{\partial \delta}(\delta_0)'[\hat{\Sigma}_\nu^{-1} \otimes Z(Z'Z)^{-1}Z'][\nu - f(\delta_0)] \right\}. \tag{8.170}$$

If $\text{SSR}(\delta_1) < \text{SSR}(\delta_0)$, the iterative process continues by linearizing the model at the revised value of the parameters $\delta_1 = \delta_0 + \Delta\delta$. If not, we shrink $\Delta\delta$ as before, dividing $\Delta\delta$ by two and reevaluating the criterion function and continuing until an improvement is found or $\max_j \Delta\delta_j/\delta_j$ is less than a convergence criterion.

The nonlinear three stage least squares estimator obtained by minimizing the criterion function (8.167) is a consistent estimator of the vector of unknown parameters δ; note that this requires taking the probability limit of the NL3SLS estimator as the number of cross-section observations K and the number of time series observations T tend to infinity. This estimator has asymptotic covariance matrix

$$V(\hat{\delta}) = \left\{ Y'(\Sigma_\varepsilon^{-1} \otimes I)Y + \frac{\partial f}{\partial \delta}(\delta)'[\Sigma_\nu^{-1} \otimes Z(Z'Z)^{-1}Z'] \frac{\partial f}{\partial \delta}(\delta) \right\}^{-1}. \tag{8.171}$$

We obtain an estimator of this matrix by inserting the estimators $\hat{\delta}, \hat{\Sigma}_\varepsilon$, and $\hat{\Sigma}_\nu$ in place of the parameters δ, Σ_ε, and Σ_ν. The conditions for identifiability of the vector of unknown parameters δ in the model for pooling time-series and cross-section data are equivalent to nonsingularity of the following matrix in the neighborhood of the true parameter vector

$$Y'(\Sigma_\varepsilon^{-1} \otimes I)Y + \frac{\partial f}{\partial \delta}(\delta)'(\Sigma_\nu^{-1} \otimes Z(Z'Z)^{-1}Z') \frac{\partial f}{\partial \delta}(\delta). \tag{8.172}$$

Under the following regularity conditions

$$\lim_{K\to\infty} \frac{X'X}{K} = \Sigma_{X'X}$$
$$\lim_{T\to\infty} \frac{Z'Z}{T} = \Sigma_{Z'Z}$$
$$\lim_{T\to\infty} \frac{1}{T} Z' \frac{\partial f_i}{\partial \delta_i} = \Sigma_{Z'\partial f_i/\partial \delta_i}, \quad (i = 1, 2, \ldots, N) \tag{8.173}$$

where $\Sigma_{X'X}$, $\Sigma_{Z'Z}$ and $\Sigma_{Z'\partial f_i/\partial\delta_i}$, $(i = 1, 2, \ldots, N)$ are positive definite matrices, the NL3SLS estimator is asymptotically efficient in the class of instrumental variables estimators using X and Z as instrumental variables.

Up to this point we have presented the pooled estimator for cross-section and time-series models as a standard application of the NL3SLS estimator. The linearity of the cross-section model resulting from exact aggregation implies that the computations can be simplified. First, the moment matrix of the cross-section model takes the form

$$Y' (\hat{\Sigma}_\varepsilon^{-1} \otimes I)Y = \hat{\Sigma}_\varepsilon^{-1} \otimes X'X \tag{8.174}$$

which depends on $\hat{\Sigma}_\varepsilon$ and on $X'X$, the moment matrix of the independent variables in the cross-section model. Similarly, the vector of moments involving the dependent variables of the cross-section model takes the form

$$Y'(\hat{\Sigma}_\varepsilon^{-1} \otimes I)(y - Y\delta) = \hat{\Sigma}_\varepsilon^{-1} \otimes (X'y - X'X\delta) \tag{8.175}$$

which depends on $\hat{\Sigma}_\varepsilon$, $X'X$, and on $X'y$, the vector of moments involving the dependent variables of the cross-section model.

The final step in pooled estimation of the unknown parameters of the translog model of aggregate consumer behavior is to estimate these parameters subject to the inequality restrictions implied by monotonicity of the individual expenditure shares. We minimize the criterion (8.167) subject to the restrictions (8.160). As before, this is a concave programming problem. We apply inequality constrained three stage least squares to the linearized model, obtaining

$$\Delta\delta * = \Delta\delta + \left\{ Y'(\hat{\Sigma}_\varepsilon^{-1} \otimes I)Y + \frac{\partial f}{\partial\delta}(\delta_0)' \right.$$
$$\left. \times (\hat{\Sigma}_v^{-1} \otimes Z(Z'Z)^{-1}Z)\frac{\partial f}{\partial\delta}(\delta_0) \right\}^{-1} \frac{\partial\phi}{\partial\delta}(\delta_0)\lambda * \tag{8.176}$$

where $\Delta\delta$ is the change in the value of the parameters for unconstrained three stage least squares (8.170) and λ^* is the solution of the linear complementarity problem

$$\frac{\partial \phi}{\partial \delta}(\delta_0)\left\{Y'(\hat{\Sigma}_\varepsilon^{-1} \otimes I)Y + \frac{\partial f}{\partial \delta}(\delta_0)'(\hat{\Sigma}_\nu^{-1} \otimes Z(Z'Z)^{-1}Z')\frac{\partial f}{\partial \delta}(\delta_0)\right\}^{-1} \frac{\partial \phi}{\partial \delta}(\delta_0)\lambda$$
$$+ \frac{\partial \phi}{\partial \delta}(\delta_0)\Delta\delta - \phi(\delta_0) \geq 0$$

where

$$\left[\frac{\partial \phi}{\partial \delta}(\delta_0)\left\{Y'(\hat{\Sigma}_\varepsilon^{-1} \otimes I)Y + \frac{\partial f}{\partial \delta}(\delta_0)'(\hat{\Sigma}_\nu^{-1} \otimes Z(Z'Z)^{-1}Z')\frac{\partial f}{\partial \delta}(\delta_0)\right\}^{-1} \frac{\partial \phi}{\partial \delta}(\delta_0)\lambda\right.$$
$$\left. + \frac{\partial \phi}{\partial \delta}(\delta_0)\Delta\delta - \phi(\delta_0)\right]' \lambda = 0, \qquad \lambda \geq 0.$$

Given an initial value of the unknown parameters δ_0 that satisfies the constraints, if $\text{SSR}(\delta_0) < \text{SSR}(\delta)$ and δ_1 satisfies the constraints, the iterative process continues by linearizing the model as in (8.169) and the constraints as in (8.164) at the revised value of the vector of unknown parameters $\delta_1 = \delta_0 + \Delta\,\delta$. If not, we shrink $\Delta\delta$ as before, continuing until an improvement is found subject to the constraints or $\max_j \Delta\delta_j/\delta_j$ is less than a convergence criterion.

We assume that the restrictions associated with monotonicity of the individual expenditure shares are valid or, more precisely, that the vector of unknown parameters δ is an interior point of the set of parameters defined by the constraints. Under this assumption the inequality constrained nonlinear three stage least squares estimator is a consistent estimator of the vector of unknown parameters. This estimator has the same asymptotic covariance matrix (8.171) as the estimator pooling time series and cross-section data.[23] As before, we obtain an estimator of this matrix by inserting the estimators $\delta, \hat{\Sigma}_\varepsilon$, and $\hat{\Sigma}_\nu$ in place of the parameters δ, Σ_ε, and Σ_ν. The conditions for identifiability of the vector of unknown parameters δ is the nonsingularity of the matrix (8.172) in the neighborhood of the true parameter vector.

8.6.D Summary and Conclusion

In this section we have discussed the econometric implementation of the translog model of aggregate consumer behavior presented in section 8.5. To formulate an econometric model of individual consumer behavior we add a stochastic component to the functions that determine the individual expenditure shares. The interpretation of the individual disturbances is that the individual consuming unit maximizes utility, subject to a budget constraint, but that the expenditure shares are chosen with a random disturbance.

We assume that the individual disturbances have expected value equal to zero. Since the individual expenditure shares for all commodities sum to unity for each consuming unit in each time period, the unobservable random disturbances for all commodities sum to zero. As a consequence, these disturbances are not distributed independently. We assume that the covariance matrix of the individual disturbances has rank equal to $N - 1$, where N is the number of commodities. Finally, we assume that disturbances corresponding to distinct observations are uncorrelated.

The aggregate expenditure shares at any point of time are equal to the individual shares multiplied by the ratio of individual expenditure to aggregate expenditure. Although the data for individual consuming units and for the aggregate of all consuming units are based on the same definitions, the methods of measurement are not the same. Accordingly, we introduce an additional random component in the equations for the aggregate expenditure shares. This component corresponds to errors of measurement in the observations on individual expenditure shares that underly the observations of the aggregate expenditure shares.

We assume that the errors of measurement that underly the aggregate expenditure shares have expected value equal to zero. These errors of measurement, like the individual disturbances, sum to zero for each unit in each time period and are not distributed independently. We assumes that the covariance matrix of the errors of observation has rank equal to $N - 1$. Finally, we assume that the errors of measurement corresponding to distinct observations are uncorrelated.

The aggregate disturbances are weighted averages of the individual disturbances and the errors of measurement. As a consequence, the aggregate disturbances corresponding to different time periods are heteroscedastic. We can correct for heteroscedasticity by transforming the observations on the aggregate expenditure shares. The transformed aggregate disturbances have expected value equal to zero for all observations and have a covariance matrix with rank $N - 1$. We assume that the errors of measurement corresponding to distinct observations are uncorrelated, so that the aggregate disturbances for distinct observations are also uncorrelated.

In our application of the translog model of aggregate consumer expenditure presented in section 8.7, we pool cross-section data on individual expenditure patterns with time-series data on aggregate expenditure patterns. We first estimate the parameters of a model for single cross section of observations on individual expenditure patterns, assuming that the prices for all consumers are the same for all individuals. This model can be regarded as a linear, multivariate, regression model, so that the parameters that can be identified from a single cross section can be estimated by applying ordinary least squares to each equation separately. These parameters are associated with total expenditures and demographic characteristics of individual households.

The second step in pooling individual cross-section data with aggregate time-series data is to estimate the parameters of a model for a time series of observations on aggregate expenditure patterns. In this model we treat the prices and the expenditure statistic $\sum M_k \ln M_{kt} / \sum M_{kt}$ as jointly dependent variables. A second complication is that too few time series observations are available to identify all the parameters of the model of aggregate consumer behavior.

To identify the unknown parameters we combine cross-section and time-series data. We introduce a sufficient number of instrumental variables to identify all parameters. Given the identification of the parameters from the model combining time series and cross-section data, we apply the methods of inequality constrained nonlinear three stage least squares to obtain an estimator of the parameters of the complete model. The resulting estimator is consistent and asymptotically efficient in the class of instrumental variables estimators utilizing the instruments we have chosen.

A substantial simplification in the computations required for the estimator pooling cross-section and time-series data results from the theory of exact aggregation. The iterative process for the pooled estimator depends only on moments computed as part of the evaluation of the least squares estimator for the cross-section model. The individual observations from the cross-section data are not required for the pooled estimator, provided that the ordinary least squares estimator of the cross-section model is computed first to obtain an initial estimator of the parameters of this model.

8.7 Aggregate Consumer Behavior in the United States, 1958–1974

In this section we present the empirical results of implementing the econometric model of aggregate consumer behavior discussed in section 8.6. For this purpose we employ cross-section observations on individual expenditure patterns in the United States during the year 1972. We combine these cross-section data with time series observations on aggregate expenditure patterns in the United States for the period 1958–1974. We first employ a model of individual expenditure allocation as a basis for estimating the parameters that can be identified from cross-section data alone. We then employ a model of aggregate expenditure allocation as a basis for estimating the remaining parameters of the model from time series, holding the values of parameters estimated from cross-section data fixed. Finally, we pool time series and cross-section data to estimate all of the parameters of our model of aggregate consumer behavior.

We begin by discussing the allocation of consumer expenditures among commodity groups. We next consider the classification of consuming units by demographic characteristics. We then describe the data sources we have employed and the assumptions we have imposed in combining the data sources. We present estimates of the parameters of the transcendental logarithmic model of aggregate consumer behavior. To characterize these estimates we analyze changes in patterns of individual expenditures with changes in demographic characteristics of individual consuming units. We also describe differences in expenditure and price elasticities of demand for consuming units with different demographic characteristics.

8.7.A Commodities and Consuming Units

Total consumer expenditure is defined as the sum of all expenditures on nondurable goods and services, plus the services of durable goods. We analyze patterns of consumer expenditures as flows of goods and services with purchases of durables treated as investment, increasing the stock of durables and replacing elements of the stock as they wear out. We divide consumer expenditures into five broad categories:

1. *Energy*. Expenditures on electricity, gas heating oil, and gasoline.
2. *Food and clothing*. Expenditures on food, beverages and tobacco, clothing expenditures, and other related expenditures.

3. *Consumer services*. Expenditures on services, such as entertainment, maintenance and repairs of automobiles and housing, tailoring, cleaning, and insurance.

4. *Capital services*. The service flow from consumer durables as well as the service flow from housing.

5. *Other nondurable expenditure*. The remainder of the budget, which includes transportation and trade margins from other expenditures.

Our allocation of the consumer budget into five commodity groups embodies a set of restrictions on the allocation of expenditures within each commodity group. We assume that the direct utility function is homothetically separable in goods within each commodity group. This implies that the indirect utility function is homothetically separable in the prices of goods within each group. More specifically, we assume that the price for each commodity group is a homogeneous translog function of its components, so that

$$\ln p_n = \ln p^{n'} \alpha_p^n + 1/2 \ln p^{n'} B_{pp}^n \ln p^n \tag{8.177}$$

where

$\ln p^n = (\ln p_{n1}, \ln p_{n2}, \ldots, \ln p_n M_n)$ Vector of logarithms of prices for the M_n goods within the nth commodity group,

and the vector α_p^n and the matrix B_{pp}^n satisfy the restrictions

$$\iota' \alpha_p^n = -1$$
$$\iota' B_{pp}^n = 0 .$$

The price index

$$\Delta \ln p_n = \bar{w}^{n'} \Delta \ln p^n , \tag{8.178}$$

is exact for the homogeneous translog functions,[24] where

$\bar{w}^n = (\bar{w}_{n1}, \bar{w}_{n2}, \ldots, \bar{w}_{nM_n})$ Vector of average budget shares for the M_n goods within the nth commodity group,

and

$$\bar{w}_{nm} = \frac{1}{2}(w_{nm,t} + w_{nm,t-1}) , \quad (m = 1, 2, \ldots, M_n) .$$

The basic consuming unit employed in this study is the household. Unrelated individuals are considered to be households of size one. All consuming units are classified by attributes that reflect differences in preferences among consuming units. We employ the following demographic characteristics as attributes of households:

1. Family size: 1,2,3,4,5,6, and 7 or more persons.
2. Age of head: 15–24, 25–34, 35–44, 45–54, 55–65, 65 and over.
3. Region of residence: Northeast, North Central, South and West.
4. Race: White, nonwhite.
5. Type of residence: Urban, rural.

Each household is assigned to one of the categories for each of the five demographic characteristics. Since these categories are discrete, integer-valued variables are required to represent the attributes.

Under exact aggregation all attributes appear linearly in the functions that determine shares of individual expenditures. We impose no *a priori* restrictions on the form of the impact on expenditure patterns of variations in demographic characteristics among consuming units. If, for example, we were to include an integer-valued variable with value equal to family size as a determinant of individual expenditure patterns, we would implicitly impose a constraint on the effects of different family sizes. To avoid these implicit constraints, we represent each family size by a qualitative or dummy variable, so that the precise pattern of the impacts of changes in family size can be estimated. To avoid singularity of the matrix of dummy variables we take all variables to be zero for unrelated individuals, age 15–24, living in the Northeast, white in race, and living in an urban area. This leaves 16 qualitative variables to be treated as separate consumer attributes in representing the effects of demographic characteristics on preferences of consuming units.

We next turn to a discussion of data sources for our study. For time series observations on aggregate expenditure patterns we take data on personal consumption expenditures from the U.S. Interindustry Transactions Accounts for the period 1958–1974.[25] These data are very similar to data from the National Income and Product Accounts (NIPA) with two exceptions. First, we consider purchases of durable goods to be investment rather than consumption; the corresponding service flow from the stock of durables is the appropriate measure of personal consumption.[26] Second, trade and transportation margins are separated from final purchases, so that all goods and services are evaluated at producers' prices.

We employ data on household expenditure patterns for the year 1972 from the 1972–1973 Survey of Consumer Expenditures (CES), collected and published by the Bureau of Labor Statistics.[27] The CES data categories correspond fairly closely to those within the NIPA accounts, so that we were able to employ a bridge between the U.S. Interindustry Accounts and the U.S. National Income and Product Accounts[28] to transform observations on individual expenditures to appropriate commodity groups.

A key feature of the exact aggregation approach is the incorporation of the distribution of individual expenditures into the determination of aggregate expenditure patterns. We have a detailed description of the distribution of total expenditures in 1972, the year of our cross-section survey, plus a detailed tabulation of before tax income for all years from *Current Population Reports, Series P–60, Consumer Income*.[29] To construct the statistics of the joint distribution of attributes and expenditures required for our model of aggregate consumer behavior, we have constructed a mapping from the distribution of before tax income to the distribution of total expenditure, using the detailed information about these distributions available from our cross-section data.[30]

First, we characterize the tax structure in each year empirically by means of a mapping between the before-tax and after-tax income distributions. This mapping is not exact so that the tax rates for demographically identical families with the same income are measured with a residual. However, the mapping is sufficiently detailed to provide statistics of the after-tax income distribution from those of the before-tax income distribution. Second, we map the distribution of after-tax income into the distribution of expenditure, by using the permanent income model. We assume that income and expenditure are joint log normally distributed, so that the marginal distribution of expenditure is lognormal. On the basis of similar assumptions for groups of the population classified by demographic characteristics we determine the distribution of expenditure over groups from the distribution of income over groups.

The translog model of aggregate consumer behavior requires variables that depend only on the distribution of individual expenditures

$$\frac{\sum_{k=1}^{K} M_{kt} \ln M_{kt}}{\sum_{k=1}^{K} M_{kt}} = \mu_M + \sigma_M^2 , \quad (t = 1, 2, \ldots, T) \tag{8.179}$$

where the logarithm of expenditure M has a normal distribution with mean μ_M and variance σ_M^2, and variables that depend on the distribution of individual attributes and expenditures of the form

$$\frac{\sum_{k=1}^{K} M_{kt} A_{kt}}{\sum_{k=1}^{K} M_{kt}} , \quad (t = 1, 2, \ldots, T) . \tag{8.180}$$

Finally, we require the heteroscedasticity correction ρ_t of section 8.6, which takes the form

$$\rho_t = \frac{\left(\sum_{k=1}^{K} M_{kt} \right)^2}{\sum_{k=1}^{K} M_{kt}^2} = \sqrt{K}\, e^{-1/2\, \sigma_M^2} , \quad (t = 1, 2, \ldots, T) \tag{8.181}$$

where, without loss of generality, we normalize population size to one in 1972. Together with the time series of prices and aggregate expenditure shares, the variables (179–181) form a complete set of aggregate data for the translog model for the period 1958–1974.

8.7.B Estimation Results

The translog model of individual expenditures described in section 8.6 can be represented in the form

$$w_{kt} = \frac{1}{D_t} (\alpha_p + B_{pp} \ln p_t - B_{pp}\iota \ln M_{kt} + B_{pA} A_k) + \varepsilon_{kt}$$

$$(k = 1, 2, \ldots, K; \; t + 1, 2, \ldots, T) \tag{8.182}$$

where

$$D_t = -1 + \iota' B_{pp} \ln p_t , \quad (t = 1, 2, \ldots, T)$$

w_{kt} is the vector of observed budget shares, M_{kt} is expenditure for the kth consuming unit at time t, $\ln p_t$ is the vector of logarithms of prices at time t, and A_k is the vector of attributes of the kth consuming unit. The unobservable random disturbance ε_{kt} is distributed normally with mean zero and covariance matrix Ω_ε.

The cross-section model for a sample of size K' in 1972 with all prices equal to unity and time equal to zero is

$$w_{k,1972} = -\alpha_p + B_{pp}\iota \ln M_{k,1972} - B_{pA} A_k + \varepsilon_{k,1972} \quad (k = 1, 2, \ldots, K') \qquad (8.183)$$

where we have set $\iota'\alpha_p = -1$; the disturbance term $\varepsilon_{k,1972}$ is assumed to be uncorrelated among consuming units.

The translog model of aggregate expenditures, corrected for heteroscedasticity, is

$$\rho_t w_t = \rho_t \frac{\sum_{k=1}^{K} M_{kt} w_{kt}}{\sum_{k=1}^{K} M_{kt}} = \frac{1}{D_t} \alpha_p \rho_t + B_{pp} \rho_t \ln p_t - B_{pp} \iota \rho_t \frac{\sum_{k=1}^{K} M_{kt} \ln M_{kt}}{\sum_{k=1}^{K} M_{kt}}$$

$$+ B_{pA} \rho_t \frac{\sum_{k=1}^{K} \mathbf{M}_{kt} \mathbf{A}_k}{\sum_{k=1}^{K} \mathbf{M}_{kt}} + \rho_t \varepsilon_t \quad (t = 1, 2, \ldots, T) \qquad (8.184)$$

where the unobservable random disturbance $\rho_t\varepsilon_t$ is normally distributed with mean zero and covariance matrix Ω_v; we assume that this disturbance is uncorrelated over time.

In our application we have five commodity groups so that we estimate four equations. As unknown parameters we have four elements of the vector α_p, four expenditure coefficients of the vector $B_{pp}\iota$, sixteen attribute coefficients for each of the four equations in the matrix B_{pA}, plus ten price coefficients in the matrix B_{pp}, which is symmetric. We have a total of 82 unknown parameters to be estimated. Since there are only seventeen time-series data points and we utilize fourteen instrumental variables, not all of the parameters can be identified from time-series data alone. Since there is no price variation in the cross section, the remaining parameters of the matrix B_{pp} cannot be identified from the cross-section model alone.

We first estimate the cross-section model by ordinary least squares from data on individual expenditures, as outlined in section 8.6. We present the results in appendix 8.1. Next, we estimate the complete model, subject to the inequality restrictions implied by monotonicity of the individual expenditure shares, pooling time series and cross-section data. The results are given in table 8.3. We now turn to a detailed discussion of the inequality constrained pooled results, utilizing the cross-section results only for comparison.

We begin our discussion of the pooled estimation results by comparing the final estimates of the impact of total expenditure and demographic characteristics to those obtained from the cross-section model alone. Next, we analyze the impact of changes in total expenditure and demographic characteristics. Finally, we present price and expenditure elasticities calculations to illustrate the character of our pooled results. As an overview of the pooled estimates, we see that most of the unknown parameters are estimated very precisely. This is largely due to the enormous quantity of data that enters the pooling process. The price coefficients that appear in the numerators of the functions giving expenditure shares for commodity groups have relatively large standard errors by comparison with the attribute coefficients; this is to be expected, since there is no price variation in the cross-section data. By contrast the price coefficients that appear in the denominators are estimated very precisely. These coefficients are estimated by pooling time series and cross-section data.

The patterns of demographic effects, such as increases in the shares of food and clothing with increases in family size, are the same in the estimates from cross section alone and the pooled estimates. This invalidates the usual criticism of pooling cross section and aggregate time series, namely, that the aggregate data reflect only short run determinants of expenditure patterns, resulting in smaller effects in the time series than the cross section.[31] It appears to be very likely that the demographic effects in the aggregate data capture the underlying dynamics of the processes determining changes in aggregate expenditure patterns.[32]

8.7.C Individual Expenditure Patterns

We next turn to a discussion of the impact of change in expenditure and demographic characteristics on individual expenditure patterns. In addition to the estimated coefficients we present the results graphically in order to bring out their implications more clearly. In the graphs employed to depict individual expenditure patterns we use a "typical" consumer unit with family size five, age of head 35–44 years, living in the Northeast, white in race, with an urban residence, having a total expenditure of $9,000 as a basis for comparison. The choice of

Table 8.3
Pooled estimation results

Notation:

W	budget share
$\ln p$	log price

In order to designate the proper good to which W or $\ln p$ refers, we append the following subscripts where appropriate:

EN	energy
FC	food and clothing
O	other nondurable goods
CAP	capital services
$SERV$	consumer services

Further notation is given as:

$\ln M$	log total expenditure
$F2$	dummy for family size 2
$F3$	dummy for family size 3
$F4$	dummy for family size 4
$F5$	dummy for family size 5
$F6$	dummy for family size 6
$F7$	dummy for family size 7 or more
$A30$	dummy for age class 25–34
$A40$	dummy for age class 35–44
$A50$	dummy for age class 45–54
$A60$	dummy for age class 55–64
$A70$	dummy for age class 65 and older
RNC	dummy for region North Central
RS	dummy for region South
RW	dummy for region West
RNW	dummy for nonwhite head
RUR	dummy for rural residence

$D(p) = -1$	$-.01814 \ln p_{EN}$	$-.06201 \ln p_{FC}$	$-.03097 \ln p_{O}$
	(.000660)	(.00137)	(.00123)
	$+.1507 \ln p_{CAP}$	$-.03965 \ln p_{SERV}$	
	(.00308)	(.00286)	

Table 8.3 (continued)

Equation	Variable	Numerator coefficicient	Standard error
WEN	Constant	−.1845	.00601
	$\ln p_{EN}$	.02659	.0125
	$\ln p_{FC}$	−.02255	.0254
	$\ln p_{O}$	.005458	.0191
	$\ln p_{CAP}$	−.008346	.0207
	$\ln p_{SERV}$	−.01929*	.0243*
	$\ln M$	.01814	.000660
	$F2$	−.01550	.000974
	$F3$	−.01900	.00114
	$F4$	−.02201	.00125
	$F5$	−.02209	.00143
	$F6$	−.02524	.00173
	$F7$	−.02372	.00182
	$A30$	−.001581	.00134
	$A40$	−.003679	.00144
	$A50$	−.005671	.00138
	$A60$	−.008287	.00137
	$A70$	−.007465	.00133
	RNC	−.008694	.000910
	RS	−.007465	.000908
	RW	.004283	.000978
	RNW	.003624	.00116
	RUR	−.01767	.000978
WFC	Constant	−.7155	.0126
	$\ln p_{EN}$	−.02255	.0254
	$\ln p_{FC}$	.07251	.110
	$\ln p_{O}$	.01702	.0906
	$\ln p_{CAP}$	−.1083	.0514
	$\ln p_{SERV}$	−.02069*	.0900*
	$\ln M$	.06201	.00137
	$F2$	−.03461	.00203
	$F3$	−.05254	.00239
	$F4$	−.06782	.00260
	$F5$	−.08293	.00299
	$F6$	−.08945	.00361
	$F7$	−.1148	.00380
	$A30$	−.02209	.00281
	$A40$	−.04021	.00302
	$A50$	−.04769	.00288
	$A60$	−.04689	.00287
	$A70$	−.03444	.00279
	RNC	.01792	.00189
	RS	.01216	.00189
	RW	.01381	.00204
	RNW	−.01138	.00242
	RUR	.007507	.00188

Table 8.3 (continued)

Equation	Variable	Numerator coefficicient	Standard error
WO	Constant	−.4452	.0110
	$\ln p_{EN}$	.005458	.0191
	$\ln p_{FC}$	.01702	.0906
	$\ln p_{O}$	.1723	.123
	$\ln p_{CAP}$	−.1710	.0362
	$\ln p_{SERV}$	−.05472*	.0357*
	$\ln M$	.03097	.00123
	*F*2	−.01588	.00182
	*F*3	−.02667	.00214
	*F*4	−.03366	.00234
	*F*5	−.03707	.00268
	*F*6	−.04314	.00324
	*F*7	−.05565	.00341
	*A*30	−.01318	.00252
	*A*40	−.01646	.00270
	*A*50	−.01928	.00258
	*A*60	−.01746	.00257
	*A*70	−.003344	.00250
	RNC	.009577	.00170
	RS	−.0001790	.00169
	RW	.008988	.00183
	RNW	−.004260	.00217
	RUR	−.0001298	.00169
WCAP	Constant	1.0906	.0273
	$\ln p_{EN}$	−.008346	.0207
	$\ln p_{FC}$	−.1083	.0514
	$\ln p_{O}$	−.1710	.0362
	$\ln p_{CAP}$	.5929	.0481
	$\ln p_{SERV}$	−.1544*	.0540*
	$\ln M$	−.1507	.00308
	*F*2	.006422	.00456
	*F*3	.01695	.00537
	*F*4	.02416	.00585
	*F*5	.02668	.00671
	*F*6	.03810	.00811
	*F*7	.06580	.00853
	*A*30	.03668	.00632
	*A*40	.04184	.00678
	*A*50	.04674	.00646
	*A*60	.03187	.00645
	*A*70	−.002706	.00627
	RNC	−.04193	.00426
	RS	−.02927	.00425
	RW	−.01785	.00458
	RNW	.02118	.00543
	RUR	−.04590	.00423

Table 8.3 (continued)

Equation	Variable	Numerator coefficicient	Standard error
WSERV	Constant	−.7452*	.0255*
	$\ln p_{EN}$	−.01929*	.0243*
	$\ln p_{FC}$	−.02069*	.0900*
	$\ln p_{O}$	−.05472*	.0357*
	$\ln p_{CAP}$	−.1544*	.0540*
	$\ln p_{SERV}$	.2094*	.105*
	$\ln M$	.03965*	.00286*
	*F*2	.05958*	.00424*
	*F*3	.08126*	.00500*
	*F*4	.09934*	.00545*
	*F*5	.1154*	.00625*
	*F*6	.1197*	.00755*
	*F*7	.1284*	.00794*
	*A*30	.0001850*	.00588*
	*A*40	.01851*	.00631*
	*A*50	.02590*	.00602*
	*A*60	.04076*	.00600*
	*A*70	.04795*	.00584*
	RNC	.02313*	.00397*
	RS	.02474*	.00396*
	RW	−.009231*	.00426*
	RNW	−.009156*	.00506*
	RUR	.05620*	.00394*

Estimate of covariance matrix $\sum_v$

	WEN	*WFC*	*WO*	*WCAP*
WEN	.000009436			
WFC	−.000003545	.00008021		
WO	−.000002289	−.00001017	.000007800	
WCAP	−.00001444	.00002593	−.000005464	.00004371

SRR = 32626.58.
Gauss Newton algorithm.
Convergence criterion = .01.
Convergence achieved after one iteration.

* Derived from estimated coefficients

another base case would shift the curves vertically, but would leave the relative impact of changes in demographic characteristics unchanged.[33]

1. *Total Expenditure*

In figure 8.1 we display the effects of changing expenditure on individual expenditure patterns on each commodity. We see that as expenditure increases, the share devoted to capital services increases, while all other shares decrease. The effect is quite strong for low expenditure values and diminishes as total expenditure grows.[34] The overall behavior of the individual expenditure shares with respect to changes in expenditure corresponds quite closely to what might be expected. The goods energy and food and clothing correspond most closely to basic necessities. As expenditure increases, the shares of energy and food and clothing decline. The dramatic growth of the capital services share as expenditure increases indicates that capital services are a luxury good. The individual expenditure shares of consumer services and other nondurables diminish at a much lower rate than those for energy and food and clothing as expenditure increases, and remain fairly constant over a large range of expenditure. This indicates that the expenditures on services and other nondurables grow at approximately the same rate as total expenditure.

Nonnegativity in our model is equivalent to the condition that all budget shares are between zero and unity. Since the equations for individual expenditure shares are linear in the logarithms of expenditure, there is a range of expenditure for each share and for each set of attributes where nonnegativity holds. We investigate the range of total expenditure for which nonnegativity holds for 1972 by presenting two sets of calculations. First, we calculate the range of admissible shares for a typical family in 1972, of family size five, age of head 35–44, Northeast region, white race, and urban residence. Second, we calculate the greatest lower bound on expenditure and the least upper bound which allows the share to fall between zero and unity. These calculations are presented in table 8.4.

For our typical family, we see that nonnegativity will hold for expenditures between $2,427 and $112,198. This range certainly includes almost all families with the typical attributes. The large lower bound is due to the capital services equation. At any rate, for the typical set of attributes, the proportion of the population on which nonnegativity fails is quite small. The greatest lower bound is $3,997

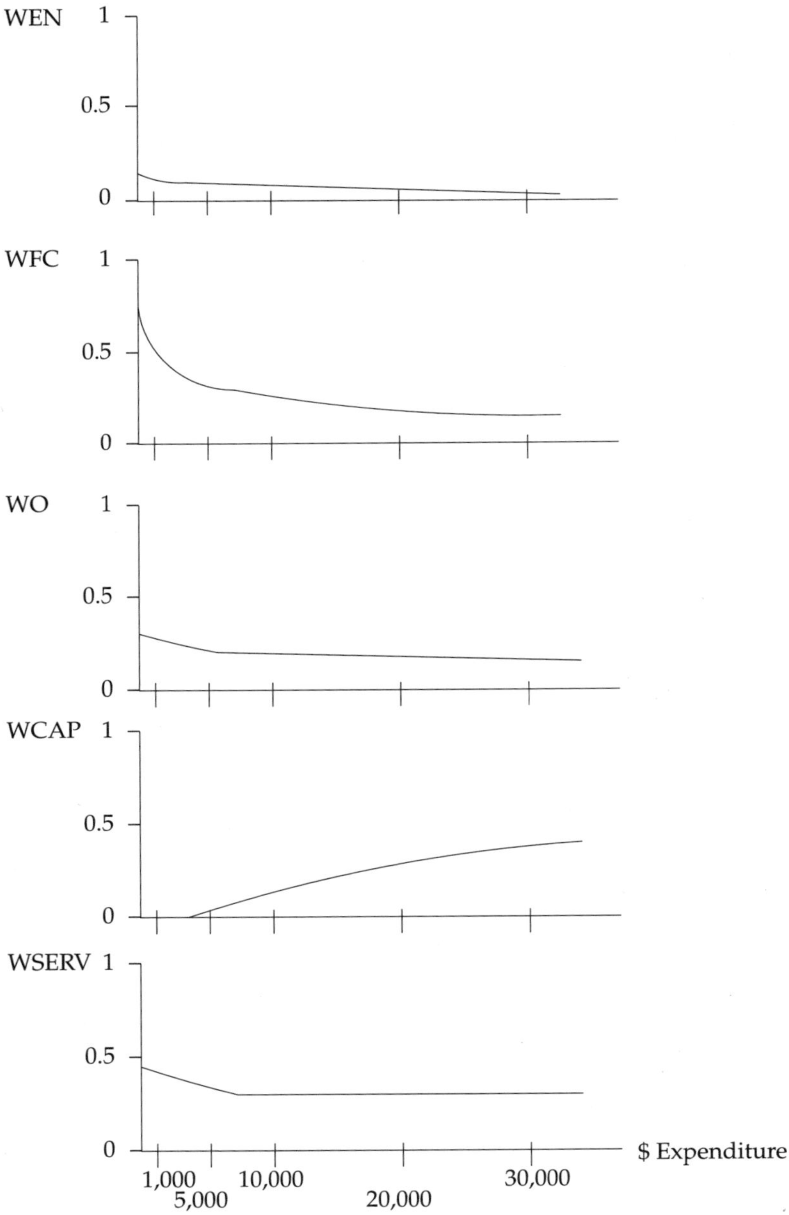

Figure 8.1
Expenditure shares as functions of total expenditure, 1972. Reference family has: family size = 5, age = 35–44, region = Northeast, race = white, residence = urban.

Table 8.4
Nonnegativity bounds, 1972*

Share	Lower bound	Upper bound
WEN	1.0×10^{-18}	112,198
WFC	0.15	492,820
WO	1.2×10^{-7}	8,588,666
WCAP	2,427	1,386,632
WSERV	9.8×10^{-8}	4,880,149

* Reference family has: family size = 5, age = 35–44; region = Northeast, race = white, residence = urban.

Greatest lower bounds, 1972

Share	Bound	Attributes
WEN	6.2×10^{-18}	FS = 7, A = 55–64, R = NC, RC = White, RES = Rural
WFC	0.40	FS = 7, A = 35–44, R = NE, RC = White, RES = Urban
WO	3.7×10^{-7}	FS = 7, A = 35–44, R = S, RC = Nonwhite, RES = Urban
WCAP	3,997	FS = 7, A = 35–44, R = NE, RC = Nonwhite, RES = Urban
WSERV	0.01	FS = 1, A = 15–24, R = W, RC = Nonwhite, RES = Urban

Least upper bounds, 1972

Share	Bound	Attributes
WEN	11,981	FS = 1, A = 15–24, R = W, RC = Nonwhite, RES = Urban
WFC	28,640	FS = 1, A = 15–24, R = NC, RC = Nonwhite, RES = Rural
WO	604,564	FS = 1, A = 15–24, R = NC, RC = White, RES = Rural
WCAP	403,061	FS = 1, A = 15–24, R = NC, RC = White, RES = Rural
WSERV	198,986	FS = 7, A = 65 and over, R = S, RC = White, RES = Rural

from capital services, for families of size seven or more, head age 35–44, living in the urban Northeast, and nonwhite in race. Thus nonnegativity fails for large nonwhite families with income less than \$3,997. The least upper bound is \$11,981, for single nonwhites, age 20 living in the urban West. Except for consumer services, all upper bounds are generated by unrelated individuals of age 15–24. Again, except for consumer services, all lower bounds are generated by families of size seven or more.

2. *Family Size*

Figure 8.2 depicts the effects of family size on relative expenditure shares. We see that as family size changes from one to seven or more, the shares of energy, food and clothing, and other nondurable expenditures increase, whereas the shares of capital services and consumer services decrease. A striking feature of these graphs is the abrupt changes from family size one to two and from six to seven or more. For families of sizes two to six the share of energy remains roughly constant, food and clothing and other nondurable expenditure show a monotonic increase, matched by smooth decreases in capital and consumer services. Larger families buy more food and clothing and employ fewer services, such as entertainment.

The movement from family size one to two involves a substantial alteration of expenditure patterns. Two person families spend a much larger proportion of their budget on necessities than unrelated individuals and spend less on capital services and consumer services with the same total expenditure. Similarly, the movement from family size six to seven or more involves a sizable change in expenditure patterns, especially in food and clothing. Expenditures on food and clothing are higher, expenditure shares of energy and other nondurable expenditures are relatively large, and expenditure shares devoted to capital services and consumer services are quite small. The abruptness of the change in expenditure patterns results from the fact that the size category seven or more includes not only families of size seven or eight, but also those of larger size, such as twelve and fifteen.

3. *Age of Head*

The impact of age of head of families on expenditure patterns is depicted in figure 8.3.[35] We see that the age of head has impacts that are not monotonic. The energy shares increases a small amount, food and clothing grows until approximately age 40, levels off and then

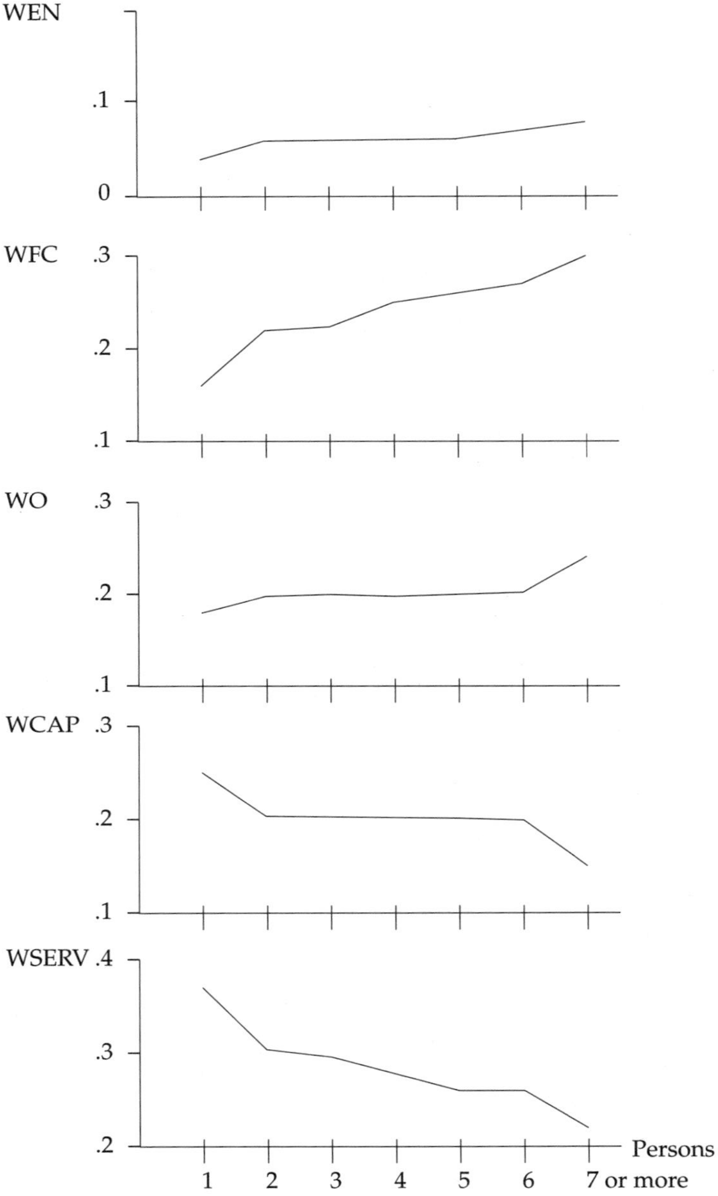

Figure 8.2
Expenditure shares as functions of family size, 1972. Reference family has: expenditure = $9,000, age = 35–44, region = Northeast, race = white, residence = urban.

decreases. The capital services share shows the opposite profile to food and clothing. Consumer services decline relatively smoothly and other nondurable expenditures rise and then fall a small amount. A plausible explanation of this behavior is that the age of head is highly correlated with the ages of children in the family. When the head is young, so are the children and so relatively small amounts are allocated to food and clothing. As the head ages, the children need more food for growth and more clothing; the family allocates more expenditure to food and clothing. This is associated with a decrease in the shares of capital services and consumer services. The food and clothing share peaks, levels off, and drops as the head ages further.

4. *Region and Race*

In figure 8.4 we present the impact of demographic characteristics: region, race, and type of residence. The region effects are rather small for energy and other nondurables, but households living in North Central and Southern regions use relatively more capital services from homes and automobiles. Increased use of capital is accompanied by a small increase in energy use. The increases are associated with a fall in the share of consumer services. The Northeast and West regions are virtually indistinguishable in individual expenditure patterns with only a slight increase in capital services and consumer services and a slight decrease in food and clothing for the West. The white-nonwhite distinction has no substantial effect on the shares of energy, food and clothing, or other nondurable expenditures. The only difference between whites and nonwhites is a smaller share devoted to capital services and a larger share devoted to consumer services for nonwhites.

5. *Type of Residence*

The final difference in demographic characteristics that we analyze, type of residence, is also depicted in figure 8.4. Food and clothing and other nondurable expenditure shares are smaller for rural families; the shares of capital services and energy are much larger and the consumer services share is much smaller for these families. Except for food and clothing, these impacts are exactly as expected. Being relatively distant from urban areas, rural families tend to employ much more capital services in the form of homes and automobiles. In order to use the increased capital services, more energy is acquired. This is associated with a reduced share of consumer services, which are less available to rural locations.

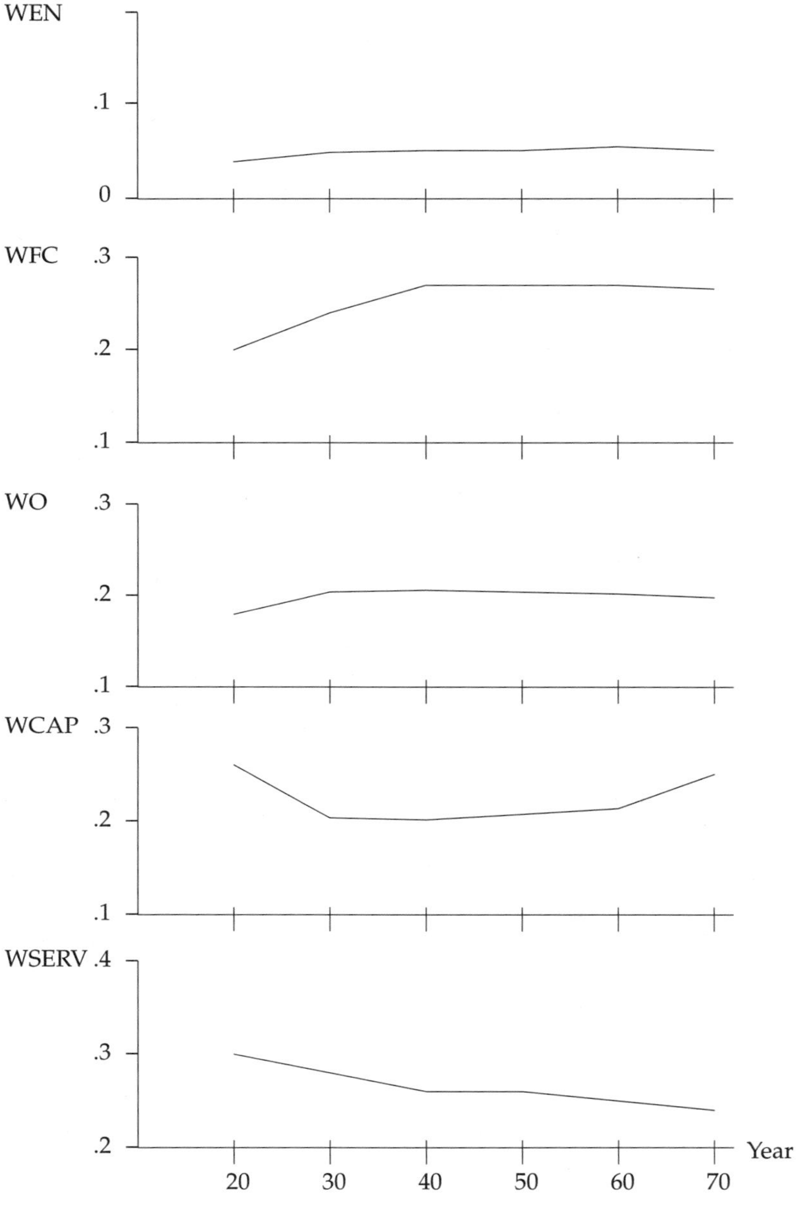

Figure 8.3
Expenditure shares as functions of age of head, 1972. Reference family has: expenditure = $9,000, family size = 5, region = Northeast, race = white, residence = urban.

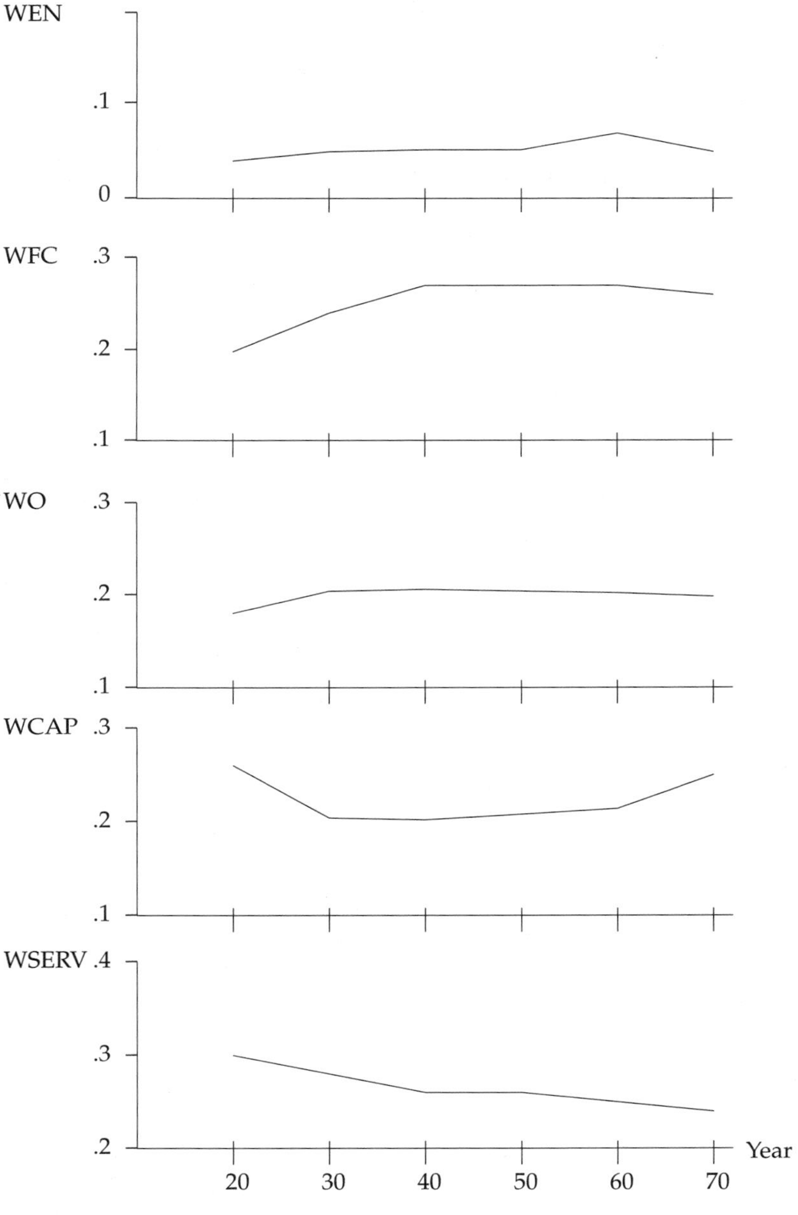

Figure 8.4
Expenditure shares as functions of region, race, and residence, 1972. Reference family has: expenditure = $9,000, family size = 5, region = Northeast, race = white, residence = urban.

We are left with the problem of explaining the decrease in the share of food and clothing for rural households. Some of the food consumed by the family may be produced at home and may be underreported in our data. Under this interpretation it is quite likely that rural families have expenditure greater than the $9,000 indicated in figure 8.4. The large increase in the share of capital services may be partly due to differences in consumption patterns and partly due to larger expenditure. Similar remarks would apply to the share of consumer services. The energy share also shows a marked difference; the effect of increased expenditure would lessen rather than increase it.

6. *Elasticity Calculation*

As a further illustration of the differences in preferences among individual consuming units represented in our model, we give budget shares, price elasticities, and expenditure elasticities for all commodities in table 8.5. Different budget shares, price elasticities, and expenditure elasticities are given by the model for each set of total expenditure levels and demographic characteristics. By varying total expenditure and each demographic characteristic, we obtain an indication of the variation in elasticities among consuming units. Unless otherwise indicated we consider consuming units with expenditure of $9,000, family size five, age of head 35–44 years, living in the Northeast region, white, and having an urban residence.

We see that as total expenditure increases, expenditure allocation becomes significantly less sensitive to changes in total expenditure and more sensitive to changes in all prices except the price of capital services. Expenditure elasticities of demand decrease with total expenditure for all commodity groups and price elasticities of demand increase with total expenditure for all commodity groups except for capital services. Variations in family size are almost, but not quite, a mirror image of variations in total expenditure. As family size increases, the expenditure elasticities of demand increase for all commodity groups except consumer services and for all family sizes except the largest. The expenditure elasticity of demand for consumer services declines with family size, possibly indicating that some services available in the market are performed within the household by members of large families. The expenditure elasticity of demand for energy peaks at family size six and declines for families of size seven or more. Price elasticities of demand decrease for all commodity groups except capital services and consumer services and for all

Table 8.5
Estimated budget shares, price and expenditure elasticities, 1972*

Expenditure	\$5,000	\$10,000	\$15,000	\$20,000	\$25,000	\$30,000	\$35,000
				Budget shares			
EN	0.055802	0.043229	0.035874	0.030655	0.026607	0.023300	0.020504
FC	0.310471	0.267483	0.242337	0.224496	0.210657	0.199350	0.189790
O	0.234992	0.213524	0.200967	0.192057	0.185146	0.179500	0.174726
CAP	0.125156	0.229674	0.290813	0.334191	0.367838	0.395330	0.418574
SERV	0.273579	0.246090	0.230010	0.218601	0.209751	0.202520	0.196407
				Income elasticities			
EN	0.674924	0.580371	0.494335	0.408253	0.318229	0.221455	0.115277
FC	0.800247	0.768144	0.744086	0.723748	0.705600	0.688902	0.673231
O	0.868205	0.854955	0.845892	0.838743	0.832724	0.827426	0.822747
CAP	2.204792	1.656527	1.518502	1.451200	1.409927	1.381420	1.360240
SERV	0.855037	0.838844	0.827577	0.818578	0.810924	0.804173	0.798078
				Price elasticities			
EN	−1.494684	−1.633294	−1.759418	−1.885610	−2.017580	−2.159447	−2.315099
FC	−1.295595	−1.333133	−1.361265	−1.385047	−1.406268	−1.425794	−1.444118
O	−1.764320	−1.838050	−1.888480	−1.928261	−1.961754	−1.991034	−2.017266
CAP	−5.586618	−3.430767	−2.888035	−2.623392	−2.461103	−2.349010	−2.265725
SERV	−1.805281	−1.890805	−1.950310	−1.997838	−2.038265	−2.073918	−2.106111

Table 8.5 (continued)

Family size	1	2	3	4	5	6	7 or more
				Budget shares			
EN	0.023044	0.038553	0.042048	0.045057	0.045140	0.048289	0.046764
FC	0.191084	0.225695	0.243628	0.258906	0.274017	0.280543	0.305953
O	0.179716	0.195603	0.206391	0.213384	0.216787	0.222865	0.235371
CAP	0.240472	0.234050	0.223513	0.216312	0.213787	0.202370	0.174666
SERV	0.365684	0.306100	0.284419	0.266340	0.250268	0.245932	0.237246
				Income elasticities			
EN	0.212801	0.529477	0.568586	0.597398	0.598138	0.624345	0.612096
FC	0.675444	0.725215	0.745442	0.760464	0.773673	0.778938	0.797297
O	0.827669	0.841666	0.849942	0.854860	0.857138	0.861035	0.868418
CAP	1.627045	1.644252	1.674622	1.697080	1.705315	1.745104	1.863287
SERV	0.891549	0.870438	0.860562	0.851097	0.841535	0.838741	0.832836
				Price elasticities			
EN	−2.172133	−1.707903	−1.650570	−1.608333	−1.607248	−1.568831	−1.586787
FC	−1.441531	−1.383332	−1.359680	−1.342115	−1.326668	−1.320512	−1.299044
O	−1.989877	−1.911994	−1.865942	−1.838579	−1.825902	−1.804222	−1.763138
CAP	−3.314841	−3.382500	−3.501918	−3.590228	−3.622607	−3.779064	−4.243776
SERV	−1.612444	−1.723941	−1.776101	−1.826091	−1.876594	−1.891351	−1.922535

Table 8.5 (continued)

Age of Head	15–24	25–34	35–44	45–54	55–64	65 & over
			Budget shares			
EN	0.041461	0.043043	0.045140	0.047132	0.049748	0.048926
FC	0.233801	0.255901	0.274017	0.281497	0.280692	0.268242
O	0.200322	0.213512	0.216787	0.219610	0.217789	0.203667
CAP	0.255627	0.218941	0.213787	0.208882	0.223749	0.258334
SERV	0.268788	0.268603	0.250268	0.242878	0.228022	0.220831
			Income elasticities			
EN	0.562479	0.578559	0.598138	0.615123	0.635362	0.629235
FC	0.734743	0.757651	0.773673	0.779687	0.779055	0.768800
O	0.845396	0.854947	0.857138	0.858975	0.857796	0.847935
CAP	1.589871	1.688711	1.705315	1.721877	1.673910	1.583690
SERV	0.852453	0.852351	0.841535	0.836713	0.826074	0.820411
			Price elasticities			
EN	−1.659523	−1.635950	−1.607248	−1.582350	−1.552681	−1.561662
FC	−1.372190	−1.345404	−1.326668	−1.319636	−1.320375	−1.332366
O	−1.891238	−1.838096	−1.825902	−1.815683	−1.822244	−1.877112
CAP	−3.168664	−3.557318	−3.622607	−3.687730	−3.499118	−3.144363
SERV	−1.818929	−1.819466	−1.876594	−1.902060	−1.958249	−1.988159

Table 8.5 (continued)

Region	Northeast	North Central	South	West
		Budget shares		
EN	0.045140	0.053835	0.052606	0.040856
FC	0.274017	0.256097	0.261848	0.260199
O	0.216787	0.207210	0.216966	0.207799
CAP	0.213787	0.255727	0.243058	0.231645
SERV	0.250268	0.227131	0.225522	0.259500
		Income elasticities		
EN	0.598138	0.663044	0.655172	0.556001
FC	0.773673	0.757836	0.763155	0.761654
O	0.857138	0.850535	0.857256	0.850959
CAP	1.705315	1.589641	1.620376	1.650940
SERV	0.841535	0.825392	0.824146	0.847172
		Price elasticities		
EN	−1.607248	−1.512100	−1.523641	−1.669020
FC	−1.326668	−1.345187	−1.338967	−1.340723
O	−1.825902	−1.862642	−1.825246	−1.860285
CAP	−3.622607	−3.167763	−3.288614	−3.408797
SERV	−1.876594	−1.961853	−1.968432	−1.846820

Race and Residence	White	Nonwhite	Urban	Rural
		Budget shares		
EN	0.045140	0.041516	0.045140	0.062818
FC	0.274017	0.285407	0.274017	0.266510
O	0.216787	0.221047	0.216787	0.216917
CAP	0.213787	0.192606	0.213787	0.259689
SERV	0.250268	0.259424	0.250268	0.194065
		Income elasticities		
EN	0.598138	0.563058	0.598138	0.711228
FC	0.773673	0.782705	0.773673	0.767298
O	0.857138	0.859892	0.857138	0.857224
CAP	1.705315	1.782879	1.705315	1.580644
SERV	0.841535	0.847127	0.841535	0.795641
		Price elasticities		
EN	−1.607248	−1.658674	−1.607248	−1.441464
FC	−1.326668	−1.316107	−1.326668	−1.334123
O	−1.825902	−1.810581	−1.825902	−1.825426
CAP	−3.622607	−3.927601	−3.622607	−3.132384
SERV	−1.876594	−1.847056	−1.876594	−2.118979

* Reference family has: expenditure = $9,000, family size = five, age = 35–44, region = Northeast, race = white, residence = urban.

family sizes except the largest. The price elasticity of demand for energy reaches a minimum at family size six.

Variations in the age of head of household result in smaller changes in expenditure and price elasticities than variations in total expenditure or family size. The expenditure elasticity of demand for energy increases up to age of head 55–64 and then declines for age of head 65 and older. The pattern for food and clothing is similar. The expenditure elasticities of demand for other nondurables and capital services peak at age of head 45–54. The expenditure elasticity of demand for consumer services declines monotonically with age of head of household. The price elasticity of demand for energy falls to age of head 55–64 and then rises for age of head 65 and over. Price elasticities for food and clothing and other nondurables fall to age of head 45–54 and then rise. The price elasticity of demand for capital services reaches a peak at age 45–54 and then falls. The price elasticity of demand for consumer services increases monotonically with age of head of household.

Expenditure and price elasticities of demand vary with region, race, and type of residence. Expenditure elasticities of demand for energy are highest in the North Central and Southern regions, the expenditure elasticity for food and clothing is highest in the Northeast, while the expenditure elasticity for other nondurables is highest in the South. The expenditure elasticity of demand for capital services is highest in the Northeast, while the expenditure elasticities for consumer services are highest in the Northeast and Western regions. Price elasticities of demand for energy are lowest in the North Central and Southern regions, the price elasticity of demand for food and clothing is lowest in the Northeast, and the price elasticity for other nondurables is lowest in the Northeast and Southern regions. The price elasticity of demand for capital services is lowest in the North Central regions while the price elasticity of demand for consumer services is lowest in the West.

The expenditure elasticity of demand for energy is lower for whites than for nonwhites. For all other commodity groups the expenditure elasticities of demand are lower for nonwhites than for whites. Price elasticities of demand for energy and capital services are higher for nonwhites than for whites, while price elasticities for food and clothing, other nondurables, and consumer services are higher for whites. Finally, expenditure elasticities of demand for energy and other nondurables are lower for urban residents than for rural residents, while expenditure elasticities of demand for food and clothing, capital services, and consumer services are lower for rural residents. Price elasticities of demand for energy, other nondurables, and capital services are higher for urban than for rural residents. Price elasticities for food and clothing and consumer services are higher for rural residents. Our overall conclusion is that both expenditure and price elasticities of demand vary considerably with total expenditure and with demographic characteristics of the household.

8.7.D Summary and Conclusion

In this section we have presented the results of implementing the translog model of aggregate consumer behavior. For this purpose we have divided consumer expenditures among five broad commodity groups—energy, food and clothing, consumer services, capital services, and other nondurable expenditure. We assume that the direct utility function is homothetically separable in goods within each category, so that we can construct price indexes for each commodity group. We define the quantity consumed for each group as the ratio of expenditure on that group to the corresponding price index.

We employ households as consuming units. Expenditures within the household are allocated so as to maximize a household welfare function, so that the household behaves in the same way as an individual maximizing a utility function. All consuming units are classified by five demographic characteristics that result in differences in preferences among households—family size, age of head, region of residence, race, and type of residence. For each of these characteristics, households are classified into exhaustive and mutually exclusive groups. Each group is represented by a qualitative or dummy variable, equal to unity when a household is in the group and zero otherwise.

Our time series observations are based on data on personal consumption expenditures from the U.S. Interindustry Transactions Accounts for the period 1958–1974. Our cross-section observations are for the year 1972 from the 1972–1973 Survey of Consumer Expenditures. We employ data on the distribution of expenditures over all households and among demographic groups based on the Current Population Survey. To complete our time-series data set we require data for our heteroscedasticity adjustment, also based on the Current Population Survey.

We first estimate the model for individual expenditures by ordinary least squares. We then estimate the combined model by pooling time series and cross-section data. We discuss the pooled estimates in detail, introducing the results from cross-section data alone only to provide additional perspective. Most of the unknown parameters in the pooled model for cross-section and time-series data are estimated very precisely.

The impacts of changes in total expenditures and in demographic characteristics of the household that appear in the numerators of the functions determining the allocation of expenditures are estimated more precisely than the impacts of changes in prices. This reflects the fact that estimates of the expenditure and demographic effects incorporate a relatively large quantity of cross-section data while estimates of the price effects incorporate a much smaller quantity of time-series data on prices. The impacts of changes in prices that appear in the denominators of the functions determining the allocation of expenditures are estimated very precisely, reflecting the fact that these changes incorporate both time series and cross-section data. The sign and order of magnitude of the expenditure and demographic effects are very similar in the cross-section and the pooled estimates.

We characterize the impact of changes in expenditure, demographic characteristics of the household, and prices on individual expenditure patterns by considering a consumer unit with five members, age of head 35–44 years, living in the Northeast, white in race, and with an urban residence, having a total expenditure of $9,000 for the year 1972. We then vary total expenditure and each of the demographic characteristics, holding constant all the demographic characteristics and total expenditure and the remaining demographic characteristics, respectively.

Individual expenditure shares for capital services increase with total expenditure, while all other shares decrease with total expenditures. As family size increases, the shares of energy, food and clothing, and other nondurable expenditures increase, while the shares of capital services and consumer services decrease. The energy share increases with age of head, while the consumer services share declines. The shares of food and clothing and of other nondurables increase and then decrease with age of head, while capital services has the opposite profile.

The effects of region of residence on patterns of individual expenditures is small for energy and other nondurables. Households living in North Central and Southern regions use relatively more capital services and slightly more energy; these households use less consumer services. The only difference between whites and nonwhites is a smaller share of capital services and a larger share of consumer services for nonwhites. Finally, shares of food and clothing, consumer services, and other nondurables are smaller for rural families, while the shares of capital services and energy are much larger.

As a final illustration of differences in preferences among individual consuming units, we have presented price and expenditure elasticities for different consuming groups. Again we consider units with five members, age of head 35–44 years, living in the Northeast, white in race, and with an urban residence, having a total expenditure of $9,000 for the year 1972. Increases in total expenditure decrease expenditure elasticities and increase price elasticities, except for capital services. Increases in family size for a given total expenditure result in decreases in price elasticities and increases in expenditure elasticities of demand, except for consumer services. Differences in price and expenditure elasticities associated with age of head, region of residence, race, and type of residence are also substantial.

Appendix 8.1 Cross-Section Estimation Results

Table 8.A1
Cross-section estimation results

Equation	Variable	Coefficient	Standard error
WEN	Constant	−.18047	.00572
	ln *M*	.01750	.00066
	F2	−.01550	.00097
	F3	−.01900	.00115
	F4	−.02201	.00125
	F5	−.02209	.00143
	F6	−.02524	.00173
	F7	−.02372	.00182
	A30	−.00158	.00134
	A40	−.00367	.00144
	A50	−.00567	.00138
	A60	−.00828	.00137
	A70	−.00746	.00134
	RNC	−.00869	.00091
	RS	−.00746	.00091
	RW	.00428	.00098
	RNW	.00362	.00116
	RUR	−.01767	.00090

$R^2 = 0.2057$. S.E. = 0.0283. Number of observations = 8,049.

Table 8.A1 (continued)

Equation	Variable	Coefficient	Standard error
WFC	Constant	−.65939	.01193
	ln *M*	.06286	.00138
	F2	−.03461	.00203
	F3	−.05254	.00239
	F4	−.06782	.00261
	F5	−.08293	.00299
	F6	−.08945	.00362
	F7	−.11486	.00381
	A30	−.02210	.00281
	A40	−.04021	.00302
	A50	−.04769	.00288
	A60	−.04689	.00287
	A70	−.03444	.00279
	RNC	.01792	.00190
	RS	.01216	.00189
	RW	.01381	.00204
	RNW	.01138	.00242
	RUR	.00750	.00189

$R^2 = 0.2909$. S.E. = 0.0591. Number of observations = 8,049.

Equation	Variable	Coefficient	Standard error
WO	Constant	−.42202	.01070
	ln *M*	.03105	.00124
	F2	−.01588	.00182
	F3	−.02667	.00215
	F4	−.03366	.00234
	F5	−.03706	.00268
	F6	−.04314	.00324
	F7	−.05565	.00341
	A30	−.01319	.00252
	A40	−.01646	.00270
	A50	−.01928	.00258
	A60	−.01746	.00257
	A70	−.00334	.00250
	RNC	.00957	.00170
	RS	−.00018	.00170
	RW	.00899	.00183
	RNW	−.00426	.00217
	RUR	−.00013	.00169

$R^2 = 0.1159$. S.E. = 0.0530. Number of observations = 8,049.

Table 8.A1 (continued)

Equation	Variable	Coefficient	Standard error
WCAP	Constant	1.09550	.02680
	ln *M*	−.15184	.00310
	F2	.00642	.00457
	F3	.01695	.00538
	F4	.02415	.00587
	F5	.02668	.00672
	F6	.03808	.00813
	F7	.06580	.00855
	A30	.03668	.00632
	A40	.04183	.00678
	A50	.04674	.00647
	A60	.03187	.00645
	A70	−.00270	.00627
	RNC	−.04194	.00426
	RS	−.02927	.00425
	RW	−.01785	.00458
	RNW	.02118	.00544
	RUR	−.04590	.00424

$R^2 = 0.2827$. S.E. = 0.1327. Number of observations = 8,049.

Equation	Variable	Coefficient	Standard error
WSERV	Constant	−.83361	.02496
	ln *M*	.04041	.00289
	F2	.05958	.00425
	F3	.08126	.00501
	F4	.09934	.00546
	F5	.11541	.00626
	F6	.11976	.00757
	F7	.12843	.00796
	A30	.00018	.00588
	A40	.01852	.00631
	A50	.02591	.00602
	A60	.04076	.00600
	A70	.04795	.00584
	RNC	.02313	.00397
	RS	.02474	.00396
	RW	−.00923	.00427
	RNW	−.00915	.00506
	RUR	.05620	.00395

$R^2 = 0.2052$. S.E. = 0.1236. Number of observations = 8,049.

Table 8.A1 (continued)

Estimate of covariance matrix $\sum_{\varepsilon}$

	WEN	*WFC*	*WO*	*WCAP*
WEN	.0008032			
WFC	−.0001561	.003494		
WO	.00002166	.001951	.002812	
WCAP	.0001231	−.002970	−.003694	.01763

Number of observations = 8,049.

Appendix 8.2 Aggregate Instrumental Variables

The variables used as instruments for the aggregate time series portion of the model are as follows:

Constant

TL—effective tax rate, labor services

TCR—effective tax rate, noncompetitive imports

LH—time available for labor services

P—U.S. population, millions of individuals

PL—implicit deflator, supply of labor service

PLG—implicit deflator, government purchases of labor services

EL-HR-RT—exogenous income, which equals government transfers to persons (excepting social insurance) less personal transfers to foreigners and personal nontax payments to government

$W(-1)$—private national wealth, lagged one period

$LH \cdot (1 + H)^T$—potential time for labor services; H—rate of Harrod neutral change

Total Imports

PCR—implicit deflator, noncompetitive imports

$PL/(1 + H)^T$—corrected deflator for labor services

T—time, set to 0 in 1972

Notes

1. Note that when we consider only a single commodity or a single consumer, we can suppress the corresponding commodity or individual subscript. This is done to keep the notation as simple as possible; any omission of subscripts will be clear from the context.
2. Note the power of the assumption that $F(p, M_1 + M_2, A_1 + A_2)$ is single-valued. In general, $F(p, M_1 + M_2, A_1 + A_2) = f_1(p, M_1, A_1) + f_2(p, M_2, A_2)$ is a correspondence; for fixed A_1 and A_2, there is an infinite number of possible combinations of M_1 and M_2 corresponding to every aggregate expenditure $M_1 + M_2$; aggregate demands are given by

$$f_1(p, M_1, A_1) + f_2(p, M_2, A_2) = f_1(p, M_1, A_1) + f_2(p, (M_1 + M_2) - M_1, A_2).$$

Since M_1 is free to change, aggregate demand can take many different values for the same value of aggregate expenditure.
3. See, for example, Houthakker (1957) and the references given there.
4. Alternative approaches to the representation of the effects of household characteristics on expenditure allocation are presented by Barten (1964b), Gorman (1976), and Prais and Houthakker (1955). Empirical evidence on the impact of variations in demographic characteristics on expenditure allocation is given by Lau, Lin, and Yotopoulos (1978), Muellbauer (1977), Parks and Barten (1973) and Pollak and Wales (1980). A review of the literature is presented by Deaton and Muellbauer (1980b), pp. 191–213.
5. Alternative approaches to the representation of the effects of total expenditure on expenditure allocation are reviewed by Deaton and Muellbauer (1980b), pp. 148–160. Gorman (1981) shows that Engel curves for an individual consumer that are linear in certain functions of total expenditure, as required in the theory of exact aggregation considered below, involve at most three linearly independent functions of total expenditure. Evidence from budget studies on the nonlinearity of Engel curves is presented by Leser (1963), Muellbauer (1976b), Pollak and Wales (1978), and Prais and Houthakker (1955).
6. See, for example, Blackorby, Boyce, and Russell (1978) and the references given there.
7. We omit the proof of this theorem, referring the interested reader to Lau (1977b).
8. Alternative approaches to the representation of the effects of prices on expenditure allocation are reviewed by Barten (1977), Deaton and Muellbauer (1980b), pp. 60–85, and Lau (1977a). The indirect translog utility function was introduced by Christensen, Jorgenson, and Lau (1975) and was extended to encompass changes in preferences over time by Jorgenson and Lau (1975).
9. The specification of a system of individual demand functions by means of Roy's Identity was first implemented empirically in a pathbreaking study by Houthakker (1960). A detailed review of econometric models of consumer behavior based on Roy's Identity is given by Lau (1977a).
10. Note that this derivation does not require differentiability of either the individual or aggregate demand functions.
11. Summability requires that $\sum_{n=1}^{N} p_n h_{n2}(p) = 0$ which implies $h_{n2}(p) = 0$, $(n = 1, 2, \ldots, N)$. For the power function case, the system of individual demand functions may not be nonnegative under summability.
12. Summability requires that $\sum_{n=1}^{N} p_n h_{n2}^*(p) = 0$, which implies that at least one function $h_{n2}^*(p)$ is negative for some prices. This is consistent with the condition $h_{n2}^*(p) \ln h_{n1}^*(p) \geqq 0$, since for that function and those prices $\ln h_{n1}^*(p)$ can be negative.
13. See Jorgenson and Lau (1979), p. 131.

14. For details, see Jorgenson and Lau (1979). The second-order interpolation property is discussed by Lau (1977a).
15. See Samuelson (1956) for details.
16. These conditions are implied by the Fundamental Theorem of Exact Aggregation presented in section 8.1, above.
17. The concepts of equivalent and compensating variations are due to Hicks (1942). Measures of compensating variations based on the translog indirect utility functions under exact aggregation were introduced by Jorgenson, Lau, and Stoker (1980). The corresponding measures of equivalent variations were introduced by Jorgenson, Lau, and Stoker (1981). Net equivalent variations correspond to Samuelson's (1974) concept of "money metric utility." Further discussion and references to the literature are provided by Deaton and Muellbauer (1980b), pp. 184–190.
18. Chipman and Moore (1976, 1980) have shown that in the absence of restrictions on price variations a necessary and sufficient condition for net compensating variations to provide a unique ordering among a number of alternative policies is that individual preferences are homothetic. These conditions are also necessary and sufficient for Hicksian and Marshallian measures of consumer's surplus to provide a unique ordering among alternative policies. In the absence of restrictions on price variations or on preferences, they recommend net equivalent variations, based on an econometric model of individual consumer expenditure allocation, to provide an ordering among policies.
19. Since budget shares are bounded dependent variables, the normality assumption cannot be strictly valid.
20. See Barten (1969).
21. See Malinvaud (1980), chapter 9, for a discussion of these techniques.
22. Nonlinear two stage least squares estimators were introduced by Amemiya (1974). Subsequently, nonlinear three stage least squares estimators were introduced by Jorgenson and Laffont (1974). For detailed discussion of nonlinear three stage least squares estimators, see Amemiya (1977), Gallant (1977), and Gallant and Jorgenson (1979).
23. See Malinvaud (1970), pp. 366–368, for more detailed discussion.
24. See Diewert (1976) for a detailed justification of this approach to price index number.
25. The preparation of these data is described in detail in Jack Faucett Associates (1977).
26. In the U.S. National Income and Product Accounts consumers' durables purchases are included in personal consumption expenditures.
27. The cross-section data are described by Carlson (1974).
28. The application of the bridge to the cross-section data involves four steps. First, the cross-section expenditure categories are associated with expenditure categories of the National Income and Product Accounts (NIPA). Second, the expenditure allocated to each commodity group is divided among five components—energy, food and clothing, trade and transportation, durables, and consumer services—on the basis of the proportion of the corresponding NIPA commodity group allocated to each Interindustry Transactions group. Third, these expenditures are added across commodity groups, providing energy, food and clothing, trade and transportation, durables purchases, and consumer services for each consumer. Finally, durables purchases are scaled to a durables service rate using the aggregate ratio of durables service flow to durables purchases. The durables service rate is added to the estimated annual rental value for owner-occupied housing to give the flow of capital services. Total expenditure is then defined as the sum of expenditures for energy, food and clothing, trade and transportation, consumer services, and durables.

Mean total expenditure in 1972 in the aggregate data was found to be \$10,326, while the cross-section value of \$9,369, resulting in a discrepancy of 9.3 percent. This can be partly attributed to underreporting of expenditures in the cross-section data, and partly to the inclusion of institutional purchases in the time-series data. Therefore, we normalized the time series of mean total expenditure to match the cross section in 1972, making the assumption that aggregate budget shares are the same across for families and institutions. The cross-section data contain 8,049 observations and the time-series data observations from 1958 to 1974.

29. This series is published annually by the U.S. Bureau of the Census. For our study, numbers 33, 35, 37, 39, 41, 43, 47, 51, 53, 59, 60, 62, 66, 72, 75, 79, 80, 84, 85, 90,96, 97, and 101 were employed together with technical report numbers 8 and 17.

30. For details, the interested reader is referred to Stoker (1979).

31. This viewpoint is presented by Kuh and Meyer (1957).

32. Alternative approaches to the representation of changes in expenditure allocation over time are presented by Darrough, Pollak, and Wales (1980), Houthakker and Taylor (1970), Jorgenson and Lau (1975), and Phlips (1974).

33. Attributes have a constant effect on the budget shares. Also, it should be kept in mind that the figures are constructed for 1972 and will differ for other years.

34. This is due to our reliance on $\ln M$ as the expenditure variable in the share equations; this choice is supported by the results of Leser (1963) and Muellbauer (1976b).

35. The reader should bear in mind that the figures are constructed holding all demographic dimensions constant except the one under study. This is particularly important for age, which holds expenditure constant at $9,000. Thus the decrease in capital services over the age range 15–44 does not imply that this behavior is typical for families whose expenditure grows with age. When expenditure is not held constant, the share for capital services increases as expected over the age range 15–44.

9 Aggregate Consumer Expenditures on Energy

Dale W. Jorgenson and
Thomas M. Stoker

9.I Aggregate Consumer Expenditures on Energy

9.I.1 Introduction

The objective of this chapter and the following two chapters is to present a new econometric model of the allocation of aggregate consumer expenditure on energy in the United States for the period 1958–1978. The model incorporates time-series data on aggregate quantities of energy consumed, and energy prices. It also includes time-series data on the level and distribution of total energy expenditure and the demographic characteristics of the population. Finally, the model incorporates individual cross-section data on the allocation of energy expenditure among types of energy for households with different demographic characteristics.

Our econometric model can be applied to the generation of projections of aggregate energy demand in the United States. For this purpose, projections of future energy prices, the future level and distribution of total energy expenditure, and the future demographic development of the population are required. The model can also be used to make projections of energy demand for groups of individuals in the United States, classified by demographic characteristics. Finally, the model can be integrated with a model for the allocation of total consumer expenditure between energy and nonenergy commodities to provide a complete model of aggregate consumer behavior.

Our econometric model is based on a theory of consumer behavior involving the allocation of total expenditure in two stages. In the first stage total expenditures are allocated between energy and nonenergy commodities. The first-stage allocation depends on the price of energy, prices of all nonenergy commodities, and the level of total expenditure. In the second stage expenditure on energy is allocated among individual types of energy. The second-stage allocation depends on the prices of individual types of energy and the level of total energy expenditure.

In section 9.I.2 we present the theory of two-stage allocation. To incorporate the implications of the theory of the individual consumer, we first specify the dependence of individual demand functions on prices and on total expenditure. We find that the transcendental logarithmic or translog indirect utility function combines flexibility in the representation of preferences with parsimony in the number of parameters that must be estimated. We derive a model of individual expenditures on energy by applying Roy's Identity (1943) to an indirect translog utility function for each consumer.

Our model of individual expenditures on energy is based on a system of demand functions giving the shares of total energy expenditure allocated to types of energy. This system of demand functions corresponds to homothetic preferences, so that expenditures on all types of energy are proportional to total energy expenditure. We can represent consumer preferences by a homothetic translog indirect utility function that is homogeneous, monotone, and quasi-convex.

To incorporate differences in individual preferences into our model of aggregate consumer expenditures on energy we allow the indirect utility function for each individual to depend on attributes that vary among individuals. We obtain a system of aggregate demand functions for all types of energy by summing over systems of individual demand functions for all consumers. We can characterize the system of aggregate demand functions by means of the theory of exact aggregation. This theory requires that individual demand functions must be linear in functions of the attributes, prices that vary among individuals, and total energy expenditures.

To construct a model of aggregate energy expenditures we weight the individual energy expenditure shares by the ratio by total energy expenditure for each individual to total energy expenditure for the population as a whole. The resulting model of aggregate energy expenditures gives the shares of aggregate energy expenditure allocated to each type of energy as a function of energy prices and the share of all individuals with each attribute in aggregate energy expenditure. We incorporate the impact of changes in the demographic composition of the population by including the shares of energy expenditure for all demographic groups as explanatory variables.

In section 9.I.3 we show how a model of aggregate energy expenditures based on the theory of exact aggregation can be implemented from individual cross-section data on energy expenditure shares, energy prices, and demographic characteristics. Alternatively, a model of aggregate energy expenditures can be implemented from time-series data on aggregate energy expenditure shares, energy prices, and shares of demographic groups in aggregate energy expenditure. Finally, such a model can be implemented by pooling time-series and cross-section data.

In our second and third chapters, below, we present a transcendental logarithmic model of aggregate demand for energy for the United States for the period 1958–1978. In the second chapter, we analyze the allocation of total energy expenditures among four types of energy—electricity, natural gas, fuel oil and other, and gasoline—on the basis of individual cross-section data. We employ a breakdown of individual consumer units by family size, age of head of household, region, race, and urban vs. rural residence. We implement this model from five cross-section surveys: the 1960/61, 1972, and 1973 Consumer Expenditure Surveys of the U.S. Bureau of Labor Statistics, and the 1973 and 1975 Lifestyle and Household Energy Use Surveys of the Washington Center for Metropolitan Studies.

In the third chapter, we incorporate a model based on cross-section data into a model of aggregate energy expenditures. We implement the combined model by pooling data from the five cross-section surveys of individual expenditures on energy for the United States and from annual time-series observations on aggregate expenditures on energy for the period 1958–1978.

9.I.2 Translog Model of Consumer Behavior

The purpose of this section is to present the implications of exact aggregation for a model of individual consumer behavior based on two stage allocation.[1] In the first stage total expenditure for each unit is allocated between energy and nonenergy commodities. In the second stage total expenditure on energy is allocated among individual types of energy. Before proceeding with a formal presentation of our model, we set down some notation. First, there are K consuming units, indexed by $k = 1, 2, \ldots, K$. At the first stage of the two-stage allocation process there are N commodities, indexed by $n = 1, 2, \ldots, N$;

one of these commodities is energy. Without loss of generality we can take energy to be the first commodity. At the second stage there are M types of energy, indexed by $m = 1, 2, \ldots, M$. We can regard each unit as consuming $M + N - 1$ commodities, where the first M are types of energy and the remaining $N - 1$ are nonenergy commodities.

9.I.2A Two-Stage Allocation

We assume that the prices of all nonenergy commodities and all types of energy are the same for all consuming units. We denote the price index of energy at the first stage by p_{1k}, $(k = 1, 2, \ldots, K)$; this price index may differ among consumers. We denote the price of the nth commodity at the first stage of the two-stage allocation process by p_n $(n = 2, 3, \ldots, N)$; similarly, we denote the price of the mth commodity at the second stage by q_m $(m = 1, 2, \ldots, M)$. The quantity of the nth commodity at the first stage demanded by the kth unit is x_{nk}, $(n = 1, 2, \ldots, N;\ k = 1, 2, \ldots, K)$; similarly, the quantity of the mth commodity at second stage demanded by this unit is y_{mk}, $(m = 1, 2, \ldots, M;$ $k = 1, 2, \ldots, K)$.

To represent our model of consumer behavior we require the following additional notation:

$M_k = \sum_{m=1}^{M} q_m y_{mk} + \sum_{n=2}^{N} p_n x_{nk}$ — total expenditure of the kth consuming unit on energy and nonenergy commodities $(k = 1, 2, \ldots, K)$;

$E_k = \sum_{m=1}^{M} q_m y_{mk}$ — total expenditure of the kth consuming unit on the m types of energy $(k = 1, 2, \ldots, K)$;

A_k — attributes of the kth consuming unit, such as demographic characteristics, that reflect differences in preferences $(k = 1, 2, \ldots, K)$;

$p_k = (p_{1k}, p_2, \ldots, p_N)$ — vector of prices at the first stage for the kth consuming unit $(k = 1, 2, \ldots, K)$.

In our model of individual consumer behavior we take households as consuming units. We assume that expenditures on energy and nonenergy commodities are allocated so as to maximize a household social welfare function. As a consequence, the household behaves in the same way as an individual maximizing a utility function, as demonstrated by Samuelson (1956) and Pollak (1981). Consumer equilibrium implies the existence of an indirect utility function for each consuming unit, say V_k, where

$$V_k = V_k(p_{1k}, p_2, \ldots, p_N, M_k, A_k)\,, \quad (k = 1, 2, \ldots, K)\,. \tag{9.I.1}$$

We can characterize the behavior of a consuming unit in terms of the following properties of an indirect utility function:

1. *Homogeneity.* The indirect utility function is homogeneous of degree zero in prices and expenditure

$$V_k = V_k\,(\lambda p_k, \lambda M_k, A_k)\,, \quad (k = 1, 2, \ldots, K) \tag{9.I.2}$$

for all prices p_k, expenditure M_k, and positive λ.

2. *Monotonicity.* The indirect utility function is nonincreasing in prices and increasing in expenditure

$$\frac{\partial V_k}{\partial p_k} \leq 0\,, \quad \frac{\partial V_k}{\partial M_k} > 0\,, \quad (k = 1, 2, \ldots, K) \tag{9.I.3}$$

for all prices p_k and expenditure M_k.

3. *Quasi-convexity.* The indirect utility function is quasi-convex in prices and expenditure for all prices p_k and expenditure M_k.

We have characterized the behavior of the individual consumer in terms of properties of the indirect utility function. In addition to the properties of homogeneity, monotonicity, and quasi-convexity, as defined above, the indirect utility function that underlies the two-stage allocation process has the following property:

4. *Homothetic separability.* The indirect utility function is homothetically separable in energy prices

$$V_k = V_k(p_{1k}(q_1, q_2, \ldots, q_M, A_k), p_2, \ldots, p_N, M_k, A_k)\,, \quad (k = 1, 2, \ldots, K) \tag{9.I.4}$$

where the function p_{1k} is homogeneous of degree 1, concave, and nondecreasing in energy prices.

We can regard the function p_{1k} as a price index for energy

$$p_{1k} = p_{1k}(q_1, q_2, \ldots, q_M, A_k)\,, \quad (k = 1, 2, \ldots, K)\,. \tag{9.I.5}$$

Although the prices of individual types of energy are the same for all consumers, the price index for energy also depends on the vector A_k of attributes of the kth consumer. This index differs among consumers with different attributes.

Total expenditure of the kth consumer on energy, say E_k, is

$$E_k = \sum_{m=1}^{M} q_m y_{mk} , \quad (k = 1, 2, \ldots, K) . \tag{9.I.6}$$

We can define a quantity index for energy, say x_{1k}, as the ratio of total expenditure on energy to the price index for energy

$$x_{1k} = \frac{E_k}{p_{1k}} , \quad (k = 1, 2, \ldots, K) . \tag{9.I.7}$$

The product of the price and quantity indexes for energy is equal to total expenditure on energy.

Given the price and quantity index for energy, we can define a two-stage allocation process for each consuming unit. Total expenditure is allocated between energy and nonenergy commodities at the first stage. This allocation process depends on the price index for energy, the prices of all nonenergy commodities, the level of total expenditure, and the attributes of the consuming unit. We can characterize the first stage of the allocation process in terms of an indirect utility function with the properties of homogeneity, monotonicity, and quasi-convexity described above.

The second stage of the two-stage allocation process for each consuming unit is to allocate total energy expenditure among the individual types of energy. This allocation depends on the prices of all types of energy and the level of total energy expenditure. We can regard the function $E_k/p_{1k}(q_1, q_2, \ldots, q_M, A_k)$ as an indirect utility function corresponding to homothetic preferences. This indirect utility function is homogeneous of degree zero in energy prices and total energy expenditure, nonincreasing in prices and increasing in expenditure. The price index for energy $p_{1k}(q_1, q_2, \ldots, q_M, A_k)$ is concave in energy prices.

Our model of the two-stage allocation process results in two systems of individual demand functions. The first stage of the process generates a system for the allocation of total expenditure among energy and $N - 1$ nonenergy commodities. The second stage of the process produces a system for the allocation of total energy expenditure among M types of energy. The system of individual demand functions for the allocation of total energy expenditure corresponds to homothetic preferences, so that demand functions for all types of energy are proportional to total energy expenditure.

The concept of homothetic separability can be employed in further simplifying the model for allocation of total energy expenditure among the M types of energy. Energy is used by consumers in two distinct sets of activities—transportation and household operations, the latter including heating, lighting, and the operation of household appliances. An important empirical issue in analyzing the demand for energy is whether these two activities can be treated separately. If, for example, energy for transportation purposes is homothetically separable from energy for household operations, the overall allocation can be broken down into three stages. In the third stage total expenditure on energy for household operations is allocated among the remaining types of energy.

Integrability of systems of individual demand functions requires that the indirect utility function for each individual must be homogeneous, monotone, and quasi-convex. To construct a system of individual demand functions for energy, we apply Roy's Identity[2] to the indirect translog utility function[3] in section 9.I.2B, below. The resulting model of individual consumer behavior consists of a system of demand functions giving the shares of total energy expenditure allocated to the individual types of energy. Given the values of prices that are the same for all individuals, the expenditures shares are linear in the attributes of individuals and logarithms of energy prices.

To represent the second stage of our model of consumer behavior we require the following additional notation:

$v_{mk} = q_m y_{mk}/E_k$ — share of the mth type of energy in total energy expenditure of the kth consumer unit ($m = 1, 2, \ldots, M$; $k = 1, 2, \ldots, K$).

$v_k = (v_{1k}, v_{2k}, \ldots, v_{Mk})$ — vector of expenditure shares for the kth consuming unit ($k = 1, 2, \ldots, K$);

$\ln(q/E_k) = [\ln(q_1/E_k), \ln(q_2/E_k), \ldots, \ln(q_M/E_k)]$ — vector of logarithms of ratios of energy prices to total energy expenditure by the kth consuming unit ($k = 1, 2, \ldots, K$);

$\ln q = (\ln q_1, \ln q_2, \ldots, \ln q_M)$ — vector of logarithms of energy prices.

We assume that the kth consuming unit allocates its total energy expenditure among types of energy in accord with the homothetic translog indirect utility function, say H_k, where

$$\ln H_k = G(A_k) + \ln q' \gamma_q + \ln E_k + \frac{1}{2} \ln q' \Delta_{qq} \ln q + \ln q' \Delta_{qA} A_k \, , \quad (k = 1, 2, \ldots, K) \, . \tag{9.I.8}$$

As before, the expenditure shares of the kth consuming unit can be derived by the logarithmic form of Roy's Identity. Applying this

Identity to the homothetic translog indirect utility function, we obtain the system of individual expenditure shares

$$-v_k = \gamma_q + \Delta_{qq} \ln q + \Delta_{qA} A_k \, , \quad (k = 1, 2, \ldots, K) \, . \tag{9.I.9}$$

The conditions for exact aggregation are that the individual expenditure shares are linear in functions of the attributes $\{A_k\}$ and total energy expenditures $\{E_k\}$ for all consuming units. These conditions are satisfied by the system of individual expenditure shares (9.I.9).

Aggregate expenditure shares, say v, are obtained by multiplying the individual expenditure shares by total energy expenditure for each consuming unit, adding over all consuming units, and dividing by aggregate energy expenditure

$$v = \frac{\sum E_k v_k}{\sum E_k} \, . \tag{9.I.10}$$

The aggregate expenditure shares can be written

$$-v = \gamma_q + \Delta_{qq} \ln q + \Delta_{qA} \frac{\sum E_k A_k}{\sum E_k} \, . \tag{9.I.11}$$

These shares depend on the logarithms of energy prices $\ln q$ and the distribution of energy expenditures among demographic groups through the functions $\{\sum E_k A_k / \sum E_k\}$, which may be regarded as statistics of the joint distribution of total energy expenditures and attributes. As before, these functions are equal to the shares of the corresponding demographic groups in aggregate energy expenditure. Aggregate energy expenditure patterns depend on the distribution of energy expenditure among demographic groups through the statistics $\{\sum E_k A_k / \sum E_k\}$.

9.I.2B Integrability

Systems of individual expenditure shares for consuming units with identical demographic characteristics can be recovered in one and only one way from the system of aggregate expenditure shares under exact aggregation. This makes it possible to employ all of the implications of the theory of individual consumer behavior in specifying an econometric model of aggregate expenditure allocation. If a system of individual expenditures shares can be generated from an indirect utility function by means of the logarithmic form of Roy's Identity, we say that the system is *integrable*. A complete set of conditions for integrability expressed in terms of the system of individual expenditure shares for the first stage of the two-stage allocation process, is the following:[4]

1. *Homogeneity*. The individual expenditure shares for all types of energy are homogeneous of degree zero in energy prices and energy expenditure.

Homogeneity implies that the parameters Δ_{qq} in the representation (9.I.9) of the individual expenditure shares must satisfy the restrictions

$$\Delta_{qq}\, i = 0 \,. \tag{9.I.12}$$

There are M restrictions implied by homogeneity.

2. *Summability*. The sum of the individual expenditure shares over all types of energy is equal to unity

$$\sum v_{mk} = 1 \,, \qquad (k = 1, 2, \ldots, K) \,.$$

Summability implies that the parameters must satisfy the restrictions

$$\begin{aligned} i'\gamma_q &= -1 \,, \\ i'\Delta_{qq} &= 0 \,, \\ i'\Delta_{qA} &= 0 \,. \end{aligned} \tag{9.I.13}$$

There are $M + P + 1$ restrictions implied by summability, where there are P components of the vector of attributes A_k.

3. *Symmetry*. The matrix of compensated own- and cross-price effects must be symmetric.

Imposing homogeneity and summability restrictions on the individual energy expenditure shares, we have

$$-v_k = \gamma_q + \Delta_{qq} \ln q + \Delta_{qA} A_k \,, \qquad (k = 1, 2, \ldots, K) \,.$$

The typical element of the matrix of uncompensated own- and cross-price substitution effects takes the form

$$\frac{\partial y_{mk}}{\partial q_n} = -\frac{E_k}{q_m q_n} (\delta_{mn} + \delta^*_{mn}\, v_{mk}) \,, \qquad (m, n = 1, 2, \ldots, M; \; k = 1, 2, \ldots, K) \,,$$

where

$$\delta^*_{mn} + \begin{cases} 0 & \text{if } m \neq n \\ 1 & \text{if } m = n \end{cases}, \qquad (m, n = 1, 2, \ldots, M) .$$

The corresponding element of the matrix of compensated own- and cross-price effects takes the form

$$\frac{\partial y_{mk}}{\partial q_n} + y_{nk} \sum \frac{\partial y_{mk}}{\partial E_k} = \frac{E_k}{q_m q_n} (-\delta_{mn} - \delta^*_{mn} - \delta^*_{mn} v_{mk} + v_{mk} v_{nk}) ,$$
$$(m, n = 1, 2, \ldots, M;\ k = 1, 2, \ldots, K) .$$

The full matrix of compensated own-and cross-price effects, say R_k, takes the form

$$R_k = E_k Q_k^{-1} (-\Delta_{qq} + v_k v_k' - V_k) Q_k^{-1} , \qquad (k = 1, 2, \ldots, K)$$

where

$$Q_k^{-1} = \begin{bmatrix} 1 & 0 & \cdots & 0 \\ 0 & \frac{1}{q_1} & \cdots & 0 \\ 0 & \frac{1}{q_2} & & \\ \vdots & \vdots & \cdots & \vdots \\ 0 & 0 & \cdots & \frac{1}{q_M} \end{bmatrix}, \quad V_k = \begin{bmatrix} v_1 & 0 & \cdots & 0 \\ 0 & v_2 & \cdots & 0 \\ \vdots & \vdots & \cdots & \vdots \\ 0 & 0 & \cdots & v_M \end{bmatrix},$$
$$(k = 1, 2, \ldots, K) .$$

If the system of individual expenditure shares for all types of energy is to be generated from a homothetic translog indirect utility function, a necessary and sufficient condition for symmetry is that the matrix Δ_{qq} must be symmetric. We can write the individual expenditure shares in the form (9.I.9) without imposing the condition that the matrix Δ_{qq} is symmetric. Symmetry implies that the parameters must satisfy the restrictions

$$\Delta_{qq} = \Delta'_{qq} .$$

The total number of symmetry restrictions is $1/2M(M-1)$.

4. *Nonnegativity*. The individual expenditure shares ... negative

$$v_{mk} \geq 0 , \quad (m = 1, 2, \ldots, M;\ k = 1, 2 \ldots$$

By summability th...
that

sented by a dummy variable equal to unity when the consuming unit has the corresponding characteristics and zero otherwise.

Given translog indirect utility functions for each consuming unit, we derive the expenditure shares for that unit by means of Roy's Identity. The second stage of the two-stage allocation process corresponds to homothetic preferences. This results in expenditure shares for all types of energy that are linear in the logarithms of energy prices and in attributes. These shares satisfy the conditions required for exact aggregation.

To derive aggregate expenditure shares for all types of energy, we multiply the individual expenditure shares by total energy expenditure for each consuming unit, sum over all units, and divide by aggregate expenditure. The aggregate energy expenditure shares, like the individual energy expenditure shares, are linear in the logarithms of energy prices and in the shares of all demographic groups in aggregate energy expenditure $\{\sum E_k A_k / \sum E_k\}$.

The individual energy expenditure shares are homogeneous of degree zero in prices and expenditure. This implies M restrictions on the parameters of the homothetic translog indirect utility functions, where M is the number of types of energy. Second, the sum of individual expenditure shares over all types of energy is equal to unity. There are $M + P + 1$ restrictions implied by summability, where P is the number of components of the vector of attributes A_k. Third, the matrix of compensated own- and cross-price effects must be symmetric, which implies $1/2M(M-1)$ additional restrictions on the parameters of the homothetic translog indirect utility functions. The individual expenditure shares for all types of energy must be nonnegative. We consider restrictions that imply that the matrix of compensated own- and cross-price effects must be nonpositive definite for all nonnegative expenditure shares.

9.I.3 Econometrics of Aggregate Energy Expenditures

In this section we outline the econometric implementation of the translog model of aggregate energy expenditures presented in section 9.I.2. Our observations on individual energy expenditure patterns are given by a number of cross sections, each providing data on energy expenditure shares and demographic characteristics for individual consuming units at a given point of time. We assume that energy prices are the same for all consuming units whereas demographic characteristics vary among units. By analyzing individual cross-section data we can obtain estimates of demographic effects on individual energy expenditure patterns.

Our observations on aggregate energy expenditure patterns include time-series data on energy expenditure shares, shares of demographic groups in aggregate energy expenditure, and energy prices. It is important to note that our econometric model can be implemented from aggregate time-series and cross-section data we can obtain more precise estimates of the effects of variations in demographic characteristics on aggregate energy expenditure allocation.

We begin our discussion of econometrics of the translog model by presenting the stochastic structure employed for cross-section and time-series data. We next discuss the identification and estimation of unknown parameters for a single cross-section, assuming that prices are the same for all consuming units. We then discuss identification and estimation for aggregate time-series and the pooling of time-series and cross-section data. This section provides the link between the theoretical model described in section 9.I.2, above, and the empirical results to be presented in the next two chapters.

9.I.3A Stochastic Structure

The model of aggregate energy expenditures just presented is generated from a homothetic translog indirect utility function for each consuming unit. To formulate an econometric model of consumer behavior we add a stochastic component to the equations for the individual expenditure shares. We associate this component with unobservable random disturbances at the level of the individual consuming unit. The consuming unit maximizes utility, but the expenditure shares are chosen with a random disturbance. This disturbance may result from errors in implementation of consumption plans, random elements in the determination of consumer preferences not reflected in our list of attributes of consuming units, or errors of measurement of the individual expenditure shares. We assume that each of the equations for the individual shares has two additive components. The first is a nonrandom function of prices and demographic characteristics. The second is an unobservable random disturbance that is functionally independent of these variables.

To represent our econometric model of consumer behavior we introduce some additional notation. We consider observations on expenditure patterns by K consuming units, indexed by $k = 1, 2, \ldots, K$, for T time periods, indexed by $t = 1, 2, \ldots, T$. The vector of expenditure shares for the kth consuming unit in the tth time period is denoted v_{kt} $(k = 1, 2, \ldots, K;\ t = 1, 2, \ldots, T)$. Similarly, expenditure for the kth unit on all types of energy in the tth time period is denoted E_{kt} $(k = 1, 2, \ldots, K; t = 1, 2, \ldots, T)$. The vector of energy prices faced by all consuming units in the tth time period is denoted q_t $(t = 1, 2, \ldots, T)$. Similarly, the vector of logarithms of energy prices in the tth time period is denoted in $\ln q_t$ $(t = 1, 2, \ldots, T)$.

Using our new notation, the individual expenditure shares can be written

$$-v_{kt} = \gamma_q + \Delta_{qq} \ln q_t + \Delta_{qA}\ A_k + \varepsilon_{kt}\ , \qquad (k = 1, 2, \ldots, K;\ t = 1, 2, \ldots, T)\,, \tag{9.I.14}$$

where ε_{kt} $(k = 1, 2, \ldots, K;\ t = 1, 2, \ldots, T)$ is the vector of unobservable random disturbances for the kth consuming unit and the tth time period. Since the individual expenditure shares for all types of energy sum to unity for each consuming unit in each time period, the unobservable random disturbances for all types of energy sum to zero for each unit in each time period

$$i'\varepsilon_{kt} = 0\ , \quad (k = 1, 2, \ldots, K; t = 1, 2, \ldots, T)\ . \tag{9.I.15}$$

These disturbances are not distributed independently.

We assume that the unobservable random disturbances for all commodities have expected value equal to zero for all observations

$$E(\varepsilon_{kt}) = 0\ , \quad (k = 1, 2, \ldots, K;\ t = 1, 2, \ldots, T)\ . \tag{9.I.16}$$

We also assume that these disturbances have the same covariance matrix for all observations

$$V(\varepsilon_{kt}) = \Omega_\varepsilon\ , \quad (k = 1, 2, \ldots, K;\ t = 1, 2, \ldots, T)\ .$$

Since the disturbances sum to zero for each observation, this matrix is nonnegative definite with rank at most equal to $M - 1$, where M is the number of types of energy. We assume that the covariance matrix has rank equal to $M - 1$.

Finally, we assume that disturbances corresponding to distinct observations are uncorrelated. Under this assumption the covariance matrix of the disturbances for all consuming units at a given point of time has the Kronecker product form

$$V \begin{bmatrix} \varepsilon_{1t} \\ \varepsilon_{2t} \\ \vdots \\ \varepsilon_{Kt} \end{bmatrix} = \Omega_\varepsilon \otimes I \, . \tag{9.I.17}$$

The covariance matrix of the disturbances for all time periods for a given individual has an analogous form. The unknown parameters of the system of equations determining the individual energy expenditure shares can be estimated from time-series data on individual energy expenditure shares, energy prices, and demographic characteristics.

Although the data for individual consuming units and for the aggregate of all consuming units are based on the same definitions, the aggregate data are not obtained by summing over the data for individuals. Observations on individual consuming units are based on a random sample from the population of all consuming units. Observations for the aggregate of all consuming units are constructed from data on production of all types of energy and on energy consumption by households and by other consuming units such as businesses, governments, and the rest of the world. Accordingly, we must introduce an additional source of random error in the equations for the aggregate energy expenditure shares, corresponding to unobservable errors of measurement in the observations that underly the aggregate shares.

We assume that each of the equations for the aggregate energy expenditure shares has three additive components. The first is a weighted average of the nonrandom functions of energy prices and demographic characteristics that determine the individual energy expenditure shares. The second is a weighted average of the unobservable random disturbances in equations for the individual energy expenditure shares. The third is a weighted average of the unobservable random errors of measurement in the observations on the aggregate energy expenditure shares.

Denoting the vector of aggregate expenditure shares at time t by v_t $(t = 1, 2, \ldots, T)$, we can express these shares in the form

$$-v_t = \gamma_q + \Delta_{qq} \ln q_t + \Delta_{qA} \frac{\sum_{k=1}^{K} E_{kt} A_{kt}}{\sum_{k=1}^{K} E_{kt}} + \varepsilon_t \, , \quad (t = 1, 2, \ldots, T) \, , \tag{9.I.18}$$

where ε_t $(t = 1, 2, \ldots, T)$ is the vector of unobservable random disturbances for the tth time period.

The aggregate disturbances ε_t can be expressed in the form

$$\varepsilon_t = \frac{\sum_{k=1}^K E_{kt}\varepsilon_{kt}}{\sum_{k=1}^K E_{kt}} + \frac{\sum_{k=1}^K E_{kt}\nu_{kt}}{\sum_{k=1}^K E_{kt}}, \quad (t = 1, 2, \ldots, T), \tag{9.I.19}$$

where v_{kt} $(k = 1, 2, \ldots, K;\ t = 1, 2, \ldots, T)$ is the vector of errors of measurement that underlie the data on the aggregate energy expenditure shares. Since the random disturbances for all commodities sum to zero in each time period,

$$i'\varepsilon_t = 0, \quad (t = 1, 2, \ldots, T), \tag{9.I.20}$$

these disturbances are not distributed independently.

We assume that the errors of measurement that underlie the data on the aggregate energy expenditure shares have expected value equal to zero for all observations

$$E(\nu_{kt}) = 0, \quad (k = 1, 2, \ldots, K;\ t = 1, 2, \ldots, T).$$

We also assume that these errors have the same covariance matrix for all observations

$$V(\nu_{kt}) = \Omega_\nu, \quad (k = 1, 2, \ldots, K;\ t = 1, 2, \ldots, T),$$

and that the rank of this matrix is equal to $M - 1$.

If the errors of measurement are distributed independently of energy expenditure and of the disturbances in the equations for the individual energy expenditure shares, the aggregate disturbances have expected value equal to zero for all time periods

$$E(\varepsilon_t) = 0, \quad (t = 1, 2, \ldots, T), \tag{9.I.21}$$

and have a covariance matrix given by

$$V(\varepsilon_t) = \frac{\sum_{k=1}^K E_{kt}^2}{\left(\sum_{k=1}^K E_{kt}\right)^2}\Omega_\varepsilon + \frac{\sum_{k=1}^K E_{kt}^2}{\left(\sum_{k=1}^K E_{kt}\right)^2}\Omega_\nu, \quad (t = 1, 2, \ldots, T),$$

so that the aggregate disturbances for different time periods are heteroscedastic.

We can correct for heteroscedasticity of the aggregate disturbances by transforming the observations on the aggregate energy expenditure shares as follows

$$-\rho_t v_t = \rho_t \left(\gamma_q + \Delta_{qq} \ln q_t + \Delta_{qA} \frac{\sum_{k=1}^{K} E_{kt} A_{kt}}{\sum_{k=1}^{K} E_{kt}} \right) + \rho_t \varepsilon_t \,, \qquad (t = 1, 2, \ldots, T) \,,$$

where

$$\rho_t^2 = \frac{\left(\sum_{k=1}^{K} E_{kt} \right)^2}{\sum_{k=1}^{K} E_{kt}^2} \,, \qquad (t = 1, 2, \ldots, T) \,.$$

The covariance matrix of the transformed disturbances, say Ω, becomes

$$V(\rho_t \varepsilon_t) = \Omega_\varepsilon + \Omega_v = \Omega \,.$$

This matrix is nonnegative definite with rank equal to $M - 1$. Finally, we assume that the errors of measurement corresponding to distinct observations are uncorrelated. Under this assumption the covariance matrix of the transformed disturbances at all points of time has the Kronecker product form

$$V \begin{bmatrix} \rho_1 \varepsilon_1 \\ \rho_2 \varepsilon_2 \\ \vdots \\ \rho_T \varepsilon_T \end{bmatrix} = \Omega \otimes I \,. \qquad (9.I.22)$$

9.I.3B Identification

We next discuss the estimation of the translog model of aggregate energy expenditures, combining cross-section observations on individual energy expenditure patterns with time-series observations on aggregate energy expenditure patterns. We first discuss application of the translog model to cross-section data only. We then present methods for pooling individual cross-section and aggregate time-series data.

Suppose first that we have a random sample of observations on individual energy expenditure patterns at a given point of time. Energy prices for all consumers are the same. The translog model (9.I.2) takes the form

$$-v_k = \delta + \Delta_{qA}\, A_k + \varepsilon_k\,, \qquad (k = 1, 2, \ldots, K)\,, \tag{9.I.23}$$

where we drop the time subscript. In this model δ is a vector of unknown parameters and Δ_{qA} is a matrix of unknown parameters. Random sampling implies that disturbances for different individuals are uncorrelated. We assume that the data matrix with $(1, A_k)$ as its kth row has full rank.

The parameters δ and Δ_{qA} are identified in the cross section. Moreover, the model (9.I.24) is a multivariate regression model, except that the vector ε_k has a singular distribution. If the vector ε_k is normally distributed, the maximum likelihood estimator is obtained by dropping one equation, estimating the remaining $M - 1$ equations by maximum likelihood.[5] Estimates of the parameters of the omitted equation from estimates of the parameters for the $M - 1$ equations not omitted are derived.[6] Consider a model where one equation has been dropped; this reduced model is a linear, multivariate regression model so the unique, minimum variance, unbiased estimator of the unknown parameters δ and Δ_{qA} is obtained by applying ordinary least squares to each equation separately.

The constants δ and the parameters associated with demographic characteristics of individual households Δ_{qA} can be estimated from a single cross-section. The remaining parameters, i.e., those associated with prices, can be estimated from time-series data on aggregate expenditure patterns. Since the model is linear in parameters for a cross-section, we can use ordinary least squares regression to estimate the impact of the demographic structure on aggregate expenditure patterns. This feature characterizes exact aggregation models in general, as indicated in section 9.I.2 above. The resulting linearity greatly simplifies computations.

After correction for heteroscedasticity, the translog model of aggregate consumer behavior is given by

$$-\rho_t v_t = \rho_t \left(\gamma_q + \Delta_{qA} \frac{\sum_{k=1}^{K} E_{kt} A_{kt}}{\sum_{k=1}^{K} E_{kt}} \right) + \rho_t \varepsilon_t\,, \qquad (t = 1, 2, \ldots, T)\,, \tag{9.I.24}$$

where ε_t is a vector of unobservable random disturbances. We have time-series observations on energy prices q_t, the vector of attribute-expenditure statistics $\{\sum E_{kt} A_{kt} / \sum E_{kt}\}$, and the heteroscedasticity correction ρ_t $(t = 1, 2, \ldots, T)$.

The translog model in (9.I.24) might appear to be a nonlinear regression model with additive errors, taking into account the symmetry of the matrix of parameters Δ_{qq}, so that nonlinear regression techniques could be employed.[7] However, the existence of supply functions for all commodities makes it more appropriate to treat some of the right-side variables as endogenous. For example, shifts in energy prices owing to demand-supply interactions may cause significant shifts in the distribution of energy expenditure. To obtain a consistent estimator for this model we could specify supply functions for all types of energy and estimate the complete model by full information maximum likelihood.

Alternatively, to estimate the model in (9.I.24) we can consider limited information techniques utilizing instrumental variables. In particular, we can introduce a sufficient number of instrumental variables to identify all parameters. We estimate the model by nonlinear three-stage least squares (NL3SLS).[8] Application of NL3SLS to our model would be straightforward except for the fact that the covariance matrix of the disturbances is singular. We obtain NL3SLS estimators of the complete system by dropping one equation and estimating the resulting system of $M - 1$ equations by NL3SLS; we derive an estimator for parameters of the remaining equation from the conditions for summability. The parameter estimates are invariant to the choice of the equation omitted in the model for aggregate time-series data and the model for individual cross-section data.

The NL3SLS estimator can be employed to estimate all parameters of the model of aggregate energy expenditures, provided that these parameters are identified. Since we wish to obtain a detailed characterization of the impact of changes in the demographic structure of the population, the model (9.I.11) contains a large number of parameters and requires a large number of time-series observations for identification. The technical conditions for identification are quite complicated. A necessary condition for identification is that the number of parameters is less than the number of instruments. For the translog model of aggregate consumer behavior, this occurs if

$$\frac{1}{2}(M-1)(M+2) + P(M-1) < (M-1) \times \min(V, T), \tag{9.I.25}$$

where M is the number of types of energy; P is the number of components of A_{kt} and V is the number of instruments. The left-hand side of (9.I.25) is the number of free parameters of the translog model under symmetry of the matrix Δ_{qq}, and the right-hand side is the number of instruments, assuming that no collinearity exists among the instruments.

Condition (9.I.25) fails to hold in our application, so that not all parameters are identified in the model for aggregate time-series data. We next consider methods utilizing individual cross-section data together with aggregate time-series data to obtain identification. As we have seen, cross-section data can be used to identify the constant δ and the demographic coefficients Δ_{qA}. The constant γ_q and the price coefficients Δ_{qq} must be identified from aggregate time-series data. A necessary condition for identification of these parameters is

$$\frac{1}{2}(M-1)(M+2) < (M-1) \times \min(V,T), \tag{9.I.26}$$

or

$$\frac{M+2}{2} < \min(V,T). \tag{9.I.27}$$

This condition is met in our application. Sufficient conditions are given in the next section; these amount to the nonlinear analog of the absence of multicollinearity. These conditions are quite weak and hold in our application.

In order to pool cross-section and time-series data, we combine the model for individual energy expenditures and the model for aggregate energy expenditures and apply the NL3SLS to the whole system. The instruments for the cross-section model are the micro data themselves; for the aggregate model the instruments are variables that can be taken to be distributed independently of the aggregate disturbances. The data sets are pooled statistically, where estimates of the covariance matrix of the aggregate disturbances from time-series data and the covariance matrix of the individual disturbances from the cross-section data are used to weight aggregate and cross-section data, respectively. The resulting estimator is consistent and asymptotically efficient in the class of instrumental variable estimators utilizing the instruments we have chosen. We next describe the pooled estimation procedure, together with the simplification of computations that results from exact aggregation.

9.I.3C Estimation

Estimation of the translog model of individual energy expenditures can be carried out by the method of least squares. Our objective is to estimate the constants δ and the unknown parameters Δ_{qA}, subject to the restriction implied by summability; by dropping the equation for one commodity in the cross-section model, we can eliminate the restrictions implied by summability. We employ these restrictions in estimating the parameters that occur in the equation that has been dropped.

We can write the cross-section model in the form:

$$\begin{aligned} y_1 &= X\beta_1 + \varepsilon_1 , \\ y_2 &= X\beta_2 + \varepsilon_2 , \\ &\cdots \\ y_{M-1} &= X\beta_{M-1} + \varepsilon_{M-1} , \end{aligned} \tag{9.I.28}$$

where y_i $(i = 1, 2, \ldots, M-1)$ is the vector of observations on the individual expenditure shares of the ith type of energy for all individuals; X is the matrix of observations on $P + 1$ independent variables, including a dummy variable corresponding to the constant term in each equation and dummy variables corresponding to individual attributes; and ε_i $(i = 1, 2, \ldots, M-1)$ is a vector of unobservable random disturbances.

We can stack the equations in (9.I.28) in the usual way, obtaining

$$y = [I \otimes X]\beta + \varepsilon , \tag{9.I.29}$$

where

$$y = \begin{bmatrix} y_1 \\ y_2 \\ \vdots \\ y_{M-1} \end{bmatrix}, \qquad I \otimes X = \begin{bmatrix} X & 0 & \cdots & 0 \\ 0 & X & \cdots & 0 \\ \vdots & \vdots & & \vdots \\ 0 & 0 & \cdots & X \end{bmatrix},$$

$$\beta = \begin{bmatrix} \beta_1 \\ \beta_2 \\ \vdots \\ \beta_{M-1} \end{bmatrix}, \qquad \varepsilon = \begin{bmatrix} \varepsilon_1 \\ \varepsilon_2 \\ \vdots \\ \varepsilon_{M-1} \end{bmatrix}. \tag{9.I.30}$$

By the assumptions listed in section 9.I.3B, the matrix X is of full rank and the random vector ε is distributed normally with mean zero and covariance matrix $\Sigma_\varepsilon \otimes I$, where Σ_ε is obtained from the covariance matrix Ω_ε in (9.I.17) by striking the row and column corresponding to the omitted equation.

The maximum likelihood estimator of the vector of parameters β from the cross-section model is

$$\hat{\beta} = [I \otimes (X'X)^{-1}X']y \,, \tag{9.I.31}$$

or

$$\hat{\beta}_i = (X'X)^{-1}X'y_i \,, \quad (i = 1, 2, \ldots, M-1) \,, \tag{9.I.32}$$

which is equivalent to the least squares estimator applied to each equation individually. This estimator has covariance matrix

$$V(\hat{\beta}) = \Sigma_\varepsilon \otimes (X'X)^{-1} \,. \tag{9.I.33}$$

The least squares estimator is a consistent estimator of the vector of unknown parameters β; the probability limit of this estimator as the number of cross-section observations K tends to infinity is equal to β.

Estimation of the translog model of aggregate energy expenditures requires application of the method of nonlinear three-stage least squares. Our objective is to estimate the unknown parameters, that is, γ_q, Δ_{qq}, Δ_{qA}, subject to the restrictions implied by summability, symmetry, and monotonicity. As before, we can drop the equation for one commodity and employ the summability restrictions to estimate the parameters that occur in this equation. We impose the restrictions implied by symmetry by requiring that the matrix Δ_{qq} be symmetric.

The restrictions implied by summability and symmetry take the form of equalities. The restrictions implied by monotonicity take the form of inequalities. The matrix Δ_{qq} is nonnegative definitive, so that all the elements of this matrix are nonnegative and at least one Cholesky value is equal to zero. In section 9.I.2B above, we have expressed these restrictions in terms of the Cholesky factorizations of the matrix Δqq. We discuss the estimation of the unknown parameters, that is, γ_q, Δ_{qq}, Δ_{qA}, subject to monotonicity restrictions below.

We can write the time-series model in the form

$$
\begin{aligned}
v_1 &= f_1(\beta, \gamma) + \nu_1 , \\
v_2 &= f_2(\beta, \gamma) + \nu_2 , \\
&\dots \\
v_{M-1} &= f_{M-1}(\beta, \gamma) + \nu_{M-1} ,
\end{aligned}
\tag{9.I.34}
$$

where v_i $(i = 1, 2, \dots, M-1)$ is the vector of observations on the aggregate expenditure shares of the ith commodity for all time periods, transformed to eliminate heteroscedasticity; f_i $(i = 1, 2, \dots, M-1)$ is a vector of nonlinear functions of the parameters β that enter the time-series model; and ν_i $(i = 1, 2, \dots, M-1)$ is a vector of unobservable random disturbances, transformed to eliminate heteroscedasticity.

As before, we can stack the equations in (9.I.34), obtaining

$$
\begin{aligned}
v &= f(\beta, \gamma) + \nu \\
&= f(\delta) + \nu ,
\end{aligned}
\tag{9.I.35}
$$

where

$$
v = \begin{bmatrix} v_1 \\ v_2 \\ \vdots \\ v_{M-1} \end{bmatrix}, \qquad f = \begin{bmatrix} f_1 \\ f_2 \\ \vdots \\ f_{M-1} \end{bmatrix}, \qquad \delta = \begin{bmatrix} \beta \\ \gamma \end{bmatrix}, \qquad \nu = \begin{bmatrix} \nu_1 \\ \nu_2 \\ \vdots \\ \nu_{M-1} \end{bmatrix}.
$$

By the assumptions listed in section 9.I.3B, the random vector ν is distributed normally with mean zero and covariance matrix $\Sigma_\nu \otimes I$, where Σ_ν is obtained from the covariance matrix Ω in (9.I.22) by striking the row and column corresponding to the omitted equation.

The nonlinear three-stage least squares estimator for the aggregate model is obtained by minimizing the weighted sum of squared residuals,

$$
\mathrm{SSR}(\delta) = [v - f(\delta)]'[\hat{\Sigma}_\nu^{-1} \otimes Z(Z'Z)^{-1}Z'][v - f(\delta)] ,
\tag{9.I.36}
$$

with respect to the vector of unknown parameters δ, where Z is the matrix of time-series observations on the R instrumental variables. Provided that the parameters are identified from the aggregate model, we can apply the Gauss-Newton method to minimize (9.I.36). First, we can linearize the model, obtaining

$$
v = f(\delta_0) + \frac{\partial}{\partial \delta}(\delta_0)\Delta\delta + u ,
\tag{9.I.37}
$$

where δ_0 is the initial value of the vector of unknown parameters δ and

$$\Delta\delta = \delta_1 - \delta_0 , \tag{9.I.38}$$

where δ_1 is the revised value of this vector. The fitted residuals u depend on the initial and revised values.

To revise the initial values we apply Zellner and Theil's (1962) three-stage least squares method to the linearized model, obtaining

$$\Delta\delta = \left\{ \frac{\partial f}{\partial \delta}(\delta_0)'[\hat{\Sigma}_v^{-1} \otimes Z(Z'Z)^{-1}Z'] \frac{\partial f}{\partial \delta}(\delta_0) \right\}^{-1} \times \frac{\partial f}{\partial \delta}(\delta_0)'[\hat{\Sigma}_v^{-1} \otimes Z(Z'Z)^{-1}Z'][v - f(\delta_0)] . \tag{9.I.39}$$

If $SSR(\delta_0) > SSR(\delta_1)$, a further iteration is performed by replacing δ_0 by δ_1 in (9.I.37) and (9.I.39), resulting in a further revised value, say δ_2, and so on. If this condition is not satisfied, we divide the revision $\Delta\delta$ by 2 and evaluate the criteria $SSR(\delta)$ again; we continue reducing the revision $\Delta\delta$ until the criterion improves or the convergence criterion $\max_j(\Delta\delta_j/\delta_j)$ is less than some prespecified limit. If the criterion improves, we continue with further iterations. If not, we stop the iterative process and employ the current value of the vector of unknown parameters δ as our NL3SLS estimator.

The final step in estimation of the aggregate model is to minimize the criterion function (9.I.36) subject to the restrictions implied by monotonicity of the individual expenditure shares. We have eliminated the restrictions implied by summability and symmetry; these restrictions take the form of equalities. Monotonicity of the individual expenditure shares implies inequality restrictions on the Cholesky values of the matrix Δ_{qq}. We can then represent these restrictions in the form

$$\phi_r(\delta) \geq 0 , \quad (r = 1, 2, \ldots, R) , \tag{9.I.40}$$

where R is the number of restrictions. We obtain the inequality constrained nonlinear three-stage least squares estimator for the aggregate model by minimizing the criterion function (9.I.36) subject to the constraints (9.I.40). This estimator corresponds to a saddlepoint of the Lagrangian function

$$L = \mathrm{SSR}(\delta) + \lambda'\phi\,, \tag{9.I.41}$$

where λ is a vector of R Lagrange multipliers and ϕ is a vector of R constraints. The Kuhn-Tucker (1951) conditions for a saddlepoint of this Lagrangian are the first-order conditions

$$\frac{\partial L}{\partial \delta} = \frac{\partial \mathrm{SSR}(\delta)}{\partial \delta} + \lambda' \frac{\partial \phi}{\partial \delta} = 0 \tag{9.I.42}$$

and the complementary slackness condition

$$\lambda'\phi = 0\,, \qquad (\lambda \geq 0)\,. \tag{9.I.43}$$

To find a saddlepoint of the Lagrangian (9.I.41) we begin by linearizing the aggregate model (9.I.35) as in (9.I.37). Second, we linearize the constraints as

$$\phi(\delta) = \frac{\partial \phi}{\partial \delta}(\delta_0)\Delta\delta + \phi(\delta_0)\,, \tag{9.I.44}$$

where δ_0 is a vector of initial values of the unknown parameters. We apply Liew's (1976) inequality-constrained three-stage least squares method to the linearized model, obtaining

$$\Delta\delta^* = \Delta\delta + \left\{\frac{\partial f}{\partial \delta}(\delta_0)'[\hat{\Sigma}_v^{-1} \otimes Z(Z'Z)^{-1}Z']\frac{\partial f}{\partial \delta}(\delta_0)\right\}^{-1} \frac{\partial \phi}{\partial \delta}(\delta_0)'\lambda^*\,, \tag{9.I.45}$$

where $\Delta\delta$ is the change in the value of parameters (9.I.39) and λ^* is the solution of the linear complexity problem

$$\frac{\partial \phi}{\partial \delta}(\delta_0)\left\{\frac{\partial f}{\partial \delta}(\delta_0)'[\hat{\Sigma}_v^{-1} \otimes Z(Z'Z)^{-1}Z']\frac{\partial f}{\partial \delta}(\delta_0)\right\}^{-1} \frac{\partial \phi}{\partial \delta}(\delta_0)\lambda$$
$$+ \frac{\partial \phi}{\partial \delta}(\delta_0)\Delta\delta - \phi(\delta_0) \geq 0\,,$$

where

$$\left[\frac{\partial \phi}{\partial \delta}(\delta_0)\left\{\frac{\partial f}{\partial \delta}(\delta_0)'[\hat{\Sigma}_v^{-1} \otimes Z(Z'Z)^{-1}Z']\frac{\partial f}{\partial \delta}(\delta_0)\right\}^{-1}\frac{\partial \phi}{\partial \delta}(\delta_0)\lambda \right.$$

$$\left. + \frac{\partial \phi}{\partial \delta}(\delta_0)\Delta\delta - \phi(\delta_0)\right]' \lambda = 0 \,, \qquad (\lambda \geq 0) \,.$$

Given an initial value of the unknown parameters δ_0 that satisfies the R constraints (9.I.40), if $\mathrm{SSR}(\delta_1) < \mathrm{SSR}(\delta_0)$ and δ_1 satisfies the constraints, the iterative process continues by linearizing the model (9.I.35) as in (9.I.37) and the constraints (9.I.40) as in (9.I.44) at the revised value of the vector of unknown parameters $\delta_1 = \delta_0 + \Delta\delta$. If not, we shrink $\Delta\delta$ as before, continuing until an improvement is found subject to the constraints or the convergence criterion $\max_j(\Delta\delta_j/\delta_{j})$ is less than some prespecified limit.

The condition for identifiability of the vector of unknown parameters δ in the aggregate model are equivalent to the nonsingularity of the following matrix in a neighborhood of the true parameter vector

$$\frac{\partial f}{\partial \delta}(\delta)'[\Sigma_v^{-1} \otimes Z(Z'Z)^{-1}Z']\frac{\partial f}{\partial \delta}(\delta) \,.$$

The condition (9.I.25) given above is necessary for the nonsingularity of this matrix.

9.I.3D Pooling Time-Series and Cross-Section Data

Since the parameters of the translog model of energy expenditures cannot be identified from cross-section or time-series data alone, we must pool both types of data to obtain estimates of the unknown parameters. Pooled estimation of the translog model requires application of the method of nonlinear three-stage least squares of Jorgenson and Stoker (1982). As before, our objective is to estimate the unknown parameters, that is, γ_q, Δ_{qq}, Δ_{qA}, subject to the restrictions implied by summability, symmetry, and monotonicity.

The pooled NL3SLS estimator is found by minimizing the following function with respect to δ

$$\mathrm{SSR}(\delta) = (y - Y\delta)'[\hat{\Sigma}_\varepsilon^{-1} \otimes I](y - Y\delta)$$

$$+ [v - f(\delta)]'[\hat{\Sigma}_\varepsilon^{-1} \otimes Z(Z'Z)^{-1}Z'][v - f(\delta)] \qquad (9.I.46)$$

where

$$Y = \begin{bmatrix} I \otimes X & 0 \\ 0 & 0 \end{bmatrix} \qquad (9.I.47)$$

is a matrix of observations on the variables that determine the individual expenditure shares in the cross-section model.

To find a minimum of the criterion function SSR(δ) in (9.I.46) we begin by linearizing the pooled system (9.I.29) and (9.I.35), respectively, as

$$y - Y\delta_0 = Y\Delta\delta + e \qquad (9.I.48)$$

and

$$v - f(\delta_0) = \frac{\partial f}{\partial \delta}(\delta_0)\Delta\delta + u \ ,$$

where δ_0 is a vector of initial values of the unknown parameters. As before, we apply ordinary three-stage least squares to the linearized model, obtaining

$$\Delta\delta = \left\{ Y'[\hat{\Sigma}_\varepsilon^{-1} \otimes I]Y + \frac{\partial f}{\partial \delta}(\delta_0)'[\hat{\Sigma}_v^{-1} \otimes Z(Z'Z)^{-1}Z'] \frac{\partial f}{\partial \delta}(\delta_0) \right\}^{-1}$$
$$\times \left\{ Y'[\hat{\Sigma}_\varepsilon^{-1} \otimes I](y - Y\delta_0) + \frac{\partial f}{\partial \delta}(\delta_0)'[\hat{\Sigma}_v^{-1} \otimes Z(Z'Z)^{-1}Z'][v - f(\delta_0)] \right\} . \qquad (9.I.49)$$

If SSR(δ_1) < SSR(δ_0), the iterative process continues by linearizing the model at the revised value of the parameters $\delta_1 = \delta_0 + \Delta\delta$. If not, we shrink $\Delta\delta$ as before, dividing $\Delta\delta$ by 2 and reevaluating the criterion. We continue until an improvement is found or the convergence criterion $\max_j(\Delta\delta_j / \delta_j)$ is less than some prespecified limit.

The nonlinear three-stage least squares estimator obtained by minimizing the criterion function (9.I.47) is a consistent estimator of the vector of unknown parameters δ; note that this is required taking the probability limit of the NL3SLS estimator as the number of cross-section observations K and the number of time-series observations T tend to infinity. This estimator has asymptotic covariance matrix

$$V(\hat{\delta}) = \left\{ Y'[\hat{\Sigma}_{\varepsilon}^{-1} \otimes I]Y + \frac{\partial f}{\partial \delta}(\delta_0)'[\hat{\Sigma}_{v}^{-1} \otimes Z(Z'Z)^{-1}Z'] \frac{\partial f}{\partial \delta}(\delta_0) \right\}^{-1} . \tag{9.I.50}$$

We obtain an estimator of this matrix by inserting the estimators $\hat{\delta}$, $\hat{\Sigma}_{\varepsilon}$, and $\hat{\Sigma}_{v}$ in place of the parameters δ, Σ_{ε}, and Σ_{v}. The conditions for identifiability of the vector of unknown parameters δ in the model for pooling time-series and cross-section data are equivalent to nonsingularity of the following matrix in the neighborhood of the true parameter vector

$$Y'[\hat{\Sigma}_{\varepsilon}^{-1} \otimes I]Y + \frac{\partial f}{\partial \delta}(\delta_0)'[\hat{\Sigma}_{v}^{-1} \otimes Z(Z'Z)^{-1}Z'] \frac{\partial f}{\partial \delta}(\delta_0) . \tag{9.I.51}$$

Under the regularity conditions

$$\lim_{K\to\infty} \frac{X'X}{K} = \Sigma_{X'X} ,$$

$$\lim_{T\to\infty} \frac{Z'Z}{T} = \Sigma_{Z'Z} ,$$

$$\lim_{T\to\infty} \frac{1}{T} Z' \frac{\partial f_i}{\partial \delta_i} = \Sigma_{Z'(\partial f_i/\partial \delta_i)} , \quad (i = 1, 2, \ldots, M) , \tag{9.I.52}$$

where $\Sigma_{X'X}$, $\Sigma_{Z'Z}$, $\Sigma_{Z'(\partial f_i/\partial \delta_i)}$ $(i = 1, 2, \ldots, M)$ are positive definite matrices, the NL3SLS estimator is asymptotically efficient in the class of instrumental variables estimators using X and Z as instrumental variables.

Up to this point we have presented the pooled estimator for cross-section and time-series models as a standard application of the NL3SLS estimator. The linearity of the cross-section model resulting from exact aggregation implies that the computations can be simplified. First, the moment matrix of the cross-section model takes the form

$$Y'[\hat{\Sigma}_{\varepsilon}^{-1} \otimes I]Y = \hat{\Sigma}_{\varepsilon}^{-1} \otimes X'X , \tag{9.I.53}$$

which depends on $\hat{\Sigma}_{\varepsilon}$ and on $X'X$, the moment matrix of the independent variables in the cross-section model. Similarly, the vector of moments involving the dependent variables of the cross-section model takes the form

$$Y'[\hat{\Sigma}_\varepsilon^{-1} \otimes I](y - Y\delta) = \hat{\Sigma}_\varepsilon^{-1} \otimes (X'y - X'X\delta) , \tag{9.I.54}$$

which depends on $\hat{\Sigma}_\varepsilon$, $X'X$, and $X'y$, the vector of moments involving the dependent variables of the cross-section model.

The final step in pooled estimation of the unknown parameters of the translog model of aggregate consumer behavior is to estimate these parameters subject to the inequality restrictions implied by monotonicity of the individual expenditure shares. We minimize the criterion (9.I.46) subject to the restrictions (9.I.40). As before, this is a concave programming problem. We apply inequality-constrained three-stage least squares to the linearized model, obtaining

$$\Delta\delta^* = \Delta\delta + \left\{ Y'[\hat{\Sigma}_\varepsilon^{-1} \otimes I]Y + \frac{\partial f}{\partial \delta}(\delta_0)'[\hat{\Sigma}_v^{-1} \otimes Z(Z'Z)^{-1}Z] \frac{\partial f}{\partial \delta}(\delta_0) \right\}^{-1} \times \frac{\partial \phi}{\partial \delta}(\delta_0)\lambda^* , \tag{9.I.55}$$

where $\Delta\delta^*$ is the change in the value of the parameters for unconstrained three-stage least squares and γ^* is the solution of the linear complementarity problem

$$\frac{\partial \phi}{\partial \delta} \left\{ Y'[\hat{\Sigma}_\varepsilon^{-1} \otimes I]Y + \frac{\partial f}{\partial \delta}(\delta_0)'[\hat{\Sigma}_v^{-1} \otimes Z(Z'Z)^{-1}Z] \frac{\partial f}{\partial \delta}(\delta_0) \right\}^{-1} \times \frac{\partial \phi}{\partial \delta}(\delta_0)\lambda + \frac{\partial \phi}{\partial \delta}(\delta_0)\Delta\delta - \phi(\delta_0) \geq 0 ,$$

where

$$\left[\frac{\partial \phi}{\partial \delta}(\delta_0) \left\{ Y'[\hat{\Sigma}_\varepsilon^{-1} \otimes I]Y + \frac{\partial f}{\partial \delta}(\delta_0)'[\hat{\Sigma}_v^{-1} \otimes Z(Z'Z)^{-1}Z] \frac{\partial f}{\partial \delta}(\delta_0) \right\}^{-1} \times \frac{\partial \phi}{\partial \delta}(\delta_0)\lambda + \frac{\partial \phi}{\partial \delta}(\delta_0)\Delta\delta - \phi(\delta_0) \right]' \lambda = 0 , \quad \lambda \geq 0 .$$

Given an initial value of the unknown parameters δ_0 that satisfies the constraints, is $\mathrm{SSR}(\delta_0) < \mathrm{SSR}(\delta)$ and δ_1 satisfies the constraints, the iterative process continues by linearizing the model as in (9.I.48) and the constraints as in (9.I.44). at the revised value of the vector of unknown parameters $\delta_1 = \delta_0 + \Delta\delta$. If not, we shrink $\Delta\delta$ as before, continuing until an improvement is found subject to the constraints or the convergence criterion $\max_j(\Delta\delta_j/\delta_j)$ is less than some prespecified limit.

We assume that the restrictions associated with monotonicity of the individual expenditure shares are valid or, more precisely, that the vector of unknown parameters δ is an interior point of the set of parameters defined by the constraints. Under this assumption the inequality-constrained nonlinear three-stage least squares estimator is a consistent estimator of the vector of unknown parameters. This estimator has the same asymptotic covariance matrix (I.9.50) as the estimator pooling time-series and cross-section data.[9] As before, we obtain an estimator of this matrix by inserting the estimators delta, $\hat{\Sigma}_\varepsilon$ and $\hat{\Sigma}_V$ in place of the parameters delta, Σ_ε and Σ_V. The conditions for identifiability of the vector of unknown parameters δ is the nonsingularity of the matrix (9.I.51) in the neighborhood of the true parameter vector.

For simplicity we have considered pooled estimation of the translog model of aggregate energy expenditures from K cross-section observations on individual energy expenditures at a single point of time and T time-series observations on aggregate expenditure patterns. If there are C cross sections at different points of time, each with K_c observations on individual expenditure patterns, we can represent the cross-section models in the form

$$y_c = [I \otimes X_c]\beta_c + \varepsilon_c\,, \qquad (c = 1, 2, .., C)\,,$$

where each model takes the form (9.I.29); the matrices X_c $(c = 1, 2, .., C)$ are of full rank; and the random vectors ε_c $(c = 1, 2, .., C)$ are distributed normally and independently with means equal to zero and covariance matrices $\Sigma_{\varepsilon_c} \otimes I$ $(c = 1, 2, .., C)$, as before. The maximum likelihood estimators of the parameters β_c $(c = 1, 2, .., C)$ from each cross-section model are equivalent to the least squares estimators applied to each equation in each model individually.

The pooled NL3SLS estimator is obtained by minimizing the following function with respect to δ

$$\begin{aligned} SSR(\delta) = &\sum_{c=1}^{C} (y_c - Y_c\delta)'[\hat{\Sigma}_{\varepsilon_c} \otimes I](y_c - Y_c\delta) \\ &+ [v + f(\delta)]'[\hat{\Sigma}_V^{-1} \otimes Z(Z'Z)^{-1}Z'][v - f(\delta)]\,, \end{aligned} \qquad (9.I.56)$$

where

$$Y_c = \begin{bmatrix} I \otimes X_c & 0 \\ 0 & 0 \end{bmatrix} \tag{9.I.57}$$

is a matrix of observations on the variables that determine the individual expenditure shares in the cross-section model. As before, we can linearize the pooled system and apply ordinary three-stage least squares to the linearized model. We can linearize the model for the revised estimator and continue the iterative process until convergence. The resulting nonlinear three-stage least squares estimator has asymptotic covariance matrix

$$V(\hat{\delta}) = \left\{ \sum_{c=1}^{C} Y_c'[\hat{\Sigma}_{\varepsilon_c}^{-1} \otimes I]Y_c + \frac{\partial f}{\partial \delta}(\delta)'[\hat{\Sigma}_{\nu}^{-1} \otimes Z(Z'Z)^{-1}Z'] \frac{\partial f}{\partial \delta}(\delta) \right\}^{-1} . \tag{9.I.58}$$

As before, the pooled estimator depends only on the moments of the cross-section data, not on the individual cross-section observations.

9.I.3E Summary and Conclusion

In this section we have discussed the econometric implementation of the translog model of aggregate energy expenditures presented in section 9.I.3B. To formulate an econometric model of individual energy expenditures we add a stochastic component to the functions that determine the individual expenditure shares. The interpretation of the individual disturbances is that the individual consuming unit maximizes utility, subject to a budget constraint, but that the expenditure shares are chosen with a random disturbances.

We assume that the individual disturbances have expected value equal to zero. Since the individual expenditure shares for all types of energy sum to unity for each consuming unit in each time period, the unobservable random disturbances for all types of energy sum to zero. As a consequence, these disturbances are not distributed independently. We assume that the covariance matrix of the individual disturbances has rank equal to $M - 1$, where M is the number of types of energy. Finally, we assume that disturbances corresponding to distinct observations are uncorrelated.

The aggregate energy expenditure shares at any point of time are equal to the individual shares multiplied by the ratio of individual energy expenditure to aggregate energy expenditure. Although the data for individual consuming units and for the aggregate of all consuming units are based on the same definitions, the methods of measurement are not the same. Accordingly, we introduce an additional random component in the equations for the aggregate energy expenditure shares. This component corresponds to errors of measurement in the observations on individual energy expenditure shares that underly the observations of the aggregate energy expenditure shares.

We assume that the errors of measurement that underly the aggregate energy expenditure shares have expected value equal to zero. These errors of measurement, like the individual disturbances, sum to zero for each unit in each time period and are not distributed independently. We assume that the covariance matrix of the errors of measurement has rank equal to $M - 1$. Finally, we assume that the errors of measurement corresponding to distinct observations are uncorrelated.

The aggregate disturbances are weighted averages of individual disturbances and the errors of measurement. As a consequence, the aggregate disturbances corresponding to different time periods are heteroscedastic. We can correct for heteroscedasticity by transforming the observations on the aggregate energy expenditure shares. The transformed aggregate disturbances have expected value equal to zero for all observations and have a covariance matrix with rank $M - 1$. We assume that the errors of measurement corresponding to distinct observations are uncorrelated, so that the aggregate disturbances for distinct observations are also uncorrelated.

In our application of the translog model of aggregate energy expenditures presented in section 9.III, below, we pool cross-section data on individual energy expenditure patterns with time-series data on aggregate energy expenditure patterns. We first estimate the parameters of models for cross sections of observations on individual energy expenditure patterns, assuming that energy prices for all consumers are the same for all individuals. These models can be regarded as linear, multivariate, regression models, so that the parameters that can be identified from a single cross section can be estimated by applying ordinary least squares to each equation separately. These parameters are associated with demographic characteristics of individual households.

The second step in pooling individual cross-section data with aggregate time-series data is to estimate the parameters of a model for a time series of observations on aggregate energy expenditure patterns. In this model we treat the energy prices as jointly dependent variables. A second complication is that too few time-series observations are available to identify all the parameters of the model of aggregate energy expenditures.

To identify the unknown parameters we combine cross-section and time-series data. We introduce a sufficient number of instrumental variables to identify all parameters. Given the identification of the parameters from the model combining time-series and cross-section data, we apply the methods of nonlinear three-stage least squares to obtain an estimator of the parameters fo the complete model. The resulting estimator is consistent and asymptotically efficient in the class of instrumental variables estimators utilizing the instruments we have chosen.

A substantial simplification in the computations required for the estimator pooling cross-section and time-series data results from the theory of exact aggregation. The iterative process for the pooled estimator depends only on moments computed as part of the evaluation of the least squares estimators for the cross-section models. The individual observations from cross-section data are not required for the pooled estimator, provided that the ordinary least squares estimator of the cross-section model is computed first to obtain an initial estimator of the parameters of this model.

9.II Individual Energy Expenditures

9.II.1 Introduction

In this chapter we present the empirical results of implementing the econometric model of individual energy expenditures discussed in the preceding chapter. For this purpose we employ five sets of cross-section observations on individual energy expenditure patterns in the United States: the Bureau of Labor Statistics (BLS) Consumer Expenditure Surveys (CES) of 1960/61, 1972, and 1973 and the Washington Center for Metropolitan Studies (WCMS) Lifestyle and Household Energy Use Surveys (LHES) for 1973 and 1975. In this chapter we employ a model of individual expenditure allocation as a basis for estimating the parameters that can be identified from cross-section data alone. In the following chapter we pool time-series and cross-section data to estimate all of the parameters of our model of aggregate energy expenditures.

We begin by discussing the allocation of consumer expenditures among commodity groups. We next consider the classification of consuming units by demographic characteristics. We then describe the data sources we have employed and the assumptions we have imposed in combining the data sources. We present estimates of the parameters of the transcendental logarithmic model of individual energy expenditures. To characterize these estimates we analyze changes in patterns of individual expenditures with changes in demographic characteristics of individual consuming units. We also describe differences in estimates among our five sets of cross-section observations on individual energy expenditure patterns.

Total energy expenditure is defined as the sum of all expenditures on electricity, natural gas, gasoline, fuel oil, and other fuels. We divide energy expenditures into four broad categories:

1. *Electricity*: Expenditures on electricity for lighting, heating, use of appliances, and so on.

2. *Natural gas*: Expenditures on natural gas for heating, use of appliances, and so on, both from main and bottled gas.

3. *Fuel oil and other*: Expenditures on fuel oil for heating and expenditures on other fuels such as coal, wood, charcoal, and so on.

4. *Gasoline*: Expenditures on gasoline for operation of automobiles and for operation of tools such as power mowers, and so on.

The basic consuming unit employed in this study is the household. Unrelated individuals are considered to be households of size 1. All consuming units are classified by attributes that reflect differences in preferences among consuming units. We employ the following demographic characteristics as attributes of households—

1. *Family size*: 1,2,3,4,5,6, and 7 or more persons

2. *Age of head*: 15–24, 25–34, 35–44, 45–54, 55–65, 65 and over

3. *Region of residence*: Northeast, North Central, South, and West

4. *Race*: White, nonwhite

5. *Type of residence*: Urban, rural

Each household is assigned to one of the categories for each of the five demographic characteristics. Since these categories are discrete, integer-valued variables are required to represent the attributes.

Under exact aggregation all attributes appear linearly in the functions that determine shares of individual energy expenditures. We impose no *a priori* restrictions on the form of the impact on expenditure patterns of variations in demographic characteristics among consuming units. We could, for example, include an integer-valued variable with value equal to family size as a determinant of individual energy expenditure patterns. However, this would impose a constraint on the effects of different family sizes. To avoid imposing these constraints, we represent each family size by a qualitative or dummy variable, so that the precise pattern of the impacts of changes in family size can be estimated. To avoid singularity of the matrix of dummy variables we take all variables to be zero for unrelated individuals, age 15–24, living in the Northeast, white in race, and living in an urban area. This leaves 16 qualitative variables to be treated as separate consumer attributes in representing the effects of demographic characteristics on preferences on consuming units.

The translog model of individual energy expenditures described in this chapter can be represented in the form

$$-v_{kt} = \delta + \Delta_{qA} A_{kt} + \varepsilon_{kt} \,, \quad (k = 1, 2, .., K; \, t = 1, 2, ..., T) \,, \tag{9.II.1}$$

where v_{kt} is the vector of observed energy expenditure shares and A_{kt} is the vector of attributes of the kth consuming unit. The observable random disturbance ε_{kt} is distributed normally with mean zero and covariance matrix Ω_ε. In our application we have four types of energy, so that we estimate three equations. As unknown parameters we have three elements of the vector δ and 16 attribute coefficients for each of the three equations in the matrix Δ_{qA}.

We estimate each of the cross-section models by ordinary least squares from data on individual energy expenditures. We present results in the appendix. We now turn to a detailed consideration of the regression results from each of the data bases. We first describe each data base in terms of the means and standard deviations of the energy expenditure shares and the attributes of the individual consumers. We then characterize the regression estimates by means of a series of figures indicating the impact of demographic characteristics of individual households on patterns of allocation of energy expenditure. The notation employed in the appendix, the tables denoting each data base, and the figures in the text are presented in table 9.II.1.

9.II.2 Consumer Expenditure Survey of 1960/61

The Consumer Expenditure Surveys (CES) employed by the BLS represent the largest and most detailed collections of individual family budget data available for the United States. The 1960/61 CES is com-

Table 9.II.1
Notation

EN	Total energy expenditures
GASELEC	Electricity and gas expenditures (1960/61 CES) Combined bills (1972, 1973 CES)
ELEC	Total electricity expenditures (1972, 1973 CES; 1973, 1975 LHES)
GAS	Total natural gas expenditures (1972, 1973 CES; 1973, 1975 LHES)
SOLID	Fuel oil and other expenditures (1960/61, 1972, 1973 CES)
FUELOIL	Fuel oil expenditures (1972, 1973 CES; 1973, 1975 LHES)
COAL	Other expenditure (1972, 1973 CES)
GASOLINE	Total gasoline expenditure (all data bases)
DF2 , DF3 ,..., DF7	Family size dummies for sizes 2, 3,..., 7 or more (all data bases)
DA30 , DA40 ,..., DA70	Age dummies for classes 25–34, 35–44,..., 65 and over (all data bases)
DRNC, DRS, DRW	Regional dummies for North Central, South and West (all data bases)
DNW	Dummy for nonwhite (all data bases)
DRUR	Dummy for rural (all data bases)
WGASELEC	Share for electricity and natural gas (1960/61 CES)
WELEC	Share for electricity (1972, 1973 CES; 1973, 1975 LHES)
WGAS	Share for natural gas (1972, 1973 CES; 1973, 1975 LHES)
WSOL	Share for fuel oil and other (1960/61, 1972, 1973 CES)
WFUEL	Share for fuel oil (1973, 1975 LHES)
WGASO	Share for gasoline (all data bases)

posed of a sample comprising 13,728 individual observations. Each data point has been checked for positive total energy expenditures, giving 13,098 observations for the 1960/61 CES. Since the survey is representative of the U.S. population, all statistics such as means and regression coefficients have been calculated from the individual observations without weighting.

The 1960/61 CES is the largest of our cross-section data sets. Its only deficiency is that expenditures on electricity and on natural gas are combined into a single category. The regression estimates for the equation for this combined share represent the sum of the coefficients of the individual electricity and natural gas equations. Since the combined shares can be used efficiently in the pooled data estimation, there was no need to separate expenditures in this category. The regression estimates for this sample are located in table 9.II.A.1 of the Appendix. Statistics summarizing the sample are given in table 9.II.2.

As a brief overview of the regression results for the 1960/61 CES, we see first from the share equation for electricity and natural gas given in appendix table 9.II.A.1 that all coefficients are estimated relatively precisely except for the dummy for the West. The most precisely estimated coefficients are those for moderate family sizes, older age classes, and rural residence. Table 9.II.A.1 shows that in the fuel oil and other share equation the family size impacts are rather small and imprecisely estimated, the age of head effects are substantial and precisely estimated, and the regional variables and race and rural dummies are even more so. Finally, table 9.II.A.1 gives the results for the gasoline shares equation, with sizable and precise effects for family sizes 2–5, all age classes, all regions, and the nonwhite variable. Virtually no difference could be attributed to the urban-rural distinction.

To portray the joint impact on all shares of each demographic characteristic, we present fitted share values for changing family size in figure 9.II.1a, for changing age of head in figure 9.II.1b, and for changing region, race, and type of residence in figure 9.II.1c. These figures are drawn by holding all demographic characteristics fixed except for that under study. The attributes held constant in these comparisons are family size 4, age of head 35–44, region Northeast, race white, and type of residence urban. The choice of basis for comparison is not critical. A different choice would change the vertical position of each graph, leaving the shape of the graph unaffected.

Table 9.II.2
Summary statistics, 1960/61 CES

	Mean	Std. Dev.
GASELEC	168.0781	107.6511
SOLID	63.6283	102.5014
GASOLINE	207.0817	198.7994
EN	438.7880	264.7352
DF2	0.2793	0.4487
DF3	0.1865	0.3895
DF4	0.1730	0.3783
DF5	0.1145	0.3185
DF6	0.0621	0.2414
DF7	0.0586	0.2349
DA30	0.1804	0.3845
DA40	0.2285	0.4199
DA50	0.2074	0.4054
DA60	0.1656	0.3717
DA70	0.1761	0.3809
DRNC	0.2978	0.4573
DRS	0.3074	0.4614
DRW	0.1622	0.3686
DNW	0.1102	0.3131
DRUR	0.3187	0.4660
WGASELEC	0.4563	0.2855
WSOL	0.1453	0.2133
WGASO	0.4002	0.2882

For increasing family size, as depicted in figure 9.II.1a, we see first a large drop in the share of electricity and natural gas together with a large gain in the share of gasoline as family size goes from 1 to 2. Further increases in family size show that these effects level off and reverse direction: an increasing gas and electricity share and a decreasing gasoline share are associated with larger families. The fuel oil and other share is less sensitive to family size, with only small increases as family size grows. On average the move from family size 1 to 2 involves the addition of a spouse who is a second driver, but it does not add appreciably to the heating and other fuel requirements. Increases in family size beyond 2 generally involve children, who tend to add more to heating and appliance use. These additions induce a reversal of the family size effect.

As depicted in figure 9.II.1b, increasing age of head involves a monotonic shift from gasoline to natural gas plus electricity and to fuel oil and other expenditure. This shift is most pronounced for both younger ages and relatively older ages, and more moderate for families with middle-aged heads. This appears to be due entirely to an increased propensity to drive for younger families, plus the fact that younger families would generally have smaller, more modest housing or other living accommodations, with small payments for heating and other energy uses for household operations.

Figure 9.II.1c shows the joint impact on all energy shares of changing region, race, and residence. Taking region first, we see that the share of fuel oil and other is by far the largest for the Northeast, declining markedly for other regions, especially the South and West. These declines are matched by increases in the shares of gasoline, which completely explains the Northeast-West difference. For the North Central region and the South, part of the decline in the share of fuel oil and other is associated with an increase in the share of gasoline, with the rest associated with an increase in the share of natural gas and electricity. This seems best explained by differences in the housing structure among regions, with the Northeast characterized by older homes using fuel oil for heat, whereas other regions mainly use natural gas as a heating fuel.

The major impact of race revealed by our analysis is in a decline in the gasoline share, matched by increases both in fuel oil and other and in gas and electricity. Nonwhites may just own fewer automobiles on average than whites, making their gasoline requirements smaller. The major impact of the urban-rural distinction is in a shift from electricity

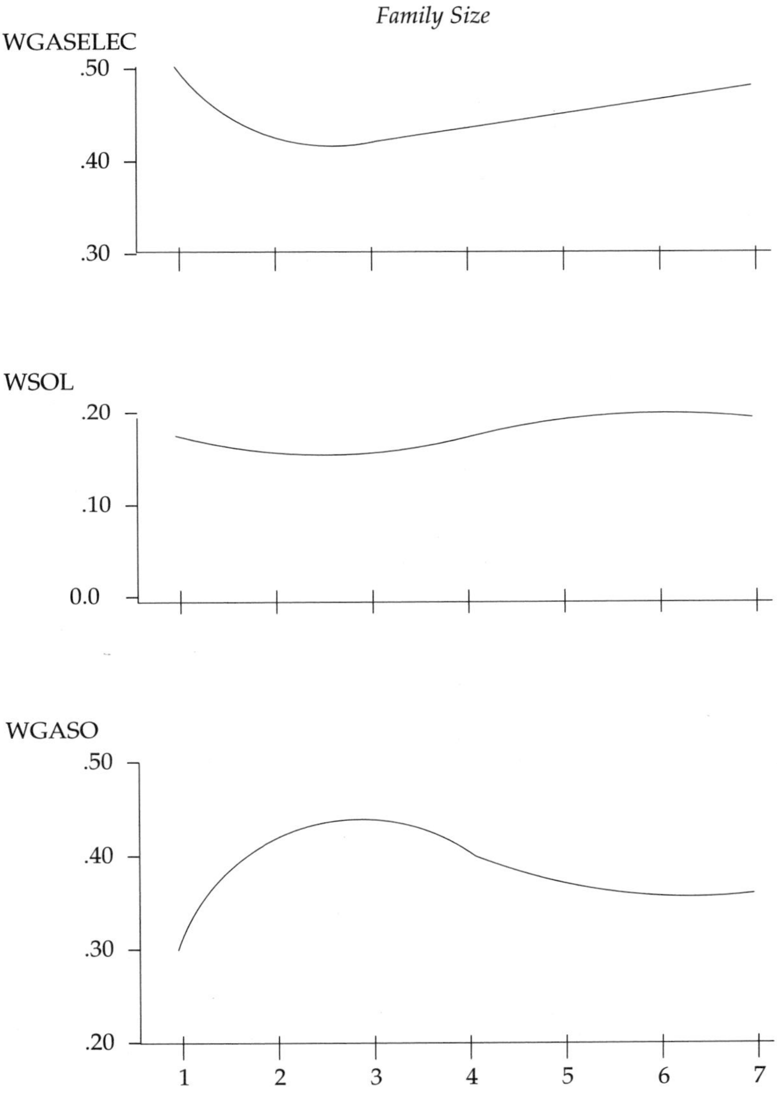

Figure 9.II.1a
Expenditure shares as a function of family size, 1960/61 CES.

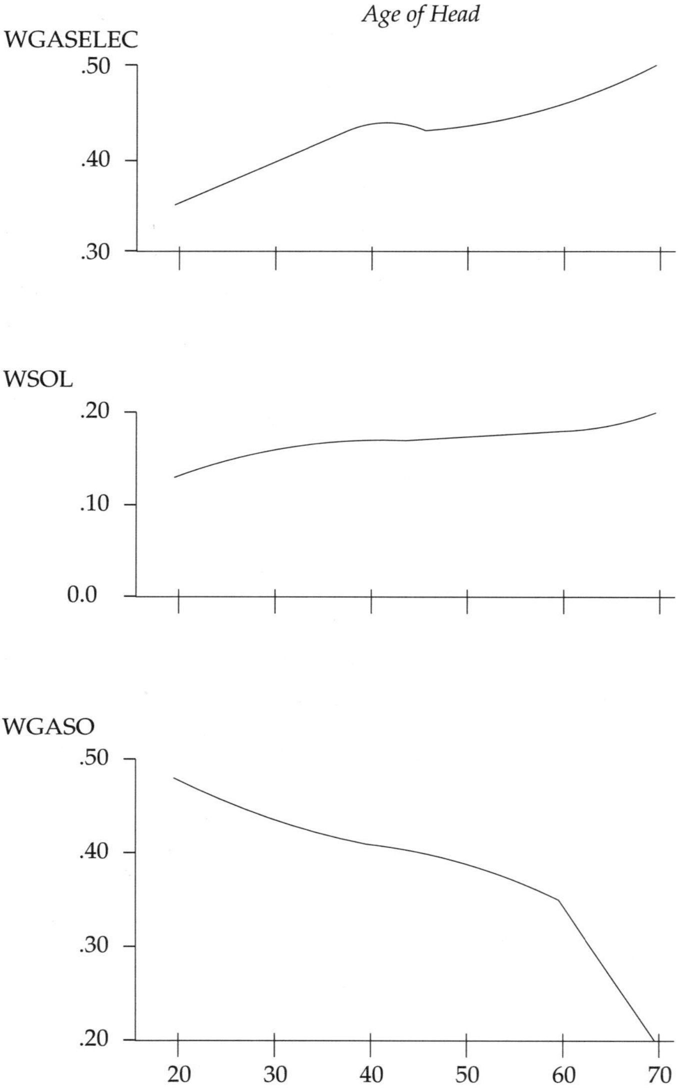

Figure 9.II.1b
Expenditure shares as a function of age of head, 1960/61 CES.

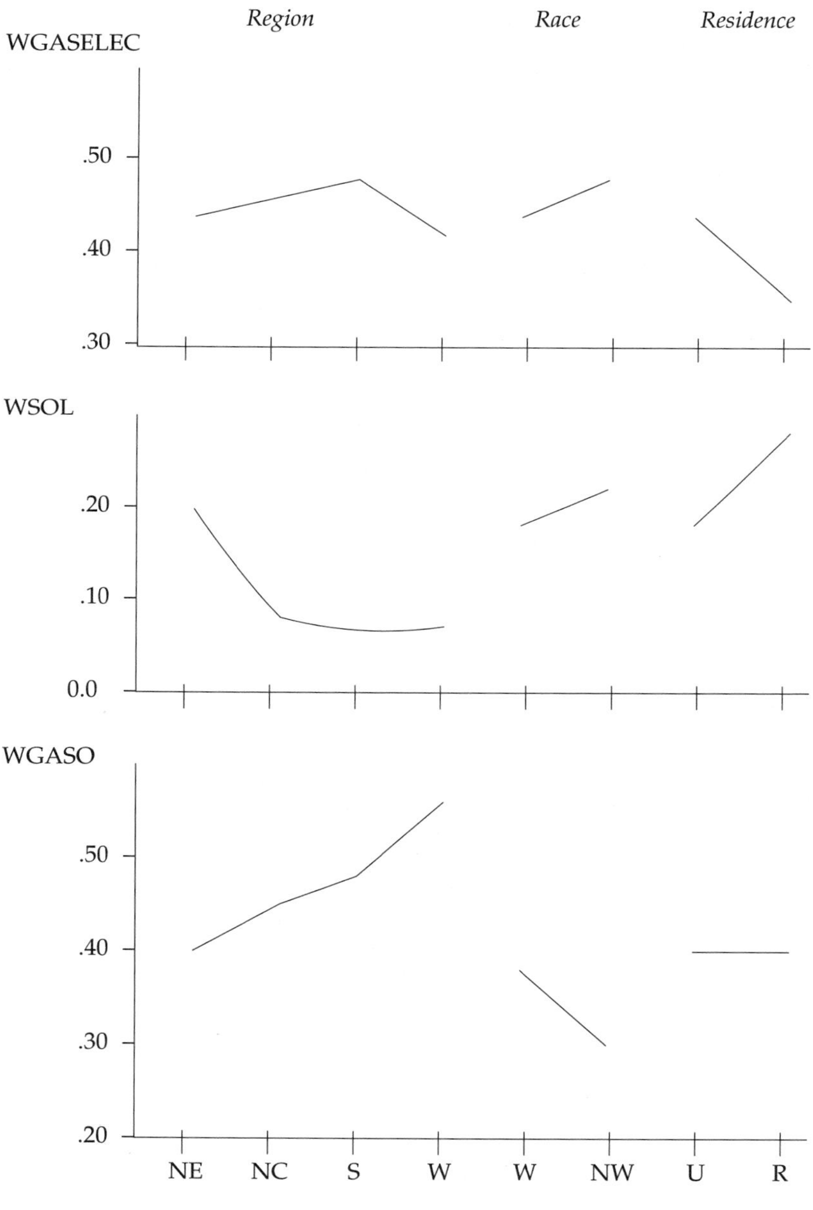

Figure 9.II.1c
Expenditure shares as a function of region, race and type of residence, 1960/61 CES.

and natural gas to fuel oil and other for home heating. There is no perceptible impact on the share of gasoline. Apparently, farms tend to have older heating units, using fuel oil, or they tend to be heated by wood or coal rather than by natural gas or electricity.

9.II.3 Consumer Expenditure Survey of 1972

The 1972/73 CES is actually two surveys, representing data from the 1972 sample and the 1973 sample, each comprising about 10,000 observations. After checking each data point for positive total energy expenditures a total of 8870 observations remains for the 1972 CES. As before, all statistics such as means and regression coefficients have been calculated from samples without weighting.

The 1972 CES data set corresponds to the first year of the 1972/73 Consumer Expenditure Interview Survey. The 1972 CES as well as the 1973 CES are the most detailed of our data bases, giving eight individual categories of energy usage: (1) gas in mains; (2) gas in bottles or tanks; (3) electricity; (4) gas and electricity (combined bills); (5) fuel oil and kerosene; (6) wood, coal, charcoal briquettes, and other such fuel; (7) gasoline (normal usage); and (8) gasoline used on vacations. The only problem posed for our analysis is the combined gas and electricity category, which was split and allocated to individual gas and electricity categories on the basis of the average ratio of mean electricity to mean natural gas observed from the individual categories. Therefore, the natural gas category is defined as the sum of gas in mains, gas in bottles or tanks, and a fraction of combined gas and electricity bills. Similarly, electricity in our analysis is the sum of the original electricity category plus a fraction of the combined gas and electricity bills. Fuel oil and other is defined as the sum of fuel oil, kerosene, wood, coal, charcoal, briquets, and other fuel expenditure. Finally gasoline is defined as the sum of gasoline (normal usage) and gasoline used on vacations. As mentioned above, the sample size is 8,879 after checking for positive total envery values. The regression estimates for the four energy share equations are located in table 9.II.A.2 of the appendix. Summary statistics of the sample are given in table 9.II.3.

For a brief overview of the results, we see from appendix table 9.II.A.2 that the family size effects on the share of electricity are appreciable and precisely estimated only for sizes 2–4; age effects are almost all estimated quite precisely; similarly, the effects of the Southern region and the nonwhite dummy variables are sizable and are precisely estimated. For natural gas, given in appendix table 9.II.A.2, the

Table 9.II.3
Summary statistics, 1972 CES

	Mean	Std. Dev.
ELEC	172.0295	128.4382
GAS	111.2381	124.3902
SOLID	53.3215	122.8348
GASOLINE	366.2232	317.9937
EN	702.8122	431.9337
GASELEC	39.5364	125.6421
FUELOIL	47.1266	118.4120
COAL	6.1949	37.0837
DF2	0.2813	0.4497
DF3	0.1666	0.3726
DF4	0.1402	0.3472
DF5	0.0872	0.2821
DF6	0.0479	0.2135
DF7	0.0421	0.2009
DA30	0.1947	0.3960
DA40	0.1700	0.3756
DA50	0.1879	0.3906
DA60	0.1604	0.3670
DA70	0.2016	0.4012
DRNC	0.2791	0.4486
DRS	0.3061	0.4609
DRW	0.2017	0.4013
DNW	0.0887	0.2844
DRUR	0.1678	0.3737
WELEC	0.2756	0.1931
WGAS	0.1777	0.1862
WSOL	0.0704	0.1549
WGASO	0.4763	0.2760

age structure is estimated precisely, as are the region, race, and type of residence impacts. Family size coefficients are all quite imprecise, except that for family size 2. In the fuel oil and other share equation given in table 9.II.A.2, age effects, region and type of residence effects are estimated precisely. Finally, the gasoline share equation estimation shows sizable coefficients for the age structure, region, race, and type of residence; only the effects of family sizes 2–3 are significant.

To study the interactions between energy expenditure shares and demographic characteristics of the consuming unit we vary each characteristic individually, holding the others fixed, in figures 9.II.2a,b,c. As before, except for the dimension under study. the demographic values are fixed at family size 4, age of head 35–44, Northeast region, white race, and urban residence.

As shown in figure 9.II.2a, the major impact of increasing family size is the reallocation of the energy budget from electricity and natural gas to gasoline as family size goes from 1 to 2. After family size 2 this effect is reversed; by family size 4 the electricity and natural gas share has returned to the size 1 level. These changes are indicated in appendix table 9.II.A.3 by the insignificant coefficients for larger family sizes. Fuel oil and other is virtually unaffected by family size. As before, this effect may be traceable to the fact that, on average, movement from family size 1 to 2 involves the addition of a second automobile drive, thus requiring relatively more gasoline, whereas further additions involve children.

As the age of head of the family is changed, we see that there is an almost monotonic reallocation from gasoline to the other three fuel categories. This reallocation is most pronounced in lower ages and higher ages, with the tendency much less evident or even reversed through the middle age levels. The reason for this may be that the youngest families have very modest housing needs and larger needs for automobile use. As age increases, families invest more heavily in housing until about age 40–50, when this tendency moderates, possibly because of increased automobile use by children. Finally, for the oldest ages, the reallocation away from gasoline continues.

As depicted in figure 9.II.2c, the most significant regional effect is the very low use of fuel oil and other by all regions except the Northeast. In the South this gap is covered by increased electricity usage. In the North Central region increased natural gas usage is observed. All regions other than the Northeast show increased use of gasoline, with the biggest increase appearing from the West. All of these effects

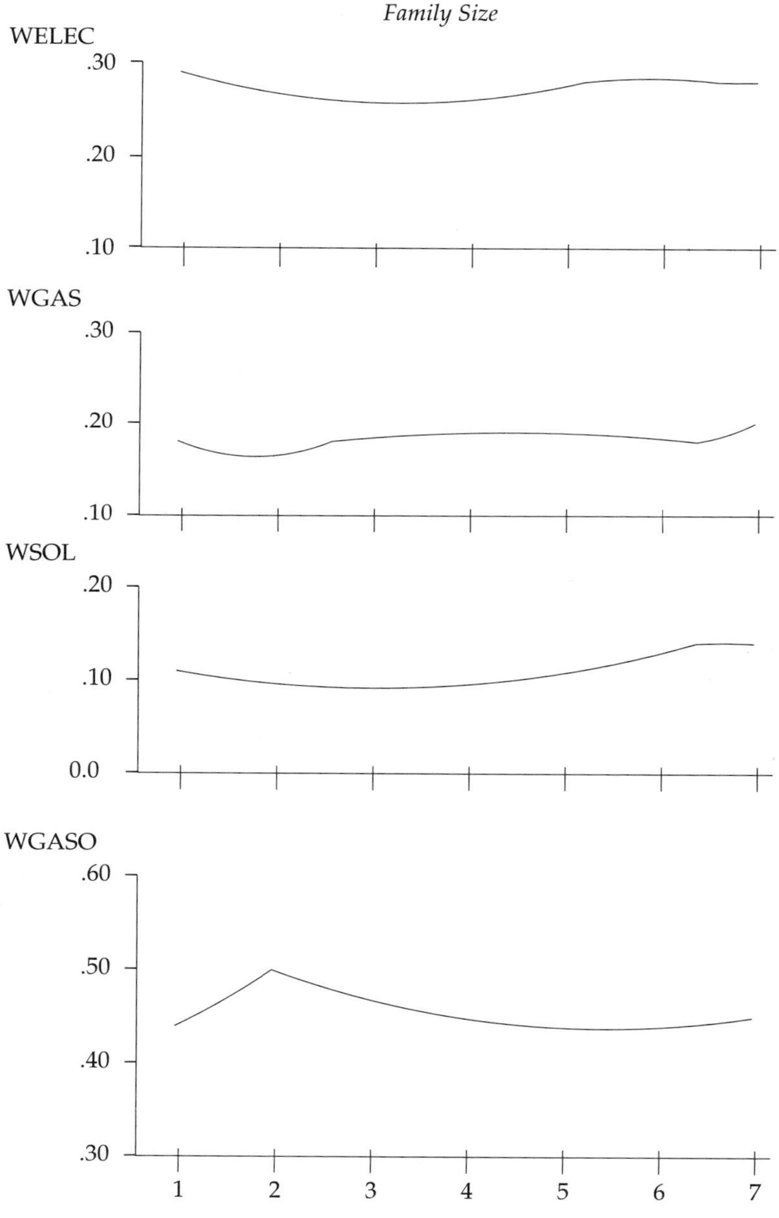

Figure 9.II.2a
Expenditure shares as functions of family size, 1972 CES.

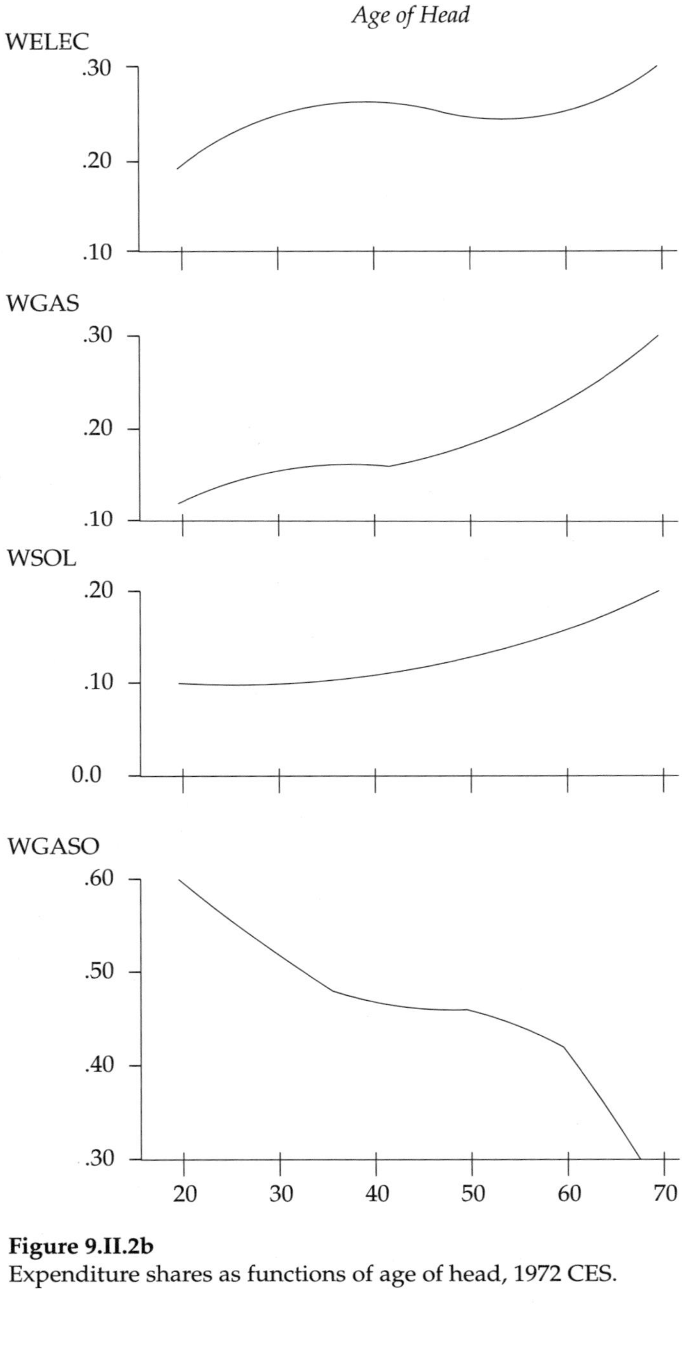

Figure 9.II.2b
Expenditure shares as functions of age of head, 1972 CES.

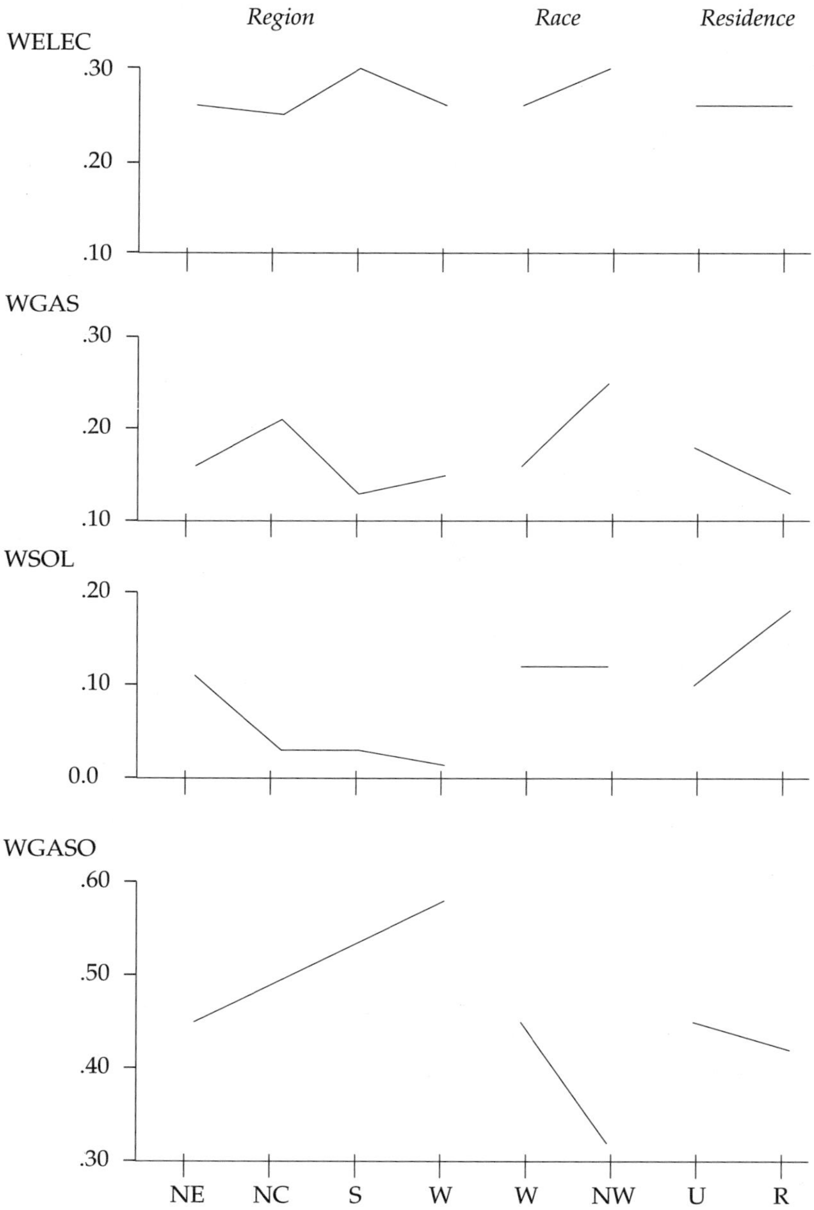

Figure 9.II.2c
Expenditure shares as functions of region, race and type of residence, 1972 CES.

appear sensible in view of the housing type available in those regions, as well as climatic considerations.

The major impact of race is a shift from gasoline to the other fuels, electricity, and natural gas. This may reflect greater automobile ownership and use by whites than by nonwhites; however, this explanation requires further investigation. By and large, the major impact of the type of residence is the switch from natural gas to fuel oil and other (wood, coal, and so on) as a major heating fuel as families change from urban to rural residences. The level of electricity usage is virtually identical—an effect we could not trace in the 1960/61 CES—whereas the level of gasoline usage is slightly less here.

9.II.4 Consumer Expenditure Survey of 1973

The definition of our four energy categories for the 1973 CES is identical to that of the 1972 CES, as the data bases were obtained using the same interview format. As before, each data point has been checked for positive total energy expenditures, giving 8898 observations for the 1973 CES. The 1972 and 1973 surveys are treated as separate data bases, and such statistics as means and regression coefficients have been calculated without weighting.

As with the 1972 CES, a split of combined electricity and gas bills for the 1973 CES was carried out by allocating this category between individual electricity and natural gas; the fraction going to electricity is slightly different owing to a change in the ratio of mean electricity consumption to mean natural gas consumption. Summary statistics from the 1973 CES sample are presented in table 9.II.4. We see that the main change from 1973 is an increase in the level of all energy expenditures, reflecting the rise in energy prices. Aside from this, the demographic structure of the sample is fairly representative of the U.S. population as a whole.

The regression estimates for this sample are located in appendix table 9.II.A.3. They are qualitatively and quantitatively very similar to the estimates obtained from the 1972 CES; therefore, we will be relatively brief in presenting them. From table 9.II.A.3, we see that in the share of elasticity only the effects of family sizes 2–4 are estimated precisely. The age, region, race, and type of residence effects are estimated quite precisely. A similar situation obtains in the equations for natural gas and for gasoline in table 9.II.A.3, except that no perceptible urban-rural effect can be found in the gasoline share equation. Finally,

Table 9.II.4
Summary statistics, 1973 CES

	Mean	Std. Dev.
ELEC	188.1160	148.1674
GAS	114.3769	32.3108
SOLID	56.3983	142.1538
GASOLINE	404.9710	345.5796
EN	763.8623	479.5934
GASELEC	38.7076	122.8542
FUELOIL	51.5262	139.2732
COAL	4.8721	29.4298
DF2	0.2814	0.4497
DF3	0.1562	0.3631
DF4	0.1514	0.3584
DF5	0.0870	0.2818
DF6	0.0445	0.2062
DF7	0.0399	0.1957
DA30	0.2143	0.4101
DA40	0.1678	0.3737
DA50	0.1793	0.3836
DA60	0.1606	0.3672
DA70	0.1893	0.3917
DRNC	0.2788	0.4484
DRS	0.3075	0.4615
DRW	0.2063	0.4047
DNW	0.1023	0.3030
DRUR	0.1677	0.3736
WGAS	0.1690	0.1845
WELEC	0.2754	0.1977
WSOL	0.0656	0.1499
WGASO	0.4900	—

the share equation for fuel oil and other shows precise but small effects of family sizes 6 and 7 or more, precise effects for ages 35 and over, and very sizable region and type of residence effects.

From figure 9.II.3a we see that the major impact of increasing family size is a shift into gasoline from electricity and natural gas for sizes 2–4, with no perceptible effect for larger family sizes. There is a slightly increased share of fuel oil and other for the largest family sizes, which may be due to increased heating requirements for larger families. These effects are very similar to those of the 1972 CES; therefore the same explanations can be applied.

Similarly, from figure 9.II.3b we find that increasing the age of head of the family involves a shift from gasoline expenditures to heating fuels, with the most dramatic changes occurring for younger and older ranges of the age spectrum. The middle age (35–60) movements are more moderate than in the 1972 CES, indicating slightly more stability in the energy consumption behavior in 1973 than in 1972. These effects can be explained by additional housing investment together with less reliance on automobiles as families age, holding all other factors constant.

From figure 9.II.3c we see that the major regional effect is in the increased use of fuel oil and other for the Northeast, matched by increases in natural gas usage for the North Central region and increases in electricity usage in the South. The Northeast is the smallest relative user of gasoline, with the West using the largest amount. Before, these effects were rationalized by the differing housing structures as well as differing climates in the various regions. It would be surprising if this underlying structure changed appreciably in the short period between 1972 and 1973. Also, the race and type of residence effects are virtually identical to those of the 1972 CES. The major difference between races is a shift from gasoline to electricity and natural gas for moving from white to nonwhite. The major urban-rural effect embodies the increased use of fuel oil and other as a fuel for household heating.

9.II.5 Lifestyle and Household Energy Use Survey of 1973

The Lifestyle and Household Energy Use Surveys (LHES) performed by the Washington Center for Metropolitan Studies (WCMS) for 1973 and 1975 represent two surveys of energy consumption and housing stock and appliance structure of roughly 3500 observations each. The

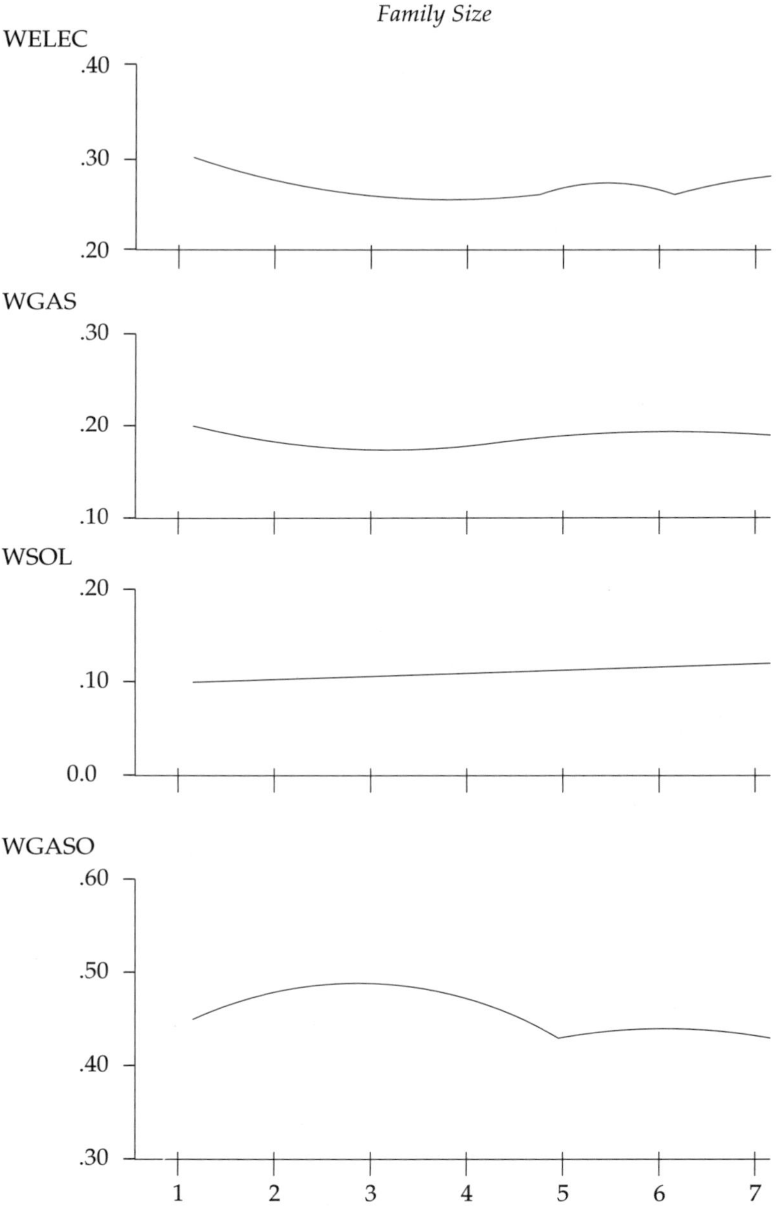

Figure 9.II.3a
Expenditure shares as functions of family size, 1973 CES.

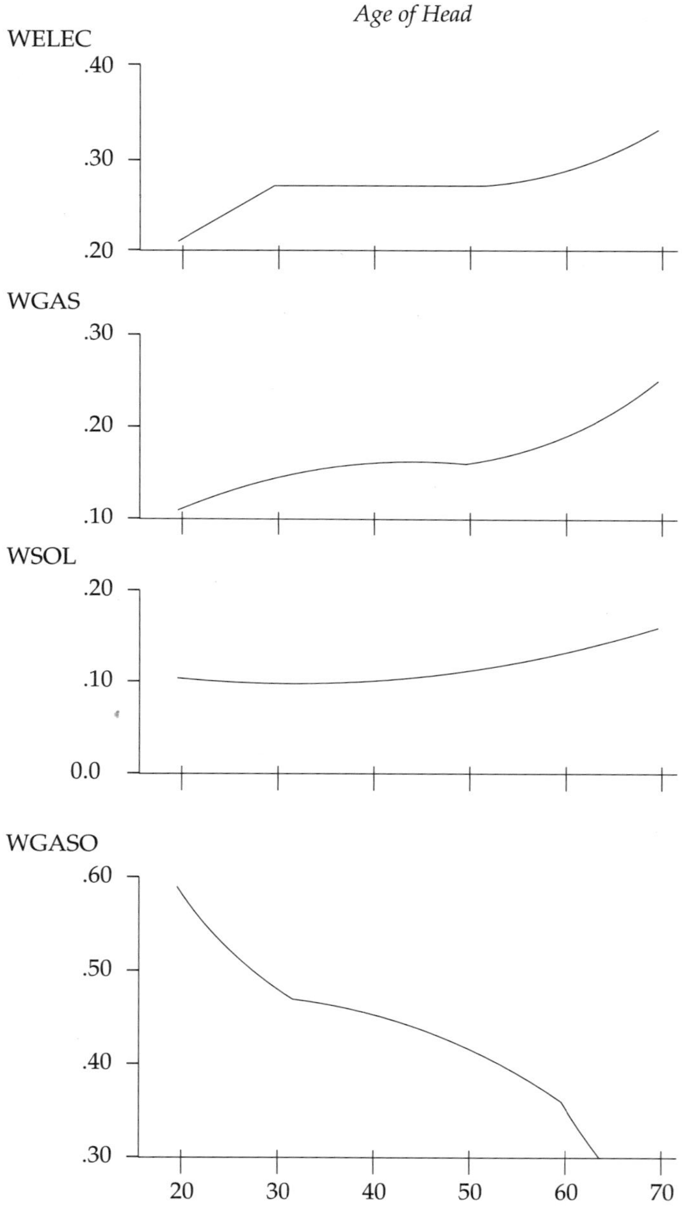

Figure 9.II.3b
Expenditure shares as functions of age of head, 1973 CES.

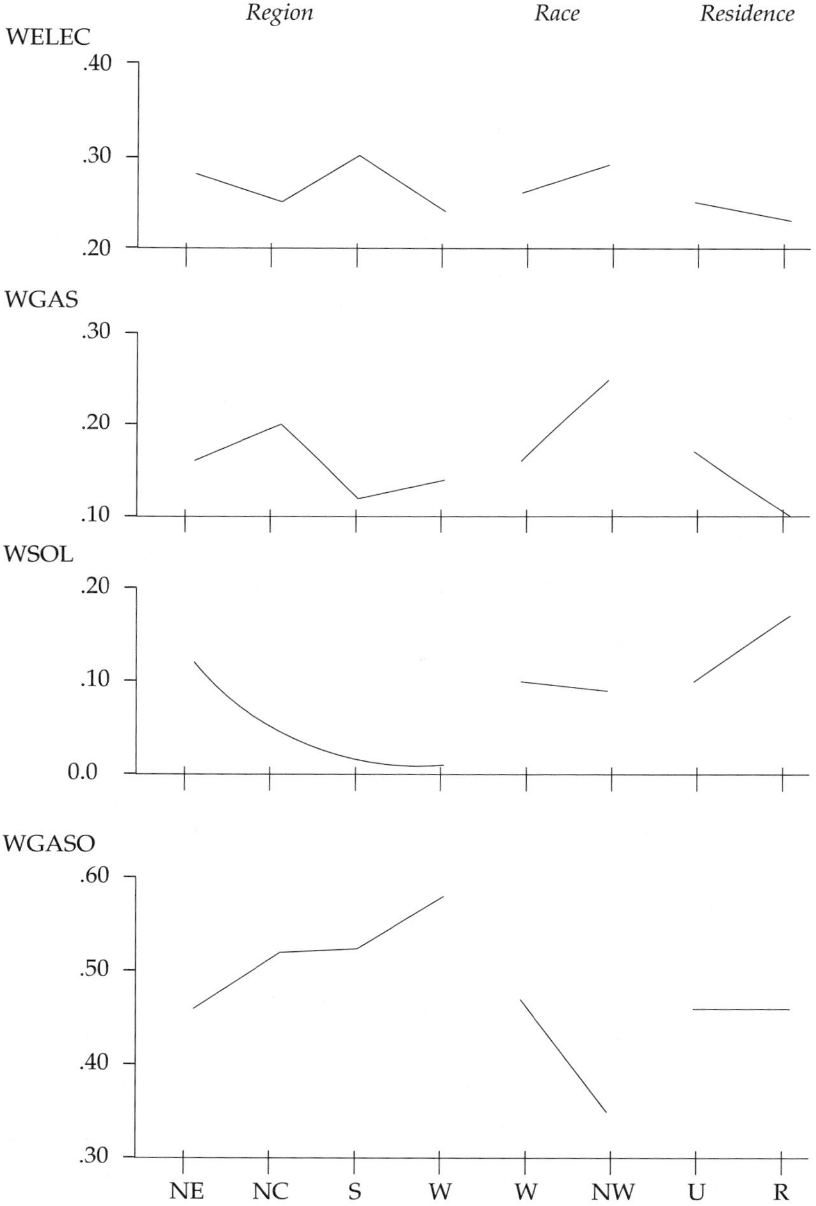

Figure 9.II.3c
Expenditure shares as functions of region, race and type of residence, 1973 CES.

data for natural gas and electricity consumption are obtained from public utility records. The data on gasoline usage are estimated from miles per gallon and mileage driven of all automobiles in the household. Unfortunately, there is no category representing other fuels, and so the fuel oil and other category here consists only of fuel oil consumption.

As with the CES, observations were checked for positive energy expenditure. In addition, ranges were published for electricity, natural gas, and gasoline use, so that observations were checked for data falling within the correct ranges. Unfortunately, after this process was completed, only 576 out of the total 3554 observations had energy data within the published ranges. Summary statistics of this sample are given in table 9.II.5. By comparing this to table 9.II.4, we can observe important differences between the 1973 LHES and the 1973 CES. The major difference in average expenditures on energy components lies in the fuel oil and gasoline categories, where substantially less expenditure is reported in the 1973 LHES.

The average fuel oil expenditure reported in the 1973 LHES is 20% of the value reported in the 1973 CES, whereas the average gasoline expenditure reported in the 1973 LHES is 50% of that of the 1973 CES. For gasoline this may be explainable by problems in the method of measurement in the LHES surveys: gasoline use was estimated from data on miles driven. Fuel oil may be underestimated because of differences in regional coverage. The LHES sample contains relatively more families of the North Central and Western regions and urban residence than did the CES. These families use less fuel oil. However, the differences in regional coverage are clearly not sufficient to explain the full discrepancy in fuel oil use. While family size and racial coverage of the two samples is very similar, the age of head coverage is biased toward older families in the LHES. Overall, the 1973 LHES appears to have a reasonably balanced demographic structure, despite the small sample size.

The results of estimating our model of individual energy expenditures from the 1973 LHES are given in appendix table 9.II.A.4. As an overview of the results we see in table 9.II.A.4 that for the electricity share the family size coefficient for size 3 is estimated precisely, as is the effect of the Southern region and race. Table 9.II.A.4 shows that in the natural gas equation the family size structure is estimated fairly precisely, as is the effect of the Western region and change in race. In table 9.II.A.4 we see that the only precisely estimated effects for the

Table 9.II.5
Summary statistics, 1973 LHES

	Mean	Std. Dev.
ELEC	170.9862	89.6479
GAS	168.7530	95.9404
FUELOIL	10.8808	69.3700
GASOLINE	202.9962	294.4753
EN	553.6162	358.4931
DF2	0.2884	0.4534
DF3	0.1693	0.3753
DF4	0.1900	0.3926
DF5	0.1209	0.3263
DF6	0.0587	0.2353
DF7	0.0449	0.2073
DA30	0.2055	0.4044
DA40	0.1641	0.3707
DA50	0.1883	0.3913
DA60	0.1693	0.3753
DA70	0.2176	0.4130
DRNC	0.3575	0.4797
DRS	0.1693	0.3753
DRW	0.2712	0.4449
DNW	0.1295	0.3361
DRUR	0.1295	0.3361
WELEC	0.3728	0.1859
WGAS	0.3689	0.2000
WFUELL	0.0141	0.0876
WGASO	0.2442	0.2816

fuel oil equation are for very large families (7 or more), the oldest age groups, and all regional differences from the Northeast. Finally, table 9.II.A.4 shows precisely estimated effects on the share of gasoline from smaller family size classes, younger age groups, the North Central and Western regions, and race.

We represent the impact of changes in demographic characteristics on the allocation of energy expenditures in figures 9.II.4a,b,c.

In figure 9.II.4a the estimated shares for differing family sizes are represented. The electricity share is roughly constant, except for substantial drops for family sizes 3 and 7 or more. The natural gas share drops from family size 1 to 2 and then levels off, excepting an increased share for family size 6. Finally, the gasoline share rises from family sizes 1–3, then declines monotonically from sizes 3–6, with a sharp rise from family size 6 to 7 or more. This sharp rise is very difficult to rationalize and appears to be a result of sampling fluctuations associated with the small sample size.

Changing age of head yields an estimated pattern of energy allocation represented in figure 9.II.4b. Changing from the youngest age class (15–24) to the next youngest (24–34) involves large downward changes in the shares of electricity, natural gas, and fuel oil, with a consequent large upward change in the gasoline share. Increasing age further shows roughly increasing trends for electricity, natural gas, and fuel oil and a decreasing trend for gasoline. The 15–24 class as well as the 35–44 class stands out as the anomaly; the remaining effects are roughly in accord with the patterns estimated from the 1973 CES.

The impacts of changing region, race, and type of residence are displayed in figure 9.II.4c. The most important regional effects are the large fuel oil share for the Northeast relative to all other regions, plus the greatly increased share of gasoline for the West relative to the other regions. The race effect is summarized as a shift from gasoline to each other fuel as race changes from white to nonwhite. Finally, there is very little evidence of an urban-rural effect, with the main change involving a shift from electricity to natural gas for rural residents. All of these patterns are consistent with those for the 1973 CES in figure 9.II.3c.

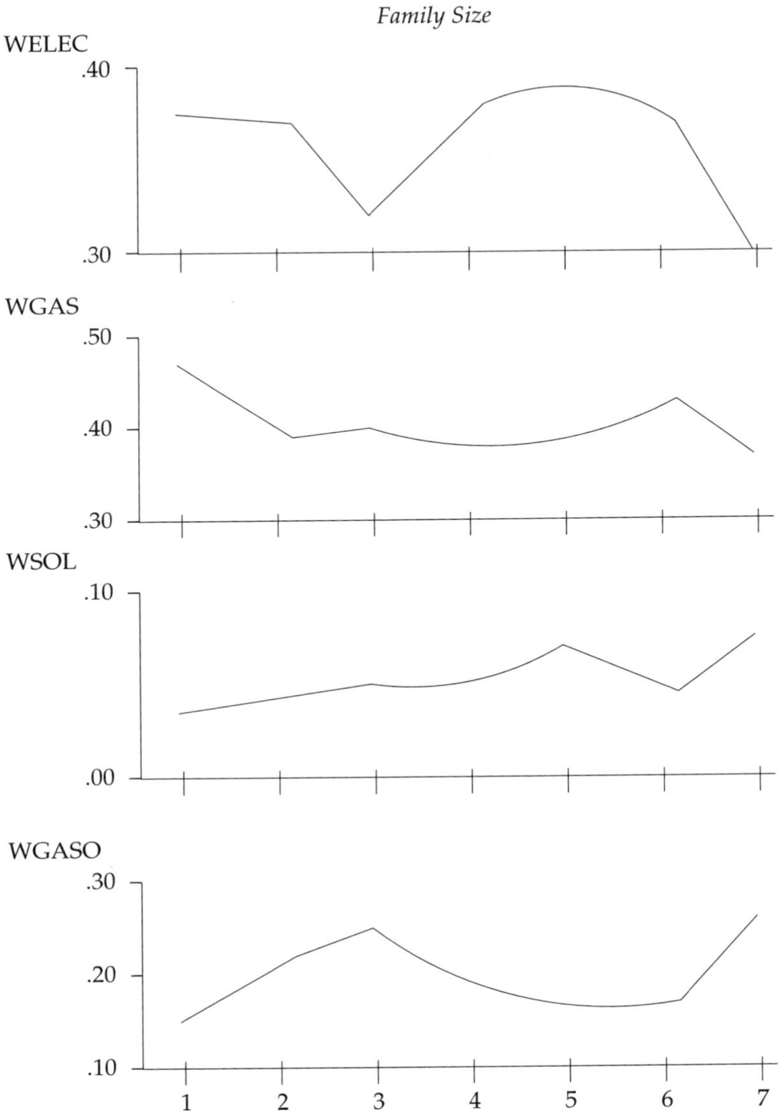

Figure 9.II.4a
Expenditure shares as functions of family size, 1973 LHES.

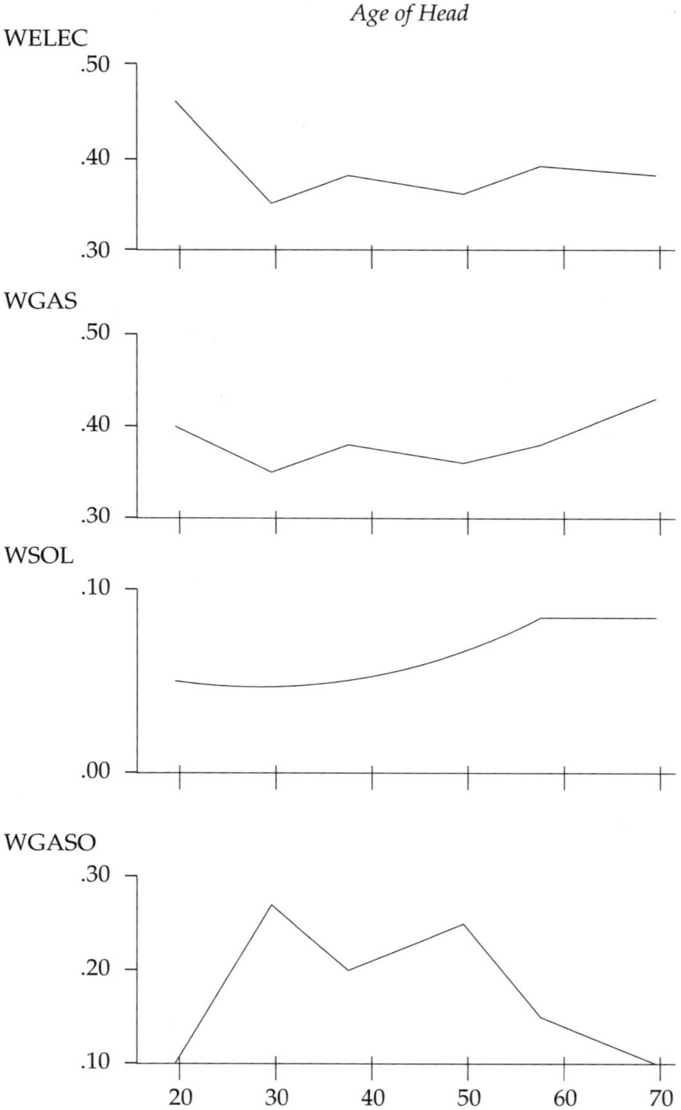

Figure 9.II.4b
Expenditure shares as functions of age of head, 1973 LHES.

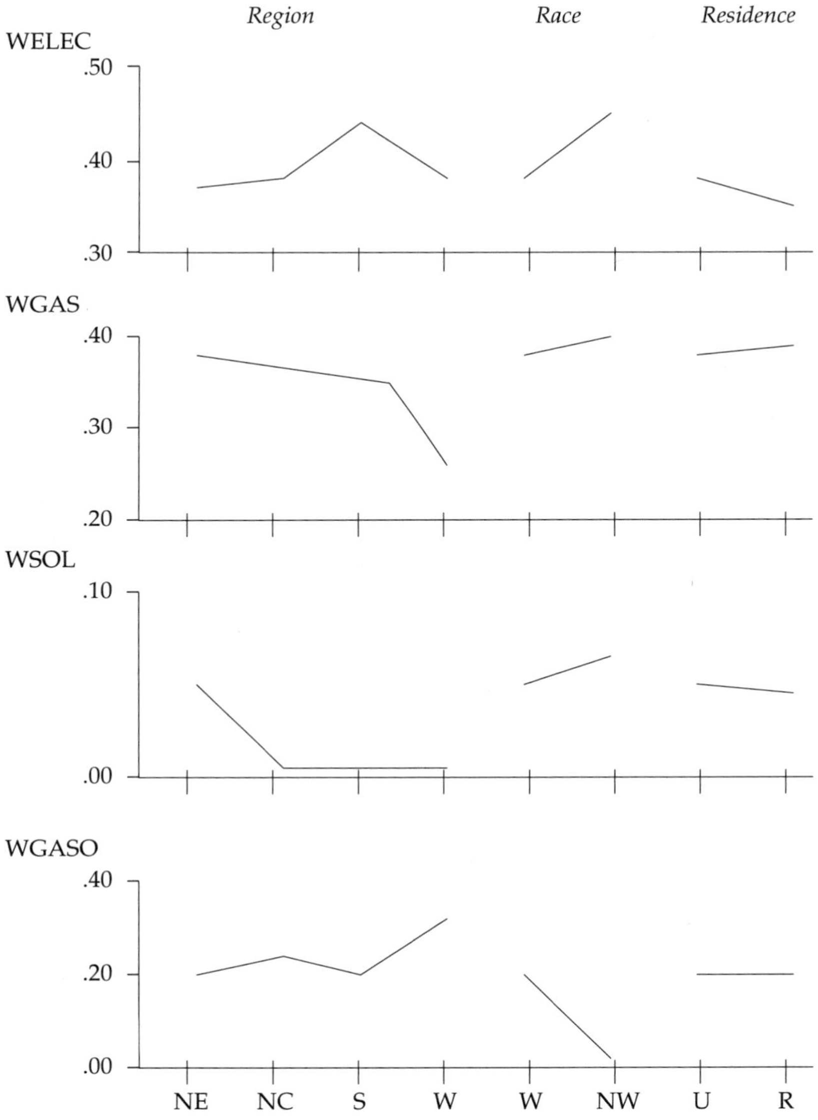

Figure 9.II.4c
Expenditure shares as functions of region, race and type of residence, 1973 LHES.

9.II.6 Lifestyle and Household Energy Use Survey of 1975

The 1975 LHES includes direct observations of expenditures on electricity, natural gas, and fuel oil usage. To construct expenditures on gasoline, data on automobile ownership, miles driven, and miles per gallon per vehicle were utilized. This procedure coincides with the method of construction for gasoline expenditures used in the 1973 LHES. All observations were checked for positive total energy expenditure, as well as for mileage and miles per gallon data. The sample conforming to these requirements consists of 2970 observations, which is much larger than the corresponding sample for the 1973 LHES summary statistics for this sample are presented in table 9.II.6.

The summary statistics indicate a potential underreporting of gasoline and fuel oil usage, as was the case of the 1973 LHES. Although there is no CES survey for 1975 to provide a basis for comparison, the gasoline and fuel oil usage levels for the 1975 LHES are less than those of the 1973 CES given in table 9.II.5. However, if the average usage displayed in table 9.II.6 for the 1973 LHES are compared to those of the 1975 LHES, the results are plausible; there is a substantial increase in gasoline and fuel oil expenditures. This supports the view that the measuring techniques of the LHES surveys result in underreporting in the gasoline and fuel oil categories relative to the CES but that they are consistent between the LHES surveys. These techniques affect only the levels of the shares of gasoline and fuel oil.

Estimates of the model of individual energy expenditures for the 1975 LHES are contained in appendix table 9.II.A.5. As an overview of the estimated effects, we see in table 9.II.A.5 that significant effects are found on the elasticity share for virtually all of the demographic variables, except for age class 25–30 and the urban-rural effect. Table 9.II.A.5 shows significant effects estimated for the natural gas share for all variables except age class 35–44, the Western region, and nonwhite race. In table 9.II.A.5, depicting the estimated coefficients for fuel oil, the only significant effects are those for regional dimensions and race. Finally, in table 9.II.A.5 we see that virtually all demographic effects are quite precisely estimated, excepting only the Southern region variable. Thus, the gains in precision afforded by the increased sample size of the 1975 LHES survey are substantial.

The movements of all shares that result from changing each demographic dimension individually are portrayed in figures 9.II.5a,b,c.

Table 9.II.6
Summary statistics, 1975 LHES

	Mean	Std. Dev.
ELEC	187.5838	188.7610
GAS	94.3788	139.1332
FUELOIL	19.5690	111.4929
GASOLINE	327.7956	212.9359
EN	629.3273	321.2503
DF2	0.3007	0.4586
DF3	0.1761	0.3810
DF4	0.1805	0.3846
DF5	0.0919	0.2890
DF6	0.0441	0.2054
DF7	0.0444	0.2061
DA30	0.2040	0.4031
DA40	0.1616	0.3682
DA50	0.1795	0.3838
DA60	0.1640	0.3703
DA70	0.2148	0.4108
DRNC	0.2687	0.4434
DRS	0.2599	0.4387
DRW	0.2721	0.4451
DNW	0.1919	0.3939
DRUR	0.2993	0.4580
WELEC	0.3074	0.3049
WGAS	0.1448	0.2150
WFUEL	0.0198	0.1119
WGASO	0.5280	0.3735

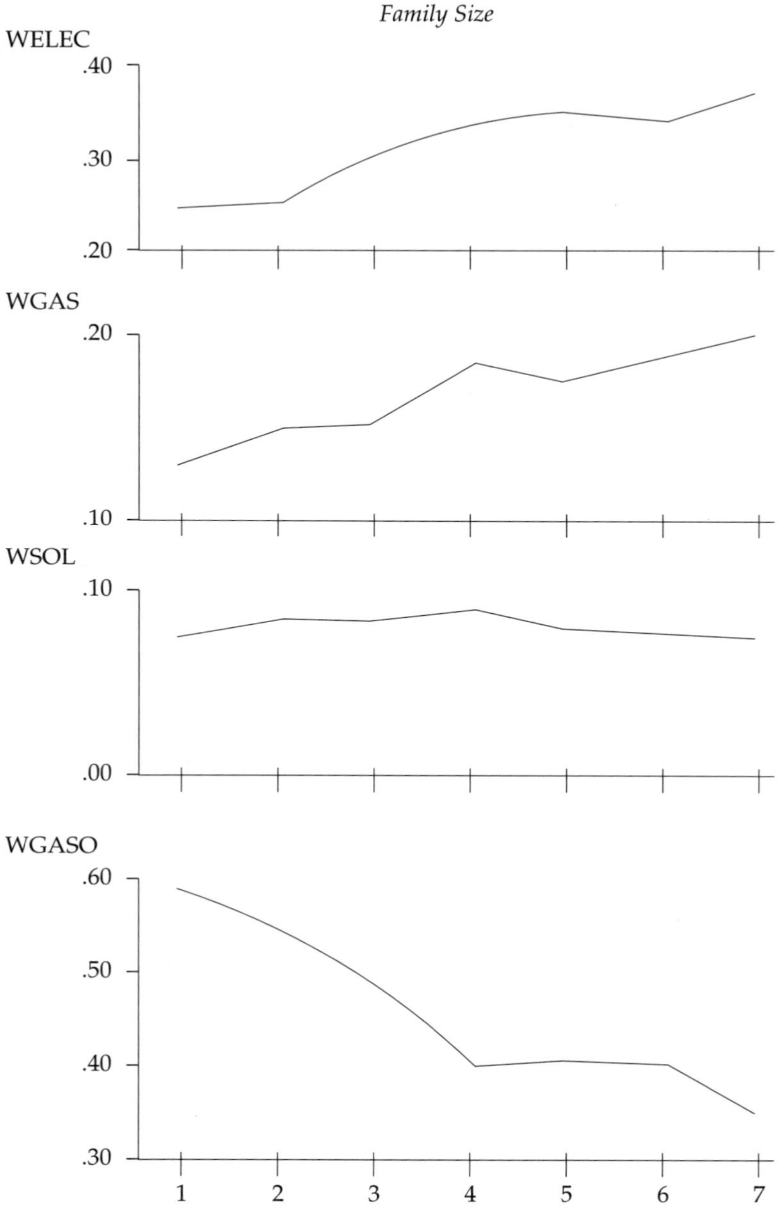

Figure 9.II.5a
Expenditure shares as functions of family size, 1975 LHES.

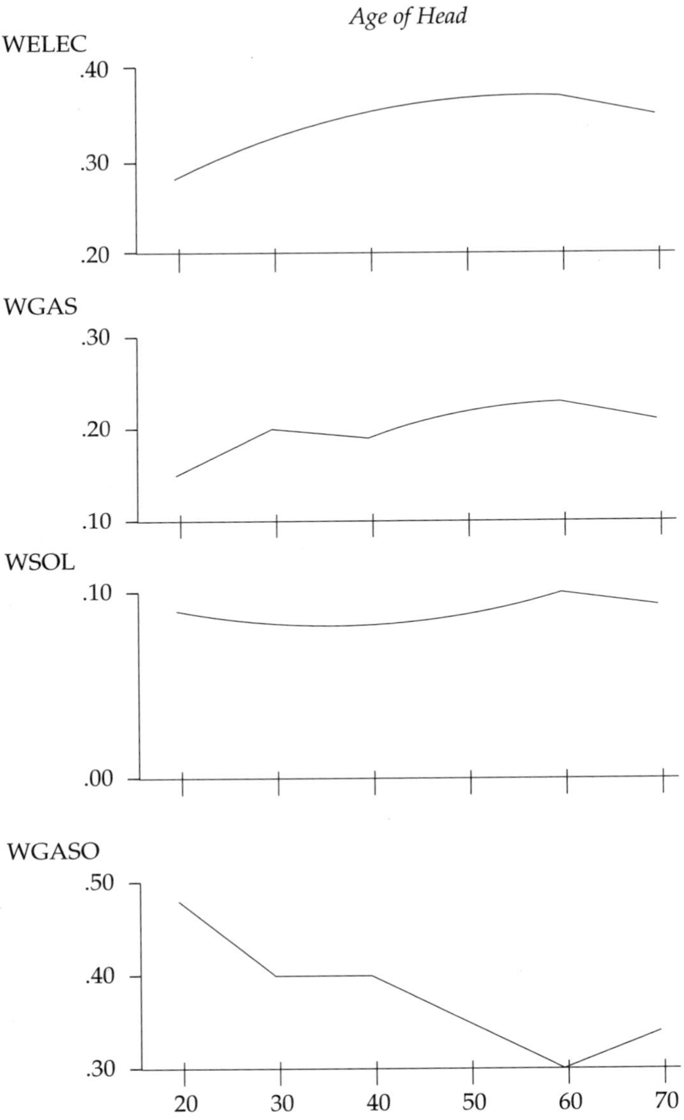

Figure 9.II.5b
Expenditure shares as functions of age of head, 1975 LHES.

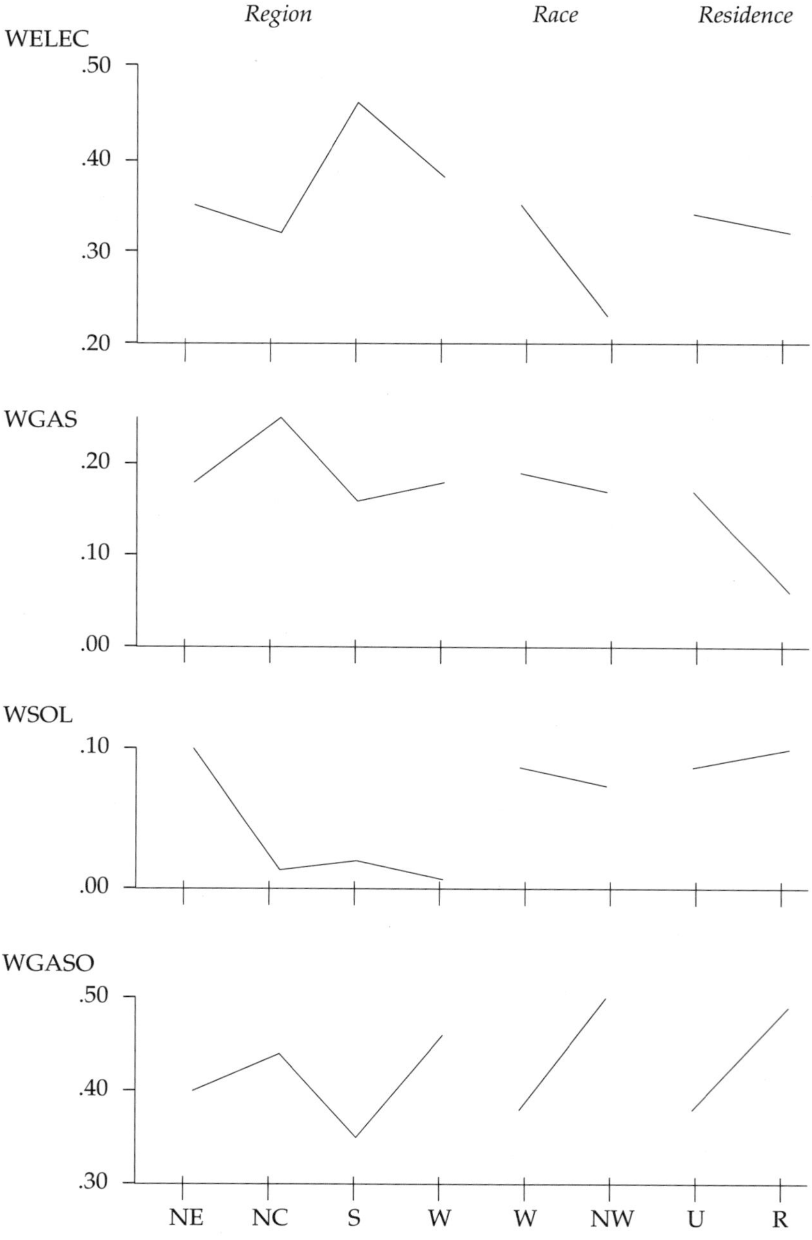

Figure 9.II.5c
Expenditure shares as functions of region, race and type of residence, 1975 LHES.

The impact of changing family size is presented in figure 9.II.5a. Here we see that as family size increases, the shares of electricity and natural gas increase, the share of fuel oil stays roughly constant, and the share devoted to gasoline decreases. Thus it appears that larger families require more heating and lighting and less gasoline relative to smaller families. These effects are much stronger in the 1975 LHES than in any of the other surveys.

The impact of changing age of head is represented in figure 9.II.5b. As age of head increases we see a general increase in the shares of electricity, natural gas, and fuel oil, with a decrease in the share of gasoline. Except for a slight reversal of this trend for the oldest age group, this is precisely the trend indicated in the CES surveys. The trend is more pronounced in the 1975 LHES.

The impact of changing region, race, and type of residence are portrayed in figure 9.II.5c. With the exception of a smaller gasoline share for the South and a consequent increase in the share devoted to electricity, the regional impacts are analogous to the regional patterns found in the CES surveys, with the major effects found as a shift away from fuel oil for all regions other than Northeast and an increased share of gasoline for the West.

To this point, all demographic patterns evident in the 1975 LHES are similar to those of the earlier surveys. This is not the case with the race and type of residence effects. In figure 9.II.5c we see a substantial increase in the share of gasoline as race changes from white to nonwhite or as type of residence changes from urban to rural. This can be contrasted with the effects estimated from other surveys.

9.II.7 Summary and Conclusion

To conclude this chapter we can compare the results from all the three CES data bases. Each of the data bases is fairly well balanced in terms of differing demographic characteristics. The regression results from each can be considered to be representative of the underlying structure of energy expenditures. Our model of individual consumer behavior implies that effects should be the same in each of the data bases. Therefore, similarity among the estimation results should be taken as support for the model, while dissimilarities indicate violations of the underlying assumptions. In the 1960/61 CES, data on natural gas and electricity consumption are combined. Therefore, the gas and electricity expenditure shares in figures 9.II.1a,b,c are comparable to vertical sums of the electricity and natural gas shares of figures 9.II.2a,b,c and 9.II.3a,b,c. The share of fuel oil and other and the share of gasoline are directly comparable.

Figures 9.II.1a,b,c, 9.II.2a,b,c, and 9.II.3a,b,c show qualitatively that the impacts of demographic characteristics on energy use are virtually identical. The only exception is the increased use of fuel oil and other by nonwhites shown for 1960/61 but absent for 1972 and 1973. Also, the decreased use of gasoline by rural families in 1972 conflicts with the finding of no effect in 1960/61 and 1973. Overall, the similarities are striking. Viewing figures 9.II.1a,b,c, 9.II.2a,b,c, and 9.II.3a,b,c more quantitatively, we see two differences between 1960/61 and 1972 and 1973. First, differences in levels of the expenditure shares are in complete accordance with the model, when we recall that the constant terms are functions of prices, which are constant for any single data base, but vary over time with varying prices. The other difference is that the actual movements of fitted shares in the 1960/61 CES in figures 9.II.1a,b,c are slightly larger in magnitude than those from the 1972 and 1973 CES. This is not consistent with the theoretical model. Overall, there are realtively few differences among the patterns of demographic variations. We therefore consider the model validated; further, the three CES bases are completely compatible for pooling under the translog model of energy expenditures.

Two substantive differences between the CES and LHES survey results are apparent. First, a substantial difference between the average gasoline and fuel oil usage is reported in the two sets of surveys; a direct comparison is possible between the 1973 CES and 1973 LHES surveys. As we have seen above, the demographic patterns indicated by these surveys are similar, which indicates that the major impact of the difference is in the average levels of the expenditure shares between the two sets of surveys. The differences in levels can be attributed to important differences in the procedures for measuring gasoline and fuel oil consumption. In order that the differences in procedures not affect the final pooled estimation process in the following chapter, we utilize mean-centered moments in the pooled estimates; these moments are unaffected by differences in the levels of the expenditure shares.

We have found that the race and type residence effects are reversed in the 1975 LHES results, relative to all other surveys. This indicates a structural change in the values of the nonwhite and rural effects between 1973 and 1975. Given the timing of the LHES surveys around the 1973/74 Arab oil embargo, it is possible that structural change has taken place in the underlying model. Therefore, when pooling the average time-series data and the CES and LHES survey results, we explicitly model structural change in the coefficients of nonwhite and rural variables.

Appendix

Table 9.II.A.1
Cross-section results, 1960/61 CES

	WELEC	WSOL	WGASO
C	−.43581(.01432)	−.12775(.01053)	−.43643(.01385)
F2	.08039(.00819)	.01140(.00602)	−.09179(.00792)
F3	.09181(.00912)	.00659(.00671)	−.09840(.00882)
F4	.07949(.00960)	.00171(.00706)	−.08119(.00928)
F5	.06272(.01060)	−.00451(.00779)	−.05821(.01025)
F6	.05393(.01248)	−.01907(.00918)	−.03486(.01207)
F7	.04165(.01277)	−.02044(.00939)	−.02121(.01235)
A30	−.03803(.01314)	−.03890(.00967)	.07693(.01271)
A40	−.06933(.01298)	−.05078(.00955)	.12011(.01256)
A50	−.07133(.01289)	−.06493(.00948)	.13626(.01247)
A60	−.11294(.01322)	−.07671(.00972)	.18965(.01279)
A70	−.20500(.01333)	−.13050(.00980)	.33550(.01290)
RNC	−.02024(.00670)	.07965(.00493)	−.05941(.00648)
RS	−.04159(.00685)	.12846(.00503)	−.08687(.00662)
RW	.00898(.00780)	.12922(.00574)	−.13821(.00755)
NW	−.04139(.00787)	−.05942(.00579)	.10080(.00761)
RUR	.08603(.00542)	−.08608(.00399)	.00005(.00525)
SSR	983.7	532.0	920.5

Table 9.II.A.2
Cross-section results, 1972 CES

	WELEC	WGAS	WSOL	WGASO
C	−.20764(.00859)	−.12060(.00805)	−.09644(.00670)	−.57533(.01145)
F2	.02500(.00566)	.01554(.00529)	−.00100(.00441)	−.03953(.00753)
F3	.02387(.00671)	−.00089(.00628)	−.00081(.00523)	−.02217(.00894)
F4	.02412(.00736)	−.00682(.00689)	−.00685(.00574)	−.01045(.00981)
F5	.01169(.00862)	.00041(.00807)	−.01791(.00672)	.00581(.01148)
F6	.02371(.01063)	.00523(.00996)	−.02520(.00829)	−.00375(.01417)
F7	.02091(.01124)	−.00564(.01052)	−.01894(.00876)	.00367(.01497)
A30	−.05865(.00847)	−.03079(.00793)	−.00217(.00660)	.09160(.01128)
A40	−.07696(.00906)	−.04861(.00848)	−.01059(.00706)	.13616(.01206)
A50	−.05782(.00853)	−.04515(.00799)	−.01966(.00665)	.12263(.01137)
A60	−.07727(.00854)	−.07644(.00799)	−.03677(.00666)	.19048(.01137)
A70	−.13217(.00823)	−.14137(.00770)	−.07141(.00641)	.34494(.01096)
RNC	.01406(.00576)	−.04696(.00539)	.08022(.00449)	.04733(.00767)
RS	−.04034(.00572)	.04199(.00536)	.08514(.00446)	−.08679(.00762)
RW	−.00033(.00623)	.02237(.00583)	.09584(.00486)	−.11789(.00830)
NW	−.03344(.00716)	−.08944(.00670)	.00276(.00558)	.12012(.00953)
RUR	.00276(.00547)	.04051(.00513)	−.06454(.00427)	.02128(.00729)
SSR	312.9	274.2	190.2	555.2

Table 9.II.A.3
Cross-section results, 1973 CES

	WELEC	WGAS	WSOL	WGASO
C	−.22681(.00859)	−.11517(.00780)	−.08766(.00632)	−.57035(.01121)
F2	.02333(.00573)	.01981(.00521)	.00163(.00422)	−.04477(.00748)
F3	.03293(.00687)	.01224(.00624)	−.00835(.00505)	−.03683(.00896)
F4	.02013(.00724)	.00335(.00657)	−.00712(.00532)	−.01635(.00945)
F5	.01088(.00872)	−.00301(.00792)	−.01493(.00641)	.00706(.01138)
F6	.02728(.01104)	−.00603(.01003)	−.02198(.00812)	.00073(.01441)
F7	.01606(.01163)	−.00227(.01057)	−.02631(.00856)	.01253(.01518)
A30	−.05075(.00837)	−.03291(.00761)	−.00901(.00616)	.09268(.01093)
A40	−.05200(.00911)	−.05246(.00827)	−.01566(.00670)	.12012(.01188)
A50	−.05255(.00862)	−.05636(.00783)	−.02585(.00634)	.13476(.01125)
A60	−.06812(.00860)	−.08028(.00781)	−.04333(.00633)	.19173(.01123)
A70	−.12862(.00838)	−.14440(.00761)	−.07639(.00616)	.34942(.01094)
RNC	.01939(.00592)	−.03489(.00537)	.08218(.00435)	−.06668(.00772)
RS	−.03894(.00588)	.03625(.00534)	.09002(.00433)	−.08733(.00768)
RW	.02237(.00635)	.02289(.00576)	.08808(.00467)	−.13334(.00828)
NW	−.03124(.00690)	−.09974(.00626)	.00707(.00507)	.12390(.00900)
RUR	.01947(.00558)	.05388(.00506)	−.06883(.00410)	−.00452(.00728)
SSR	327.2	270.0	177.0	557.2

Table 9.II.A.4
Cross-section results, 1973 LHES

	WELEC	WGAS	WSOL	WGASO
C	−.45972(.04107)	−.49333(.04275)	−.02083(.01898)	−.02613(.05931)
F2	.00506(.02587)	.08711(.02693)	−.01275(.01196)	−.07942(.03737)
F3	.06268(.02977)	.07503(.03099)	−.01865(.01376)	−.11905(.04299)
F4	.00018(.03106)	.08910(.03233)	−.02228(.01436)	−.06699(.04486)
F5	.00010(.03438)	.07782(.03579)	−.03167(.01589)	−.04625(.04966)
F6	.01119(.04148)	.04864(.04318)	−.01656(.01917)	−.04326(.05990)
F7	.06922(.04432)	.09820(.04614)	−.04257(.02049)	−.12485(.06401)
A30	.11300(.03766)	.05325(.03920)	−.00262(.01741)	−.16363(.05439)
A40	.08571(.03971)	.02929(.04133)	−.00824(.01835)	−.10676(.05735)
A50	.10605(.03721)	.05371(.03873)	−.01733(.01720)	−.14243(.05373)
A60	.07596(.03758)	.01315(.03912)	−.04060(.01737)	−.04851(.05427)
A70	.09068(.03753)	−.04004(.03906)	−.03642(.01735)	−.01423(.05420)
RNC	−.00384(.02130)	.02337(.02217)	.05678(.00985)	−.07630(.03076)
RS	−.06156(.02618)	.03263(.02725)	.05789(.01210)	−.02896(.03780)
RW	−.00292(.02262)	.11672(.02355)	.05952(.01046)	−.17332(.03267)
NW	−.07694(.02340)	−.06429(.02435)	−.01613(.01081)	.15736(.03379)
RUR	.02885(.02406)	−.02748(.02504)	.00267(.01112)	−.00404(.03474)
SSR	18.6	20.2	4.0	38.9

Table 9.II.A.5
Cross-section results, 1973 LHES

	WELEC	WGAS	WSOL	WGASO
C	−.16873(.02674)	−.08674(.01857)	−.06865(.00975)	−.67588(.03270)
F2	−.04223(.01688)	−.02343(.01172)	−.00598(.00615)	.07165(.02064)
F3	−.07776(.01997)	−.02804(.01386)	−.00601(.00728)	.11182(.02442)
F4	−.11108(.02080)	−.06035(.01444)	−.02058(.00758)	.19201(.02544)
F5	−.12001(.02442)	−.05455(.01696)	−.01317(.00890)	.18773(.02986)
F6	−.09799(.03087)	−.07421(.02143)	−.01306(.01125)	.18526(.03775)
F7	−.12895(.03072)	−.09766(.02133)	−.00707(.01120)	.23367(.03757)
A30	−.04477(.02347)	−.04427(.01629)	.00537(.00855)	.08368(.02870)
A40	−.06035(.02498)	−.03074(.01734)	−.00174(.00911)	.09283(.03054)
A50	−.07393(.02372)	−.06192(.01647)	−.01383(.00865)	.14967(.02900)
A60	−.07876(.02374)	−.07528(.01649)	−.01894(.00866)	.17298(.02903)
A70	−.07399(.02338)	−.06925(.01623)	−.00817(.00852)	.15141(.02858)
RNC	.03069(.01603)	−.06516(.01113)	.08292(.00584)	−.04845(.01960)
RS	−.13444(.01678)	.02772(.01165)	.07245(.00612)	.03427(.02052)
RW	−.02717(.01612)	.01374(.01119)	.08009(.00588)	−.06666(.01972)
NW	.10473(.01421)	.01763(.00986)	.01354(.00518)	−.13590(.01737)
RUR	.01260(.01267)	.11020(.00880)	−.00492(.00462)	−.11787(.01549)
SSR	254.2	122.5	33.8	380.0

9.III Aggregate Energy Expenditures

9.III.1 Introduction

In the preceding sections, we have estimated the parameters of our econometric model of aggregate energy expenditures that can be identified from cross-section data alone. For this purpose we have utilized five sets of cross-section observations on individual energy expenditure patterns—the 1960/61, 1972, and 1973 Consumer Expenditure Surveys (CES) of the U.S. Bureau of Labor Statistics (BLS) and the 1973 and 1975 Lifestyle and Household Energy Use Surveys (LHES) of the Washington Center for Metropolitan Studies (WCMS). In the present section we estimate all the parameters of our econometric model by pooling the individual cross-section data employed in the foregoing section with aggregate time-series data. For this purpose we utilize annual data on prices and aggregate quantities consumed of four types of energy—electricity, natural gas, fuel oil and other, and gasoline—from the U.S. National Income and Product Accounts for the period 1958 to 1978.

A key feature of our econometric model of aggregate energy expenditures is the incorporation of the distribution of energy expenditures among demographic groups into the determination of the allocation of aggregate energy expenditure among types of energy. In the preceding section we have given a detailed description of the distribution of energy expenditures among demographic groups for 1960/61, 1972, 1973 and 1975, the years of our cross-section surveys. Annual time-series data for the statistics that describe the distribution of energy expenditures among groups are constructed on the basis of the methodology developed by Stoker (1979). This methodology utilizes a detailed tabulation of before-tax income for all years from *Current Population Reports, Series P-60, Consumer Income*,[10] and a bridging equation estimated from cross-section data on energy expenditures.[11] This results in an annual time series of proportions of aggregate energy expenditure for all demographic groups. The instrumental variables used in our estimation procedure are given in appendix table 9.III.A.1.

The translog model of aggregate energy expenditures requires variables that depend on the joint distribution of individual attributes and expenditures

$$\frac{\sum_{k=1}^{K} E_{kt}\, A_k}{\sum_{k=1}^{K} E_{kt}}\,, \qquad (t = 1, 2, \ldots, T)\,. \tag{9.III.1}$$

Second, we require the heteroscedasticity correction ρ_t of section 9.I, which takes the form

$$\rho_t = \frac{\left(\sum_{k=1}^{K} E_{kt}\right)^2}{\sum_{k=1}^{K} E_{kt}^2} = \sqrt{K}\, \exp\left(-1/2\, \sigma_E^2\right)\,, \qquad (t = 1, 2, \ldots, T)\,, \tag{9.III.2}$$

where the logarithm of energy expenditure E has a normal distribution with mean μ_E and variance σ_E^2. Together with the time series of prices and aggregate energy expenditure shares for each type of energy, the variables (9.III.1) and (9.III.2) form a complete set of aggregate data for the translog model for the period 1958–1978.

The translog model of aggregate energy expenditures, corrected for heteroscedasticity, is

$$-\rho_t v_t = \gamma_q \rho_t + \Delta_{qq} \rho_t \ln q_t + \Delta_{qA} \rho_t \frac{\sum_{k=1}^{K} E_{kt}\, A_k}{\sum_{k=1}^{K} E_{kt}} + \rho_t \varepsilon_t\,, \qquad (t = 1, 2, \ldots, T)\,, \tag{9.III.3}$$

where the unobservable random disturbance $\rho_t \varepsilon_t$ is normally distributed with mean zero and covariance matrix Ω_v; we assume that this disturbance is uncorrelated over time. In our application we have four types of energy, so that we estimate the parameters of three equations. The parameters of the remaining equation are estimated from the restrictions implied by summability of the system of individual demand functions. As unknown parameters we have three elements of the vector γ_q, sixteen attribute coefficients for each of the three equations in the matrix Δ_{qA}, and six price coefficients in the matrix Δ_{qq}, which is symmetric, for a total of 57 unknown parameters. Not all of these parameters can be identified from time-series data alone. We present the results of pooling the time-series data with data from all five cross-section data set in table 9.III.1.

9.III.2 Pooled Estimation Results

The main results of estimating our econometric model of aggregate energy expenditures are presented in table 9.III.1. The results employ aggregate time-series data and cross-section data from five surveys:

Table 9.III.1
Pooled estimation results: Five cross-section data sets[a]

	WELEC	WGAS	WSOL	WGASO
C	−.19408(.00613)	−.05933(.00548)	−.17494(.00497)	−.57164(.00783)
P_{ELEC}	.19525(.0247)	−.07742(.0154)	−.11574(.0129)	−.00235(.0215)
P_{GAS}	−.07742(.0154)	.03816(.0194)	.04478(.0100)	−.00552(.0151)
P_{SOL}	−.11547(.0129)	.04478(.0100)	.09950(.0176)	−.02881(.0116)
P_{GASO}	−.00235(.0215)	−.00552(.0151)	−.02881(.0116)	.03669(.0221)
F2	.00875(.00385)	.01164(.00346)	.00578(.00264)	−.02617(.00505)
F3	.01695(.00458)	.00615(.00412)	−.01074(.00313)	−.01236(.00600)
F4	.00506(.00491)	−.00067(.00440)	−.00272(.00333)	−.00166(.00643)
F5	.00102(.00582)	−.00949(.00522)	−.01294(.00393)	.02142(.00762)
F6	.02728(.00727)	.00186(.00654)	−.02758(.00493)	−.00156(.00953)
F7	.01838(.00765)	.01886(.00686)	−.03629(.00515)	−.00095(.0100)
A30	−.04510(.00568)	−.03069(.00510)	−.01483(.00386)	.09062(.00744)
A40	−.03043(.00611)	−.05132(.00548)	−.02067(.00414)	.10242(.00800)
A50	−.03483(.00578)	−.04415(.00518)	−.03410(.00392)	.11308(.00756)
A60	−.02949(.00577)	−.05081(.00518)	−.05428(.00391)	.13457(.00756)
A70	−.06154(.00560)	−.08582(.00502)	−.10288(.00381)	.25023(.00733)
RNC	.00837(.00391)	−.07277(.00351)	.09628(.00264)	−.03188(.00512)
RS	−.04519(.00392)	−.03384(.00352)	.11666(.00268)	−.03763(.00513)
RW	.00613(.00419)	−.05045(.00374)	.10529(.00278)	−.06097(.00547)
NW	−.01645(.00456)	−.08812(.00401)	.00493(.00289)	.09965(.00594)
RUR	.01297(.00367)	.11150(.00325)	−.11128(.00240)	−.01318(.00478)

[a] Convergence after three iterations. SSR = 8537.79.

1960/61 CES, 1972 CES, 1973 CES, 1973 LHES, and 1975 LHES. The estimates were obtained by fitting the equations for electricity, natural gas and fuel oil, with the coefficients for the gasoline equation derived from the summability restrictions.

As an overview of the results, we see that most coefficients are estimated precisely. Utilizing a one percent normal critical value for ratios of each coefficient to its standard error, we see that all price coefficients are significant except for the coefficients of the price of gasoline, and the own-price coefficient of natural gas. This leads us to suspect that gasoline and the other types of energy are separable; we perform a formal test of this hypothesis in section 9.III.4.

Turning to the demographic coefficients, we see that all are significant except for the following: family sizes 2, 4, 5, North Central and

Western regions, in the electricity equation; family sizes 3 through 7 or more in the natural gas equation; family sizes 2 and 4 and nonwhite in the fuel oil equation; and family sizes 4, 6 and 7 or more in the gasoline equation. The insignificance of these coefficients poses no problem for our model, since they indicate no difference in families of these types from a family of size one, age of head 15–24, region Northeast, race white and residence urban. For all the demographic coefficients the standard errors are quite small, so that an insignificant coefficient can be interpreted as a precisely estimated small effect.

In order to interpret the estimated values of the demographic parameters, we have plotted the fitted expenditure shares for changing demographic effects in figures 9.III.1a,b,c. Each figure is constructed by varying the relevant demographic characteristic while holding the other characteristics constant at family size 4, age of head 35–44, region Northeast, race white and type of residence urban. The choice of the attributes held constant is not critical. Only the levels of each graph would be affected by a change in the attributes held constant, while the shape of the graphs would remain the same.

Considering family size first, we see that the relative share of electricity in the energy budget is nearly the same for small and moderate-size families with a slight decline in the share of electricity for large families. Natural gas displays roughly the same pattern, again with a slight decline in the intensity of use for larger families. The use of fuel oil and other energy sources is greater on average for larger families, with no other substantial effects. Finally, we see that relative gasoline usage increases from family size one to two, and declines thereafter, with the graph flattening out and slightly reversing slope for the largest families. The interpretation of these effects is that heating fuel usage is relatively unaffected by family size, holding age of head constant, but the change in size from 1 to 2 in general involves more gasoline usage, since the second family member, a spouse, is likely to be an additional driver. The decline in *relative* gasoline usage for family sizes greater than two is due to those additional family members being children, who are less intensive users of gasoline.

Changing the age of head variable yields patterns of energy expenditure shares as represented in figure 9.III.1b. The general pattern is a moderate increase in the relative use of heating fuels, with the strongest gain registered for fuel oil and other. Accompanying this is a strong decline in gasoline usage from age classes 15–24 to 25–34, followed by a uniform decline from age classes 25–34 to 55–64. Finally a

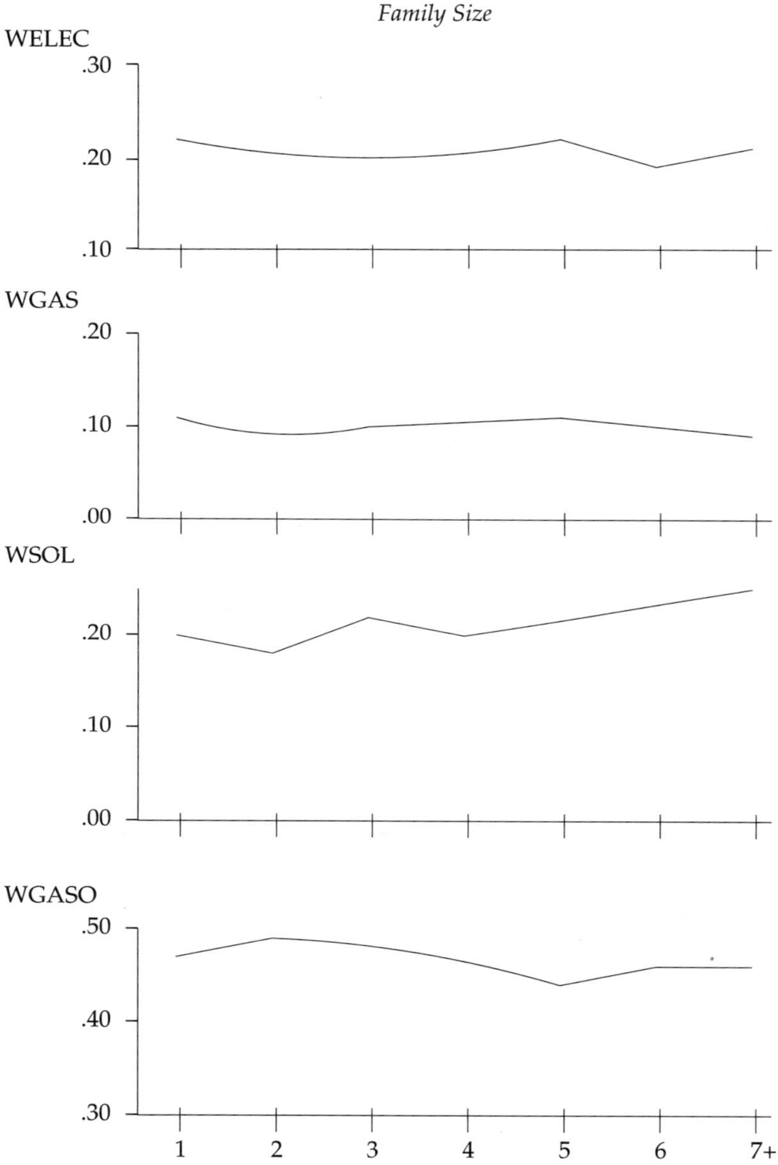

Figure 9.III.1a
Expenditure shares as functions of family size: Five cross-section data sets.

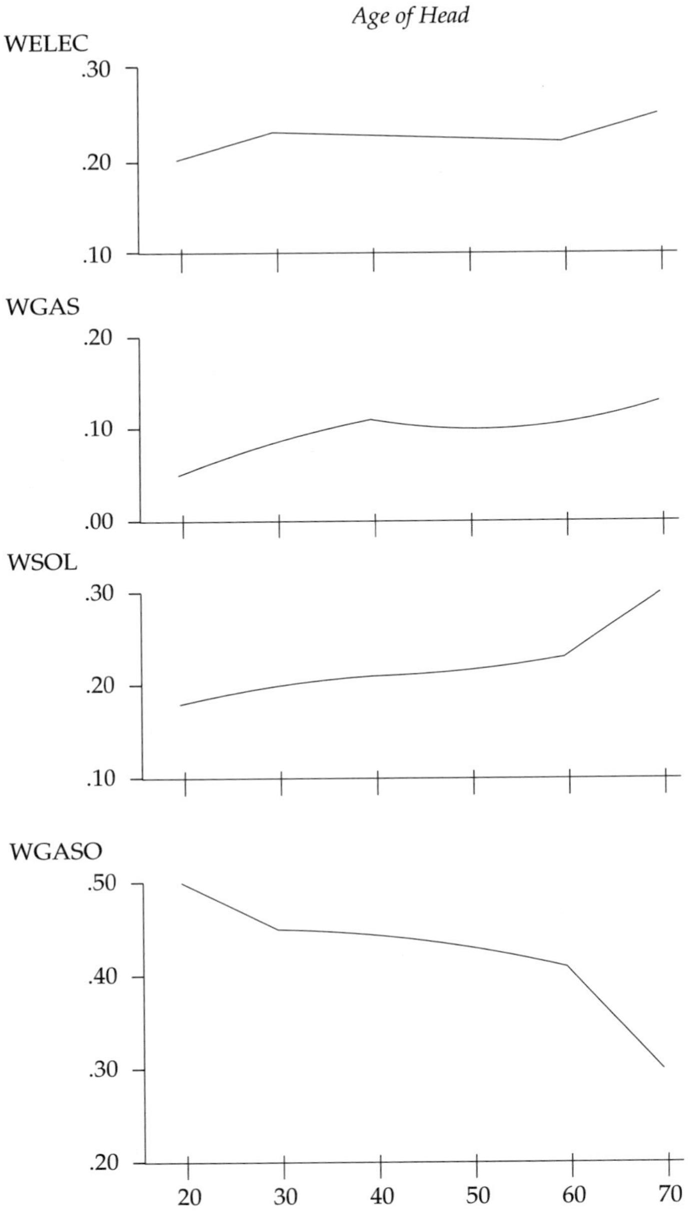

Figure 9.III.1b
Expenditure shares as functions of age of head: Five cross-section data sets.

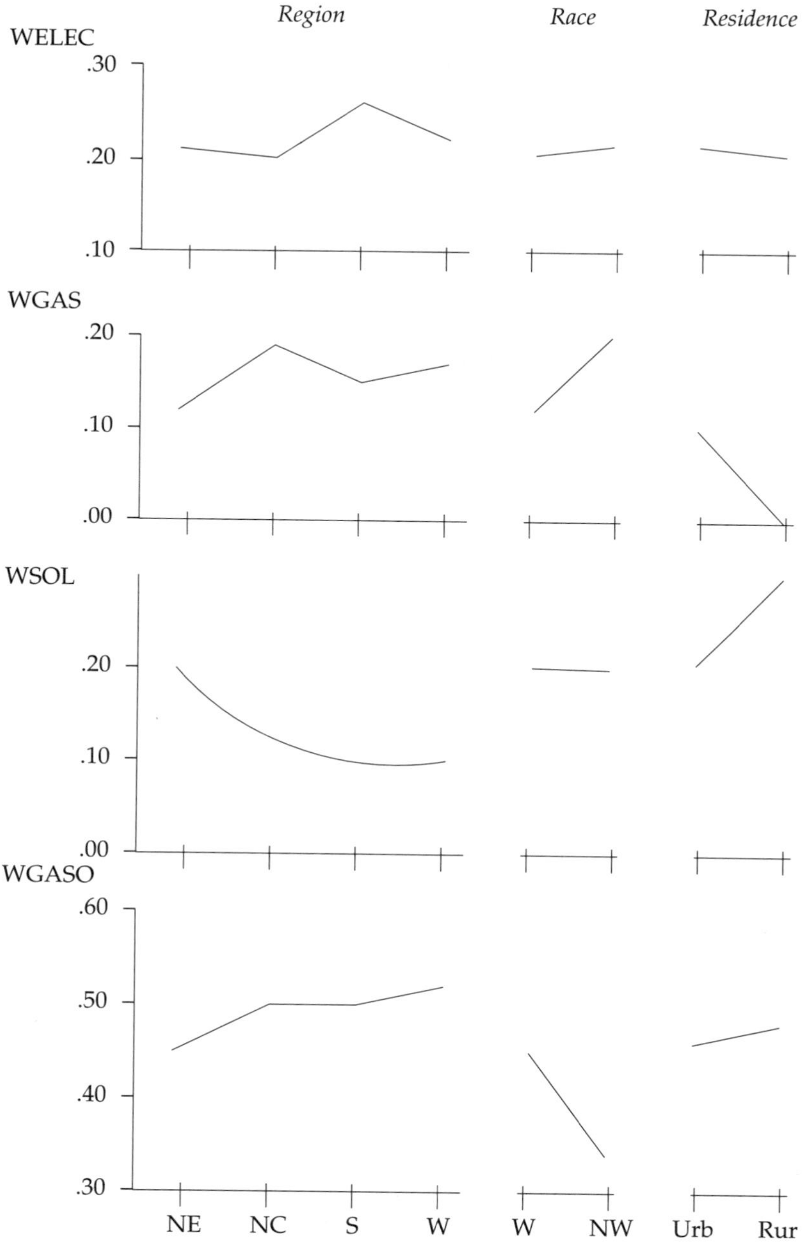

Figure 9.III.1c
Expenditure shares as functions of region, race and type of residence: Five cross-section data sets.

substantial drop for the oldest age group represents the effect of older homes, where fuel oil is more likely the dominant heating fuel.

The regional impacts of figure 9.III.1c reflect the regional housing structure. In the Northeast there is a greater number of houses using fuel oil. Since heating requirements are substantial, a relatively smaller amount of gasoline is consumed. The North Central housing structure is similar, only with natural gas as the dominant heating fuel. The greater use of electricity by Southern homes reflects cooling needs. Finally, the West is characterized by moderately heavy use of gasoline, indicating relatively more energy use for automobiles than for heating or cooling.

The major race effect indicates a shift away from gasoline to natural gas for nonwhites. It is possible that nonwhite families own fewer automobiles, and thus use relatively more fuel for household operation. Finally, the only effect perceptible in changing from urban to rural residence is the increased usage of fuel oil and other relative to natural gas. Rural communities are likely to be characterized by older homes, utilizing fuel oil or by a heavier reliance on alternative fuels such as coal or wood.

The price effects implied by the estimates in table 9.III.1 are most easily interpreted in elasticity form. Since preferences vary with the demographic structure of the individual consuming unit, there are different price elasticities for each type of family. A complete display of all own- and cross-price elasticities for a given price vector would require elasticities for each of the 672 different types of families. As this would be quite cumbersome and difficult to assimilate, we present the own-price elasticities in the same format as the figures representing demographic effects. In table 9.III.2 we present own-price elasticities for all four energy types, while varying each demographic dimension individually with prices held at 1972 values.

A word of caution is required in reading these tables. A quick perusal indicates that all of our estimated own-price elasticities are greater than one in absolute value. In interpreting these values, one must bear in mind that they represent elasticities of each energy type, holding total energy expenditure constant but not fixing total expenditure on energy and nonenergy commodities. For example, the effect of an increase in the price of electricity on a given family's electricity consumption will reflect only substitution among energy types. In addition, electricity consumption will be effected by substitution among energy and nonenergy commodities.

Table 9.III.2
Estimated price elasticities, 1972

	A. Family size						
	1	2	3	4	5	6	7+
ELEC	−1.869633	−1.904912	−1.940665	−1.889669	−1.873597	−1.989919	−1.947184
GAS	−1.344908	−1.385455	−1.365207	−1.342846	−1.317651	−1.350807	−1.415780
SOL	−1.508691	−1.524186	−1.482221	−1.501704	−1.477117	−1.445825	−1.429082
GASO	−1.508691	−1.524186	−1.482221	−1.501704	−1.477117	−1.445825	−1.429082

	B. Age of head					
	16–24	25–34	35–44	45–54	55–64	65+
ELEC	−2.011307	−1.819802	−1.873597	−1.856728	−1.877320	−1.766870
GAS	−1.554514	−1.383495	−1.317651	−1.337803	−1.319017	−1.246789
SOL	−1.529601	−1.490855	−1.477117	−1.448246	−1.410884	−1.342216
GASO	−1.066697	−1.079848	−1.081952	−1.083952	−1.088292	−1.122332

	C. Region			
	NE	NC	S	W
ELEC	−1.873597	−1.907592	−1.726674	−1.898251
GAS	−1.317651	−1.197832	−1.247840	−1.223714
SOL	−1.477117	−1.886279	−2.082895	−1.963586
GASO	−1.081952	−1.076505	−1.075599	−1.072131

	D. Race		E. Residence	
	W	NW	URB	RUR
ELEC	−1.873597	−1.813694	−1.873597	−1.927420
GAS	−1.317651	−1.183245	−1.317651	−5.413400
SOL	−1.477117	−1.488659	−1.477117	−1.311106
GASO	−1.081952	−1.105410	−1.081952	−1.079608

The principal effects of changes in family size are increases in the price elasticity of electricity and natural gas, and a corresponding decrease in the own-price elasticity for fuel oil and other energy. As previously noted, larger families use more fuel oil and other on average, which accounts for the relative inelasticity of the price responses. Changing age of head indicates the change from the youngest age class to the next youngest, with the price elasticities for household fuels decreasing rather dramatically in absolute value. Also, we find a similar change in proceeding from the 55–64 age class to the 65 and older class. This reflects a pronounced shift toward heating fuels and away from gasoline that we have already noted.

The region, race and type of residence elasticity tables reflect the relative intensity of use of the various fuel types. The most striking differences among regional price elasticities are the low elasticities for fuel oil and other for Northeastern families and for electricity among Southern families; both categories of energy are heavily used in those regions. The race effects are quite small. The only difference is a slightly lower natural gas price elasticity for nonwhites, together with a slightly higher gasoline elasticity. Finally, type of residence elasticities indicate a lower price elasticity for fuel oil and other owing to greater use of this fuel and an extremely high natural gas elasticity owing to the extremely small use of this type of energy. This concludes the presentation and interpretation of the main results of pooling time-series data with all five cross-section surveys.

9.III.3 Consumer Expenditure Surveys

The results presented in section 9.III.2 above utilize all five cross-section surveys, embodying 34,424 observations on individual energy expenditures. In this section we compare our previous results to those obtained by pooling only one data base, 1972 CES, with the time-series data, and those obtained by pooling three data bases—1960/61 CES, 1972 CES, 1973 CES—with the time-series data. The estimates obtained from using only the 1972 CES data are presented in table 9.III.3, and those using the 1960/61 CES, 1972 CES and 1973 CES are given in table 9.III.4. The reader should bear in mind that values of the objective function values (SSR) are not comparable among tables 9.III.1, 3 and 4.

In an overall comparison of these results, we find first the expected result that the asymptotic standard errors decrease substantially for

Table 9.III.3
Pooled estimation results: 1972 CES[a]

	WELEC	WGAS	WSOL	WGASO
P_{ELEC}	.17376(.0248)	−.05782(.0155)	−.12535(.0129)	.00940(.0216)
P_{GAS}	−.05782(.0155)	.02990(.0194)	.03937(.0101)	−.01144(.0151)
P_{SOL}	−.12535(.0129)	.03937(.0101)	.10453(.0176)	−.01855(.0117)
P_{GASO}	.00940(.0216)	−.01144(.0151)	−.01855(.0117)	.02058(.0223)
CONST	−.18806(.00878)	−.08670(.00818)	−.17193(.00730)	−.55331(.0115)
F2	.02332(.00565)	.01981(.00529)	.00160(.00440)	−.04472(.00752)
F3	.03290(.00670)	.01221(.00628)	−.00837(.00523)	−.03674(.00892)
F4	.02011(.00735)	.00335(.00689)	−.00718(.00573)	−.01628(.00979)
F5	.01086(.00860)	−.00303(.00806)	−.01498(.00671)	.00714(.0114)
F6	.02731(.0106)	−.00607(.00994)	−.02200(.00828)	.00075(.0141)
F7	.01603(.0112)	−.00228(.0105)	−.02634(.00875)	.01258(.0149)
A30	−.05069(.00846)	−.03287(.00792)	−.00891(.00660)	.09247(.0112)
A40	−.05196(.00903)	−.05243(.00846)	−.01555(.00705)	.11994(.0120)
A50	−.05252(.00852)	−.05631(.00798)	−.02574(.00665)	.13457(.0113)
A60	−.06809(.00852)	−.08026(.00798)	−.04323(.00665)	.19158(.0113)
A70	−.12859(.00821)	−.14439(.00769)	−.07631(.00641)	.34929(.0109)
RNC	.01933(.00575)	−.03491(.00538)	.08220(.00448)	−.06662(.00765)
RS	−.03898(.00571)	.03623(.00535)	.09004(.00446)	−.08729(.00759)
RW	.02232(.00622)	.02289(.00583)	.08807(.00485)	−.13328(.00828)
NW	−.03120(.00715)	−.09974(.00669)	.00703(.00557)	.12391(.00951)
RUR	.01946(.00546)	.05388(.00512)	−.06887(.00426)	−.00447(.00727)

[a] Convergence after one iteration. SSR = 26,784.88.

Table 9.III.4
Pooled estimation results: Three CES cross-section data sets[a]

	WELEC	WGAS	WSOL	WGASO
P_{ELEC}	.19881(.0247)	−.07862(.0154)	−.11618(.0129)	−.00400(.0215)
P_{GAS}	−.07862(.0154)	.03828(.0194)	.04391(.0100)	−.00356(.0151)
P_{SOL}	−.11618(.0129)	.04391(.0100)	.09966(.0176)	−.02738(.0115)
P_{GASO}	−.00400(.0215)	−.00356(.0151)	−.02738(.0116)	.03496(.0222)
CONS	−.19168(.00636)	−.05616(.00581)	−.18046(.00545)	−.57169(.00818)
F2	.00516(.00402)	.00820(.00371)	.00451(.00304)	−.01787(.00530)
F3	.01073(.00479)	.00244(.00442)	−.01194(.00363)	−.00123(.00631)
F4	−.00539(.00515)	−.00579(.00475)	−.00696(.00390)	.01813(.00679)
F5	−.00665(.00612)	−.01399(.00564)	−.01375(.00463)	.03438(.00806)
F6	.02072(.00764)	−.00230(.00705)	−.02652(.00579)	.00810(.0100)
F7	.01287(.00806)	.01325(.00744)	−.03582(.00611)	.00970(.0106)
A30	−.04052(.00595)	−.03134(.00548)	−.01180(.00450)	.08365(.00783)
A40	−.02603(.00640)	−.04811(.00591)	−.01782(.00485)	.09196(.00844)
A50	−.03063(.00605)	−.04104(.00558)	−.03285(.00458)	.10452(.00798)
A60	−.02294(.00605)	−.04588(.00558)	−.05179(.00458)	.12061(.00797)
A70	−.04473(.00586)	−.07229(.00540)	−.08957(.00444)	.20659(.00772)
RNC	.00724(.00412)	−.08003(.00378)	.10100(.00312)	−.02821(.00543)
RS	−.05340(.00409)	−.04303(.00378)	.12074(.00310)	−.02430(.00539)
RW	.00284(.00444)	−.05454(.00409)	.10924(.00336)	−.05754(.00585)
NW	.00142(.00496)	−.06340(.00457)	−.00045(.00375)	.06242(.00652)
RUR	.00697(.00390)	.12287(.00360)	−.10188(.00295)	−.02795(.00513)

[a] Convergence after three iterations. SSR = 74,327.49.

the demographic variables as additional cross-section data are added. The decreases in the asymptotic standard errors of the price coefficients are slight, since they are primarily determined by time-series data.

Comparing the estimated price coefficients, we find some differences among the estimated results; however, none is significantly different. The only substantial coefficient change is the own-price gasoline coefficient, which is not estimated very precisely in any of the results. The demographic coefficients vary somewhat across tables 9.III.1, 3 and 4. Overall, the least precise values are obtained by pooling only one cross section, here the 1972 CES. Pooling all three CES data sets results in more precise estimates, and pooling all five data sets produces the most precise estimates.

9.III.4 Separability of Transportation and Household Operations

A natural structure for the allocation of relative energy expenditures would involve the separability of gasoline for transportation from the fuels for household operation. Testing this type of separability within the translog model amounts to testing the hypothesis that cross-price coefficients for the price of gasoline are zero. Failure to reject separability restrictions implies that each family's indirect utility function can be represented with gasoline separable from the other fuels. This implies that price and quantity indexes for energy for household operation could be constructed for each family. However, demographic differences in the estimated equations imply that the aggregate price of energy for household operations would vary from household to household. The restrictions required for a common aggregate price for all households are much stronger, implying that all demographic effects vanish from the electricity, natural gas and fuel oil and other equations; these restrictions are certainly in conflict with the estimates of the demographic coefficients presented in section 9.II.

The test for separability in the translog model involves the restriction of two gasoline price coefficients to zero. Summability restrictions guarantee that the remaining gasoline price coefficients must be equal to zero. The test is performed as follows: Let $\hat{\theta}$ be the unrestricted parameter estimates in table 9.III.1 and let $(\hat{\theta}^R)$ be the estimates subject to the separability restrictions. Then the statistic SSR $(\hat{\theta}^R)$ – SSR $(\hat{\theta})$ is distributed asymptotically as chi-squared with two degrees of freedom; comparison with chi-squared critical values permits us to carry out the test.

Table 9.III.5 contains the nonlinear three-stage least squares (NL3SLS) estimates constrained by separability of gasoline from energy used for household operations. Comparing the results with those presented in table 9.III.1, we see that the coefficients estimates for demographic effects are nearly identical. Second, we see that the coefficients of the price of electricity all increase in absolute value, with the remaining coefficients declining somewhat in absolute value.

The test of separability is performed as follows: $SSR(\hat{\theta}^R) = 85,432.23$; $SSR(\hat{\theta}) = 85,370.79$ so that $SSR(\hat{\theta}^R) - SSR(\hat{\theta}) = 61.44$. The 1% critical

Table 9.III.5
Pooled estimation results for separability: Five cross-section data sets[a]

	WELEC	WGAS	WSOL	WGASO
P_{ELEC}	.12698(.0109)	–.06869(.0138)	–.05829(.00629)	.00000(.000)
P_{GAS}	–.06869(.0138)	.01943(.0206)	.04925(.0101)	.00000(.000)
P_{SOL}	–.05829(.00629)	.04925(.0101)	.00904(.00763)	.00000(.000)
P_{GASO}	.00000(.000)	.00000(.000)	.00000(.000)	.00000(.000)
CONS	–.19926(.00608)	–.06001(.00545)	–.16754(.00480)	.57318(.00780)
F2	.00866(.00385)	.01158(.00346)	.00568(.00264)	.02592(.00504)
F3	.01684(.00458)	.00604(.00412)	–.01099(.00313)	.01189(.00600)
F4	.00496(.00491)	–.00077(.00440)	–.00300(.00333)	.00119(.00642)
F5	.00072(.00582)	–.00974(.00522)	–.01342(.00393)	.02244(.00761)
F6	.02681(.00727)	.00151(.00654)	–.02826(.00493)	.00006(.00952)
F7	.01777(.00764)	.01841(.00685)	–.03712(.00514)	.00094(.00999)
A30	–.04503(.00568)	–.03063(.00510)	–.01470(.00386)	.09036(.00744)
A40	–.03015(.00611)	–.05122(.00548)	–.02068(.00414)	.10204(.00800)
A50	–.03483(.00578)	–.04416(.00518)	–.03414(.00392)	.11312(.00756)
A60	–.02945(.00577)	–.05080(.00518)	–.05436(.00391)	.13460(.00756)
A70	–.06149(.00560)	–.08582(.00502)	–.10299(.00381)	.25029(.00733)
RNC	.00832(.00391)	–.07276(.00351)	.09639(.00264)	.03195(.00512)
RS	–.04522(.00392)	–.03378(.00352)	.11694(.00267)	.03793(.00512)
RW	.00618(.00419)	–.05039(.00374)	.10542(.00278)	.06120(.00547)
NW	–.01641(.00456)	–.08806(.00401)	.00508(.00289)	.09938(.00594)
RUR	.01299(.00366)	.11147(.00325)	–.11137(.00240)	.01309(.00478)

[a] Convergence after three iterations. SSR = 85,432.23.

level for a chi-squared tese with two degrees of freedom is 9.21; we reject separability at this level of significance. Further evidence on the acceptability of separability is presented in table 9.III.6, where we present elasticities calculated from the estimates of table 9.III.5. A comparison with table 9.III.2 indicates that the two sets of elasticities are substantially different, with the own-price elasticities of gasoline constrained to 1.00 under separability.

9.III.5 Tests of Structural Change

In analyzing the regression results of the previous section we noted that the LHES data of 1975 suggest substantially different race and type of residence effects than the other cross-section data sets. This raises the possibility of structural change in the coefficients of the translog model of individual energy expenditures between 1973 and 1975, owing to the shock of the Arab oil embargo. In order to test for this possibility, we first extend the translog model to include two additional variables per equation. In place of the expenditure statistics for nonwhite and rural residence, we include four series: two series represent the nonwhite and rural expenditure statistics up to and including 1973, and zero thereafter; two additional series are zero until 1974 and are equal to the nonwhite and rural expenditure statistics afterward.

Differences between the coefficients of the two nonwhite series and of the two rural series indicate structural change. The moments of all cross-section data bases except the 1975 LHES influence the coefficients of the earlier expenditures statistic series, while the 1975 LHES moments influence the coefficients of the two later series. The results of estimating this extended model are presented in table 9.III.7. Restricting the model to no structural change produces the estimates presented in table 9.III.1. The test of structural change is performed as follows: $SSR(\hat{\theta}^R) = 85{,}370.79$ and $SSR(\hat{\theta}) = 85{,}034.97$, so that $SSR(\hat{\theta}^R) - SSR(\hat{\theta}) = 355.82$. The 1% critical level for chi squared with three degrees of freedom is 24.0, so that this hypothesis is soundly rejected.

On comparing the coefficient values, we see that the price coefficients given in tables 9.III.1 and 9.III.7 are quite similar. The demographic coefficients do show some differences, but on close inspection we find that the demographic coefficients of table 9.III.4 for three cross sections are virtually identical to those of table 9.III.7, excepting the

Table 9.III.6
Estimated price elasticities: Separability, 1972

A. Family size

	1	2	3	4	5	6	7+
ELEC	−1.553509	−1.575213	−1.597352	−1.565737	−1.555246	−1.626753	−1.599971
GAS	−1.174717	−1.195027	−1.184755	−1.173518	−1.160653	−1.177124	−1.209379
SOL	−1.048053	−1.049548	−1.045402	−1.047299	−1.044854	−1.041780	−1.040136
GASO	−1.000000	−1.000000	−1.000000	−1.000000	−1.000000	−1.000000	−1.000000

B. Age of head

	16–24	25–34	35–44	45–54	55–64	65+
ELEC	−1.639574	−1.521343	−1.555246	−1.544125	−1.556971	−1.488329
GAS	−1.278619	−1.193592	−1.160653	−1.170608	−1.161207	−1.124918
SOL	−1.049979	−1.046224	−1.044854	−1.042047	−1.038434	−1.031852
GASO	−1.000000	−1.000000	−1.000000	−1.000000	−1.000000	−1.000000

C. Region

	NE	NC	S	W
ELEC	−1.555246	−1.576206	−1.463583	−1.570663
GAS	−1.160653	−1.100317	−1.125583	−1.113411
SOL	−1.044854	−1.085928	−1.106773	−1.093990
GASO	−1.000000	−1.000000	−1.000000	−1.000000

	D. Race		E. Residence	
	W	NW	URB	RUR
ELEC	−1.555246	−1.518063	−1.555246	−1.588685
GAS	−1.160653	−1.092974	−1.160653	−1.046868
SOL	−1.044854	−1.046013	−1.044854	−1.028895
GASO	−1.000000	−1.000000	−1.000000	−1.000000

Table 9.III.7
Pooled estimation results for structural change: Five cross-section data sets[a]

	WELEC	WGAS	WSOL	WGASO
P_{ELEC}	.21712(.0248)	–.04270(.0156)	–.17107(.0135)	–.00335(.0216)
P_{GAS}	–.04270(.0156)	.03269(.0194)	.02620(.0104)	–.01618(.0152)
P_{SOL}	–.17107(.0135)	–.02620(.0104)	.07673(.0177)	.04859(.0128)
P_{GASO}	–.00335(.0216)	–.01618(.0152)	.06813(.0128)	–.56470(.0227)
CONS	–.19372(.00614)	–.06159(.00548)	–.17999(.00498)	–.56470(.00783)
F2	.00940(.00385)	.01176(.00346)	.00554(.00264)	–.02670(.00505)
F3	.01698(.00458)	.00592(.00412)	–.01094(.00313)	–.01195(.00600)
F4	.00517(.00491)	–.00075(.00440)	–.00293(.00333)	–.00149(.00643)
F5	.00187(.00582)	–.00987(.00523)	–.01356(.00394)	.02155(.00762)
F6	.02779(.00727)	.00214(.00654)	–.02798(.00493)	–.00194(.00953)
F7	.01886(.00765)	.01866(.00686)	–.03686(.00515)	–.00066(.0100)
A30	–.04536(.00568)	–.03119(.00510)	–.01489(.00386)	.09143(.00744)
A40	–.03154(.00611)	–.05193(.00548)	–.02057(.00414)	.10404(.00800)
A50	–.03533(.00578)	–.04449(.00518)	–.03406(.00392)	.11387(.00756)
A60	–.02988(.00577)	–.05146(.00518)	–.05446(.00391)	.13579(.00756)
A70	–.06181(.00560)	–.08642(.00502)	–.10314(.00381)	.25136(.00733)
RNC	.00796(.00391)	–.07299(.00351)	.09645(.00264)	–.03142(.00512)
RS	–.04672(.00392)	–.03381(.00353)	.11743(.00268)	–.03690(.00513)
RW	.00702(.00419)	–.04761(.00375)	.10579(.00279)	–.06519(.00548)
NW	.00082(.00482)	–.06744(.00445)	.00329(.00351)	.06333(.00635)
RUR	.00068(.00384)	.12447(.00354)	–.10407(.00283)	–.02708(.00505)
NW(74–78)	.15495(.0137)	.03771(.00960)	.01184(.00509)	–.20450(.01670)
RUR(74–78)	.08985(.0119)	.13439(.00832)	–.01265(.00440)	–.21158(.0145)

[a] Convergence after three iterations. SSR = 85,034.97.

nonwhite and rural variables from 1974–1978. This is not surprising since these three cross sections underlying table 9.III.5 represent almost all of the individual data prior to 1974; LHES data for 1973 contain only 579 observations. Further evidence on the acceptability of structural change is presented in table 9.III.8, where we present price elasticities calculated from estimates in table 9.III.7.

Effectively, the test of structural change provides validation of the differences in coefficients noted in section II. Consequently, this test relies heavily on the comparability of the 1975 LHES with the other surveys. Even though we have made every effort to make the data definitions as closely comparable as possible, there is always the possibility of noncomparability of data on energy expenditures from the 1975 LHES to the CES surveys. This would lead to the interpretations of our rejection of the hypothesis of no structural change as a reflection of differences in procedures for measurement of energy consumption.

9.III.6 Summary and Conclusion

In this section we have presented pooled estimation results for aggregate time-series data on energy expenditures and individual cross-section data from five surveys: 1960/61 CES, 1972 CES, 1973 CES, 1973 LHES, and 1975 LHES. We have discussed the precision of the resulting estimates of all the parameters that enter into our model of aggregate energy expenditures. We have represented the effects of demographic characteristics of individual households on energy use diagrammatically. We have described the effects of prices on aggregate energy expenditures through tables of estimated price elasticities.

We have compared our pooled estimation results for all five cross-section surveys with three alternative specifications to indicate how changes in the treatment of the data sources or changes in specification of the equations can affect our estimated results. First, we compare the overall results to those employing fewer cross-section data. Next, we analyze the price structure of the model by testing the separability of gasoline from other energy types. Finally, we test for the possibility of structural change in the demographic structure, as suggested by the results of section 9.III.5, by allowing the race and type of residence to change after 1973.

We have consistently found strong demographic effects in the determination of aggregate energy expenditures, which invalidates

Table 9.III.8
Estimated price elasticities: Structural change, 1972

	A. Family size						
	1	2	3	4	5	6	7+
ELEC	−1.963833	−2.005795	−2.042387	−1.986489	−1.971886	−2.099487	−2.051887
GAS	−1.287973	−1.321262	−1.303814	−1.286089	−1.264942	−1.293506	−1.344621
SOL	−1.382593	−1.393466	−1.362806	−1.377091	−1.358367	−1.335746	−1.323201
GASO	−0.894500	−0.900280	−0.897169	−0.894842	−0.889320	−0.894944	−0.894651

	B. Age of head					
	16–24	25–34	35–44	45–54	55–64	65+
ELEC	−2.131681	−1.915273	−1.971886	−1.955699	−1.979199	−1.855915
GAS	−1.457484	−1.318489	−1.264942	−1.281953	−1.265945	−1.207067
SOL	−1.396463	−1.368144	−1.358367	−1.337128	−1.309408	−1.258636
GASO	−0.910522	−0.892410	−0.889320	−0.886786	−0.880694	−0.833437

	C. Region			
	NE	NC	S	W
ELEC	−1.971886	−2.007818	−1.803786	−2.003418
GAS	−1.264942	−1.166470	−1.207963	−1.191173
SOL	−1.358367	−1.652089	−1.793603	−1.708310
GASO	−0.889320	−0.896712	−0.897900	−0.903629

	D. Race		E. Residence	
	W	NW	URB	RUR
ELEC	−1.971886	−1.975471	−1.971886	−2.001855
GAS	−1.264942	−1.171305	−1.264942	29.172414
SOL	−1.358367	−1.363962	−1.358367	−1.241156
GASO	−0.889320	−0.870666	−0.889320	−0.895750

the use of an economy-wide price index of energy that does not incorporate differences among expenditure patterns among demographic groups. We have found that gasoline is not separable from other types of energy consumed, so that we are unable to break down energy demand into transportation use and household use components. Finally, we noted the strong possibility of structural change in demographic patterns during the later years of our sample.

Appendix

Table 9.III.A1
Instrumental variables, 1958–1978

Notation	Definition
I1	Constant
I2	Effective tax rate, labor services
I3	Effective tax rate, noncompetitive imports
I4	Time available for labor services
I5	U.S. population, millions of individuals
I6	Implicit deflator, supply of labor services
I7	Implicit deflator, government purchases of labor services
I8	Exogenous income, which equals government transfers to persons (excepting social insurance) less personal transfers to foreigners and personal nontax payments to government
I9	Private national wealth, lagged one period
I10	Potential time for labor services; rate of Harrod neutral change
I11	Total imports
I12	Implicit deflator, noncompetitive imports
I13	Corrected deflator for labor services
I14	Time, set to 0 in 1972

Notes

1. A comprehensive review of the theory of two-stage allocation and references to the literature are given by Blackorby *et al.* (1978, esp. pp. 173–216).
2. The specification of a system of individual demand functions by means of Roy's Identity was first implemented empirically in a pathbreaking study by Houthakker (1960). A detailed review of econometric models of consumer behavior based on Roy's Identity is given by Lau (1977a).

3. Alternative approaches to the representation of the effects of prices on expenditure allocation are reviewed by Barten (1977), Deaton and Muellbauer (1980b, pp. 60–85), and Lau (1977a). The indirect translog utility function was introduced by Christensen *et al.* (1975) and was extended to encompass changes in preferences over time by Jorgenson and Lau (1975).
4. Integrability is discussed in greater detail by Jorgenson and Lau (1979).
5. Since budget shares are bounded dependent variables, the normality assumption cannot be strictly valid.
6. See Barten (1969).
7. See Malinvaud (1980, chap. 9) for a discussion of these techniques.
8. Nonlinear two-stage least squares estimators were introduced by Amemiya (1974). Subsequently, nonlinear three-stage squares estimators were introduced by Jorgenson and Laffont (1974). For detailed discussion of nonlinear three-stage least squares estimators, see Amemiya (1977), Gallant (1977), and Gallant and Jorgenson (1979). A survey of these techniques is given by Malinvaud (1980, chap. 20).
9. See Malinvaud (1980, pp. 380–382) for a more detailed discussion.
10. This series is published annual by the U.S. Bureau of the Census. For our study, nos. 33, 35, 37, 39, 41, 43, 47, 51, 53, 59, 60, 62, 66, 72, 75, 79, 80, 84, 85, 90, 96, 97, and 101 were employed together with technical report Nos. 8 and 17.
11. For details, the interested reader is referred to Stoker (1979).

10 Nonlinear Three-Stage Least Squares Pooling of Cross-Section and Time-Series Observations

Dale W. Jorgenson and
Thomas M. Stoker

10.1 Introduction

The purpose of this chapter is to discuss the pooling of cross-section and average time-series data by the method of nonlinear three-stage least squares (NL3SLS) introduced by Jorgenson and Laffont (1974).[1] We consider applications of this method to exact aggregation models, where there is a unique correspondence between individual and aggregate behavior. This correspondence makes exact aggregation models appropriate for the analysis of individual data, average data, or both in combination.[2]

We consider observations on K individuals, indexed by $k = 1, 2, \ldots, K$, for T time periods, indexed by $t = 1, 2, \ldots, T$. We can represent the structural form of an exact aggregation model for the kth individual in the tth time period by

$$y_{nkt} = x'_{kt}\, \beta_n(p_t, \theta)\,, \qquad (n = 1, 2, \ldots, N)\,.$$

The observations y_{nkt} and x_{kt} vary over both individuals and time periods, while the vector of observations p_t varies over time periods, but is the same for all individuals in a given time period. The coefficients $\beta_n(p_t, \theta)$ are functions of the observations p_t and the vector of L structural parameters $\theta' = (\theta_1, \theta_2, \ldots, \theta_L)$. Restrictions on the parameters that take the form of equalities are embodied in the forms of these functions.

We can write the exact aggregation model for the kth individual in vector form

$$y_{kt} = (I_N \otimes x'_{kt})\, \beta(p_t, \theta)\,, \tag{10.1}$$

where y_{kt} is a vector of N observations; $\beta(p_t, \theta)$ is a vector of all coefficients; and I_N is the identity matrix of order N. By averaging the model (10.1) over all individuals for each time period, we obtain the structural form of the exact aggregation model for averaged data,

$$\bar{y}_t = (I_N \otimes \overline{x_t'})\, \beta(p_t, \theta)\,, \tag{10.2}$$

where $\bar{y}_t$ and $\overline{x_t'}$ are vectors of N observations on averages of y_{kt} and x_{kt}' over all individuals.

The models for individual cross-section and average time-series observations contain the same parameter vector θ and the same coefficient vector $\beta(p_t, \theta)$. This reflects the correspondence between individual and aggregate behavior that characterizes exact aggregation models. The forms of the individual and aggregate model (10.1) and (10.2) are necessary and sufficient for exact aggregation, provided that the population distribution of x_{kt} is unrestricted.[3]

As an example of exact aggregation models we first consider the linear model that underlies previous discussions of pooling cross-section and time-series data[4]

$$y_{nkt} = p_t'\, \theta_{1n} + z_{kt}'\, \theta_{2n}\,, \qquad (n = 1, 2, \ldots, N)\,,$$

where θ_{1n} and θ_{2n} are vectors of parameters. In this example the vector of parameters θ of models (10.1) and (10.2) includes the elements of θ_{1n} and θ_{2n} $(n = 1, 2, \ldots, N)$. The vector of coefficients $\beta_n(p_t, \theta)'$ is $(p_t'\, \theta_{1n}, \theta'_{2n})$ and the vector of observations x_{kt}' is $(1, z_{kt}')$.

Demand analysis provides many examples of nonlinear exact aggregation models. In each of these examples the theory of consumer behavior implies constraints on the parameters of the model that are incorporated through the form of the coefficients $\beta_n(p_t, \theta)$ $(n = 1, 2, \ldots, N)$. Demand systems generated by the Gorman polar form of the indirect utility function are nonlinear exact aggregation models. Specific examples include the linear expenditure system introduced by Klein and Rubin (1947–1948) and implemented by Stone (1954), the S-branch utility tree of Brown and Heien (1972), and the generalization of the S-branch utility tree of Blackorby, Boyce, and Russell (1978).

As an illustration, the linear expenditure system can be written in exact aggregation form as follows

$$y_{nkt} = (p_{nt}\, c_n - b_n \sum c_j\, p_{jt}) + b_n\, M_{kt}\,, \qquad (n = 1, 2, \ldots, N)\,,$$

where y_{nkt} denotes expenditure on the nth commodity by the kth individual in period t and p_{nt} is the price of this commodity ($n = 1, 2, \ldots, N$); M_{kt} is total expenditure on all commodities. The vector of parameters θ includes the parameters b_n and c_n ($n = 1, 2, \ldots, N$), the vector of coefficients $\beta_n(p_t, \theta)'$ is $(p_{nt}c_n - b_n \sum_j c_j p_{jt}, b_n)$ and the vector of observations x'_{kt} is $(1, M_{kt})$.

More complex nonlinear exact aggregation models have recently been introduced by Deaton and Muellbauer (1980a, b) and by Jorgenson, Lau, and Stoker (1980, 1981, 1982). The AIDS models of Deaton and Muellbauer can be written

$$y_{nkt} = \left(a_n + \sum c_{nj} \ln p_{jt}\right) M_{kt} + b_n \frac{M_{kt} \ln M_{kt}}{\ln P_t}, \qquad (n = 1, 2, \ldots, N),$$

where y_{nkt}, M_{kt}, and p_{nt} are defined as in the linear expenditure system and

$$\ln P_t = \sum a_j \ln p_{jt} + \frac{1}{2} \sum \sum c_{nj} \ln p_{nt} \cdot \ln p_{jt}$$

is a price index. The vector of parameters θ includes the parameters a_n, b_n, c_{nj} ($n, j = 1, 2, \ldots, N$), the vector of coefficients $\beta_n(p_t, \theta)'$ is $(a_n + \sum c_{nj} \ln p_{jt}, \; b_n / \ln P_t)$ and the vector of observations x'_{kt} is $(M_{kt}, M_{kt} \ln M_{kt})$.

The translog model of Jorgenson, Lau and Stoker can be represented in the form

$$y_{nkt} = \left(\frac{a_n + \sum b_{nj} \ln p_{jt}}{D(p_t)}\right) M_{kt} - \frac{b_{Mn}}{D(p_t)} M_{kt} \ln M_{kt} + \sum \frac{b^A_{ns} M_{kt} A_{skt}}{D(p_t)}, \qquad n = 1, 2, \ldots, N,$$

where y_{nkt}, M_{kt} and p_{nt} are defined as above, A_{skt} ($s = 1, 2, \ldots, S$) represents demographic characteristics such as family size, age of head of household, and so on; and

$$D(p_t) = -1 + \sum b_{Mj} \ln p_{jt}.$$

In this example the vector θ consists of the parameters a_n, b_{nj}, b_{Mj}, b^A_{ns} ($n, j = 1, 2, \ldots, N$; $s = 1, 2, \ldots, S$), the vector of coefficients $\beta_n(p_t, \theta)'$ is

$$\left(\frac{a_n + \sum b_{nj} \ln p_{jt}}{D(p_t)}, \frac{b_{Mj}}{D(p_t)}, \frac{b^A_{n1}}{D(p_t)}, \frac{b^A_{n2}}{D(p_t)}, \ldots, \frac{b^A_{nS}}{D(p_t)}\right)$$

and the vector of observations x'_{kt} is

$(M_{kt}, M_{kt} \ln M_{kt}, M_{kt} A_{1kt}, M_{kt} A_{2kt}, \ldots, M_{kt} A_{Skt})$.

In this chapter we focus on the implications of nonlinearity for the pooling of cross-section and average time-series data. In section 10.2 we consider the stochastic specification of exact aggregation models (10.1) and (10.2). In section 10.3 we present and characterize the nonlinear three-stage least squares estimator for pooled time-series and cross-section observations. In section 10.4 we discuss hypothesis testing and in section 10.5 we consider estimation subject to inequality constraints. In section 10.6 we illustrate the application of our methodology with a model of residential demand for energy. We close with a brief summary of the results.

10.2 Stochastic Specification

We begin by considering average observations for T time periods and a single cross section of K' individual observations. We assume that the observations are generated by exact aggregation models (10.1) and (10.2) with additive disturbance terms. Given the stochastic specification of the disturbance terms, the observations must be transformed to obtain disturbances that are homoscedastic and uncorrelated across observations.

For pooling of cross-section and average time-series data the transformation of observations to obtain homoscedastic and uncorrelated disturbances can be divided into two steps. The first step separates the data sets by transforming the average data so that time-series disturbances are uncorrelated with cross-section disturbances. The second step transforms the resulting data sets to a form where disturbances in each data set are homoscedastic and uncorrelated. We present the transformation for the first step explicitly, indicating the features of this transformation that result in increased efficiency. The second step involves standard techniques for transformation, which we illustrate by example.

We assume that individual observations are generated by the exact aggregation model (10.1) with an additive random component, say ε_{kt}

$$y_{kt} = (I_N \otimes x'_{kt})\, \beta(p_t, \theta) + \varepsilon_{kt}\,. \qquad (10.1')$$

We assume that the disturbance term ε_{kt} is distributed with mean zero and is uncorrelated across individuals, so that

$$E(\varepsilon_{kt}\ \varepsilon'_{k't'}) = 0\,, \qquad k \neq k'\,.$$

Any systematic correlation among individuals is assumed to be captured by selection of the variables x_{kt}. The disturbance term ε_{kt} is assumed to have variance Ω_ε and time-series covariance structure $E(\varepsilon_{kt}\ \varepsilon'_{kt'}) = C_{tt'}\ \Omega_\varepsilon$. A wide variety of alternative time-series structures for ε_{kt} can be represented by choosing an appropriate form for the matrix $C_{tt'}$.

We could obtain a stochastic version of the exact aggregation model (10.2) by averaging the individual observations in eq. (10. 1′) for each time period. This would be the appropriate procedure if the average data were constructed by averaging the individual observations. However, we must allow for alternative methods for constructing the aggregate data. In demand analysis, for example, data on aggregate personal consumption expenditures are obtained from production accounts for the economy as a whole rather than by direct observation of quantities consumed by the entire population of individual households.

To allow for differences in methods of construction of the individual and aggregate data we introduce an additive random component ν_t into the exact aggregation model (10.2) for each time period. The model relating the averaged data $\bar{y}_t$ to $\bar{x}_t$ and p_t is then

$$\bar{y}_t = (I_N \otimes \overline{x'_t})\ \beta(p_t, \theta) + u_t, \tag{10.2′}$$

where $u_t = \nu_t + \bar{\varepsilon}_t$ and $\bar{\varepsilon}_t$ is a vector of N averaged disturbances $\{\varepsilon_{kt}\}$. The stochastic term ν_t is assumed to be distributed independently of ε_{kt} with mean zero, variance Ω_ν^{tt}, and time-series covariance structure $E(\nu_t\ \nu'_{t'}) = \Omega_\nu^{tt'}$ for $t \neq t'$. To accommodate a variety of time-series covariance structures for u_t we have

$$E(u_t\ u'_{t'}) = \Omega_\nu^{tt'} + \frac{1}{K}\ C_{tt'}\ \Omega_\varepsilon\,.$$

In order to present methods for pooling cross-section and time-series data we consider a sample of K' individual observations. We can "stack" the equations (10. 1′) to obtain

$$Y = (I_N \otimes X)\ \beta(p_{t_0}, \theta) + \varepsilon\,, \tag{10.3}$$

where Y is the vector of observations $\{y_{nkt_0}\}$, X is the matrix with rows $\{x'_{kt_0}\}$ and ε is the vector of disturbances with mean zero and covariance matrix $\Omega_\varepsilon \otimes I_{K'}$. Similarly, we can represent the equations (10. 2′) in the form

$$\bar{Y} = f(\theta) + \bar{u}, \tag{10.4}$$

where $\bar{Y}$ is the vector of averaged observations $\{\bar{y}_t\}$,

$$f(\theta) = \begin{bmatrix} \overline{x_1'}\ \beta(p_1, \theta) \\ \overline{x_2'}\ \beta(p_2, \theta) \\ \cdots\cdots\cdots\cdots \\ \overline{x_T'}\ \beta(p_T, \theta) \end{bmatrix},$$

and $\bar{u}$ is the vector of disturbances.

The first step in the transformation of observations eliminates the correlation between of ε and $\bar{u}$

$$E(u_t\ \varepsilon_{kt_0'}) = \frac{K'}{K}\ C_{tt_0}\ \Omega_\varepsilon\,, \qquad (k = 1, 2, \ldots, K';\ t = 1, 2, \ldots, T)\,. \tag{10.5}$$

This correlation is removed by a nonsingular transformation of (10.3) and (10.4), which is equivalent to replacing $\bar{y}_t$, $\bar{x}_t$ and $\bar{u}_t$ in (10. 2′), respectively, by

$$\begin{aligned} \bar{y}_t^0 &= \bar{y}_t - \frac{K'}{K}\ C_{tt_0}\ \bar{y}_{cs}, \\ \bar{x}_t^0 &= \bar{x}_t - \frac{K'}{K}\ C_{tt_0}\ \bar{x}_{cs}, \\ \bar{u}_t^0 &= \bar{u}_t - \frac{K'}{K}\ C_{tt_0}\ \bar{\varepsilon}_{cs}, \end{aligned} \tag{10.6}$$

where $\bar{y}_{cs}$, $\bar{x}_{cs}$ and $\bar{\varepsilon}_{cs}$ denote the cross-section averages of y_{kt_0} , x_{kt_0} and ε_{kt_0}. The resulting disturbances $\bar{u}_t^0$ are now uncorrelated with ε_{kt_0} $(k = 1, 2, \ldots, K')$, but have a more complicated time-series structure than the original disturbances

$$E(u_t^0\ u_{t'}^{0'}) = \Omega_\nu^{tt'} + \frac{1}{K}\ C_{tt'}\ \Omega_\varepsilon - \frac{K'}{K^2}\ [C_{t_0t'} + C_{tt_0}]\ \Omega_\varepsilon\,. \tag{10.7}$$

The second step in the transformation of observations is to apply a nonsingular transform to the average data in (10.4) to obtain disturbances that are homoscedastic and uncorrelated. We illustrate this transformation below by example. We assume that the transformation has been performed, altering the model (10.4) to

$$\bar{Y}^* = f^*(\theta^*) + \bar{u}^*, \tag{10.8}$$

where $\bar{u}^*$ is distributed with mean zero and variance $\Omega_{u^*} \otimes I_T$. For estimation, we stack the equation systems (10.3) and (10.8)

$$\mathbf{Y} = \psi(\theta) + U, \tag{10.9}$$

where $U' = (\varepsilon', \bar{u}^{*'})$, which is distributed with mean zero and variance

$$\Sigma = E(U\,U') = \begin{bmatrix} \Omega_\varepsilon \otimes I_{K'} & 0 \\ 0 & \Omega_{u^*} \otimes I_T \end{bmatrix}. \tag{10.10}$$

The implementation of the transformations described above requires consistent estimates of the variances and covariances Ω_ε, $C_{tt'}$, $\Omega_\nu^{tt'}$ $(t, t' = 1, 2, \ldots, T)$. In general, these estimates require specific models of the processes generating the disturbances. The purpose of the transformations is to ensure efficiency in estimation. Equation (10. 2′) shows that the contribution of the individual errors ε_{kt} to the covariance structure of u_t is likely to be negligible unless the matrices $\Omega_\nu^{tt'}$ are the same order of magnitude as $1/K\, C_{tt'}\, \Omega_\varepsilon$, where K is population size. The benefits of performing the transformation (10.6) depend on the size of the cross section relative to the population. In many applications, K'/K will be extremely small so that the transformation (10.6) leaves the observations unaffected. Typical numbers for an analysis of U.S. household demand behavior are $K' = 10{,}000$ and $K = 70$ million. Consequently, only when the cross-section sample size is of the same order of magnitude as the size of the population will the correction yield significant benefits; otherwise it can be ignored.

The following examples illustrate different error structures, where we assume K'/K is very small. We take $C_{tt'} = 0$, $t \neq t'$, for simplicity, deferring further discussion of this time-series structure until we have presented the examples. In examples 10.1 and 10.2 we take $\Omega_\nu^{tt'} = 0$ for $t \neq t'$.

Example 10.1 (Random Individual Errors). Suppose that ν_t arises because of an additional random component ν_{kt} at the individual level, distributed with mean zero and variance Ω_ν, so that $\nu_t = \sum \nu_{kt}/K$. Then $u_t = \sum(\nu_{kt} + \varepsilon_{kt})/K$, with

$$E(u_t\, u_{t'}') = \begin{cases} \dfrac{1}{K(\Omega_\nu + \Omega_\varepsilon)} & t = t' \\ 0 & t \neq t'. \end{cases}$$

The second-stage transformation is just a grouping correction, with u_t^* of (10.8) given as $u_t^* = \sqrt{K}\, u_t$, with $\Omega_{u^*} = \Omega_\nu + \Omega_\varepsilon$.[5]

Example 10.2 (Common Time Effect). Suppose that ν_t represents a common disturbance in the aggregate data with $\Omega_\nu^{tt} = \Omega_\nu$ for all t. In practice one will usually encounter $K\, \Omega_\nu \gg \Omega_\varepsilon$, so that $u_t \cong \nu_t$ for purposes of estimation. Here no second-stage correction is necessary, with $u_t^* = u_t$, $\Omega_{u^*} = \Omega_\nu$.

Example 10.3 (Autocorrelated Common Time Effect). Suppose that example 10.2 is modified to $\nu_t = \gamma\nu_{t-1} + \omega_t$, where ω_t is distributed with mean zero, variance Ω_ω and uncorrelated over time, with $K\, \Omega_\omega \gg \Omega_\varepsilon$. Then $\Omega_\nu^{tt} = \Omega_\omega/1 - \gamma^2$. As above, the contribution of $\sum \varepsilon_{kt} / K$ to u_t is negligible, so that $u_t \cong \nu_t$. The second-stage correction is now quasi-first differencing, replacing $\bar{y}_t$ and $\bar{x}_t$ by $\bar{y}_t - \gamma\bar{y}_{t-1}$ and $\bar{x}_t - \gamma\bar{x}_{t-1}$ (with the standard adjustment to the first observation). Of course, $u_t^* = \omega_t$ and $\Omega_{u^*} = \Omega_\omega$ in this case.

Now suppose that $C_{tt'} \neq 0$ so that we have a nontrivial time series correlation structure for ε_{kt}. In examples 10.2 and 10.3 above, the effect of $C_{tt'} \neq 0$ would be negligible, due to the unimportance of $\sum \varepsilon_{kt}/K$ in u_t.[6] In example 10.1, however, the time-series structure is potentially important, since $\sqrt{K}\, u_t$ will have the same time-series covariance structure as ε_{kt} and would require consideration in the second stage of the transformation of observations.

Example 10.3 illustrates the cost of pooling with very general error structures. In particular, example 10.3, the parameter γ is best relabeled as a component of θ, with the transformed error covariance structure now determined by Ω_ε and $\Omega_{u^*} = \Omega_\omega$. The treatment of autocorrelation will involve augmenting the list of parameters to be estimated with the remaining error structure characterized by Ω_ε and Ω_{u^*}. This modeling approach is standard practice in time-series analysis. Consequently, in section 10.3 we discuss only the consistent estimation of the parameters Ω_ε and Ω_{u^*}, which we will regard as positive definite but otherwise unrestricted.

Before discussing the additional assumptions required for estimation of the complete model, we introduce instrumental variables. It is often appropriate to treat the variables x_{kt} and p_t as endogenous for the individual observations, the aggregate observations, or both. This can occur when the model is a simultaneous equations model in exact aggregation form or part of a larger system of simultaneous equations. For example, in demand analysis observations on prices can reflect both supply and demand influences, requiring aggregate instruments. Alternatively, in a study of savings, errors in variables may necessitate instruments for the individual data, while in the average data such errors may be negligible.[7]

We assume that there are vectors of observations on instrumental variables, say $\{z_{kt}\}$. Denote as Z_0 and $\bar{Z}$ the matrices with rows z'_{kt} and $\overline{z'_t}$ respectively, and as Z the matrix

$$Z = \begin{bmatrix} I_q \otimes Z_0 & 0 \\ 0 & I_q \otimes \bar{Z} \end{bmatrix}.$$

Finally, we must introduce regularity assumptions in order to characterize the NL3SLS estimator. We include these in appendix 10.A. The assumptions are that the coefficient functions $\beta(p_t, \theta)$ are twice continuously differentiable in the components of θ, that the moment matrices defining the NL3SLS objective function converge to stable, well-behaved limits, and that the parameter vector θ is identified. We collect all components of θ identified in the cross section in a set Θ^0, all parameters identified in the time series in a set $\bar{\Theta}$, and all the remaining parameters in a set Θ^1.

10.3 The Nonlinear Three-Stage Least Squares Estimator

Denote the true value of θ as θ^*. The NL3SLS estimator $\hat{\theta}$ of θ^* is found as the value of θ which minimizes

$$S(\theta) = (\mathbf{Y} - \psi(\theta))' [\hat{\Sigma}^{-1} \otimes Z(Z'Z)^{1} Z'] (\mathbf{Y} - \psi(\theta)) \tag{10.11}$$

where

$$\hat{\Sigma} = \begin{bmatrix} \hat{\Omega}_{\varepsilon} \otimes I_{K'} & 0 \\ 0 & \hat{\Omega}_{u*} \otimes I_T \end{bmatrix},$$

is a consistent estimator of Σ as K', $T \to \infty$. The objective function

$S(\theta)$ can be written more explicitly as

$$S(\theta) = S^0(\theta) + \bar{S}(\theta), \qquad (10.12)$$

with

$$S^0 = (Y - (I_q \otimes X)\beta(p_{t_0}, \theta))'[\hat{\Omega}_\varepsilon^{-1} \otimes Z_0(Z_0'Z_0)^{-1}Z_0'](Y - (I_q \otimes X)\beta(p_{t_0}, \theta))$$
$$\bar{S}(\theta) = (\bar{Y}^* - f^*(\theta))'[\hat{\Omega}_{u*}^{-1} \otimes \bar{Z}(\bar{Z}'\bar{Z})^{-1}\bar{Z}'](\bar{Y}^* - f^*(\theta)),$$

where $S^0(\theta)$ and $\bar{S}(\theta)$ are NL3SLS objective functions for the cross-section and average models individually.[8] Obviously, the function $S^0(\theta)$ could be minimized to estimate the elements of Θ^0, for fixed values of the remaining parameters; similarly, $\bar{S}(\theta)$ could be minimized to estimate the elements of $\bar{\Theta}$. If $\Theta^0 = \bar{\Theta}$ and $\Theta^1 = \varnothing$, then all parameters could be estimated from either data set. Minimizing (10.11) constrains the estimated values from cross-section and time-series data sets to be equal, which results in efficiency gains.

Note that the function $S^0(\theta)$ can be evaluated using only $\hat{\Omega}_\varepsilon$ and the moment matrices $Z_0'X$, $Z_0'Z_0$ and $(I_q \otimes Z_0')Y$. Thus for estimating θ or other more restricted parameterizations of $\beta(p_t, \theta)$, only one pass through the cross-section data is required to construct these moments. This computational simplification results from exact aggregation.

The estimation procedure consists of three steps: First, find consistent estimators of Ω_ε and Ω_{u*}; second, minimize (10.11) to obtain $\hat{\theta}$; third, calculate the asymptotic covariance matrix of $\hat{\theta}$. If Θ^1 is not empty, then we cannot improve upon previous suggestions in the literature for finding consistent estimators of Ω_ε and Ω_{u*}; for example, Gallant (1977) suggests estimating each equation of the model by NL2SLS. This involves pooling both data sources on a single equation basis, forming $\hat{\Omega}_\varepsilon$ as the estimated residual covariance from the cross-section data, and forming $\hat{\Omega}_{u*}$ as the estimated residual covariance from the transformed average time-series data.

The more usual situation is that Θ^1 is empty, which suggests a simpler procedure. First, obtain consistent estimates of $\beta(p_{t_0}, \theta)$ by linear two-stage least squares (2SLS) estimation of each equation using the cross-section data. The estimated residual covariance matrix $\hat{\Omega}_\varepsilon$ provides a consistent estimator of Ω_ε even if Θ^1 is not empty. Using the consistent estimators of $\beta(p_{t_0}, \theta^*)$, solve for consistent estimates of the elements of θ^0, say $\hat{\theta}^0$. Holding these parameters fixed at $\hat{\theta}^0$, estimate the remaining parameters of θ by applying NL2SLS to each equation of the model or NL3SLS to the system as a whole, using only the time-series data. The estimated covariance matrix of the NL2SLS residuals, $\hat{\Omega}_{u*}$ provides a consistent estimator of Ω_{u*}. In addition, this procedure usually produces good starting values for θ used in minimizing (10.11).

The objective function (10.11) can be minimized using a variety of well-known computational methods. A convenient method that illustrates pooling cross-section and time-series data is the Gauss-Newton process.[9] To discuss this method we require the following notation: Let $B_0(\theta)$ and $\psi(\theta)$ denote the matrices

$$B_0(\theta) = \begin{bmatrix} B_{01}(\theta) \\ B_{02}(\theta) \\ \cdot \\ \cdot \\ \cdot \\ B_{0q}(\theta) \end{bmatrix} \quad \text{and} \quad \psi(\theta) = \begin{bmatrix} \psi_1(\theta) \\ \psi_2(\theta) \\ \cdot \\ \cdot \\ \cdot \\ \psi_q(\theta) \end{bmatrix}$$

and $\psi_i\ (\theta)$ is the matrix with elements $\{\sqrt{K}\ \overline{x_t'}\beta_i^j(p_t, \theta)\}$.[10]

The Gauss-Newton process is an iterative procedure for finding $\hat{\theta}$ from an initial value $\hat{\theta}_1$. At the ith iteration, the current value $\hat{\theta}_i$ is updated to $\hat{\theta}_{i+1} = \hat{\theta}_i + \Delta\hat{\theta}_i$ by first linearizing the system (10.9) with respect to θ as

$$\begin{aligned} &Y - (I_q \otimes X)\ \beta\ (p_{t_0}, \hat{\theta}_i) = (I_q \otimes X)\ B_0\ (\hat{\theta}_i)\ \Delta\theta_i + \varepsilon\,, \\ &\bar{Y}^* - f^*(\hat{\theta}_i) \cong \psi(\hat{\theta}_i)\Delta\theta_i + u^*\,. \end{aligned} \tag{10.13}$$

We then apply Zellner and Theil's (1962) linear three-stage least squares method to the model (10.13), obtaining

$$\Delta\hat{\theta}_i = (M_{x0} + \bar{M}_x)^{-1}(M_{\varepsilon 0} + \bar{M}_u)\,, \tag{10.14}$$

where

$$\begin{aligned} M_{x0} &= B_0(\hat{\theta}_i)'(\hat{\Omega}_\varepsilon^{-1} \otimes X'Z_0(Z_0'Z_0)^{-1}\ Z_0'X)B_0(\hat{\theta}_i) \\ M_{\varepsilon 0} &= B_0(\hat{\theta}_i)'(\hat{\Omega}_\varepsilon^{-1} \otimes X'Z_0(Z_0{}'Z_0)^{-1}Z_0')(Y - (I_q \otimes X)\beta(p_{t_0}, \hat{\theta}_i)) \\ \bar{M}_x &= \psi(\hat{\theta}_i)'(\hat{\Omega}_{u*}^{-1} \otimes \bar{Z}(\bar{Z}'\bar{Z})^{-1}\bar{Z}')\psi(\hat{\theta}_i) \\ \bar{M}_u &= \psi(\hat{\theta}_i)'(\hat{\Omega}_{u*}^{-1} \otimes \bar{Z}(\bar{Z}'\bar{Z})^{-1}\bar{Z}')\bar{Y}^* - f^*(\hat{\theta}_i))\,. \end{aligned}$$

Convergence to $\hat{\theta}$ is achieved when $\Delta\hat{\theta}_i$ becomes sufficiently small.

Following Hartley (1961) we check whether $S(\hat{\theta}_i + \Delta\hat{\theta}_i) < S(\hat{\theta}_i)$; if not, we shrink $\Delta\hat{\theta}_i$ by forming $\hat{\theta}_{i+1} = \hat{\theta}_i + \Delta\hat{\theta}_i / 2$. We continue until improvement in S is found, where a new iteration is performed; alternatively, if the current increment falls below a convergence criterion, we have found the minimum.

Under our assumptions the NL3SLS estimator $\hat{\theta}$ is consistent for θ * as $K', T \to \infty$, and asymptotically normal with asymptotic covariance matrix

$$\text{AVAR}\ (\hat{\theta}) = (M^*_{x0} + \bar{M}^*_x)^{-1}\ , \tag{10.15}$$

where the moment matrices are evaluated at the true values Ω_ε and Ω_u. A consistent estimator of AVAR($\hat{\theta}$) is given by $(M_{x0} + \bar{M}_x)^{-1}$.

Closer inspection of (10.14) indicates the relationship of NL3SLS to linear pooling estimators; for example, if $\Theta^0 = \bar{\Theta}$, $\Theta^1 = \varnothing$, then

$$\Delta\hat{\theta}_i = (M_{x0} + \bar{M}_x)^{-1}(M_{x0}\Delta\hat{\theta}^0_i + \bar{M}_x\Delta\hat{\bar{\theta}}_i)\,,$$

where $\Delta\hat{\theta}^0_i$ and $\Delta\hat{\bar{\theta}}_i$ are the Gauss-Newton increments from minimizing $S^0(\theta)$ and $\bar{S}(\theta)$ respectively. Thus, $\Delta\hat{\theta}_i$ is just a matrix weighted average of the individual increments.[11]

Second, if the cross-section data are exogenous, then $Z_0 = X$, and both M_{x0} and $M_{\varepsilon 0}$ can be evaluated using the moments $X'X$ and $(I_q \otimes X)'Y$. In this case one can obtain $\hat{\Omega}_\varepsilon$ from the cross-section residuals of each equation estimated by ordinary least squares (OLS).

Third, additional cross-section data sets can be incorporated in a straightforward manner. If an additional cross section is available for time t_1, (or t_0, for that matter) with data Y_1, X_1 and Z_1, then $B_1(\theta)$, M_{x1} and $M_{\varepsilon 1}$ are formed as above, and M_{x1} and $M_{\varepsilon 1}$ enter additively into the first and second term of (10.14). The proper correction (10.7) must be applied to the aggregate data series.[12] In this way all of the available cross-section information can be used in estimating the vector of parameters θ.

10.4 Parametric Hypothesis Tests

Statistical hypotheses take the form $\theta^* = g(\rho^*)$, for some $\rho = \rho^*$, where ρ is a vector with dimensionality R less than that of θ, say L. Our interest is in testing the hypothesis that $\theta^* = g(\rho^*)$ against the alternative $\theta^* \neq g(\rho^*)$ for any ρ^*. For this task, we require two additional assumptions, listed in appendix 10.A, which indicate that ρ is identified and that the disturbances ε_{kt} and u_t^* are normally distributed.

The test statistic, analogous to a likelihood ratio, is found as follows: Let $S_r(\rho)$ denote the objective function

$$S_r(\rho) = (\mathbf{Y} - \psi(g(\rho)))'[\hat{\Sigma}^{-1} \otimes Z(Z'Z)^{-1}Z'](\mathbf{Y} - \psi(g(\rho)))\,. \tag{10.16}$$

Denote by $\hat{\rho}$ the value of ρ which minimizes $S_r(\rho)$. Under our assumptions Gallant and Jorgenson (1979) have shown that the statistic,

$$\tau = S_r(\hat{\rho}) - S(\hat{\theta}), \tag{10.17}$$

is asymptotically distributed as chi-square with $L - R$ degrees of freedom under the null hypothesis. The appropriate test statistic is provided by τ.

The minimization of $S_r(\rho)$ to find $\hat{\rho}$ is analogous to the procedure for finding $\hat{\theta}$, and requires only moment matrices from the cross section. Although any consistent estimator of Σ can be used in evaluating (10.16), the monotonicity condition $S_r(\hat{\rho}) - S(\hat{\theta}) > 0$ will be guaranteed only if the same $\hat{\Sigma}$ is used to evaluate both S_r and S. Thus, the original consistent estimates $\hat{\Omega}_\varepsilon$ and $\hat{\Omega}_{u*}$ used in estimating $\hat{\theta}$ should be used in finding estimators for restricted versions of the model.

10.5 Estimation Subject to Inequality Restrictions

The final topic we consider is the estimation of the parameter θ subject to inequality restrictions. For example, an integrable demand system must obey the condition that the Slutsky matrix of compensated price derivatives is negative semidefinite. The unconstrained estimator $\hat{\theta}$ need not obey these restrictions for finite samples; thus, it may be desirable to impose them. We represent such restrictions formally as

$$\phi_m(\theta^*) \geq 0\,, \quad (m = 1, 2, \ldots, M')\,, \tag{10.18}$$

where we assume ϕ_m to be twice continuously differentiable in each component of θ.

The inequality constrained estimator $\hat{\hat{\theta}}$ minimizes $S(\theta)$ subject to the constraints (10.18). This estimator may be obtained from a saddlepoint of the Lagrangian function

$$L = S(\theta) + \lambda'\phi\,, \tag{10.19}$$

where λ is a vector of M′ Lagrange multipliers and ϕ is the M' vector of constraint functions. The Kuhn-Tucker (1951) conditions for a saddlepoint of this Lagrangian are

$$\frac{\partial L}{\partial \theta} = \frac{\partial S(\theta)}{\partial \theta} + \lambda'(\Phi(\theta)) = 0\,,$$

and the complementary slackness condition

$$\lambda'\phi = 0\,, \qquad \lambda \geq 0\,,$$

where $\Phi(\theta)$ is the matrix with elements $\{\partial\phi_i / \partial\theta_j\}$.

To obtain the estimator $\hat{\hat{\theta}}$ we begin by linearizing the model as in (10.13). Next, we linearize the constraints as

$$\phi(\theta_{i+1}) = \Phi(\hat{\hat{\theta}}_i)\ \Delta\ \theta_i + \phi(\hat{\hat{\theta}}_i)\,,$$

where $\hat{\hat{\theta}}_i$ is the current iteration value of the unknown parameters. We then apply Liew's (1976) inequality constrained linear three-stage least squares method to the linear model, obtaining

$$\Delta\hat{\hat{\theta}}_i = \Delta\hat{\theta}_i + (M_{\otimes} + \bar{M}_x)^{-1}\Phi(\hat{\hat{\theta}}_i)'\lambda\,^*\,,$$

where $\Delta\hat{\theta}_i$ is given by (10.14) and $\lambda\,^*$ is the solution of the linear complementarity problem

$$\Phi(\hat{\hat{\theta}}_i)(M_{\otimes} + \bar{M}_x)^{-1}\Phi(\hat{\hat{\theta}}_i)'\lambda + [\Phi(\hat{\hat{\theta}}_i)\Delta\hat{\theta}_i - \phi(\hat{\hat{\theta}}_i)]'\lambda = 0\,, \qquad \lambda \geq 0.$$

Given $\hat{\hat{\theta}}_i$ that satisfies the constraints (10.18), we update to $\hat{\hat{\theta}}_{i+1} = \hat{\hat{\theta}}_i + \Delta\hat{\theta}_i$ and check that both $S(\hat{\hat{\theta}}_{i+1}) < S(\hat{\hat{\theta}}_i)$, and that $\phi_m(\hat{\theta}_{i+1}) \geq 0$, $m = 1, 2, \ldots, M'$. If not, we shrink the increment vector as before, until either improvement is found or the increment values fall in absolute value below a convergence criterion. This concludes our discussion of the NL3SLS estimator.

10.6 Illustration: Residential Demand for Energy

To illustrate nonlinear three-stage least squares pooling of cross-section and time-series observations, we consider a model of residential demand for energy. In the first stage of this model total expenditure is allocated between energy and nonenergy commodities. In the second stage total expenditure on energy is allocated among four types of energy. The model of energy expenditures is generated from a homothetic translog indirect utility function for each consuming unit.[13]

To represent our econometric model of consumer behavior we introduce some additional notation. We consider observations on expenditure patterns by K consuming units, indexed by $k = 1, 2, \ldots, K$, for T time periods, indexed by $t = 1, 2, \ldots, T$. The vector of expenditure shares for the kth consuming unit in the tth time period is denoted v_{kt} $(k = 1, 2, \ldots, K;\ t = 1, 2, \ldots, T)$. Similarly, expenditure for the kth unit on all types of energy in the tth time period is denoted E_{kt} $(k = 1, 2, \ldots, K;\ t = 1, 2, \ldots, T)$. The vector of energy prices faced by all consuming units in the tth time period is denoted q_t $(t = 1, 2, \ldots, T)$. Similarly, the vector of logarithms of energy prices in the tth time period is denoted in $\ln q_t$ $(t = 1, 2, \ldots, T)$.

Using our new notation, the individual expenditure shares can be written

$$-v_{kt} = \gamma_q + \Delta_{qq} \ln q_t + \Delta_{qA} A_{kt} + \varepsilon_{kt}\,, \quad (k = 1, 2, \ldots, K;\, t = 1, 2, \ldots, T)\,, \qquad (10.20)$$

where ε_{kt} $(k = 1, 2, \ldots, K;\ t = 1, 2, \ldots, T)$ is the vector of unobservable random disturbances for the kth consuming unit and the tth time period. Since the individual expenditure shares for all types of energy sum to unity for each consuming unit in each time period, the unobservable random disturbances for all types of energy sum to zero for each unit in each time period

$$i'\varepsilon_{kt} = 0\,, \quad (k = 1, 2, \ldots, K;\ t = 1, 2, \ldots, T)\,. \qquad (10.21)$$

These disturbances are not distributed independently.

We assume that the unobservable random disturbances for all commodities have expected value equal to zero for all observations

$$E(\varepsilon_{kt}) = 0\,, \quad (k = 1, 2, \ldots, K;\ t = 1, 2, \ldots, T)\,. \qquad (10.22)$$

We also assume that these disturbances have the same covariance matrix for all observations

$$V(\varepsilon_{kt}) = \Omega_\varepsilon\,, \quad (k = 1, 2, \ldots, K;\ t = 1, 2, \ldots, T)\,. \tag{10.23}$$

Since the disturbances sum to zero for each observation, this matrix is nonnegative definite with rank at most equal to $M - 1$, where M is the number of types of energy. We assume that the covariance matrix has rank equal to $M - 1$.

Finally, we assume that disturbances corresponding to distinct observations are uncorrelated. Under this assumption the covariance matrix of the disturbances for all consuming units at a given point of time has the Kronecker product form

$$V \begin{bmatrix} \varepsilon_{1t} \\ \varepsilon_{2t} \\ \cdot \\ \cdot \\ \cdot \\ \varepsilon_{Kt} \end{bmatrix} = \Omega_\varepsilon \otimes I\,. \tag{10.24}$$

The covariance matrix of the disturbances for all time periods for a given individual has an analogous form. The unknown parameters of the system of equations determining the individual energy expenditure shares can be estimated from time-series data on individual energy expenditure shares, energy prices, and demographic characteristics.

We assume that each of the equations for the aggregate energy expenditure shares has three additive components. The first is a weighted average of the nonrandom functions of energy prices and demographic characteristics that determine the individual energy expenditure shares. The second is a weighted average of the unobservable random disturbances in equations for the individual energy expenditure shares. The third is a weighted average of the unobservable random errors of measurement in the observations on the aggregate energy expenditure shares.

Denoting the vector of aggregate expenditure shares at time t by v_t $(t = 1, 2, \ldots, T)$, we can express these shares in the form

$$-v_t = \gamma_q + \Delta_{qq} \ln q_t + \Delta_{qA} \frac{\sum_{k=1}^{K} E_{kt} A_{kt}}{\sum_{k=1}^{K} E_{kt}} + \varepsilon_t\,, \qquad (t = 1, 2, \ldots, T)\,,$$

where ε_t $(t = 1, 2, \ldots, T)$ is the vector of unobservable random disturbances for the tth time period.

The aggregate disturbances ε_t can be expressed in the form

$$\varepsilon_t = \frac{\sum_{k=1}^{K} E_{kt}\varepsilon_{kt}}{\sum_{k=1}^{K} E_{kt}} + \frac{\sum_{k=1}^{K} E_{kt}\nu_{kt}}{\sum_{k=1}^{K} E_{kt}}, \qquad (t = 1, 2, \ldots, T), \tag{10.25}$$

where ν_{kt} $(k = 1, 2, \ldots, K;\ t = 1, 2, \ldots, T)$ is the vector of errors of measurement that underly the data on the aggregate energy expenditure shares. Since the random disturbances for all commodities sum to zero in each time period

$$i'\varepsilon_t = 0, \qquad (t = 1, 2, \ldots, T), \tag{10.26}$$

these disturbances are not distributed independently.

We assume that the errors of measurement that underly the data on the aggregate energy expenditure shares have expected value equal to zero for all observations

$$E(\nu_{kt}) = 0, \qquad (k = 1, 2, \ldots, K;\ t = 1, 2, \ldots, T).$$

We also assume that these errors have the same covariance matrix for all observations

$$V(\nu_{kt}) = \Omega_\nu, \qquad (k = 1, 2, \ldots, K;\ t = 1, 2, \ldots, T),$$

and that the rank of this matrix is equal to $M - 1$.

If the errors of measurement are distributed independently of energy expenditure and of the disturbances in the equations for the individual energy expenditure shares, the aggregate disturbances have expected value equal to zero for all time periods

$$E(\varepsilon_t) = 0, \qquad (t = 1, 2, \ldots, T), \tag{10.27}$$

and have a covariance matrix given by

$$V(\varepsilon_t) = \frac{\sum_{k=1}^{K} E_{kt}^2}{\left(\sum_{k=1}^{K} E_{kt}\right)^2}\Omega_\varepsilon + \frac{\sum_{k=1}^{K} E_{kt}^2}{\left(\sum_{k=1}^{K} E_{kt}\right)^2}\Omega_\nu, \qquad (t = 1, 2, \ldots, T),$$

so that the aggregate disturbances for different time periods are heteroscedastic.

We can correct for heteroscedasticity of the aggregate disturbances by transforming the observations on the aggregate energy expenditure shares as follows

$$-\rho_t v_t = \rho_t \left(\gamma_q + \Delta_{qq} \ln q_t + \Delta_{qA} \frac{\sum_{k=1}^{K} E_{kt} A_{kt}}{\sum_{k=1}^{K} E_{kt}} \right) + \rho_t \varepsilon_t \,, \qquad (t = 1, 2, \ldots, T) \,,$$

where

$$\rho_t^2 = \frac{\left(\sum_{k=1}^{K} E_{kt} \right)^2}{\sum_{k=1}^{K} E_{kt}^2} \,, \qquad (t = 1, 2, \ldots, T) \,.$$

The covariance matrix of the transformed disturbances, say Ω, becomes

$$V(\rho_t \varepsilon_t) = \Omega_\varepsilon + \Omega_v = \Omega \,.$$

This matrix is nonnegative definite with rank equal to $M - 1$. Finally, we assume that the errors of measurement corresponding to distinct observations are uncorrelated. Under this assumption the covariance matrix of the transformed disturbances at all points of time has the Kronecker product form

$$V \begin{bmatrix} \rho_1 \varepsilon_1 \\ \rho_2 \varepsilon_2 \\ \cdot \\ \cdot \\ \cdot \\ \rho_T \varepsilon_T \end{bmatrix} = \Omega \otimes I \,. \qquad (10.28)$$

To estimate the parameters of our econometric model of residential demand for energy we utilize five sets of cross-section observations on individual energy expenditure patterns—the 1960–1961, 1972, and 1973 Consumer Expenditure Surveys (CES) of the Bureau of Labor Statistics (BLS) and the 1973 and 1975 Lifestyle and Household Energy Use Surveys (LHES) of the Washington Center for Metropolitan Studies (WCMS). We estimate the parameters of our model by pooling the individual cross-section data with aggregate time-series data. For this purpose we utilize annual data on prices and aggregate quantities consumed of four types of energy—electricity, natural gas, fuel oil, and other, and gasoline—from the U.S. National Income and Product Accounts for the period 1958 to 1978.

A key feature of our econometric model of residential demand for energy is the incorporation of the distribution of energy expenditures among demographic groups into the determination of the allocation of aggregate energy expenditure among types of energy. For this purpose we assigned each household to one of the categories for each of five demographic characteristics:

1. *Family size*: 1, 2, 3, 4, 5, 6, 7 or more persons
2. *Age of head*: 15–24, 25–34, 35–44, 45–54, 55–65, 65 and over
3. *Region of residence*: Northeast, North Central, South and West
4. *Race*: White, nonwhite
5. *Type of residence*: Urban, rural

Annual time-series data for the statistics that describe the distribution of energy expenditures among groups are constructed on the basis of methodology developed by Stoker (1979). This methodology utilizes a detailed tabulation of before-tax income for all years from *Current Population Reports, Series P-60, Consumer Income*,[14] and a bridging equation estimated from cross-section data on energy expenditures.[15] This results in an annual time series of proportions of aggregate energy expenditures for all demographic groups. A list of instrumental variables used in our estimation procedure is given in appendix 10.B.

In our application we have four types of energy, so that we estimate the parameters of three equations. The parameters of the remaining equations are estimated from the restrictions implied by summability, that is, by the fact that the shares of all four types of energy in total energy expenditure must sum to unity. As unknown parameters we have three elements of the vector γ_q, sixteen attribute coefficients for each of the three equations in the matrix Δ_{qA}, and six price coefficients in the matrix Δ_{qq}, which is symmetric, for a total of 57 unknown parameters.

The main results of estimating our econometric model of residential demand for energy are presented in table 10.1. The results employ aggregate time-series data and cross-section data from five surveys—1960–1961 CES, 1972 CES, 1973 CES, 1973 LHES, and 1975 LHES. The estimates were obtained by fitting the equations for electricity, natural gas, and fuel oil, with coefficients for the gasoline equation derived from the summability restrictions.

When we examine the results we see that most of the coefficients are estimated very precisely. Utilizing a one percent normal critical value for ratios of each coefficient to its standard error, we see that all price coefficients are significant except for the coefficients of the price of gasoline, and the own-price coefficient of natural gas. This leads us to suspect that gasoline and the other types of energy are separable; we perform a formal test of this hypothesis.

Turning to the demographic coefficients, we see that all are significant except for family sizes 2, 4, 5, North Central and West regions in the electricity equations, family sizes 3 through 7 or more in the natural gas equation, family sizes 2 and 4 and nonwhite in the fuel oil equation, and family sizes 4, 6 and 7 or more in the gasoline equation. The insignificance of these coefficients poses no problem for our model, since they indicate no difference of families of these types from a family of size one, age of head 15–24, region Northeast, race white, and residence urban.

A natural structure for the allocation of relative energy expenditures would involve the separability of gasoline for transportation from the fuels for household operation. Testing this type of separability within the translog model amounts to testing the hypothesis that cross-price coefficients for the price of gasoline are zero. Failure to reject separability restrictions implies that each family's indirect utility function can be represented with gasoline separable from the other fuels. This implies that price and quantity indexes for energy for household operation could be constructed for each family. However, demographic differences in the estimated equations imply that the aggregate price of energy for household operations would vary from household to household. The restrictions required for a common aggregate price for all households are much stronger, implying that all demographic effects vanish from the electricity, natural gas and fuel oil equations and other; these restrictions are certainly in conflict with the estimates of the demographic coefficients presented in table 10.1.

The test for separability in the translog model involves the restriction of two gasoline price coefficients to zero. Summability restrictions guarantee that the remaining gasoline price coefficients must be equal to zero. The test is performed as follows: Let $\hat{\theta}$ be the unrestricted parameter estimates in table 10.1 and let $\hat{\theta}^R$ be the estimates subject to the separability restrictions. Then the statistic $SSR(\hat{\theta}^R) - SSR(\hat{\theta})$ is distributed asymptotically as chi-squared with two degrees of freedom; comparison with chi-squared critical values permits us to carry out the test.

Table 10.2 contains the NL3SLS estimates constrained by separability of gasoline from energy used for household operations. Comparing the results with those presented in table 10.1, we see that

Table 10.1
Residential demand for energy

Notation	Definition
ELEC	Total electricity expenditures
GAS	Total natural gas expenditures
SOL	Fuel oil and other expenditures
GASO	Total gasoline expenditures
F2,F3,...,F7	Family sizes 2,3,...,7 or more
A30,A40,...,A70	Age classes 25–34, 35–44, ..., 65 or over
RNC, RS, RW	North Central, South, and West regions
NW	Nonwhite
RUR	Rural
C	Constant term
P	Price
W	Share in total energy expenditures

Pooled estimation results: Five cross-section data sets[a]

	W_{ELEC}	W_{GAS}	W_{SOL}	W_{GASO}
C	–.19408(.00613)	–.05933(.00548)	–.17494(.00497)	–.57164(.00783)
P_{ELEC}	.19525(.0247)	–.07742(.0154)	–.11574(.0129)	–.00235(.0215)
P_{GAS}	–.07742(.0154)	.03816(.0194)	.04478(.0100)	–.00552(.0151)
P_{SOL}	–.11547(.0129)	.04478(.0100)	.09950(.0176)	–.02881(.0116)
P_{GASO}	–.00235(.0215)	–.00552(.0151)	–.02881(.0116)	.03669(.0221)
F2	.00875(.00385)	.01164(.00346)	.00578(.00264)	–.02617(.00505)
F3	.01695(.00458)	.00615(.00412)	–.01074(.00313)	–.01236(.00600)
F4	.00506(.00491)	–.00067(.00440)	–.00272(.00333)	–.00166(.00643)
F5	.00102(.00582)	–.00949(.00522)	–.01294(.00393)	.02142(.00762)
F6	.02728(.00727)	.00186(.00654)	–.02758(.00493)	–.00156(.00953)
F7	.01838(.00765)	.01886(.00686)	–.03629(.00515)	–.00095(.0100)
A30	–.04510(.00568)	–.03069(.00510)	–.01483(.00386)	.09062(.00744)
A40	–.03043(.00611)	–.05132(.00548)	–.02067(.00414)	.10242(.00800)
A50	–.03483(.00578)	–.04415(.00518)	–.03410(.00392)	.11308(.00756)
A60	–.02949(.00577)	–.05081(.00418)	–.05428(.00391)	.13457(.00756)
A70	–.06154(.00560)	–.08582(.00502)	–.10288(.00381)	.25023(.00733)
RNC	.00837(.00391)	–.07277(.00351)	.09628(.00264)	–.03188(.00512)
RS	–.04519(.00392)	–.03384(.00352)	.11666(.00368)	–.03763(.00513)
RW	.00613(.00419)	–.05045(.00374)	.10529(.00278)	–.06097(.00547)
NW	–.01645(.00456)	–.08812(.00401)	.00493(.00289)	.09965(.00594)
RUR	.01297(.00367)	.11150(.00325)	–.11128(.00240)	–.01318(.00478)

[a] Convergence after three iterations. SSR = 8537.79.

Table 10.2
Residential demand for energy with gasoline separable from other types of energy[a]

	W_{ELEC}	W_{GAS}	W_{SOL}	W_{GASO}
P_{ELEC}	.12698(.0109)	–.06869(.0138)	–.05829(.00629)	.00000(.000)
P_{GAS}	–.06869(.0138)	.01943(.0206)	.04925(.0101)	.00000(.000)
P_{SOL}	–.05829(.00629)	.04925(.0101)	.00904(.00763)	.00000(.000)
P_{GASO}	.00000(.000)	.00000(.000)	.00000(.000)	.00000(.000)
C	–.19926(.00608)	–.06001(.00545)	–.16754(.00480)	–.57318(.00780)
F2	.00866(.00385)	.01158(.00346)	.00568(.00264)	–.02592(.00504)
F3	.01684(.00458)	.00604(.00412)	–.01099(.00313)	–.01189(.00600)
F4	.00496(.00491)	–.00077(.00440)	–.00300(.00333)	–.00119(.00642)
F5	.00072(.00582)	–.00974(.00522)	–.01342(.00393)	.02244(.00761)
F6	.02681(.00727)	.00151(.00654)	–.02826(.00493)	–.00006(.00952)
F7	.01777(.00764)	.01841(.00685)	–.03712(.00514)	.00094(.00999)
A30	–.04503(.00568)	–.03063(.00510)	–.01470(.00386)	.09036(.00744)
A40	–.03015(.00611)	–.05122(.00548)	–.02068(.00414)	.10204(.00800)
A50	–.03483(.00578)	–.04416(.00518)	–.03414(.00392)	.11312(.00756)
A60	–.02945(.00577)	–.05080(.00518)	–.05436(.00391)	.13460(.00756)
A70	–.06149(.00560)	–.08582(.00502)	–.10299(.00381)	.25029(.00733)
RNC	.00832(.00391)	–.07276(.00351)	.09639(.00264)	–.03195(.00512)
RS	–.04522(.00392)	–.03378(.00352)	.11694(.00267)	–.03793(.00512)
RW	.00618(.00419)	–.05039(.00374)	.10542(.00278)	–.06120(.00547)
NW	–.01641(.00456)	–.08806(.00401)	.00508(.00289)	.09938(.00594)
RUR	.01299(.00366)	.11147(.00325)	–.11137(.00240)	–.01309(.00478)

[a] Convergence after three iterations. SSR = 85,432.23.

the coefficient estimates for demographic effects are nearly identical. Second, we see that the coefficients of the price of electricity all increase in absolute value, with the remaining coefficients declining somewhat in absolute value. The test of separability is performed as follows: $SSR(\hat{\theta}^R) = 85415.50$, $SSR(\hat{\theta}) = 85375.56$ so that $SSR(\hat{\theta}^R) - SSR(\hat{\theta}) = 39.94$. The one percent critical level for a chi-squared test with two degrees of freedom is 9.21; we reject separability at this level of significance.

10.7 Conclusion

In this chapter we have discussed the nonlinear three-stage least squares method of pooling average time-series and cross-section data. There are two major advantages of this technique:

The first is the identification of parameters and the gains in efficiency in estimation. For example, by pooling average time-series and cross-section data, models can be estimated that account for a large number of specific demographic effects in consumer behavior in both microeconomic and macroeconomic settings. Such effects are difficult to identify or estimate precisely using aggregate time-series data alone. Alternatively, the effects of time varying factors such as price levels that are constant across consumers in each time period may be impossible to identify using only data from a single cross-section survey. Both effects can be estimated when cross-section observations are pooled with average time-series observations.

The second major advantage of the nonlinear three-stage least squares technique is ease of computation. While exact aggregation models can allow for substantial nonlinearities in variables representing common influences on behavior as well as in parameters, cross-section data are employed in pooled estimation through moment matrices. These matrices can be constructed utilizing only one pass through each cross-section data source. This feature substantially reduces the time and expense of performing iterations to estimate a nonlinear model and the cost of estimating several restricted versions of the same model for hypothesis testing.

Appendix 10.A Technical Assumptions

Below we list the assumptions required to establish consistency and asymptotic normality for the NL3SLS estimator. Assumptions 10.1–10.5 follow Gallant (1977) and assumptions 10.6–10.7 follow Jorgenson and Gallant (1979).

Assumption 10.1: The parameter space of θ, say Θ, is compact, with the true value an interior point.

Assumption 10.2: The components of $\beta_n\ (p_t, \theta)\ (n = 1, 2, \ldots, N)$ are twice continuously differentiable in θ_j.

For the next two assumptions, we use the notation $\beta_n^j\ (p_t, \theta)$ and β_n^{1j} (p_t, θ) to refer to the vectors

$$\beta_n^j(p_t, \theta) = \left(\frac{\partial \beta_{n1}}{\partial \theta_j}, \frac{\partial \beta_{n2}}{\partial \theta_j}, \ldots, \frac{\partial \beta_{nN}}{\partial \theta_j}\right)',$$

$$\beta_n^{1j}(p_t, \theta) = \left(\frac{\partial^2 \beta_{n1}}{\partial \theta_1 \partial \theta_j}, \frac{\partial^2 \beta_{n2}}{\partial \theta_1 \partial \theta_j}, \ldots, \frac{\partial^2 \beta_{nN}}{\partial \theta_1 \partial \theta_j}\right)',$$

where β_{nm} is the mth component of $\beta_n\ (p_t, \theta)$.

Assumption 10.3A (Cross Section): The matrix $(1/N)Z_0'Z_0$ converges to a positive definite matrix as $N \to \infty$. The Cesaro sums,

$$\frac{1}{N}\sum_k (y_{nkt_0} - x_{kt_0}'\beta_n(p_{t_0},\theta))(y_{jkt_0} - x_{kt_0}'\beta_j(p_{t_0},\theta))$$
$$\frac{1}{N}\sum_k z_{kt_0}(y_{nkt} - x_{kt}'\beta_n(p_{t_0},\theta))$$
$$\frac{1}{N}\sum_k z_{kt_0}(x_{kt_0}'\beta_n^1(p_{t_0},\theta))$$

converge almost surely uniformly in θ $(n, j = 1, 2, \ldots, N)$. The sums

$$\frac{1}{N}\sum_k \sup_\theta | z_{s'kt_0}(\bar{x}'_{kt_0}\beta_n^1(p_{t_0},\theta))|$$
$$\frac{1}{N}\sum_k \sup_\theta | z_{s'kt_0}(\bar{x}_{kt_0'}\beta_n^{j1}(p_{t_0},\theta))|$$

are bounded almost surely for all $(n, j = 1, 2, \ldots, N;\ s' = 1, 2, \ldots, S)$, where z_{skt_0}' is the sth component of $\bar{z}_{kt_0}$.

Assumption 10.3B (Time Series): The matrix $(1/T)\bar{Z}'\bar{Z}$ converges to a positive definite matrix as $T \to \infty$. The Cesaro sums

$$\frac{1}{T}\sum_t K_t(\bar{y}_{it} - \bar{x}'_t\beta_n(p_t,\theta))(\bar{y}_{jt} - \bar{x}'_t\beta_j(p_t,\theta))$$
$$\frac{1}{T}\sum_t \sqrt{K_t}\,\bar{z}_t(\bar{y}_{nt} - \bar{x}'_t\beta_n(p_t,\theta))$$
$$\frac{1}{T}\sum_t \sqrt{K_t}\,\bar{z}_t(\bar{x}'_t\beta_n^1(p_t,\theta))$$

converge almost surely in θ $(n, j = 1, 2, \ldots, N)$. The sums,

$$\frac{1}{T}\sum_t \sup_\theta|\bar{z}_{s't}(\bar{x}'_t\beta_n^1(p_t,\theta))|$$
$$\frac{1}{T}\sum_t \sup_\theta|\bar{z}_{s't}(\bar{x}'_t\beta_n^{1j}(p_t,\theta))|$$

are bounded almost surely $(n, j = 1, 2, \ldots, N)$, where $\bar{z}_{s't}$ is the sth component of $\bar{z}_t$.

Assumption 10.4: The matrix

$$\lim_{N,T\to\infty} \frac{1}{N+T}(M_{x0}^* + \bar{M}_x^*)$$

is nonsingular, where M_{x0}^* and $\bar{M}_x^*$ are defined in equations (10.14) and (10.15).

Assumption 10.5 (Identification): The parameter θ of (10.11) is identified by the instrumental variables z_{kt_0} and $\bar{z}_t$; that is, the only solution of the equations defined by the almost sure limits

$$\lim_{N\to\infty} \frac{1}{N} \sum_k z_{kt_0}(y_{nkt} - x'_{kt}\beta_n(p_{t_0}, \theta)) = 0\,, \qquad (n = 1, 2, \ldots, N)\,, \qquad (10.A.1)$$

$$\lim_{T\to\infty} \frac{1}{T} \sum_t \sqrt{K_t}\, \bar{z}_t(\bar{y}_{nt} - \overline{x'_t}\beta_n(p_t, \theta)) = 0\,, \qquad (n = 1, 2, \ldots, N)\,, \qquad (10.A.2)$$

is the true value θ^*.

Assumption 10.6 (Parameter Restriction): The function $g(\rho)$ is a twice continuously differentiable mapping of a compact set P into the parameter space Θ. There is only one point ρ^* in P which satisfies $g(\rho) = \theta^*$ and ρ^* is an interior point of P. The $L \times R$ matrix $G(\rho^*)$ has rank R, where the (n, j)th element of G is $\partial g_n / \partial \rho_j$, where g_n is the nth component of $g(\rho)$ and ρ_j is the jth component of ρ.

Assumption 10.7: (Normality). The disturbances ε_{kt} and ν_{kt} are normally distributed for all k and t.

Appendix 10.B

Table 10.B.1
Instrumental variables, 1958–1978

Notation	Definition
I1	Constant
I2	Effective tax rate, labor services
I3	Effective tax rate, noncompetitive services
I4	Time available for labor services
I5	U.S. population, millions of individuals
I6	Implicit deflator, supply of labor services
I7	Implicit deflator, government purchases of labor services
I8	Exogeneous income, which equals government transfers to persons (excepting social insurance) less personal transfers to foreigners and personal nontax payments to government
I9	Private national wealth, lagged one period
I10	Potential time for labor services; rate of Harrod neutral change
I11	Total imports
I12	Implicit deflator, noncompetitive imports
I13	Corrected deflator for labor services
I14	Time, set to 0 in 1972

Notes

1. For detailed discussion of nonlinear three stage least squares estimators, see Amemiya (1977), Gallant (1977), and Gallant and Jorgenson (1979).
2. The correspondence between individual and aggregate behavior is discussed by Lau (1977b, 1982) and Stoker (1982, 1984).
3. An alternative approach to aggregation is based on restrictions on the distribution of the variables x_{kt}. See, for example, Stoker (1984).
4. See for example, Balestra and Nerlove (1966), Kmenta (1978), and Mundlak (1978). Much of the discussion of the linear model focuses on the stochastic specification rather than the structural model; see, for example, Amemiya (1978). The literature on pooling cross-section and average time-series data in a linear model has been surveyed by Dielman (1983).
5. This stochastic specification is used in an exact aggregation model by Jorgenson, Lau, and Stoker (1980, 1981, 1982).
6. The exclusion of ν_t from the cross-section disturbances in examples 10.2 and 10.3 may appear to be somewhat arbitrary. Suppose instead that $\nu_{t_0} + \varepsilon_{kt_0}$ represent the cross-section disturbances. The ν_{t_0} can be estimated as the difference between the estimate of the cross-section constant term and the constant term applicable to the time series. Correlation between resulting cross-section and time-series disturbances is then due only to the ε_{kt_0} terms, so that the effect of the transformation separating the two data sets is negligible.
7. This excludes the possibility that $\bar{x}_t$ is subject to measurement error; aggregate instruments would be required to deal with errors of measurement.
8. We assume that the variance of the disturbance, conditional on the instrumental variables, is constant for both cross-section and average time-series models. If this assumption is relaxed, efficiency gains are possible by adjusting the weighting matrix of equations (10.11) and (10.12). See White (1980a, b, 1982) and Hansen (1982) for details.
9. The Gauss-Newton method for systems of nonlinear regression equations is discussed by Malinvaud (1980).
10. If the observations are transformed, the transformed data should be used here.
11. Matrix-weighted averages are discussed in Chamberlain and Leamer (1976) and Mundlak (1978), among others.
12. This assumes that disturbances in different cross sections are uncorrelated, which requires transformations of the average data only. Overlapping cross sections require panel data techniques that are beyond the scope of this article.
13. This model is presented in much greater detail by Jorgenson and Stoker (1984). Jorgenson, Slesnick and Stoker (1983) have presented models of two-stage budgeting.
14. This series is published annually by the U.S. Bureau of the Census. For our study, numbers 33, 35, 37, 39, 41, 43, 47, 51, 53, 59, 60, 62, 66, 72, 75, 79, 80, 84, 85, 90, 96, 97, and 101 were employed together with technical report numbers 8 and 17.
15. For details, the interested reader is referred to Stoker (1979).

11 Two-Stage Budgeting and Consumer Demand for Energy

Dale W. Jorgenson,
Daniel T. Slesnick, and
and Thomas M. Stoker

11.1 Introduction

The purpose of this chapter is to present individual and aggregate models of consumer demand for energy. Our model of individual behavior is based on a two-stage allocation process that results in two systems of individual demand functions. In the first stage total expenditure for each consuming unit is allocated between energy and nonenergy commodities. In the second stage total expenditure on energy is allocated among individual types of energy.

Our model of aggregate consumer behavior is based on exact aggregation over individual demand functions. To be consistent with exact aggregation, individual demand functions must be linear in functions of individual attributes such as demographic characteristics, prices that vary among individuals, and total expenditure. Aggregate demand functions depend on statistics of the joint distribution of total expenditures, demographic characteristics, and prices that vary among individuals.

The primary objective of consumer demand modeling is to determine empirically the price and income elasticities of demand for specific commodities. These elasticities play a critical role in projecting demand and in evaluating the impact of economic policies on consumer welfare. For example, the own-price and cross-price elasticities of demand for energy and nonenergy commodities and for specific types of energy are essential to the analysis of energy policies.

Unfortunately, the number of own-price and cross-price elasticities of demand increases with the square of the number of commodity groups. This fact has necessitated the development of modeling strategies based on two-stage budgeting. At each stage the number of commodity groups can be kept relatively small. The usefulness of the two-stage budgeting approach is considerably enhanced by Gorman's

(1959) detailed characterization of the corresponding restrictions on preferences.

Gorman's theory of two-stage budgeting suggests two alternative approaches to modeling consumer behavior. The first is based on a utility function for each consuming unit that is additive in subutility functions for all commodity groups. Under this restriction the group utility functions must correspond to indirect utility functions having the generalized Gorman polar form of Blackorby, Primont, and Russell (1978).

The first approach to two-stage budgeting has been employed in econometric applications by Blackorby, Boyce, and Russell (1978), Braithwait (1975), Brown and Heien (1972), Deaton (1975a), Hausman and Trimble (1984), and Heien (1973). An important advantage of this approach is the possibility of exact aggregation over consumers at the second stage of the budgeting process. A significant disadvantage is the imposition of the restrictions on elasticities of demand implied by additivity at the first stage of the process.

The second approach to consumer demand modeling suggested by the theory of two-stage budgeting is based on homothetic separability. The utility function for each consuming unit is not required to be additive, but subutility functions for all commodity groups must be homothetic. This approach is implicit in many models of consumer demand for energy, for example, in the studies of consumer response to time of day pricing presented in Aigner (1984).

Our model of consumer demand treats individual types of energy as homothetically separable from nonenergy commodities. In modeling consumer demand for the resulting energy aggregate and for nonenergy commodities we permit price and income elasticities to be determined empirically. The cost of this flexibility at the first stage is that consumer demands for individual types of energy at the second stage are required to be proportional to total energy expenditure.

11.2 Translog Model of Consumer Behavior

In our model of consumer behavior the individual consuming units are households. We assume that household expenditures on commodity groups are allocated so as to maximize a household welfare function. As a consequence, the household behaves in the same way as an individual maximizing a utility function.[1] We require that both of the two systems of individual demand functions that result from the two-stage allocation process are integrable. These demand functions can be generated by Roy's (1943) Identity from indirect utility functions for each consuming unit.[2]

Before proceeding with a formal presentation of our model, we set down some notation. First, there are K consuming units, indexed by $k = 1, 2, \ldots, K$. At the first stage of the two-stage allocation process there are N commodities, indexed by $n = 1, 2, \ldots, N$; one of these commodities is energy. Without loss of generality we can take energy to be the first commodity. At the second stage there are M types of energy, indexed by $m = 1, 2, \ldots, M$. We can regard each unit as consuming $M + N - 1$ commodities, where the first M are types of energy and the remaining $N - 1$ are nonenergy commodities.

We assume that the prices of all nonenergy commodities and all types of energy are the same for all consuming units. We denote the price index of energy at the first stage by p_{1k} $(k = 1, 2, \ldots, K)$; this price index may differ among consumers. We denote the price of the nth commodity at the first stage of the two-stage allocation process by p_n $(n = 2, 3, \ldots, N)$; similarly, we denote the price of the mth commodity at the second stage by q_m $(m = 1, 2, \ldots, M)$. The quantity of the nth commodity at the first stage demanded by the kth unit is x_{nk} $(n = 1, 2, \ldots, N;\ k = 1, 2, \ldots, K)$; similarly, the quantity of the mth commodity at the second stage demanded by this unit is y_{mk} $(m = 1, 2, \ldots, M;\ k = 1, 2, \ldots, K)$.

To represent our model of consumer behavior we require the following additional notation:

$M_k = \sum_{m=1}^{M} q_m\, y_{mk} + \sum_{n=2}^{N} p_n\, x_{nk}$ — total expenditure of the kth consuming unit on energy and nonenergy commodities $(k = 1, 2, \ldots, K)$.

$E_k = \sum_{m=1}^{M} q_m\, y_{mk}$ — total expenditure of the kth consuming unit on the m types of energy $(k = 1, 2, \ldots, K)$.

A_k — attributes of the kth consuming unit, such as demographic characteristics, that reflect differences in preferences $(k = 1, 2, \ldots, K)$.

$p_k = (p_{1k}, p_2, \cdots, p_N)$ — vector of prices at the first stage for the kth consuming unit $(k = 1, 2, \ldots, K)$.

Our model of the two-stage allocation process results in two systems of individual demand functions. The first stage of the process generates a system for the allocation of total expenditure among energy and

$N-1$ nonenergy commodities. The second stage of the process produces a system for the allocation of total energy expenditure among M types of energy. The system of individual demand functions for the allocation of total energy expenditure corresponds to homothetic preferences, so that demand functions for all types of energy are proportional to total energy expenditure.

11.2.1 First Stage

To represent the first stage of our model of consumer behavior we require the following additional notation:

$w_{1k} = p_{1k}\, x_{1k}/M_k$ — expenditure share of energy in the budget of the kth consuming unit $(k = 1, 2, \ldots, K)$.

$w_{nk} = p_{nk}\, x_{nk}/M_k$ — expenditure share of the nth nonenergy commodity in the budget of the kth consuming unit $(n = 2, 3, \ldots, N;\ k = 1, 2, \ldots, K)$.

$w_k = (w_{2k}, w_{3k}, \ldots, w_{Nk})$ — vector of expenditure shares on nonenergy commodities for the kth consuming unit $(k = 1, 2, \ldots, K)$.

$\ln \frac{p_{1k}}{M_k}$ — logarithm of the ratio of the price index for energy to expenditure by the kth consuming unit $(k = 1, 2, \ldots, K)$.

$\ln \frac{p}{M_k} = \left(\ln \frac{p_2}{M_k}, \ln \frac{p_3}{M_k}, \ldots, \ln \frac{p_N}{M_k}\right)$ — vector of logarithms of ratios of prices of nonenergy commodities to expenditure by the kth consuming unit $(k = 1, 2, \ldots, K)$.

$\ln p_{1k}$ — logarithm of the price index for energy by the kth consuming unit $(k = 1, 2, \ldots, K)$.

$\ln p = (\ln p_2, \ln p_3, \ldots, \ln p_N)$ — vector of logarithms of prices of nonenergy commodities.

We assume that the kth consuming unit allocates its expenditures among energy and nonenergy commodities in accord with the transcendental logarithmic or translog indirect utility function,[3] say V_k, where

$$\ln V_k = F(A_k) + \begin{bmatrix} \ln \frac{p_{1k}}{M_k} & \ln \frac{p'}{M_k} \end{bmatrix} \begin{bmatrix} \alpha_1 \\ \alpha_p \end{bmatrix} + \frac{1}{2} \begin{bmatrix} \ln \frac{p_{1k}}{M_k} & \ln \frac{p'}{M_k} \end{bmatrix} \begin{bmatrix} \beta_{11} & \beta'_{1p} \\ \beta_{1p} & B_{pp} \end{bmatrix} \begin{bmatrix} \ln \frac{p_{1k}}{M_k} \\ \ln \frac{p}{M_k} \end{bmatrix} + \begin{bmatrix} \ln \frac{p_{1k}}{M_k} & \ln \frac{p'}{M_k} \end{bmatrix} \begin{bmatrix} \beta'_{1A} \\ B_{pA} \end{bmatrix} A_k, \quad (k = 1, 2, \ldots, K). \tag{11.1}$$

In this representation the function F depends on the attribute vector A_k but is independent of the prices p_{1k} and p and of total expenditure M_k. The scalars α_1 and β_{11}, the vectors α_p, β_{1p}, β_{1A}, and β_{p1} and the matrices B_{pp} and B_{pA} are constant parameters that are the same for all consuming units.

The expenditure shares of the kth consuming unit can be derived by the logarithmic form of Roy's Identity

$$w_{nk} = \frac{\partial \ln V_k}{\partial \ln (p_n/M_k)} \Big/ \sum \frac{\partial \ln V_k}{\partial \ln (p_n/M_k)}, \quad (n = 1, 2, \ldots, N;\ k = 1, 2, \ldots, K). \tag{11.2}$$

Applying this Identity to the translog indirect utility function, we obtain the system of individual expenditure shares

$$w_{1k} = \frac{1}{D_k}\left(\alpha_1 + \beta_{11} \ln \frac{p_{1k}}{M_k} + \beta'_{1p} \ln \frac{p}{M_k} + \beta'_{1A} A_k\right),$$
$$w_k = \frac{1}{D_k}\left(\alpha_p + \beta_{p1} \ln \frac{p_{1k}}{M_k} + B_{pp} \ln \frac{p}{M_k} + B_{pA} A_k\right), \quad (k = 1, 2, \ldots, K), \tag{11.3}$$

where the denominators $\{D_k\}$ take the form

$$D_k = i' \begin{bmatrix} \alpha_1 \\ \alpha_p \end{bmatrix} + i' \begin{bmatrix} \beta_{11} \\ \beta_{p1} \end{bmatrix} \ln \frac{p_{1k}}{M_k} + i' \begin{bmatrix} \beta'_{1p} \\ B_{pp} \end{bmatrix} \ln \frac{p}{M_k} + i' \begin{bmatrix} \beta'_{1A} \\ B_{pA} \end{bmatrix} A_k, \quad (k = 1, 2, \ldots, K). \tag{11.4}$$

and i is a vector of ones.

We first observe that the function F that appears in the translog indirect utility function does not enter into the determination of the individual expenditure shares. In the absence of further restrictions this function is not identifiable from observed patterns of individual expenditure allocation. Second, since the individual expenditure shares can be expressed as ratios of functions that are homogeneous and linear in the unknown parameters—α_1, α_p, β_{11}, β_{1p}, β_{p1}, B_{pp}, β_{1A}, B_{pA}—these shares are homogeneous of degree zero in the parameters.

By multiplying a given set of the unknown parameters by a constant we obtain another set of parameters that generates the same system of individual budget shares. Accordingly, we can choose a normalization for the parameters without affecting observed patterns of individual expenditure allocation. We find it convenient to employ the normalization

$$i'\begin{bmatrix}\alpha_1\\ \alpha_p\end{bmatrix} = -1 .$$

Under this restriction any change in the set of unknown parameters will be reflected in a change in individual expenditure patterns.

The conditions for exact aggregation are that the individual expenditure shares are linear in functions of the attributes $\{A_k\}$ and total expenditures $\{M_k\}$ for all consuming units.[4] These conditions will be satisfied if and only if the terms involving the individual attributes, prices that vary among individuals, and expenditures do not appear in the denominators of the expressions given above for the individual expenditure shares, so that

$$i'\begin{bmatrix}\beta_{11}\\ \beta_{p1}\end{bmatrix} = 0 ,$$

$$i'\begin{bmatrix}\beta'_{1p}\\ B_{pp}\end{bmatrix} i = 0 ,$$

$$i'\begin{bmatrix}\beta_{1A}\\ B_{pA}\end{bmatrix} = 0 .$$

These restrictions imply that the denominators $\{D_k\}$ reduce to

$$D = -1 + i'\begin{bmatrix}\beta'_{1p}\\ B_{pp}\end{bmatrix} \ln p ,$$

where the subscript k is no longer required, since the denominator is the same for all consuming units. Under these restrictions the individual expenditure shares can be written

$$w_{1k} = \frac{1}{D}\left(\alpha_1 + \beta_{11} \ln \frac{p_{1k}}{M_k} + \beta'_{1p} \ln \frac{p}{M_k} + \beta'_{1A} A_k\right),$$
$$w_k = \frac{1}{D}\left(\alpha_p + \beta_{p1} \ln \frac{p_{1k}}{M_k} + B_{pp} \ln \frac{p}{M_k} + B_{pA} A_k\right),$$
$$(k = 1, 2, \ldots, K). \quad (11.5)$$

The individual expenditure shares are linear in the logarithms of total expenditure $\{\ln M_k\}$, attributes $\{A_k\}$, and the logarithms of prices $\{\ln p_{1k}\}$ that vary among individuals, as required by exact aggregation.

Aggregate expenditure shares, say w_1 and w, are obtained by multiplying the corresponding individual shares, w_{1k} and w_k, respectively, by total expenditure for each consuming unit, adding over all consuming units, and dividing by aggregate expenditure

$$w_1 = \frac{\sum M_k w_{1k}}{\sum M_k}, \quad (11.6)$$
$$w = \frac{\sum M_k w_k}{\sum M_k}.$$

The aggregate expenditure shares can be written

$$w_1 = \frac{1}{D}\left(\alpha_1 + \beta_{11} \frac{\sum M_k \ln p_{1k}}{\sum M_k} + \beta'_{1p} \ln p + \beta'_{1A} \frac{\sum M_k A_k}{\sum M_k}\right),$$
$$w = \frac{1}{D}\left(\alpha_p + \beta_{p1} \frac{\sum M_k \ln p_{1k}}{\sum M_k} + B_{pp} \ln p \right.$$
$$\left. - [\beta_{p1}\ B_{pp}]i \frac{\sum M_k \ln M_k}{\sum M_k} + B_{pA} \frac{\sum M_k A_k}{\sum M_k}\right). \quad (11.7)$$

Aggregate expenditure shares depend on the logarithms of price indexes for energy that vary among individuals through the function $\sum M_k \ln p_{1k} / \sum M_k$. This statistic summarizes the impact of changes in energy prices on aggregate expenditure allocation. Second, the aggregate shares depend on the logarithms of prices of nonenergy commodities $\ln p$; we treat these prices as the same for all consumers. Third, the aggregate shares depend on the distribution of expenditures over all consuming units through the function $\sum M_k \ln M_k / \sum M_k$, which may be regarded as a statistic of the distribution; this statistic summarizes the impact of changes in the distribution of expenditures. Finally, the aggregate shares depend on the distribution of expenditures among demographic groups through the functions $\{\sum M_k A_k / \sum M_k\}$, which may be regarded as statistics of the joint distribution of expenditures and attributes. Since the attributes are represented as dummy variables, equal to one for a consuming unit with that characteristic and zero otherwise, these functions are equal to the shares of the corresponding demographic groups in aggregate expenditure. We conclude that aggregate expenditure patterns depend on the distribution of expenditure over all consuming units through the statistic $\sum M_k \ln M_k / \sum M_k$ and the distribution among demographic groups through the statistics $\{\sum M_k A_k / \sum M_k\}$.

11.2.2 Second Stage

To represent the second stage of our model of consumer behavior we require the following additional notation:

$v_{mk} = q_m y_{mk} / E_k$ — share of the mth type of energy in total energy expenditure of the kth consuming unit $(m = 1, 2, \ldots, M; k = 1, 2, \ldots, K)$.

$v_k = (v_{1k}, v_{2k}, \ldots, v_{Mk})$ — vector of expenditure shares for the kth consuming unit $(k = 1, 2, \ldots, K)$.

$\ln \frac{q}{E_k} = \left(\ln \frac{q_1}{E_k}, \ln \frac{q_2}{E_k}, \ldots, \ln \frac{q_M}{E_k}\right)$ — vector of logarithms of ratios of energy prices to total energy expenditure by the kth consuming unit $(k = 1, 2, \ldots, K)$.

$\ln q = (\ln q_1, \ln q_2, \ldots, \ln q_M)$ — vector of logarithms of energy prices.

We assume that the kth consuming unit allocates its total energy expenditure among types of energy in accord with the homothetic translog indirect utility function, say H_k, where

$$\ln H_k = G(A_k) + \ln q'\gamma_q + \ln E_k + \frac{1}{2} \ln q'\Delta_{qq} \ln q + \ln q'\Delta_{qA} A_k \, , \quad (k = 1, 2, \ldots, K) . \tag{11.8}$$

As before, the expenditure shares of the kth consuming unit can be derived by the logarithmic form of Roy's Identity, equation (11.2). Applying this Identity to the homothetic translog indirect utility function, we obtain the system of idividual expenditure shares

$$-v_k = \gamma_q + \Delta_{qq} \ln q + \Delta_{qA} A_k \,, \qquad (k = 1, 2, \ldots, K) \,. \tag{11.9}$$

The conditions for exact aggregation are that the individual expenditure shares are linear in functions of the attributes $\{A_k\}$ and total energy expenditures $\{E_k\}$ for all consuming units. These conditions are satisfied by the system of individual expenditure shares (equation (11.9)).

Aggregate expenditure shares, say v, are obtained by multiplying the individual expenditure shares by total energy expenditure for each consuming unit, adding over all consuming units, and dividing by aggregate energy expenditure

$$v = \frac{\sum E_k \, v_k}{\sum E_k} \,. \tag{11.10}$$

The aggregate expenditure shares can be written

$$-v = \gamma_q + \Delta_{qq} \ln q + \Delta_{qA} \frac{\sum E_k A_k}{\sum E_k} \,. \tag{11.11}$$

These shares depend on the logarithms of energy prices $\ln q$ and the distribution of energy expenditures among demographic groups through the functions $\{\sum E_k A_k / \sum E_k\}$, which may be regarded as statistics of the joint distribution of total energy expenditures and attributes. As before, these functions are equal to the shares of the corresponding demographic groups in aggregate energy expenditure. Aggregate energy expenditure patterns depend on the distribution of energy expenditure among demographic groups through the statistics $\{\sum E_k A_k / \sum E_k\}$.

11.2.3 Two-Stage Allocation

We have presented a model of aggregate consumer expenditures based on a two-stage allocation process. The first stage generates a system of individual demand functions for the allocation of total expenditure among energy and all nonenergy commodities. Under exact aggregation this system is linear in the logarithms of total expenditures $\{\ln M_k\}$, attributes of individual consumers $\{A_k\}$, and the logarithms of price indexes for energy $\{\ln p_{1k}\}$ that vary among consumers. The problem that remains in implementing the model is to derive an appropriate energy price index for each consumer.

The second stage of the two-stage allocation process generates a system of individual demand functions for the allocation of total energy expenditure among the individual types of energy. Under exact aggregation this system of demand functions is linear in attributes of the individual consumers $\{A_k\}$. The corresponding system of aggregate demand functions is linear in the shares of demographic groups in total energy expenditure $\{\sum E_k A_k / \sum E_k\}$. To implement this model we derive the shares of demographic groups in energy expenditure from the model of the first stage of the two-stage process.

We can express the energy price index for each consumer in terms of the homothetic translog utility function in equation (11.8)

$$\begin{aligned}\ln p_{1k} &= \ln E_k - \ln H_k \\ &= -\left[G(A_k) + \ln q'\gamma_q + \frac{1}{2}\ln q'\Delta_{qq}\ln q + \ln q'\Delta_{qA}A_k\right], \\ &\qquad\qquad (k = 1, 2, \ldots, K). \qquad (11.12)\end{aligned}$$

If we normalize the price index for each consumer so that it is equal to unity when the vector of energy prices q has components equal to unity, the function $G(A_k)$ is equal to zero for all consumers, so that the price index for energy becomes

$$-\ln p_{1k} = \ln q'\gamma_q + \frac{1}{2}\ln q'\Delta_{qq}\ln q + \ln q'\Delta_{qA}A_k\,, \quad (k=1,2,\ldots,K). \qquad (11.13)$$

The first stage model in equation (11.3) depends on the energy price index for each consumer, which summarizes the impact of changes in the prices of individual types of energy on the allocation of total expenditure. Using the price index in equation (11.13), the individual expenditure shares can be written

$$w_{1k} = \frac{1}{D}\left[\alpha_1 - \beta_{11}\left(\ln q'\gamma_q + \frac{1}{2}\ln q'\Delta_{qq}\ln q + \ln q'\Delta_{qA}A_k\right)\right.$$
$$\left. + \beta'_{1p}\ln p + \beta'_{1A}A_k\right], \qquad (11.14)$$
$$w_k = \frac{1}{D}\left[\alpha_p - \beta_{p1}\left(\ln q'\gamma_q + \frac{1}{2}\ln q'\Delta_{qq}\ln q + \ln q'\Delta_{qA}A_k\right)\right.$$
$$\left. + B_{pp}\ln p - \{\beta_{p1}\ B_{pp}\}i\ \ln M_k + B_{pA}A_k\right], \quad (k = 1, 2, \ldots, K).$$

The first stage model in equation (11.7) depends on the weighted average of the logarithms of energy price indexes for all consumers $\sum M_k \ln p_{1k} / \sum M_k$. This statistic can be regarded as an aggregate energy price index, since it summarizes the impact of changes in the prices of individual types of energy on the allocation of aggregate expenditure. Using the individual energy price indexes in equation (11.13) we can express the aggregate energy price index in the form

$$-\frac{\sum M_k \ln p_{1k}}{\sum M_k} = \ln q'\gamma_q + \frac{1}{2}\ln q'\Delta_{qq}\ln q + \ln q'\Delta_{qA}\frac{\sum M_k A_k}{\sum M_k}. \qquad (11.15)$$

This price index depends on the vector of energy prices q and the shares of demographic groups in total expenditure $\{\sum M_k A_k / \sum M_k\}$.

We can express the first stage model of aggregate consumer behavior in equation (11.7) in terms of the aggregate price index for energy in equation (11.15), as follows

$$w_1 = \frac{1}{D}\left[\alpha_1 - \beta_{11}\left(\ln q'\gamma_q + \frac{1}{2}\ln q'\Delta_{qq}\ln q + \ln q'\Delta_{qA}\frac{\sum M_k A_k}{\sum M_k}\right)\right.$$
$$\left. + \beta'_{1p}\ln p + \beta'_{1A}\frac{\sum M_k A_k}{\sum M_k}\right],$$
$$w = \frac{1}{D}\left[\alpha_p - \beta_{p1}\left(\ln q'\gamma_q + \frac{1}{2}\ln q'\Delta_{qq}\ln q + \ln q'\ \Delta_{qA}\frac{\sum M_k A_k}{\sum M_k}\right)\right.$$
$$\left. + B_{pp}\ln p - \{\beta_{p1}\ B_{pp}\}i\ \frac{\sum M_k \ln M_k}{\sum M_k} + B_{pA}\frac{\sum M_k A_k}{\sum M_k}\right]. \qquad (11.16)$$

The system of aggregate demand functions in equation (11.11) for individual types of energy depends on the shares of total energy expenditure among demographic groups $\{\sum E_k A_k / \sum E_k\}$. The problem that remains in implementing this model is to derive these shares from the model of the first stage of the two-stage allocation process. We first determine the expenditure on energy by the ith household from the first equation of the first stage model, namely

$$E_k = M_k w_{1k}\,, \quad (k = 1, 2, \ldots, K)\,. \tag{11.17}$$

The share of energy in aggregate total expenditure takes the form

$$w_1 = \frac{\sum E_k}{\sum M_k}\,. \tag{11.18}$$

Similarly, we can determine the vector of ratios of energy expenditures for specific demographic groups to total expenditure. First, for the kth household we obtain

$$\begin{aligned} E_k A_k &= M_k w_{1k} A_k\,, \\ &= \frac{1}{D}\left[\alpha_1 - \beta_{11}\left(\ln q'\gamma_q + \frac{1}{2}\ln q'\Delta_{qq}\ln q + \ln q'\Delta_{qA}A_k\right)\right. \\ &\quad \left. + \beta'_{1p}\ln p + \beta'_{1A}\,A_k\right] M_k A_k\,, \quad (k = 1, 2, \ldots, K)\,. \end{aligned} \tag{11.19}$$

The vector of ratios of energy expenditures for specific demographic groups to total expenditure is

$$\begin{aligned} \frac{\sum E_k A_k}{\sum M_k} &= \frac{1}{D}\left[\alpha_1 - \beta_{11}\left(\ln q'\gamma_q + \frac{1}{2}\ln q'\Delta_{qq}\ln q\right) + \beta'_{1p}\ln p\right] \\ &\quad \times \frac{\sum M_k A_k}{\sum M_k} + \frac{1}{D}\left[\frac{\sum(-\beta_{11}\ln q'\Delta_{qA}A_k)M_k A_k}{\sum M_k}\right. \\ &\quad \left. + \frac{\sum(\beta'_{1A}A_k)M_k A_k}{\sum M_k}\right]. \end{aligned} \tag{11.20}$$

Although these shares cannot be observed directly, they can be expressed as functions of the vector of prices of all nonenergy commodities p, the vector of prices of individual types of energy q, the shares of demographic groups in total expenditure $\{\sum M_k A_k / \sum M_k\}$ and the unknown parameters.

Finally, we can determine the shares of demographic groups in energy expenditure by dividing the ratios of energy expenditures for specific demographic groups to total expenditure in equation (11.20) to the shares of energy in total expenditure in equation (11.18), obtaining

$$\frac{\sum E_k A_k}{\sum E_k} = \frac{1}{D} \cdot \frac{1}{w_1} \left\{ \left[\alpha_1 - \beta_{11}\left(\ln q'\gamma_q + \frac{1}{2} \ln q'\Delta_{qq} \ln q \right) + \beta'_{1p} \ln p \right] \right.$$
$$\times \frac{\sum M_k A_k}{\sum M_k} + \frac{\sum(-\beta_{11} \ln q'\Delta_{qA} A_k) M_k A_k}{\sum M_k}$$
$$\left. + \frac{\sum(\beta'_{1A} A_k) M_k A_k}{\sum M_k} \right\}. \tag{11.21}$$

We can replace these shares in our aggregate model for the second stage of the two-stage allocation process in equation (11.11) to obtain a model for the allocation of aggregate energy expenditure among individual types of energy.

11.3 Econometrics of Exact Aggregation

In this section we outline the econometric implementation of the translog model of aggregate consumer behavior presented in section 11.2. Our observations on individual expenditure patterns on energy and all nonenergy commodities are given by a single cross section. This cross section provides data on expenditure shares for each commodity group, demographic characteristics for individual consuming units, and total expenditure for these units at a single point of time. We assume that prices of individual types of energy and all nonenergy commodities are the same for all consuming units, while demographic characteristics and total expenditures vary among units.

Our observations on aggregate consumer behavior include time-series data on expenditure shares for energy and all nonenergy commodities, shares of demographic groups in aggregate expenditure, the level and distribution of total expenditure, and prices of individual types of energy and all nonenergy commodities. By pooling time-series and cross-section data we obtain more precise estimates of the effects of demographic characteristics and total expenditure on aggregate expenditure allocation.

11.3.1 Stochastic Structure

The model of a two-stage allocation process presented in section 11.2 is generated from translog indirect utility functions for each consuming unit. We formulate an econometric model of consumer behavior by adding a stochastic component to the equations for the individual expenditure shares. We associate this component with unobservable random disturbances at the level of the individual consuming unit. The consuming unit maximizes utility, but the expenditure shares are chosen with a random disturbance. This disturbance may result from errors in implementation of consumption plans or errors of measurement of the individual expenditure shares.

To represent our econometric model we introduce some additional notation. We consider observations on expenditure patterns by K consuming units, indexed by $k = 1, 2, \ldots, K$, for T time periods indexed by $t = 1, 2, \ldots, T$. The expenditure share of energy for the kth consuming unit in the tth time period is denoted w_{1kt} $(k = 1, 2, \ldots, K;$ $t = 1, 2, \ldots, T)$; the vector of expenditure shares on nonenergy commodities for the kth consuming unit in the tth time period is denoted w_{kt} $(k = 1, 2, \ldots, K; t = 1, 2, \ldots, T)$. Total expenditure for the kth unit on energy and all nonenergy commodities in the tth time period is denoted M_{kt} $(k = 1, 2, \ldots, K; t = 1, 2, \ldots, T)$. The price index for energy for the kth consuming unit in the tth time period is denoted p_{1kt} $(k = 1, 2, \ldots, K;\ t = 1, 2, \ldots, T)$; the vector of prices of all nonenergy commodities faced by all consuming units in the tth time period is denoted p_t $(t = 1, 2, \ldots, T)$. Similarly, the logarithm of the ratio of the price index for energy to expenditure by the kth consuming unit in the tth time period is denoted $\ln p_{1kt} / M_{kt}$ $(k = 1, 2, \ldots, K;\ t = 1, 2, \ldots, T)$; the vector of logarithms of the ratios of prices of all nonenergy commodities to expenditure by the kth consuming unit in the tth time period is denoted $\ln p_t / M_{kt}$ $(k = 1, 2, \ldots, K; t = 1, 2, \ldots, T)$.

Using our new notation, the individual expenditure shares for energy and all nonenergy commodities can be written

$$w_{1kt} = \frac{1}{D_t}\left[\alpha_1 - \beta_{11}\left(\ln q_t'\gamma_q + \frac{1}{2}\ln q_t'\Delta_{qq}\ln q_t + \ln q_t'\Delta_{qA}A_k\right)\right.$$
$$\left. + \beta'_{1p}\ln p_t + \beta'_{1A}A_k\right] + \mu_{1kt}\,,$$

$$w_{kt} = \frac{1}{D_t}\left[\alpha_p - \beta_{p1}\left(\ln q_t'\gamma_q + \frac{1}{2}\ln q_t'\Delta_{qq}\ln q_t + \ln q_t'\Delta_{qA}A_k\right)\right.$$
$$\left. + B_{pp}\ln p_t - \{\beta_{p1}B_{pp}\}i\ln M_{kt} + B_{pA}A_k\right] + \mu_{kt}\,,$$
$$(k = 1, 2, \ldots, K;\ t = 1, 2, \ldots, T)\,, \qquad (11.22)$$

where μ_{1kt} $(k = 1, 2, \ldots, K;\ t = 1, 2, \ldots, T)$ is the unobservable random disturbance for the allocation of energy and μ_{kt} $(k = 1, 2, \ldots, K;\ t = 1, 2, \ldots, T)$ is the vector of unobservable random disturbances for the allocation of all nonenergy commodities for the kth consuming unit and the tth time period. Since the individual expenditure shares for energy and all nonenergy commodities sum to unity for each consuming unit in each time period, the unobservable random disturbances sum to zero for each unit in each time period

$$\mu_{1kt} + i'\mu_{kt} = 0\,, \qquad (k = 1, 2, \ldots, K;\ t = 1, 2, \ldots, T). \tag{11.23}$$

The disturbances are not distributed independently.

We assume that the unobservable random disturbances for energy and all nonenergy commodities have expected value equal to zero for all observations

$$E\begin{bmatrix} \mu_{1kt} \\ \mu_{kt} \end{bmatrix} = 0\,, \qquad (k = 1, 2, \ldots, K;\ t = 1, 2, \ldots, T)\,. \tag{11.24}$$

We also assume that these disturbances have the same covariance matrix for all observations

$$V\begin{bmatrix} \mu_{1kt} \\ \mu_{kt} \end{bmatrix} = \Omega_{\mu}\,, \qquad (k = 1, 2, \ldots, K;\ t = 1, 2, \ldots, T)\,.$$

Since the disturbances sum to zero for each observation, this matrix is nonnegative definite with rank at most equal to $N - 1$, the number of nonenergy commodities. We assume that the covariance matrix has rank equal to $N - 1$.

We assume that disturbances corresponding to distinct observations are uncorrelated. Under this assumption the covariance matrix of the disturbances for energy and all nonenergy commodities for all consuming units at a given point of time has a Kronecker product form. The covariance matrix of the disturbances for all time periods for given individual has a similar form.

The data for individual consuming units and for the aggregate of all consuming units are based on the same definitions, but the aggregate data are not obtained by summing over the data for individuals. Individual observations are based on a random sample from the population of all consuming units, while aggregate observations are constructed from data on production of energy and all nonenergy commodities and on consumption by households and other consuming units such as businesses, governments, and the rest of the world. Accordingly, we introduce an additional source of random error in the equations for the aggregate expenditure shares, corresponding to errors of measurement.

Denoting the aggregate expenditure share on energy at time t by w_{1t} and the vector of aggregate expenditure shares on nonenergy commodities at time t by w_t $(t = 1, 2, \ldots, T)$, we can express these shares in the form

$$w_{1t} = \frac{1}{D_t}\left[\alpha_1 - \beta_{11}\left(\ln q_t'\gamma_q + \frac{1}{2}\ln q_t'\,\Delta_{qq}\ln q_t + \ln q_t'\,\Delta_{qA}\frac{\sum M_{kt}A_k}{\sum M_{kt}}\right)\right.$$
$$\left. + \beta'_{1p}\ln p_t + \beta'_{1A}\frac{\sum M_{kt}A_k}{\sum M_{kt}}\right] + \mu_{1t}\,, \qquad (11.25)$$
$$w_t = \frac{1}{D_t}\left[\alpha_p - \beta_{p1}\left(\ln q_t'\,\gamma_q + \frac{1}{2}\ln q_t'\,\Delta_{qq}\ln q_t + \ln q_t'\,\Delta_{qA}\frac{\sum M_{kt}A_k}{\sum M_{kt}}\right)\right.$$
$$\left. + B_{pp}\ln p_t - \{\beta_{p1}\;B_{pp}\}i\,\frac{\sum M_{kt}\ln M_{kt}}{\sum M_{kt}} + B_{pA}\frac{\sum M_{kt}A_k}{\sum M_{kt}}\right] + \mu_t\,,$$
$$(t = 1, 2, \ldots, T)\,.$$

where μ_{1t} $(t = 1, 2, \ldots, T)$ is the unobservable random disturbance for the allocation of energy and μ_t $(t = 1, 2, \ldots, T)$ is the vector of unobservable random disturbances for the tth time period.

The aggregate disturbances can be expressed in the form

$$\mu_{1t} = \frac{\sum_{k=1}^{K} M_{kt}\,\mu_{1kt}}{\sum_{k=1}^{K} M_{kt}} + \frac{\sum_{k=1}^{K} M_{kt}\,\eta_{1kt}}{\sum_{k=1}^{K} M_{kt}}\,,$$
$$\mu_t = \frac{\sum_{k=1}^{K} M_{kt}\,\mu_{kt}}{\sum_{k=1}^{K} M_{kt}} + \frac{\sum_{k=1}^{K} M_{kt}\,\eta_{kt}}{\sum_{k=1}^{K} M_{kt}}\,, \qquad (t = 1, 2, \ldots, T)\,, \qquad (11.26)$$

where η_{1kt} $(k = 1, 2, \ldots, K;\ t = 1, 2, \ldots, T)$ is the error of measurement for the allocation of energy and η_{kt} $(k = 1, 2, \ldots, K;\ t = 1, 2, \ldots, T)$ is the vector of errors of measurement for the allocation of all nonenergy commodities that underly the data on the aggregate expenditure shares. Since the random disturbances for all commodities sum to zero in each time period

$$\eta_{1t} + i'\eta_t = 0\,, \qquad (t = 1, 2, \ldots, T)\,. \qquad (11.27)$$

These disturbances are not distributed independently.

We assume that the errors of measurement that underly the data on the aggregate expenditure shares for energy and all nonenergy commodities have expected value equal to zero for all observations

$$E\begin{bmatrix}\eta_{1kt}\\ \eta_{kt}\end{bmatrix}=0\,,\qquad (k=1,2,\ldots,K;\quad t=1,2,\ldots,T)\,.$$

We also assume that these errors have the same covariance matrix for all observations

$$V\begin{bmatrix}\eta_{1kt}\\ \eta_{kt}\end{bmatrix}=\Omega_\eta\,,\qquad (k=1,2,\ldots,K;\, t=1,2,\ldots,T)\,,$$

and that the rank of this matrix is equal to $N-1$.

If the errors of measurement are distributed independently of total expenditure and of the disturbances in the equations for the individual expenditure shares of energy and all nonenergy commodities, the aggregate disturbances have expected value equal to zero for all time periods

$$E\begin{bmatrix}\mu_{1t}\\ \mu_{t}\end{bmatrix}=0\,,\qquad (t=1,2,\ldots,T)\,, \tag{11.28}$$

and have a covariance matrix given by

$$V\begin{bmatrix}\mu_{1t}\\ \mu_{t}\end{bmatrix}=\frac{\sum_{k=1}^{K}M_{kt}^2}{\left(\sum_{k=1}^{K}M_{kt}\right)^2}\,\Omega_\mu+\frac{\sum_{k=1}^{K}M_{kt}^2}{\left(\sum_{k=1}^{K}M_{kt}\right)^2}\,\Omega_\eta\,,\qquad (t=1,2,\ldots,T)\,,$$

so that the aggregate disturbances for different time periods are heteroscedastic.

We can correct the aggregate disturbances for heteroscedasticity by transforming the observations on the aggregate expenditure shares of energy and all nonenergy commodities as follows

$$\sigma_t w_{1t} = \frac{\sigma_t}{D_t}\left[\alpha_1 - \beta_{11}\left(\ln q_t'\gamma_q + \frac{1}{2}\ln q_t'\Delta_{qq}\ln q_t + \ln q_t'\Delta_{qA}\frac{\sum M_{kt}A_k}{\sum M_{kt}}\right)\right.$$
$$\left. + \beta'_{1p}\ln p_t + \beta'_{1A}\frac{\sum M_{kt}A_k}{\sum M_{kt}}\right] + \sigma_t\,\mu_{1t}\,, \qquad (11.29)$$
$$\sigma_t w_t = \frac{\sigma_t}{D_t}\left[\alpha_p - \beta_{p1}\left(\ln q_t'\,\gamma_q + \frac{1}{2}\ln q_t'\,\Delta_{qq}\ln q_t + \ln q_t'\,\Delta_{qA}\frac{\sum M_{kt}A_k}{\sum M_{kt}}\right)\right.$$
$$\left. + B_{pp}\ln p_t - \{\beta_{p1}\ B_{pp}\}i\ \frac{\sum M_{kt}\ln M_{kt}}{\sum M_{kt}} + B_{pA}\frac{\sum M_{kt}A_k}{\sum M_{kt}}\right] + \sigma_t\,\mu_t\,,$$
$$(t = 1, 2, \ldots, T)\,,$$

where

$$\sigma_t^2 = \frac{\left(\sum_{k=1}^{K} M_{kt}\right)^2}{\sum_{k=1}^{K} M_{kt}^2}\,, \qquad (t = 1, 2, \ldots, T)\,.$$

The covariance matrix of the transformed disturbances, say Ω_σ, becomes

$$V\begin{bmatrix}\sigma_t & \mu_{1t}\\ \sigma_t & \mu_t\end{bmatrix} = \Omega_\mu + \Omega_\eta = \Omega_\sigma\,.$$

This matrix is nonnegative definite with rank equal to $N - 1$. We assume that errors of measurement corresponding to distinct observations are uncorrelated. Under this assumption the covariance matrix of the transformed disturbances at all points of time has a Kronecker product form.

To represent the second stage of our econometric model of consumer behavior we introduce some additional notation. As before, we consider observations on expenditure patterns by K consuming units, indexed by $k = 1, 2, \ldots, K$, for T time periods, indexed by $t = 1, 2, \ldots, T$. The vector of energy expenditure shares for the kth consuming unit in the tth time period is denoted v_{kt} $(k = 1, 2, \ldots, K;$ $t = 1, 2, \ldots, T)$. Similarly, expenditure for the kth unit on all types of energy in the tth time period is denoted E_{kt} $(k = 1, 2, \ldots, K;$ $t = 1, 2, \ldots, T)$. The vector of energy prices faced by all consuming units in the tth time period is denoted q_t $(t = 1, 2, \ldots, T)$. Similarly, the vector of logarithms of energy prices in the tth time period is denoted $\ln q_t$ $(t = 1, 2, \ldots, T)$.

Using our new notation, the individual expenditure shares can be written

$$-v_{kt} = \gamma_q + \Delta_{qq} \ln q_t + \Delta_{qA} A_{kt} + \varepsilon_{kt}\,, \quad (k=1,2,\ldots,K;\ t=1,2,\ldots,T)\,, \tag{11.30}$$

where ε_{kt} $(k = 1,2,\ldots,K;\ t = 1,2,\ldots,T)$ is the vector of unobservable random disturbances for the kth consuming unit and the tth time period. Since the individual expenditure shares for all types of energy sum to unity for each consuming unit in each time period, the unobservable random disturbances for all types of energy sum to zero for each unit in each time period

$$i'\varepsilon_{kt} = 0\,, \quad (k = 1,2,\ldots,K;\ t = 1,2,\ldots,T)\,. \tag{11.31}$$

These disturbances are not distributed independently.

We assume that the unobservable random disturbances for all commodities have expected value equal to zero for all observations

$$E(\varepsilon_{kt}) = 0\,, \quad (k = 1, 2,\ldots,K;\ t = 1,2,\ldots,T)\,. \tag{11.32}$$

We also assume that these disturbances have the same covariance matrix for all observations

$$V(\varepsilon_{kt}) = \Omega_\varepsilon\,, \quad (k = 1,2,\ldots,K;\ t = 1,2,\ldots,T)\,,$$

and that the covariance matrix has rank equal to $M - 1$. As before, we assume that disturbances corresponding to distinct observations are uncorrelated. Under this assumption the covariance matrix of the disturbances for all consuming units at a given point of time and the covariance matrix of the disturbances for all time periods for a given individual have Kronecker product forms.

We introduce an additional source of random error in the equations for the aggregate energy expenditure shares, corresponding to unobservable errors of measurement in the observations that underly the aggregate shares. Denoting the vector of aggregate expenditure shares at time t by v_t $(t = 1,2,\ldots,T)$, we can express these shares in the form

$$
\begin{aligned}
-v_t = \gamma_q + \Delta_{qq} \ln q_t + \Delta_{qA} \frac{1}{D_t} \frac{1}{w_{1t}} \\
\times \left\{ \left[\alpha_1 - \beta_{11} \left(\ln q_t' \gamma_q + \frac{1}{2} \ln q_t' \, \Delta_{qq} \ln q_t + \beta'_{1p} \ln p_t \right) \right] \right. \\
\times \frac{\sum M_{kt} A_k}{\sum M_{kt}} + \frac{\sum(-\beta_{11} \ln q_t' \, \Delta_{qA} A_k) M_{kt} A_k}{\sum M_{kt}} \\
\left. + \frac{\sum (\beta'_{1A} A_k) \, M_{kt} A_k}{\sum M_{kt}} \right\} + \varepsilon_t \,, \quad (t = 1, 2, \ldots, T) \,, \qquad (11.33)
\end{aligned}
$$

where ε_t $(t = 1, 2, \ldots, T)$ is the vector of unobservable random disturbances for the tth time period.

The aggregate disturbances ε_t can be expressed in the form

$$
\varepsilon_t = \frac{\sum_{k=1}^{K} E_{kt} \varepsilon_{kt}}{\sum_{k=1}^{K} E_{kt}} + \frac{\sum_{k=1}^{K} E_{kt} \gamma_{kt}}{\sum_{k=1}^{K} E_{kt}} \,, \qquad (t = 1, 2, \ldots, T) \,, \qquad (11.34)
$$

where γ_{kt} $(k = 1, 2, \ldots, K; \; t = 1, 2, \ldots, T)$ is the vector of errors of measurement that underly the data on the aggregate energy expenditure shares. Since the random disturbances for all commodities sum to zero in each time period

$$
i' \varepsilon_t = 0 \,, \qquad (t = 1, 2, \ldots, T) \,, \qquad (11.35)
$$

these disturbances are not distributed independently.

We assume that the errors of measurement that underly the data on the aggregate energy expenditure shares have expected value equal to zero for all observations, the same covariance matrix for all observations, and that the rank of this matrix is $M - 1$.

If the errors of measurement are distributed independently of energy expenditure and of the disturbances in the equations for the individual energy expenditure shares, the aggregate disturbances have expected value equal to zero for all time periods

$$
E(\varepsilon_t) = 0 \,, \quad (t = 1, 2, \ldots, T) \,, \qquad (11.36)
$$

and have a covariance matrix given by

$$
V(\varepsilon_t) = \frac{\sum_{k=1}^{K} E_{kt}^2}{\left(\sum_{k=1}^{K} E_{kt} \right)^2} \Omega_\varepsilon + \frac{\sum_{k=1}^{K} E_{kt}^2}{\left(\sum_{k=1}^{K} E_{kt} \right)^2} \Omega_\gamma \,, \qquad (t = 1, 2, \ldots, T) \,,
$$

so that the aggregate disturbances for different time periods are heteroscedastic.

We can correct for heteroscedasticity of the aggregate disturbances, as before, by transforming the observations on the aggregate energy expenditure shares. The covariance matrix of the transformed disturbance becomes

$$V\ (\rho_t \varepsilon_t) = \Omega_\varepsilon + \Omega_\gamma = \Omega\,,$$

where

$$\rho_t^2 = \frac{\left(\sum_{k=1}^K E_{kt}\right)^2}{\sum_{k=1}^K E_{kt}^2}\,, \qquad (t = 1, 2, \ldots, T)\,.$$

The covariance matrix is nonnegative definite with rank equal to $M - 1$.

Finally, we assume that the covariance matrix of the transformed disturbances at all points of time has a Kronecker product form and that these disturbances are independent of the corresponding disturbances in the first stage model in equation (11.22).

11.3.2 Identification and Estimation

We can now discuss the estimation of the translog model of aggregate consumer behavior, combining cross-section observations on individual expenditure patterns on all types of energy and all nonenergy commodities with time-series observations on aggregate expenditure patterns. We first consider a random sample of observations on individual expenditure patterns on energy and all nonenergy commodities at a given point of time. The translog model for individual expenditures in equation (11.22) takes the form

$$\begin{aligned} -\,w_{1k} &= \delta_1 + \beta'_{1A} A_k + \mu_{1k}\,, \\ -\,w_k &= \delta_p - [\beta_{p1}\ B_{pp}] i \ln M_k + B_{pA} A_k + \mu_k\,, \qquad (k = 1, 2, \ldots, K)\,, \end{aligned} \tag{11.37}$$

where we drop the time subscript. The prices for all types of energy and all nonenergy commodities are the same for all consumers; we consider cross-section observations for a single year, taken to be the base period for the prices, so that the energy price indexes in equation (11.13) are also the same for all consumers. In the model in equation

(11.37) δ_1 is an unknown parameter, δ_p, β_{1A} and β_{1p} are vectors of unknown parameters and B_{pp} and B_{pA} are matrices of unknown parameters. We assume that the data matrix with $(1, \ln M_k, A_k)$ as its kth row is of full rank.

The translog model for individual expenditures on all types of energy takes the form

$$-v_k = \delta + \Delta_{qA} A_k + \varepsilon_k\,, \quad (k = 1, 2, \ldots, K)\,, \tag{11.38}$$

where we drop the time subscript. In this model δ is a vector of unknown parameters and Δ_{qA} is a matrix of unknown parameters. The data matrix with $(1, A_k)$ as its kth row is of full rank.

The translog model of aggregate consumer expenditure on energy and all nonenergy commodities is given by the vector equation in equation (11.29), while the corresponding model of aggregate expenditures on all types of energy is obtained from equation in equation (11.33) by transforming this equation to eliminate heteroscedasticity. To estimate these models we employ time-series observations on prices of all nonenergy commodities p_t, prices of all types of energy q_t, the shares of demographic groups in total expenditure $\{\sum M_{kt} A_k / \sum M_{kt}\}$, and the heteroscedasticity corrections ρ_t and σ_t $(t = 1, 2, \ldots, t)$.

The translog model of the two-stage allocation process given by equations (11.29) and (11.33) might appear to be a nonlinear regression model with additive errors. However, prices of all nonenergy commodities and all types of energy may be treated as endogenous, so that we can consider limited information techniques utilizing instrumental variables. We introduce a sufficient number of instrumental variables to identify all parameters. The list of instrumental variables we have employed is given in the appendix table. We assume that each of these variables is exogenous to the household sector. The list of instrumental variables includes variables determined by government and rest-of-the-world sectors, the time endowment of the household sector, and the lagged wealth of the sector. We drop one equation from the model in equation (11.29) for expenditures on energy and all nonenergy commodities; similarly, we drop one equation from the model in equation (11.33) for energy expenditures.

The NL3SLS estimator introduced by Jorgenson and Laffont (1974) can be employed to estimate all parameters of the translog model of aggregate expenditures on all nonenergy commodities and all types of energy, provided that these parameters are identified. Our detailed characterization of the impact of changes in the demographic structure of the population would require a large number of observations for identification of the parameters from aggregate data alone. A necessary condition for identification is the following

$$\frac{1}{2}(M-1)(M+2)+P(M-1)+(N-1)(1+P)\,\frac{(N+1)\,N}{2}-2$$
$$<(M+N-2)\times\min(V,T)\,, \qquad (11.39)$$

where M is the number of types of energy, $N-1$ is the number of nonenergy commodities, P is the number of components of A_k, and V is the number of additional instruments. The instruments for the cross-section models are the micro data themselves; for the aggregate models we employ the list of additional instruments given in the appendix table. The left-hand side of equation (11.39) is the number of free parameters of the translog model and the right-hand side is the number of instruments, assuming, as before, that no multicollinearity exists among the instruments. Equation (11.39) fails to hold in our application, so that not all parameters are identified in the model for aggregate time-series data on energy and nonenergy expenditures.

11.3.3 Pooling Time Series and Cross Sections

We next consider methods utilizing individual cross-section data together with aggregate time-series data on energy and nonenergy expenditures to obtain identification. Cross-section data can be used to identify the constants δ_1, δ_p, the coefficients of total expenditure $[\beta_{p1} B_{pp}]i$, and the demographic coefficients Δ_{qA} and B_{pA}. The constants γ_q, α_1 and α_p and the price coefficients Δ_{qq} and B_{pp} must be identified from aggregate time-series data. A necessary condition for identification of these parameters is

$$\frac{1}{2}(M-1)(M+2)+\frac{1}{2}(N-1)(N+1)<(M+N-2)\times\min(V,T)\,. \qquad (11.40)$$

This condition is met in our application. Sufficient conditions that hold in our application are given below.

Estimation of the complete model requires application of the method of nonlinear three-stage least squares for pooling time-series and cross-section data introduced by Jorgenson and Stoker (1986).

Our objective is to estimate the unknown parameters—α_1, α_p, γ_q, β_{11}, β_{1p}, β_{1A}, β_{p1}, B_{pp}, B_{pA}, Δ_{qq}, and Δ_{qA}—subject to the restrictions implied by summability, symmetry, and monotonicity for both stages of the two-stage model.

If a system of individual expenditure shares can be generated from an indirect utility function, we say that the systems is *integrable*. The final step in pooled estimation of the unknown parameters of the translog model of aggregate consumer behavior is to estimate the parameters—α_1, α_p, γ_q, β_{11}, β_{1p}, β_{1A}, B_{pp}, Δ_{qq}, and Δ_{qA}—subject to the restrictions implied by integrability of systems of individual expenditure shares at both stages of our model of the two-stage allocation process. As before, we can drop the equation for one commodity and employ the summability restrictions to estimate the parameters that occur in this equation. The restrictions that the vectors β_{1p} and β_{p1} are the same and that the matrices B_{pp} and Δ_{qq} are symmetric take the form of equalities. We can represent the remaining restrictions implied by integrability in the form of inequalities.[5]

We assume that the restrictions associated with integrability of the individual expenditure shares are valid or, more precisely, that the vector of unknown parameters is an interior point of the set of parameters defined by the constraints. Under this assumption the inequality constrained three-stage least squares estimator is a consistent estimator of the vector of unknown parameters. This estimator has the same asymptotic covariance matrix as the estimator pooling time-series and cross-section data presented by Jorgenson and Stoker (1986).[6]

11.4 Empirical Results

In this section we present the empirical results of implementing the two-stage econometric model of aggregate consumer behavior outlined in section 11.3. The first stage of this model includes the allocation of total expenditure among energy and all nonenergy commodities. The second stage incorporates the allocation of total energy expenditure among individual types of energy. To implement this model we employ individual cross-section data from the 1972 Consumer Expenditure Survey of the Bureau of Labor Statistics.[7] We also employ aggregate time-series data from the U.S. National Income and Product Accounts for the period 1958 to 1978.[8] We employ time-series data on the distribution of expenditures over all households and among demographic groups based on *Current Population Reports*.[9]

We begin by discussing the allocation of consumer expenditures among commodity groups. We first divide total expenditure into five broad categories:

1. *Energy*. Expenditures on energy include electricity, natural gas, fuel oil and other, and gasoline.
2. *Food*. Expenditures on food include all food products, together with tobacco and alcohol.
3. *Consumer Goods*. Expenditures on consumer goods include all non-durable expenditures other than energy and food.
4. *Capital Services*. Expenditures on capital services include the flow of capital services from consumers' durables and from housing.
5. *Consumer Services*. Expenditures on consumer services includes all expenditures on services other than energy and capital services.

We divide energy expenditures into four categories:

1. *Electricity*. Expenditures on electricity for lighting, heating, use of appliances, and so on.
2. *Natural gas*. Expenditures on natural gas for heating, use of appliances, and so on, both from main and bottled gas.
3. *Fuel oil and other*. Expenditures on fuel oil for heating and expenditures on other fuels such as coal, wood, charcoal, and so on.
4. *Gasoline*. Expenditures on gasoline for operation of automobiles and for operation of tools such as power mowers, and so on.

The basic consuming unit employed in this study is the household. Unrelated individuals are considered to be households of size one. All consuming units are classified by attributes that reflect differences in preferences among consuming units. We employ the following demographic characteristics as attributes of households:

1. *Family size*: 1, 2, 3, 4, 5, 6, 7 or more persons.
2. *Age of head*: 15–24, 25–34, 35–44, 45–54, 55–65, 65 and over.
3. *Region of residence*: Northeast, North Central, South and West.
4. *Race*: White, nonwhite.
5. *Type of residence*: Urban, rural.

Each household is assigned to one of the categories for each of the five demographic characteristics. Since these categories are discrete, integer-valued variables are required to represent the attributes.

Under exact aggregation all attributes appear linearly in the functions that determine shares of individual energy expenditures. We impose no *a priori* restrictions on the form of the impact on expenditure patterns of variations in demographic characteristics among consuming units. We could, for example, include an integer-valued variable with value equal to family size as a determinant of individual energy expenditure patterns. However, this would impose a constraint on the effects of different family sizes. To avoid imposing these constraints, we represent each family size by a qualitative or dummy variable, so that the precise pattern of the impacts of changes in family size can be estimated. To avoid singularity of the matrix of dummy variables we take all variables to be zero for unrelated individuals, age 16–24, living in the Northeast, white in race, and living in an urban area. This leaves 16 qualitative variables to be treated as separate consumer attributes in representing the effects of demographic characteristics on preferences on consuming units.

Before proceeding with a presentation of our empirical results, it is important to note that we treat quantities of both energy and nonenergy commodities as continuous variables. In particular, we represent capital by the consumption of services and not by the purchase of stocks. We do not explicitly model the impact of characteristics of specific types of capital on the demand for energy and other nonenergy commodities. An alternative approach that we do not consider would be to model the purchase of capital stocks and to incorporate the characteristics of types of capital into the determination of demands for other commodities. This would require aggregate data on the joint distribution of total expenditures and types of capital that are unavailable for the time period we have considered.

11.4.1 Pooled Estimates for Aggregate Consumer Behavior

We turn next to the discussion of pooled estimation results for our two-stage model of aggregate consumer behavior. In this section we consider the first stage of our two-stage model, which determines the allocation of total expenditure among energy and all nonenergy commodity groups. In the following section we consider the second stage model, which determines the allocation of total energy expenditure among individual types of energy. We represent the demographic effects on the allocation of consumer expenditures diagrammatically. In section 11.3 we describe the price effects through tables of estimated elasticities corresponding to individual demographic groups.

The results of estimating the unknown parameters of the first stage of our econometric model of aggregate consumer behavior, using the

Table 11.1
Pooled estimation results for aggregate consumer behavior

	WF	WCG	WK	WEN	WCS
P_F	.012651 (.108)	−.000989 (.108)	.00023 (.0457)	−.00192 (.0453)	−.21407 (.223)
P_{CG}	−.00098 (.108)	.21532 (.142)	−.00177 (.0571)	−.00104 (.0384)	−.13702 (.223)
P_K	.00023 (.0457)	−.00177 (.0571)	.15485 (.0509)	−.00128 (.0162)	−.14643 (.102)
P_{EN}	−.00192 (.0434)	−.00104 (.0384)	−.00128 (.0162)	.09282 (.0221)	−.08856 (.0513)
P_{CS}	−.21407 (.223)	−.13702 (.223)	−.14643 (.102)	−.08856 (.0513)	.59627 (.459)
CONST	−.97040 (.0331)	.52520 (.0292)	−.39724 (.0288)	−.08193 (.00753)	−.07562 (.0537)
Log M	.09023 (.00234)	−.07448 (.00215)	−.00559 (.00303)	.00000 (.0000)	−.01016 (.00255)
F2	−.05222 (.00333)	−.00118 (.00300)	.07637 (.00422)	−.01162 (.00145)	−.01135 (.00364)
F3	−.07267 (.00390)	.00076 (.00352)	.10372 (.00494)	−.01223 (.00168)	−.01958 (.00426)
F4	−.09543 (.00427)	.00663 (.00385)	.11965 (.00542)	−.01052 (.00182)	−.02034 (.00467)
F5	−.11880 (.00494)	.01513 (.00446)	.13086 (.00627)	−.00983 (.00212)	−.01736 (.00541)
F6	−.12805 (.00597)	.02199 (.00538)	.13433 (.00757)	−.01245 (.00259)	−.01583 (.00653)
F7	−.15750 (.00638)	.02662 (.00575)	.14284 (.00808)	−.00692 (.00279)	−.00505 (.00698)
A30	−.04449 (.00474)	−.02151 (.00426)	.04527 (.00599)	.00651 (.00212)	.01422 (.00518)
A40	−.08382 (.00504)	−.01578 (.00454)	.08695 (.00637)	.00253 (.00225)	.01012 (.00551)
A50	−.09883 (.00478)	−.00147 (.00431)	.11936 (.00605)	−.00049 (.00213)	−.01855 (.00523)
A60	−.10509 (.00477)	−.00683 (.00429)	.14051 (.00603)	−.00850 (.00214)	−.02007 (.00521)
A70	−.08747 (.00470)	−.01811 (.00423)	.12832 (.00595)	−.00840 (.00212)	−.01433 (.00514)
RNC	.01984 (.00315)	−.02284 (.00283)	.02689 (.00398)	−.00652 (.00141)	−.01737 (.00344)
RS	.01363 (.00314)	−.03849 (.00283)	.05425 (.00397)	−.00410 (.00141)	−.02530 (.00344)
RW	.01877 (.00337)	−.01070 (.00304)	−.00442 (.00427)	.01376 (.00152)	−.01740 (.00369)
NW	.00912 (.00408)	−.03086 (.00368)	−.00582 (.00517)	.00434 (.00182)	.02322 (.00447)
RUR	.00188 (.00322)	−.01464 (.00290)	.05357 (.00408)	−.04179 (.00141)	.000975 (.00352)

Notes: Convergence after 3 iterations. SSR = 64351.57.

time-series data for the period 1958–1978 and cross-section data from the 1972 Consumer Expenditure Survey, are presented in table 11.1. Estimates of the unknown parameters for the first stage of our two-stage model are obtained by fitting equations for energy, food, consumer goods, and capital services. Estimates for parameters of the equation for consumer services are derived from the summability restrictions. In analyzing the results, it is useful to recall that the effects of total expenditure and demographic characteristics of individual households can be identified from cross-section data alone, while the effects of prices can be identified only by pooling cross-section and time-series data.

Estimates of the effects of changes in total expenditure on patterns of consumer behavior are very similar for the pooled estimates given in table 11.1. The expenditure shares for energy and food increase with total expenditure, while the shares for consumer goods, capital services, and other consumer services decline. The effects of increases in family size are the reverse of increases in total expenditure. The expenditure shares for energy and food decrease with family size, while the shares for other commodity groups rise. The qualitative effects of age of head, region, race, and urban versus rural residence are very substantial for most commodity groups.

Under exact aggregation the expenditure share for each commodity group is determined by the ratio of two functions. The denominators of these ratios depend on prices and are the same for all commodity groups and all consumers. The numerators are different for each commodity group and incorporate total expenditure and consumer attributes as well as prices. In the function that appears as a denominator for all five commodity groups the price effects are equal to the negative of the total expenditure effects in the functions that appear as numerators for each commodity group. For example, the price effect of food in the denominator is equal to the negative of the total expenditure effect in the numerator of the expenditure share for food.

We have already seen that the total expenditure effects are highly significant for all commodity groups, except for capital services. The effects of changes in the prices of all commodities, except for the price of capital services, are highly significant in the function that appears as a denominator in the ratios that determine expenditure shares for all five commodity groups. Considering the functions that appear as numerators in these ratios, we find that own- and cross-price effects are highly significant for almost all commodity groups. The exceptions are cross-price effects of consumer goods and capital services prices in the share of consumer services. By symmetry the cross-price effects of consumer services prices in the share equations for consumer goods and capital services are relatively insignificant.

The most striking effect of an increase in family size is a sharp rise in the proportion of total expenditure devoted to food. There is a very substantial increase from family size one to family size two, probably the consequence of the fact that the second member of the family is usually an adult. The increases from family size two to larger family sizes are positive but less substantial, since these members of the family are likely to be children. The same phenomenon can be seen in somewhat attenuated form in the expenditure shares for energy. The increase from one family member to two of ten corresponds to the addition of a second driver; increases in energy consumption as family size increases further are more moderate. The decline in the energy share for families with seven or more members results from a shift in the composition of the budget away from energy toward food.

The impact of age of head of household can be interpreted through the implied age of other members of the household. The most substantial impact can be seen in the transition between ages 16–24 and 25–34, when the family enters into childbearing years. As children grow up and develop consumption patterns more similar to those of adults, the household budget shifts toward to that of a larger family. In particular, there is an increase in the expenditure shares for energy and food as the household head ages, while the share of capital services declines. The age group sixty-five and over has a highly distinctive consumption pattern. The expenditure shares of energy and food decline while those of consumer goods, capital services, and consumer services increase.

Regional differences in expenditure shares for energy and food are very small, although energy consumption is less important in the West and food consumption is somewhat higher in the Northeast. Nonwhite families have lower expenditure shares for energy and consumer services and a higher share for consumer goods than white families. Rural families have substantially larger expenditure shares for energy than urban families, reflecting the need for greater utilization of energy to provide transportation services. Finally, urban families have a much higher expenditure share for capital services than for rural families.

11.4.2 Pooled Estimates for Aggregate Energy Expenditure

The results of estimating the unknown parameters of the second stage of our econometric model of aggregate consumer behavior are presented in table 11.2. The estimates for this model were obtained by fitting equations for electricity, natural gas, and fuel oil with coefficients for the gasoline equation derived from the summability restrictions. We recall from section 11.3 that the effects of changes in the demographic composition of the population can be identified from cross-section data alone, while the effects of prices can be identified only by pooling cross-section and time-series data.

Estimates of the effects of changes in the demographic composition of the population from pooled cross-section and time-series data given in table 11.2. The share of electricity in total energy expenditure decreases from families of size one to families of size two. There is no consistent pattern in this expenditure share as family size increases

Table 11.2
Pooled estimation results for aggregate energy expenditures

	WELEC	WGAS	WSOL	WGASO
P_{ELEC}	.19221 (.0204)	−.04556 (.0171)	−.16256 (.0146)	.01591 (.0195)
P_{GAS}	−.04556 (.0171)	.04302 (.0306)	.01307 (.0169)	−.01053 (.0307)
P_{SOL}	−.16256 (.0146)	.01307 (.0169)	.16155 (.0188)	−.01206 (.0176)
P_{GASO}	.01591 (.0195)	−.01053 (.0307)	−.01206 (.0176)	.00668 (.0350)
CONST	−.15580 (.0102)	−.07008 (.0104)	−.24258 (.0130)	−.53153 (.0115)
F2	.00368 (.00544)	−.00411 (.00502)	.03355 (.00651)	−.03312 (.00755)
F3	.00563 (.00630)	−.01744 (.00580)	.03189 (.00753)	−.02008 (.00874)
F4	.00429 (.00686)	−.02083 (.00631)	.02283 (.00819)	−.00629 (.00954)
F5	−.00533 (.00801)	−.01426 (.00735)	.01013 (.00956)	.00947 (.0111)
F6	.00837 (.00981)	−.00890 (.00900)	−.00145 (.0116)	.00198 (.0136)
F7	−.00001 (.0105)	−.02454 (.00967)	.01333 (.0125)	.01121 (.0146)
A30	−.04984 (.00766)	−.03066 (.00725)	.01124 (.00931)	.06926 (.0105)
A40	−.06258 (.00816)	−.04948 (.00769)	.00520 (.00989)	.10687 (.0112)
A50	−.04374 (.00768)	−.04299 (.00726)	−.00610 (.00932)	.09285 (.0105)
A60	−.05796 (.00772)	−.06698 (.00729)	−.03152 (.00937)	.15647 (.0105)
A70	−.10194 (.00756)	−.12105 (.00719)	−.07967 (.00921)	.30267 (.0103)
RNC	.00046 (.00525)	−.04339 (.00487)	.11880 (.00630)	−.07587 (.00727)
RS	−.04800 (.00523)	.04051 (.00486)	.12978 (.00628)	−.12229 (.00725)
RW	−.00777 (.00566)	.01955 (.00524)	.13004 (.00678)	−.14182 (.00784)
NW	−.01455 (.0691)	−.06949 (.00633)	−.03118 (.00822)	.11523 (.00962)
RUR	.01273 (.00536)	.04072 (.00491)	−.06785 (.00638)	.01440 (.00747)

Notes: Convergence after 3 iterations. SSR = 64351.57.

further. The shares of natural gas and fuel oil also fall from families of size one to families of size two, but then rise as family size increases further. The effects of changes in family size on the share of gasoline in total energy expenditure are highly significant. As family size increases from one to two, the share of gasoline rises. Further increases in family size are accompanied by a gradual decline in the gasoline share.

The effects of age of head of household on the share of electricity in total energy expenditure is positive and increases monotonically through the highest age range. The pattern for natural gas is very similar to that for electricity. The share of fuel oil increases with age of head, but the age effect is smaller than for electricity and natural gas. The share of gasoline drops substantially from families with age of head from 16 to 24 to families with age of head 25 to 34. The share of gasoline continues to decline as age of head increases, ultimately declining by about a third of the total energy budget between the youngest and oldest age groups.

There are significant regional differences in shares of energy in total energy expenditure with higher consumption in the South and lower consumption in the North Central and West, all relative to the Northeast. The share of natural gas consumption is higher in the North Central region and lower in the South and West than in the Northeast. All regions have lower shares of fuel oil than the Northeast and higher shares of gasoline. Nonwhite households have higher shares of electricity and natural gas in total energy expenditure and lower shares of fuel oil and gasoline than white households. Finally, rural residents have higher shares of fuel oil and gasoline and lower shares of electricity and natural gas.

We can summarize the effects of changes in the demographic composition of the population by saying that the effects of family size are substantial only for gasoline. The addition of a second member of the family usually involves a second driver and increases the share of gasoline considerably. As additional members are added to the family unit, mainly children, the share of gasoline gradually declines. By contrast with family size, the impact of the age of head of household on the composition of the energy budget is quite dramatic. The share of gasoline declines gradually throughout the age range with corresponding increases in the shares of electricity, natural gas, and fuel oil. Effects of region, race, and rural versus urban residence are all quite substantial.

11.4.3 Estimated Price Effects

We have summarized the results of estimation of our two-stage model of consumer demand for energy in sections 11.2 and 11.3. In this concluding section we provide additional perspective on these results by calculating price elasticities of demand. Since there are four individual types of energy and four nonenergy commodity groups included in our model, a complete set of own- and cross-price elasticities of demand would require a total of sixty-four elasticities.

To reduce the price effects to manageable dimensions, we have limited our calculations to own-price elasticities of demand for individual types of energy. Our model of aggregate consumer behavior incorporates models of consumer demand for 672 types of consuming units. Using models for all types of consuming units, we can express own-price elasticities of demand for individual types of energy as functions of the demographic characteristics of individual households.

As a starting point for our calculations we take a household of size five, with age of head 35–44, living in the Northeast region, of white race and urban residence, and with total expenditure of $10,000 in 1972. We present own-price elasticities of demand for individual types of energy for seven family size categories, six age groups, four regions, two races, and urban versus rural residence.

In table 11.3 we present own-price elasticities of demand for all four types of energy, holding total energy expenditure fixed. These elasticities are calculated from second stage models for all types of consuming units. In table 11.4 we analyze the impact of changes in prices of individual types of energy by combining first stage and second stage models. We calculate own-price elasticities of demand for individual types of energy, holding total expenditure rather than total energy expenditure fixed.

The price elasticities of demand presented in table 11.3 are limited to substitution among different types of energy, while those given in table 11.4 also encompass substitution among energy and nonenergy commodities. As expected, the price elasticities of demand for individual types of energy presented in table 11.4 are uniformly larger in absolute value than those iven in table 11.3.

In analyzing the differences among households with different sets of demographic characteristics, we focus attention on the price response with total expenditure held constant presented in table 11.4. For all types of consuming units, gasoline is the least price elastic,

Table 11.3
Estimated own-price elasticities, 1972, holding total energy expenditure fixed

	A. Family size			
	1	2	3	4
ELEC	–1.880153	–1.895237	–1.903482	–1.897792
GAS	–1.359857	–1.347873	–1.314028	–1.306465
SOL	–1.680576	–1.792632	–1.786193	–1.753027
GASO	–1.015734	–1.014596	–1.015024	–1.015504
	5	6	7+	
ELEC	–1.859150	–1.915268	–1.880122	
GAS	–1.321506	–1.334914	–1.298565	
SOL	–1.710914	–1.676424	–1.721093	
GASO	–1.016093	–1.015808	–1.016161	
	B. Age of head			
	16–24	25–34	35–44	45–54
ELEC	–2.192842	–1.911047	–1.859150	–1.938145
GAS	–1.510152	–1.374117	–1.321506	–1.337890
SOL	–1.695006	–1.730342	–1.710914	–1.677214
GASO	–0.012798	–1.014756	–1.016093	–1.015567
	55–64	65+		
ELEC	–1.877261	–1.730636		
GAS	–1.284343	–1.209481		
SOL	–1.612007	–1.517599		
GASO	–1.018276	–1.030455		
	C. Region			
	NE	NC	S	W
ELEC	–1.859150	–1.860950	–1.707381	–1.830306
GAS	–1.321506	–1.242781	–1.461089	–1.376518
SOL	–1.710914	–2.489657	–2.657457	–2.661907
GASO	–1.016093	–1.013606	–1.012431	–1.011995
	D. Race		E. Residence	
	W	NW	URB	RUR
ELEC	–1.859150	–1.806678	–1.859150	–1.910989
GAS	–1.321506	–1.211617	–1.321506	–1.462110
SOL	–1.710914	–1.625124	–1.710914	–1.547455
GASO	–1.016093	–1.022276	–1.016093	–1.016671

Table 11.4
Estimated own-price elasticities, 1972, holding total expenditure fixed

	A. Family size			
	1	2	3	4
ELEC	−2.135454	−2.114194	−2.118997	−2.118798
GAS	−1.499632	−1.474005	−1.452825	−1.451391
SOL	−1.958079	−2.000486	−1.994355	−1.974490
GASO	−1.512159	−1.481422	−1.465533	−1.460356
	5	6	7+	
ELEC	−2.091881	−2.127498	−2.114964	
GAS	−1.460720	−1.464743	−1.453528	
SOL	−1.947309	−1.917785	−1.962006	
GASO	−1.447979	−1.442940	−1.460727	
	B. Age of head			
	16–24	25–34	35–44	45–54
ELEC	−2.355844	−2.140767	−2.091881	−2.144279
GAS	−1.595467	−1.499339	−1.460720	−1.466003
SOL	−1.930142	−1.971191	−1.947309	−1.917223
GASO	−1.540878	−1.507754	−1.447979	−1.447374
	55–64	65+		
ELEC	−2.080092	−1.974415		
GAS	−1.424421	−1.399808		
SOL	−1.856372	−1.806824		
GASO	−1.356697	−1.233744		
	C. Region			
	NE	NC	S	W
ELEC	−2.091881	−2.077382	−1.977628	−2.115028
GAS	−1.460720	−1.414585	−1.553896	−1.517065
SOL	−1.947309	−2.594791	−2.754398	−2.781467
GASO	−1.447979	−1.489636	−1.546969	−1.697050
	D. Race		E. Residence	
	W	NW	URB	RUR
ELEC	−2.091881	−2.067236	−2.091881	−2.060471
GAS	−1.460720	−1.433949	−1.460720	−1.528073
SOL	−1.947309	−1.907722	−1.947309	−1.756522
GASO	−1.447979	−1.350260	−1.447979	−1.300603

which electricity is the most price elastic form of energy. Price elasticities of natural gas are similar to these for gasoline, while price elasticities for fuel oil are intermediate between price elasticities for gasoline and for electricity.

The price elasticity of demand for electricity fluctuates with changes in family size with the largest elasticity for families of size one and the smallest elasticity for families of size five. The price elasticity of demand for natural gas is also a maximum for families of size one and reaches a minimum for families of size four. The price elasticity of demand for fuel oil is a maximum for families of size two and a minimum for families of size six. The price elasticities of demand vary more uniformly with age of head, declining almost monotonically with age for all types of energy.

The price elasticity of demand for electricity is lowest in the South, while elasticities of demand for electricity are very similar among Northeast North Central, and West regions. Price elasticities of demand for natural gas are very similar for Northeast, North Central, and West; this elasticity is highest for the South. Demand for fuel oil is most price elastic in the South and East and least price elastic in the Northeast. There are sizable differences in elasticities of demand for gasoline among regions with demand being most price elastic in the West. Finally, price elasticities of demand are lower for nonwhites than for whites and lower for rural residents than for urban residents, except for natural gas.

11.A Appendix: Intrumental Variables, 1958–1978

Table 11.A
Instrumental variables, 1958–1978

	Notation
I1	Constant
I2	Effective tax rate, labor services
I3	Effective tax rate, noncompetitive imports
I4	Time available for labor services
I5	U.S. population, millions of individuals
I6	Implicit deflator, supply of labor services
I7	Implicit deflator, government purchases of labor services

Table 11.A (continued)

	Notation
I8	Exogenous income, which equals government transfers to persons (excepting social insurance) less personal transfers to foreigners and personal nontax payments to government
I9	Private national wealth, lagged one period
I10	Potential time for labor services; rate of Harrod neutral change
I11	Total imports
I12	Implicit deflator, noncompetitive imports
I13	Corrected deflator for labor services
I14	Time, set to 0 in 1972

Notes

1. See Samuelson (1956) and Pollak (1981) for details.

2. The specification of a system of individual demand functions by means of Roy's Identity was first implemented empirically in a pathbreaking study by Houthakker (1960). A detailed review of econometric models of consumer behavior based on Roy's Identity is given by Lau (1977a).

3. The translog indirect utility function was introduced by Christensen, Jorgenson, and Lau (1975) and was extended to encompass changes in preferences over time by Jorgenson and Lau (1975). Alternative approaches to the representation of the effects of prices on expenditure allocation are reviewed by Barten (1977), Deaton and Muellbauer (1980b), pp. 60–85, and Lau (1977a).

4. These conditions are implied by the theory of exact aggregation presented by Lau (1977b, 1982).

5. Integrability is discussed in greater detail by Jorgenson and Lau (1979) and Jorgenson, Lau, and Stoker (1982).

6. See Malinvaud (1980) for more detailed discussion.

7. The 1972–1973 Survey of Consumer Expenditures is discussed by Carlson (1974).

8. We employ data on the flow of services from durable goods rather than purchases of durable goods. Personal consumption expenditures in the U.S. National Income and Product Accounts are based on purchases of durables goods.

9. This series is published annually by the U.S. Bureau of the Census.

References

Aigner, Dennis J. 1984. The Welfare Econometrics of Peak-Load Pricing for Electricity. Annals. *Journal of Econometrics* 26, nos. 1/2 (September/October): 1–252.

Amemiya, Takeshi. 1974. The Nonlinear Two-Stage Least Squares Estimator. *Journal of Econometrics* 2, no. 2 (July): 105–110.

———. 1977. The Maximum Likelihood and the Nonlinear Three-Stage Least Squares Estimator in the General Nonlinear Simultaneous Equation Model. *Econometrica* 45, no. 4 (May): 955–968.

———. 1978. A Note on a Random Coefficients Model. *International Economic Review* 19, no. 3 (October): 793–796.

Antonelli, Giovanni. B. 1971. On the Mathematical Theory of Political Economy. (Translated by John S. Chipman and Alan P. Kirman.) In *Preferences, Utility, and Demand*, eds. John S. Chipman, Leonid Hurwicz, Marcel K. Richter, and Hugo F. Sonnenschein, pp. 333–364. New York: Harcourt-Brace-Jovanovich, original in Italian, 1886.

Atkinson, Scott E. 1983. Discussion: The Implications of Homothetic Separability for Share Equation Price Elasticities. *Journal of Business and Economic Statistics* 1, no. 3 (July): 211–214.

Balestra, Pietro, and Marc Nerlove. 1966. Pooling Cross Section and Time Series Data in the Estimation of a Dynamic Model: The Demand for Natural Gas. *Econometrica* 34, no. 3 (July): 585–612.

Barnett, William A. 1983. Discussion: The Recent Reappearance of the Homotheticity Restriction on Preferences. *Journal of Business and Economic Statistics* 1, no. 3 (July): 215–218.

Barten, A. P. 1964a. Consumer Demand Functions Under Conditions of Almost Additive Preferences. *Econometrica* 32, no. 1 (January/April): 1–38.

———. 1964b. Family Composition, Prices and Expenditure Patterns. In *Econometric Analysis for National Economic Planning: 16th Symposium of the Colston Society*, eds. P. Hart, G. Mills, and J.K. Whitaker, 277–292. London: Butterworth.

———. 1967. Evidence on the Slutsky Conditions for Demand Equations. *Review of Economics and Statistics* 49, no. 1 (February): 77–84.

———. 1969. Maximum Likelihood Estimation of a Complete System of Demand Equations. *European Economic Review* 1 (Fall): 7–23.

———. 1974. Complete Systems of Demand Equations: Some Thoughts About Aggregation and Functional Form. *Récherches Economiques de Louvain* 40, no. 1: 1–18.

———. 1977. The Systems of Consumer Demand Functions Approach: A Review. In *Frontiers of Quantitative Economics*, vol. 3, ed. Michael D. Intriligator, 23–58. Amsterdam: North-Holland.

Barten, A. P., and E. Geyskens. 1975. The Negativity Condition in Consumer Demand. *European Economic Review* 6, no. 3 (July): 227–260.

Basmann, Robert L. 1968. Hypothesis Formulation in Quantitative Economics: A Contribution to Demand Analysis. In *Papers in Quantitative Economics*, eds. J. Quirk and H. Zarley, 143–202.

Basmann, Robert L., R. C. Battalio, and John H. Kagel. 1973. Comment on R. P. Byron's "The Restricted Aitken Estimation of Sets of Demand Relations." *Econometrica* 41, no. 1 (March): 365–370.

Bergson, Abram. 1936. Real Income, Expenditure Proportionality, and Frisch's 'New Methods of Measuring Marginal Utility.' *Review of Economic Studies* 4, no. 1 (October): 33–52.

Berndt, Ernst R., Masako N. Darrough, and W. Erwin Diewert. 1977. Flexible Functional Forms and Expenditure Distributions: An Application to Canadian Consumer Demand Functions. *International Economic Review* 18, no. 3 (October): 651–676.

Blackorby, Charles, Richard Boyce, and Robert R. Russell. 1978. Estimation of Demand Systems Generated by the Gorman Polar Form: A Generalization of the S-Branch Utility Tree. *Econometrica* 46, no. 2 (March): 345–364.

Blackorby, Charles, Daniel Primont, and Robert R. Russell. 1978. *Duality, Separability, and Functional Structure*. Amsterdam: North-Holland. Blundell, Richard. 1986. Consumer Behavior: Theory and Empirical Evidence— A Survey. *Economic Journal* 98, no. 389 (March): 16–65.

Braithwait, S. 1975. Consumer Demand and Cost of Living Indexes for the U.S.: An Empirical Comparison of Alternative Multi-Level Demand Systems. Bureau of Labor Statistics Working Paper 45.

Brown, James Alexander Campbell, and Angus S. Deaton. 1972. Models of Consumer Behaviour: A Survey. *Economic Journal* 82, no. 328 (December): 1145–1236.

Brown, Murray, and Dale M. Heien. 1972. The S-Branch Utility Tree: A Generalization of the Linear Expenditure System. *Econometrica* 40, no. 4 (July): 737–747.

Browning, Martin. 1992. Children and Household Economic Behavior. *Journal of Economic Literature* 30, no. 3 (September): 1434–1475.

Bureau of the Census. Various dates. *Current Population Reports*, Series P-60, Consumer Income. Washington, D.C.: U.S. Department of Commerce.

Byron, R. P. 1968. Methods for Estimating Demand Equations Using Prior Information: A Series of Experiments with Australian Data. *Australian Economic Papers* 7 (December): 227–248.

———. 1970a. A Simple Method for Estimating Demand Systems Under Separable Utility Assumptions. *Review of Economic Studies* 37, no. 110 (April): 261–274.

———. 1970b. The Restricted Aitken Estimation of Sets of Demand Relations. *Econometrica* 38, no. 6 (November): 816–830.

———. 1973. Reply to Basmann, Battalio, and Kagel. *Econometrica* 41, no. 1 (March): 371–374.

Carlson, Michael D. 1974. The 1972–1973 Consumer Expenditure Survey. *Monthly Labor Review* 97, no. 12 (December): 16–23.

Caves, Douglas W., and Laurits R. Christensen. 1983. Discussion. *Journal of Business and Economic Statistics* 1, no. 3 (July): 219–220.

Chamberlain, Gary, and Edward Leamer. 1976. Matrix Weighted Averages and Posterior Bounds. *Journal of the Royal Statistical Society* 38, Series B, no. 1: 73–84.

Chipman, John S. 1971. Introduction to Part II. In *Preferences, Utility, and Demand*, eds. John S. Chipman, Leonid Hurwicz, Marcel K. Richter, and Hugo F. Sonnenschein, 321–331. New York: Harcourt-Brace-Jovanovich.

———. Homothetic Preferences and Aggregation 1974. *Journal of Economic Theory* 8, no. 1 (May): 26–38.

Chipman, John S., Leonid Hurwicz, Marcel K. Richter, and Hugo F. Sonnenschein, eds. 1971. *Preferences, Utility, and Demand*. New York: Harcourt-Brace-Jovanovich.

Chipman, John S., and J. C. Moore. 1976. The Scope of Consumer's Surplus Arguments. In *Evolution, Welfare and Time in Economics: Essays in Honor of Nicholas Georgescu-Roegen*, eds. A.M. Tang, *et al.*, 69–123. Lexington: Heath-Lexington Books.

———. 1980. Compensating Variation, Consumer's Surplus, and Welfare. *American Economic Review* 70, no. 5 (December): 933–99.

Christensen, Laurits R., and Dale W. Jorgenson. 1973. U.S. Income, Saving and Wealth, 1929–1969. *Review of Income and Wealth*, ser. 19, no. 4 (December): 329–362.

Christensen, Laurits R., Dale W. Jorgenson, and Lawrence J. Lau. 1971. Conjugate Duality and the Transcendental Logarithmic Production Function. *Econometrica* 39, no. 4 (July): 255–256.

———. 1973. Transcendental Logarithmic Production Frontiers. *Review of Economics and Statistics* 55, no. 1 (February): 28–45.

———. 1975. Transcendental Logarithmic Utility Functions. *American Economic Review* 65, no. 3 (June): 367–383.

———. 1975. Cost of Living Indexes and Price Indexes for U.S. Meat and Produce, 1947–1971. In *Household Production and Consumption*, ed. N. Terleckyj, 399–446. New York: National Bureau of Economic Research.

Christensen, Laurits R., and M.E. Manser. 1977. Estimating U.S. Consumer Preferences for Meat with a Flexible Utility Function. *Journal of Econometrics* 5, no. 1 (January): 37– 54.

Conrad, Klaus. 1977. Gewohnheitsbildung und dynamische Nutzen- und Nachfragefunktionen. *Jahrbücher für Nationalökonomie und Statistik* 191, nos. 5–6 (April): 464–491.

———. 1978. Dynamic Utility and Aggregator Functions for the Allocation of Private Consumption in Input-Output Models, An Econometric Analysis. In *Theory and Applications of Economic Indices*, eds. W. Eichhorn, R. Henn, O. Opitz, and Ronald W. Shephard, 623–655. Würzburg: Physica-Verlag.

Conrad, Klaus, and Dale W. Jorgenson. 1975. *Measuring Performance in the Private Economy of the Federal Republic of Germany, 1950–73*. Tübingen: J.C.B. Mohr.

———. 1978. The Structure of Consumer Performance in the Private Economy of the Federal Republic of Germany, 1950–73. *Zeitschrift für Nationalökonomie* 38, nos. 1–2: 42–60.

———. 1979. Testing the Integrability of Consumer Demand Functions, Federal Republic of Germany, 1950–1973. *European Economic Review* 12, no. 2 (April): 149–169.

Cottle, R.W., and J.A. Ferland. 1972. Matrix-Theoretic Criteria for the Quasi-Convexity and Pseudo-Convexity of Quadratic Functions. *Linear Algebra and Its Applications* 5: 123–136.

Courant, Richard. 1936. *Differential and Integral Calculus*. New York: Interscience.

Court, Robin H. 1967. Utility Maximization and the Demand for New Zealand Meats. *Econometrica* 35, nos. 3/4 (July/October): 424–446.

Darrough, Masako, Robert A. Pollak, and Terence J. Wales. 1980. Taste Change and Stochastic Structure: An Analysis of Three Time Series of Household Budget Studies. Unpublished manuscript, September.

Deaton, Angus S. 1974. Analysis of Consumer Demand in the United Kingdom, 1900–1970. *Econometrica* 42, no. 2 (March): 341–367.

———. 1975. *Models and Projections of British Demand in Postwar Britain.* London: Chapman and Hall.

———. 1986. Demand Analysis. In *Handbook of Econometrics,* vol. 3, eds. Z. Griliches and M.D. Intriligator, 1767–1840. Amsterdam: North-Holland.

Deaton, Angus S., and John S. Muellbauer. 1980a. An Almost Ideal Demand System. *American Economic Review* 70, no.3 (June): 312–326.

———. 1980b. *Economics and Consumer Behavior.* Cambridge: Cambridge University Press.

Debreu, Gerard. 1952. Definite and Semidefinite Quadratic Forms. *Econometrica* 20, no. 2 (April): 295–300.

———. 1974. Excess Demand Functions. *Journal of Mathematical Economics* 1, no. 1 (March): 15–21.

Dielman, Terry E. 1983. Pooled Cross-Sectional and Time Series Data: A Survey of Current Statistical Methodology. *American Statistician* 37, no. 2 (May): 111–122.

Diewert, W. Erwin. 1976. Exact and Superlative Index Numbers. *Journal of Econometrics* 4, no. 2 (May): 115–146.

———. 1977. Generalized Slutsky Conditions for Aggregate Consumer Demand Functions, *Journal of Economic Theory* 15, no. 2 (August): 353–362.

Jack Faucett Associates. 1977. Development of 35 Order Input-Output Tables, 1958–1974. Final Report (October). Washington, D.C.: Federal Emergency Management Agency.

Gallant, A. Ronald. 1977. Three-Stage Least-Squares Estimation for a System of Simultaneous Nonlinear, Implicit Equations. *Journal of Econometrics* 5, no. 1 (January): 71–88.

Gallant, A. Ronald, and Dale W. Jorgenson. 1979. Statistical Inference for a System of Simultaneous, Nonlinear, Implicit Equations in the Context of Instrumental Variable Estimation. *Journal of Econometrics* 11, nos. 2/3 (October/December): 275–302.

Goldberger, Arthur S. 1969. Directly Additive Utility and Constant Marginal Budget Shares. *Review of Economic Studies* 36, no. 106 (April): 251–254.

Goldberger, Arthur S., and T. Gamaletsos. 1970. A Cross-Country Comparison of Consumer Expenditure Patterns. *European Economic Review* 1, no. 3 (Spring): 357–400.

Goldman, Steven M., and Hirofumi Uzawa. 1964. A Note on Separability in Demand Analysis. *Econometrica* 32, no. 3 (July): 387–398.

Gollnick, H. G. L. 1975. *Dynamic Structure of Household Expenditures in the Federal Republic of Germany.* Amsterdam: North-Holland.

Gorman, William M. 1953. Community Preference Fields. *Econometrica* 21, no. 1 (January): 63–80.

———. 1959. Separable Utility and Aggregation. *Econometrica* 27, no. 3 (July): 469–481.

———. 1971. Two Stage Budgeting. Unpublished paper, London School of Economics, Dept. of Economics.

———. 1976. Tricks with Utility Functions. In *Essays in Economic Analysis: Proceedings of the 1975 AUTE Conference, Sheffield*, eds. M.J. Artis and A.R. Nobay, 211–243. Cambridge: Cambridge University Press.

———. 1981. Some Engel Curves. In *Essays in the Theory and Measurement of Consumer Behavior*, ed. Angus S. Deaton. Cambridge: Cambridge University Press.

Göttinger, Hans-Werner. 1969. Beiträge zur funktionalen Separabilität bei Nutzenfunktionen. *Zeitschrift für die gesamte Staatswissenschaft* 125, no. 3 (July): 406–446.

———. 1969/70. Die Existenz einiger Klassen deterministischer Nutzenfunktionen. *Jahrbücher für Nationalökonomie und Statistik* 183, no. 2 (July): 97–124.

Hansen, Lars P. 1982. Large Sample Properties of Generalized Methods of Moments Estimators. *Econometrica* 50, no. 4 (July): 1029–1054.

Hartley, H.O. 196l. The Modified Gauss-Newton Method for the Fitting of Nonlinear Regression Functions by Least Squares. *Technometrics* 3: 269–280.

Hausman, Jerry A., and John Trimble. 1984. Appliance Purchase and Usage Adaptation to a Permanent Time-of-Day Electricity Rate Schedule. *Journal of Econometrics* 26, nos. 1/2 (September/October): 115–140.

Heien, Dale. 1973. Some Further Results on Estimation of the S-Branch Utility Tree. Bureau of Labor Statistics Working Paper 10.

Hicks, John R. 1942. Consumers' Surplus and Index-Numbers. *Review of Economic Studies* 9, no. 2 (Summer): 126–137.

———. 1946. *Value and Capital*, 2nd edition. Oxford: Oxford University Press (1st ed., 1939).

———. 1969. Direct and Indirect Additivity. *Econometrica* 37, no. 2 (April): 353–354.

Hotelling, Harold S. 1932. Edgeworth's Taxation Paradox and the Nature of Demand and Supply Functions. *J. Polit. Econ.* 40 (October): 577–616.

———. 1935. Demand Functions with Limited Budgets. *Econometrica* 3, no. 1 (January): 66–78.

Houthakker, Hendrik S. 1957. An International Comparison of Household Expenditure Patterns Commemorating the Centenary of Engel's Law. *Econometrica* 25, no. 4 (October): 532–551.

———. 1960. Additive Preferences. *Econometrica* 28, no. 2 (April): 244–257.

———. 1965a. A Note on Self-Dual Preferences. *Econometrica* 33, no. 4 (October): 797–801.

———. 1965b. New Evidence on Demand Elasticities. *Econometrica* 33, no. 2 (April): 277–288.

Houthakker, Hendrik S., and Lester D. Taylor. 1970. *Consumer Demand in the United States, Analyses and Projections*, 2nd. ed. Cambridge, MA: Harvard University Press.

Hurwicz, Leonid. 1971. On the Problem of Integrability of Demand Functions. In *Preferences, Utility, and Demand*, eds. John S. Chipman, Leonid Hurwicz, Marcel K. Richter, and H.F. Sonnenschein, 174–214. New York: Harcourt-Brace-Jovanovich.

Johansen, Leif. 1969. On the Relationships Between Some Systems of Demand Functions. *Liiketeloudellinen Aikakauskirja* 18, no. 1: 30–41.

Jorgenson, Dale W. 1986. Econometric Methods for Modeling Producer Behavior. In *Handbook of Econometrics*, vol. 3, eds. Z. Griliches and M.D. Intriligator, 1841–1915. Amsterdam: North Holland.

Jorgenson, Dale W. 1990. Aggregate Consumer Behavior and the Measurement of Social Welfare. *Econometrica*, vol. 58, no. 5 (September): 1007–1040.

Jorgenson, Dale W., and Jean-Jacques Laffont. 1974. Efficient Estimation of Nonlinear Simultaneous Equations with Additive Disturbances. *Annals of Social and Economic Measurement* 3, no. 1 (January): 615–640.

Jorgenson, Dale W., and Lawrence J. Lau. 1975. The Structure of Consumer Preferences. *Annals of Economic and Social Measurement* 4, no. 1 (January): 49–101.

———. 1977. Statistical Tests of the Theory of Consumer Behavior. In *Quantitative Wirtschaftsforschung*, eds. H.L. Albach, E. Helmstädter, and R. Henn, 383–394. Tübingen: J.C.B. Mohr.

———. 1979. The Integrability of Consumer Demand Functions. *European Economic Review* 12, no. 2 (April): 115–147.

———. 1986. Testing the Integrability of Consumer Demand Functions, United States, 1947–1971. In *Advances in Econometrics*, vol. 5, ed. Slottje, 3–48. Greenwich, CT: JAI Press.

Jorgenson, Dale W., Lawrence J. Lau, and Thomas M. Stoker. 1980. Welfare Comparison Under Exact Aggregation. *American Economic Review* 70, no. 2 (May): 268–272.

———. 1981. Aggregate Consumer Behavior and Individual Welfare. In *Macroeconomic Analysis*, eds. D. Currie, R. Nobay, and D. Peel, 35–61. London: Croom-Helm.

———. 1982. The Transcendental Logarithmic Model of Aggregate Consumer Behavior. In *Advances in Econometrics*, vol. 1, eds. Robert L. Basmann and G. Rhodes, 97–238. Greenwich, CT: JAI Press.

Jorgenson, Dale W., and Daniel T. Slesnick. 1983. Individual and Social Cost-of-Living Indexes. In *Price Level Measurement*, eds. W.E. Diewert and C. Montmarquette. Ottawa: Statistics Canada.

———. 1987. Aggregate Consumer Behavior and Household Equivalence Scales, *Journal of Business and Economic Statistics* 5, no. 2 (April): 219–232.

Jorgenson, Dale W., Daniel T. Slesnick, and Thomas M. Stoker. 1983. Two-Stage Budgeting and Exact Aggregation. *Journal of Business and Economic Statistics* 6, no. 3 (July): 313–326.

Jorgenson, Dale W., and Thomas M. Stoker. 1984. Aggregate Consumer Expenditures on Energy. In *Advances in the Economics of Energy and Resources*, vol. 5, ed. J.R. Moroney, 1–84. Greenwich, CT: JAI Press.

———. 1986. Nonlinear Three Stage Least Squares Pooling of Time Series and Cross Section Data. In *Advances in Statistical Analysis and Statistical Computing*, vol. 1, ed. R.S. Mariano, 87–115. Greenwich, CT: JAI Press.

Jorgenson, Dale W., and Peter J. Wilcoxen. 1990. Environmental Regulation and the U.S. Economic Growth. *Rand Journal of Economcis*, vol. 21, no. 2 (Summer): 314–340.

———. 1993. Energy, the Environment, and Economic Growth. In *Handbook of Natural Resource and Energy Economics*, vol. 3, eds. A.V. Kneese and J. Sweeney, 1267–1349. Amsterdam: North-Holland.

Kamke, E. 1950. *Differentialgleichungen: Lösungmethoden und Lösungen, Vol. II (Partielle Differentialgleichungen erster Ordnung für eine gesuchte Funktion)*. Leipzig: Geest and Portig.

Klein, Lawrence R., and H. Rubin. 1947–1948. A Constant-Utility Index of the Cost of Living. *Review of Economic Studies* 15, no. 2: 84–87.

Kmenta, Jan. 1978. Some Problems of Inference from Economic Survey Data. In *Survey Sampling and Measurement*, ed. N.K. Namboodiri, 107–120. New York: Academic Press.

Kohler, D.F. 1983a. The Bias in Price Elasticity Estimates under Homothetic Separability: Implications for Analysis for Peak-Load Electricity Pricing. *Journal of Business and Economic Statistics* 1, no. 3 (July): 202–210.

———. 1983b. Response. *Journal of Business and Economic Statistics* 1, no. 3 (July): 226–228.

Kuh, Edwin, and John Meyer. 1957. How Extraneous are Extraneous Estimates? *Review of Economics and Statistics* 39, no. 4 (November): 380–393.

Kuhn, H.W., and A.W. Tucker. 1951. Nonlinear Programming. In *Proceedings of the Second Berkeley Symposium on Mathematical Statistics and Probability*, ed. J. Neyman, 481–492. Berkeley, CA: University of California Press.

Lau, Lawrence J. 1969a. Direct and Indirect Utility Functions: Theory and Applications. Working Paper No. 149, Institute of Business and Economic Research, University of California, Berkeley.

———. 1969b. Duality and the Structure of Utility Functions. *Journal of Economic Theory* 1, no. 4 (December): 374–396.

———. 1977a. Complete Systems of Consumer Demand Functions Through Duality. In *Frontiers of Quantitative Economics*, vol. 3, eds. Michael D. Intriligator and David A. Kendrick, 59–86. Amsterdam: North Holland.

———. 1977b. Existence Conditions for Aggregate Demand Functions: The Case of Multiple Indexes. Technical report no. 248 (October). Stanford, CA: Institute for Mathematical Studies in the Social Sciences, Stanford University (revised 1980 and 1982).

———. 1978. Testing and Imposing Monotonicity, Convexity and Quasiconvexity. In *Production Economics: A Dual Approach to Theory and Applications*, vol. 1, eds. Melvyn Fuss and Daniel McFadden, 409–453. Amsterdam: North-Holland.

———. 1982. A Note on the Fundamental Theorem of Exact Aggregation. *Economics Letters* 9, no. 2: 119–126.

———. 1986. Functional Forms in Econometric Model Building. In *Handbook of Econometrics*, vol. 3, eds. Z. Griliches and M.D. Intriligator, 1515–1566. Amsterdam: North-Holland.

Lau, Lawrence J., W.L. Lin, and P.A. Yotopoulos. 1978. The Linear Logarithmic Expenditure System: An Application to Consumption-Leisure Choice. *Econometrica* 46, no. 4 (July): 843–868.

Lau, Lawrence J. and B.M. Mitchell. 1971. A Linear Logarithmic Expenditure System: An Application to U.S. Data. *Econometrica* 39, no. 4 (July): 87–88.

Lewbel, Arthur. 1991. The Rank of Demand Systems: Theory and Nonparametric Estimation. *Econometrica*, vol. 59, no. 3 (May): 711–730.

Leontief, Wassily. 1936. Composite Commodities and the Problem of Index Numbers. *Econometrica* 4 (January): 39–59.

———. 1947. Introduction to a Theory of the Internal Structure of Functional Relationships. *Econometrica* 15, no. 4 (October): 361–373.

Leser, Conrad E.V. 1941. Family Budget Data and Price Elasticities of Demand. *Review of Economic Studies* 9, no. 1 (November): 40–57.

———. 1963. Forms of Engel Functions. *Econometrica* 31, no. 4 (October): 694–703.

Liew, Chong K. 1976. A Two-Stage Least Squares Estimator with Inequality Restrictions on Parameters. *Review of Economics and Statistics* 58, no. 2 (May): 234–238.

Lluch, Constantino. 1971. Consumer Demand Functions, Spain, 1958–1964. *European Economic Review* 2, no. 3 (Spring): 277–302.

Malinvaud, Edmond. 1980. *Statistical Methods of Econometrics*, 3rd ed. Amsterdam: North-Holland.

Mantel, Rolf. 1974. On the Characterization of Aggregate Excess Demand. *Journal of Economic Theory* 7, no. 3 (March): 348–353.

Martos, B. 1969. Subdefinite Matrices and Quadratic Forms. *SIAM Journal of Applied Mathematics* 17: 1215–1223.

McFadden, Daniel L. 1964. Existence Conditions for Theil-Type Preferences. Working Paper, Department of Economics, University of California, Berkeley.

McFadden, Daniel L., Rolf Mantel, Andreu Mas-Colell, and Marcel K. Richter. 1974. A Characterization of Community Excess Demand Functions. *Journal of Economic Theory* 9, no. 4 (December): 361–374.

Muellbauer, John S. 1975. Aggregation, Income Distribution, and Consumer Demand. *Review of Economic Studies* 42, no. 132 (October): 525–543.

———. 1976a. Community Preferences and the Representative Consumer. *Econometrica* 44, no. 5 (September): 979–999.

———. 1976b. Economics and the Representative Consumer. In *Private and Enlarged Consumption*, eds. L. Solari and J.N. Du Pasquier, 29–54. Amsterdam: North-Holland.

———. 1977. Testing the Barten Model of Household Composition Effects and the Cost of Children. *Economic Journal* 87, no. 347 (September): 460–487.

Mundlak, Yair. 1978. On the Pooling of Time Series and Cross Section Data. *Econometrica* 46, no. 1 (January): 69–86.

Parks, Richard W. 1969. Systems of Demand Equations: An Empirical Comparison of Alternative Functional Forms. *Econometrica* 37, no. 4 (October): 629–650.

———. 1983. Discussion. *Journal of Business and Economic Statistics* 1, no. 3 (July): 22–225.

Parks, Richard W., and A.P. Barten. 1973. A Cross Country Comparison of the Effects of Prices, Income and Population Compensation on Consumption Patterns. *Economic Journal* 83, no. 331 (September): 834–852.

Phlips, L. 1974. *Applied Consumption Analysis*. Amsterdam: North-Holland.

Pollak, Robert A. 1981. The Social Cost of Living Index. *Journal of Public Economics* 15, no. 3 (June): 311–336.

Pollak, Robert A., and Terence J. Wales. 1978. Estimation of Complete Demand Systems from Household Budget Data: The Linear and Quadratic Expenditure Systems. *American Economic Review* 68, no. 3 (June): 348–359.

———. 1980. Comparisons of the Quadratic Expenditure System and Translog Demand Systems with Alternatives Specifications of Demographic Effects. *Econometrica* 48, no. 3 (April): 595–612.

Prais, S.J., and Hendrik S. Houthakker. 1971. *The Analysis of Family Budgets*, 2nd ed. Cambridge, England: Cambridge University Press.

Roy, René. 1943. *De l'Utilité: Contribution à la Théorie des Choix*. Paris: Hermann et Cie.

Samuelson, Paul A. 1950. The Problem of Integrability in Utility Theory. *Economica*, N.S. 17 (November): 355–385.

———. 1956. Social Indifference Curves. *Quarterly Journal of Economics* 70, no. 1 (February): 1–22.

———. 1965. Using Full Duality to Show that Simultaneously Additive Direct and Indirect Utilities Implies Unitary Price Elasticity of Demand. *Econometrica* 33, no. 4 (October): 781–796.

———. 1969. Corrected Formulation of Direct and Indirect Additivity. *Econometrica* 37, no. 2 (April): 355–359.

———. 1974. Complementarity — An Essay on the 40th Anniversary of the Hicks-Allen Revolution in Demand Theory. *Journal of Economic Literature* 12, no. 4 (December): 1255–1289.

Sato, Kazuo. 1972. Additive Utility Functions with Double-Log Consumer Demand Functions. *Journal of Political Economy* 80, no. 1 (January/February): 102–124.

Schultz, Henry. 1938. *The Theory and Measurement of Demand*. Chicago: University of Chicago Press.

Slutsky, Eugen E. 1952. On the Theory of the Budget of the Consumer. In *Readings in Price Theory*, eds. G. J. Stigler and K. E. Boulding, 27–56. Homewood, original in Italian, 1915.

Somermeyer, W.H., J.G.M. Hilhorst, and J.W.W.A. Wit. 1961. A Method for Estimating Price and Income Elasticities from Time Series and its Application of Consumers' Expenditures in the Netherlands, 1949–59. *Statistical Studies* 13: 30–53.

Sonnenschein, Hugo. 1972. Market Excess Demand Functions. *Econometrica* 40, no. 3 (May): 549–563.

———. 1973a. Do Walras' Identity and Continuity Characterize the Class of Community Excess Demand Functions. *Journal of Economic Theory* 6, no. 4 (August): 345–354.

———. 1973b. The Utility Hypothesis and Market Demand Theory. *Western Economic Journal* 11, no. 4 (December): 404–410.

Sono, Masazo. 1961. The Effect of Price Changes on the Demand and Supply of Separable Goods. *International Economic Review* 2, no. 3 (September): 239–271.

Stoker, Thomas M. 1979. Aggregation Over Individuals and Demand Analysis. Unpublished doctoral dissertation, Harvard University.

———. 1982. The Use of Cross Section Data to Characterize Macro Functions. *Journal of the American Statistical Association* 77, no. 378 (June): 369–380.

———. 1984. Completeness, Distribution Restrictions and the Form of Aggregate Functions. *Econometrica* 52, no. 4 (July): 887–907.

Stone, Richard. 1954a. Linear Expenditure Systems and Demand Analysis: An Application to the Pattern of British Demand. *Economic Journal* 64, no. 255 (September): 511–527.

———. 1954b. *Measurement of Consumer's Expenditures and Behavior in the United Kingdom*, vol. 1. Cambridge: Cambridge University Press.

Strotz, Robert H. 1959. The Utility Tree — A Correction and Further Appraisal. *Econometrica* 27, no. 3 (July): 482–489

Theil, Henri. 1965. The Information Approach to Demand Analysis. *Econometrica* 33, no. 1 (January): 67–87.

———. 1967. *Economics and Information Theory*. Amsterdam: North-Holland.

———. 1971. *Principles of Econometrics*. New York: John Wiley and Sons.

———. 1975, *Theory and Measurement of Consumer Demand*, vol. 1. Amsterdam: North-Holland.

White, Halbert. 1980a. Nonlinear Regression on Cross-Section Data. *Econometrica* 48, no. 3 (April): 721–746.

———. 1980b. A Heteroscedasicity-Consistent Covariance Matrix Estimator with a Direct Test for Heteroscedasticity. *Econometrica* 48, no. 4 (May): 817–838.

———. 1982. Instrumental Variables Regression with Independent Observations. *Econometrica* 50, no. 2 (March): 483–500.

Wolak, Frank A. 1989. Local and Global Testing of Nonlinear Inequality Constraints in Nonlinear Econometric Models. *Econometric Theory*, vol. 5, no. 1 (April): 1–35.

Wold, Herman. 1953. *Demand Analysis: A Study in Econometrics*. New York: John Wiley and Sons.

Working, H. 1943. Statistical Laws of Family Expenditure. *Journal of the American Statistical Association* 38, (March): 43–56.

Zellner, Arnold, and Henri Theil. 1962. Three-Stage Least Squares: Simultaneous Estimation of Simultaneous Equations. *Econometrica* 30, no. 1 (January): 54–78.

Index

Note: Pages tagged with *t* locate tables.

Addilog system. *See* Direct addilog system; Indirect addilog system
Additivity restrictions
  in demand theory, 2, 8–9, 10–12
  direct translog utility function, 9, *66t*
  direct utility function, 57, *66t*
  explicit, 9, 15, 18, 24, 59, *66t*, *75t*, 160–161, 169
  homothetic, 62
  indirect utility function, 57, *75t*, 160–161
  in linear expenditure systems, 30
  tests for, 2, 14–15, *16*, 18, 24, *25t*, *26t*, 59, 62, 168–169, 174, 176
  validity of, 27
Aggregate consumer behavior model. *See also* Econometric model of aggregate consumer behavior; Translog model of aggregate consumer behavior
  age of household head, 337, 339, *340*, 347
  based on representative consumer, 204, 208, 214
  changes in total expenditures affecting, 334, 336*t*, 337, 502
  commodity groups, xxiii, 323–329
  conditions for identification, 376–377
  consuming units, 323–329
  correction for heteroscedasticity, 375, 491–492
  econometric, xii
  elasticity calculation, 342, 343–346*t*, 347–348
  exact aggregation approach, xii, xxix, 475
  expenditure shares, 219
  family size, 337, *338*
  individual preferences in, xix, 368
  integrability, 214–216
  in intertemporal general equilibrium model, xxix
  pooled cross-section and time-series data, xiii, 204, 219–220, 500, 501*t*, 502–503
  race, region, and residence type, 339, *341*, 342
  transcendental logarithmic, 220
  two-stage allocation, 500, 501*t*, 502–503
  U.S. (1958–1974), 220, 323–350
  unknown parameters, xxi
Aggregate consumer demand
  allocation categories, xxi
  econometric consumer behavior model applied to, 203
  price and total expenditures as determinants of, xii
  zero, 240, 242–243
Aggregate demand functions
  additivity, 220
  dependence on individual expenditures, 204, 217
  depending on two index functions, 241
  differentiability assumption, 207
  homogeneity conditions, 245–246
  homogeneous of degree zero, 204
  as index functions, 209, 212, 242–243
  for individual energy types, 485–486
  individual expenditures and, xiii
  nonlinearity, 208
  price dependence, 218
  restrictions on, 221

Aggregate demand functions (*cont.*)
as sum of individual demand functions, 216, 218, 280
with three index functions, 248–255
Aggregate energy expenditure shares
additive components, 464–465
errors of measurement, 372–373, 389, 465–466, 493–494
estimation, 388–389
heteroscedasticity correction, 389
integrability restrictions, 369
linearity, xxv
Aggregate energy expenditures. *See also* Energy expenditure shares
age of household head and, 431, *433*, 435, 437, 502–503, 505
chosen with random disturbance, 370–371
demographic coefficients, 430–431
demographic effects, 429–437, 430*t*, 438*t*, 439*t*, 441*t*, 444*t*, 445, 447, 467, 504–505
econometrics, 369–370, 428–447
family size effects, 431, *432*, 437
heteroscedasticity correction, 429
pooled estimation results, 429–437, 430*t*, 438*t*, 439*t*, 441*t*, 444*t*, 445, 504*t*, 504–505
price coefficients, 430
regional differences affecting, *434*, 435
time-series data, 379–380
Aggregate energy expenditures model, 357
based on exact aggregation theory, 359
combined with individual energy expenditures model, 377
demographic coefficients, 440
estimation, 379–383
heteroscedasticity correction, 380
identification, 374–377
minimizing criterion function, 381, 384
pooled cross-section and time-series data, 359, 383–388, 389–390
price coefficients, 440
stochastic structure, 370–374
two-stage, xxvii
Aggregate expenditure model
combined with individual expenditures model, 311
nonlinear three-stage least squares estimation, 310
two-stage allocation, 483–487
Aggregate expenditure shares
in aggregate consumer behavior model, 219
calculating, 300–301
corresponding to errors of measurement, 490–491
demographic changes impacting, 219, 309, 310
dependent factors, 481–482, 483
in energy demand model, 364
equations for, 304–305, 321
errors of measurement, 305–306, 321
exact aggregation conditions, 286
heteroscedasticity of aggregate disturbances, 306–307, 321, 491–492
in representative consumer model, 208
zero, 240, 242–243
AIDS system, 274, 275, 279, 451
Aigner, Dennis J., 476
Alternative economic policies, welfare impact, 283–286, 300
Antonelli matrix of own- and cross-quantity substitution, 141
Autocorrelated common time effect, 456
Autocorrelation, 456

Barten, A.P., 27, 30
consumer behavior theory, 196
integrability tests, 156
Rotterdam demand functions, xvii, 1, 91, 95, 104, 137
Basmann, Robert L., 3, 27, 30
Behavioral equations, unrestricted, 17–18
Berndt, Ernst R., xiv, 208
Blackorby, Charles, 450, 476
Boyce, Richard, 450, 476
Braithwait, S., 476
Brown, James Alexander Campbell, 91
Brown, Murray, 450, 476
Budget constraint
direct translog utility function, 4, 5, 33, 155
econometric demand model, 37
in estimating parameters of behavioral equation, 17
indirect translog utility function, 7, 36, 155
Budget shares. *See also* Constant budget shares
corresponding to translog demand systems, 189–190

in demand theory, 12–13
equations for, 34, 37, 38, 143, 145, 155
restrictions on equations for, 13
Rotterdam demand functions, 97, 99, 100–101
total expenditure and demographic characteristics affecting, 342, 343–346*t*

Capital service expenditures, 324
individual expenditure patterns and, 354
CES. *See* Consumer Expenditure Surveys
Cholesky factorization, 106, 139, 142
of compensated own- and cross-quantity effects, 122
of matrix B_{pp}, 294, 296, 298, 301
parameters of, 187, 188
Christensen, Laurits R., xvi, 29, 105, 153, 156
Commodity augmentation, 31
direct translog utility function, 66*t*, 85
direct vs. indirect utility functions, 57–58
equal rates, 53–56, 64, 85, 86
indirect translog utility function, 75*t*, 85
level of significance, 86
zero rates, 55, 56, 85
Common time effect, 456
Composite demand function
compensated own-price substitution effect, 215
monotonicity condition, 215
Conrad, Klaus, xvii, 153
Constant budget shares
as condition for summability, 113
for direct and indirect demand systems, 110–111
symmetry of Slutsky matrix and, 124, 127–132
Consumer behavior theory. *See also* Translog model of aggregate consumer behavior
based on aggregate quantities consumed, 205–206
based on direct and indirect demand functions, 138
German four-commodity model, 196
implications of, xiii
integrability conditions, 91
parametric representation of preferences, 137
system of demand functions satisfying, xiii
testing methodology, 137
two-stage allocation, 357–358
Consumer demand functions. *See also* Integrability
additive, 93–95, 101
additivity of corresponding utility functions, 179
double logarithmic system, 1, 94, 95
estimation and testing, 189–194
integrability conditions, 103, 123, 139–143
tests for, 156
linear in unknown parameters, 104
nonlinear in unknown parameters, 104
as ratios of two first-order polynomials, 180
summability condition, 123
tests of, 1
uniformity property, 183, 196
Consumer demand model
consumption expenditures, Federal Republic of Germany, 172–177, 175*t*-176*t*
durable and nondurable equations, 172
empirical results, 143–150, 171–177
stochastic specification, 171–172
test statistics
critical values, 173, 174*t*
level of significance, 173
Consumer Expenditure Surveys, xxv–xxvi
combined electricity and natural gas expenditures, 394, 406
comparison of data bases, 423–424, 425–427*t*
cross-section data, 348, 498
vs. Lifestyle and Household Energy Use Survey, 424–425, 428*t*
1973, 406, 407*t*, 408
1972, 400, 401*t*, 402, 406
1960–1961, 392, 395*t*, 396, 400
pooled estimates, 437, 438–439*t*, 440
residential energy demand data, 466
Consumer expenditures
categories of, xxi, 323–324
commodity groups, 348, 499
defined, 323
demographic effects, xxi, 220
family size effects, xxi
impact of age on, xxi–xxii
ratio of nonlinear to attribute, 253

Consumer expenditures (*cont.*)
role of prices and total expenditures on, 203
Consumer preferences. *See also* Individual preferences
in aggregate consumer behavior model, 218
approximation, 38–39
demographic effects, 500
duality, 56–58
econometric methodology, 29
unknown parameters, 65
equality restrictions, 157
groupwise equal rate of commodity augmentation, 53–56
groupwise homotheticity and homogeneity, 161–162
groupwise linear logarithmic utility, 50–53, 165–167
groupwise separability, 39–44, 158–161
homogeneity, 157–158
homothetic, 208
identical, xiv, 208
exact aggregation for, 220–242
identical homothetic, xiii–xiv, 206, 207
integrable demand system and corresponding utility, 156–157
represented by translog utility functions, 153
restrictions on, 38–39
separability of goods and time, 31
statistical tests, 85–90, 88*t*-89*t*, 168–171
critical values, 87*t*
symmetry restrictions, 157
tests for, 58–64, 87
estimation, 64–65, 84–85
Consumer services
cross-price effects, 503
estimates for parameters, 502
expenditures on, 324
Consuming unit
attributes of, 499
demographic characteristics, 348
effects of demographic characteristics on preferences of, 500
household as, 325, 348, 391, 499
individual vs. aggregate, 304
in terms of indirect utility function, 361
Cottle, R.W., 292
Covariance matrix of disturbances, Kronecker product form, 304, 307, 371–374, 464, 466, 489, 492, 493, 495
Criterion function, minimizing, 315, 317–318, 381, 384
Cross-price substitution
for all commodity groups, 502–503
compensated, 114, 120–121, 288–289, 365, 366
Slutsky matrix, 141
uncompensated, 114, 288
Cross-quantity substitution
Antonelli matrix, 141
compensated, 122, 188
Cross-section data. *See also* Pooled cross-section and time-series data
in aggregate demand model, xiii
estimation, 328, 350–353*t*
individual energy expenditures, 374–375
pooled estimation results, 430*t*
stochastic structure, 302–311
technical assumptions, 472
for U.S. individual energy expenditures, 390
Current Population Reports, 498
Current Population Survey, 348

Darrough, Masako N., xiv, 208
Deaton, Angus S., xiv
aggregate consumer behavior model, 208
AIDS system, 274, 279, 451
integrability of demand functions, 91
two-stage budgeting, 476
Demand functions. *See* Direct demand function; Indirect demand function
Demand system. *See also* Econometric demand model
with constant budget shares, 101
double-logarithmic, 91, 101, 103
generated by polar form of indirect utility function, 450
integrability conditions, 137
linear logarithmic, xvii
restrictions implied by utility maximization, 31
unknown parameters, 34
Demand theory
additivity, 8–9
duality between prices and quantities in, 2
empirical tests, 13–26
equality and symmetry restrictions, 7–8
estimation, 16–18, 23

statistical tests, 3–4, 23–26
stochastic specification, 7
tests of, 2, 7–13
Demographic characteristics
as determinants of household demand, xii
of energy expenditure, 486–487
influencing aggregate energy expenditures, 429–437, 430*t*, 438*t*, 439*t*, 441*t*, 444*t*
influencing individual energy expenditures, 391, 392, 396–408
Diewert, W. Erwin, xiii, xiv, 204, 208
Differentiability assumption, 231, 233
Direct addilog system, 2, 27
degree of homogeneity, 30
Direct demand function, 35
compensated own-price substitution, 109
homogeneity, 107, 110–111
integrability conditions, 138
monotonicity, 109, 120–122, 142–143, 188
nonlinear in parameters, 138
nonnegativity, 108, 120–122, 141–142
summability, 107–108, 111–113
symmetry restriction, 108, 113–114
Direct translog demand function
critical values, 191*t*, 194
dynamic version, 156
equality restriction, 147
estimates of parameters, 144*t*, 147–149, 190, 199–200*t*
German personal consumption expenditures, 193
homogeneity, 144–145*t*, 183
integrability conditions, 140–143, 195
nonnegativity, 187
restrictions on parameters, 181
summability, 183–184
symmetry restrictions, 184–186
in terms of expenditure shares, 181
test statistics, 151*t*, 191*t*
Direct translog utility function, 3, 4–6. *See also* Direct utility function
additive and homothetic, 12
additivity, 9
for consumer preferences, 29
estimates of parameters, 18, 19–20*t*
groupwise homogeneity, 49–50
groupwise homotheticity, 47–49
homogeneity, 46–47
homotheticity, 44–46
intrinsically groupwise homothetic, 47–48
neutral linear logarithmic, 46
normalization of parameters, 5–6, 34
parameter estimates, 65, 66–74*t*, 84–85
self-dual, 23
without time-varying preferences, 29
with time-varying preferences, 32–35
Direct utility function. *See also* Direct translog utility function
additive and homothetic, 10–12
additivity, 27, 57
characterized by commodity augmentation
groupwise equal rates, 53–56, 57
groupwise zero rates, 55, 56
direct demand system and, 110, 153
duality, 56–58
explicitly neutral, 40
groupwise commodity separable, 57
groupwise homothetically separable, 50–53
groupwise linear logarithmic, 51–53
groupwise separability restriction, 56
groupwise time separable, 57
homothetic, 9
homothetic separability, 324
neutral, 57
quasi-concave, 154
self-dual, 12–13, 58, 89–90
Duality
in consumer preferences, 56–58
in demand theory, 2, 12–13
between direct and indirect utility functions, 3
Durables
expenditure shares, 182, 189
restrictions on preference structures, 172

Econometric demand model. *See also* Demand system
equality and symmetry restrictions, 38
stochastic specification, 37–38
Econometric model of aggregate consumer behavior. *See also* Individual consumer behavior model; Residential energy demand model
empirical results, 498–509
heteroscedasticity corrections, 465–466

Econometric model (*cont.*)
  homogeneity restrictions, 157–158
  pooled estimates, 500, 501*t*, 502–503
  vs. representative consumer model, xxviii
  second stage, 492–493
  stochastic specification, 189
  two-stage, 498
  U.S. (1958–1974), 203
Elasticity of substitution
  constant, 10–11
  among pairs of commodities, 30
  unitary, 11
Energy demand model
  aggregate demand functions, xxvi–xxvii
  pooled cross-section and time-series data, xxv–xxvi
  two-stage allocation process, 475
    price effects, 506–509
Energy expenditure shares
  demographic effects, 486–487
  as function of energy prices, 358
  in translog model of consumer behavior, 478–479
Energy expenditures, 323. *See also* Aggregate energy expenditures model; Individual energy expenditures; Residential energy demand model
  allocation among energy types, xxiv
  categories of, 391, 400, 499
  family size and, 502–503
  gasoline vs. fuel oil usage, 412, 418, 468, 470*t*, 505
  Germany (1950–1973), 189
  to maximize household social welfare function, 360
  restrictions on preference structures, 172
  for transportation and household operations, 363, 440–442
  two-stage allocation of, xxiv–xxv
Energy price index, 477
  aggregate, 485
  in terms of homothetic translog utility function, 484
Engel curves, 248
  identical linear, 213
  parallel linear, 213
Engel's Law, xiii, 208
Equal rates
  direct translog utility function, 74*t*
  indirect translog utility function, 83*t*
Equality restrictions, 113
  for consumer demand functions, 7, 140–141
  direct translog demand function, 147, 190, 199*t*
  direct translog utility function, 34, 38, 66*t*, 85
  explicit, 88*t*
  on homogeneity, 157–158
  indirect translog demand function, 146*t*-147*t*, 147, 190, 196–197*t*
  indirect translog utility function, 37, 38, 75*t*
  level of significance, 194
  for monotonicity, 120–122, 187
  for nonnegativity, 186
  on summability condition, 183–184
  for symmetry, 186
  tests for, 14, 191*t*, 192
Euler's equation, 236
  for homogeneous function, 225
Exact aggregation theory, xiv–xv
  additive random component, 453
  in aggregate consumer behavior model, 209–213
  in aggregate energy expenditures model, 359
  for consumers with identical preferences, 220–242
  Corollary 8.1, 229
  Corollary 8.2, 229–230
  corresponding individual and aggregate behavior, 449–450
  with differences in individual preferences, 242–258
  econometrics of, 487–498
  homoscedastic and uncorrelated disturbances, 452, 454
  household attributes, 325
  individual consumer behavior theory and, 256
  instrumental variables, 456–457
  linearity of demand function in, xix
  nonlinear models, 450–451
  in representative consumer model, xv
  restrictions derived from, 216, 241, 312
  stochastic specification, 452–457
  Theorem 8.2, 223–224, 230
  Theorem 8.3, 228–229

Theorem 8.4, 239–240, 249
Theorem 8.5, 242–243
Theorem 8.6, 268
in translog consumer behavior model, 280–286
Expenditure elasticity
demand model, xxiii
for different consuming groups, 350
vs. price elasticities, demographic differences, xii
total expenditure and demographic characteristics affecting, 342, 343–346*t*, 347–348
Expenditure function
in assessing alternative policy impact, 300
equivalent vs. compensating variation in, 300
impact of alternative economic policies on, 283
Expenditure share functions
implications of integrability for, 105
from monotone transformations of indirect utility functions, 118
ratios of first-order polynomial functions, 123, 276
summability and nonnegativity conditions, 276
Expenditure shares
attribute effects, 247–248
chosen with random disturbance, 302
constant, 276–277
demand functions in terms of, 181
under exact aggregation, 502
as function of prices, xix
as function of quantities, 181
as function of total expenditure, *335*
integrability conditions, 181–188
price effect, 502
random disturbances, 321
summability of, 182
system of two equations, 182
total expenditure effect, 247–248, 502
Expenditure system. *See* Linear expenditure system; Nonlinear expenditure system

Family budget studies, 204
Family size
aggregate energy expenditures and, 431, *432*, 437, 502–503
individual energy expenditures and, 394, 396, *397*, 400, 402, *403*, 406, 408, *409*, 413, 414, *415*, *420*, 423
price elasticity of energy demand and, 509
relative expenditure shares and, 337, *338*
Federal Republic of Germany
consumption expenditures (1950–1973), 172–177, 175*t*-176*t*
dynamic structure of household expenditures, 156
personal consumption expenditures (1950–1973), 189–194
Ferland, J.A., 292
Function *g*
logarithmic function form, 119, 125, 126, 127–132, 138
power function form, 119, 126, 127, 133–134, 138
Function $H^{*(p)}$ and $H^{*}_{l}(p)$, polynomial specification, 268–276, 279
Fundamental Theorem of Exact Aggregation, xv, 210–211, 220, 222
implications of, 212
specializations of, 213

Gallant, A. Ronald, xix
nonlinear simultaneous equation systems, xxviii, 458, 461, 471
Gauss-Newton method, 314, 380, 459
Germany. *See* Federal Republic of Germany
Geyskens, E., 156, 196
Gini coefficient, 212
Goldman, Steven M., 156
Gollnick, H.G.L., 156
Gorman, Terence, xiii, xiv, xv, xxi, xxiii, xxviii
Gorman, William M.
preference restrictions, 475–476
utility function, 156, 206, 207, 450
Group homotheticity restriction
explicit, 60
inclusive, 60
Groupwise equal rates
of commodity augmentation, 64, *65*
tests for, 64, *65*, 88*t*
Groupwise homogeneity
direct translog utility function, 49–50
indirect translog utility function, 84, 165

Groupwise homogeneity (*cont.*)
- statistical tests, 174, 175t
- tests for, 60–61, *89t*, 169–170

Groupwise homothetic separability
- of consumer preferences, 165–166
- direct translog utility function, 50–53, 85
- explicit, 51, 62, 166, 176
- intrinsic, 51
- statistical tests, 176
- tests for, 61–62, 63, 168, 170–171, 174

Groupwise homotheticity
- of consumer preferences, 158
- direct translog utility function, 47–49, 84, 85, 156
- explicit, 48, 84, 88t, 164, 169, 174, 175t
- explicit inclusive, 49, 165, 170, 174
- inclusive, 48–49, 84, 88t, 164–165, 169, 170
- indirect utility function, 156, 161–162, 163–164
- intrinsic, 47–48
- level of significance, 86, 174
- statistical tests, 174, 175t
- tests for, 59–61, 88t, 169–170, 174

Groupwise linear logarithmic utility
- of consumer preferences, 158, 165–166
- direct translog utility function, 48, 50–53, 85
- explicit, 52, 63, 85, 166–167, 171, 174, 176t
- explicit neutral, 63, 171
- intrinsic, 51–52
- level of significance, 86, 173
- neutral, 48, 50–53, 85
- statistical tests, 174, 176t
- tests for, 62–63, 89t, 168, 171

Groupwise separability
- in consumer preferences, 39–44
- direct and indirect utility functions, 56–57, 156, 158–161
- direct translog utility function, 84, 85
- explicit, 59, 84, 86, 88t, 160, 169, 173
- indirect translog utility function, 84
- level of significance, 86, 173
- statistical tests, 175t
- tests for, 58, 88t, 168–169, 170–171
- time, 57

Hartley, H.O., 460

Hausman, Jerry A., 476

Head of household, age of
- aggregate energy expenditures and, 431, *433*, 435, 437, 502–503, 505
- individual energy expenditures and, 337, 339, *340*, 347, 396, *398*, 402, *404*, 408, *410*, 414, *416*, *421*, 423

Heien, Dale M., 450, 476

Heteroscedasticity corrections, 309, 321, 328
- for aggregate disturbances, 306–307, 373–374, 375, 465–466, 491–492, 495
- in aggregate energy expenditure model, 429
- Gauss-Newton method, 313–314
- in individual energy expenditures model, 380
- in residential energy demand model, 465–466

Hicks, John, xxii

Homogeneity
- in addilog utility function, 2
- of aggregate demand functions, 245–246
- degree minus one, 235–236, 237
- degree one, 239
- degree zero, 224, 225, 232, 234, 237–239, 241, 244–245, 287
- direct demand functions, 107, 110–111, 140, 195
- direct translog demand functions, 144–145t, 183, 190, 199t
- direct translog utility functions, 46–47, 67t, 71t
- equality and symmetry restrictions, 157–158
- functions $H^*(p)$ and $H^*_j(p)$, 268–276
- indirect demand functions, 107, 111, 140, 195
- indirect translog demand functions, 144–145t, 146–147t, 183, 190, 196–197t
- indirect translog utility functions, 76t, 80t, 163
- indirect utility functions, 216, 361
- individual demand functions, xvi, 214, 218, 224–230, 241, 249–253, 255
- individual expenditure shares, 287, 288–289, 365
- integrability conditions, 92
- level of significance, 194
- monotonicity and, 120–122, 187

nonnegativity and, 186
restrictions for budget shares, 145
statistical tests, 174, 175*t*
symmetry and, 186
tests for, 15, 18, 24, 89*t*, 169–170, 191*t*, 192
Homoscedasticity correction in exact aggregation models, 452, 454
Homothetic separability
in allocation of energy expenditure, 362–363
direct translog utility functions, 72*t*
direct utility functions, 324
in energy prices, xxiv
explicitly inclusive, 87
indirect translog utility functions, 81*t*
indirect utility functions, xxiii, 324, 361
tests for, 61–62, 87, 170–171
in two-stage budgeting, 476
Homotheticity. *See also* Groupwise homotheticity
in demand theory, 2, 9–12
direct translog utility functions, 44–50, 67*t*, 70–71*t*
direct vs. indirect utility functions, 56, 57
explicit, 46, 59–60, 67*t*, 70*t*, 76*t*, 79*t*, 88*t*, 163
inclusive, 71*t*, 80*t*
indirect translog utility functions, 44–50, 76*t*, 79*t*
intrinsic, 45–46
level of significance, 86, 173, 174
of preferences, 158
tests for, 15, *16*, 18, 24, 25*t*, 25–26, 26*t*, 59–60, 88*t*, 174
Household
aggregate price of energy, 440–442
attributes under exact aggregation, 391–392
budget studies, xii
as consuming unit, 325, 348, 360, 391, 499
demographic characteristics, xxii, xxvii, 325, 391, 499
identical preferences for, 208
maximization of welfare, 476
total expenditure and demographic characteristics as determinants of demand, xii
Household expenditures
Germany, 156
to maximize household welfare function, 280
Houthakker, Hendrik S., xii, 27
consumer demand analysis, 3, 30
direct addilog system, 2
family budget studies, 204
linear expenditure system, 1
Hurwicz, Leonid, xvi

Income elasticity of demand, 475
Index functions
depending on attributes and expenditures, 243–248, 256, 258
nondependent on individual expenditures, 242–243
Indirect addilog system, 3, 27, 30
Indirect demand function, 32
compensated own-price substitution effect, 109
homogeneity, 107, 111
integrability conditions, 105–106, 138
monotonicity, 109, 122, 142–143
nonnegativity, 108, 141–142
summability, 108, 113
symmetry restrictions, 108, 114, 120
Indirect translog demand function
equality restriction, 147
estimates of parameters, 146–147*t*, 196–198*t*
German personal consumption expenditures, 193
homogeneity, 144–145*t*, 183
homothetic, 367
integrability conditions, 140–143, 181, 195
monotonicity, 188
nonnegativity, 187
summability, 183–184
symmetry restrictions, 184–186
test statistics, 151*t*, 191*t*
unrestricted equations, 146–147*t*
Indirect translog utility function, xvii, 3, 6–7, 105
additive and homothetic, 12
in aggregate consumer behavior model, 368
in aggregate demand model, xxiii
to allocate energy and nonenergy expenditures, 478–479
as cardinal and ordinal measure of welfare, 283, 300
for consumer preferences, 29

Indirect translog utility function (*cont.*)
exact aggregation conditions, xxii, 300
explicit groupwise separability, 166
groupwise homothetic separability, 166
groupwise linear logarithmic, 166
groupwise separability, 158, 173–174, 175*t*
homogeneity, 163–164
homotheticity, 162–163
individual demand functions and, xviii
lacking second-order interpolation property, 278
monotonicity, 290, 367
neutral linear logarithmic, 167
normalization, 36–37
number of parameters, 18, 21–22*t*, 75–83*t*, 84–85, 118–119
parametric restrictions, 218
to represent consumer preferences, 358
second-order interpolation property, 279
self-dual, 23
tests for preference restrictions based on, 173, 175–176*t*
without time-varying preferences, 29
with time-varying preferences, 35–37
Indirect utility function
additivity, 27, 57, 160–161
in assessing alternative policy impact, 300
bordered Hessian, 123
in demand theory, 2–3
depending on attributes, 300
direct demand system and, 153
duality, 56–58
in energy allocation process, 362
exact aggregation conditions, 283
explicitly groupwise separable, 160
generated from individual demand functions, 477
groupwise commodity separable, 57
groupwise equal rate of commodity augmentation, 57
groupwise homogeneous, 165
groupwise homothetically separable, 165–166
groupwise homotheticity, 163–164
groupwise separability, 56, 158–159
groupwise time separable, 57
groupwise zero rates of commodity augmentation, 55
homogeneity, 163, 216
homogeneous of degree zero, 236, 237–239
homothetic, 161–163
homothetic separability, xxiii, 324
impact of alternative economic policies on, 283
incorporating restrictions on individual behavior, 298, 300
indirect demand system and, 110
individual demand function derived from, 256–257, 277, 278
integrability conditions, xix
lacking second-order interpolation property, 278–279
linear logarithmic, 166–167, 171
monotone transformation, 118
monotonicity, 216
neutral, 57, 161
nonnegativity, 216
polynomial specification, 260–268, 278
properties of, 361
quasiconvexity, 154, 216
self-dual, 58, 89–90
as solution to partial differential equation, 259
Individual consumer behavior model, xii
exact aggregation approach, xii
stochastic component, 320–321
two-stage allocation process, 368
Individual demand functions
in aggregate consumer behavior model, 475
aggregate demand function implications, 248–249
characterizing aggregate demand, xv
conforming to exact aggregation theory, xv–xvi
continuous differentiability assumption, 231, 233
dependence on individual expenditures, 217
depending on attributes and expenditures, 217–218, 220, 241
derived from indirect utility function, 277, 278
for energy allocation process, 362, 363
estimating unknown parameters, 259–260
functional forms, 258–259
homogeneity, 218, 224–230, 241, 249–253, 255

homogeneous of degree zero, 244–245, 256
implied by utility maximization, 221
incorporating differences in individual preferences, 217
integrability conditions, xvi, 214–216, 241, 256–257
linearity, 216–217
logarithmic form, 278, 279
nonlinear constraints, 275
power form, 278, 279
price dependence, xvi, 220, 258–279
rational specification, 276–278
reduced to AIDS system, 274
summability, 213, 218, 221–224, 241, 249, 251–252
symmetry restrictions, 230–241, 246–247, 250–251
with three index functions, 257
total expenditure and attribute effects, 248
with two index functions, 243–248, 256
in two-stage allocation process, 477–478

Individual energy expenditures
age of household head and, 396, *398*, 402, *404*, 408, *410*, 414, *416*, *421*, 423
cross-section data, 374–375, 378–379, 390
demand functions, 358
demographic changes affecting, 370, 391, 392, 396–408, 412, 413*t*, 414
family size impacts, 394, 396, *397*, 400, 402, *403*, 408, *409*, 412, 414, *415*, *420*, 423

Individual energy expenditures model
combined with aggregate energy expenditures model, 377
estimation, 378–379
stochastic component, 388
tests of structural change, 442, 444*t*, 445

Individual expenditure shares
additive components, 303
applied to translog indirect utility function, 281–282
in consumer behavior model, 479–480
for energy, 463, 488–489
equal to unity, 301
exact aggregation conditions, 364, 480–481, 483
homogeneous of degree zero, 282, 301, 480
integrability conditions, 287–291, 364–368, 498
linear in logarithms of expenditures and attributes, 282
monotonicity, 290–291, 315, 319–320, 387
for nonenergy commodities, 488–489
nonnegativity, 289–290, 291
second-stage model, 493
stochastic component, 488
summability restrictions, 291

Individual expenditures
combined with aggregate expenditures, 311
demographic changes affecting, 329–350
effect of changing expenditures on, 329–350
logarithmic function, 279
nonlinearity, 217
ordinary least squares estimation, 348
power function, 278, 279

translog model, 307–308

Individual preferences. *See also* Consumer preferences
in aggregate consumer behavior model, 368
exact aggregation with differences in, 242–258

Individual welfare
household maximization of, 280, 476
indirect translog utility function, 283, 300
ordinal measures, xxviii

Inequality restrictions
asymptotic distribution, 149
estimation subject to, 461–462
monotonicity conditions, 188
nonnegativity conditions, 193–194
pooled cross-section and time-series data, 319

Instrumental variables
aggregate, 311
in exact aggregation model, 456–457
pooled cross-section and time-series data, 322
two-stage allocation process, 496, 509–510*t*

Integrability
of aggregate demand functions, 214–216

Integrability (*cont.*)
conditions for, 92–93, 101, 106–110, 181–188
of demand functions, xvi, 139–143
generated by neutral linear logarithmic utility, 91–92, 101, 103, 104, 137
global, 93
implying restrictions on demand functions, 137
of individual demand functions, 218, 241, 256–257, 363
of individual expenditure shares, 287–291, 364–368, 498
local, 93, 101
in representative consumer model, xvii
restrictions on unknown parameters, 106
of Rotterdam demand system, 102
statistical tests, 91, 148–149
critical values, 150*t*
stochastic specification, 181–183
tests for, xvii–xviii, 102, 148–149, 156, 180, 191*t*, 192
Intertemporal general equilibrium model, aggregate consumer behavior model and, xxix
Invertibility assumption, 212

Johansen, Leif, 2, 3, 27, 30
Jorgenson, Dale W.
consumer demand functions, 104, 105, 123
econometric model of consumer behavior, 179
energy demand model, xxvi, xxvii
integrability conditions, 156
logarithmic demand functions, 153
nonlinear simultaneous equation systems, xxviii, 143, 449
translog model, 29, 451
U.S. preference structures, 177

Klein, Lawrence R., xiv, 208, 450
Kuhn-Tucker conditions for Lagrangian saddlepoint, 315–316, 382, 462

Laffont, Jean-Jacques, xix, xxviii, 143, 449
Lagrangian function saddlepoint, 315–316, 381–382, 461–462
Lau, Lawrence J., xii, xvi
consumer demand functions, 104, 105, 123, 153
econometric model of consumer behavior, 179
energy demand model, xxvii
exact aggregation theory, xiv–xv, xxviii, 209
integrability conditions, 106, 139, 156
time-varying preferences, xvii
translog model, 29, 451
U.S. preference structures, 177
Leontief, Wassily, 156
Leser, Conrad E.V., xii, 204
Level of significance
consumer preferences, 86, 173
in demand theory testing, 23–24
for equality restrictions, 173, 194
groupwise homotheticity, 86, 174
groupwise separability, 86, 123
homogeneity, 194
homotheticity, 86, 174
linear logarithmic utility, 86, 173
monotonicity, 149, 194
nonnegativity, 149, 194
symmetry, 194
Lewbel, Arthur, xv
LHES. *See* Lifestyle and Household Energy Use Surveys
Liew, Chong K., 316, 382, 462
Lifestyle and Household Energy Use Surveys, xxv–xvi
vs. Consumer Expenditure Surveys, 424–425, 428*t*
1975, 418, 419*t*, 423
1973, 408, 412, 413*t*, 414
residential energy demand data, 466
Likelihood ratio
consumer preferences, 85–86
in demand theory, 23, 172
Limited information techniques, 376
Linear expenditure system, xiv, 27, 208, 300
direct or indirect additivity hypotheses, 30
exact aggregation form, 450–451
Linear logarithmic utility, 1–2, 27. *See also* Neutral linear logarithmic utility
direct translog utility function, 67*t*, 72–73*t*, 84
explicit, 67*t*, 73*t*, 76*t*, 82*t*, 87, 167, 170
indirect translog utility function, 76*t*, 81–82*t*, 84
self-dual, 12–13
tests for, 15, 60–61, *64*, 87, 170, 171

Manser, M.E., 29
Martos, B., 292
Matrix B_{pp}
  elements of, 296, 297–298*t*, 299*t*
  monotonicity restrictions, 294, 301
  nonpositivity constraints, 296, 299*t*
Maximum likelihood estimator, 37, 375
  in demand theory, 17
  individual energy expenditures model, 378
  to obtain consistent estimators, 309
Merely positive subdefinite matrix, 292, 293
Mitchell, B.M., 29
Moment matrix
  cross-section model of aggregate energy expenditures, 385–386
  pooled cross-section and time-series data, 319, 322
Monotonicity, 93
  direct demand functions, 106, 109, 142–143
  direct translog utility function, 32–33, 38
  homogeneity and equality restrictions, 147
  indirect demand functions, 106, 109, 142–143
  indirect translog utility function, 36, 38, 367
  indirect utility function, 216, 290, 301, 361
  individual demand function, 214–215
  of individual energy expenditures, 379, 381
  of individual expenditure shares, 290–291, 315, 319–320, 387
  inequality restrictions, 188, 193–194
  level of significance, 149, 194
  in pooled cross-section time-series data, 312
  tests for, xviii, 58, 120–122, 139, 150–151, 187–188, 190, 191*t*, 192, 195
Muellbauer, John S.
  AIDS system, 274, 279, 451
  individual demand function form, 228
  representative consumer model, xiv, xv, xxi, 208, 213, 217

National Income and Product Accounts, time-series data, 325
Net equivalent variation, 285–286
Neutral linear logarithmic utility, 53, 61, 67*t*, 73*t*, 76*t*, 82*t*, 84, 103, 167, 170. *See also* Linear logarithmic utility
  integrability of demand system generated by, 91, 103, 104, 137
  self-duality, 58
  tests for, 106
Neutrality
  in consumer preferences, 40
  direct translog utility function, 66*t*
  direct utility function, 40
  explicit, 40, 59, 66*t*, 75*t*, 161, 169
  groupwise, 40
  indirect translog utility function, 75*t*
  indirect utility functions, 161
  tests for, 59, 169
NIPA, 325
Nondurables
  expenditure shares, 182
  expenditures for, 189, 324
  restrictions on preference structures, 172
Nonenergy commodities
  in consumer behavior model, 478–479
  prices of, 477
Nonlinear expenditure system, xiv
Nonlinear simultaneous equations model, xix
Nonlinear three-stage least squares estimator
  for aggregate energy expenditures model, 376, 380
  asymptotic covariance matrix, 384–385, 388
  for consumer demand, 143
  estimation procedure, 458–459
  for household energy expenditures, 441–442
  inequality-constrained, xx, 316, 319, 381, 382, 387, 462, 498
  iterations, xx
  null hypothesis, 149
  objective function, 457–458, 459
  regularity assumptions, 457
  relation to linear pooled estimators, 460
  technical assumptions, 471–473
  translog aggregate expenditures model, 496–497
  translog consumer behavior model, 310, 322

Nonlinear three-stage least squares pooling of cross-section and time-series data, 383–388, 390, 449, 457–460, 497–498
advantages, 470
on consumers, 311
example, 463–470
Nonnegativity
bounds of, 334, 336*t*
condition for integrability, 93
direct demand functions, 108, 141–142
expenditure share functions, 276
homogeneity and equality restrictions, 147
indirect demand functions, 108, 141–142
individual demand functions, xvi, 214–215, 230, 237, 242–243
individual energy expenditures, 379
individual expenditure shares, 289–290, 291, 301, 366–367
inequality restrictions, 193–194
level of significance, 149, 194
for Rotterdam demand functions, 100–101
tests for, xviii, 120, 187, 190, 191*t*, 195
Nonpositive definiteness condition, 291
Nonsingularity condition, 320
Nonzero commitments, 2, 30
Normalization of parameters
direct translog utility function, 5–6, 34
indirect translog utility function, 36–37
in pooled time-series cross-section model, 312
for residential energy demand model, 473
translog model of aggregate consumer behavior, 308
Null hypothesis, 23, 24, 86

Ordinary least squares estimation, 460
Own-price elasticity of energy demand, 507–508*t*, 509
Own-price substitution
for all commodity groups, 502–503
compensated, 109, 114, 120–121, 215, 288–289, 365, 366
Slutsky matrix, 141
uncompensated, 114, 288
Own-quantity substitution
Antonelli matrix, 141
compensated, 122, 188

Parametric hypothesis tests, 460–461
Partial differential equation
to derive individual demand function, 237
indirect utility function as solution to, 259
second-order ordinary, 263
Personal consumption expenditures, Germany (1950–1973), 189–194. *See also* Energy expenditures
Pollark, Robert A., 360
Polynomial specification
first-order, 123, 180, 271–273, 274–275, 278, 279
of functions $H^*(p)$ and $H^*_I(p)$, 268–276
homogeneous functions with, 269–270
of indirect utility function, 260–268
Lemma 8.1, 269–270
power vs. logarithmic form, 270
second-order, 278, 279
second-order generalized, 265, 268
Pooled cross-section and time-series data
of aggregate consumer behavior, 329, 330–333*t*
in aggregate demand model, xx, 204, 219–220
aggregate energy expenditures model, 374, 377, 383–388, 389–390, 428
CES vs. LHES surveys, 424–425, 428*t*
cross-section model, 312–313, 321
eliminating summability restrictions, 312
energy and nonenergy expenditures, 497–498
in energy use surveys, xxv–xxvi
error structures, 455–457
estimation, 328–329, 348–349
inequality restrictions, 319
instrumental variables, 322
linearizing, 317
methods of, 453–454
moment matrix, 319, 322
in residential energy demand model, 466, 467–468, 469*t*, 470*t*
statistical methods, xxviii
time-series model, 313, 321
transformation of observations, 454–455
in translog model of consumer behavior, 311–320
Power functions
function *g*, 119, 126, 127

individual demand functions, 278, 279
polynomial specification, 270
symmetry restrictions, 119–120
Prais, Sigmund J., xii, 204
Price elasticity, 475
in aggregate energy expenditures, 435, 436*t*, 443*t*, 445, 446*t*
demand model, xxiii
for different consuming groups, 350
own- and cross-, xxvii
total expenditure and demographic characteristics affecting, 342, 343–346*t*, 347–348
Price index
for energy, xxiv, 362
homogeneous translog functions, 324–325
Prices
consumer expenditure and, xix, 203
demands as functions of, 258–279
as determinants of aggregate demand, xii, 218
individual demand function and, xvi, 220, 258–279
of nonenergy commodities, 477
two-stage allocation model, 502, 506–509

Quantity index of energy, xxiv, 362
Quasiconcavity of direct utility function, 154
Quasiconvexity
direct translog utility function, 32–33, 38
indirect utility function, 36, 38, 154, 216, 290, 301, 361
tests for, 58

Random individual errors, 455–456
Regional differences
aggregate energy expenditures and, *434*, 435, 437, 503, 505
individual energy expenditures and, 396, *399*, 400, 402, *405*, 408, *411*, 414, *417*, *422*, 423
Representative consumer model, 203, 205–208
aggregate consumer behavior model based on, 204
conditions for, 213
deficiencies in, xii
vs. econometric model of aggregate consumer behavior, xxviii
individual and household preferences, 207–208
time-varying preferences in, xvii
Residential energy demand model
distribution of energy expenditures, 466–467
errors of measurement, 465–466
estimating parameters, 466
heteroscedasticity correction, 465–466
nonlinear three-stage least squares estimation, 463
parameter restrictions, 473
pooled cross-section and time-series data, 466, 467–468, 469*t*, 470*t*
random disturbances, 463–464
Rotterdam demand functions, xvii, 1, 91
additivity, homotheticity, and stationarity assumptions, 30
integrability, 102, 104, 137
implications of, 95–101
tests for, 156
Roy, Rene. *See* Roy's Identity
Roy's Identity, xix, 105
applied to indirect translog utility function, 218, 363, 364
to generate individual demand functions, 232, 236, 268, 477
logarithmic form, 154, 281
to obtain individual expenditure shares, 479–480, 483
Rubin, Herman, xiv, 208, 450
Russell, Robert R., 450, 476

Samuelson, Paul A., 360
Sato, Kazuo, 2, 3, 27, 30
S-branch utility tree, 450
Schultz, Henry, xii, xvii, 30, 91, 151
consumer demand studies, 1, 203
double-logarithmic system, 94, 137
statistical demand analysis, 103
Self-duality of utility functions, 12–13, 23, 58, 89–90
Separability restriction
direct translog utility function, 68–69*t*
explicit, 69*t*, 77*t*, 78*t*
indirect translog utility function, 77*t*, 78*t*
tests for, 58

Slackness condition, 316
  complementary, 382
Slesnick, Daniel T., xii, xxii, xxix
  energy demand model, xxvi
Slutsky substitution matrix, 187
  compensated price derivatives, 461
  nonpositive definiteness, 239, 241
  symmetry of, 116, 124–127, 133, 141, 231, 232–233, 241, 246, 250, 253, 277
Social welfare
  economic policies affecting, 283–286, 300
  energy expenditures and, 360
  indicators of, xxviii–xxix
Sonnenschein, Hugo, xiii, 204
Sono, Masazo, 156
Statistical demand analysis, 103
Statistical inference methods, xix
Stochastic specification
  aggregate energy expenditures model, 301–311, 370–374
  consumer demand model, 7, 171–172, 189, 320–321, 487–495
  cross-section data, 302–311
  for econometric demand model, 37–38
  exact aggregation theory, 452–453
  individual energy expenditures model, 388, 488
  for integrability, 181–183
  time-series data, 302–311
Stoker, Thomas M., xii, xix, xxiv, 428
  energy demand model, xxvi, xxvii
  individual welfare measures, xxviii
  time-series data analysis, 467
  translog model, 451
Stone, Richard, xii, xiii, xvii, 27
  consumer demand studies, 1, 91, 103
  demand analysis, 30
  double-logarithmic system, 137
  linear expenditure system, xiv, 1
  representative consumer model, 203
  test for homogeneity, 101
Strictly merely positive subdefinite matrix, 292, 293
Strotz, Robert H., 156
Substitution effects. *See* Cross-price substitution; Own-price substitution
Summability
  condition for integrability, 92
  direct demand functions, 92, 107–108, 111–113, 195, 196
  direct translog demand functions, 147, 183–184
  of energy expenditures, 378, 379
  equality restrictions, 190
  of expenditure shares, 182, 276, 287–288, 291, 365
  indirect demand functions, 92, 108, 113, 123, 140, 195, 196
  indirect translog demand functions, 147, 183–184
  individual demand functions, xvi, 213, 214–215, 218, 221–224, 228–230, 232, 237, 241, 243, 249, 251–252
  of individual expenditure shares, 301
  in pooled cross-section and time-series model, 312
  Rotterdam demand functions, 95, 97–98, 100
Symmetry
  alternative sets of, 116–118, 119, 132
  in demand theory, 7–8, 141
  direct demand functions, 108
  direct translog demand functions, 145*t*, 184, 190, 200*t*
  direct translog utility functions, 34, 38, 66*t*, 85
  of energy expenditures, 379
  homogeneity and equality conditions, 157–158, 186
  indirect demand functions, 108
  indirect translog demand functions, 146–147*t*, 184–186, 190, 197–198*t*
  indirect translog utility functions, 37, 38, 75*t*
  of individual demand functions, xvi, 214–215, 230–241, 246–247, 250–251, 276–277
  of individual expenditure shares, 288, 301, 365–366
  integrability conditions, 92–93, 141–142
  level of significance, 194
  for matrix of compensated own- and cross-price substitution, 115
  in pooled time-series cross-section model, 312
  of Slutsky matrix, 116, 124–127, 133, 141
  tests for, 14, 113–120, 139, 184, 191*t*, 195
    based on double-logarithmic demand system, 101

Taylor's series expansion, 39
Theil, Henri, 30

least squares estimation method, 315, 381, 459–460
Rotterdam demand functions, xvii, 1, 91, 95, 104, 137
Time of day pricing, 476
Time-series data. *See also* Pooled cross-section and time-series data
in aggregate demand model, xiii
for distribution of energy expenditures, 375, 428
sources of, 325–326
stochastic structure, 302–311
technical assumptions, 472
Translog model of aggregate consumer behavior, 359–360, 476–478. *See also* Aggregate consumer behavior model; Consumer behavior theory
commodity groups, 348
consistent estimators, 309–310
cross-section model parameters and, 308–309
econometrics, 301–307, 320–321, 487
exact aggregation conditions, 280–286
first stage, 478–482, 484–485
heteroscedasticity corrections, 491–492
identification and estimation, 307–311, 317
integrability conditions, 287–291
minimizing criterion function, 315, 317
normalization of parameters, 308
second stage, 482–483
stochastic structure, 302–311, 487–495
two-stage allocation, 360–364
underidentification condition, 310–311
unknown parameters, xx–xxi, 317
Translog model of aggregate expenditures
for energy and nonenergy commodities, 496
heteroscedasticity correction, 328
identification and estimation, 495–497
nonlinear three-stage least squares estimator, 496–497
pooled cross-section and time-series data, 497–498
two-stage allocation process, 496
Translog model of individual expenditures, identification and estimation, 495–496
Translog utility function
additivity, 14–15
consumer preferences represented by, 153
equality restrictions, 14
explicit additivity, 9, 15
groupwise homotheticity and homogeneity, 44–50
homogeneity, 15
homotheticity, 10, 15
linear logarithmic utility, 15
local approximation property, 39
symmetry restrictions, 14
with time-varying preferences, 38, 153, 154–157
Trimble, John, 476
Two-stage allocation process, 358
aggregate consumer expenditures model, 483–487
of energy demand, xxiv–xxv, 360–364, 475
energy price index, 484–485
individual consumer behavior model, 368
individual demand functions, xxv, 476–478
instrumental variables, 496, 509–510*t*
methods of, xxviii
pooled estimates, 500, 501*t*, 502–503
Two-stage budgeting, xxiii, 475–476

Underidentification condition, 310–311
Uniformity property, 183, 196
U.S. Interindustry Transactions Accounts (1958–1974)
personal consumption expenditures, 325
time-series data, 348
U.S. National Income and Product Accounts, 428, 466
time-series data, 498
Unobservable random disturbances, 372–373
for all commodities, 303–304, 371, 489, 493
for all energy types, 388, 463–464, 493
equal to zero, 321, 489
Utility functions
corresponding demand functions generated by, 180
testing validity of restrictions on, 24–25
transcendental logarithmic, 4–7
Utility maximization, 38
by individual consumers, 206
restrictions on demand functions implied by, 243

Uzawa, Hirofumi, 156

Washington Center for Metropolitan Studies, 408, 412, 413*t*, 414
WCMS. *See* Washington Center for Metropolitan Studies
Wilcoxen, Peter, xxix
Wold, Herman, xii, xiii, xvii, 27, 30
  consumer demand studies, 1, 91, 103
  double-logarithmic system, 137
  representative consumer model, 203
  test for symmetry, 101
Working, Holbrook, xii

Zellner, Arnold, 315, 381, 459–460
Zero rates
  of aggregate consumer demand, 240, 242–243
  of commodity augmentation, 55, 56, 85
  indirect translog utility function, 83*t*
  tests for, 89*t*